TOYOTA
PICK-UPS/LAND CRUISER/4RUNNER
1970-88 REPAIR MANUAL

Covers all U.S. and Canadian models of Toyota Pick-Up, Land Cruiser and 4Runner; 2 and 4 wheel drive, gasoline and diesel engines

by Tony Tortorici

CHILTON *Automotive Books*

PUBLISHED BY **HAYNES NORTH AMERICA**, Inc.

Manufactured in USA
© 1994 Haynes North America, Inc.
ISBN 0-8019-8578-1
Library of Congress Catalog Card No. 93-074297
0123456789 9876543210

Haynes Publishing Group
Sparkford Nr Yeovil
Somerset BA22 7JJ England

Haynes North America, Inc
861 Lawrence Drive
Newbury Park
California 91320 USA

ABCDE
FGH

Contents

Contents

SAFETY NOTICE

Proper service and repair procedures are vital to the safe, reliable operation of all motor vehicles, as well as the personal safety of those performing repairs. This manual outlines procedures for servicing and repairing vehicles using safe, effective methods. The procedures contain many NOTES, CAUTIONS and WARNINGS which should be followed, along with standard procedures to eliminate the possibility of personal injury or improper service which could damage the vehicle or compromise its safety.

It is important to note that repair procedures and techniques, tools and parts for servicing motor vehicles, as well as the skill and experience of the individual performing the work vary widely. It is not possible to anticipate all of the conceivable ways or conditions under which vehicles may be serviced, or to provide cautions as to all possible hazards that may result. Standard and accepted safety precautions and equipment should be used when handling toxic or flammable fluids, and safety goggles or other protection should be used during cutting, grinding, chiseling, prying, or any other process that can cause material removal or projectiles.

Some procedures require the use of tools specially designed for a specific purpose. Before substituting another tool or procedure, you must be completely satisfied that neither your personal safety, nor the performance of the vehicle will be endangered.

Although information in this manual is based on industry sources and is complete as possible at the time of publication, the possibility exists that some car manufacturers made later changes which could not be included here. While striving for total accuracy, the authors or publishers cannot assume responsibility for any errors, changes or omissions that may occur in the compilation of this data.

PART NUMBERS

Part numbers listed in this reference are not recommendations by Haynes North America, Inc. for any product brand name. They are references that can be used with interchange manuals and aftermarket supplier catalogs to locate each brand supplier's discrete part number.

SPECIAL TOOLS

Special tools are recommended by the vehicle manufacturer to perform their specific job. Use has been kept to a minimum, but where absolutely necessary, they are referred to in the text by the part number of the tool manufacturer. These tools can be purchased, under the appropriate part number, from your local dealer or regional distributor, or an equivalent tool can be purchased locally from a tool supplier or parts outlet. Before substituting any tool for the one recommended, read the SAFETY NOTICE at the top of this page.

ACKNOWLEDGMENTS

The publisher expresses appreciation to Toyota Motor Corporation for their generous assistance.

1

GENERAL INFORMATION AND MAINTENANCE

HOW TO USE THIS BOOK

This Chilton's Total Car Care manual is intended to help you learn more about the inner workings of your Toyota truck while saving you money on its upkeep and operation.

The beginning of the book will likely be referred to the most, since that is where you will find information for maintenance and tune-up. The other sections deal with the more complex systems of your vehicle. Systems (from engine through brakes) are covered to the extent that the average do-it-yourselfer can attempt. This book will not explain such things as rebuilding a differential because the expertise required and the special tools necessary make this uneconomical. It will, however, give you detailed instructions to help you change your own brake pads and shoes, replace spark plugs, and perform many more jobs that can save you money and help avoid expensive problems.

A secondary purpose of this book is a reference for owners who want to understand their vehicle and/or their mechanics better.

Where to Begin

• Before removing any bolts, read through the entire procedure. This will give you the overall view of what tools and supplies will be required. So read ahead and plan ahead. Each operation should be approached logically and all procedures thoroughly understood before attempting any work.

If repair of a component is not considered practical, we tell you how to remove the part and then how to install the new or rebuilt replacement. In this way, you at least save labor costs.

Avoiding Trouble

Many procedures in this book require you to "label and disconnect . . ." a group of lines, hoses or wires. Don't be think you can remember where everything goes—you won't. If you hook up vacuum or fuel lines incorrectly, the vehicle may run poorly, if at all. If you hook up electrical wiring incorrectly, you may instantly learn a very expensive lesson.

You don't need to know the proper name for each hose or line. A piece of masking tape on the hose and a piece on its fitting will allow you to assign your own label. As long as you remember your own code, the lines can be reconnected by matching your tags. Remember that tape will dissolve in gasoline or solvents; if a part is to be washed or cleaned, use another method of identification. A permanent felt-tipped marker or a metal scribe can be very handy for marking metal parts. Remove any tape or paper labels after assembly.

Maintenance or Repair?

Maintenance includes routine inspections, adjustments, and replacement of parts which show signs of normal wear. Maintenance compensates for wear or deterioration. Repair implies that something has broken or is not working. A need for a repair is often caused by lack of maintenance. for example: draining and refilling automatic transmission fluid is maintenance recommended at specific intervals. Failure to do this can shorten the life of the transmission/transaxle, requiring very expensive repairs. While no maintenance program can prevent items from eventually breaking or wearing out, a general rule is true: MAINTENANCE IS CHEAPER THAN REPAIR.

Two basic mechanic's rules should be mentioned here. First, whenever the left side of the vehicle or engine is referred to, it means the driver's side. Conversely, the right side of the vehicle means the passenger's side. Second, screws and bolts are removed by turning counterclockwise, and tightened by turning clockwise unless specifically noted.

Safety is always the most important rule. Constantly be aware of the dangers involved in working on an automobile and take the proper precautions. Please refer to the information in this section regarding SERVICING YOUR VEHICLE SAFELY and the SAFETY NOTICE on the acknowledgment page.

Avoiding the Most Common Mistakes

Pay attention to the instructions provided. There are 3 common mistakes in mechanical work:

1. Incorrect order of assembly, disassembly or adjustment. When taking something apart or putting it together, performing steps in the wrong order usually just costs you extra time; however, it CAN break something. Read the entire procedure before beginning. Perform everything in the order in which the instructions say you should, even if you can't see a reason for it. When you're taking apart something that is very intricate, you might want to draw a picture of how it looks when assembled in order to make sure you get everything back in its proper position. When making adjustments, perform them in the proper order. One adjustment possibly will affect another.

2. Overtorquing (or undertorquing). While it is more common for overtorquing to cause damage, undertorquing may allow a fastener to vibrate loose causing serious damage. Especially when dealing with aluminum parts, pay attention to torque specifications and utilize a torque wrench in assembly. If a torque figure is not available, remember that if you are using the right tool to perform the job, you will probably not have to strain yourself to get a fastener tight enough. The pitch of most threads is so slight that the tension you put on the wrench will be multiplied many times in actual force on what you are tightening.

There are many commercial products available for ensuring that fasteners won't come loose, even if they are not torqued just right (a very common brand is Loctite_). If you're worried about getting something together tight enough to hold, but loose enough to avoid mechanical damage during assembly, one of these products might offer substantial insurance. Before choosing a threadlocking compound, read the label on the package and make sure the product is compatible with the materials, fluids, etc. involved.

3. Crossthreading. This occurs when a part such as a bolt is screwed into a nut or casting at the wrong angle and forced. Crossthreading is more likely to occur if access is difficult. It helps to clean and lubricate fasteners, then to start threading the bolt, spark plug, etc. with your fingers. If you encounter resistance, unscrew the part and start over again at a different angle until it can be inserted and turned several times without much effort. Keep in mind that many parts have tapered threads, so that gentle turning will automatically bring the part you're threading to the proper angle. Don't put a wrench on the part until it's been tightened a couple of turns by hand. If you suddenly encounter resistance, and the part has not seated fully, don't force it. Pull it back out to make sure it's clean and threading properly.

Be sure to take your time and be patient, and always plan ahead. Allow yourself ample time to perform repairs and maintenance.

TOOLS AND EQUIPMENT

▶ **See Figures 1 thru 15**

Without the proper tools and equipment it is impossible to properly service your vehicle. It would be virtually impossible to catalog every tool that you would need to perform all of the operations in this book. It would be unwise for the amateur to rush out and buy an expensive set of tools on the theory that he/she may need one or more of them at some time.

The best approach is to proceed slowly, gathering a good quality set of those tools that are used most frequently. Don't be misled by the low cost of bargain tools. It is far better to spend a little more for better quality. Forged wrenches, 6

or 12-point sockets and fine tooth ratchets are by far preferable to their less expensive counterparts. As any good mechanic can tell you, there are few worse experiences than trying to work on a vehicle with bad tools. Your monetary savings will be far outweighed by frustration and mangled knuckles.

Begin accumulating those tools that are used most frequently: those associated with routine maintenance and tune-up. In addition to the normal assortment of screwdrivers and pliers, you should have the following tools:

• Wrenches/sockets and combination open end/box end wrenches in sizes ⅛–¾ in. and/or 3mm–19mm ¹³⁄₁₆ in. or ⅝ in. spark plug socket (depending on plug type).

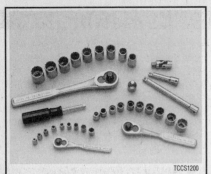

TCCS1200

Fig. 1 All but the most basic procedures will require an assortment of ratchets and sockets

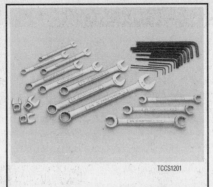

TCCS1201

Fig. 2 In addition to ratchets, a good set of wrenches and hex keys will be necessary

TCCS1202

Fig. 3 A hydraulic floor jack and a set of jackstands are essential for lifting and supporting the vehicle

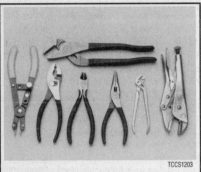

TCCS1203

Fig. 4 An assortment of pliers, grippers and cutters will be handy for old rusted parts and stripped bolt heads

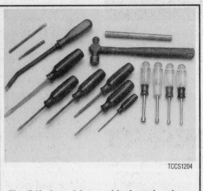

TCCS1204

Fig. 5 Various drivers, chisels and prybars are great tools to have in your toolbox

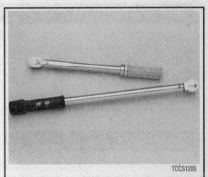

TCCS1205

Fig. 6 Many repairs will require the use of a torque wrench to assure the components are properly fastened

TCCS1209

Fig. 7 Although not always necessary, using specialized brake tools will save time

TCCS1210

Fig. 8 A few inexpensive lubrication tools will make maintenance easier

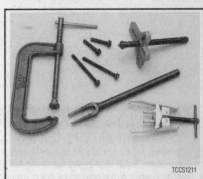

TCCS1211

Fig. 9 Various pullers, clamps and separator tools are needed for many larger, more complicated repairs

TCCS1212

Fig. 10 A variety of tools and gauges should be used for spark plug gapping and installation

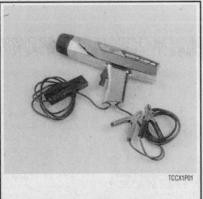

TCCX1P01

Fig. 11 Inductive type timing light

TCCX1P02

Fig. 12 A screw-in type compression gauge is recommended for compression testing

Fig. 13 A vacuum/pressure tester is necessary for many testing procedures

TCCX1P03

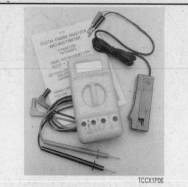

Fig. 14 Most modern automotive multimeters incorporate many helpful features

TCCX1P06

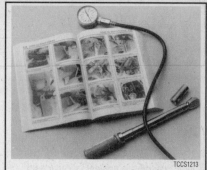

Fig. 15 Proper information is vital, so always have a Chilton Total Car Care manual handy

TCCS1213

→If possible, buy various length socket drive extensions. Universal-joint and wobble extensions can be extremely useful, but be careful when using them, as they can change the amount of torque applied to the socket.

- Jackstands for support.
- Oil filter wrench.
- Spout or funnel for pouring fluids.
- Grease gun for chassis lubrication (unless your vehicle is not equipped with any grease fittings).
- Hydrometer for checking the battery (unless equipped with a sealed, maintenance-free battery).
- A container for draining oil and other fluids.
- Rags for wiping up the inevitable mess.

In addition to the above items there are several others that are not absolutely necessary, but handy to have around. These include an equivalent oil absorbent gravel, like cat litter, and the usual supply of lubricants, antifreeze and fluids. This is a basic list for routine maintenance, but only your personal needs and desire can accurately determine your list of tools.

After performing a few projects on the vehicle, you'll be amazed at the other tools and non-tools on your workbench. Some useful household items are: a large turkey baster or siphon, empty coffee cans and ice trays (to store parts), a ball of twine, electrical tape for wiring, small rolls of colored tape for tagging lines or hoses, markers and pens, a note pad, golf tees (for plugging vacuum lines), metal coat hangers or a roll of mechanic's wire (to hold things out of the way), dental pick or similar long, pointed probe, a strong magnet, and a small mirror (to see into recesses and under manifolds).

A more advanced set of tools, suitable for tune-up work, can be drawn up easily. While the tools are slightly more sophisticated, they need not be outrageously expensive. There are several inexpensive tach/dwell meters on the market that are every bit as good for the average mechanic as a professional model. Just be sure that it goes to a least 1200–1500 rpm on the tach scale and that it works on 4, 6 and 8-cylinder engines. The key to these purchases is to make them with an eye towards adaptability and wide range. A basic list of tune-up tools could include:

- Tach/dwell meter.
- Spark plug wrench and gapping tool.

- Feeler gauges for valve adjustment.
- Timing light.

The choice of a timing light should be made carefully. A light which works on the DC current supplied by the vehicle's battery is the best choice; it should have a xenon tube for brightness. On any vehicle with an electronic ignition system, a timing light with an inductive pickup that clamps around the No. 1 spark plug cable is preferred.

In addition to these basic tools, there are several other tools and gauges you may find useful. These include:

- Compression gauge. The screw-in type is slower to use, but eliminates the possibility of a faulty reading due to escaping pressure.
- Manifold vacuum gauge.
- 12V test light.
- A combination volt/ohmmeter
- Induction Ammeter. This is used for determining whether or not there is current in a wire. These are handy for use if a wire is broken somewhere in a wiring harness.

As a final note, you will probably find a torque wrench necessary for all but the most basic work. The beam type models are perfectly adequate, although the newer click types (breakaway) are easier to use. The click type torque wrenches tend to be more expensive. Also keep in mind that all types of torque wrenches should be periodically checked and/or recalibrated. You will have to decide for yourself which better fits your pocketbook, and purpose.

Special Tools

Normally, the use of special factory tools is avoided for repair procedures, since these are not readily available for the do-it-yourself mechanic. When it is possible to perform the job with more commonly available tools, it will be pointed out, but occasionally, a special tool was designed to perform a specific function and should be used. Before substituting another tool, you should be convinced that neither your safety nor the performance of the vehicle will be compromised.

Special tools can usually be purchased from an automotive parts store or from your dealer. In some cases special tools may be available directly from the tool manufacturer.

SERVICING YOUR VEHICLE SAFELY

▶ **See Figures 16, 17 and 18**

It is virtually impossible to anticipate all of the hazards involved with automotive maintenance and service, but care and common sense will prevent most accidents.

The rules of safety for mechanics range from "don't smoke around gasoline," to "use the proper tool(s) for the job." The trick to avoiding injuries is to develop safe work habits and to take every possible precaution.

Do's

- Do keep a fire extinguisher and first aid kit handy.
- Do wear safety glasses or goggles when cutting, drilling, grinding or prying, even if you have 20–20 vision. If you wear glasses for the sake of vision, wear safety goggles over your regular glasses.
- Do shield your eyes whenever you work around the battery. Batteries contain sulfuric acid. In case of contact with, flush the area with water or a mixture of water and baking soda, then seek immediate medical attention.
- Do use safety stands (jackstands) for any undervehicle service. Jacks are for raising vehicles; jackstands are for making sure the vehicle stays raised until you want it to come down.
- Do use adequate ventilation when working with any chemicals or hazardous materials. Like carbon monoxide, the asbestos dust resulting from some brake lining wear can be hazardous in sufficient quantities.
- Do disconnect the negative battery cable when working on the electrical

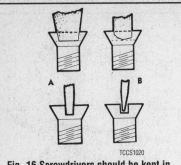

Fig. 16 Screwdrivers should be kept in good condition to prevent injury or damage which could result if the blade slips from the screw

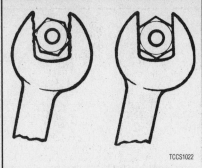

Fig. 17 Using the correct size wrench will help prevent the possibility of rounding off a nut

Fig. 18 NEVER work under a vehicle unless it is supported using safety stands (jackstands)

system. The secondary ignition system contains EXTREMELY HIGH VOLTAGE. In some cases it can even exceed 50,000 volts.

• Do follow manufacturer's directions whenever working with potentially hazardous materials. Most chemicals and fluids are poisonous.

• Do properly maintain your tools. Loose hammerheads, mushroomed punches and chisels, frayed or poorly grounded electrical cords, excessively worn screwdrivers, spread wrenches (open end), cracked sockets, slipping ratchets, or faulty droplight sockets can cause accidents.

• Likewise, keep your tools clean; a greasy wrench can slip off a bolt head, ruining the bolt and often harming your knuckles in the process.

• Do use the proper size and type of tool for the job at hand. Do select a wrench or socket that fits the nut or bolt. The wrench or socket should sit straight, not cocked.

• Do, when possible, pull on a wrench handle rather than push on it, and adjust your stance to prevent a fall.

• Do be sure that adjustable wrenches are tightly closed on the nut or bolt and pulled so that the force is on the side of the fixed jaw.

• Do strike squarely with a hammer; avoid glancing blows.

• Do set the parking brake and block the drive wheels if the work requires a running engine.

Don'ts

• Don't run the engine in a garage or anywhere else without proper ventilation—EVER! Carbon monoxide is poisonous; it takes a long time to leave the human body and you can build up a deadly supply of it in your system by simply breathing in a little at a time. You may not realize you are slowly poisoning yourself. Always use power vents, windows, fans and/or open the garage door.

• Don't work around moving parts while wearing loose clothing. Short

sleeves are much safer than long, loose sleeves. Hard-toed shoes with neoprene soles protect your toes and give a better grip on slippery surfaces. Watches and jewelry is not safe working around a vehicle. Long hair should be tied back under a hat or cap.

• Don't use pockets for toolboxes. A fall or bump can drive a screwdriver deep into your body. Even a rag hanging from your back pocket can wrap around a spinning shaft or fan.

• Don't smoke when working around gasoline, cleaning solvent or other flammable material.

• Don't smoke when working around the battery. When the battery is being charged, it gives off explosive hydrogen gas.

• Don't use gasoline to wash your hands; there are excellent soaps available. Gasoline contains dangerous additives which can enter the body through a cut or through your pores. Gasoline also removes all the natural oils from the skin so that bone dry hands will suck up oil and grease.

• Don't service the air conditioning system unless you are equipped with the necessary tools and training. When liquid or compressed gas refrigerant is released to atmospheric pressure it will absorb heat from whatever it contacts. This will chill or freeze anything it touches.

• Don't use screwdrivers for anything other than driving screws! A screwdriver used as an prying tool can snap when you least expect it, causing injuries. At the very least, you'll ruin a good screwdriver.

• Don't use an emergency jack (that little ratchet, scissors, or pantograph jack supplied with the vehicle) for anything other than changing a flat! These jacks are only intended for emergency use out on the road; they are NOT designed as a maintenance tool. If you are serious about maintaining your vehicle yourself, invest in a hydraulic floor jack of at least a 1½ ton capacity, and at least two sturdy jackstands.

SERIAL NUMBER IDENTIFICATION

Vehicle Identification Number

▶ See Figures 19, 20, 21 and 22

The vehicle serial number is stamped on the left side of the frame behind the front wheel (Pick-Ups) or on the right side of the firewall (Land Cruiser) on 1970–79 models. It can also be found stamped on a metal tag, fastened to the driver's side door pillar (all models).

On 1980–83 models, the number is located both on the right front fender apron in the engine compartment (Pick-Ups) or on the right side of the firewall (Land Cruiser), and on the driver's side door pillar.

All 1984–88 models have the vehicle identification number stamped on a plate attached to the left side of the instrument panel. The plate is visible through the windshield. The VIN is also stamped on a plate attached to the right front fender apron with the exception of the Land Cruiser where it still found on the right side of the firewall and additionally on the driver's side door pillar.

The serial number on all 1970–80 models consists of a series identification (see chart) followed by a six digit production number. The serial number on all 1981–88 models has been changed to the 17-digit format. The first three digits are the World Manufacturer Identification number. The next five digits are the

Vehicle Description Section (same as the series identification number above). The remaining nine digits are the production numbers.

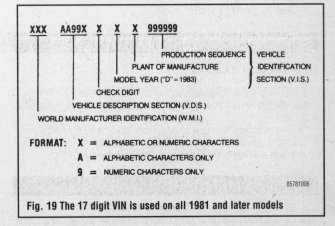

Fig. 19 The 17 digit VIN is used on all 1981 and later models

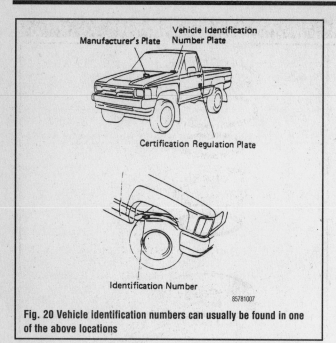

Fig. 20 Vehicle identification numbers can usually be found in one of the above locations

Engine

♦ See Figure 23

The engine serial number consists of an engine series identification number followed by a six digit production number.

8R-C, F, 2F AND 3F-E ENGINES

The serial number is stamped on the right side of the engine block beside the fuel pump (except on fuel injected engines).

18R-C ENGINES

The 2000cc model 18R-C engine has its serial number stamped on the left side of the engine below the number one spark plug.

20R, 22R, 22R-E, 22R-TE AND 3VZ-E ENGINES

On these engines the serial number is stamped on the left side of the cylinder block, behind the alternator.

1L, 2L AND 2L-T ENGINES

On these engines the serial number is stamped on the left side of the cylinder block, under the manifold.

Fig. 21 Vehicle model number

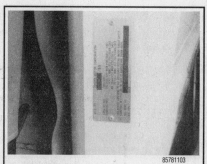

Fig. 22 Vehicle identification number and production date

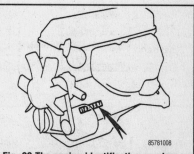

Fig. 23 The engine identification number is stamped somewhere on the side of the engine block

Engine Identification

Year	Model	Engine Displacement cu. in. (cc)	Engine Series Identification	No. of Cylinders	Engine Type
1970–71	Pick-Up	113.8 (1858)	8R-C	4	SOHC
1972–74	Pick-Up	120.7 (1980)	18R-C	4	SOHC
1975–80	Pick-Up	133.3 (2189)	20R	4	SOHC
1981–83	Pick-Up	144.4 (2367)	22R	4	SOHC
		133.5 (2188)	1L	4	Diesel/SOHC
1984–88	Pick-Up/4 Runner	144.4 (2367)	22R, 22R-E	4	SOHC
		144.4 (2367)	22R-TE	4	Turbo/SOHC
		149.3 (2447)	2L	4	Diesel/SOHC
		149.3 (2447)	2L-T	4	Turbo Diesel/SOHC
		180.0 (2950)	3VZ-E	6	SOHC
1970–74	Land Cruiser	236.7 (3878)	F	6	OHV
1975–87	Land Cruiser	257.9 (4200)	2F	6	OHV
1988	Land Cruiser	241.3 (3955)	3F-E	6	OHV

SOHC: Single Overhead Camshaft
OHV: Overhead Valve

85781C02

ROUTINE MAINTENANCE

Air Cleaner

REMOVAL & INSTALLATION

Oil Bath Type

▶ See Figure 24

Clean the element and replace the oil in the oil bath type air cleaner every 3,000 miles (4,800 km) or sooner in dusty areas.

Remove the air cleaner assembly from the vehicle and disassemble the various parts. Remove any rubber or plastic hoses that are connected to the air cleaner. Remove the oil from the oil cup and scrape out all the dirt inside and the bottom. Wash the cup with a safe solvent, such as kerosene. Refill the oil cup to the level mark with the same weight (SAE) oil as is being used in the engine at that particular time. If it is cold and you are using a light viscosity oil in the engine, use a light viscosity oil in the air filter. If you are using a heavier oil in the crankcase for warm weather, use the same, heavier oil in the oil bath air cleaner. Soak the filter element in the same safe solvent as the oil cup. Agitate the element thoroughly in the cleaning solution to remove all dirt particles. Dry the element thoroughly with compressed air. Reassemble the air cleaner assembly and reinstall it on the engine to the reverse order of disassembly and removal.

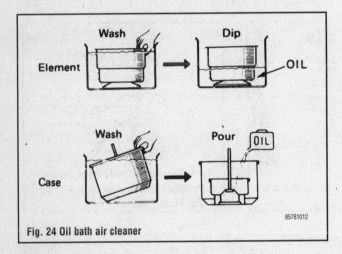

Fig. 24 Oil bath air cleaner

Dry Type

▶ See Figure 25

The element should be replaced at the recommended intervals shown in the Maintenance Intervals chart later in this section. If your truck is operated under severely dusty conditions or severe operating conditions, more frequent changes will certainly be necessary. Inspect the element at least twice a year. Early spring and early fall are always good times for inspection. Remove the element and check for any perforations or tears in the filter. Check the cleaner housing for signs of dirt or dust that may have leaked through the filter element or in through the snorkel tube. Position a droplight on one side of the element and look through the filter at the light. If no glow of light can be seen through the element material, replace the filter. If holes in the filter element are apparent or signs of dirt seepage through the filter are evident, replace the filter.

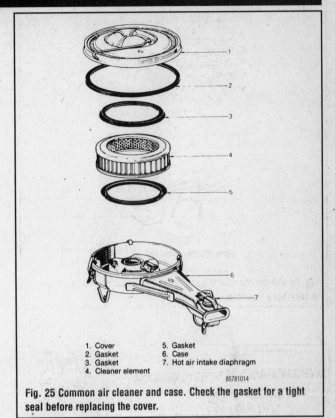

1. Cover
2. Gasket
3. Gasket
4. Cleaner element
5. Gasket
6. Case
7. Hot air intake diaphragm

Fig. 25 Common air cleaner and case. Check the gasket for a tight seal before replacing the cover.

AIR CLEANER ASSEMBLY

▶ See Figures 26 thru 36

1. Disconnect all hoses, ducts and vacuum tubes from the air cleaner assembly.
2. Remove the top cover wing nut (two on the Land Cruiser) and grommet (if equipped). Most models will also utilize three or four side clips to further secure the top of the assembly, simply pull the wire tab and release the clip; in fact air cleaners on fuel injected engines are secured solely by means of clips (air box-to-cleaner housing). Remove the cover and lift out the filter element. On fuel injected engines, simply lift up on the air box and slide out the filter.
3. Remove any side mount brackets and/or retaining bolts and lift off the air cleaner assembly. Remove only the lower filter housing box on fuel injected engines.

To install:

4. Clean or replace the filter element as detailed previously. Wipe clean all surfaces of the air cleaner housing and cover. Check the condition of the mounting gasket and replace it if it appears worn or broken.
5. Reposition the air cleaner assembly and install the mounting bracket and/or bolts.
6. Reposition the filter element in the case and install the cover being careful not to overtighten the wingnut(s). On round-style cleaners (carbureted engines), be certain that the arrows on the cover lid and the snorkel match up properly.

➡**Filter elements on fuel injected engines have a TOP and BOTTOM side, be sure they are inserted correctly.**

7. Reconnect all hoses, ductwork and vacuum lines.

➡**Never operate the engine without the air filter element in place.**

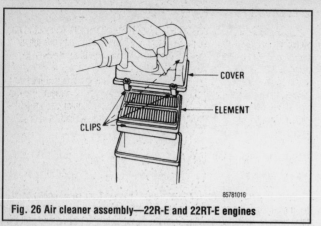

Fig. 26 Air cleaner assembly—22R-E and 22RT-E engines

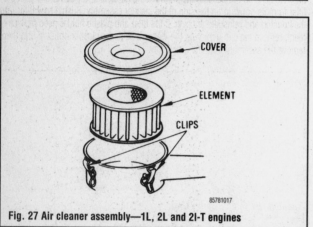

Fig. 27 Air cleaner assembly—1L, 2L and 2I-T engines

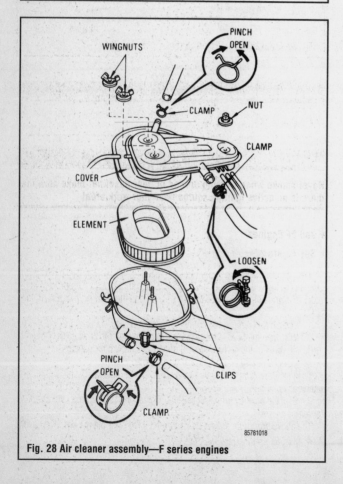

Fig. 28 Air cleaner assembly—F series engines

Fig. 29 Remove the wing nut on the air cleaner assembly

Fig. 30 Remove the side clips on the air cleaner assembly

Fig. 31 Remove the emission hose on the air cleaner assembly

Fig. 32 Remove the air cleaner element

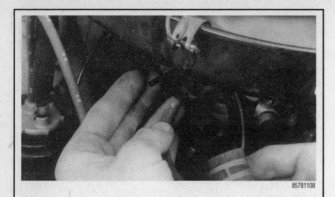

Fig. 33 Install the related hoses on the air cleaner assembly

Fig. 34 Remove the hold down bolt on air cleaner assembly

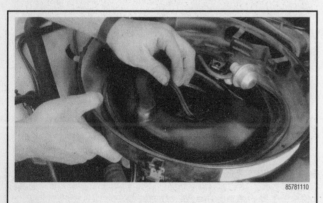

Fig. 35 Remove the center gasket on the air cleaner assembly

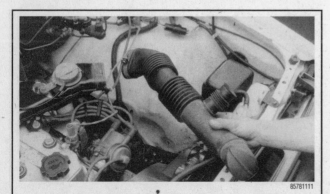

Fig. 36 Remove the duct work on the air cleaner assembly

AIR CLEANER ELEMENT

The element can, in most cases be replaced by removing the wingnut(s) and side clips as already detailed. Remember that on fuel injected engines the air box should not be removed, just lifted upward carefully until the element is accessible.

On certain Land Cruisers with diesel engines that utilize a cyclone-type air cleaner, there is also a dust cup that should be cleaned. It's underneath the regular air cleaner assembly and can be opened just like the regular cleaner (side-clips!). Once the top is off, carefully clean out any dust or accumulated crud with a rag.

Crankcase Ventilation Filter

▶ See Figure 37

Certain models may also utilize a cleaner-mounted crankcase ventilation filter, if so, it should also be cleaned or replaced at the same time as the regular filter element. To replace the filter, remove the air cleaner top cover and pull the filter from its housing on the side of the cleaner assembly. Push a new filter into the housing and reinstall the cover. If the filter and plastic holder need replacement, remove the clip mounting the feeder tube to the cleaner housing and then remove the assembly from the air cleaner.

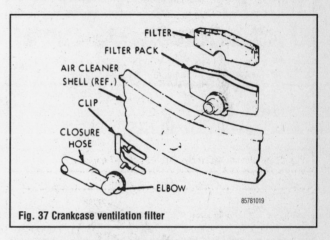

Fig. 37 Crankcase ventilation filter

Fuel Filter

REMOVAL & INSTALLATION

❋❋ CAUTION

Never smoke when working around or near gasoline! Make sure that there is no active ignition source near your work area!

F and 2F Engines

▶ See Figure 38

The Land Cruiser uses a cartridge type fuel filter with a disposable element. The filter is located in the fuel line. It should not be necessary to remove it in order to change the disposable element. To replace the element, proceed as follows:

1. Loosen and remove the nut on the filter bowl bail.
2. Withdraw the bowl, element spring, element and the bowl gasket.
3. Wash all of the parts in solvent and examine them for damage.
4. Install a new filter element and bowl gasket.
5. Install the components in the reverse order of removal. Do not fully tighten the bail nut.
6. Seat the bowl by turning it slightly. Tighten the bail nut fully and check for leaks.

The above procedure should be performed if the clear glass bowl fills up with water or every 12,000 miles (20,000 km).

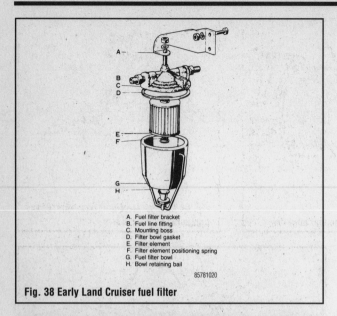

A. Fuel filter bracket
B. Fuel line fitting
C. Mounting boss
D. Filter bowl gasket
E. Filter element
F. Filter element positioning spring
G. Fuel filter bowl
H. Bowl retaining bail

Fig. 38 Early Land Cruiser fuel filter

✳✳ CAUTION

Do not have any open flame nearby while servicing the fuel filter because of the presence of flammable gasoline vapors.

3F-E Engines

1. Unbolt the retaining screws and remove the protective shield from the fuel filter.
2. Place a pan under the delivery pipe (large connection) to catch the dripping fuel and SLOWLY loosen the union bolt to bleed off the fuel pressure.
3. Remove the union bolt and drain the remaining fuel.
4. Disconnect and plug the inlet line.
5. Unbolt and remove the fuel filter.

➡**When tightening the fuel line bolts to the fuel filter, you must use a torque wrench. The tightening torque is very important, as under or over tightening may cause fuel leakage. Insure that there is not fuel line interference and that there is sufficient clearance between it and any other components.**

6. Coat the flare unit, union nut and all bolt threads with engine oil.
7. Hand tighten the inlet line to the fuel filter.
8. Install the fuel filter and then tighten the inlet line nut to 22 ft. lbs. (29 Nm).
9. Reconnect the delivery pipe using new gaskets and then tighten the union bolt to 22 ft. lbs. (29 Nm).
10. Run the engine for a few minutes and check for any fuel leaks.
11. Install the protective shield.

8R-C Engines

▶ **See Figure 39**

It is not necessary to remove the filter unit to replace the element.
1. Loosen and remove the nut on the filter bowl bail.
2. Take out the bowl, element spring, element, and bowl gasket.
3. Wash the parts (except for the element—discard that) in solvent and inspect for damage. Install a new filter element, and if its condition warrants, a new gasket.
4. After reinstalling the parts, do not fully tighten the bail nut.
5. Seat the bowl by turning it slightly, pressing gently against the gasket. Tighten the bail nut fully and check for leaks.

18R-C Engines

▶ **See Figure 40**

The entire fuel filter is replaced on these engines.
1. Unfasten the fuel intake hose. Use a wrench to loosen the attachment nut, and another wrench on the opposite side to keep the filter from turning.
2. Remove the flexible fuel line from the other side of the filter. Unfasten the attaching screws from the filter bracket.
3. Install the new filter and reconnect the fuel lines. Start the engine and check for leaks.

20R and 22R Engines

▶ **See Figure 41**

The entire fuel filter is replaced on these engines.
1. Using a pair of pliers, expand the hose clamp on one side of the filter, and slide the clamp further down the hose, past the point to which the filter pipe extends. Remove the other clamp in the same manner.
2. Grasp the hoses near the ends and twist them gently to pull them free from the filter pipes.
3. Pull the filter from the clip and discard.
4. Install the new filter into the clip. The arrow must point towards the hose that runs to the carburetor. Push the hoses onto the filter pipes, and slide the clamps back into position. Start the engine and check for leaks.

22R-E, 22R-TE and 3VZ-E Engines

▶ **See Figures 42, 43, 44 and 45**

1. Unbolt the retaining screws and remove the protective shield from the fuel filter.
2. Place a pan under the delivery pipe (large connection) to catch the dripping fuel and SLOWLY loosen the union bolt to bleed off the fuel pressure.
3. Remove the union bolt and drain the remaining fuel.
4. Disconnect and plug the inlet line.
5. Unbolt and remove the fuel filter.

➡**When tightening the fuel line bolts to the fuel filter, you must use a torque wrench. The tightening torque is very important, as under or over tightening may cause fuel leakage. Insure that there is not fuel line interference and that there is sufficient clearance between it and any other components.**

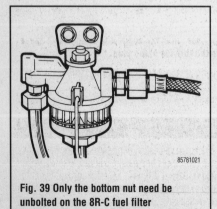

Fig. 39 Only the bottom nut need be unbolted on the 8R-C fuel filter

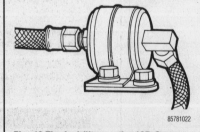

Fig. 40 The fuel filter on the 18R-C engines will either have two nuts, as illustrated here, or a nut on one side and a clamp on the other. Be sure you get the correct replacement filter for your truck

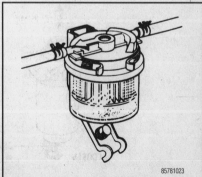

Fig. 41 The arrow on the 20R fuel filter must point toward the carburetor line

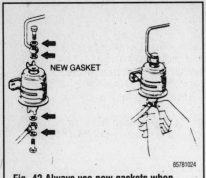

Fig. 42 Always use new gaskets when installing the fuel filter on fuel injected engines

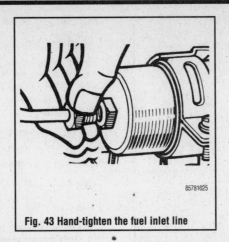

Fig. 43 Hand-tighten the fuel inlet line

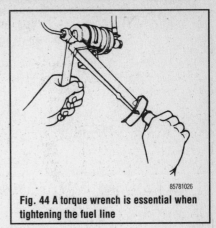

Fig. 44 A torque wrench is essential when tightening the fuel line

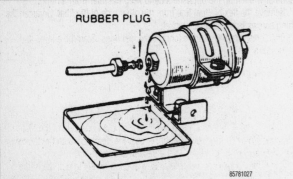

Fig. 45 When removing the fuel lines, it is always a good idea to place a pan underneath to catch any dripping fuel

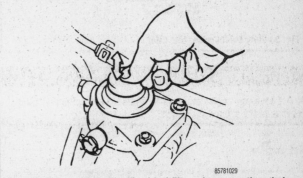

Fig. 47 When replacing the diesel fuel filter, always use the priming pump to fill the filter with fuel before starting the engine

6. Coat the flare unit, union nut and all bolt threads with engine oil.

7. Hand tighten the inlet line to the fuel filter.

8. Install the fuel filter and then tighten the inlet line nut to 22 ft. lbs. (29 Nm).

9. Reconnect the delivery pipe using new gaskets and then tighten the union bolt to 22 ft. lbs. (29 Nm).

10. Run the engine for a few minutes and check for any fuel leaks.

11. Install the protective shield.

1L, 2L and 2L-T Engines

▶ See Figures 46 and 47

1. Disconnect the fuel level warning switch connector at the lower end of the filter.

2. Drain the fuel from the filter (see Section 5), loosen the two mounting bolts and remove the filter.

3. Remove the water level warning switch from the filter housing and then

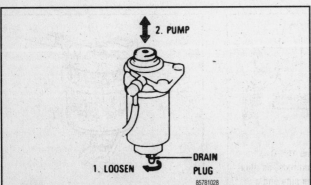

Fig. 46 When draining water from the diesel fuel filter, turn the drain plug counterclockwise

unscrew the filter from the housing. An oil filter strap wrench may come in handy when removing the filter.

4. Install the water level warning switch using a new O-ring.

5. Coat the filter gasket lightly with diesel fuel and then screw it in hand tight. Next, use the strap wrench and turn the filter ¾ turn more.

6. Mount the filter assembly, tighten the bolts and connect the warning switch.

7. Using the priming pump on top of the filter, fill the filter with fuel and check for leaks.

DRAINING THE DIESEL FUEL FILTER

✷✷ CAUTION

When the fuel filter warning light or buzzer comes on, the water in the fuel filter must be drained immediately.

1. Raise the hood and position a small pan or jar underneath the drain plug to catch the water about to be released.

2. Reach under the fuel filter and turn the drain plug counterclockwise about 2-2½ turns.

➡Loosening the drain plug more than the suggested amount will cause water to ooze from around the threads of the plug.

3. Depress the priming pump on top of the filter housing until fuel is the only substance being forced out.

4. Retighten the drain plug by hand only, do not use a wrench.

PCV Valve

The PCV valve regulates crankcase ventilation during various engine operating conditions. At high vacuum (idle speed and partial load range) it will open slightly and at low vacuum (full throttle) it will open fully. This causes vapor to be removed from the crankcase by the engine vacuum and then sucked into the combustion chamber where it is dissipated.

➡ The PCV system will not function properly unless the oil filler cap is tightly sealed. Check the gasket on the cap and be certain it is not leaking. Replace the cap or gasket or both if necessary to ensure proper sealing.

REMOVAL & INSTALLATION

▶ See Figures 48 thru 53

1. Check the ventilation hoses and lines for leaks or clogging. Clean or replace as necessary.
2. Locate the PCV valve in the cylinder head cover and remove it by pulling it upward.
3. Blow into the crankcase end of the valve. There should be free passage of air through the valve.
4. Blow into the intake manifold end of the valve. There should be little or no passage of air through the valve.
5. If the PCV valve failed either of the preceding two checks, it will require replacement.
6. To install, simply slip the hose back onto the proper end of the PCV valve and then press it into the retaining grommet in the cylinder head cover.
7. For further information on the PCV system, please refer to Section 4.

➡ On models with fuel injection, there is no PCV valve. Vapor passage in the ventilation lines is controlled by two orifices. To check the PCV system on these models, inspect the hoses for cracks, leaks or other visible damage. Blow through the orifices to make sure they are not blocked. Replace any components as necessary.

Heat Riser

SERVICING

Certain early models may have been equipped with exhaust control valves (heat risers) which would be located near the head pipe connection in the exhaust manifold. The valves aid initial warm-up during particularly cold weather by slightly restricting the gas flow. The resultant heat generated by this restriction is transferred to the intake manifold where it results in improved fuel vaporization.

The operation of this valve should be checked every 6 months or 6,000 miles (9,600 km). If the valve appears to be sticking, lubricate the shaft bushings lightly with penetrating oil and then operate the valve manually a few times to work in the lubricant. If this is no help, replace the entire valve.

Evaporative Emission Control Canister

▶ See Figures 54 and 55

There is no charcoal canister for 1970-71 engines. It can be found on the front of the left fender on late 1971-74 trucks and at the rear of the engine compartment, on or near the firewall on 1975 and later trucks (if so equipped).

The canister functions to cycle the fuel vapor from the fuel tank and carburetor float chambers into the intake manifold and eventually into the cylinders for combustion. The activated charcoal element within the canister acts as a storage device for the fuel vapors at times when the engine operating conditions are not conducive to the efficient burning of the vapors.

The only required service for the canister inspection at the intervals specified in the Maintenance Chart at the end of this section. If the charcoal element is gummed up, the entire canister will require replacement. Disconnect the canister purge hoses, loosen the retaining bracket bolt(s) and lift out the canister. Installation is simply the reverse of the removal process.

Case Storage System

1970–71 trucks use a case storage system in lieu of the charcoal canister. This system's basic function is to prevent the escape of fuel vapors by routing them into a storage case for later combustion. The only scheduled maintenance for this system is the replacement of the system's air filter every 12,000 miles (20,000 km). The filter is located above the fuel vapor storage case, next to the fuel filler cap. Unplug the old filter from the hose, discard it, and insert the new filter.

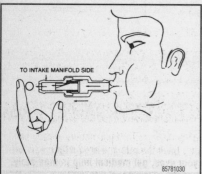

Fig. 48 Air should pass through the PCV valve when blowing into the crankcase side

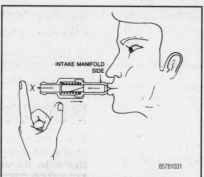

Fig. 49 Air should not pass through the PCV valve when blowing through the intake manifold side

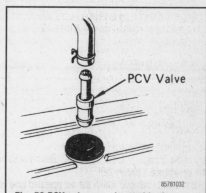

Fig. 50 PCV valves are located in the cylinder head cover

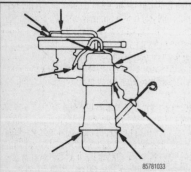

Fig. 51 Check all PCV valve hoses, connections and cracks for cracks and brittleness

Fig. 52 Removing the PCV valve hose

Fig. 53 Removing the PCV valve

Fig. 54 Using compressed air to clean the charcoal canister

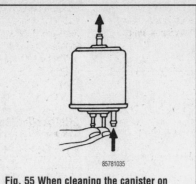

Fig. 55 When cleaning the canister on later models, blow air into the outer vent pipe while plugging the other two

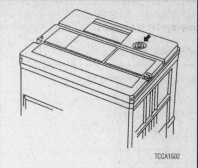

Fig. 56 Maintenance-free batteries usually contain a built-in hydrometer to check fluid level

Battery

PRECAUTIONS

Always use caution when working on or near the battery. Never allow a tool to bridge the gap between the negative and positive battery terminals. Also, be careful not to allow a tool to provide a ground between the positive cable/terminal and any metal component on the vehicle. Either of these conditions will cause a short circuit, leading to sparks and possible personal injury.

Do not smoke or all open flames/sparks near a battery; the gases contained in the battery are very explosive and, if ignited, could cause severe injury or death.

All batteries, regardless of type, should be carefully secured by a battery hold-down device. If not, the terminals or casing may crack from stress during vehicle operation. A battery which is not secured may allow acid to leak, making it discharge faster. The acid can also eat away at components under the hood.

Always inspect the battery case for cracks, leakage and corrosion. A white corrosive substance on the battery case or on nearby components would indicate a leaking or cracked battery. If the battery is cracked, it should be replaced immediately.

GENERAL MAINTENANCE

Always keep the battery cables and terminals free of corrosion. Check and clean these components about once a year.

Keep the top of the battery clean, as a film of dirt can help discharge a battery that is not used for long periods. A solution of baking soda and water may be used for cleaning, but be careful to flush this off with clear water. DO NOT let any of the solution into the filler holes. Baking soda neutralizes battery acid and will de-activate a battery cell.

Batteries in vehicles which are not operated on a regular basis can fall victim to parasitic loads (small current drains which are constantly drawing current from the battery). Normal parasitic loads may drain a battery on a vehicle that is in storage and not used for 6–8 weeks. Vehicles that have additional accessories such as a phone or an alarm system may discharge a battery sooner. If the vehicle is to be stored for longer periods in a secure area and the alarm system is not necessary, the negative battery cable should be disconnected to protect the battery.

Remember that constantly deep cycling a battery (completely discharging and recharging it) will shorten battery life.

BATTERY FLUID

▶ **See Figure 56**

Check the battery electrolyte level at least once a month, or more often in hot weather or during periods of extended vehicle operation. On non-sealed batteries, the level can be checked either through the case (if translucent) or by removing the cell caps. The electrolyte level in each cell should be kept filled to the split ring inside each cell, or the line marked on the outside of the case.

If the level is low, add only distilled water through the opening until the level is correct. Each cell must be checked and filled individually. Distilled water should be used, because the chemicals and minerals found in most drinking water are harmful to the battery and could significantly shorten its life.

If water is added in freezing weather, the vehicle should be driven several miles to allow the water to mix with the electrolyte. Otherwise, the battery could freeze.

Although some maintenance-free batteries have removable cell caps, the electrolyte condition and level on all sealed maintenance-free batteries must be checked using the built-in hydrometer "eye." The exact type of eye will vary. But, most battery manufacturers, apply a sticker to the battery itself explaining the readings.

➡**Although the readings from built-in hydrometers will vary, a green eye usually indicates a properly charged battery with sufficient fluid level. A dark eye is normally an indicator of a battery with sufficient fluid, but which is low in charge. A light or yellow eye usually indicates that electrolyte has dropped below the necessary level. In this last case, sealed batteries with an insufficient electrolyte must usually be discarded.**

Checking the Specific Gravity

▶ **See Figures 57, 58 and 59**

A hydrometer is required to check the specific gravity on all batteries that are not maintenance-free. On batteries that are maintenance-free, the specific gravity is checked by observing the built-in hydrometer "eye" on the top of the battery case.

※ CAUTION

Battery electrolyte contains sulfuric acid. If you should splash any on your skin or in your eyes, flush the affected area with plenty of clear water. If it lands in your eyes, get medical help immediately.

The fluid (sulfuric acid solution) contained in the battery cells will tell you many things about the condition of the battery. Because the cell plates must be kept submerged below the fluid level in order to operate, the fluid level is extremely important. And, because the specific gravity of the acid is an indication of electrical charge, testing the fluid can be an aid in determining if the battery must be replaced. A battery in a vehicle with a properly operating charging system should require little maintenance, but careful, periodic inspection should reveal problems before they leave you stranded.

At least once a year, check the specific gravity of the battery. It should be between 1.20 and 1.26 on the gravity scale. Most auto stores carry a variety of inexpensive battery hydrometers. These can be used on any non-sealed battery to test the specific gravity in each cell.

The battery testing hydrometer has a squeeze bulb at one end and a nozzle at the other. Battery electrolyte is sucked into the hydrometer until the float is lifted from its seat. The specific gravity is then read by noting the position of the float. If gravity is low in one or more cells, the battery should be slowly charged and checked again to see if the gravity has come up. Generally, if after charging, the specific gravity between any two cells varies more than 50 points (0.50), the battery should be replaced, as it can no longer produce sufficient voltage to guarantee proper operation.

Fig. 57 On non-sealed batteries, the fluid level can be checked by removing the cell caps

Fig. 58 If the fluid level is low, add only distilled water until the level is correct

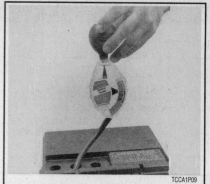

Fig. 59 Check the specific gravity of the battery's electrolyte with a hydrometer

CABLES

▶ **See Figures 60, 61, 62 and 63**

Once a year (or as necessary), the battery terminals and the cable clamps should be cleaned. Loosen the clamps and remove the cables, negative cable first. On top post batteries, the use of a puller specially made for this purpose is recommended. These are inexpensive and available in most parts stores. Side terminal battery cables are secured with a small bolt.

Clean the cable clamps and the battery terminal with a wire brush, until all corrosion, grease, etc., is removed and the metal is shiny. It is especially important to clean the inside of the clamp thoroughly (an old knife is useful here), since a small deposit of oxidation there will prevent a sound connection and inhibit starting or charging. Special tools are available for cleaning these parts, one type for conventional top post batteries and another type for side terminal

Fig. 60 The underside of this special battery tool has a wire brush to clean post terminals

batteries. It is also a good idea to apply some dielectric grease to the terminal, as this will aid in the prevention of corrosion.

After the clamps and terminals are clean, reinstall the cables, negative cable last; DO NOT hammer the clamps onto battery posts. Tighten the clamps securely, but do not distort them. Give the clamps and terminals a thin external coating of grease after installation, to retard corrosion.

Check the cables at the same time that the terminals are cleaned. If the cable insulation is cracked or broken, or if the ends are frayed, the cable should be replaced with a new cable of the same length and gauge.

CHARGING

✳✳ CAUTION

The chemical reaction which takes place in all batteries generates explosive hydrogen gas. A spark can cause the battery to explode and splash acid. To avoid personal injury, be sure there is proper ventilation and take appropriate fire safety precautions when working with or near a battery.

A battery should be charged at a slow rate to keep the plates inside from getting too hot. However, if some maintenance-free batteries are allowed to discharge until they are almost "dead," they may have to be charged at a high rate to bring them back to "life." Always follow the charger manufacturer's instructions on charging the battery.

REPLACEMENT

When it becomes necessary to replace the battery, select one with an amperage rating equal to or greater than the battery originally installed. Deterioration and just plain aging of the battery cables, starter motor, and associated wires makes the battery's job harder in successive years. This makes it prudent to install a new battery with a greater capacity than the old.

Fig. 61 Place the tool over the battery posts and twist to clean until the metal is shiny

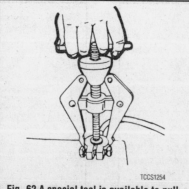

Fig. 62 A special tool is available to pull the clamp from the post

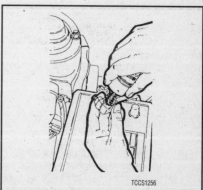

Fig. 63 The cable ends should be cleaned as well

Drive Belts

INSPECTION

▶ **See Figures 64 thru 71**

Check the condition of the drive belts and check the belt tension at least every 15,000 miles (24,000 km).

1. Inspect the belts for signs of glazing or cracking. A glazed belt will be perfectly smooth from slippage, while a good belt will have a slight texture of fabric visible. Cracks will generally start at the inner edge of the belt and run outward. Replace the belt at the first sign of cracking or if the glazing is severe.

2. Belt tension does not refer to play or droop. By placing your thumb midway between the two pulleys, it should be possible to depress the belt ¼-½ in.. If any of the belts can be depressed more than this, or cannot be depressed this much, adjust the tension. Inadequate tension will always result in slippage or wear, while excessive tension will damage pulley bearings and cause belts to fray and crack.

3. Its not a bad idea to replace all drive belts at 60,000 miles (96,000 km) regardless of their condition.

ADJUSTMENT

▶ **See Figures 72 thru 77**

Alternator

To adjust the tension of the alternator drive belt, loosen the pivot and mounting bolts on the alternator. Using a wooden hammer handle or a broomstick, or even your hand if you're strong enough, move the alternator one way or the other until the tension is within acceptable limits.

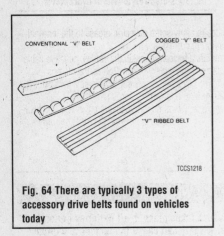

Fig. 64 There are typically 3 types of accessory drive belts found on vehicles today

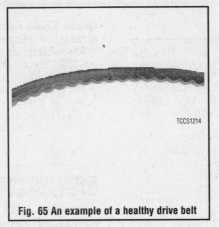

Fig. 65 An example of a healthy drive belt

Fig. 66 Deep cracks in this belt will cause flex, building up heat that will eventually lead to belt failure

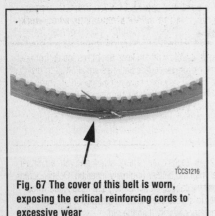

Fig. 67 The cover of this belt is worn, exposing the critical reinforcing cords to excessive wear

Fig. 68 Installing too wide a belt can result in serious belt wear and/or breakage

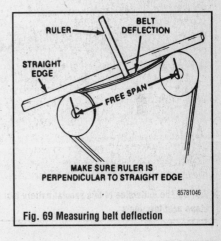

Fig. 69 Measuring belt deflection

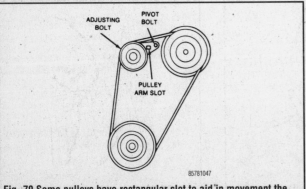
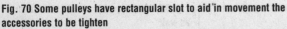

Fig. 70 Some pulleys have rectangular slot to aid in movement the accessories to be tighten

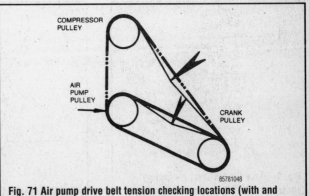

Fig. 71 Air pump drive belt tension checking locations (with and without A/C)

Fig. 72 To adjust the alternator drive belt, loosen the bottom bolt . . .

Fig. 73 . . . then loosen the adjusting (top) bolt and move the alternator as necessary to obtain the proper tension

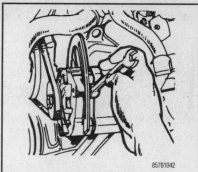

Fig. 74 To adjust belt tension or to replace belts, first loosen the components mounting and adjusting bolts slightly

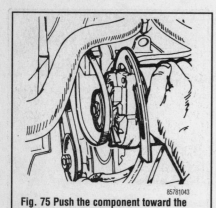

Fig. 75 Push the component toward the engine and slip off the belt

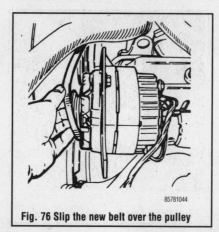

Fig. 76 Slip the new belt over the pulley

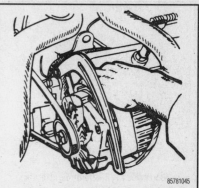

Fig. 77 Pull outward on the component and tighten the mounting bolts

✳✳ CAUTION

Never use a screwdriver or any other metal device such as a prybar, as a lever when adjusting the alternator belt tension.

Tighten the mounting bolts securely. If a new belt has been installed, always recheck the tension after a few hundred miles of driving.

Air Conditioning Compressor

A/C compressor belt tension can be adjusted by turning the tension adjusting bolt which is located on the compressor tensioner bracket. Turn the bolt clockwise to tighten the belt and counterclockwise to loosen it.

Air Pump

To adjust the tension of the air pump drive belt, loosen the adjusting lever bolt and then the pivot bolt. Move the pump in or out until the desired tension is achieved.

➡The tension should always be checked between the air pump and the crankshaft pulley on all trucks without air conditioning. On trucks with air conditioning, tension should be checked between the A/C compressor and the crankshaft pulley.

Power Steering Pump

Tension on the power steering belt is adjusted by means of an idler pulley. Turn the adjusting bolt on the idler pulley until the desired tension is achieved and the retighten the idler pulley lockbolt.

Hoses

✳✳ CAUTION

On models equipped with an electric cooling fan, disconnect the negative battery cable, or fan motor wiring harness connector before replacing any radiator/heater hose. The fan may come on, under certain circumstances, even though the ignition is Off.

INSPECTION

▶ **See Figures 78, 79, 80 and 81**

Inspect the condition of the radiator and heater hoses periodically. Early spring and at the beginning of the fall or winter, when you are performing other maintenance, are good times. Make sure the engine and cooling system are cold. Visually inspect for cracking, rotting or collapsed hoses, replace as necessary. Run your hand along the length of the hose. If a weak or swollen spot is noted when squeezing the hose wall, replace the hose.

REPLACEMENT

▶ **See Figures 82, 83, 84 and 85**

1. Drain the cooling system into a suitable container (if the coolant is to be reused).
2. Loosen the hose clamps at each end of the hose that requires replacement.
3. Twist, pull and slide the hose off the radiator, water pump, thermostat or heater connection.

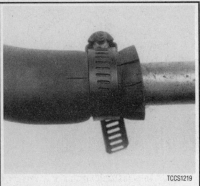

Fig. 78 The cracks developing along this hose are a result of age-related hardening

Fig. 79 A hose clamp that is too tight can cause older hoses to separate and tear on either side of the clamp

Fig. 80 A soft spongy hose (identifiable by the swollen section) will eventually burst and should be replaced

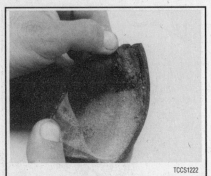

Fig. 81 Hoses are likely to deteriorate from the inside if the cooling system is not periodically flushed

Fig. 82 Removing the upper radiator hose

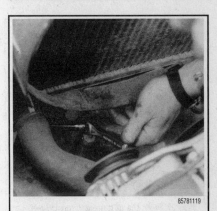

Fig. 83 Removing the lower radiator hose

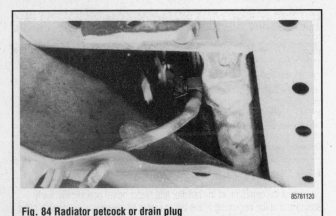

Fig. 84 Radiator petcock or drain plug

Fig. 85 Check or refill the coolant bottle after all repairs

To install:

4. Clean the hose mounting connections. Position the hose clamps on the new hose.

5. Coat the connection surfaces with a water resistant sealer and slide the hose into position. Make sure the hose clamps are located beyond the raised bead of the connector (if equipped) and centered in the clamping area of the connection.

6. Tighten the clamps to 20-30 inch lbs. Do not overtighten.

7. Fill the cooling system.

8. Start the engine and allow it to reach normal operating temperature. Check for leaks.

Air Conditioning System

SYSTEM SERVICE & REPAIR

➡ **It is recommended that the A/C system be serviced by an EPA Section 609 certified automotive technician utilizing a refrigerant recovery/recycling machine.**

The do-it-yourselfer should not service his/her own vehicle's A/C system for many reasons, including legal concerns, personal injury, environmental damage and cost.

According to the U.S. Clean Air Act, it is a federal crime to service or repair (involving the refrigerant) a Motor Vehicle Air Conditioning (MVAC) system for money without being EPA certified. It is also illegal to vent R-12 refrigerant into the atmosphere. State and/or local laws may be more strict than the federal regulations, so be sure to check with your state and/or local authorities for further information.

➡ **Federal law dictates that a fine of up to $25,000 may be levied on people convicted of venting refrigerant into the atmosphere.**

When servicing an A/C system you run the risk of handling or coming in contact with refrigerant, which may result in skin or eye irritation or frostbite.

Although low in toxicity (due to chemical stability), inhalation of concentrated refrigerant fumes is dangerous and can result in death; cases of fatal cardiac arrhythmia have been reported in people accidentally subjected to high levels of refrigerant. Some early symptoms include loss of concentration and drowsiness.

Also, some refrigerants can decompose at high temperatures (near gas heaters or open flame), which may result in hydrofluoric acid, hydrochloric acid and phosgene (a fatal nerve gas).

It is usually more economically feasible to have a certified MVAC automotive technician perform A/C system service on your vehicle.

PREVENTIVE MAINTENANCE

Although the A/C system should not be serviced by the do-it-yourselfer, preventive maintenance should be practiced to help maintain the efficiency of the vehicle's A/C system. Be sure to perform the following:

• The easiest and most important preventive maintenance for your A/C system is to be sure that it is used on a regular basis. Running the system for five minutes each month (no matter what the season) will help ensure that the seals and all internal components remain lubricated.

➡**Some vehicles automatically operate the A/C system compressor whenever the windshield defroster is activated. Therefore, the A/C system would not need to be operated each month if the defroster was used.**

• In order to prevent heater core freeze-up during A/C operation, it is necessary to maintain proper antifreeze protection. Be sure to properly maintain the engine cooling system.

• Any obstruction of or damage to the condenser configuration will restrict air flow which is essential to its efficient operation. Keep this unit clean and in proper physical shape.

➡**Bug screens which are mounted in front of the condenser (unless they are original equipment) are regarded as obstructions.**

• The condensation drain tube expels any water which accumulates on the bottom of the evaporator housing into the engine compartment. If this tube is obstructed, the air conditioning performance can be restricted and condensation buildup can spill over onto the vehicle's floor.

SYSTEM INSPECTION

Although the A/C system should not be serviced by the do-it-yourselfer, system inspections should be performed to help maintain the efficiency of the vehicle's A/C system. Be sure to perform the following:

The easiest and often most important check for the air conditioning system consists of a visual inspection of the system components. Visually inspect the system for refrigerant leaks, damaged compressor clutch, abnormal compressor drive belt tension and/or condition, plugged evaporator drain tube, blocked condenser fins, disconnected or broken wires, blown fuses, corroded connections and poor insulation.

A refrigerant leak will usually appear as an oily residue at the leakage point in the system. The oily residue soon picks up dust or dirt particles from the surrounding air and appears greasy. Through time, this will build up and appear to be a heavy dirt impregnated grease.

For a thorough visual and operational inspection, check the following:

• Check the surface of the radiator and condenser for dirt, leaves or other material which might block air flow.

• Check for kinks in hoses and lines. Check the system for leaks.

• Make sure the drive belt is properly tensioned. During operation, make sure the belt is free of noise or slippage.

• Make sure the blower motor operates at all appropriate positions, then check for distribution of the air from all outlets.

➡**Remember that in high humidity, air discharged from the vents may not feel as cold as expected, even if the system is working properly. This is because moisture in humid air retains heat more effectively than dry air, thereby making humid air more difficult to cool.**

Windshield Wipers

ELEMENT (REFILL) CARE & REPLACEMENT

▶ **See Figures 86, 87 and 88**

For maximum effectiveness and longest element life, the windshield and wiper blades should be kept clean. Dirt, tree sap, road tar and so on will cause streaking, smearing and blade deterioration if left on the glass. It is advisable to wash the windshield carefully with a commercial glass cleaner at least once a month. Wipe off the rubber blades with the wet rag afterwards. Do not attempt to move wipers across the windshield by hand; damage to the motor and drive mechanism will result.

To inspect and/or replace the wiper blade elements, place the wiper switch in the **LOW** speed position and the ignition switch in the **ACC** position. When the wiper blades are approximately vertical on the windshield, turn the ignition switch to **OFF**.

Examine the wiper blade elements. If they are found to be cracked, broken or torn, they should be replaced immediately. Replacement intervals will vary with usage, although ozone deterioration usually limits element life to about one year. If the wiper pattern is smeared or streaked, or if the blade chatters across the glass, the elements should be replaced. It is easiest and most sensible to replace the elements in pairs.

If your vehicle is equipped with aftermarket blades, there are several different types of refills and your vehicle might have any kind. Aftermarket blades and arms rarely use the exact same type blade or refill as the original equipment.

Regardless of the type of refill used, be sure to follow the part manufacturer's instructions closely. Make sure that all of the frame jaws are engaged as the refill is pushed into place and locked. If the metal blade holder and frame are allowed to touch the glass during wiper operation, the glass will be scratched.

Tires and Wheels

Common sense and good driving habits will afford maximum tire life. Make sure that you don't overload the vehicle or run with incorrect pressure in the

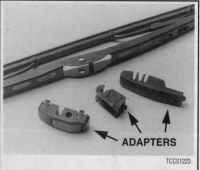

TCCS1223

Fig. 86 Most aftermarket blades are available with multiple adapters to fit different vehicles

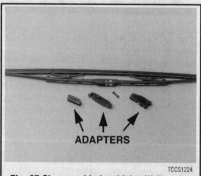

TCCS1224

Fig. 87 Choose a blade which will fit your vehicle, and that will be readily available next time you need blades

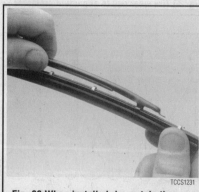

TCCS1231

Fig. 88 When installed, be certain the blade is fully inserted into the backing

tires. Either of these will increase tread wear. Fast starts, sudden stops and sharp cornering are hard on tires and will shorten their useful life span.

➡**For optimum tire life, keep the tires properly inflated, rotate them often and have the wheel alignment checked periodically.**

Inspect your tires frequently. Be especially careful to watch for bubbles in the tread or sidewall, deep cuts or underinflation. Replace any tires with bubbles in the sidewall. If cuts are so deep that they penetrate to the cords, discard the tire. Any cut in the sidewall of a radial tire renders it unsafe. Also look for uneven tread wear patterns that may indicate the front end is out of alignment or that the tires are out of balance.

TIRE ROTATION

▶ See Figures 89 and 90

Tires must be rotated periodically to equalize wear patterns that vary with a tire's position on the vehicle. Tires will also wear in an uneven way as the front steering/suspension system wears to the point where the alignment should be reset.

Rotating the tires will ensure maximum life for the tires as a set, so you will not have to discard a tire early due to wear on only part of the tread. Regular rotation is required to equalize wear.

When rotating "unidirectional tires," make sure that they always roll in the same direction. This means that a tire used on the left side of the vehicle must not be switched to the right side and vice-versa. Such tires should only be rotated front-to-rear or rear-to-front, while always remaining on the same side of the vehicle. These tires are marked on the sidewall as to the direction of rotation; observe the marks when reinstalling the tire(s).

Some styled or "mag" wheels may have different offsets front to rear. In these cases, the rear wheels must not be used up front and vice-versa. Furthermore, if these wheels are equipped with unidirectional tires, they cannot be rotated unless the tire is remounted for the proper direction of rotation.

➡**The compact or space-saver spare is strictly for emergency use. It must never be included in the tire rotation or placed on the vehicle for everyday use.**

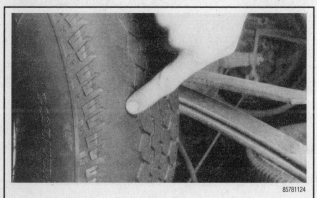

Fig. 89 Tire wear due to alignment problems

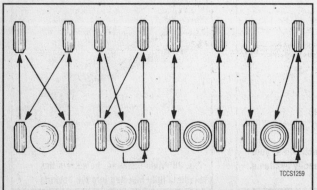

Fig. 90 Common tire rotation patterns for 4 and 5-wheel rotations

TIRE DESIGN

▶ See Figure 91

For maximum satisfaction, tires should be used in sets of four. Mixing of different brands or types (radial, bias-belted, fiberglass belted) should be avoided. In most cases, the vehicle manufacturer has designated a type of tire on which the vehicle will perform best. Your first choice when replacing tires should be to use the same type of tire that the manufacturer recommends.

When radial tires are used, tire sizes and wheel diameters should be selected to maintain ground clearance and tire load capacity equivalent to the original specified tire. Radial tires should always be used in sets of four.

✳✳ CAUTION

Radial tires should never be used on only the front axle.

When selecting tires, pay attention to the original size as marked on the tire. Most tires are described using an industry size code sometimes referred to as P-Metric. This allows the exact identification of the tire specifications, regardless of the manufacturer. If selecting a different tire size or brand, remember to check the installed tire for any sign of interference with the body or suspension while the vehicle is stopping, turning sharply or heavily loaded.

Snow Tires

Good radial tires can produce a big advantage in slippery weather, but in snow, a street radial tire does not have sufficient tread to provide traction and control. The small grooves of a street tire quickly pack with snow and the tire behaves like a billiard ball on a marble floor. The more open, chunky tread of a snow tire will self-clean as the tire turns, providing much better grip on snowy surfaces.

To satisfy municipalities requiring snow tires during weather emergencies, most snow tires carry either an M + S designation after the tire size stamped on the sidewall, or the designation "all-season." In general, no change in tire size is necessary when buying snow tires.

Most manufacturers strongly recommend the use of 4 snow tires on their vehicles for reasons of stability. If snow tires are fitted only to the drive wheels, the opposite end of the vehicle may become very unstable when braking or turning on slippery surfaces. This instability can lead to unpleasant endings if the driver can't counteract the slide in time.

Note that snow tires, whether 2 or 4, will affect vehicle handling in all non-snow situations. The stiffer, heavier snow tires will noticeably change the turning and braking characteristics of the vehicle. Once the snow tires are installed, you must re-learn the behavior of the vehicle and drive accordingly.

➡**Consider buying extra wheels on which to mount the snow tires. Once done, the "snow wheels" can be installed and removed as needed. This eliminates the potential damage to tires or wheels from seasonal removal and installation. Even if your vehicle has styled wheels, see if inexpensive steel wheels are available. Although the look of the vehicle will change, the expensive wheels will be protected from salt, curb hits and pothole damage.**

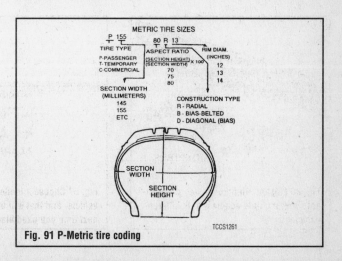

Fig. 91 P-Metric tire coding

TIRE STORAGE

If they are mounted on wheels, store the tires at proper inflation pressure. All tires should be kept in a cool, dry place. If they are stored in the garage or basement, do not let them stand on a concrete floor; set them on strips of wood, a mat or a large stack of newspaper. Keeping them away from direct moisture is of paramount importance. Tires should not be stored upright, but in a flat position.

INFLATION & INSPECTION

▶ **See Figures 92 thru 97**

The importance of proper tire inflation cannot be overemphasized. A tire employs air as part of its structure. It is designed around the supporting strength of the air at a specified pressure. For this reason, improper inflation drastically reduces the tire's ability to perform as intended. A tire will lose some air in day-to-day use; having to add a few pounds of air periodically is not necessarily a sign of a leaking tire.

Two items should be a permanent fixture in every glove compartment: an accurate tire pressure gauge and a tread depth gauge. Check the tire pressure (including the spare) regularly with a pocket type gauge. Too often, the gauge on the end of the air hose at your corner garage is not accurate because it suffers too much abuse. Always check tire pressure when the tires are cold, as pressure increases with temperature. If you must move the vehicle to check the tire inflation, do not drive more than a mile before checking. A cold tire is generally one that has not been driven for more than three hours.

A plate or sticker is normally provided somewhere in the vehicle (door post, hood, tailgate or trunk lid) which shows the proper pressure for the tires. Never counteract excessive pressure build-up by bleeding off air pressure (letting some air out). This will cause the tire to run hotter and wear quicker.

> ※※ **CAUTION**
>
> **Never exceed the maximum tire pressure embossed on the tire! This is the pressure to be used when the tire is at maximum loading, but it is rarely the correct pressure for everyday driving. Consult the owner's manual or the tire pressure sticker for the correct tire pressure.**

Once you've maintained the correct tire pressures for several weeks, you'll be familiar with the vehicle's braking and handling personality. Slight adjustments in tire pressures can fine-tune these characteristics, but never change the cold pressure specification by more than 2 psi. A slightly softer tire pressure will give a softer ride but also yield lower fuel mileage. A slightly harder tire will give crisper dry road handling but can cause skidding on wet surfaces. Unless you're fully attuned to the vehicle, stick to the recommended inflation pressures.

All automotive tires have built-in tread wear indicator bars that show up as ½ in. (13mm) wide smooth bands across the tire when 1/16 in. (1.5mm) of tread remains. The appearance of tread wear indicators means that the tires should be replaced. In fact, many states have laws prohibiting the use of tires with less than this amount of tread.

You can check your own tread depth with an inexpensive gauge or by using a Lincoln head penny. Slip the Lincoln penny (with Lincoln's head upside-down) into several tread grooves. If you can see the top of Lincoln's head in 2 adjacent grooves, the tire has less than 1/16 in. (1.5mm) tread left and should be replaced. You can measure snow tires in the same manner by using the "tails" side of the Lincoln penny. If you can see the top of the Lincoln memorial, it's time to replace the snow tire(s).

Fig. 92 Tires with deep cuts, or cuts which bulge, should be replaced immediately

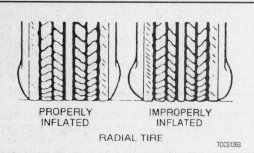

Fig. 93 Radial tires have a characteristic sidewall bulge; don't try to measure pressure by looking at the tire. Use a quality air pressure gauge

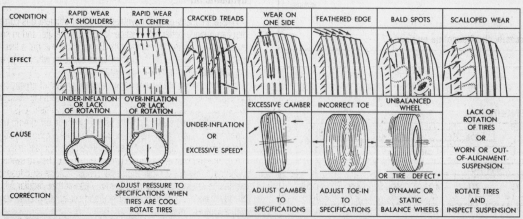

CONDITION	RAPID WEAR AT SHOULDERS	RAPID WEAR AT CENTER	CRACKED TREADS	WEAR ON ONE SIDE	FEATHERED EDGE	BALD SPOTS	SCALLOPED WEAR
EFFECT							
CAUSE	UNDER-INFLATION OR LACK OF ROTATION	OVER-INFLATION OR LACK OF ROTATION	UNDER-INFLATION OR EXCESSIVE SPEED*	EXCESSIVE CAMBER	INCORRECT TOE	UNBALANCED WHEEL OR TIRE DEFECT *	LACK OF ROTATION OF TIRES OR WORN OR OUT-OF-ALIGNMENT SUSPENSION.
CORRECTION	ADJUST PRESSURE TO SPECIFICATIONS WHEN TIRES ARE COOL ROTATE TIRES		ADJUST CAMBER TO SPECIFICATIONS	ADJUST TOE-IN TO SPECIFICATIONS	DYNAMIC OR STATIC BALANCE WHEELS	ROTATE TIRES AND INSPECT SUSPENSION	

*HAVE TIRE INSPECTED FOR FURTHER USE.

Fig. 94 Common tire wear patterns and causes

Fig. 95 Tread wear indicators will appear when the tire is worn

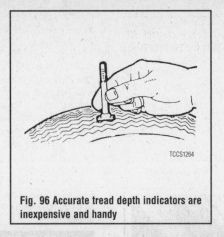

Fig. 96 Accurate tread depth indicators are inexpensive and handy

Fig. 97 A penny works well for a quick check of tread depth

FLUIDS AND LUBRICANTS

Oil and Fuel Recommendations

OIL

▶ See Figures 98 thru 105

The SAE (Society of Automotive Engineers) grade number indicates the viscosity of the engine oil; its resistance to flow at a given temperature. The lower the SAE grade number, the lighter the oil. For example, the mono-grade oils begin with SAE 5 weight, which is a thin light oil, and continue in viscosity up to SAE 80 or 90 weight, which are heavy gear lubricants. These oils are also known as "straight weight", meaning they are of a single viscosity, and do not vary with engine temperature.

Multi-viscosity oils offer the important advantage of being adaptable to temperature extremes. These oils have designations such as 10W-40, 20W-50, etc. The "10W-40" means that in winter (the "W" in the designation) the oil acts like

a thin 10 weight oil, allowing the engine to spin easily when cold and offering rapid lubrication. Once the engine has warmed up, the oil acts like a straight 40 weight, maintaining good lubrication and protection for the engine's internal components. A 20W-50 oil would therefore be slightly heavier than and not as ideal in cold weather as the 10W-40, but would offer better protection at higher rpm and temperatures because when warm it acts like a 50 weight oil. Whichever oil viscosity you choose when changing the oil, make sure you are anticipating the temperatures your engine will be operating in until the oil is changed again. Refer to the oil viscosity chart for oil recommendations according to temperature.

The API (American Petroleum Institute) designation indicates the classification of engine oil used under certain given operating conditions. Only oils designated for use "Service SF" should be used. Oils of the SF type perform a variety of functions inside the engine in addition to the basic function as a lubricant. Through a balanced system of metallic detergents and polymeric dispersants, the oil prevents the formation of high and low temperature deposits and also keeps sludge and particles of dirt in suspension. Acids, particularly sulfuric acid, as well as other by-products of combustion, are neutralized. Both the SAE grade number and the APE designation can be found on top of the oil can.

Diesel engines also require SF engine oil. In addition, the oil must qualify for a CC rating. The API has a number of different diesel engine ratings, including CB, CC, and CD. Any of these other oils are fine as long as the designation CC appears on the can along with them. Do not use oil labeled only SF or only CC. Both designations must always appear together.

For recommended oil viscosities, refer to the chart. Note that 10W-30 and 10W-40 grade oils are not recommended for sustained high speed driving when the temperature rises above the indicated limit.

Synthetic Oil

There are many excellent synthetic and fuel-efficient oils currently available that can provide better gas mileage, longer service life, and in some cases better engine protection. These benefits do not come without a few hitches, however; the main one being the price of synthetic oils, which is three or four times the price per quart of conventional oil.

Synthetic oil is not for every truck and every type of driving, so you should consider your engine's condition and your type of driving. Also, check your truck's warranty conditions regarding the use of synthetic oils.

Generally, it is best to avoid the use of synthetic oil in both brand new and older, high mileage engines. New engines require a proper break-in, and the synthetics are so slippery that they can impede this; most manufacturers recommend that you wait at least 5,000 miles (8,000 km) before switching to a synthetic oil. Conversely, older engines are looser and tend to lose more oil; synthetics will slip past worn parts more readily than regular oil. If your truck already leaks oil, (due to worn parts or bad seals/gaskets), it may leak more with a synthetic inside.

Consider your type of driving. If most of your accumulated mileage is high speed, highway type driving, the more expensive synthetic oils may be a benefit. Extended highway driving gives the engine a chance to warm up, accumulating less acids in the oil and putting less stress on the engine over the long run.

GASOLINE ENGINE

	15W-40		20W-40		20W-50	
	10W-30		10W-40		10W-50	
5W-30						

°F	−20	0	20	40	60	80	100
°C	−29	−18	−7	4	16	27	38

TEMPERATURE RANGE ANTICIPATED BEFORE NEXT OIL CHANGE

85781059

Fig. 98 Oil viscosity chart-gasoline engines

DIESEL ENGINE

	15W-40		20W-40		20W-50
	10W-30				
5W-30					

°F	−20	0	20	40	60	80	100
°C	−29	−18	−7	4	16	27	38

TEMPERATURE RANGE ANTICIPATED BEFORE NEXT OIL CHANGE

85781060

Fig. 99 Oil viscosity chart-diesel engines

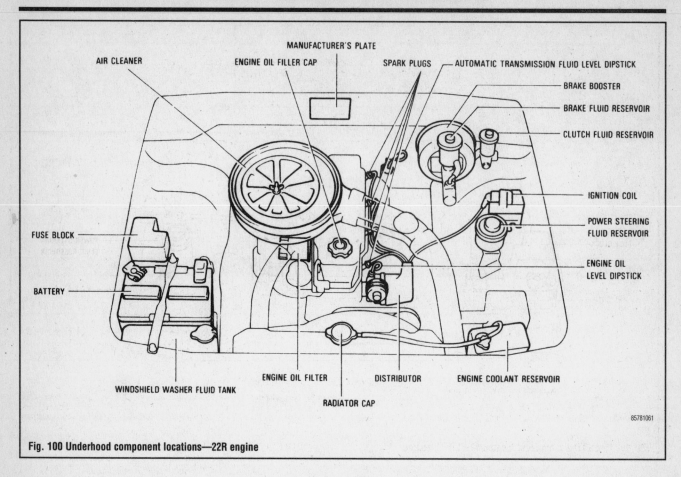

Fig. 100 Underhood component locations—22R engine

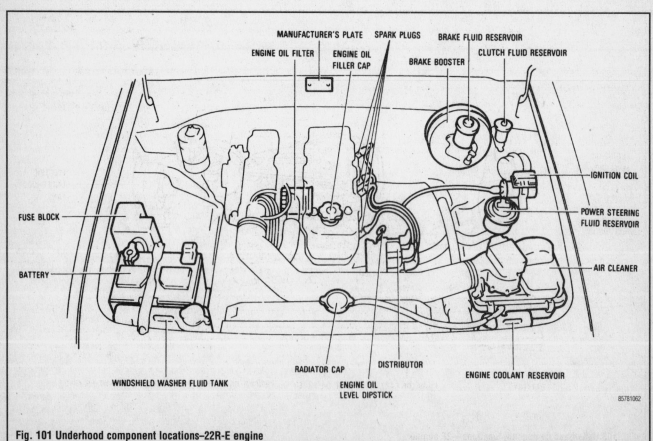

Fig. 101 Underhood component locations–22R-E engine

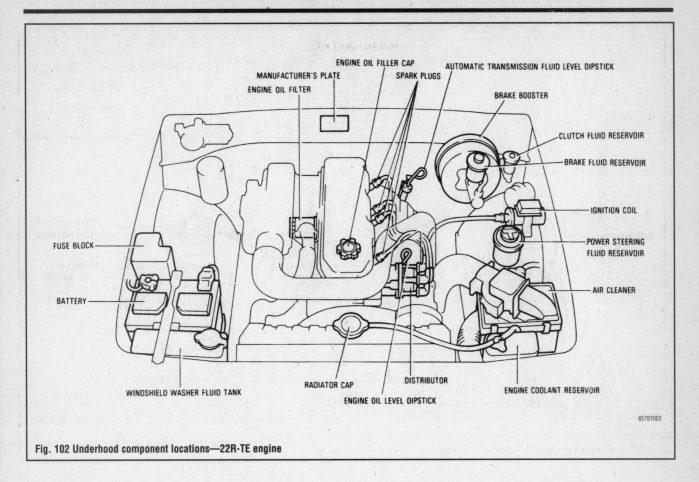

Fig. 102 Underhood component locations—22R-TE engine

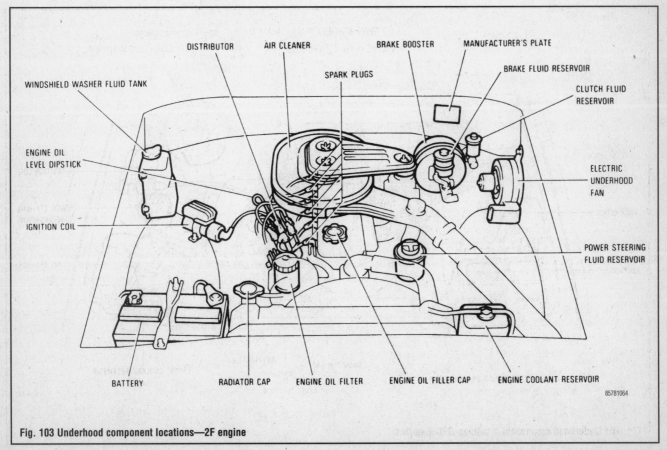

Fig. 103 Underhood component locations—2F engine

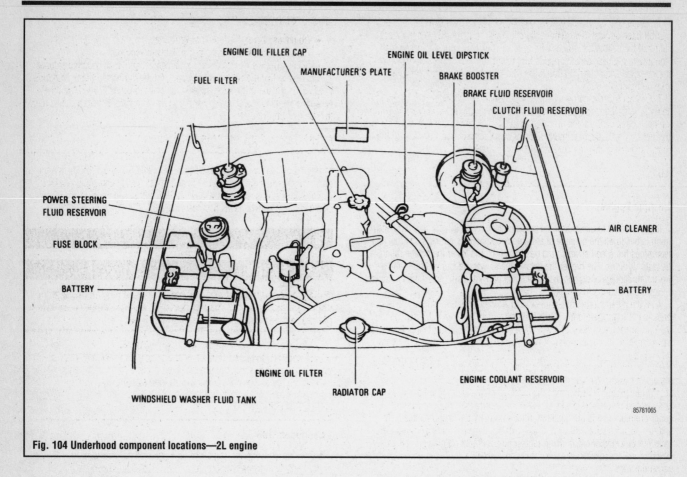

Fig. 104 Underhood component locations—2L engine

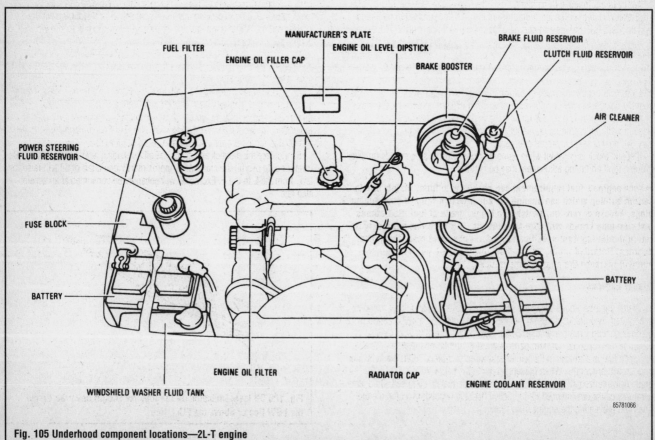

Fig. 105 Underhood component locations—2L-T engine

Under these conditions, the oil change interval can be extended (as long as your oil filter can last the extended life of the oil) up to the advertised mileage claims of the synthetics. Trucks with synthetic oils may show increased fuel economy in highway driving, due to less internal friction. However, many automotive experts agree that 50,000 miles (80,000 km) is too long to keep any oil in your engine.

Trucks used under harder circumstances, such as stop-and-go, city type driving, short trips, or extended idling, should be serviced more frequently. For the engines in these trucks, the much greater cost of synthetic or fuel-efficient oils may not be worth the investment. Internal wear increase much quicker on these trucks, causing greater oil consumption and leakage.

FUEL

Gasoline Engines

It is important to use fuel of the proper octane rating in your truck. Octane rating is based on the quantity of anti-knock compounds added to the fuel and it determines the speed at which the gas will burn. The lower the octane rating, the faster it burns. The higher the octane, the slower the fuel will burn and a greater percentage of compounds in the fuel prevent spark ping (knock), detonation and pre-ignition (dieseling).

As the temperature of the engine increases, the air/fuel mixture exhibits a tendency to ignite before the spark plug is fired. If fuel of an octane rating too low for the engine is used, this will allow combustion to occur before the piston has completed its compression stroke, thereby creating a very high pressure very rapidly.

Fuel of the proper octane rating, for the compression ratio and ignition timing of your truck, will slow the combustion process sufficiently to allow the spark plug enough time to ignite the mixture completely and smoothly. Many non-catalyst models are designed to run on regular fuel. The use of some super-premium fuel is no substitution for a properly tuned and maintained engine. Chances are that if your engine exhibits any signs of spark ping, detonation or pre-ignition when using regular fuel, the ignition timing should be checked against specifications or the cylinder head should be removed for decarbonizing.

Vehicles equipped with catalytic converters must use UNLEADED GASOLINE ONLY. Use of unleaded fuel shortened the life of spark plugs, exhaust systems and EGR valves and can damage the catalytic converter. Most converter equipped models are designed to operate using unleaded gasoline with a minimum rating of 87 octane. Use of unleaded gas with octane ratings lower than 87 can cause persistent spark knock which could lead to engine damage.

Light spark knock may be noticed when accelerating or driving up hills. The slight knocking may be considered normal (with 87 octane) because the maximum fuel economy is obtained under condition of occasional light spark knock. Gasoline with an octane rating higher than 87 may be used, but it is not necessary (in most cases) for proper operation.

If spark knock is constant when using 87 octane, at cruising speeds on level ground, ignition timing adjustment may be required.

➡️ **Your engine's fuel requirement can change with time, mainly due to carbon buildup which can change the compression ratio. If your engine pings, knocks or runs on, switch to a higher grade of fuel. Sometimes just changing brands will cure the problem. If it becomes necessary to retard the timing from specifications, don't change it more than a few degrees. Retarded timing will reduce power output and fuel mileage and will increase the engine temperature.**

Diesel Engines

Diesel engines require the use of diesel fuel. At no time should gasoline be substituted. Two grades of diesel fuel are manufactured, #1 and #2, although #2 grade is generally more available. Better fuel economy results from the use of #2 grade fuel. In some northern parts of the U.S. and in most parts of Canada, #1 grade fuel is available in the winter or a winterized blend of #2 grade is supplied in winter months. When the temperature falls below 20°F (–7°C), #1 grade or winterized #2 grade fuel are the only fuels that can be used. Cold temperatures cause unwinterized #2 to thicken (it actually gels), blocking the fuel lines and preventing the engine from running.

DIESEL CAUTIONS:

- Do not use home heating oil in your truck.
- Do not use ether or starting assist fluids in your truck.
- Do not use any fuel additives recommended for use in gasoline engines.

It is normal that the engine noise level is louder during the warm-up period in winter. It is also normal that whitish-blue smoke may be emitted from the exhaust after starting and during warm-up. The amount of smoke depends upon the outside temperature.

OPERATION IN FOREIGN COUNTRIES

If you plan to drive your truck outside the United States or Canada, there is a possibility that fuels will be too low in anti-knock quality and could produce engine damage. It is wise to consult with local authorities upon arrival in a foreign country to determine the best fuels available.

Engine

✳️ CAUTION

Prolonged and repeated skin contact with used engine oil, with no effort to remove the oil, may be harmful. Always follow these simple precautions when handling used motor oil:

- Avoid prolonged skin contact with used motor oil.
- Remove oil from skin by washing thoroughly with soap and water or waterless hand cleaner. Do not use gasoline, thinners or other solvents.
- Avoid prolonged skin contact with oil-soaked clothing.

OIL LEVEL CHECK

▶ **See Figure 106**

Every time you stop for fuel, check the engine oil as follows:
1. Park the truck on level ground.
2. When checking the oil level it is best for the engine to be at operating temperature, although checking the oil immediately after a stopping will lead to a false reading. Wait a few minutes after turning off the engine to allow the oil to drain back into the crankcase.
3. Open the hood and locate the dipstick which is on the left side of all engines but the 8R and 18R-C, where it is on the right. Pull the dipstick from its tube, wipe it clean and reinsert it.
4. Pull the dipstick out again and, holding it horizontally, read the oil level. The oil should be between the **F** and **L** marks on the dipstick. If the oil is below the **L** mark, add oil of the proper viscosity through the capped opening on the top of the cylinder head cover. See the "Oil and Fuel Recommendations" chart in this section for the proper viscosity and rating of oil to use.
5. Replace the dipstick and check the oil level again after adding any oil. Be careful not to overfill the crankcase. Approximately one quart of oil will raise the level from the **L** to the **F**. Excess oil will generally be consumed at an accelerated rate.

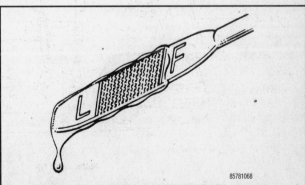

85781068

Fig. 106 Oil level indicated on the dipstick should never be below the LOW line or above the FULL line

OIL AND FILTER CHANGE

▶ **See Figures 107 thru 113**

The oil should be changed every 6000 miles (10,000 km) on models built between 1970-77. All 1978-88 models should have the oil changed every 7500 miles (12,000 km). ALWAYS read the oil filter package for any additional installation instructions.

✳✳ CAUTION

Prolonged and repeated skin contact with used engine oil, with no effort to remove the oil, may be harmful. Always follow these simple precautions when handling used motor oil.

- Avoid prolonged skin contract with used motor oil.
- Remove oil from skin by washing thoroughly with soap and water or waterless hand cleaner. Do not use gasoline, thinners or other solvents.
- Avoid prolonged skin contact with oil-soaked clothing.

The oil drain plug is located on the bottom, rear of the oil pan (bottom of the engine, underneath the truck). The oil filter is located on the right side of the engine on all models.

The mileage figures given are the Toyota recommended intervals assuming normal driving and conditions. If your truck is being used under dusty, polluted or off-road conditions, change the oil and filter more frequently than specified. The same goes for trucks driven in stop-and-go traffic or only for short distances. Always drain the oil after the engine has been running long enough to bring it to normal operating temperature. Hot oil will flow easier and more contaminants will be removed along with the oil than if it were drained cold. To change the oil and filter:

All Except 1970–72 Land Cruiser With Canister-Type Filter

1. Run the engine until it reaches normal operating temperature.
2. Jack up the front of the truck and support it on safety stands.
3. Slide a drain pan of at least 6 quarts capacity under the oil pan.

Fig. 109 Location of oil drain plug

Fig. 110 Removing the oil filter with the correct tool

Fig. 107 Location of the oil dipstick

Fig. 111 Location of oil cap

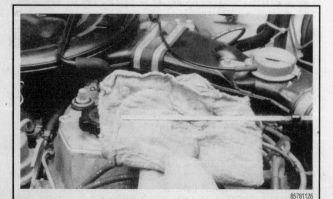
Fig. 108 Checking the oil dipstick

Fig. 112 Adding oil to the engine

Fig. 113 After adding oil to the engine, start the engine. The oil warning light should go out after a few seconds

4. Loosen the drain plug. Turn the plug out by hand. By keeping an inward pressure on the plug as you unscrew it, oil won't escape past the threads and you can remove it without being burned by hot oil.

5. Allow the oil to drain completely and then install the drain plug. Don't overtighten the plug, or you'll be buying a new pan or a trick replacement plug for stripped threads.

6. Using a strap wrench, remove the oil filter. Keep in mind that it's holding about one quart of dirty, hot oil.

7. Empty the old filter into the drain pan and dispose of the filter.

8. Using a clean rag, wipe off the filter adapter on the engine block. Be sure that the rag doesn't leave any lint which could clog an oil passage.

9. Coat the rubber gasket on the filter with fresh oil. Spin it onto the engine by hand; when the gasket touches the adapter surface give it another ½-¾ turn. No more, or you'll squash the gasket and it will leak.

10. Refill the engine with the correct amount of fresh oil. See the "Capacities" chart.

11. Check the oil level on the dipstick. It is normal for the level to be a bit above the full mark. Start the engine and allow it to idle for a few minutes.

✳ CAUTION

Do not run the engine above idle speed until it has built up oil pressure, indicated when the oil light goes out.

12. Shut off the engine, allow the oil to drain for a minute, and check the oil level. Check around the filter and drain plug for any leaks, and correct as necessary.

1970–72 Land Cruiser With Canister-Type Filter

▶ See Figure 114

The oil filter on the earlier models is a replaceable element type of oil filter. Change this type of filter along with the oil in the crankcase as follows:
1. Drain the oil as outlined previously.
2. Place the drain pan under the drain plug on the filter case and remove the plug. Allow all of the oil to drain from the oil filter case.
3. Remove the two oil lines from the filter case.
4. Unfasten the mounting bolts which attach the filter bracket to the intake manifold. Remove the entire filter assembly.
5. Unscrew the securing bolt from the cap. Remove the large cap gasket, collar, small gasket and the filter element.
6. Remove the gasket, element support spring, and washer from the element guide.
7. Clean the sludge out of the bottom of the case with solvent. Allow the case to dry completely.
8. Replace the element and all of the gaskets with new ones.
9. Install the element support spring and the washer from the element guide.
10. Install the collar and then position the filter cap and tighten the securing bolt.
11. Install the filter assembly and reconnect the two oil lines.
12. Make sure that the crankcase drain plug is installed and fill the crankcase with the proper amount and type of oil.

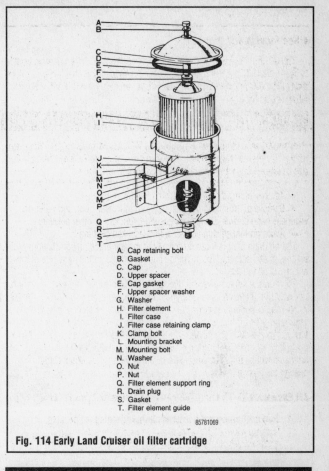

A. Cap retaining bolt
B. Gasket
C. Cap
D. Upper spacer
E. Cap gasket
F. Upper spacer washer
G. Washer
H. Filter element
I. Filter case
J. Filter case retaining clamp
K. Clamp bolt
L. Mounting bracket
M. Mounting bolt
N. Washer
O. Nut
P. Nut
Q. Filter element support ring
R. Drain plug
S. Gasket
T. Filter element guide

Fig. 114 Early Land Cruiser oil filter cartridge

Manual Transmission

FLUID RECOMMENDATIONS

- Pick-Ups and 4Runner—multipurpose gear oil API GL-4 or GL-5; SAE 75W-90 or 80W-90
- Land Cruiser—multipurpose gear oil API GL-4 or GL-5; SAE 90W.

FLUID LEVEL CHECK

The oil in the manual transmission should be checked at least every 7500 miles (12,000 km) and replaced every 25,000-30,000 miles (40,000-48,000 km), even more frequently if driven in deep water.
1. With the truck parked on a level surface, remove the filler plug (17mm) from the side of the transmission housing.
2. If the lubricant begins to trickle out of the hole, there is enough. Otherwise, carefully insert your finger (watch out for sharp threads) and check to see if the oil is up to the edge of the hole.

✳ CAUTION

Prolonged and repeated skin contact with used engine oil, with no effort to remove the oil, may be harmful. Always follow these simple precautions when handling used motor oil.

- Avoid prolonged skin contact with used motor oil.
- Remove oil from skin by washing thoroughly with soap and water or waterless hand cleaner. Do not use gasoline, thinners or other solvents.
- Avoid prolonged skin contact with oil-soaked clothing.
3. If not, add oil through the hole until the level is at the edge of the hole. Most gear lubricants come in a plastic squeeze bottle with a nozzle; making additions simple. You can also use a common everyday kitchen baster.
4. Replace the filler plug, run the engine and check for leaks.

DRAIN AND REFILL

♦ **See Figures 115 and 116**

Once every 24,000 miles (1970-78) or once every 30,000 miles (1979-88), the oil in the manual transmission should be changed.

1. The transmission oil should be hot before it is drained. If the engine is at normal operating temperature, the transmission oil should be hot enough.

2. Raise the truck and support it properly on jackstands so that you can safely work underneath. You will probably not have enough room to work if the truck is not raised.

3. The drain plug is located on the bottom of the transmission. It is on the passenger side on four speeds, and on the bottom center of five speeds. Place a pan under the drain plug and remove it. Keep a slight upward pressure on the plug while unscrewing it, this will keep the oil from pouring out until the plug is removed.

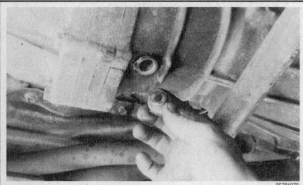

Fig. 115 Drain the manual transmission

Fig. 116 Typical manual transmission drain plug location

✳✳ CAUTION

The oil will be HOT. Be careful when you remove the plug so that you don't take a bath in hot gear oil.

4. Allow the oil to drain completely. Clean off the plug and replace it, tightening it until it is just snug.

5. Remove the filler plug from the side of the transmission case. It is on the driver's side of four speeds, and on the passenger side on five speeds. There will be a gasket underneath this plug. Replace it if damaged.

6. Fill the transmission with gear oil through the filler plug hole as detailed previously. Refer to the Capacities Chart for the amount of oil needed to refill your transmission.

7. The oil level should come right up to the edge of the hole. You can stick your finger in to verify this. Watch out for sharp threads.

8. Replace the filler plug and gasket, lower the truck, and check for leaks. Dispose of the old oil in the proper manner.

Automatic Transmission

FLUID RECOMMENDATIONS

- 1970-83—ATF Type F
- 1984-88—ATF DEXRON®II

FLUID LEVEL CHECK

Check the automatic transmission fluid level at least every 15,000 miles (more if possible). The dipstick is in the rear of the engine compartment. The fluid level should be checked only when the transmission is hot (normal operating temperature). The transmission is considered hot after about 20 miles of highway driving.

1. Park the truck on a level surface with the engine idling. Shift the transmission into Neutral and set the parking brake.

2. Remove the dipstick, wipe it clean and reinsert if firmly. Be sure that it has been pushed all the way in. Remove the dipstick and check the fluid level while holding it horizontally. With the engine running, the fluid level should be between the second and third notches on the dipstick.

3. If the fluid level is below the second notch, use Type F automatic transmission fluid through the dipstick tube on all 1970–83 models. On 1984–88 models use only Dexron®II Automatic transmission fluid. This is easily done with the aid of a funnel. Check the level often as you are filling the transmission. Be extremely careful not to overfill it. Overfilling will cause slippage, seal damage and overheating. Approximately one pint of ATF will raise the level from one notch to the other.

➡**Always use the proper transmission fluid when filling your truck's transmission. All 1971–83 models use Type F. All 1984–88 models use Dexron® or Dexron®II. Always check with the owner's manual to be sure. NEVER use Dexron® in a transmission requiring Type F or vice versa, as severe damage will result.**

✳✳ CAUTION

The fluid on the dipstick should always be a bright red color. It if is discolored (brown or black), or smells burnt, serious transmission troubles, probably due to overheating, should be suspected. The transmission should be inspected by a qualified service technician to locate the cause of the burnt fluid.

DRAIN AND REFILL

The automatic transmission fluid should be changed at least every 25,000–30,000 miles (40,000–48,000 km). If the truck is normally used in severe service, such as stop-and-go driving, trailer towing or the like, the interval should be halved. The fluid should be hot before it is drained; a 20 minute drive will accomplish this.

Toyota automatic transmissions have a drain plug in them so that if you are in a hurry, you can simply remove the plug, drain the fluid, replace the plug and then refill the transmission. Although this method is fine, a more thorough procedure is recommended.

Pan and Filter Service

♦ **See Figure 117**

1. Remove the plug and drain the fluid. When the fluid stops coming out of the drain hole, loosen the pan retaining screws until the pan can be pulled down at one corner. Lower a corner of the pan and allow any remaining fluid to drain out.

2. After the pan has drained completely, remove the pan retaining screws and then remove the pan and gasket.

To install:

3. Clean the pan thoroughly and allow it to air dry. If you wipe it out with a rag you run the risk of leaving bits of lint in the pan which will clog the tiny hydraulic passages in the transmission.

4. Install the pan using a new gasket.

5. Install the drain plug.

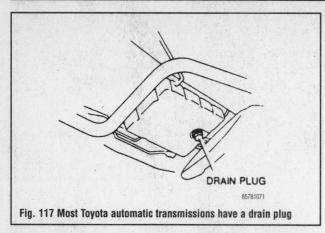

Fig. 117 Most Toyota automatic transmissions have a drain plug

6. It is a good idea to measure the amount of fluid drained from the transmission to determine the correct amount of fresh fluid to add. This is because some parts of the transmission may not drain completely and using the dry refill amount specified in the "Capacities" chart could lead to overfilling. Fluid is added only through the dipstick tube. Use only the proper automatic transmission fluid; do not overfill.

7. Replace the dipstick after filling. Start the engine and allow it to idle. DO NOT race the engine.

8. After the engine has idled for a few minutes, shift the transmission slowly through the gears and then return it to Park. With the engine still idling, check the fluid level on the dipstick. If necessary, add more fluid to raise the level to where it is supposed to be.

Transfer Case

FLUID RECOMMENDATIONS

- Pick-Ups and 4Runner w/MT—multipurpose gear oil API GL-4 or GL-5; SAE 75W-90 or 80W-90
- Pick-Ups and 4Runner w/AT—ATF DEXRON®II
- Land Cruiser—multipurpose gear oil API GL-4 or GL-5; SAE 90W.

FLUID LEVEL CHECK

▶ **See Figure 118**

The oil in the transfer case should be checked at least every 7500 miles (12,000 km) and replaced every 25,000–30,000 miles (40,000–48,000 km), even more frequently if driven in deep water.

1. With the truck parked on a level surface, remove the filler plug from the side of the transmission housing.

2. If the lubricant begins to trickle out of the hole, there is enough. Otherwise, carefully insert your finger (watch out for sharp threads) and check to see if the oil is up to the edge of the hole.

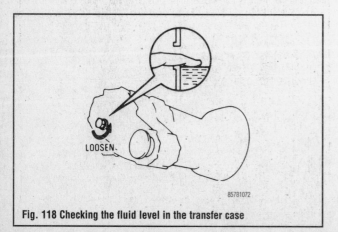

Fig. 118 Checking the fluid level in the transfer case

3. If not, add oil through the hole until the level is at the edge of the hole. Most gear lubricants come in a plastic squeeze bottle with a nozzle; making additions simple. You can also use a common everyday kitchen baster.

4. Replace the filler plug, run the engine and check for leaks.

DRAIN AND REFILL

Once every 24,000 miles (1970–78) or once every 30,000 miles (1979–88), the oil in the transfer case should be changed.

1. The transfer case oil should be hot before it is drained. If the engine is at normal operating temperature, the oil should be hot enough.

2. Raise the truck and support it properly on jackstands so that you can safely work underneath. You will probably not have enough room to work if the truck is not raised.

3. The drain plug is located on the bottom of the transfer case. Place a pan under the drain plug and remove it. Keep a slight upward pressure on the plug while unscrewing it, this will keep the oil from pouring out until the plug is removed.

✳✳ **CAUTION**

The oil will be HOT. Be careful when you remove the plug so that you don't take a bath in hot gear oil.

4. Allow the oil to drain completely. Clean off the plug and replace it, tightening it until it is just snug.

5. Remove the filler plug from the side of the case. There will be a gasket underneath this plug. Replace it if damaged.

6. Fill the transfer case with gear (or ATF) oil through the filler plug hole as detailed previously. Refer to the Capacities Chart for the amount of oil needed to refill your transfer case.

7. The oil level should come right up to the edge of the hole. You can stick your finger in to verify this. Watch out for sharp threads.

8. Replace the filler plug and gasket, lower the truck, and check for leaks. Dispose of the old oil in the proper manner.

Drive Axles (Differentials)

FLUID RECOMMENDATIONS

- All models—Hypoid gear oil API GL-5; below 0°F (−18°C): SAE 90W, above 0°F (−18°C): SAE 80W or 80W-90.

FLUID LEVEL CHECK

▶ **See Figure 119**

The oil in the front and/or rear differential should be checked at least every 7500 miles (12,000 km) and replaced every 25,000–30,000 miles (40,000–48,000 km). If driven in deep water it should be replaced immediately.

1. With the truck parked on a level surface, remove the filler plug from the back of the differential.

➡**The plug on the bottom is the drain plug.**

2. If the oil begins to trickle out of the hole, there is enough. Otherwise, carefully insert your finger (watch out for sharp threads) into the hole and check to see if the oil is up to the bottom edge of the filler hole.

3. If not, add oil through the hole until the level is at the edge of the hole. Most gear oils come in a plastic squeeze bottle with a nozzle, making additions simple. You can also use a common kitchen baster. Use standard

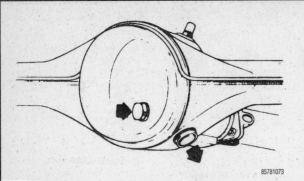

Fig. 119 Filler (upper) and drain (lower) plug locations on the differential assembly

GL-5 hypoid type gear oil; SAE 90 or SAE 80 if you live in a particularly cold area.

4. Replace the filler plug and drive the truck for a while. Stop the truck and check for leaks.

DRAIN AND REFILL

▶ **See Figures 120 thru 125**

The gear oil in the front or rear axle should be changed at least every 25,000-30,000 miles (40,000-48,000 km); immediately if driven in deep water.

To drain and fill the rear axle, proceed as follows:

1. Park the vehicle on a level surface. Set the parking brake.
2. Remove the filler (upper) plug. Place a container which is large enough to catch all of the differential oil, under the drain plug.
3. Remove the drain (lower) plug and gasket, if so equipped. Allow all of the oil to drain into the container.

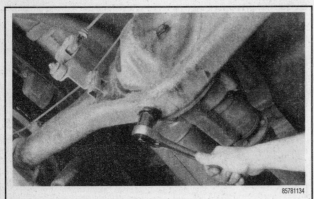

Fig. 120 Removing the rear axle assembly drain plug

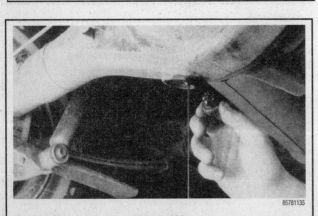

Fig. 121 Draining the rear axle assembly

Fig. 122 Rear axle assembly drain plug

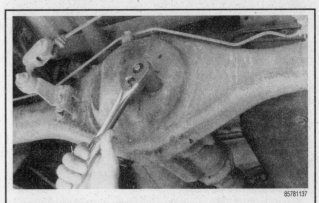

Fig. 123 Removing the rear axle assembly filler plug

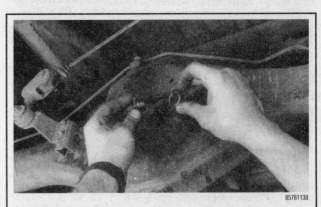

Fig. 124 Rear axle assembly filler plug—replace gasket

Fig. 125 Refill the rear axle assembly

4. Install the drain plug. Tighten it so that it will not leak, but do not over-tighten.

➡ Its usually a good idea to replace the drain plug gasket at this time.

5. Refill with the proper grade and viscosity of axle lubricant (see "Recommended Lubricants" chart). Be sure that the level reaches the bottom of the filler plug. DO NOT overfill.
6. Install the filler plug and check for leakage.

Cooling System

FLUID RECOMMENDATIONS

When additional coolant is required to maintain the proper level, always add a 50/50 mixture of ethylene glycol antifreeze/coolant and water.

FLUID LEVEL CHECK

Dealing with the cooling system can be a tricky matter unless the proper precautions are observed. It is best to check the coolant level in the radiator when the engine is cold. This is done by removing the radiator cap and seeing that the coolant is within ¾ in. of the bottom of the filler neck. On later models, the cooling system has, as one of its components, an expansion tank. If coolant is visible above the **Low** or **Min** mark on the tank, the level is satisfactory. Always be certain that the filler caps on both the radiator and the reservoir are tightly closed.

In the event that the coolant level must be checked when the engine is warm or on engines without the expansion tank, place a thick rag over the radiator cap and slowly turn the cap counterclockwise until it reaches the first detent. Allow all the hot steam to escape. This will allow the pressure in the system to drop gradually, preventing an explosion of hot coolant. When the hissing noise stops, remove the cap the rest of the way.

It's a good idea to check the coolant every time that you stop for fuel. If the coolant level is low, add equal amount of ethylene glycol based antifreeze and clean water. On models without an expansion tank, add coolant through the radiator filler neck. Fill the expansion tank to the **Full** level on trucks with that system.

❋ CAUTION

Never add cold coolant to a hot engine unless the engine is running, to avoid cracking the engine block.

Avoid using water that is known to have a high alkaline content or is very hard, except in emergency situations. Drain and flush the cooling system as soon as possible after using such water.

The radiator hoses and clamps and the radiator cap should be checked at the same time as the coolant level. Hoses which are brittle, cracked, or swollen should be replaced. Clamps should be checked for tightness (screwdriver tight only! Do not allow the clamp to cut into the hose or crush the fitting). The radiator cap gasket should be checked for any obvious tears, cracks or swelling, or any signs of incorrect seating in the radiator neck.

DRAIN AND REFILL

▸ **See Figures 126, 127, 128, 129 and 130**

❋ CAUTION

When draining the coolant, keep in mind that cats and dogs are attracted by the ethylene glycol antifreeze, and are quite likely to drink any that is left in an uncovered container or in puddles on the ground. This will prove fatal in sufficient quantity. Always drain the coolant into a sealable container. Coolant should be reused unless it is contaminated or several years old.

Completely draining and refilling the cooling system every two years at least will remove accumulated rust, scale and other deposits.

➡ **Use a good quality antifreeze with water pump lubricants, rust inhibitors and other corrosion inhibitors along with acid neutralizers. Use a permanent type coolant that meets specification ESE-M97B44A or the equivalent.**

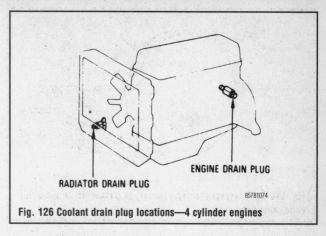

Fig. 126 Coolant drain plug locations—4 cylinder engines

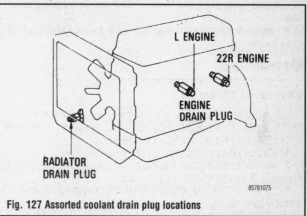

Fig. 127 Assorted coolant drain plug locations

Fig. 128 Removing the radiator cap—only when the engine is COLD

Fig. 129 Refill the cooling system

Fig. 130 Windshield washer fluid bottle—do not mistake it for the coolant recovery bottle

1. Drain the existing antifreeze and coolant. Open the radiator and engine drain petcocks (models equipped), or disconnect the bottom radiator hose, at the radiator outlet. Set the heater temperature controls to the full HOT position.

➡**Before opening the radiator petcock, spray it with some penetrating lubricant.**

2. Close the petcock or reconnect the lower hose and fill the system with water.

3. Add a can of quality radiator flush. Be sure the flush is safe to use in engines having aluminum components.

4. Idle the engine until the upper radiator hose gets hot.

5. Drain the system again.

6. Repeat this process until the drained water is clear and free of scale.

7. Close all petcocks and connect all the hoses.

8. If equipped with a coolant recovery system, flush the reservoir with water and leave empty.

9. Determine the capacity of your cooling system (see Capacities specifications). Add a 50/50 mix of quality antifreeze (ethylene glycol) and water to provide the desired protection.

SYSTEM INSPECTION

Most permanent antifreeze/coolant have a colored dye added which makes the solution an excellent leak detector. When servicing the cooling system, check for leakage at:
- All hoses and hose connections.
- Radiator seams, radiator core, and radiator draincock.
- All engine block and cylinder head freeze (core) plugs, and drain plugs.
- Edges of all cooling system gaskets (head gaskets, thermostat gasket).
- Transmission fluid cooler.
- Heating system components, water pump.
- Check the engine oil dipstick for signs of coolant in the engine oil.
- Check the coolant in the radiator for signs of oil in the coolant.

Investigate and correct any indication of coolant leakage.

Check the Radiator Cap

♦ **See Figure 131**

While you are checking the coolant level, check the radiator cap for a worn or cracked gasket. If the cap doesn't seal properly, fluid will be lost and the engine will overheat.

A worn cap should be replaced with a new one.

Clean Radiator of Debris

Periodically clean any debris such as leaves, paper, insects, etc., from the radiator fins. Pick the large pieces off by hand. The smaller pieces can be washed away with water pressure from a hose.

Carefully straighten any bent radiator fins with a pair of needle nose pliers. Be careful, the fins are very soft. Don't wiggle the fins back and forth too much. Straighten them once and try not to move them again.

CHECKING SYSTEM PROTECTION

♦ **See Figure 132**

A 50/50 mix of coolant concentrate and water will usually provide protection to −35°F (−37°C). Freeze protection may be checked by using a cooling system hydrometer. Inexpensive hydrometers (floating ball types) may be obtained from a local department store (automotive section) or an auto supply store. Follow the directions packaged with the coolant hydrometer when checking protection.

Master Cylinders

All models utilize both a brake and a clutch master cylinder. Both are located above the brake booster unit at the driver's side firewall.

FLUID RECOMMENDATIONS

Use only Heavy Duty Brake fluid meeting DOT 3 or SAE J1703 specifications.

FLUID LEVEL CHECK

♦ **See Figures 133, 134, 135 and 136**

The fluid in the brake and/or clutch master cylinders should be checked every 6 months or 6,000 miles (9,600 km).

Check the fluid level on the side of the reservoir. If fluid is required, remove the filler cap and gasket from the master cylinder. Fill the reservoir to the full line in the reservoir. Install the filler cap, making sure the gasket is properly seated in the cap.

➡**It is normal for the fluid level to fall as the disc brake pads wear. However, if the master cylinder requires filling frequently, you should check the system for leaks in the hoses, master cylinder, or wheel cylinders. Brake fluid dissolves paint. It also absorbs moisture from the air; never leave a container or the master cylinder or the clutch cylinder uncovered any longer than necessary. The clutch master cylinder uses the same fluid as the brakes, and should be checked at the same time as the brake master cylinder.**

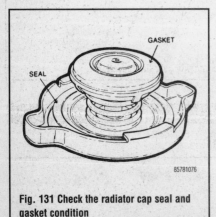

Fig. 131 Check the radiator cap seal and gasket condition

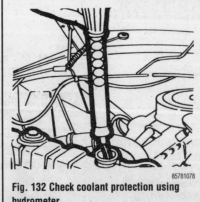

Fig. 132 Check coolant protection using hydrometer

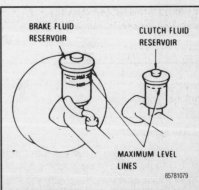

Fig. 133 Brake and clutch master cylinder locations-typical

Fig. 134 Brake master cylinder assembly

Fig. 135 Checking the brake master cylinder—note level indicator

Fig. 136 Removing the brake master cylinder cap—do not remove the gasket

Power Steering Pump

FLUID RECOMMENDATIONS

Use only ATF DEXRON® or DEXRON®II in the power steering system.

FLUID LEVEL CHECK

◗ See Figure 137

Check the power steering fluid level every 6 months or 6,000 miles (9,600 km).
1. Park the vehicle on a level surface. Run the engine until normal operating temperature is reached.
2. Turn the steering all the way to the left and then all the way to the right several times. Center the steering wheel and shut off the engine.

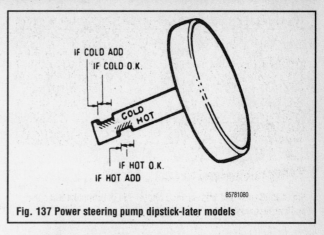

Fig. 137 Power steering pump dipstick-later models

3. Open the hood and check the power steering reservoir fluid level.
4. Remove the filler cap and wipe the dipstick attached clean.
5. Re-insert the dipstick and tighten the cap. Remove the dipstick and note the fluid level indicated on the dipstick.
6. The level should be at any point below the Full mark, but not below the Add mark (in the HOT or COLD ranges).
7. Add fluid as necessary. Do not overfill.

Steering Gear

FLUID RECOMMENDATIONS

Use standard hypoid-type gear oil GL-4, SAE 90W when refilling the steering gear.

FLUID LEVEL CHECK

◗ See Figure 138

Every year or 15,000 miles (24,000 km) you should check the steering gear housing lubricating oil. The filler plug is on top of the housing and requires a 14mm wrench for removal. The level should be 18—28mm from the top on 2WD models and 14—17mm from the top on 4WD models.

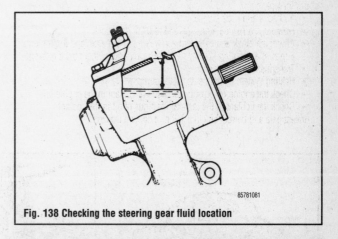

Fig. 138 Checking the steering gear fluid location

Electric Winch

FLUID RECOMMENDATIONS

- Pick-Ups & 4Runner—ATF DEXRON®II
- Land Cruiser—ATF Type F

FLUID LEVEL CHECK

▶ **See Figures 139 and 140**

Park the truck on level ground, remove the filler plug and check the fluid level. On Land Cruisers, the fluid level should be 5–10mm from the lower edge of the hole. On Pick-Ups and 4Runners, the fluid level should be 50–60mm from the lower edge of the hole.

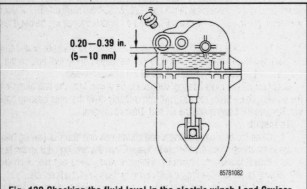

Fig. 139 Checking the fluid level in the electric winch-Land Cruiser

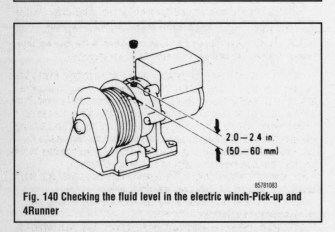

Fig. 140 Checking the fluid level in the electric winch-Pick-up and 4Runner

Steering Knuckle

4-WHEEL DRIVE

▶ **See Figure 141**

Check the amount and condition of the lubricant in the steering knuckle every 6 months or 12,000 miles (20,000 km), whichever comes first. The steering knuckle should be packed with multi-purpose grease (NLGI No. 2)

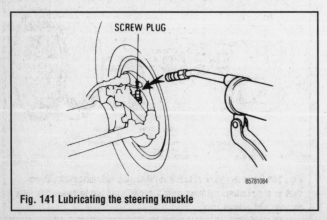

Fig. 141 Lubricating the steering knuckle

Chassis Greasing

▶ **See Figure 142**

Complete chassis greasing should include an inspection of all rubber suspension bushings, lubrication of all body hinges, as well as proper greasing of the front suspension upper and lower ball joints and control arm bushings. To provide correct operation, the chassis should be greased every 6 months or 6000 miles (10,000 km) on 1970—78 trucks. The 1979—88 trucks should be greased every 7500 miles (12,000 km).

If you wish to perform this operation yourself you should purchase a cartridge type grease gun and several cartridges of multipurpose lithium base grease. You will also need to purchase grease fittings from your Toyota dealer, as the front end components are fitted with screw-in plugs to prevent entry of foreign material.

Remove the plug, using a 10mm wrench and install the grease fitting. Push the nozzle of the grease gun down firmly onto the fitting and while applying pressure, force the new grease into the boot. Force sufficient grease into the fitting to cause the old grease to be expelled. When this has been accomplished, remove the fitting and replace the plug. Follow this procedure on each front suspension lubrication point.

Long Bed Pick-Ups have a two piece driveshaft which must be greased at the same 6 month/7,500 mile interval. The driveshaft is equipped with a grease fitting, located on the shaft just behind the center support bearing. Simply wipe off the fitting and pump in two or three shots of grease. There is no built in escape hole for the old grease to exit, so don't keep pumping in grease until the seal gives way. The factory recommends 5—10 grams of lithium base grease at the specified interval.

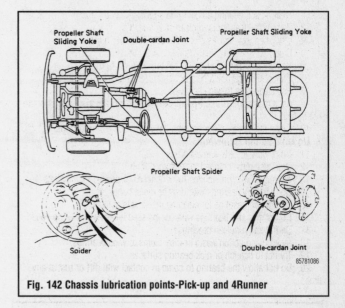

Fig. 142 Chassis lubrication points-Pick-up and 4Runner

STEERING ARM STOPS

The steering arm stops are attached to the lower control arm. They are located between each steering arm and the upturned end of the front suspension strut.

1. Park the vehicle on a level surface, set the parking brake, block the rear wheels, raise the front end and support it with jackstands.
2. Clean the friction points and apply multi-purpose grease.
3. Lower the vehicle.

MANUAL TRANSMISSION AND CLUTCH LINKAGE

On models so equipped, apply a small amount of chassis grease to the pivot points of the transmission and clutch linkage as per the chassis lubrication diagram.

AUTOMATIC TRANSMISSION LINKAGE

On models so equipped, apply a small amount of 10W engine oil to the kickdown and shift linkage at the pivot points.

PARKING BRAKE LINKAGE

At yearly intervals or whenever binding is noticeable in the parking brake linkage, lubricate the cable guides, levers and linkage with a suitable chassis grease.

Wheel Bearings

ADJUSTMENT AND LUBRICATION

♦ See Figure 143

Only the front wheel bearings require periodic service. The lubricant to use is high temperature disc brake wheel bearing grease meeting NLGI No. 2 specifications. (This grease should be used even if the truck is equipped with drum brakes; it has superior protection characteristics.) This service is recommended at the specified period in the Maintenance Intervals chart or whenever the truck has been driven in water up to the hub.

Before handling the bearings there are a few things that you should remember:

Remember to DO the following:

1. Remove all outside dirt from the housing before exposing the bearing.
2. Treat a used bearing as gently as you would a new one.
3. Work with clean tools in clean surroundings.
4. Use clean, dry canvas gloves, or at least clean, dry hands.
5. Clean solvents and flushing fluids are a must.
6. Use clean paper when laying out the bearings to dry.
7. Protect disassembled bearings from rust and dirt. Cover them up.
8. Use clean rags to wipe bearings
9. Keep the bearings in oil-proof paper when they are to be stored or are not in use.
10. Clean the inside of the housing before replacing the bearings.

Do NOT do the following:

11. Don't work in dirty surroundings.
12. Don't use dirty, chipped, or damaged tools.
13. Try not to work on wooden work benches or use wooden mallets.
14. Don't handle bearings with dirty or moist hands.
15. Do not use gasoline for cleaning; use a safe solvent.
16. Do not spin dry bearings with compressed air. They will be damaged.
17. Do not spin unclean bearings.
18. Avoid using cotton waste or dirty cloths to wipe bearings.
19. Try not to scratch or nick bearing surfaces.
20. Do not allow the bearing to come in contact with dirt or rust at any time.

2 Wheel Drive

♦ See Figure 144

You will need a special claw type puller for this job to remove the inner bearing and the steering knuckle grease retainer if you truck has drum brakes.

Procedures are basically the same for either disc or drum brakes.

1. Remove the brake drum or brake caliper, following the procedure outlined in Section 9.
2. It is not necessary to remove the drum or disc from the hub. The outer wheel bearing will come off with the hub. Simply pull the hub and disc or drum assembly towards you off the spindle. Be sure to catch the bearing before it falls to the ground.
3. Drum brakes: The inner bearing and grease retainer must be pulled from the spindle with the claw puller. Be sure that the fingers of the tool pull on the seal, and not on the bearing itself. Discard the grease retainer.

Disc brakes: The inner bearing will have to be driven from the hub along with the oil seal. Use a brass rod as a drift and carefully drive the inner bearing cone out. Remove the bearing and the oil seal. Discard the seal.

To install:

4. Clean the bearings in solvent and allow to air dry. You risk leaving bits of lint in the races if you dry them with a rag. Clean the bearing cups in the hub.
5. Inspect the bearings carefully. If they are worn, pitted, burned, or scored, they should be replaced, along with the bearing cups in which they run.
6. You can use a brass rod as a drift, or a large socket or piece of pipe to drive the inner and outer bearing cups out of the hub.
7. Install the new inner cup, and then the outer cup, in that order, into the hub, using either the brass drift or socket method outlined earlier.

➡**Use care not to cock the bearing cups in the hub. If they are not fully seated, the bearings will be impossible to adjust properly.**

8. Drum brakes: Press a new grease retainer onto the spindle. Place a large glob of grease into one palm and force the edge of the inner bearing into it so that the grease fills the bearing. Do this until the whole bearing is packed. Press the inner bearing into the spindle, seating it firmly against the grease retainer.

Disc brakes: Coat the inner bearing cup with grease. Pack the inner bearing with grease as outlined for drum brakes, and press the inner bearing into the cup. Press a new oil seal into place on top of the bearing. You may have to give the seal a few gentle taps with a soft drift to get it to seat properly.

9. Install the hub and drum or disc assembly onto the spindle. With drum brakes, first thoroughly coat the inner cup with grease.
10. Coat the outer bearing cup with grease. Pack the outer bearing with grease and install into the cup.
11. Pack the grease cap with grease and set it aside. It will be replaced last, after the preload adjustment. You can put the grease away now.
12. Install the lock washer, and castellated nut (lock washer, nut, and adjusting castle nut with disc brakes) loosely, and go on to the preload adjustment following.

BEARING PRELOAD ADJUSTMENT

1. While turning the hub forward, tighten the castellated nut (plain nut on disc brakes) to 35 ft. lbs. (21 ft. lbs. with disc brakes).

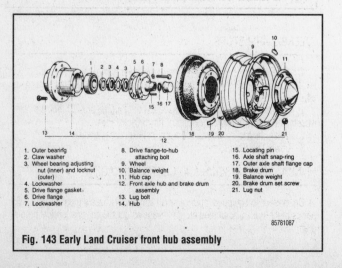

1. Outer bearing
2. Claw washer
3. Wheel bearing adjusting nut (inner) and locknut (outer)
4. Lockwasher
5. Drive flange gasket
6. Drive flange
7. Lockwasher
8. Drive flange-to-hub attaching bolt
9. Wheel
10. Balance weight
11. Hub cap
12. Front axle hub and brake drum assembly
13. Lug bolt
14. Hub
15. Locating pin
16. Axle shaft snap-ring
17. Outer axle shaft flange cap
18. Brake drum
19. Balance weight
20. Brake drum set screw
21. Lug nut

85781087

Fig. 143 Early Land Cruiser front hub assembly

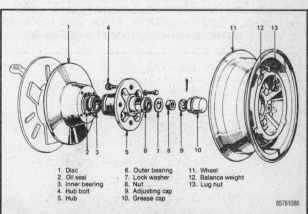

1. Disc
2. Oil seal
3. Inner bearing
4. Hub bolt
5. Hub
6. Outer bearing
7. Lock washer
8. Nut
9. Adjusting cap
10. Grease cap
11. Wheel
12. Balance weight
13. Lug nut

85781088

Fig. 144 Exploded view of the front disc and hub assembly. Drum brakes are similar, but have only 1 castellated nut between the lock washer and grease cap

2. Rotate the hub a few more times to snug down the bearings.

3. Retighten the nut to the above specification. Unscrew it ⅙ of a turn and lock it in place with a new cotter pin. On disc brakes, snug the adjusting nut up against the nut and then back it off the required distance to insert a new cotter pin. You should not have to back it off more than ⅙ of a turn.

4. Install the grease cap, and wipe off any grease that oozes out.

5. Install the front wheel and a couple of lug nuts. Check the axial play of the wheel by shaking it back and forth; the bearing free-play should feel close to zero, but the wheel should spin freely. With drum brakes, be sure that the shoes are not dragging against the drum.

6. If the bearing play is correct with drum brakes you can install the rest of the lug nuts. With disc brakes, remove the wheel, replace the caliper, then install the wheel.

4 Wheel Drive

➡ **The following applies to early models without free wheeling hubs. For models with free wheel hubs, see the front drive axle section in Section 7.**

The front wheel bearings should be repacked every 12,000 miles (20,000 km), or once a year, whichever comes first.

REMOVAL

1. Remove the hub cap and loosen the lug nuts.
2. Raise the front of the Cruiser and support it with jackstands.
3. Remove the lug nuts and the wheel.
4. Remove the cap from the axle shaft outer flange. Remove the snapring from the shaft.
5. Remove the bolts which secure the axle shaft outer flange to the hub.
6. Install two service bolts into the holes provided in the flange. Tighten the bolts evenly in order to loosen the flange. Withdraw the flange and the sealing gasket.

➡ **The flange should never be removed by prying it off; damage to the sealing surface could result in oil leaks.**

7. Remove the set screws and remove the brake drum.
8. Straighten out the lockwasher and remove the adjusting nut, using a spindle nut wrench.

➡ **Removing the adjusting nut with a hammer and chisel will result in damage to the nut and the spindle threads.**

9. Remove the hub assembly, complete with the washer, bearings and oil seal.
10. Remove the bearings from the hub.

CLEANING, INSPECTION, AND PACKING

Place all of the bearings, nuts, washer, and dust caps in a container of solvent. Cleanliness is basic to wheel bearing maintenance. Use a soft brush to thoroughly clean each part. Make sure that every bit of dirt and grease is rinsed of, then place each cleaned part on an absorbent cloth and let them dry completely.

Inspect the bearings for pitting, flat spots, rust, and rough areas. Check the races on the hub and the spindle for the same defects and rub them clean with a rag that has been soaked in solvent. If the races show hairline cracks or worn, shiny areas, they must be replaced with new parts. Replacement seals, bearings, and other required parts can be bought at an auto parts store. The old parts that are to be replaced should be taken along to be compared with the replacement part to ensure a perfect match.

Pack the wheel bearings with grease. There are special devices made for the specific purpose of greasing bearings, but, if one is not available, pack the wheel bearings by hand. Put a large dab of grease in the palm of your hand and push the bearing through it with a sliding motion. The grease must be forced through the side of the bearing and in between each roller. Continue until the grease begins to ooze out the other side and through the gaps between the rollers; the bearing must be completely packed with grease.

INSTALLATION

1. Install the inner bearing cone and the oil seal.
2. Pack the hub with grease, and install the outer bearing cup.
3. Assemble the brake drum to the hub.
4. Install the hub and drum assembly over the spindle and then install the outer bearing.
5. Install the claw washer and adjusting nut with the spindle nut wrench.
6. Adjust the bearing preload in the following manner:

   a. After tightening the adjusting nut with the spindle nut wrench, rotate the wheel back-and-forth in order to seat the bearing.

   b. Loosen the adjusting nut ⅛-⅙ of a turn.

   c. Check the brake drum for free rotation.

   d. Install the lockwasher and the locknut. Use the spindle nut wrench to tighten the locknut.

   e. Bend up the tabs on the lockwasher.

7. Install the axle shaft flange and gasket. Tighten the retaining bolts to 11–16 ft. lbs.

8. Install the bolt on the end of the outer shaft. Pull out on the shaft while installing the snapring.

9. Install the flange cap.

10. Install the wheel and the hub cap. Lower the vehicle.

OUTSIDE VEHICLE MAINTENANCE

Lock Cylinders

Apply graphite lubricant sparingly thought the key slot. Insert the key and operate the lock several times to be sure that the lubricant is worked into the lock cylinder.

Door Hinges and Hinge Checks

Spray a silicone lubricant on the hinge pivot points to eliminate any binding conditions. Open and close the door several times to be sure that the lubricant is evenly and thoroughly distributed.

Tailgate

Spray a silicone lubricant on all of the pivot and friction surfaces to eliminate any squeaks or binds. Work the tailgate to distribute the lubricant

Body Drain Holes

Be sure that the drain holes in the doors and rocker panels are cleared of obstruction. A small screwdriver can be used to clear them of any debris.

TRAILER TOWING

Factory trailer towing packages are available on most Toyota trucks. However, if you are installing a trailer hitch and wiring on your truck, there are a few thing that you ought to know.

Trailer Weight

Trailer weight is the first, and most important, factor in determining whether or not your vehicle is suitable for towing the trailer you have in mind. The horsepower-to-weight ratio should be calculated. The basic standard is a ratio of 35:1. That is, 35 pounds of GVW for every horsepower.

To calculate this ratio, multiply you engine's rated horsepower by 35, then subtract the weight of the vehicle, including passengers and luggage. The resulting figure is the ideal maximum trailer weight that you can tow. One point to consider: a numerically higher axle ratio can offset what appears to be a low trailer weight. If the weight of the trailer that you have in mind is somewhat higher than the weight you just calculated, you might consider changing your rear axle ratio to compensate.

Hitch Weight

There are three kinds of hitches: bumper mounted, frame mounted, and load equalizing.

Bumper mounted hitches are those which attach solely to the vehicle's bumper. Many states prohibit towing with this type of hitch, when it attaches to the vehicle's stock bumper, since it subjects the bumper to stresses for which it was not designed. Aftermarket rear step bumpers, designed for trailer towing, are acceptable for use with bumper mounted hitches.

Frame mounted hitches can be of the type which bolts to two or more points on the frame, plus the bumper, or just to several points on the frame. Frame mounted hitches can also be of the tongue type, for Class I towing, or, of the receiver type, for Classes II and III.

Load equalizing hitches are usually used for large trailers. Most equalizing hitches are welded in place and use use equalizing bars and chains to level the vehicle after the trailer is hooked up.

The bolt-on hitches are the most common, since they are relatively easy to install.

Check the gross weight rating of your trailer. Tongue weight is usually figured as 10% of gross trailer weight. Therefore, a trailer with a maximum gross weight of 2000 lb. will have a maximum tongue weight of 200 lb. Class I trailers fall into this category. Class II trailers are those with a gross weight rating of 2000–3500 lb., while Class III trailers fall into the 3500–6000 lb. category. Class IV trailers are those over 6000 lb. and are for use with fifth wheel trucks, only.

When you've determined the hitch that you'll need, follow the manufacturer's installation instructions, exactly, especially when it comes to fastener torques. The hitch will subjected to a lot of stress and good hitches come with hardened bolts. Never substitute an inferior bolt for a hardened bolt.

Wiring

Wiring your Toyota for towing is fairly easy. There are a number of good wiring kits available and these should be used, rather than trying to design your own. All trailers will need brake lights and turn signals as well as tail lights and side marker lights. Most states require extra marker lights for overly wide trailers. Also, most states have recently required back-up lights for trailers, and most trailer manufacturers have been building trailers with back-up lights for several years.

Additionally, some Class I, most Class II and just about all Class III trailers will have electric brakes.

Add to this number an accessories wire, to operate trailer internal equipment or to charge the trailer's battery, and you can have as many as seven wires in the harness.

Determine the equipment on your trailer and buy the wiring kit necessary. The kit will contain all the wires needed, plus a plug adapter set which included the female plug, mounted on the bumper or hitch, and the male plug, wired into, or plugged into the trailer harness.

When installing the kit, follow the manufacturer's instructions. The color coding of the wires is standard throughout the industry.

One point to note, most imported vehicles, have separate turn signals. On most domestic vehicles, the brake lights and rear turn signals operate with the same bulb. For those vehicles with separate turn signals, you can purchase an isolation unit so that the brake lights won't blink whenever the turn signals are operated, or, you can go to your local electronics supply house and buy four diodes to wire in series with the brake and turn signal bulbs. Diodes will isolate the brake and turn signals. The choice is yours. The isolation units are simple and quick to install, but far more expensive than the diodes. The diodes, however, require more work to install properly, since they require the cutting of each bulb's wire and soldering in place of the diode.

One final point, the best kits are those with a spring loaded cover on the vehicle mounted socket. This cover prevents dirt and moisture from corroding the terminals. Never let the vehicle socket hang loosely. Always mount it securely to the bumper or hitch.

Cooling

ENGINE

One of the most common, if not THE most common, problem associated with trailer towing is engine overheating.

With factory installed trailer towing packages, a heavy duty cooling system is usually included. Heavy duty cooling systems are available as optional equipment, with or without a trailer package. If you have one of these extra-capacity systems, you shouldn't have any overheating problems.

If you have a standard cooling system, without an expansion tank, you'll definitely need to get an aftermarket expansion tank kit, preferably one with at least a 2 quart capacity. These kits are easily installed on the radiator's overflow hose, and come with a pressure cap designed for expansion tanks.

Another helpful accessory is a Flex Fan. These fans are large diameter units are designed to provide more airflow at low speeds, with blades that have deeply cupped surfaces. The blades then flex, or flatten out, at high speed, when less cooling air is needed. These fans are far lighter in weight than stock fans, requiring less horsepower to drive them. Also, they are far quieter than stock fans.

If you do decide to replace your stock fan with a flex fan, note that if your truck has a fan clutch, a spacer between the flex fan and water pump hub will be needed.

Aftermarket engine oil coolers are helpful for prolonging engine oil life and reducing overall engine temperatures. Both of these factors increase engine life. While not absolutely necessary in towing Class I and some Class II trailers, they are recommended for heavier Class II and all Class III towing.

Engine oil cooler systems consist of an adapter, screwed on in place of the oil filter, a remote filter mounting and a multi-tube, finned heat exchanger, which is mounted in front of the radiator or air conditioning condenser.

TRANSMISSION

An automatic transmission is usually recommended for trailer towing. Modern automatics have proven reliable and, of course, easy to operate, in trailer towing.

The increased load of a trailer, however, causes an increase in the temperature of the automatic transmission fluid. Heat is the worst enemy of an automatic transmission. As the temperature of the fluid increases, the life of the fluid decreases.

It is essential, therefore, that you install an automatic transmission cooler.

The cooler, which consists of a multi-tube, finned heat exchanger, is usually installed in front of the radiator or air conditioning compressor, and hooked inline with the transmission cooler tank inlet line. Follow the cooler manufacturer's installation instructions.

Select a cooler of at least adequate capacity, based upon the combined gross weights of the truck and trailer.

Cooler manufacturers recommend that you use an aftermarket cooler in addition to, and not instead of, the present cooling tank in your radiator. If you do want to use it in place of the radiator cooling tank, get a cooler at least two sizes larger than normally necessary.

➡**A transmission cooler can sometimes cause slow or harsh shifting in the transmission during cold weather, until the fluid has a chance to come up to normal operating temperature. Some coolers can be purchased with or retrofitted with a temperature bypass valve which will allow fluid flow through the cooler only when the fluid has reached operating temperature, or above.**

JACKING AND HOISTING

▶ **See Figures 145, 146, 147 and 148**

Your truck is equipped with either a scissors type jack, or a bumper jack. The scissor-type jack is placed under the side of the truck so that it fits into the notch in the vertical rocker panel flange nearest the wheel to be changed. These jacking notches are located approximately 8 inches from the wheel opening on the rocker panel flanges. Bumper jack slots or flats are provided on the front and rear bumper. Be sure the jack is inserted firmly and is straight before raising the vehicle.

When raising the truck with a scissors or bumper jack follow these precautions: Park the truck on level spot, put the selector in **P** (PARK) with an automatic transmission or in reverse if your truck has a manual transmission, apply the parking brake and block the front and the back of the wheel that is diagonally opposite the wheel being changed. These jacks are fine for changing a tire,

Fig. 145 Vehicle lift and support locations—Front

Fig. 146 Vehicle lift and support locations—Rear

but never crawl under the truck when it is supported only by the scissors or bumper jack.

✶✶ CAUTION

If you're going to work beneath the vehicle, always support it on jackstands.

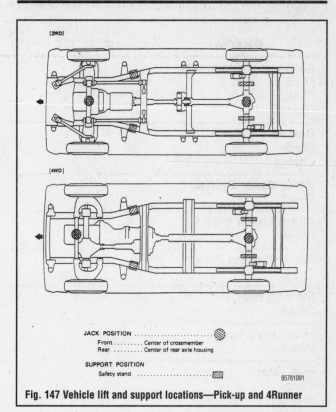

Fig. 147 Vehicle lift and support locations—Pick-up and 4Runner

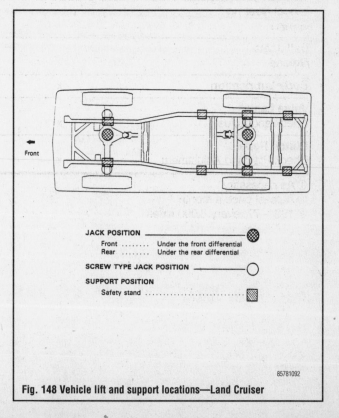

Fig. 148 Vehicle lift and support locations—Land Cruiser

Maintenance Intervals Chart

Intervals are for thousands of miles or number of months, whichever comes first.

NOTE: *Heavy-duty operation (trailer towing, prolonged idling, severe stop-and-go driving and winter operation on salted roads) should be accompanied by a 50% increase in maintenance. Cut the interval in half for these conditions. Operation in extremely dirty or dusty conditions may require immediate changes of engine oil and all filters.*

Maintenance	7.5 (6)	15 (12)	22.5 (18)	30 (24)	37.5 (30)	45 (36)	52.5 (42)	60 (48)	See Chapter
Automatic Transmission Fluid									
Check		x		x		x		x	1
Change				x				x	
Rear Axle									
Check		x		x		x		x	1
Change				x				x	
Brake Master Cylinder									
Check		x		x		x		x	1
Clutch Master Cylinder									
Check		x		x		x		x	1
Power Steering Fluid									
Check		x		x		x		x	1
Steering Gear									
Check		x		x		x		x	1
Wheels and Tires									
Check	②	②	②	②	②	②	②	②	1
Fuel Filter									
Check		x		x		x		x	1
Replace				x				x	
Wheel Bearing									
Grease				x				x	9
Ball Joints									
Grease				x				x	1 & 8
Body Lubrication		x		x		x		x	1
Valve Lash									
Check and Adjust		x		x		x		x	2
Clutch Pedal									
Check Play and Adjustment		x		x		x		x	6

① As necessary
② At least once a month
③ 1971–77; every 6,000 miles

85781R94

Capacities

Year	Model	Engine	Engine Displacement Cu. In. (cc)	Engine Crankcase (qts) With Filter	Without Filter	Transmission (qts) Manual 4-spd	5-spd	Automatic	Transfer Case (qts)	Drive Axle (qts) Front	Rear	Gasoline Tank (gals)	Cooling System (qts)
1970	Pick-Up	8R-C	113.8 (1858)	5.3	4.3	1.8	—	7.4	—	—	1.1	12.1	7.8
	Land Cruiser	F	236.7 (3878)	8.5	6.5	3.3	—	—	1.8	2.6	2.6	16.5①	17.7
1971	Pick-Up	8R-C	113.8 (1858)	5.3	4.3	1.8	—	7.4	—	—	1.1	12.1	7.8
	Land Cruiser	F	236.7 (3878)	8.5	6.5	3.3	—	—	1.8	2.6	2.6	16.5①	17.7
1972	Pick-Up	18R-C	120.7 (1980)	5.3	4.3	1.8	—	7.4	—	—	1.1	12.1	7.8
	Land Cruiser	F	236.7 (3878)	8.5	6.5	3.3	—	—	1.8	2.6	2.6	16.5①	17.7
1973	Pick-Up	18R-C	120.7 (1980)	5.3	4.3	1.8	—	7.4	—	—	1.1	12.1	7.8
	Land Cruiser	F	236.7 (3878)	8.5	6.5	3.3	—	—	1.8	2.6	2.6	16.5①	17.7
1974	Pick-Up	18R-C	120.7 (1980)	5.3	4.3	2.0	—	6.8	—	—	1.6	13.7	9.0
	Land Cruiser	F	236.7 (3878)	8.5	6.5	3.3	—	—	1.8	2.6	2.6	16.5①	17.7
1975	Pick-Up	20R	133.3 (2189)	4.8	3.9	2.0	2.8	7.0	—	—	1.6	12.1	8.5
	Land Cruiser	2F	257.9 (4200)	8.4	7.4	3.3	—	—	2.6	2.6	2.6	22.2②	17.5
1976	Pick-Up	20R	133.3 (2189)	4.8	3.9	2.0	2.8	7.0	—	—	1.6	12.1①	8.5
	Land Cruiser	2F	257.9 (4200)	8.4	7.4	3.3	—	—	2.6	2.6	2.6	22.2②	17.5
1977	Pick-Up	20R	133.3 (2189)	4.8	3.9	2.0	2.8	7.0	—	—	1.6	12.1①	8.5
	Land Cruiser	2F	257.9 (4200)	8.4	7.4	3.3	—	—	2.6	2.6	2.6	22.2②	17.5
1978	Pick-Up	20R	133.3 (2189)	4.8	3.9	2.0	2.8	6.7	—	—	1.6	12.1①	7.4
	Land Cruiser	2F	257.9 (4200)	8.4	7.4	3.3	—	—	2.6	2.6	2.6	22.2②	19.9
1979	Pick-Up	20R	133.3 (2189)	4.9	4.0	3.3	2.8	6.7	1.7	2.0	2.1	13.7	7.4
	Land Cruiser	2F	257.9 (4200)	8.4	7.4	3.3	—	—	2.6	2.6	2.6	22.2②	19.9
1980	Pick-Up	20R	133.3 (2189)	4.9	4.0	2.0	2.8	6.7	1.7	2.4	2.3	13.7②	8.9
	Land Cruiser	2F	257.9 (4200)	8.4	7.4	3.3	—	—	2.6	2.6	2.6	22.2②	19.9
1981	Pick-Up (2 wd)	22R	144.4 (2367)	4.9	4.0	2.1	2.7	6.7	—	—	1.8	13.7②	8.9
	Pick-Up (4 wd)	22R	144.4 (2367)	4.9	4.0	2.1	1.9	—	1.7	2.3	2.3	13.7②	8.9
	Land Cruiser	1L	133.5 (2188)	6.1	5.1	2.3	—	—	2.3	1.8	1.8	16.0	11.1
1982	Pick-Up (2 wd)	22R	144.4 (2367)	4.9	4.0	2.1	2.7	6.9	—	—	1.8	13.7②	8.9
	Pick-Up (4 wd)	22R	144.4 (2367)	4.9	4.0	2.1	1.9	—	1.7	2.3	2.3	13.7②	8.9
	Land Cruiser	1L	133.5 (2188)	6.1	5.1	2.3	—	—	2.6	1.8	1.8	16.0	11.1
1983	Pick-Up (2 wd)	22R	144.4 (2367)	4.9	4.2	2.9	2.7	6.9	—	—	1.8	13.7②	8.9
	Pick-Up (4 wd)	22R	144.4 (2367)	4.9	4.2	2.1	1.9	—	1.7	2.3	2.3	13.7②	8.9
	Pick-Up	1L	133.5 (2188)	6.1	5.3	—	2.3	—	1.7	2.4	2.3	17.2②	11.1
	Land Cruiser	2F	257.9 (4200)	8.2	7.4	3.3	4.7	—	2.6	2.6	2.6	22.2②	16.9

85781C09

Capacities (cont.)

Year	Model	Engine	Engine Displacement Cu. In. (cc)	Engine Crankcase (qts) With Filter	Without Filter	Transmission (qts) Manual 4-spd	5-spd	Automatic	Transfer Case (qts)	Drive Axle (qts) Front	Rear	Gasoline Tank (gals)	Cooling System (qts)
1984	Pick-Up (2 wd)	22R	144.4 (2367)	4.9	4.2	2.9	2.7	6.9	—	—	1.8	13.7③	8.9
	Pick-Up (4 wd)	22R	144.4 (2367)	4.9	4.2	2.4	4.1	—	1.7	2.4	2.3	17.2③	8.9
	Pick-Up	2L, 2L-T	149.3 (2447)	6.1	5.1	—	4.1	—	1.7	2.4	2.3	17.2③	11.1
	Land Cruiser	2F	257.9 (4200)	8.2	7.4	3.3	4.7	—	2.6	2.6	2.6	22.2③	16.9
1985	Pick-Up (2 wd)	22R	144.4 (2367)	4.9	4.2	2.5	2.7	6.9	—	—	1.9	13.7③	8.9
	Pick-Up (4 wd)	22R	144.4 (2367)	4.9	4.2	⑥	4.1	—	1.7	2.4	2.3	17.2③	8.9
	Pick-Up	2L, 2L-T	149.3 (2447)	⑥	5.1	⑥	—	—	1.7	2.4	2.6	17.2③	11.1
	Land Cruiser	2F	257.9 (4200)	8.2	7.4	3.7	2.5	15.9	2.2	3.2	2.6	23.8	17.4
1986	Pick-Up (2 wd)	22R	144.4 (2367)	4.9	4.2	2.5	2.7	⑨	—	—	1.9	13.7③	⑨
	Pick-Up (4 wd)	22R	144.4 (2367)	4.9	4.2	3.7	5.2	10.9	⑬	1.7	2.6	⑨	17.4
	Land Cruiser	2F	257.9 (4200)	8.2	7.4	3.7	5.2	15.9	2.2	3.2	2.6	23.8	17.4
1987–88	Pick-Up (2 wd)	22R	144.4 (2367)	4.5	4.0	2.5	2.5	6.9	—	—	1.9	13.7③	8.9
	Pick-Up (4 wd)	22R	144.4 (2367)	4.5	4.0	⑥	⑥	10.9	⑬	1.7	2.5	17.2③	⑨
	Pick-Up	3VZ-E	180.0 (2950)	4.8	4.4	—	3.2	—	1.2	1.7	2.5	17.2	NA
	Land Cruiser	2F	257.9 (4200)	8.2	7.4	3.7	5.2	15.9	2.2	3.2	2.6	23.8	17.4
	Land Cruiser	3F-E	241.3 (3955)	8.2	7.4	3.7	5.2	15.9	2.2	3.2	2.6	23.8	17.4

① Station Wagon: 23.8
② Station Wagon: 21.7
③ Long Bed: 16.1
④ Large Type: 19.3
⑤ Exc. Calif.: 6.1
⑥ 2.5
⑦ 2 wd: 2.5 / 4 wd: 3.2
⑧ 2 wd: 1.8 / 4 wd: 2.3
⑨ w/MT: 8.9 / w/AT: 9.6
⑩ 22R: 4.1 / 22R-E, 22R-TE: 3.2
⑪ w/MT: 1.7 / w/AT: 22R-E—0.8, 22R-TE—1.2
⑫ 22R, 22R-E: 2.3 / 22R-TE: 2.5
⑬ Pick-Up: Short bed—17.2, Long Bed—19.3 / 4 Runner: Standard—14.8, Large—17.2

85781CA9

Recommended Lubricants

Component		Lubricant
Engine Oil		API SF/CC
Manual Transmission	Pick-Up & 4 Runner	API GL-4 or GL-5, SAE 75W-90 or 80W-90
	Land Cruiser	API GL-4 or GL-5, SAE 90W
Automatic Transmission	1970–83	ATF Type F
	1984–88	ATF DEXRON® II
Transfer Case	Pick-Up & 4 Runner w/MT	API GL-4 or GL-5, SAE 75W-90 or 80W-90
	Pick-Up & 4 Runner w/AT	ATF DEXRON® or DEXRON® II
	Land Cruiser	API GL-4 or GL-5, SAE 90W
Drive Axles		API GL-5, SAE 90W
Brake Master Cylinder	Under 0°F (−18°C)	API GL-5, SAE 80W or 80W-90
Clutch Master Cylinder	Above 0°F (−18°C)	DOT 3, SAE J1703
Power Steering		DOT 3, SAE J1703
Steering Gear		ATF DEXRON® or DEXRON® II
Electric Winch		ATF DEXRON® or DEXRON® II
	Pick-Up & 4 Runner	ATF DEXRON® or DEXRON® II
	Land Cruiser	ATF Type F
Steering Knuckle		NLGI #2
Ball Joints		NLGI #1 / NLGI #2
Wheel Bearings		NLGI #2
Coolant		Ethylene Glycol-based Anti-freeze

85781067

2

ENGINE PERFORMANCE AND TUNE-UP

TUNE-UP PROCEDURES

In order to extract the best performance and economy from your engine it is essential that it be properly tuned at regular intervals. A regular tune-up will keep your Toyota's engine running smoothly and will prevent the annoying minor breakdowns and poor performance associated with an untuned engine.

➡**All Toyota Pick-Ups use a conventional breaker points ignition system through 1974. In 1975 Toyota switched to a transistorized ignition system. This system was much like the previous system with one basic difference; instead of the breaker points switching the primary current to the coil on and off, they triggered an igniter which did it for them. This igniter contains two transistors and an assortment of resistors which together serve as a switching device to turn the coil primary current on and off. The advantage of this type of circuitry is a reduced current through the distributor breaker points, thus prolonging their expected life and reducing scheduled maintenance. The transistorized igniter is found next to the coil on the right fender panel (as you face the truck) in 1975, and mounted on top of the coil in the same location in 1976–77. In 1977, a few models sold in California came equipped with a fully transistorized electronic ignition system. In 1978, this system became standard on all models.**

A complete tune-up should be performed every 15,000 miles (24,000 km) or twelve months, whichever comes first. This interval should be halved if the truck is operated under severe conditions, such as trailer towing, prolonged idling, continual stop and start driving, or if starting or running problems are noticed. It is assumed that the routine maintenance described in Section 1 has been kept up, as this will have a decided effect on the results of a tune-up. All of the applicable steps of a tune-up should be followed in order, as the result is a cumulative one.

If the specifications on the tune-up sticker in the engine compartment of your Toyota disagree with the "Tune-Up Specifications" chart in this section, the figures on the sticker must be used. The sticker often reflects changes made during the production run.

Spark Plugs

◆ **See Figures 1 and 2**

Spark plugs ignite the air and fuel mixture in the cylinder as the piston reaches the top of the compression stroke. The controlled explosion that results forces the piston down, turning the crankshaft and the rest of the drive train.

The average life of a spark plug is 15,000 miles (24,000 km), although manufacturers are now claiming spark plug lives of up to 30,000 miles (48,000 km) or more with the new platinum tipped plugs. This is, however, dependent on a

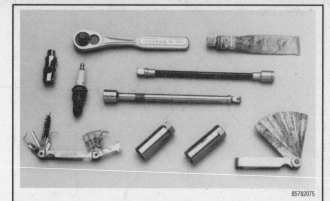
Fig. 2 Tune-up tools and feeler gauges

number of factors: the mechanical condition of the engine; the type of fuel; the driving conditions; and the driver.

When you remove the spark plugs, check their condition. They are a good indicator of the condition of the engine. It is a good idea to remove the spark plugs every 6,000 miles (9,600 km) or so to keep an eye on the mechanical state of the engine.

A small deposit of light tan or gray material (or rust red with unleaded fuel) on a spark plug that has been used for any period of time is to be considered normal. Any other color, or abnormal amounts of deposit, indicates that there is something amiss in the engine.

The gap between the center electrode and the side or ground electrode can be expected to increase not more than 0.0254mm every 1,000 miles (1600 km) under normal conditions.

When a spark plug is functioning normally or, more accurately, when the plug is installed in an engine that is functioning properly, the plugs can be taken out, cleaned, regapped, and reinstalled in the engine without doing the engine any harm.

When, and if, a plug fouls and begins to misfire, you will have to investigate, correct the cause of the fouling, and either clean or replace the plug.

There are several reasons why a spark plug will foul and you can learn which is at fault by just looking at the plug.

Spark plugs suitable for use in your Toyota's engine are offered in a number of different heat ranges. The amount of heat which the plug absorbs is determined by the length of the lower insulator. The longer the insulator the hotter the plug will operate; the shorter the insulator, the cooler it will operate. A spark plug that absorbs (or retains) little heat and remains too cool will accumulate deposits of lead, oil, and carbon, because it is not hot enough to burn them off. This leads to fouling and consequent misfiring. A spark plug that absorbs too much heat will have no deposits, but the electrodes will burn away quickly and, in some cases, preignition may result. Preignition occurs when the spark plug tips get so hot that they ignite the air/fuel mixture before the actual spark fires. This premature ignition will usually cause a pinging sound under conditions of low speed and heavy load. In severe cases, the heat may become high enough to start the air/fuel mixture burning throughout the combustion chamber rather than just to the front of the plug. In this case, the resultant explosion will be strong enough to damage pistons, rings, and valves.

In most cases the factory recommended heat range is correct; it is chosen to perform well under a wide range of operating conditions. However, if most of your driving is long distance, high speed travel, you may want to install a spark plug one step colder than standard. If most of your driving is of the short trip variety, when the engine may not always reach operating temperature, a hotter plug may help burn off the deposits normally accumulated under those conditions.

REMOVAL

◆ **See Figures 3, 4, 5 and 6**

1. Number the wires so that you won't cross them when you replace them.

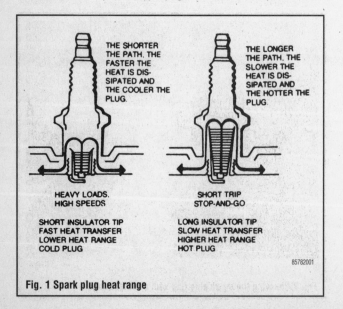

THE SHORTER THE PATH, THE FASTER THE HEAT IS DISSIPATED AND THE COOLER THE PLUG.

THE LONGER THE PATH, THE SLOWER THE HEAT IS DISSIPATED AND THE HOTTER THE PLUG.

HEAVY LOADS, HIGH SPEEDS

SHORT TRIP STOP-AND-GO

SHORT INSULATOR TIP
FAST HEAT TRANSFER
LOWER HEAT RANGE
COLD PLUG

LONG INSULATOR TIP
SLOW HEAT TRANSFER
HIGHER HEAT RANGE
HOT PLUG

Fig. 1 Spark plug heat range

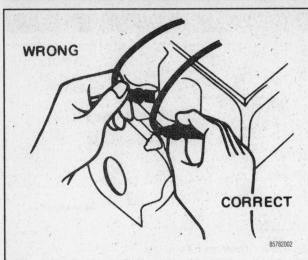

Fig. 3 When removing the spark plug wire always grasp it by the rubber boot

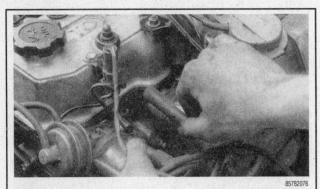

Fig. 4 Remove the spark plug wire—mark if necessary for correct installation

Fig. 5 Removing the spark plug

2. Remove the wire from the end of the spark lug by grasping the wire by the rubber boot. If the boot sticks to the plug, remove it by twisting and pulling at the same time. Do not pull wire itself or you will damage the core.

3. Use a $13/16$ in. spark plug socket to loosen all of the plugs about two turns.

➡**The cylinder head is cast from aluminum. Remove the spark plugs when the engine is cold, to prevent damage to the threads. If removal of the plugs is difficult, apply a few drops of penetrating oil or silicone**

Fig. 6 Check the spark plug wires in the distributor cap for correct installation

spray to the area around the base of the plug, and allow it a few minutes to work.

4. If compressed air is available, apply it to the area around the spark plug holes. Otherwise, use a rag or a brush to clean the area. Be careful not to allow any foreign material to drop into the spark plug holes.

5. Remove the plugs by unscrewing them the rest of the way from the engine.

INSPECTION & GAPPING

⬧ **See Figures 7, 8, 9 and 10**

Check the plugs for deposits and wear. If they are not going to be replaced, clean the plugs thoroughly. Remember that any kind of deposit will decrease the efficiency of the plug. Plugs can be cleaned on a spark plug cleaning machine, which can sometimes be found in service stations, or you can do an acceptable job of cleaning with a stiff brush. If the plugs are cleaned, the electrodes must be filed flat. Use an ignition points file, not an emery board or the like, which will leave deposits. The electrodes must be filed perfectly flat with sharp edges; rounded edges reduce the spark plug voltage by as much as 50%.

Check spark plug gap before installation. The ground electrode (the L-shaped one connected to the body of the plug) must be parallel to the center electrode and the specified size wire gauge (please refer to the Tune-Up Specifications chart for details) must pass between the electrodes with a slight drag.

➡**NEVER adjust the gap on a used platinum type spark plug.**

Always check the gap on new plugs as they are not always set correctly at the factory. Do not use a flat feeler gauge when measuring the gap on a used plug,

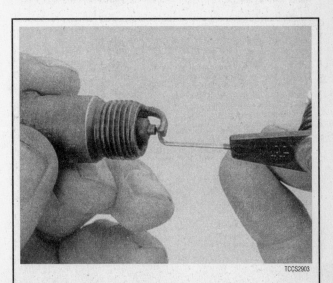

Fig. 7 Checking the spark plug gap with a feeler gauge

A normally worn spark plug should have light tan or gray deposits on the firing tip.

A carbon fouled plug, identified by soft, sooty, black deposits, may indicate an improperly tuned vehicle. Check the air cleaner, ignition components and engine control system.

This spark plug has been **left in the engine too long,** as evidenced by the extreme gap- Plugs with such an extreme gap can cause misfiring and stumbling accompanied by a noticeable lack of power.

An oil fouled spark plug indicates an engine with worn poston rings and/or bad valve seals allowing excessive oil to enter the chamber.

A physically damaged spark plug may be evidence of severe detonation in that cylinder. Watch that cylinder carefully between services, as a continued detonation will not only damage the plug, but could also damage the engine.

A bridged or almost bridged spark plug, identified by a build-up between the electrodes caused by excessive carbon or oil build-up on the plug.

TCCA1P40

Fig. 8 Inspect the spark plug to determine engine running conditions

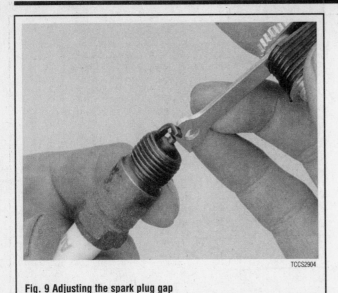

Fig. 9 Adjusting the spark plug gap

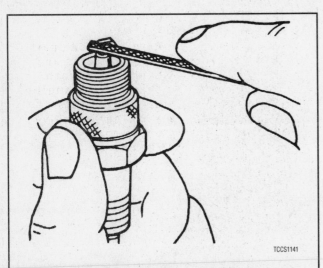

Fig. 10 If the standard plug is in good condition, the electrode may be filed flat—WARNING: do not file platinum plugs

because the reading may be inaccurate. A round-wire type gapping tool is the best way to check the gap. The correct gauge should pass through the electrode gap with a slight drag. If you're in doubt, try one size smaller and one larger. The smaller gauge should go through easily, while the larger one shouldn't go through at all. Wire gapping tools usually have a bending tool attached. Use that to adjust the side electrode until the proper distance is obtained. Absolutely never attempt to bend the center electrode. Also, be careful not to bend the side electrode too far or too often as it may weaken and break off within the engine, requiring removal of the cylinder head to retrieve it.

INSTALLATION

1. Lubricate the threads of the spark plugs with a drop of oil. Install the plugs and tighten them hand tight. Take care not to cross-thread them.
2. Tighten the spark plugs with the socket. Do not apply the same amount of force you would use for a bolt; just snug them in. If a torque wrench is available, tighten to 11–15 ft. lbs.
3. Install the wires on their respective plugs. Make sure the wires are firmly connected. You will be able to feel them click into place.

Spark Plug Wires

CHECKING & REPLACEMENT

▶ **See Figures 11 and 12**

At every tune-up, visually inspect the spark plug cables for burns, cuts, or breaks in the insulation. Check the boots and the nipples on the distributor cap and coil. Replace any damaged wiring.

Every 36,000 miles (58,000 km) or so, the resistance of the wires should be checked with an ohmmeter. Wires with excessive resistance will cause misfiring, and may make the engine difficult to start in damp weather. Generally, the useful life of the cables is 36,000-50,000 miles (58,000-80,000 km).

To check resistance, remove the distributor cap, leaving the wires attached. Connect one lead of an ohmmeter to an electrode within the cap; connect the other lead to the corresponding spark plug terminal (remove it from the plug for this test). Replace any wire which shows a resistance over 25,000 ohms. Test the high tension lead from the coil by connecting the ohmmeter between the center contact in the distributor cap and either of the primary terminals of the coil. If resistance is more than 25,000 ohms, remove the cable from the coil and check the resistance of the cable alone. Anything over 15,000 ohms is cause for replacement. It should be remembered that resistance is also a function of length; the longer the cable, the greater the resistance. Thus, if the cables on your truck are longer than the factory originals, resistance will be higher, quite possibly outside these limits.

When installing new cables, replace them one at a time to avoid mix-ups. Start by replacing the longest one first. Install the boot firmly over the spark plug. Route the wire over the same path as the original. Insert the nipple firmly into the tower on the cap or the coil.

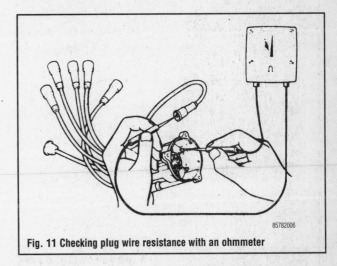

Fig. 11 Checking plug wire resistance with an ohmmeter

Fig. 12 Check the distributor cap for cracks; check the cable ends for wear

GASOLINE ENGINE TUNE-UP SPECIFICATIONS

When analyzing compression test results, look for uniformity among cylinders, rather than specific pressures.

Year	Engine Type	Spark Plugs Type	Spark Plugs Gap (in.)	Point Dwell (deg.)	Point Gap (in.)	Ignition Timing (deg.) ▲ MT	Ignition Timing (deg.) ▲ AT	Compression Pressure (psi)**	Fuel Pump Pressure (psi)	Idle Speed (rpm) ▲ MT	Idle Speed (rpm) ▲ AT	Valve Clearance (in.)‡ In.	Valve Clearance (in.)‡ Ex.
1970	8R-C	W20-EP	0.031	52	0.018	TDC	TDC	164	2.8-4.3	650	650	0.008	0.014
	F	B5-ES	0.030	41	0.018	7B	—	150	3.4-4.8	650	—	0.008	0.014
1971	8R-C	W20-EP	0.031	52	0.018	10B	10B	164	2.8-4.3	650	650	0.008	0.014
	F	B5-ES	0.030	41	0.018	7B	—	150	3.4-4.8	650	—	0.008	0.014
1972	18R-C	W20-EP	0.031	52	0.018	7B	7B	164	2.8-4.3	650	650	0.008	0.014
	F	B5-ES	0.030	41	0.018	7B	—	150	3.4-4.8	650	—	0.008	0.014
1973	18R-C	W20-EP	0.031	52	0.018	7B	7B	164	2.8-4.3	650	650	0.008	0.014
	F	B5-ES	0.030	41	0.018	7B	—	150	3.4-4.8	650	—	0.008	0.014
1974	18R-C	W20-EP	0.031	52	0.018	7B	7B	164	2.8-4.3	650	650	0.008	0.014
	F	B5-ES	0.030	41	0.018	7B	—	150	3.4-4.8	650	—	0.008	0.014
1975	20R	W16-EP	0.031	52	0.018	8B⊙	8B⊙	156	2.1-4.3	850	850	0.008	0.012
	2F	W14-EX	0.037	41	0.018	7B	—	150	3.4-4.8	650	—	0.008	0.014
1976	20R	W16-EP	0.031	52	0.018	8B⊙	8B⊙	156	2.1-4.3	850	850	0.008	0.012
	2F	W14-EX	0.037	41	0.018	7B	—	150	3.4-4.8	650	—	0.008	0.014
1977	20R	W16-EP	0.031	52	0.018	8B⊙	8B⊙	156	2.1-4.3	850	850	0.008	0.012
	2F	W14-EX	0.037	41	0.018	7B	—	150	3.4-4.8	650	—	0.008	0.014
1978	20R	W16-EP	0.031	⊚	0.012②	8B⊙	8B⊙	156	2.1-4.3	800	800	0.008	0.012
	2F	W14-EX	0.039	⊚	0.012②	8B	8B	150	3.4-4.8	800	800	0.008	0.014
1979	20R	W16-EXU	0.031	⊚	0.012②	8B	8B	156	2.1-4.3	800	800	0.008	0.010
	2F	W14-EX	0.039	⊚	0.012②	8B	8B	150	3.4-4.8	800	800	0.008	0.014
1980	20R	W16-EXU	0.031	⊚	0.012②	8B	8B	156	2.1-4.3	850	850	0.008	0.012
	2F	W14-EXU	0.031	⊚	0.012②	7B	—	150	3.4-4.8	800	—	0.008	0.014
1981	22R	W16-EXRU	0.031	⊚	0.012②	8B⊙	8B⊙	156	2.1-4.3	700	750	0.008	0.012
	2F	W14-EXRU	0.031	⊚	0.012②	7B	—	150	3.4-4.8	700	—	0.008	0.014
1982	22R	W16-EXRU	0.031	⊚	0.012②	8B⊙	8B⊙	156	2.1-4.3	700	750	0.008	0.012
	2F	W14-EXRU	0.031	⊚	0.012②	7B	—	150	3.4-4.8	700	—	0.008	0.014
1983	22R	W16-EXRU	0.031	⊚	0.012②	5B	5B	171	2.1-4.3	700	750	0.008	0.012
	2F	W14-EXRU	0.031	⊚	0.012②	7B	—	150	3.4-4.8	650	—	0.008	0.014
1984	22R	W16-EXRU	0.031	⊚	0.012②	5B	5B	171	2.1-4.3	700	750	0.008	0.012
	22R-E	W16-EXRU	0.031	⊚	0.012②	5B	5B	171	33-38	750	750	0.008	0.012
	2F	W16-EXRU	0.031	⊚	0.012②	7B	—	150	3.4-4.8	700	—	0.008	0.014
1985	22R	W16-EXRU	0.031	⊚	0.012②	0	0	171	2.1-4.3	700	750	0.008	0.012
	22R-E	W16-EXRU	0.031	⊚	0.012②	5B	5B	171	33-38	750	750	0.008	0.012
	2F	W14-EXRU	0.031	⊚	0.012②	7B	—	150	3.4-4.8	650	—	0.008	0.014
1986	22R	W16-EXRU	0.031	⊚	0.012②	0	0	171	2.1-4.3	700	750	0.008	0.012
	22R-E	W16-EXRU	0.031	⊚	0.012②	5B	5B	171	33-38	750	750	0.008	0.012
	22R-TE	W16-EXRU	0.031	⊚	0.012②	5B	5B	171	33-38	800	800	0.008	0.012
	2F	W16-EXRU	0.031	⊚	0.012②	7B	—	150	3.4-4.8	650	—	0.008	0.014
1987	22R	W16-EXRU	0.031	⊚	0.012②	0	0	171	2.1-4.3	700	750	0.008	0.012
	22R-E	W16-EXRU	0.031	⊚	0.012②	5B	5B	171	33-38	750	750	0.008	0.012
	22R-TE	W16-EXRU	0.031	⊚	0.012②	5B	5B	171	33-38	800	800	0.008	0.012
	2F	W14-EXRU	0.031	⊚	0.012②	7B	—	150	3.4-4.8	650	—	0.008	0.014

85782C01

GASOLINE ENGINE TUNE-UP SPECIFICATIONS

When analyzing compression test results, look for uniformity among cylinders, rather than specific pressures.

Year	Engine Type	Spark Plugs Type	Spark Plugs Gap (in.)	Point Dwell (deg.)	Point Gap (in.)	Ignition Timing (deg.) ▲ MT	Ignition Timing (deg.) ▲ AT	Compression Pressure (psi)**	Fuel Pump Pressure (psi)	Idle Speed (rpm) ▲ MT	Idle Speed (rpm) ▲ AT	Valve Clearance (in.)‡ In.	Valve Clearance (in.)‡ Ex.
1988	22R	W16-EXRU	0.031	⊚	0.012①	0	0	171	2.1-4.3	700	700	0.008	0.012
	22R-E	W16-EXRU	0.031	⊚	0.012①	5B	5B	171	33-38	750	750	0.008	0.012
	22R-TE	W16-EXRU	0.031	⊚	0.012①	5B	5B	171	33-38	800	800	0.008	0.012
	3VZ-E	Q6R-U	0.031	⊚	0.012①	10B	10B	171	38-44	800	800	0.012	0.013
	3F-E	W16-EXRU	0.031	⊚	0.008	7B	7B	149	37-46	650	650	0.008	0.014

85782C1A

NOTE: The underhood specifications sticker often reflects tune-up specification changes in production. Sticker figures must be used if they disagree with those in this chart.

▲ With the manual transmission in Neutral and the automatic transmission in Drive (D)

** The difference between cylinders should not exceed 14 psi

‡ Valve clearances checked with the engine HOT
MT—Manual transmission
AT—Automatic transmission
B—Before top dead center
In.—Intake
Ex.—Exhaust
① w/HAC—13B (see text)
② Electronic Ignition; refers to air gap, not point gap
⊚ Electronic ignition; dwell is pre-set at factory and not adjustable

Diesel Engine Tune-Up Specifications

Injector Opening Pressure (psi)	Idle Speed (rpm)	Valve Clearance (in.) Intake	Valve Clearance (in.) Exhaust	Cranking Compression Pressure @ 250 rpm (psi)	Maximum Compression Variance ③	Firing Order
1636–1778 ①	700	.010	.014	284–455 psi	71 psi	1-3-4-2
1493–1777 ②						

① New
② Used
③ Between highest & lowest readings

85782C02

FIRING ORDER

▶ **See Figures 13, 14, 15 and 16**

➡ **To avoid confusion, remove and tag the spark plug wires one at a time, for replacement.**

If a distributor is not keyed for installation with only one orientation, it could have been removed previously and rewired. The resultant wiring would hold the correct firing order, but could change the relative placement of the plug towers in relation to the engine. For this reason it is imperative that you label all wires before disconnecting any of them. Also, before removal, compare the current wiring with the accompanying illustrations. If the current wiring does not match, make notes in your book to reflect how your engine is wired.

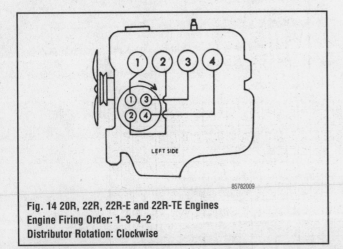

Fig. 13 8R-C and 18R-C Engines
Engine Firing Order: 1–3–4–2
Distributor Rotation: Clockwise

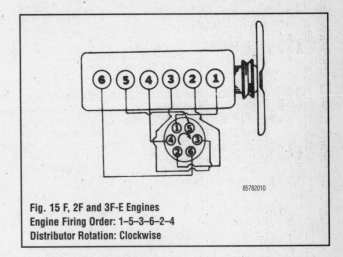

Fig. 15 F, 2F and 3F-E Engines
Engine Firing Order: 1–5–3–6–2–4
Distributor Rotation: Clockwise

Fig. 14 20R, 22R, 22R-E and 22R-TE Engines
Engine Firing Order: 1–3–4–2
Distributor Rotation: Clockwise

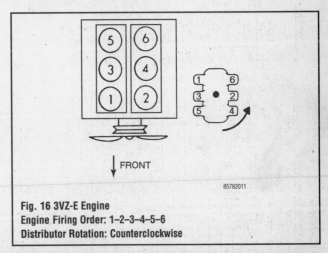

Fig. 16 3VZ-E Engine
Engine Firing Order: 1–2–3–4–5–6
Distributor Rotation: Counterclockwise

POINT TYPE IGNITION

Breaker Points and Condenser

The points function as a circuit breaker for the primary circuit of the ignition system. The ignition coil must boost the 12 volts of electrical pressure supplied by the battery to as much as 25,000 volts in order to fire the plugs. To do this, the coil depends on the points and the condenser to make a clean break in the primary circuit.

The coil has both primary and secondary circuits. When the ignition is turned on, the battery supplies voltage through the coil and onto the points. The points are connected to ground, completing the primary circuit. As the current passes through the coil, a magnetic field is created in the iron center core of the coil. When the cam in the distributor turns, the points open, breaking the primary circuit. The magnetic field in the primary circuit of the coil then collapses and cuts through the secondary circuit windings around the iron core. Because of the physical principle called "electromagnetic induction", the battery voltage is increased to a level sufficient to fire the spark plugs.

When the points open, the electrical charge in the primary circuit tries to jump the gap created between the two open contacts of the points. If this electrical charge were not transferred elsewhere, the metal contacts of the points would start to change rapidly.

The function of the condenser is to absorb excessive voltage from the points when they open and thus prevent the points from becoming pitted or burned.

If you have ever wondered why it is necessary to tune your engine occasionally, consider the fact that the ignition system must complete the above cycle each time a spark plug fires. On a 4-cylinder, 4-cycle engine, two of the four plugs must fire once for every engine revolution. If the idle speed of your engine is 800 revolutions per minute (800 rpm), the breaker points open and close two times for each revolution. For every minute your engine idles, your points open and close 1,600 times (2 x 800 = 1,600). And that is just at idle. What about at 3,000 rpm?

There are two ways to check breaker point gap; with a feeler gauge or with a dwell meter. Either way you set the points, you are adjusting the amount of time (in degrees of distributor rotation) that the points will remain open. If you adjust the points with a feeler gauge, you are setting the maximum amount the points will open when the rubbing block on the points is on a high point of the distributor cam. When you adjust the points with a dwell meter, you are measuring the number of degrees (of distributor cam rotation) that points will remain closed before they start to open as a high point of the distributor cam approaches the rubbing block of the points.

If you still do not understand how the points function, take a friend, go outside, and remove the distributor cap from your engine. Have your friend operate the starter (make sure that the transmission is not in gear) as you look at the exposed parts of the distributor.

There are two rules that should always be followed when adjusting or replacing points. The points and condenser are a matched set; never replace one without replacing the other. If you change the point gap or dwell of the engine, you also change the ignition timing. Therefore, if you adjust the points, you must also adjust the timing.

INSPECTION AND CLEANING

▶ **See Figures 17 and 18**

The breaker points should be inspected and cleaned at 6,000 mile (9,600 km) intervals. To do so, perform the following steps:
1. Disconnect the high tension lead from the coil.
2. Unsnap the two distributor cap retaining clips and lift the cap straight up. Leave the leads connected to the cap and position it out of the way.
3. Remove the rotor and dust cover by pulling them straight up.
4. Place a screwdriver against the breaker points and pry them open. Examine their condition. If they are excessively worn, burned, or pitted, they should be replaced.
5. Polish the points with a point file. Do not use emery cloth or sandpaper; these may leave particles on the points causing them to arc.
6. Clean the distributor cap and rotor with alcohol. Inspect the cap terminals for looseness and corrosion. Check the rotor tip for excessive burning. Inspect both cap and rotor for cracks. Replace either if they show any of the above signs of wear or damage.
7. Check the operation of the centrifugal advance mechanism by turning the rotor clockwise. Release the rotor; it should return to its original position. If it doesn't, check for binding parts.

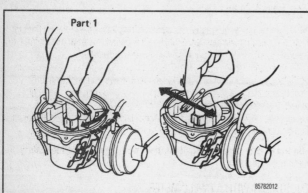

Fig. 17 The rotor should return to its original position when rotated slightly and then let go

Fig. 18 Pull straight up on the rotor to remove—when replacing, make certain that it is fully seated

8. Check the vacuum advance unit, but removing the plastic cap and pressing on the octane selector. It should return to its original position. Check for binding if it doesn't.
9. If the points do not require replacement, proceed with the adjustment section below. Otherwise perform the point and condenser replacement procedures.

POINT REPLACEMENT

1970–77

The points should be replaced every 12,000 miles (19,200 km), or if they are badly pitted, worn, or burned. To replace them, proceed as follows:
1. If you have not already done so, perform Steps 1–3 of the preceding "Inspection and Cleaning" procedure.
2. Unfasten the point lead connector.
3. Remove the point retaining clip and unfasten the point hold-down screw(s). It is a good idea to use a magnetic or locking screwdriver to remove the small screws inside the distributor, since they are almost impossible to find once they have been dropped.
4. Lift out the point set.
5. Install the new point set in the reverse order of removal. Adjust the points as detailed below, after completing installation.

CONDENSER REPLACEMENT

1970–77

Replace the condenser whenever the points are replaced, or if it is suspected of being defective. On Toyota trucks the condenser is located on the outside of the distributor (except the F, where it is inside the distributor). To replace it, proceed as follows:
1. Carefully remove the nut and washer from the condenser lead terminal. On the F, you must first remove the distributor cap.
2. Use a magnetic or locking screwdriver to remove the condenser mounting screw.
3. Remove the condenser.
4. Installation of a new condenser is performed in the reverse order of removal.

ADJUSTMENT

▶ **See Figures 19, 20, 21, 22 and 23**

Perform the gap adjustment procedure whenever new points are installed, or as part of routing maintenance. If you are adjusting an old set of points, you must check the dwell as well, since the feeler gauge is really only accurate with

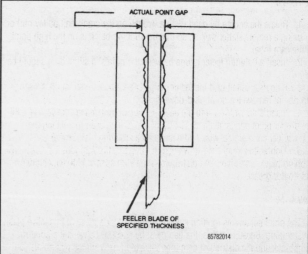

Fig. 19 The feeler gauge method of checking point gap is less accurate than the dwell meter method

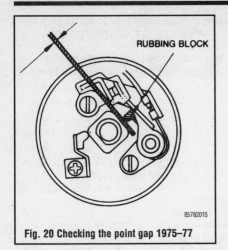

Fig. 20 Checking the point gap 1975–77

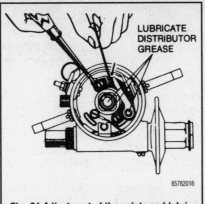

Fig. 21 Adjustment of the points and lubrication of the distributor cam

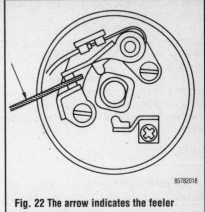

Fig. 22 The arrow indicates the feeler gauge used to set the point gap

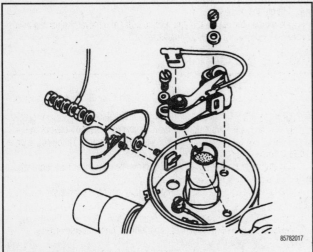

Fig. 23 Location of points and condenser. The screw below the points wire clip also serves to locate the ground wire, seen attached incorrectly here

a new point set. The points on 1975–77 trucks are adjusted in a slightly different manner than you may be familiar with so make sure that you follow the correct adjustment procedure below.

1970–74

1. Rotate the engine by hand (with a wrench on the crankshaft pulley nut) or by using a remote starter switch, so that the rubbing block is on the high point of the cam lobe.
2. Insert a 0.46mm feeler gauge between the points; a slight drag should be felt.
3. If no drag is felt or if the feeler gauge cannot be inserted at all, loosen, but do not remove the point hold-down screw.
4. Insert a screwdriver into the adjustment slot. Rotate the screwdriver until the proper point gap is attained. The point gap is increased by rotating the screwdriver counterclockwise and decreased by rotating it clockwise.
5. Tighten the point hold-down screw. Lubricate the cam lobes, breaker arm, rubbing block, arm pivot, and distributor shaft with special high temperature distributor grease.

1975–77

The point set on this ignition system is covered by a piece of protective plastic shielding. Because of this, the gap must be checked between the point rubbing block and the distributor cam lobe instead of between the two points. Do not try to remove the plastic shielding as it will damage the point set.

1. Using your hands, a wrench on the crankshaft pulley nut, or a remote

starter switch, rotate the engine so that the rubbing block is resting on the low point (flat side) of the cam lobe.
2. Insert a 0.46mm flat feeler gauge between the rubbing block and the cam lobe; a slight drag should be felt.
3. If no drag can be felt or if the feeler gauge cannot be inserted at all, loosen, but do not remove, the point hold-down screw.
4. Insert a screwdriver into the point adjustment slot. Rotate the screwdriver until the proper gap is achieved. The gap is increased by rotating the screwdriver counterclockwise and decreased by rotating it clockwise.
5. Tighten the point hold-down screw. Lubricate the cam lobes, breaker arm, rubbing block, arm pivot and distributor shaft with special high temperature distributor grease.

Dwell Angle

◊ See Figures 24 and 25

The dwell angle is the number of degrees of distributor cam rotation through which the points remain closed (conducting electricity). Increasing the point gap decreases dwell, while decreasing the gap increases dwell.

The dwell angle may be checked with the distributor cap and rotor installed and the engine running, or with the cap and rotor removed and the engine cranking at starter speed. The meter gives a constant reading with the engine running. With the engine cranking, the meter will fluctuate between zero degrees dwell and the maximum figure for that setting. Never attempt to adjust the points when the ignition is on, or you may receive a shock.

➡ **On trucks with electronic ignition, the dwell is pre-set at the factory and is not adjustable.**

ADJUSTMENT WITH A DWELL METER

➡ **When working on a 1975–77 truck, be sure to see the precautions noted in the following Transistorized Ignition section.**

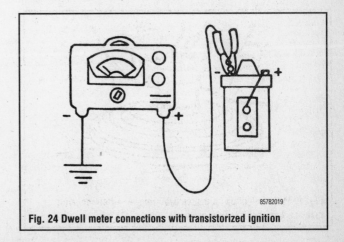

Fig. 24 Dwell meter connections with transistorized ignition

1. Connect a dwell meter to the ignition system, according to the manufacturer's instructions.

   a. When checking the dwell on a conventional ignition system, connect one meter lead (usually black) to a metallic part of the truck to ground the meter; the other lead (usually red) is connected to the coil primary post (the one with the small lead which runs to the distributor body).

   b. When checking dwell on a model with transistorized ignition, ground one meter lead (usually black) to a metallic part of the truck; hook up the other lead (usually red) to the negative (−) coil terminal. Under no circumstances should the meter be connected to the distributor or the positive (+) side of the coil. (See the "Service Precautions").

2. If the dwell meter has a set line, adjust the needle until it rests on the line.

3. Start the engine. It should be warmed up and running at the specified idle speed.

✳✳ CAUTION

Be sure to keep fingers, tools, clothes, hair, and wires clear of the engine fan. The transmission should be in Neutral (or Park), parking brake set, and running in a well ventilated area.

4. Check the reading on the dwell meter. If your meter doesn't have a 4-cylinder scale, multiply the 8-cylinder reading by two.

5. If the meter reading is within the range specified in the "Tune-Up Specifications" chart, shut the engine off and disconnect the dwell meter.

6. If the dwell is not within specifications, shut the engine off and adjust the point gap as previously outlined. Increasing the point gap decreases the dwell angle and vice versa.

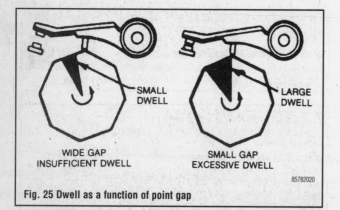

Fig. 25 Dwell as a function of point gap

ELECTRONIC IGNITION SYSTEM

Electronic Ignition

▶ **See Figures 26 thru 37**

Electronic ignition systems offer many advantages over the conventional breaker points ignition system. By eliminating the points, maintenance requirements are greatly reduced. An electronic ignition system is capable of producing much higher voltage which in turn aids in starting, reduces spark plug fouling and provides better emission control.

In 1977, certain models made for California came equipped with electronic ignition. In 1978, Toyota decided to make electronic ignition standard equipment on all models and that same basic system is still used on trucks today.

The system Toyota uses consists of a distributor with a signal generator, an ignition coil and an electronic igniter. The signal generator is used to activate the electronic components of the igniter. It is located in the distributor and consists of three main components; the signal rotor, the pick-up coil and the permanent magnet. The signal rotor (not to be confused with the normal rotor) revolves with the distributor shaft, while the pick-up coil and the permanent magnet are stationary. As the signal rotor spins, the teeth on it pass a projection leading from the pick-up coil. When this happens, voltage is allowed to flow through the system, firing the spark plugs. There is not physical contact and no electrical arcing, hence no need to replace burnt or worn parts.

7. Adjust the points until dwell is within specifications, then disconnect the dwell meter. Adjust the timing as detailed in the following section.

Transistorized Ignition

In 1975, Toyota introduced its transistorized ignition system. This system works very much like the conventional system previously described. Regular breaker points are used, but instead of switching primary current to the coil off-and-on, they are used to trigger a switching transistor. The transistor, in turn, switches the coil primary current on and off.

Since only a very small amount of current is needed to operate the transistor, the points will not become burned or pitted, as they would if they had full primary current passing through them. This also allows the primary current to be higher than usual because the use of a higher current would normally cause the points to fail much more rapidly.

As already stated, the condenser is used to absorb any extra high voltage passing through the points. Since, in the transistorized system, there is no high current, no condenser is needed or used.

As a result of the lower stress placed on them, the points only have to be replaced every 24,000 miles (38,000 km) instead of the usual 12,000 miles (19,200 km).

The Toyota transistorized ignition system may be quickly identified by the lack of a condenser on the outside of the distributor and by the addition of a control box, which is connected between the distributor and the primary side of the coil. This system was available on all 1975–77 models.

SERVICE PRECAUTIONS

Basically, the transistorized ignition is serviced just like its conventional counterpart. The points must be checked, adjusted, and replaced in the same manner. Point gap and dwell must be checked and set. The points should also be kept clean and should be replaced at 24,000 mile (38,000 km) intervals. Of course, since there is no condenser, it does not have to be replaced when the points are.

However, there are several precautions to observe when servicing the transistorized ignition system:

1. Use only pure alcohol to clean the points. Shop solvent or an oily rag will leave a film on the points which will not allow the low current to pass.

2. Hook up a tachometer, dwell meter, or a combination dwell/tachometer to the negative (−) side of the coil; NOT to the distributor or the positive (+) side. Damage to the switching transistor will result if the meter is connected in the usual manner.

3. See the previous section for the remaining service procedures which are identical to those for the conventional ignition system.

Service consists of inspection of the distributor cap, rotor and the ignition wires; replacing them as necessary. In addition, the air gap between the signal rotor and the projection on the pick-up coil should be checked periodically.

Fig. 26 Removing the coil wire from the coil assembly

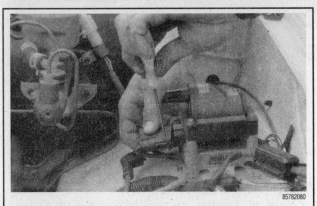

Fig. 27 Removing the coil assembly electrical locking connectors

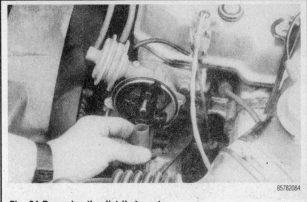

Fig. 31 Removing the distributor rotor

Fig. 28 Removing the coil assembly electrical connector

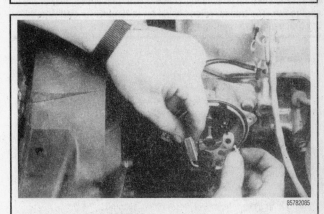

Fig. 32 Removing the distributor pick-up coil retaining screw

Fig. 29 Removing the distributor cap hold-down screws

Fig. 33 Removing the distributor pick-up coil

Fig. 30 Removing the distributor cap

Fig. 34 Removing the distributor advance unit retaining E-clip

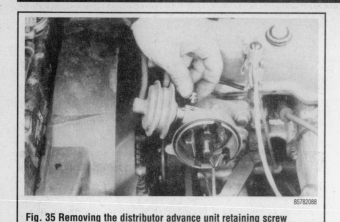

Fig. 35 Removing the distributor advance unit retaining screw

Fig. 36 Removing the distributor advance unit

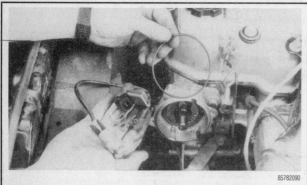

Fig. 37 View of electronic ignition components and O-ring gasket for the distributor assembly

AIR GAP ADJUSTMENT

▶ **See Figures 38 and 39**

1. Remove the distributor cap as detailed earlier. Inspect the cap for cracks, carbon tracks or a worn center contact. Replace it if necessary, transferring the wires one at a time from the old cap to the new one.
2. Pull the ignition rotor (not the signal rotor) straight up and remove it. Replace it if the contact are worn, burned or pitted. Do not file the contacts.
3. Turn the engine using a socket wrench on the front pulley bolt until the projection on the pickup coil is directly opposite the signal rotor tooth.
4. Get a non-ferrous (paper, brass, or plastic) feeler gauge of 0.30mm, and insert it into the pick-up air gap. DO NOT USE AN ORDINARY METAL FEELER GAUGE! The gauge should just touch either side of the gap. The permissible range is 0.20–0.40mm.

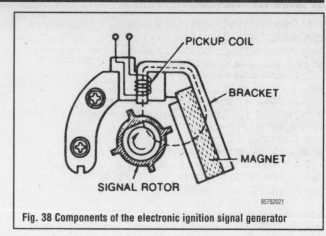

Fig. 38 Components of the electronic ignition signal generator

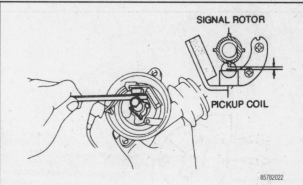

Fig. 39 Use a non-ferrous feeler gauge when checking the air gap on the electronic ignition system

➡ **The air gap on all 1987–88 engines is NOT adjustable. If the gap is not within specifications, the distributor must be replaced.**

5. If the gap is either too wide or too narrow, loosen the two Phillips screws mounting the pick-up coil onto the distributor base plate. Then, wedge a screwdriver between the notch in the pick-up coil assembly and the two dimples on the base plate, and turn the screwdriver back and forth until the pick-up gap is correct.
6. Tighten the screws and recheck gap, readjusting if necessary.

Troubleshooting the Fully Transistorized Electronic Ignition System

PRECAUTIONS

1. Do not allow the ignition switch to be ON for more than ten minutes if the engine will not start.
2. When a tachometer is connected to the system, always connect the tachometer positive lead to the ignition coil negative terminal. As some tachometers are not compatible with this system, it is recommended that you consult with the manufacturer.
3. NEVER allow the ignition coil terminals to touch ground as it could result in damage to the igniter and/or the ignition coil itself.
4. Do not disconnect the battery when the engine is running.
5. Make sure that the igniter is always properly grounded to the body.

TROUBLESHOOTING

▶ **See Figure 40**

Troubleshooting this system is easy, but you must have an accurate ohmmeter and voltmeter. The numbers in the diagram correspond to the numbers of the following troubleshooting steps. Be sure to perform each step in order.

1. Check for spark at the spark plugs by hooking up a timing light in the usual manner. If the light flashes, it can be assumed that voltage is reaching the plugs, which should then be inspected, along with the fuel system. If no flash is generated, go on to the following ignition checks.

2. Check all wiring and plastic connectors for tight and proper connections.

3. (1) With an ohmmeter, check between the positive (+) and negative (−) primary terminals of the ignition coil. The resistance (cold) should be 1.3–1.7 ohms. Between the (+) primary terminal and the high tension terminal, the resistance (cold) should be 12–16 ohms.(2) The insulation resistance between the (+) primary terminal and the ignition coil case should be infinite.

4. The resistor wire (brown and yellow) resistance should be 1.2 ohms (cold). To measure, disconnect the plastic connector at the igniter and connect one wire of the ohmmeter to the yellow wire and one to the brown.

5. Remove the distributor cap and ignition rotor.(1) Check the air gap between the timing rotor spoke and the pick-up coil. When aligned, the air gap should be 0.008–0.016 in. You will probably have to bump the engine around with the starter to line up the timing rotor.(2) Unplug the distributor connector at the distributor. Connect one wire of the ohmmeter to the white wire, and one wire to the pink wire. The resistance of the signal generator should be 130–190 ohms.

6. (1) Checking the igniter last, connect the (−) voltmeter wire to the (−) ignition coil primary terminal, and the (+) voltmeter wire to the yellow resistor wire at the connector unplugged in Step 4. With the ignition switch turned to **On** (not Start) the voltage should measure 12 volts. (2) Check the voltage between the (−) ignition coil primary terminal and the yellow resistor wire again, but this time use the ohmmeter as resistance. Using the igniter end of the distributor connector unplugged in Step 5, connect the positive (+) ohmmeter wire to the pink distributor wire, and the negative (−) ohmmeter wire to the white wire.

❋❋ CAUTION

Do not intermix the (+) and (−) terminals of the ohmmeter.

Select either the 1 ohms or 10 ohms range of the ohmmeter. With the voltmeter connected as in Step 6 (1), and the ignition switch turned to **On** (not Start), the voltage should measure nearly zero.

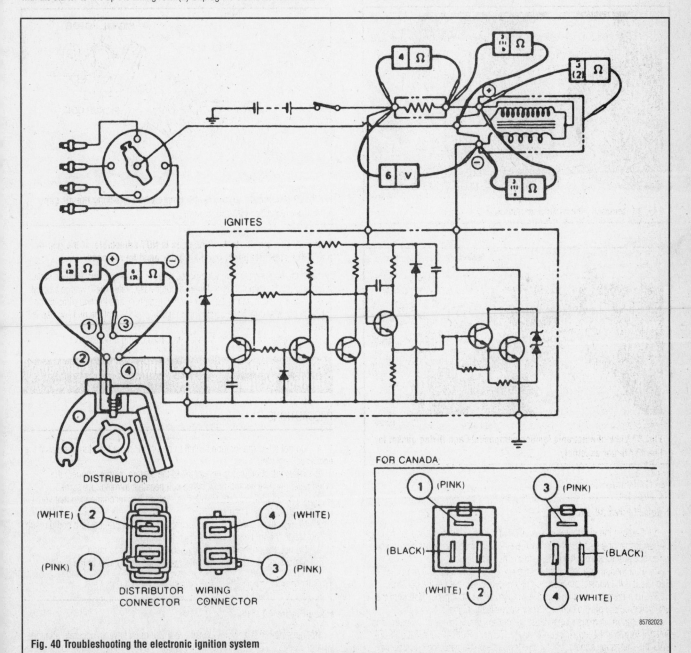

Fig. 40 Troubleshooting the electronic ignition system

IGNITION TIMING

Ignition Timing

▶ **See Figures 41 thru 47**

Ignition timing is the measurement in degrees of crankshaft rotation of the instant the spark plugs in the cylinders fire, in relation to the location of the piston, while the piston is on its compression stroke.

Ignition timing is adjusted by loosening the distributor locking device and turning the distributor in the engine.

Ideally, the air/fuel mixture in the cylinder will be ignited (by the spark plug) and just beginning its rapid expansion as the piston passes top dead center (TDC) of the compression stroke. If this happens, the piston will be beginning the power stroke just as the compressed (by the movement of the piston)

air/fuel mixture starts to expand. The expansion of the air/fuel mixture will then force the piston down on the power stroke and turn the crankshaft.

It takes a fraction of a second for the spark from the plug to completely ignite the mixture in the cylinder. Because of this, the spark plug must fire before the piston reaches TDC, if the mixture is to be completely ignited as the piston passes TDC. This measurement is given in degrees (of crankshaft rotation) before the piston reaches top dead center (BTDC). If the ignition timing setting for your engine is seven (7°) BTDC, this means that the spark plug must fire at a time when the piston for that cylinder is 7° before top dead center of its compression stroke. However, this only holds true while your engine is at idle speed.

As you accelerate from idle, the speed of your engine (rpm) increases. The increase in rpm means that the pistons are now traveling up and down much

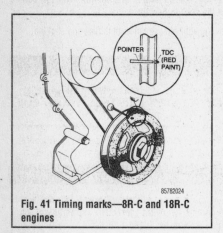

Fig. 41 Timing marks—8R-C and 18R-C engines

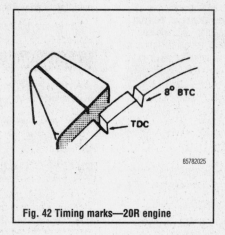

Fig. 42 Timing marks—20R engine

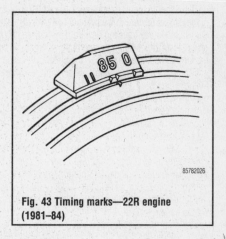

Fig. 43 Timing marks—22R engine (1981–84)

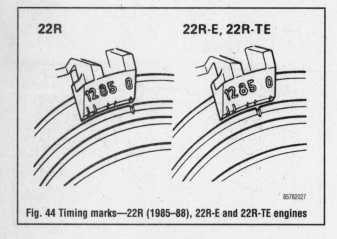

Fig. 44 Timing marks—22R (1985–88), 22R-E and 22R-TE engines

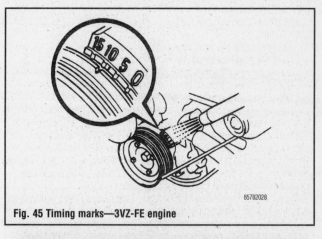

Fig. 45 Timing marks—3VZ-FE engine

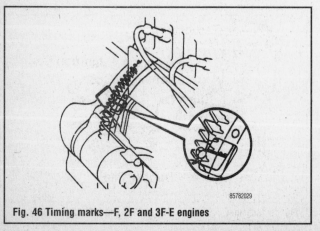

Fig. 46 Timing marks—F, 2F and 3F-E engines

Fig. 47 Timing marks on crankshaft pulley

faster. Because of this, the spark plugs will have to fire even sooner if the mixture is to be completely ignited as the piston passes TDC. To accomplish this, the distributor incorporates means to advance the timing of the spark as engine speed increases.

The distributor in your Toyota has two means of advancing the ignition timing. One is called centrifugal advance and is actuated by weights in the distributor. The other is called vacuum advance and is controlled by that larger circular housing on the side of the distributor.

In addition, some distributors have a vacuum retard mechanism which is contained in the same housing on the side of the distributor as the vacuum advance. The function of this mechanism is to retard the timing of the ignition spark under certain engine conditions. This causes more complete burning of the air/fuel mixture in the cylinder and consequently lowers exhaust emissions.

Because these mechanisms change ignition timing, it is necessary to disconnect and plug the one or two vacuum lines from the distributor when setting the basic ignition timing.

If ignition timing is set too far advanced (BTDC), the ignition and expansion of the air/fuel mixture in the cylinder will try to force the piston down the cylinder while it is still traveling upward. This causes engine "ping", a sound which resembles marbles being dropped into an empty tin can. If the ignition timing is too far retarded (after, or ATDC), the piston will have already started down on the power stroke when the air/fuel mixture ignites and expands. This will cause the piston to be forced down only a portion of its travel. This will result in poor engine performance and lack of power.

Ignition timing adjustment is checked with a timing light. This instrument is connected to the number one (No. 1) spark plug of the engine. The timing light flashes every time an electrical current is sent from the distributor, through the No. 1 spark plug wire, to the spark plug. The crankshaft pulley and the front cover of the engine are marked with a timing pointer and a timing scale. When the timing pointer is aligned with the **0** mark on the timing scale, the piston in the No. 1 cylinder is at TDC of its compression stroke. With the engine running, and the timing light aimed at the timing pointer and timing scale, the stroboscopic flashes from the timing light will allow you to check the ignition timing setting of the engine. The timing light flashes every time the spark plug in the No. 1 cylinder of the engine fires. Since the flash from the timing light makes the crankshaft pulley seem stationary for a moment you will be able to read the exact position of the piston in the No. 1 cylinder on the timing scale on the front of the engine.

There are three basic types of timing lights available. The first is a simple neon bulb with two wire connections (one for the spark plug and one for the plug wire, connecting the light in series). This type of light is quite dim, and must be held closely to the marks to be seen, but it is inexpensive. The second type of light operates from the battery. Two alligator clips connect to the battery terminals, while a third wire connects to the spark plug with an adapter. This type of light is more expensive, but the xenon bulb provides a nice bright flash which can even be seen in sunlight. The third type replaces the battery source with 110 volt house current. Some timing lights have other functions built into them, such as dwell meters, tachometers, or remote starting switches. These are convenient, in that they reduce the tangle of wires under the hood, but may duplicate the functions of tools you already have.

If your Toyota has electronic ignition, you should use a timing light with an inductive pickup. This pickup simply clamps onto the No. 1 plug wire, eliminating the adapter. It is not susceptible to crossfiring or false triggering, which may occur with a conventional light, due to the greater voltages produced by electronic ignition.

CHECKING & ADJUSTMENT

Carbureted Engines

▶ See Figures 48 thru 54

1. Warm-up the engine. Connect a tachometer and check the engine idle speed to be sure that it is within the specification given in the "Tune-Up Specifications" chart at the beginning of the section.

➡Before hooking up a tachometer to a 1975-77 truck with a transistorized ignition system see the preceding "service precautions" in the "Breaker Points and Condenser" section. On models with electronic ignition, hook the positive (+) terminal of the dwell meter or tachometer to the negative (–) side of the coil, not to the distributor primary lead, on the 22R, hook the positive lead to the service connector on the

igniter; damage to the ignition control unit will result. See illustrations.

2. Clean off the timing marks. On the 2F, the timing marks are a ball on the flywheel and a pointer on the bellhousing. On all other engines, the marks are on the crankshaft pulley and timing cover. The timing notches in the crankshaft pulley are normally marked at the factory with red or white paint. You may want to retouch them if they are dark, using chalk or paint. Fluorescent (dayglow) paint is excellent for this purpose. You might have to bump the engine around with the starter to find the pulley marks.

3. Connect a timing light according to the manufacturer's instructions.

4. Disconnect the vacuum line(s) from the distributor vacuum unit. Plug it (them) with a pencil or golf tee(s).

➡On 20R and 22R engines with HAC (High Altitude Compensation system) there are two vacuum hoses which connect to the distributor. Both must be disconnected and plugged. These systems require an extra step in the timing procedure, found at the end of this section. You can obtain more information about the HAC in Section 4.

5. Be sure that the timing light wires are clear of the fan and start the engine.

✳✳ CAUTION

Keep fingers, clothes, tools, hair, and leads clear of the spinning engine fan. Be sure that you are running the engine in a well ventilated area!

6. Allow the engine to run at the specified idle speed with the gearshift in Neutral with manual transmission and Drive (D) with automatic transmission.

✳✳ CAUTION

Be sure that the parking brake is set and that the front wheels are blocked to prevent the truck from rolling forward, especially when Drive is selected with an automatic!

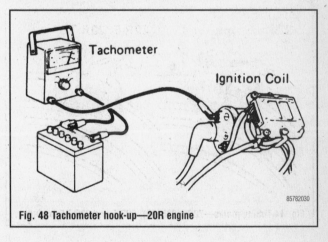

Fig. 48 Tachometer hook-up—20R engine

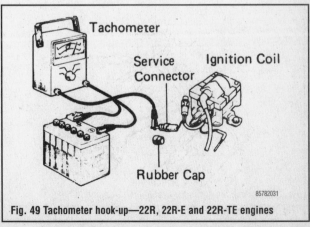

Fig. 49 Tachometer hook-up—22R, 22R-E and 22R-TE engines

7. Point the timing light at the marks indicated in the chart and illustrations. With the engine at idle, timing should be at the specification given on the "Tune-Up Specifications" chart at the beginning of the section.

8. If the timing is not at the specification, loosen the pinch bolt (hold-down bolt) at the base of the distributor just enough so that the distributor can be turned. Turn the distributor to advance or retard the timing as required. Once the proper marks are seen to align with the timing light, timing is correct. If only minor corrections in the timing are necessary, adjustment can be made with the octane selector, rather than by moving the distributor. See the Octane Selector section following for further information.

9. Stop the engine and tighten the pinch bolt. Start the engine and recheck the timing. Stop the engine; disconnect the tachometer and timing light. Connect the vacuum line(s) to the distributor vacuum unit. Except on engines with HAC.

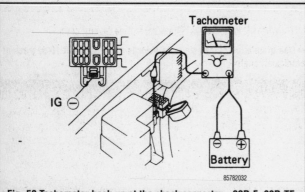

Fig. 50 Tachometer hook-up at the check connector—22R-E, 22R-TE and 3VZ-E engines

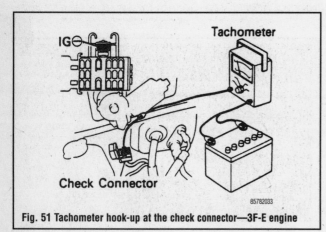

Fig. 51 Tachometer hook-up at the check connector—3F-E engine

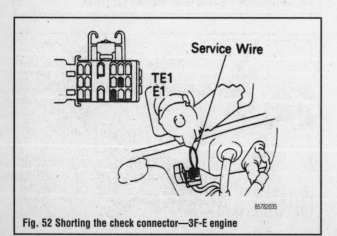

Fig. 52 Shorting the check connector—3F-E engine

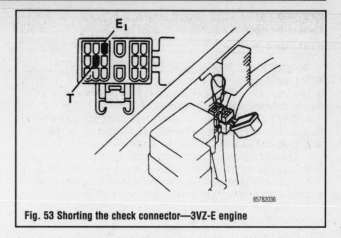

Fig. 53 Shorting the check connector—3VZ-E engine

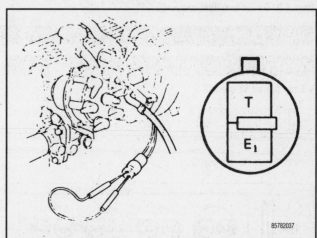

Fig. 54 Short circuit the terminals of the timing check connector T-E and check and adjust the timing, then unshort the connector—22R-E and 22R-TE engines

10. On engines with HAC (identified in the NOTE earlier) after setting the initial timing, reconnect the vacuum hose at the distributor. Recheck the timing. It should now be about 13° BTDC.

11. If the advance is still about 8°, pinch the hose between the HAC valve and the three way connector. It should now be about 13°. If not, the HAC valve should be checked for proper operation.

Fuel Injected Engines

1. Connect a timing light to the engine following the manufacturer's instructions.

➡These engines require a special type of tachometer which hooks up to the service connector wire coming out of the distributor. You may also obtain an rpm reading by hooking the tachometer lead to the IG (−) terminal in the check connector found on the inner fender well. As many tachometers are not compatible with this hook-up, we recommend that you consult with the manufacturer before purchasing a certain type.

2. Start the engine and run it at idle.

3. Remove the rubber cap from the check connector and short the connector at terminals (T-E), as shown.

4. Loosen the distributor pinch bolt just enough that the distributor can be turned. Aim the timing light at the marks on the crankshaft pulley and slowly turn the distributor until the timing mark is at the desired readings as listed in the "Tune-Up Specifications" chart. Tighten the distributor pinch bolt.

5. Unshort the connector.

Octane Selector

▶ **See Figure 55**

The octane selector is used as a fine adjustment to match the ignition timing to the grade of gasoline being used. It is located near the distributor vacuum advance unit, under a plastic cover. Normally the octane selector should not require adjustment, however, adjustment is as follows:

1. Align the setting line with the threaded end of the housing and then align the center line with the setting mark on the housing.
2. Drive the truck at 16–22 mph in High gear on a level road.
3. Depress the accelerator pedal all the way to the floor. A slight pinging sound should be heard. As the vehicle accelerates, the sound should go away.
4. If the pinging sound is loud, or if it fails to disappear as the vehicle accelerates, retard the timing by turning the knob toward **R** (retard).
5. If there is no pinging sound at all, advance the timing by turning the knob toward **A** (advance).

➡**On 1973-79 models, do not turn the octane selector more than ½ turn toward R. Do not turn it toward A at all.**

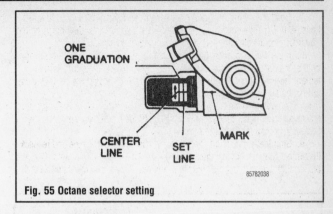

Fig. 55 Octane selector setting

6. When the adjustment is completed, replace the dust cover.

➡**One graduation of the octane selector is equal to about 10 degrees of crankshaft angle.**

VALVE LASH

Valve Lash Adjustment

▶ **See Figures 56 thru 62**

As part of every major tune-up or once every 6000 miles (1970–74) 12,500 miles (1975–78 20R engine), and 15,000 miles (1979–88) the valve clearance should be checked and adjusted if necessary.

Valve lash is one factor which determines how far the intake and exhaust valves will open into the cylinder.

If the valve clearance is too large, part of the lift of the camshaft will be used up in removing the excessive clearance, thus the valves will not be opened far enough. This condition has two effects, the valve train components will emit a tapping noise as they take up the excessive clearance, and the engine will perform poorly, since the less the intake valves open, the smaller the amount of air/fuel mixture admitted to the cylinders will be. The less the exhaust valves open, the greater the back-pressure in the cylinder which prevents the proper air/fuel mixture from entering the cylinder.

If the valve clearance is too small, the intake and exhaust valves will not fully seat on the cylinder head when they close. When a valve seats on the cylinder head it does two things; it seals the combustion chamber so none of the gases

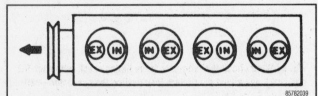

Fig. 56 Valve arragement-8R-C and 18R-C engines

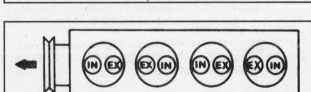

Fig. 57 Valve arragement-20R, 22R, 22R-E and 22R-TE engines

Fig. 59 Removing the valve cover retaining nut gasket

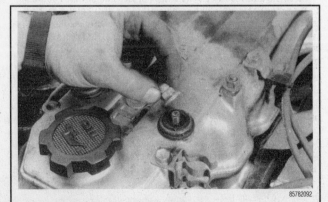

Fig. 58 Removing the valve cover nuts

Fig. 60 Removing the valve cover

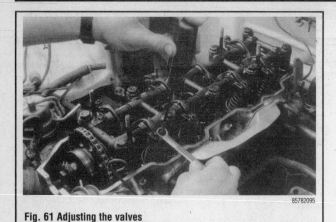

Fig. 61 Adjusting the valves

Fig. 62 Check the valve cover gasket for proper alignment before installation

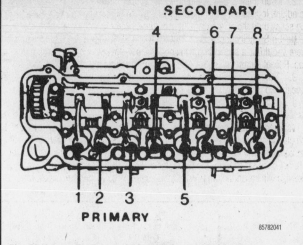

Fig. 63 Valve adjusting sequence-8R-C and 18R-C engines

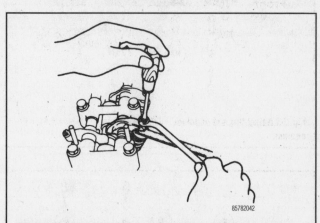

Fig. 64 Measure the clearance between the valve stem and adjusting nut—there should be a slight drag on the feeler gauge when properly adjusted

in the cylinder can escape and it cools itself by transferring some of the heat it absorbed from the combustion process through the cylinder head and into the engine cooling system. Therefore, if the valve clearance is too small, the engine will run poorly (due to gases escaping from the combustion chamber), and the valves will overheat and warp (since they cannot transfer heat unless they are touching the seat in the cylinder head).

➡**Although Toyota recommends that the valve lash on certain models be set while the engine is running, we feel that for the average owner/mechanic it is more convenient to adjust the valves statically (engine off). Thus, running valve lash and adjustment procedures have been omitted from the manual. While all valve adjustments must be as accurate as possible, it is better to have the valve adjustment slightly loose than slightly tight, as burnt valves may result from overly tight adjustments.**

ADJUSTMENT

8R-C and 18R-C

▶ **See Figures 63 and 64**

1. Start the engine and allow it to run until it reaches normal operating temperature.

➡**Be careful not to touch the engine as it will be quite hot.**

2. Turn the engine off and remove the air cleaner assembly; the housing, hoses and bracket.

3. Remove any other hoses, cables or wires which are attached to the cylinder head cover.

4. Check that the rocker arm bolts, the camshaft bearing cap bolts and the bearing cap union bolts are all tightened to the proper torque.

5. Set the No. 1 cylinder at TDC. Turn the crankshaft pulley until the pointer on the front cover lines up with the notch on the pulley.

➡Do not attempt to align the marks by cranking the engine with the starter. Valve clearances are checked with the engine stopped to prevent hot oil from being splashed out by the timing chain.

6. Check that the rocker arms on the No. 1 cylinder are loose and that the rockers on the No. 4 cylinder are tight. If not, rotate the crankshaft 360° until the marks line up again.

7. Valve clearance is checked between the end of the valve stem (it sticks out of the valve spring) and the bottom of the adjusting screw on the rocker arm.

8. Insert a feeler gauge and check for proper clearance on the No. 1 valve. To adjust, loosen the lock nut on the end of the rocker arm and turn the adjusting screw until the clearance is in accordance with the figures given in the "Tune-Up Specifications" chart. Tighten the lock nut and recheck the clearance; there should be a slight drag felt when the feeler gauge is pulled through the gap. Repeat the procedure for the Nos. 2, 3, and 5 valves.

9. Turn the crankshaft 360° until the marks align with each other again and repeat Step 8 for valves 4, 6, 7, and 8.

10. Installation of the remaining components is in the reverse order of removal.

20R, 22R, 22R-E and 22R-TE

▶ **See Figures 65, 66 and 67**

1. Disconnect the HAI and MC hoses, and follow Steps 1–7 of the 18R-C adjustment procedure. Disregard Step 5. When setting the No. 1 cylinder to TDC, align the notch on the crankshaft pulley with the **0** mark on the pointer scale.

2. Insert a feeler gauge and check for proper clearance on the No. 1 valve. To adjust, loosen the lock nut on the end of the rocker arm and turn the adjusting screw until the clearance is in accordance with the figures given in the "Tune-Up Specifications" chart. Tighten the lock nut and recheck the clearance; there should be a slight drag felt when the feeler gauge is pulled through the gap. Repeat the procedure for Nos. 2, 4 and 6 valves.

3. Turn the crankshaft 360° until the marks align with each other again and repeat Step 2 for valves 3, 5, 7, and 8.

4. Installation of the remaining components is in the reverse order of removal.

Valve adjustment determines how far the valves will open into the cylinder. If the clearance between the rocker arm and the valve is too great, part of the lift of the camshaft will be used up in removing the excess clearance; thus the valve will not open far enough into the cylinder. This will cause the valve to tap and likewise will cause the other valve train components to make an excessive amount of noise. Since the intake valves open less, the quality of air/fuel mixtures introduced into the cylinder will be less and the less the exhaust valves open, the greater the exhaust backpressure. These factors add up to a significant loss of power.

If the valve clearance is too small, the intake and exhaust valves will not fully seat on the cylinder head valve seats when they close. When the valve is tight against the valve seat it performs two functions: it seals the combustion chamber so that none of the gases in the cylinder can escape and the valve is cooled by the transference of heat to the cylinder head, which is in turn cooled by the cooling system of the engine. Therefore, if the valve clearance is too small the engine will run poorly due to the escape of gases from the combustion chambers on the compression and power strokes of the engine and the valves will overheat and burn because they cannot transfer heat properly.

Valve adjustments must be made as accurate as possible, however, it is better to have the valve clearance somewhat larger than smaller if there is any doubt.

3VZ-E Engines

▶ See Figures 68 thru 79

1. Remove the air intake chamber:
   a. Tag and disconnect the throttle position sensor connector.
   b. Tag and disconnect the canister vacuum hose from the throttle body.
   c. Tag and disconnect the vacuum and fuel hoses from the pressure regulator.
   d. Tag and disconnect the PCV hose at the union.
   e. Tag and disconnect the No. 4 water by-pass hose from the union of the intake manifold.
   f. Tag and disconnect the No. 5 water by-pass hose from the water by-pass pipe.
   g. Tag and disconnect the cold start injector wire.
   h. Tag and disconnect the vacuum hose at the fuel filter.
   i. Remove the union bolt and two gaskets and then remove the cold start injector tube.

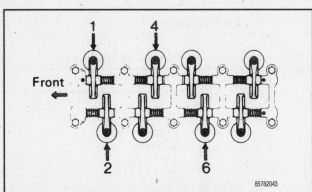

Fig. 65 Adjust this set of valves FIRST-20R, 22R, 22R-E and 22R-TE engines

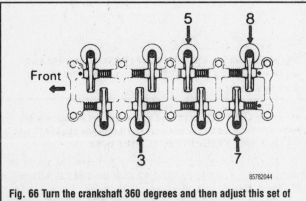

Fig. 66 Turn the crankshaft 360 degrees and then adjust this set of valves—20R, 22R, 22R-E and 22R-TE engines

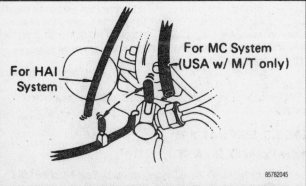

Fig. 67 Disconnect and plug the Hot Air Intake and Mixture Control (if equipped) hoses on the 22R-E engine before adjusting the valves

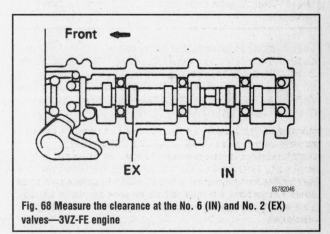

Fig. 68 Measure the clearance at the No. 6 (IN) and No. 2 (EX) valves—3VZ-FE engine

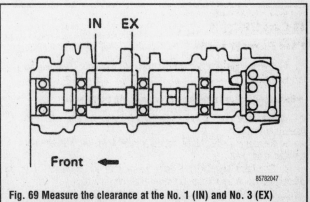

Fig. 69 Measure the clearance at the No. 1 (IN) and No. 3 (EX) valves—3VZ-FE engine

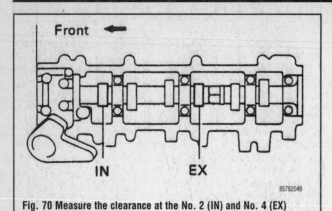

Fig. 70 Measure the clearance at the No. 2 (IN) and No. 4 (EX) valves—3VZ-FE engine

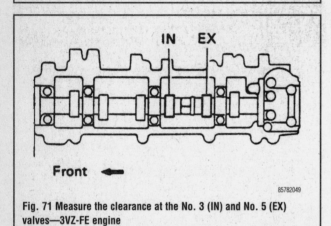

Fig. 71 Measure the clearance at the No. 3 (IN) and No. 5 (EX) valves—3VZ-FE engine

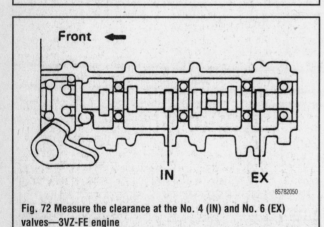

Fig. 72 Measure the clearance at the No. 4 (IN) and No. 6 (EX) valves—3VZ-FE engine

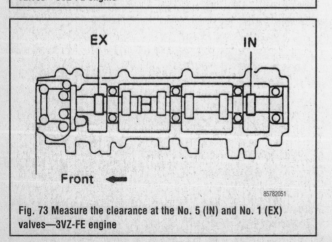

Fig. 73 Measure the clearance at the No. 5 (IN) and No. 1 (EX) valves—3VZ-FE engine

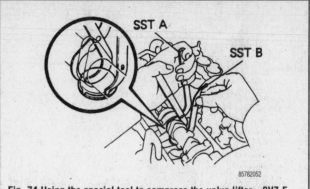

Fig. 74 Using the special tool to compress the valve lifter—3VZ-E engine

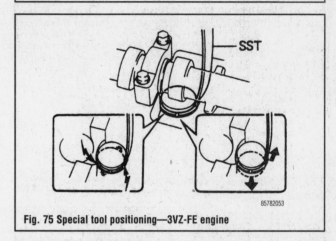

Fig. 75 Special tool positioning—3VZ-FE engine

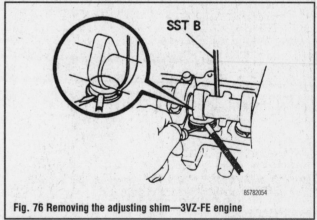

Fig. 76 Removing the adjusting shim—3VZ-FE engine

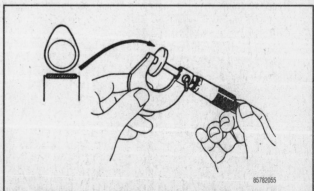

Fig. 77 Measuring the valve shim with a micrometer—3VZ-FE engine

SHIM SELECTION CHART

Intake

Measured Clearance (mm)	Installed Shim Thickness (mm)																																																
	2.200	2.225	2.250	2.275	2.300	2.325	2.350	2.375	2.400	2.425	2.450	2.475	2.500	2.525	2.550	2.575	2.600	2.625	2.650	2.675	2.700	2.725	2.750	2.775	2.800	2.825	2.850	2.875	2.900	2.925	2.950	2.975	3.000	3.025	3.050	3.075	3.100	3.125	3.150	3.175	3.200	3.225	3.250	3.275	3.300	3.325	3.350	3.375	3.400
0.000-0.025											01	01	01	03	03	05	05	07	07	09	09	11	11	13	13	15	15	17	17	19	19	21	21	23	23	25	25	27	27	29	29	31	31	33	33	35	35	37	37
0.026-0.050										01	01	01	03	03	05	05	07	07	09	09	11	11	13	13	15	15	17	17	19	19	21	21	23	23	25	25	27	27	29	29	31	31	33	33	35	35	37	37	39
0.051-0.075									01	01	01	03	03	05	05	07	07	09	09	11	11	13	13	15	15	17	17	19	19	21	21	23	23	25	25	27	27	29	29	31	31	33	33	35	35	37	37	39	39
0.076-0.100								01	01	01	03	03	05	05	07	07	09	09	11	11	13	13	15	15	17	17	19	19	21	21	23	23	25	25	27	27	29	29	31	31	33	33	35	35	37	37	39	39	41
0.101-0.125							01	01	01	03	03	05	05	07	07	09	09	11	11	13	13	15	15	17	17	19	19	21	21	23	23	25	25	27	27	29	29	31	31	33	33	35	35	37	37	39	39	41	41
0.126-0.150						01	01	01	03	03	05	05	07	07	09	09	11	11	13	13	15	15	17	17	19	19	21	21	23	23	25	25	27	27	29	29	31	31	33	33	35	35	37	37	39	39	41	41	43
0.151-0.175					01	01	01	03	03	05	05	07	07	09	09	11	11	13	13	15	15	17	17	19	19	21	21	23	23	25	25	27	27	29	29	31	31	33	33	35	35	37	37	39	39	41	41	43	43
0.176-0.200				01	01	01	03	03	05	05	07	07	09	09	11	11	13	13	15	15	17	17	19	19	21	21	23	23	25	25	27	27	29	29	31	31	33	33	35	35	37	37	39	39	41	41	43	43	45
0.201-0.225			01	01	01	03	03	05	05	07	07	09	09	11	11	13	13	15	15	17	17	19	19	21	21	23	23	25	25	27	27	29	29	31	31	33	33	35	35	37	37	39	39	41	41	43	43	45	45
0.226-0.249		01	01	01	03	03	05	05	07	07	09	09	11	11	13	13	15	15	17	17	19	19	21	21	23	23	25	25	27	27	29	29	31	31	33	33	35	35	37	37	39	39	41	41	43	43	45	45	47
0.250-0.350																																																	
0.351-0.375	03	05	05	07	07	09	09	11	11	13	13	15	15	17	17	19	19	21	21	23	23	25	25	27	27	29	29	31	31	33	33	35	35	37	37	39	39	41	41	43	43	45	45	47	47	49	49	49	
0.376-0.400	05	05	07	07	09	09	11	11	13	13	15	15	17	17	19	19	21	21	23	23	25	25	27	27	29	29	31	31	33	33	35	35	37	37	39	39	41	41	43	43	45	45	47	47	49	49	49		
0.401-0.425	05	07	07	09	09	11	11	13	13	15	15	17	17	19	19	21	21	23	23	25	25	27	27	29	29	31	31	33	33	35	35	37	37	39	39	41	41	43	43	45	45	47	47	49	49	49			
0.426-0.450	07	07	09	09	11	11	13	13	15	15	17	17	19	19	21	21	23	23	25	25	27	27	29	29	31	31	33	33	35	35	37	37	39	39	41	41	43	43	45	45	47	47	49	49	49				
0.451-0.475	07	09	09	11	11	13	13	15	15	17	17	19	19	21	21	23	23	25	25	27	27	29	29	31	31	33	33	35	35	37	37	39	39	41	41	43	43	45	45	47	47	49	49	49					
0.476-0.500	09	09	11	11	13	13	15	15	17	17	19	19	21	21	23	23	25	25	27	27	29	29	31	31	33	33	35	35	37	37	39	39	41	41	43	43	45	45	47	47	49	49	49						
0.501-0.525	09	11	11	13	13	15	15	17	17	19	19	21	21	23	23	25	25	27	27	29	29	31	31	33	33	35	35	37	37	39	39	41	41	43	43	45	45	47	47	49	49	49							
0.526-0.550	11	11	13	13	15	15	17	17	19	19	21	21	23	23	25	25	27	27	29	29	31	31	33	33	35	35	37	37	39	39	41	41	43	43	45	45	47	47	49	49	49								
0.551-0.575	11	13	13	15	15	17	17	19	19	21	21	23	23	25	25	27	27	29	29	31	31	33	33	35	35	37	37	39	39	41	41	43	43	45	45	47	47	49	49	49									
0.576-0.600	13	13	15	15	17	17	19	19	21	21	23	23	25	25	27	27	29	29	31	31	33	33	35	35	37	37	39	39	41	41	43	43	45	45	47	47	49	49	49										
0.601-0.625	13	15	15	17	17	19	19	21	21	23	23	25	25	27	27	29	29	31	31	33	33	35	35	37	37	39	39	41	41	43	43	45	45	47	47	49	49	49											
0.626-0.650	15	15	17	17	19	19	21	21	23	23	25	25	27	27	29	29	31	31	33	33	35	35	37	37	39	39	41	41	43	43	45	45	47	47	49	49	49												
0.651-0.675	15	17	17	19	19	21	21	23	23	25	25	27	27	29	29	31	31	33	33	35	35	37	37	39	39	41	41	43	43	45	45	47	47	49	49	49													
0.676-0.700	17	17	19	19	21	21	23	23	25	25	27	27	29	29	31	31	33	33	35	35	37	37	39	39	41	41	43	43	45	45	47	47	49	49	49														
0.701-0.725	17	19	19	21	21	23	23	25	25	27	27	29	29	31	31	33	33	35	35	37	37	39	39	41	41	43	43	45	45	47	47	49	49	49															
0.726-0.750	19	19	21	21	23	23	25	25	27	27	29	29	31	31	33	33	35	35	37	37	39	39	41	41	43	43	45	45	47	47	49	49	49																
0.751-0.775	19	21	21	23	23	25	25	27	27	29	29	31	31	33	33	35	35	37	37	39	39	41	41	43	43	45	45	47	47	49	49	49																	
0.776-0.800	21	21	23	23	25	25	27	27	29	29	31	31	33	33	35	35	37	37	39	39	41	41	43	43	45	45	47	47	49	49	49																		
0.801-0.825	21	23	23	25	25	27	27	29	29	31	31	33	33	35	35	37	37	39	39	41	41	43	43	45	45	47	47	49	49	49																			
0.826-0.850	23	23	25	25	27	27	29	29	31	31	33	33	35	35	37	37	39	39	41	41	43	43	45	45	47	47	49	49	49																				
0.851-0.875	23	25	25	27	27	29	29	31	31	33	33	35	35	37	37	39	39	41	41	43	43	45	45	47	47	49	49	49																					
0.876-0.900	25	25	27	27	29	29	31	31	33	33	35	35	37	37	39	39	41	41	43	43	45	45	47	47	49	49	49																						
0.901-0.925	25	27	27	29	29	31	31	33	33	35	35	37	37	39	39	41	41	43	43	45	45	47	47	49	49	49																							
0.926-0.950	27	27	29	29	31	31	33	33	35	35	37	37	39	39	41	41	43	43	45	45	47	47	49	49	49																								
0.951-0.975	27	29	29	31	31	33	33	35	35	37	37	39	39	41	41	43	43	45	45	47	47	49	49	49																									
0.976-1.000	29	29	31	31	33	33	35	35	37	37	39	39	41	41	43	43	45	45	47	47	49	49	49																										
1.001-1.025	29	31	31	33	33	35	35	37	37	39	39	41	41	43	43	45	45	47	47	49	49	49																											
1.026-1.050	31	31	33	33	35	35	37	37	39	39	41	41	43	43	45	45	47	47	49	49	49																												
1.051-1.075	31	33	33	35	35	37	37	39	39	41	41	43	43	45	45	47	47	49	49	49																													
1.076-1.100	33	33	35	35	37	37	39	39	41	41	43	43	45	45	47	47	49	49	49																														
1.101-1.125	33	35	35	37	37	39	39	41	41	43	43	45	45	47	47	49	49	49																															
1.126-1.150	35	35	37	37	39	39	41	41	43	43	45	45	47	47	49	49	49																																
1.151-1.175	35	37	37	39	39	41	41	43	43	45	45	47	47	49	49	49																																	
1.176-1.200	37	37	39	39	41	41	43	43	45	45	47	47	49	49	49																																		
1.201-1.225	37	39	39	41	41	43	43	45	45	47	47	49	49	49																																			
1.226-1.250	39	39	41	41	43	43	45	45	47	47	49	49	49																																				
1.251-1.275	39	41	41	43	43	45	45	47	47	49	49	49																																					
1.276-1.300	41	41	43	43	45	45	47	47	49	49	49																																						
1.301-1.325	41	43	43	45	45	47	47	49	49	49																																							
1.326-1.350	43	43	45	45	47	47	49	49	49																																								
1.351-1.375	43	45	45	47	47	49	49	49																																									
1.376-1.400	45	45	47	47	49	49	49																																										
1.401-1.425	45	45	47	49	49	49																																											
1.426-1.450	47	47	49	49	49																																												
1.451-1.475	47	49	49	49																																													
1.476-1.500	49	49	49																																														
1.501-1.525	49	49																																															
1.526-1.550	49																																																

Shim Thickness

Shim No.	Thickness mm (in.)	Shim No.	Thickness mm (in.)
01	2.20 (0.0866)	27	2.85 (0.1122)
03	2.25 (0.0886)	29	2.90 (0.1142)
05	2.30 (0.0906)	31	2.95 (0.1161)
07	2.35 (0.0925)	33	3.00 (0.1181)
09	2.40 (0.0945)	35	3.05 (0.1201)
11	2.45 (0.0965)	37	3.10 (0.1220)
13	2.50 (0.0984)	39	3.15 (0.1240)
15	2.55 (0.1004)	41	3.20 (0.1260)
17	2.60 (0.1024)	43	3.25 (0.1280)
19	2.65 (0.1043)	45	3.30 (0.1299)
21	2.70 (0.1063)	47	3.35 (0.1319)
23	2.75 (0.1083)	49	3.40 (0.1339)
25	2.80 (0.1102)		

Intake valve clearance (Cold):
0.25–0.35 mm (0.010–0.014 in.)
Example: 2.700 mm (0.1063 in.) shim installed
Measured clearance is 0.350 mm (0.0138 in.)
Replace 2.700 mm (0.1063 in.) shim with
shim No. 25.

85782056

Fig. 78 Shim selection chart—3VZ-FE engine

SHIM SELECTION CHART
Exhaust

Measured Clearance (mm)	Installed Shim Thickness (mm)																																																
	2.200	2.225	2.250	2.275	2.300	2.325	2.350	2.375	2.400	2.425	2.450	2.475	2.500	2.525	2.550	2.575	2.600	2.625	2.650	2.675	2.700	2.725	2.750	2.775	2.800	2.825	2.850	2.875	2.900	2.925	2.950	2.975	3.000	3.025	3.050	3.075	3.100	3.125	3.150	3.175	3.200	3.225	3.250	3.275	3.300	3.325	3.350	3.375	3.400
0.000-0.020													01	01	03	03	05	05	07	07	09	09	11	11	13	13	15	15	17	17	19	19	21	21	23	23	25	25	27	27	29	29	31	31	33	33	35	35	37
0.021-0.045												01	01	03	03	05	05	07	07	09	09	11	11	13	13	15	15	17	17	19	19	21	21	23	23	25	25	27	27	29	29	31	31	33	33	35	35	37	37
0.046-0.070											01	01	03	03	05	05	07	07	09	09	11	11	13	13	15	15	17	17	19	19	21	21	23	23	25	25	27	27	29	29	31	31	33	33	35	35	37	37	39
0.071-0.095										01	01	03	03	05	05	07	07	09	09	11	11	13	13	15	15	17	17	19	19	21	21	23	23	25	25	27	27	29	29	31	31	33	33	35	35	37	37	39	39
0.096-0.120									01	01	03	03	05	05	07	07	09	09	11	11	13	13	15	15	17	17	19	19	21	21	23	23	25	25	27	27	29	29	31	31	33	33	35	35	37	37	39	39	41
0.121-0.145								01	01	03	03	05	05	07	07	09	09	11	11	13	13	15	15	17	17	19	19	21	21	23	23	25	25	27	27	29	29	31	31	33	33	35	35	37	37	39	39	41	41
0.146-0.170							01	01	03	03	05	05	07	07	09	09	11	11	13	13	15	15	17	17	19	19	21	21	23	23	25	25	27	27	29	29	31	31	33	33	35	35	37	37	39	39	41	41	43
0.171-0.195						01	01	03	03	05	05	07	07	09	09	11	11	13	13	15	15	17	17	19	19	21	21	23	23	25	25	27	27	29	29	31	31	33	33	35	35	37	37	39	39	41	41	43	43
0.196-0.220					01	01	03	03	05	05	07	07	09	09	11	11	13	13	15	15	17	17	19	19	21	21	23	23	25	25	27	27	29	29	31	31	33	33	35	35	37	37	39	39	41	41	43	43	45
0.221-0.245				01	01	03	03	05	05	07	07	09	09	11	11	13	13	15	15	17	17	19	19	21	21	23	23	25	25	27	27	29	29	31	31	33	33	35	35	37	37	39	39	41	41	43	43	45	45
0.246-0.269			01	01	03	03	05	05	07	07	09	09	11	11	13	13	15	15	17	17	19	19	21	21	23	23	25	25	27	27	29	29	31	31	33	33	35	35	37	37	39	39	41	41	43	43	45	45	47
0.270-0.370																																																	
0.371-0.395	03	05	05	07	07	09	09	11	11	13	13	15	15	17	17	19	19	21	21	23	23	25	25	27	27	29	29	31	31	33	33	35	35	37	37	39	39	41	41	43	43	45	45	47	47	49	49		
0.396-0.420	05	05	07	07	09	09	11	11	13	13	15	15	17	17	19	19	21	21	23	23	25	25	27	27	29	29	31	31	33	33	35	35	37	37	39	39	41	41	43	43	45	45	47	47	49	49			
0.421-0.445	05	07	07	09	09	11	11	13	13	15	15	17	17	19	19	21	21	23	23	25	25	27	27	29	29	31	31	33	33	35	35	37	37	39	39	41	41	43	43	45	45	47	47	49	49				
0.446-0.470	07	07	09	09	11	11	13	13	15	15	17	17	19	19	21	21	23	23	25	25	27	27	29	29	31	31	33	33	35	35	37	37	39	39	41	41	43	43	45	45	47	47	49	49
0.471-0.495	07	09	09	11	11	13	13	15	15	17	17	19	19	21	21	23	23	25	25	27	27	29	29	31	31	33	33	35	35	37	37	39	39	41	41	43	43	45	45	47	47	49	49
0.496-0.520	09	09	11	11	13	13	15	15	17	17	19	19	21	21	23	23	25	25	27	27	29	29	31	31	33	33	35	35	37	37	39	39	41	41	43	43	45	45	47	47	49	49
0.521-0.545	09	11	11	13	13	15	15	17	17	19	19	21	21	23	23	25	25	27	27	29	29	31	31	33	33	35	35	37	37	39	39	41	41	43	43	45	45	47	47	49	49
0.546-0.570	11	11	13	13	15	15	17	17	19	19	21	21	23	23	25	25	27	27	29	29	31	31	33	33	35	35	37	37	39	39	41	41	43	43	45	45	47	47	49	49
0.571-0.595	11	13	13	15	15	17	17	19	19	21	21	23	23	25	25	27	27	29	29	31	31	33	33	35	35	37	37	39	39	41	41	43	43	45	45	47	47	49	49
0.596-0.620	13	13	15	15	17	17	19	19	21	21	23	23	25	25	27	27	29	29	31	31	33	33	35	35	37	37	39	39	41	41	43	43	45	45	47	47	49	49
0.621-0.645	13	15	15	17	17	19	19	21	21	23	23	25	25	27	27	29	29	31	31	33	33	35	35	37	37	39	39	41	41	43	43	45	45	47	47	49	49
0.646-0.670	15	15	17	17	19	19	21	21	23	23	25	25	27	27	29	29	31	31	33	33	35	35	37	37	39	39	41	41	43	43	45	45	47	47	49	49
0.671-0.695	15	17	17	19	19	21	21	23	23	25	25	27	27	29	29	31	31	33	33	35	35	37	37	39	39	41	41	43	43	45	45	47	47	49	49
0.696-0.720	17	17	19	19	21	21	23	23	25	25	27	27	29	29	31	31	33	33	35	35	37	37	39	39	41	41	43	43	45	45	47	47	49	49
0.721-0.745	17	19	19	21	21	23	23	25	25	27	27	29	29	31	31	33	33	35	35	37	37	39	39	41	41	43	43	45	45	47	47	49	49
0.746-0.770	19	19	21	21	23	23	25	25	27	27	29	29	31	31	33	33	35	35	37	37	39	39	41	41	43	43	45	45	47	47	49	49
0.771-0.795	19	21	21	23	23	25	25	27	27	29	29	31	31	33	33	35	35	37	37	39	39	41	41	43	43	45	45	47	47	49	49
0.796-0.820	21	21	23	23	25	25	27	27	29	29	31	31	33	33	35	35	37	37	39	39	41	41	43	43	45	45	47	47	49	49
0.821-0.845	21	23	23	25	25	27	27	29	29	31	31	33	33	35	35	37	37	39	39	41	41	43	43	45	45	47	47	49	49
0.846-0.870	23	23	25	25	27	27	29	29	31	31	33	33	35	35	37	37	39	39	41	41	43	43	45	45	47	47	49	49
0.871-0.895	23	25	25	27	27	29	29	31	31	33	33	35	35	37	37	39	39	41	41	43	43	45	45	47	47	49	49
0.896-0.920	25	25	27	27	29	29	31	31	33	33	35	35	37	37	39	39	41	41	43	43	45	45	47	47	49	49
0.921-0.945	25	27	27	29	29	31	31	33	33	35	35	37	37	39	39	41	41	43	43	45	45	47	47	49	49
0.946-0.970	27	27	29	29	31	31	33	33	35	35	37	37	39	39	41	41	43	43	45	45	47	47	49	49
0.971-0.995	27	29	29	31	31	33	33	35	35	37	37	39	39	41	41	43	43	45	45	47	47	49	49
0.996-1.020	29	29	31	31	33	33	35	35	37	37	39	39	41	41	43	43	45	45	47	47	49	49
1.021-1.045	29	31	31	33	33	35	35	37	37	39	39	41	41	43	43	45	45	47	47	49	49
1.046-1.070	31	31	33	33	35	35	37	37	39	39	41	41	43	43	45	45	47	47	49	49
1.071-1.095	31	33	33	35	35	37	37	39	39	41	41	43	43	45	45	47	47	49	49
1.096-1.120	33	33	35	35	37	37	39	39	41	41	43	43	45	45	47	47	49	49
1.121-1.145	33	35	35	37	37	39	39	41	41	43	43	45	45	47	47	49	49
1.146-1.170	35	35	37	37	39	39	41	41	43	43	45	45	47	47	49	49
1.171-1.195	35	37	37	39	39	41	41	43	43	45	45	47	47	49	49
1.196-1.220	37	37	39	39	41	41	43	43	45	45	47	47	49	49
1.221-1.245	37	39	39	41	41	43	43	45	45	47	47	49	49
1.246-1.270	39	39	41	41	43	43	45	45	47	47	49	49
1.271-1.295	39	41	41	43	43	45	45	47	47	49	49
1.296-1.320	41	41	43	43	45	45	47	47	49	49
1.321-1.345	41	43	43	45	45	47	47	49	49
1.346-1.370	43	43	45	45	47	47	49	49
1.371-1.395	43	45	45	47	47	49	49
1.396-1.420	45	45	47	47	49	49
1.421-1.445	45	47	47	49	49
1.446-1.470	47	47	49	49
1.471-1.495	47	49	49
1.496-1.520	49	49
1.521-1.545	49

Shim Thickness

Shim No.	Thickness mm (in.)	Shim No.	Thickness mm (in.)
01	2.20 (0.0866)	27	2.85 (0.1122)
03	2.25 (0.0886)	29	2.90 (0.1142)
05	2.30 (0.0906)	31	2.95 (0.1161)
07	2.35 (0.0925)	33	3.00 (0.1181)
09	2.40 (0.0945)	35	3.05 (0.1201)
11	2.45 (0.0965)	37	3.10 (0.1220)
13	2.50 (0.0984)	39	3.15 (0.1240)
15	2.55 (0.1004)	41	3.20 (0.1260)
17	2.60 (0.1024)	43	3.25 (0.1280)
19	2.65 (0.1043)	45	3.30 (0.1299)
21	2.70 (0.1063)	47	3.35 (0.1319)
23	2.75 (0.1083)	49	3.40 (0.1339)
25	2.80 (0.1102)		

Exhaust valve clearance (Cold):
0.27–0.37 mm (0.011–0.015 in.)
Example: 2.700 mm (0.1063 in.) shim installed
Measured clearance is 0.450 mm (0.0177 in.)
Replace 2.700 mm (0.1063 in.) shim with shim No. 27.

85782057

Fig. 79 Shim selection chart—3VZ-FE engine

j. Tag and disconnect the EGR gas temperature sensor wire.

k. Tag and disconnect the EGR vacuum hoses at the air pipe and vacuum modulator.

l. On California trucks, remove the nut and bolt and then remove the intake chamber stay.

m. Remove the EGR valve with the pipes still connected.

n. Disconnect the No. 1 air hose at the reed valve.

o. Remove the six bolts and two nuts and lift off the air intake chamber and gasket.

2. Remove the engine wire.

3. Remove the cylinder head covers.

4. Remove the spark plugs.

5. Use a wrench and turn the crankshaft until the notch in the pulley aligns with the timing mark **0** of the No. 1 timing belt cover. This will insure that engine is at TDC.

➡**Check that the valve lifters on the No. 1 cylinder are loose and those on No. 4 cylinder are tight. If not, turn the crankshaft one complete revolution (360°) and then realign the marks.**

6. Using a flat feeler gauge measure the clearance between the camshaft lobe and the valve lifter. This measurement should correspond to the one given in the "Tune-Up Specifications" chart. Check only the No. 6 intake valve and the No. 2 exhaust valve.

➡**If the measurement is within specifications, go on to the next step. If not, record the measurement taken for each individual valve. They will be used later to determine the required replacement shim sizes.**

7. Turn the crankshaft ⅓ of a revolution (120°) and measure the clearance at the No. 1 intake and the No. 3 exhaust valves. Record any measurement that is out of specification.

8. Turn the crankshaft ⅓ of a revolution (120°) and measure the clearance at the No. 2 intake and the No. 4 exhaust valves. Record any measurement that is out of specification.

9. Turn the crankshaft ⅓ of a revolution (120°) and measure the clearance at the No. 3 intake and the No. 5 exhaust valves. Record any measurement that is out of specification.

10. Turn the crankshaft ⅓ of a revolution (120°) and measure the clearance at the No. 4 intake and the No. 6 exhaust valves. Record any measurement that is out of specification.

11. Turn the crankshaft ⅓ of a revolution (120°) and measure the clearance at the No. 5 intake and the No. 1 exhaust valves. Record any measurement that is out of specification.

➡**If the measurements for the previous six sets of valves are within specifications, you need go no further, the procedure is finished. If not, to Step 12.**

12. Turn the crankshaft to position the intake camshaft lobe of the cylinder to be adjusted, upward.

13. Using a small awl, turn the valve lifter so that the notch is easily accessible.

14. Install SST No. 09248-55010 (the scissors type) on the lifter and then squeeze the handle so that the tool presses down the valve lifter evenly. Hold the valve lifter down with the single tool.

➡**For easy removal of the shim, set the special tool on the lifter so there is adequate space in the removal direction.**

15. Using a small screwdriver and a magnet, remove the valve shim.

16. Measure the thickness of the old shim with a micrometer. Locate that particular measurement in the "Installed Shim Thickness" column of the accompanying charts, then locate the previously recorded measurement (from Step 6-11) for that valve in the "Measured Clearance " column of the charts. Index the two columns to arrive at the proper replacement shim thickness.

➡**Replacement shims are available in 25 sizes, in increments of 0.05mm, from 2.200mm to 3.400mm.**

17. Install the new shim, remove the special tool and then recheck the valve clearance.

18. Install the spark plugs.

19. Install the cylinder head covers.

20. Install the engine wire.

21. Install the air intake chamber and then check the ignition timing and idle speed.

F, 2F and 3F-E Engines

▶ **See Figures 80, 81 and 82**

1. Start the engine and allow it to reach normal operating temperature (above 165°F).

2. Stop the engine. Remove the air cleaner assembly with related components. Remove any cables, hoses, wires, etc., which are attached to the valve cover and remove the valve cover.

3. Tighten the cylinder head bolts as detailed in Section 3. Also torque the manifold attaching nuts to 28–37 ft. lbs. for trucks outside of California, or 37–51 ft. lbs. for California trucks, and the rocker support fasteners to 15–21 ft. lbs. on 8mm bolts and 22–32 ft. lbs. on 10mm bolts.

4. Start the engine and adjust the idle speed as described in the following procedure.

5. Check the clearance between each of the rocker arms and valve stems while the engine is at slow idle, using a feeler gauge of the proper size (See the Tune-Up Specifications chart).

6. If the clearance is incorrect, loosen the locknut and turn the adjusting screw as required. Tighten the locknut and recheck the clearance.

7. After adjusting all of the valves, install the valve cover and any other components which were removed during Step 2.

8. Recheck the engine idle speed and adjust if necessary.

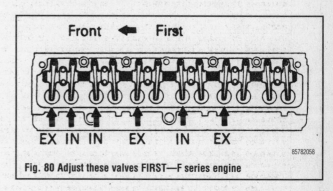

Fig. 80 Adjust these valves FIRST—F series engine

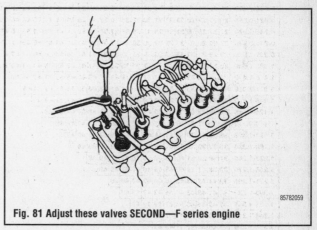

Fig. 81 Adjust these valves SECOND—F series engine

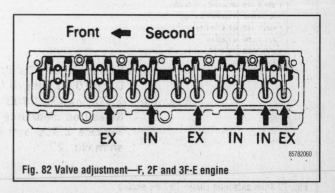

Fig. 82 Valve adjustment—F, 2F and 3F-E engine

1L, 2L and 2L-T Engines

◆ **See Figure 83**

The valves are adjusted in basically the same manner as the 20R, 22R and 22R-E engines, in that the engine must be OFF during the adjustment and that the clearance is checked with a feeler gauge between the rocker arm and the valve stem end.

➡**The engine must be at normal operating temperature to obtain the proper valve clearances.**

1. Remove the valve cover and rotate the crankshaft to align the TDC mark on the crankshaft pulley with the corresponding pointer. The valves of the number one cylinder should be closed (rocker arms should feel loose). If the rocker arms of the number one cylinder are tight, rotate the engine another 360° and again align the TDC marks.
2. Adjust the clearances of the following valves:
- No.1 cylinder: intake and exhaust
- No.2 cylinder: intake
- No.3 cylinder: exhaust
3. Rotate the crankshaft 360° and adjust the remaining valves:
- No.2 cylinder: exhaust
- No.3 cylinder: intake
- No.4 cylinder: intake and exhaust

Remember that the cylinder numbering from the front of the engine to the rear is No. 1 through No. 4, and that the valve arrangement from the front of the engine is E-I-E-I-E-I-E-I, with E designating each exhaust valve and I designating each intake valve. Choose your specifications from the Diesel Tune-Up Chart accordingly.
4. Reinstall the valve cover.

➡**Never operate the engine with the valve cover removed.**

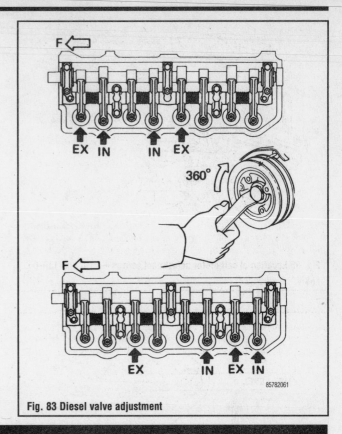

Fig. 83 Diesel valve adjustment

ADJUSTMENTS

Carburetor

This section contains only carburetor adjustments as they normally apply to engine tune-up. Descriptions of the carburetor and complete adjustment procedures can be found in Section 5.

When the engine in your Toyota is running, air/fuel mixture from the carburetor is being drawn into the engine by a partial vacuum which is created by the downward movement of the pistons on the intake stroke of the 4-stroke cycle of the engine. The amount of air/fuel mixture that enters the engine is controlled by throttle plates in the bottom of the carburetor. When the engine is not running, the throttle plates are closed, completely blocking off the bottom of the carburetor from the inside of the engine. The throttle plates are connected, through the throttle linkage, to the gas pedal in the passenger compartment of the truck. After you start the engine and put the transmission in gear, you depress the gas pedal to start the truck moving. What you actually are doing when you depress the gas pedal is opening the throttle plate in the carburetor to admit more of the air/fuel mixture to the engine. The further you open the throttle plates in the carburetor, the higher the engine speed becomes.

As previously stated, when the engine is not running, the throttle plates in the carburetor are closed. When the engine is idling, it is necessary to open the throttle plates slightly. To prevent having to keep your foot on the gas pedal when the engine is idling, an idle speed adjusting screw was added to the carburetor. This screw has the same effect as keeping your foot slightly depressed on the gas pedal. The idle speed adjusting screw contacts a lever (the throttle lever) on the outside of the carburetor. When the screw is turned in, it opens the throttle plate on the carburetor, raising the idle speed of the engine. This screw is called the curb idle adjusting screw, and the procedures in this section tell you how to adjust it.

Since it is difficult for the engine to draw the air/fuel mixture from the carburetor with the small amount of throttle plate opening that is present when the engine is idling, an idle mixture passage is provided in the carburetor. This passage delivers air/fuel mixture to the engine from a hole which is located in the bottom of the carburetor below the throttle plates. This idle mixture passage contains an adjusting screw which restricts the amount of air/fuel mixture that enters the engine at idle.

IDLE SPEED AND MIXTURE ADJUSTMENTS

◆ **See Figures 84 thru 92**

1970–74

➡**Perform the following adjustments with the air cleaner in place. When adjusting the idle speed and mixture, the gear selector should be placed in Drive (D) on 1970–73 models equipped with an automatic transmission. Be sure to set the parking brake and block the front wheels. On all trucks equipped with manual transmissions and all 1974 automatics, adjust the idle speed with the gearshift in Neutral (N).**

1. Run the engine until it reaches normal operating temperature. Stop the engine.
2. Connect a tachometer to the engine as detailed in the manufacturer's instructions.

Vacuum At Idle
(in. Hg)

Year	Engine	Transmission	Minimum Vacuum Gauge Reading
1970–71	8R-C	All	15.7
1972–73	18R-C	MT	17.7
		AT	15.7
1974	18R-C	All	17.7

MT—Manual Transmission
AT—Automatic Transmission

Fig. 84 Vacuum at idle chart

3. Remove the plug and install a vacuum gauge in the manifold vacuum port by using a suitable metric adapter.

4. Start the engine and allow it to stabilize at idle.

5. Turn the mixture screw in or out, until the engine runs smoothly at the lowest possible engine speed without stalling.

6. Turn the idle speed screw until the vacuum gauge indicates the highest specified reading (see the "Vacuum At Idle" chart) at the specified idle speed. (See the "Tune-Up Specifications" chart at the beginning of the section).

7. Tighten the idle speed screw to the point just before the engine rpm and vacuum readings drop off.

8. Remove the tachometer and the vacuum gauge. Install the plug back in the manifold vacuum port. Road-test the vehicle.

9. In some states, emission inspection is required. In such cases, you should take your truck to a diagnostic center which has an HC/CO meter, and have the idle emission level checked to be sure that it is in accordance with state regulations. Starting 1974, CO levels at idle are given on the engine tune-up decal under the hood.

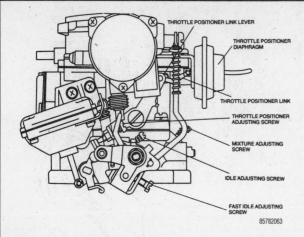

Fig. 85 Location of carburetor adjustment screws—8R-C and 18R-C engine

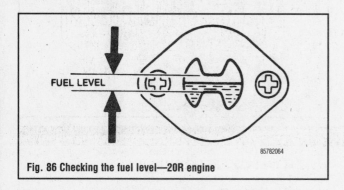

Fig. 86 Checking the fuel level—20R engine

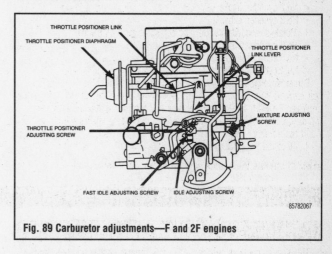

Fig. 89 Carburetor adjustments—F and 2F engines

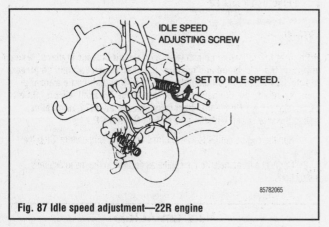

Fig. 87 Idle speed adjustment—22R engine

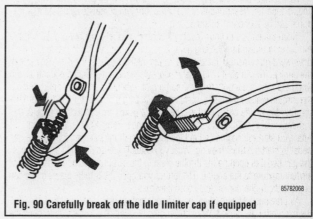

Fig. 90 Carefully break off the idle limiter cap if equipped

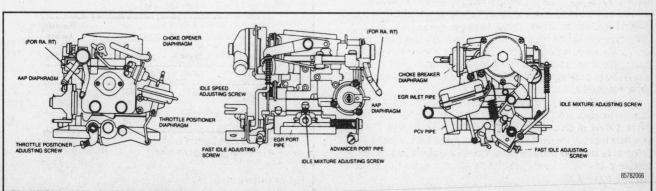

Fig. 88 Carburetor adjustments—20R engine

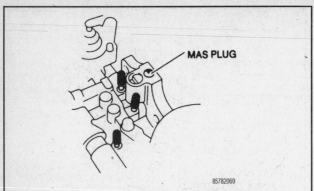

Fig. 91 Cap or plug all vacuum ports before attempting to drill the plug—carburetor shown on its side

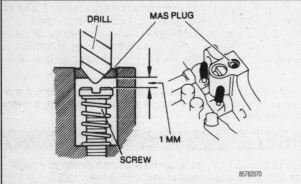

Fig. 92 Use a variable speed or hand drill on the plug—there is 1mm clearance between the plug and the top of the screw

Fig. 93 Idle speed adjustment

Fig. 94 Idle mixture adjustment

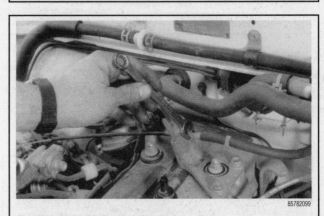

Fig. 95 Loosen the throttle cable nuts to adjust

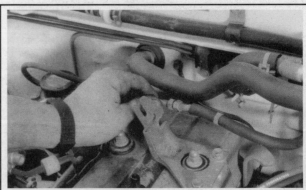

Fig. 96 Removing the throttle cable from bracket

1975–77

The idle speed and mixture should be adjusted under the following conditions: the air cleaner must be installed, the choke fully opened, the transmission should be in Neutral (N), all accessories should be turned off, all vacuum lines should be connected, and the ignition timing should be set to specification.

1. Start the engine and allow it to reach normal operating temperature (180°F).
2. Check the float setting; the fuel level should be just about even with the spot on the sight glass. If the fuel level is too high or low, adjust the float level. (See Section 5).
3. Connect a tachometer in accordance with the manufacturer's instructions. However, connect the tachometer positive (+) lead to the coil Negative (–) terminal. Do NOT hook it up to the distributor or positive (+) side; damage to the transistorized ignition will result. In some cases there is a service connector at the igniter and the tachometer may be connected to this.
4. Adjust the speed to the highest rpm it will attain with the idle mixture adjusting screw.
5. Set the rpm to the idle mixture speed of 900 rpm, by turning the idle speed adjusting screw. You may have to repeat Steps 4 and 5 a few times until the highest idle reached in Step 4 will go no further.
6. Now set the speed to the initial idle speed of 850 plus or minus 50 rpm, by turning the idle mixture adjusting screw in (clockwise).
7. Disconnect the tachometer.

1978–88

▶ **See Figures 93, 94, 95, 96 and 97**

Use the same procedure as given for 1975–77 models, described above. However, substitute different idle mixture and idle speeds as specified below:

➥Certain models may have an idle limiter cap on the idle adjusting screw; if so, use pliers to break it off. Be sure to install a new cap after adjustment.

To meet U.S. emissions regulations, the idle mixture adjusting screw on the later models covered here is preadjusted and plugged by Toyota. When

Fig. 97 Removing the throttle cable

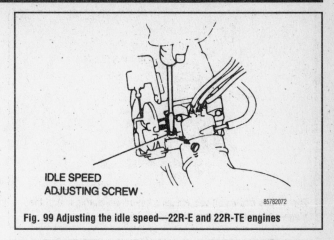

IDLE SPEED
ADJUSTING SCREW

Fig. 99 Adjusting the idle speed—22R-E and 22R-TE engines

troubleshooting a rough idle, check all other possible causes before attempting to adjust the idle mixture; the plug should not be removed and the adjusting screw tampered with in the course of a normal tune-up. Toyota recommends all mixture adjustments be handled by a professional mechanic equipped with the proper emissions test equipment. If all other trouble causes have been checked, then on 1978-83 models the carburetor must be removed while the plug is removed form the mixture screw hole. Plug all vacuum ports to keep metal chips out before drilling. After the plug is removed, remove the mixture screw to inspect the tip for wear, and blow out the hole with compressed air. Reinstall the adjusting screw by screwing it in fully until it just seats, then unscrewing it 2½ full turns (4 turns on 1983 models). Reinstall the carburetor and proceed with the mixture adjustment only if necessary. 1984-88 models require an HC/CO meter for mixture adjustments.

Fuel Injection

IDLE SPEED ADJUSTMENT

22R-E, 22R-TE, 3F-E and 3VZ-E Engines

▶ **See Figures 98 and 99**

1. Make sure that the air cleaner is installed properly, all air intake system pipes and hoses are connected, all vacuum lines are connected properly.
2. Make sure that all EFI system wiring connectors are fully plugged.

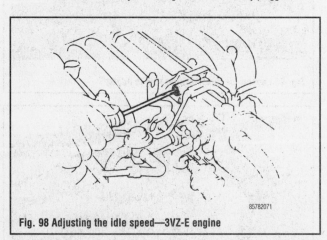

Fig. 98 Adjusting the idle speed—3VZ-E engine

3. Run the engine until it reaches normal operating temperature, switch off all accessories and put the transmission in Neutral. Turn off the engine.
4. Connect a tachometer to the engine. Be sure to connect the positive (+) terminal of the tachometer to the negative (–) terminal of the ignition coil (or as detailed in the Ignition Timing section) or else damage to the igniter will result.

➡ **Not all tachometers are compatible with this ignition system, it is recommended that you check with the manufacturer before using a particular tachometer.**

❊❊ CAUTION

NEVER allow the tachometer terminal to touch ground as it could result in damage to the igniter and/or the ignition coil!

5. Restart the engine and run it at 2,500 rpm for about 2 minutes.
6. Remove the plug and turn the idle speed adjusting screw until the idle speed agrees with the appropriate figure given in the "Tune-Up Specifications" chart.
7. Recheck the idle speed once more and then disconnect the tachometer.

Diesel Fuel System

IDLE AND MAXIMUM SPEED ADJUSTMENTS

▶ **See Figures 100 and 101**

➡ **The following adjustments are made with the transmission in neutral and the parking brake applied fully.**

1. Warm the engine to normal operating temperature and allow it to idle.
2. Turn the idle adjuster knob counterclockwise; the knob should return to its unlocked position.
3. Turn the engine off and remove the accelerator connection rod.
4. Connect a tachometer to the engine according the tachometer manufacturer's instructions.
5. Start the engine and check the engine rpm at idle. The idle rpm should be 700 rpm.
6. If adjustment is necessary, turn the idle adjusting screw on the fuel injection pump as required to obtain the 700 rpm idle speed.
7. Fully depress the injection pump lever, note the maximum engine speed and release the accelerator pedal immediately. The maximum rpm should be 4900.
8. If adjustment is necessary:

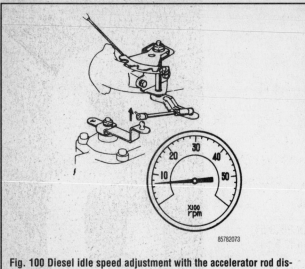

85782073

Fig. 100 Diesel idle speed adjustment with the accelerator rod dis-connected at the pump lever

85782074

Fig. 101 After making speed adjustments on the diesel, attach the accelerator cable and adjust it to remove all slack

a. Remove the wire seal of the maximum speed adjusting screw, if so equipped.

b. Using Toyota special service tool #09275-54020 or its equivalent, loosen the locknut of the maximum speed adjusting screw.

c. Turn the maximum speed adjusting screw until the proper maximum rpm is obtained.

9. Install the accelerator connecting rod and adjust its length so that there is no slack in the accelerator cable.

10. Check that the idle speed increases as the idle adjuster knob is pulled outward. Then turn the knob counterclockwise so that the rpm returns to the idle specifications.

11. Turn the engine off and disconnect the tachometer from the engine.

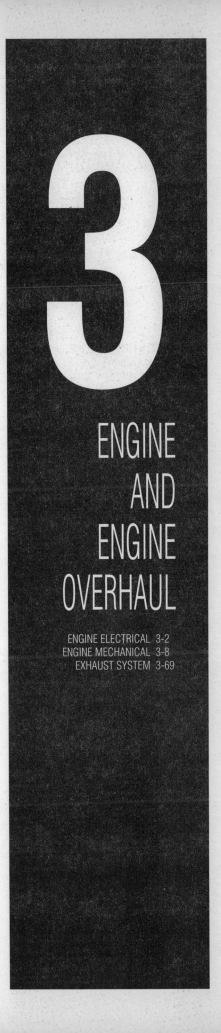

3

ENGINE AND ENGINE OVERHAUL

ENGINE ELECTRICAL

➡ For information on understanding electricity and troubleshooting electrical circuits, please refer to Section 6 of this manual.

Ignition Coil

TESTING

◆ See Figures 1 and 2

Primary Resistance Check

In order to check the coil primary resistance, you must first disconnect all wires from the ignition coil terminals. Using an ohmmeter, check the resistance between the positive (15) and the negative (1) terminals on the coil. The resistance should be:

- 8R-C and 18R-C—1.3–1.7 ohms
- 20R (1975-79)—1.3–1.7 ohms
- 20R (1980)—0.5–0.6 ohms
- 22R (1981)—0.8–1.0 ohms
- 22R (1982-88)—0.4–0.5 ohms
- 22R-E (1984-85)—0.8–1.1 ohms
- 22R-E and 22R-TE (1986-88)—0.5–0.7 ohms
- 3VZ-E—0.5–0.7 ohms
- F and 2F—0.5–0.7 ohms
- 3F-E—0.5–0.7 ohms

If the resistance is not within these tolerances, the coil will require replacement.

Secondary Resistance Check

In order to check the coil secondary resistance, you must first disconnect all wires from the ignition coil terminals. Using an ohmmeter, check the resistance between the positive (15) terminal and the coil wire (4) terminal. The resistance should be:

- 8R-C and 18R-C—6500-10,500 ohms
- 20R (1975-79)—6500-10,500 ohms
- 20R (1980)—11,500-15,500 ohms
- 22R (1981)—11,500-15,500 ohms
- 22R (1982-88)—8500-11,500 ohms
- 22R-E (1984-85)—10,700-14,500 ohms
- 22R-E and 22R-TE (1986-88)—11,400-15,600 ohms
- 3VZ-E—11,400-15,600 ohms
- F and 2F—11,500-15,500 ohms
- 3F-E—11,500-15,500 ohms

If the resistance is not within these tolerances, the coil will require replacement.

REMOVAL & INSTALLATION

1. Disconnect the negative battery cable.
2. Tag and disconnect all electrical leads at the coil.
3. Remove the two mounting bolts and lift off the ignition coil.
4. Installation is the reverse of the removal procedure.

Distributor

REMOVAL

◆ See Figures 3 thru 8

On the 8R-C and 18R-C, the distributor is on the right (passenger's) side. On all other engines, the distributor is located at the front of the engine on the left (driver's) side. To remove the distributor, proceed in the following order:

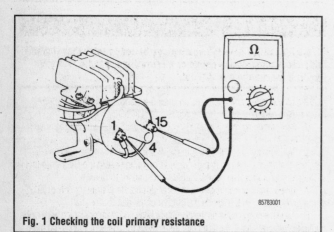

Fig. 1 Checking the coil primary resistance

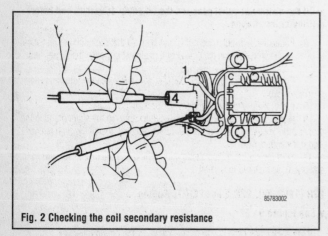

Fig. 2 Checking the coil secondary resistance

Fig. 3 Mark distributor rotor position to distributor housing

Fig. 4 Mark distributor housing position to engine mounting

Fig. 5 Removing the distributor hold down bolt

Fig. 6 Remove and mark all hoses from the distributor assembly

Fig. 7 Remove the distributor assembly

Fig. 8 Removing the distributor O-ring

1. Unfasten the retaining clips and lift the distributor cap straight off. It will be easier to install the distributor if the wiring is left connected to the cap. If the wires must be removed from the cap, mark their positions to aid in installation.

2. Remove the dust cover and mark the position of the rotor relative to the distributor body; then mark the position of the body relative to the block.

3. Disconnect the coil primary wire and the vacuum lines, mark which is which for installation.

4. Remove the pinch-bolt and lift the distributor straight out, away from the engine. The rotor and body are marked so that they can be returned to the position from which they were removed. Do not turn or disturb the engine (unless absolutely necessary, such as for engine rebuilding), after the distributor has been removed.

INSTALLATION—TIMING NOT DISTURBED

1. Insert the distributor in the block and align the matchmarks made during removal.

2. Engage the distributor driven gear with the distributor drive.

3. Install the distributor clamp and secure it with the pinch-bolt.

4. Install the cap, primary wire, and vacuum line(s).

5. Install the spark plug leads. Consult the marks made during removal to be sure that the proper lead goes to each plug. Install the high tension wire if it was removed.

6. Start the engine. Check the timing and adjust it with the octane selector (if equipped), as outlined in Section 2.

INSTALLATION—TIMING LOST

8R-C, 18R-C, 20R, 22R (1981-82), F and 2F Engines

If the engine has been cranked, dismantled, or the timing otherwise lost, proceed as follows:

1. Determine the top dead center (TDC) of the No. 1 cylinder's compression stroke by removing the spark plug from the No.1 cylinder and placing your finger on a vacuum gauge over the spark plug hole. This is important because the timing marks will also line up with the cylinder in the firing order in its exhaust stroke.

> ✷✷ **CAUTION**

On engines which have the spark plugs buried in the exhaust manifold, use a compression gauge or a screwdriver handle, not your finger, if the manifold is still hot.

Crank the engine until compression pressure starts to build up. Continue cranking the engine until the timing marks indicate **TDC** or **0**.

2. Next, align the timing marks to the specifications given in the Ignition Timing column of the Tune-Up Specifications chart at the beginning of Section 2.

3. Temporarily install the rotor in the distributor without the dust cover. Turn the distributor shaft so that the rotor is pointing toward the No. 1 terminal in the distributor cap. The points should be just about to open.

4. Use a small screwdriver to align the slot on the distributor drive (oil pump driveshaft) with the key on the bottom of the distributor shaft.

5. Align the matchmarks on the distributor body and the block which were made during the removal. Install the distributor in the block by rotating it slightly (no more than one gear tooth in either direction) until the driven gear meshes with the drive.

➡ **Oil the distributor spiral gear and the oil pump driveshaft end before distributor installation.**

6. Rotate the distributor, once it is installed, so that the point are just about to open or the projection on the pickup coil is almost opposite the signal rotor tooth. Temporarily tighten the pinchbolt.

7. Remove the rotor and install the dust cover. Replace the rotor and the distributor cap.

8. Install the primary wire and the vacuum line(s).

9. Install the No.1 spark plug. Connect the cables to the spark plugs in the proper order by using the marks made during removal. Install the high tension lead if it was removed.

10. Start the engine. Adjust the ignition timing and the octane selector (if equipped), as outlined in Section 2.

22R (1983–88), 22R-E and 22R-TE Engine

▶ **See Figure 9**

If the engine has been cranked, dismantled, or the timing otherwise lost, proceed as follows:

1. Determine top dead center (TDC) of the No. 1 cylinder's compression stroke by removing the spark plug from the No. 1 cylinder and placing your finger or a vacuum gauge over the spark plug hole. This is important because the timing marks will also line up with the cylinder in the firing order in its exhaust stroke.

❊❊ CAUTION

On engines which have the spark plugs buried in the exhaust manifold, use a compression gauge or a screwdriver handle, not your finger, if the manifold is still hot.

Crank the engine until compression pressure starts to build up. Continue cranking the engine until the timing marks indicate **TDC** or **0**.

2. Follow Step 2 of the above procedure.

3. Check that the rocker arms on the No. 1 cylinder are loose. If not, turn the crankshaft one complete revolution (360°).

4. Temporarily install the rotor.

5. Slowly insert the distributor into the cylinder block. The rotor should be pointing upward and the distributor mounting hole should be approximately at the center position of the bolt hole.

6. When the distributor is fully installed, the rotor should rotate to the position shown in the illustration.

7. Remove the rotor and the dust cap. Install the pinch-bolt and tighten it slightly.

8. Align on of the teeth on the signal rotor with the projection on the signal generator (pick-up coil).

9. Tighten the pinch-bolt to 14 ft. lbs. (19 Nm).

10. Install the dust cover and the rotor. Replace the distributor cap and wires and check the ignition timing.

3VZ-E Engines

▶ **See Figures 10 and 11**

If the engine has been cranked, dismantled, or the timing otherwise lost, proceed as follows:

1. Determine top dead center (TDC) of the No. 1 cylinder's compression stroke by removing the spark plug from the No. 1 cylinder and placing your finger on a vacuum gauge over the spark plug hole. This is important because the timing marks will also line up with the cylinder in the firing order in its exhaust stroke.

❊❊ CAUTION

On engines which have the spark plugs buried in the exhaust manifold, use a compression gauge or a screwdriver handle, not your finger, if the manifold is still hot.

Crank the engine until compression pressure starts to build up. Continue cranking the engine until the timing marks indicate **TDC** or **0**.

2. Next, align the timing marks to the specifications given in the Ignition Timing column of the Tune-Up Specifications chart at the beginning of Section 2.

3. Replace the distributor shaft O-ring.

4. Align the protrusion on the distributor driven gear with the groove on the lower edge of the distributor housing.

5. Insert the distributor into the hole so that the groove on the lower edge of the distributor housing is in alignment with the groove on the No. 4 camshaft bearing cap.

6. Lightly tighten the distributor hold-down bolts.

7. Install the dust proof packing and then the distributor cap.

8. Connect the distributor line and the high tension wires to the cap.

9. Run the engine until it reaches normal operating temperature and then check the ignition timing.

3F-E Engines

▶ **See Figures 12, 13 and 14**

If the engine has been cranked, dismantled, or the timing otherwise lost, proceed as follows:

1. Determine top dead center (TDC) of the No. 1 cylinder's compression

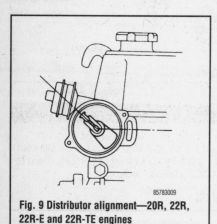

Fig. 9 Distributor alignment—20R, 22R, 22R-E and 22R-TE engines

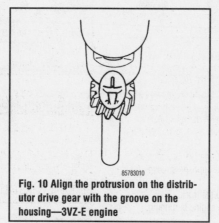

Fig. 10 Align the protrusion on the distributor drive gear with the groove on the housing—3VZ-E engine

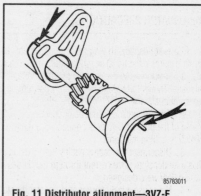

Fig. 11 Distributor alignment—3VZ-E engine

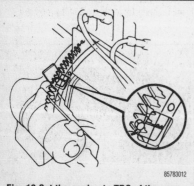

Fig. 12 Set the engine to TDC of the compression stroke—3F-E engine

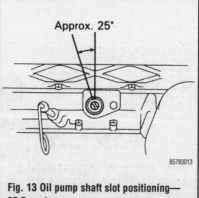

Fig. 13 Oil pump shaft slot positioning—3F-E engine

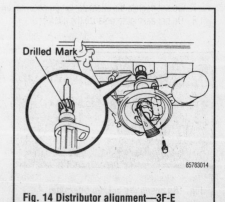

Fig. 14 Distributor alignment—3F-E engine

stroke by removing the spark plug from the No. 1 cylinder and placing your finger on a vacuum gauge over the spark plug hole. This is important because the timing marks will also line up with the cylinder in the firing order in its exhaust stroke.

✳✳ CAUTION

On engines which have the spark plugs buried in the exhaust manifold, use a compression gauge or a screwdriver handle, not your finger, if the manifold is still hot.

Crank the engine until compression pressure starts to build up. Continue cranking the engine until the timing marks indicate **TDC** or **0**.

2. Next, align the timing marks to the specifications given in the Ignition Timing column of the Tune-Up Specifications chart at the beginning of Section 2.

3. Position the oil pump shaft slot so that it is in roughly the 11 and 5 position.

4. Lightly coat a new O-ring with engine oil and then install it onto the distributor shaft.

5. With the drilled mark on the distributor driven gear facing upward, insert the distributor into its hole so that the center of the flange aligns with center of the bolt hole in the cylinder head.

6. When the distributor is fully inserted, the rotor should be pointing in the direction shown.

7. Lightly tighten the distributor hold-down bolt and then install the distributor cap and high tension lines.

8. Run the engine until it reaches normal operating temperature and then check the ignition timing.

Alternator

All models use a 12 volt alternator. Amperage ratings vary according to the year and model. 1970-79 models utilize a separate, adjustable regulator, while 1980-88 models have a transistorized, non-adjustable regulator, integral with the alternator.

ALTERNATOR PRECAUTIONS

To prevent damage to the alternator and regulator, the following precautionary measures must be taken when working with the electrical system.

1. Never reverse the battery connections. Always check the battery polarity visually. This is to be done before any connections are made to ensure that all of the connections correspond to the battery ground polarity of the truck.

2. Booster batteries must be connected properly. Make sure the positive cable of the booster battery is connected to the positive terminal of the battery which is getting the boost.

3. Disconnect the battery cables before using a fast charger; the charger has a tendency to force current through the diodes in the opposite direction for which they were designed.

4. Never use a fast charger as a booster for starting the truck.

5. Never disconnect the voltage regulator while the engine is running, unless as noted for testing purposes.

6. Do not ground the alternator output terminal.

7. Do not operate the alternator on an open circuit with the field energized.

8. Do not attempt to polarize the alternator.

9. Disconnect the battery cables and remove the alternator before using an electric arc welder on the truck.

10. Protect the alternator from excessive moisture. If the engine is to be steam cleaned, cover or remove the alternator.

REMOVAL & INSTALLATION

▶ See Figures 15, 16, 17 and 18

➡On some models, the alternator assembly is mounted very low on the engine. On these models, it may be necessary to remove the gravel shield and work from beneath the truck in order to gain access to the alternator.

1. Disconnect the negative battery cable.

2. Remove the alternator pivot bolt. Push the alternator in and remove the drive belt.

3. Pull back the rubber boots and disconnect the wiring from the back of the alternator.

4. Remove the alternator mounting bolt and then withdraw the alternator from its bracket.

To install:

5. Position the alternator in its mounting bracket and lightly tighten the mounting and adjusting bolts.

6. Connect the electrical leads at the rear of the alternator.

7. Adjust the belt tension as detailed in Section 1.

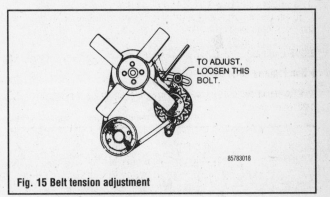

TO ADJUST, LOOSEN THIS BOLT.

85783018

Fig. 15 Belt tension adjustment

Regulator

All 1970–79 models are equipped with a separate, adjustable regulator. 1980-88 models are equipped with a transistorized regulator which is attached to the brush assembly on the side of the alternator housing. If faulty, it must be replaced; there are no adjustments which can be made.

REMOVAL & INSTALLATION

1970–79

1. Disconnect the negative battery cable.

2. Disconnect the wiring harness connector at the back of the regulator.

85783225

Fig. 16 Loosen the bottom alternator adjusting bolt

85783226

Fig. 17 Remove the bottom alternator adjusting bolt—note the location of the top alternator bolt

85783227

Fig. 18 Remove the alternator assembly

3. Remove the regulator mounting bolts.
4. Remove the regulator.
5. Installation is the reverse of the removal procedure.

1980–88

1. Remove the alternator as detailed earlier.
2. Remove the two screws on the back of the alternator housing and then remove the regulator end cover.
3. Underneath the end cover there are three terminal screws, remove them.
4. Remove the two regulator mounting screws and remove the regulator.
5. Using a small screwdriver, pry out the plastic housing and the rubber seal around the regulator terminals.
6. Installation is in the reverse order of removal.

VOLTAGE ADJUSTMENT

1970–79

1. Connect a voltmeter up to the battery terminals. Negative (black) lead to the negative (–) terminal; positive (red) lead to positive (+) terminal.
2. Start the engine and gradually increase its speed to about 1,500 rpm.
3. At this speed, the voltage reading should fall within the range specified in the Alternator and Regulator Specifications chart.
4. If the voltage does not fall within the specifications, remove the cover from the regulator and adjust it by bending the adjusting arm.
5. Repeat Steps 2 and 3 if the voltage cannot be brought to specification, proceed the mechanical adjustments which follow.

MECHANICAL ADJUSTMENTS

▶ See Figures 19, 20, 21 and 22

1970–79

➡Perform the voltage adjustment outlined above, before beginning the mechanical adjustments.

FIELD RELAY

1. Remove the cover from the regulator assembly.
2. Use a feeler gauge to check the amount that the contact spring is deflected while the armature is being depressed.
3. If the measurement is not within specifications (see the Alternator and Regulator Specifications chart), adjust the regulator by bending the point holder P_2 (see the illustration).
4. Check the point gap with a feeler gauge against the specifications in the chart.
5. Adjust the point gap, as required, by bending the point holder P_1 (see the illustration).
6. Clean off the points with emery cloth if they are dirty and wash them with solvent.

VOLTAGE REGULATOR

1. Use a feeler gap to measure the air (armature) gap. If it is not within specification (see the Alternator and Regulator Specifications Chart), adjust it by bending the low speed point holder (see the illustration).
2. Check the point gap with a feeler gauge. If it is not within specifications, adjust it by bending the high speed point holder (see the illustration). Clean the points with emery cloth and wash them off with solvent.
3. Check the amount of contact spring deflection while depressing the armature. The specification should be the same as that for the contact spring on the field relay.

Starter

REMOVAL & INSTALLATION

▶ See Figures 23 thru 30

➡On some models with automatic transmission, it may be necessary to disconnect the throttle rod.

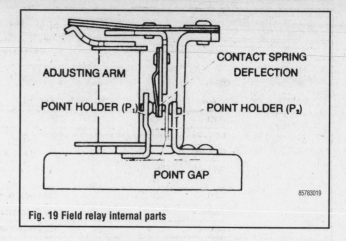

Fig. 19 Field relay internal parts

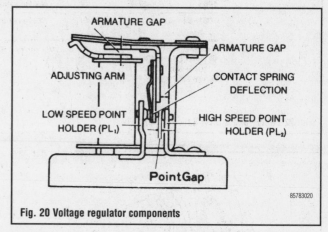

Fig. 20 Voltage regulator components

Alternator and Regulator Specifications

Year	Engine Type	Alternator Output (amps)	Regulator — Field Relay — Contact Spring Deflection (in.)	Point Gap (in.)	Volts to Close	Regulator — Air Gap (in.)	Point Gap (in.)	Volts
1970–71	8R-C	40	0.008–0.010	0.016–0.047	4.5–5.8	0.008	0.001–0.008	13.8–14.8
1972–74	18R-C	45	0.008–0.024	0.016–0.047	4.5–5.8	0.012	0.012–0.018	13.8–14.8
1975–79	20R	40	0.008–0.024	0.016–0.047	4.5–5.8	0.012	0.012–0.018	13.8–14.8
		55	0.008–0.024	0.016–0.047	4.5–5.8	0.012	0.012–0.018	14.0–14.7
1980	20R	40, 55, 60	①	①	①	①	①	14.0–14.7
1981–84	22R, 22R-E	40, 55, 60	①	①	①	①	①	14.0–14.7
1985–88	22R, 22R-E, 22R-TE	60	①	①	①	①	①	13.9–15.1
1988	3VZ-E	60	①	①	①	①	①	13.9–15.1
1970–74	F	40	0.008–0.024	0.016–0.047	4.5–5.8	0.012	0.012–0.018	13.8–14.8
1975–79	2F	40, 50, 55	0.008–0.024	0.016–0.047	4.5–5.8	0.012	0.012–0.018	13.8–14.8
1980–87	2F	50, 60, 70	①	①	①	①	①	13.8–14.8
1988	3F-E	80	①	①	①	①	①	13.8–14.5
1981–85	1L, 2L, 2L-T	55	①	①	①	①	①	13.8–14.8

① Regulator not adjustable

Fig. 21 Alternator and Regulator Specifications Chart

1. Disconnect the negative (–) battery cable at the battery, then disconnect the positive (+) battery cable at the starter.
2. Disconnect the remaining electrical connections at the starter solenoid.

Battery and Starter Specifications

All cars use 12 volt, negative ground electrical systems

			Starter							
		Battery Amp Hour Capacity	Lock Test			No Load Test			Brush Spring Tension (oz)	Min. Brush Length (in.)
Year	Engine Type		Amps	Volts	Torque (ft. lbs.)	Amps	Volts	RPM		
1970–71	8R-C	50	550	7.7	10	45	11	6,000	21	0.47
1972–74	18R-C	50	550	7.7	10	45	11	6,000	21	0.47
1975–80	20R	60	Not Recommended			50	11.5	5,000	21	0.47
1981–88	22R, 22R-E, 22R-TE	①	Not Recommended			90	11.5	3,500	64	0.39 ②
1988	3VZ-E	①	Not Recommended			90	11.5	3,500	64	②
1970–74	F	50	Not Recommended			50	11.5	5,000	64	0.51
1975–87	2F	①	Not Recommended			50	11	5,000	64	0.51 ③
1988	3F-E	①	Not Recommended			90	11.5	3,000	64	0.34
1981–85	1L, 2L, 2L-T	①	Not Recommended			180	11	3,500	84–96	0.47

① Replace w/battery of at least same capacity; consult application chart at battery dealer
② 1983–84: 1.0 KW—0.335; 1.4 KW—0.354
1985–88: 1.0 KW—0.335; 1.4 KW—0.394
③ 1980–87: 0.394

85783022

Fig. 22 Battery and Starter Specifications Chart

85783023

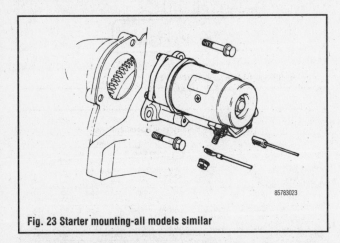

Fig. 23 Starter mounting-all models similar

85783228

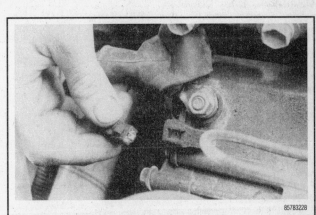

Fig. 24 Removing the starter electrical connection

85783229

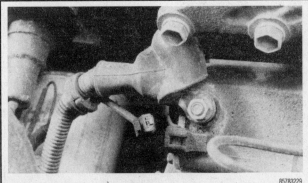

Fig. 25 View of the starter electrical connection (lower) and battery connection (upper)

85783230

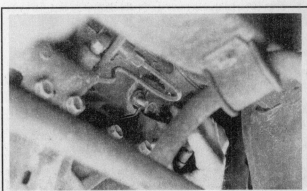

Fig. 26 Removing the battery electrical connection

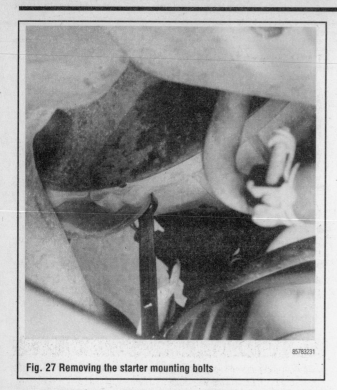

Fig. 27 Removing the starter mounting bolts

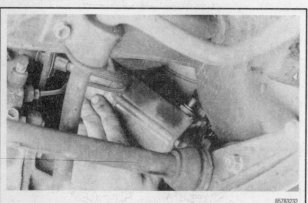

Fig. 28 Removing the starter assembly from the vehicle

Fig. 29 Installing the starter assembly

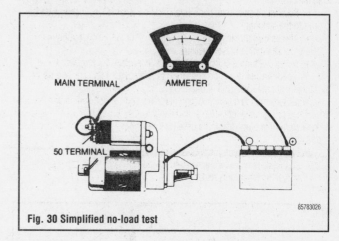

Fig. 30 Simplified no-load test

3. Remove the two nuts holding the starter to the bell housing and pull the starter toward the front of the vehicle.

4. To install the unit, insert the starter into the bell housing being sure that the starter drive is not jammed against the flywheel. Tighten the attaching nuts and replace all electrical connections making the battery connection the last.

ENGINE MECHANICAL

Engine Overhaul

Most engine overhaul procedures are fairly standard. In addition to specific parts replacement procedures and complete specifications for your individual engine, this section also is a guide to accept rebuilding procedures. Examples of standard rebuilding practice are shown and should be used along with specific details concerning your particular engine.

Competent and accurate machine shop services will ensure maximum performance, reliability and engine life. Procedures marked with the symbol shown above should be performed by a competent machine shop, and are provided so that you will be familiar with the procedures necessary to a successful overhaul.

In most instances it is more profitable for the do-it-yourself mechanic to remove, clean and inspect the component, buy the necessary parts and deliver these to a shop for actual machine work.

On the other hand, much of the rebuilding work (crankshaft, block, bearings, piston rods, and other components) is well within the scope of the do-it-yourself mechanic.

TOOLS

The tools required for an engine overhaul or parts replacement will depend on the depth of your involvement. With a few exceptions, they will be the tools found in a mechanic's tool kit (see Section 1). More in-depth work will require any or all of the following:

- a dial indicator (reading in thousandths) mounted on a universal base
- micrometers and telescope gauges
- jaw and screw type pullers
- scraper
- valve spring compressor
- ring groove cleaner
- piston ring expander and compressor
- ridge reamer
- cylinder hone or glaze breaker
- Plastigage®
- engine stand

Use of most of these tools is illustrated in this section. Many can be rented for a one-time use from a local parts jobber or tool supply house specializing in automotive work.

Occasionally, the use of special tools is called for. See the information on Special Tools and Safety Notice in the front of this book before substituting another tool.

INSPECTION TECHNIQUES

Procedures and specifications are given in this section for inspecting, cleaning and assessing the wear limits of most major components. Other procedures such as Magnaflux® and Zyglo® can be used to locate material flaws and stress cracks. Magnaflux® is a magnetic process applicable only to ferrous materials. The Zyglo® process coats the material with a fluorescent dye penetrant and can be used on any material Check for suspected surface cracks can be more readily made using spot check dye. The dye is sprayed onto the suspected area, wiped off and the area sprayed with a developer. Cracks will show up brightly.

OVERHAUL TIPS

Aluminum has become extremely popular for use in engines, due to its low weight. Observe the following precautions when handling aluminum parts:
• Never hot tank aluminum parts (the caustic hot-tank solution will eat the aluminum.
• Remove all aluminum parts (identification tag, etc.) from engine parts prior to the tanking.
• Always coat threads lightly with engine oil or anti-seize compounds before installation, to prevent seizure.
• Never overtorque bolts or spark plugs especially in aluminum threads.
Stripped threads in any component can be repaired using any of several commercial repair kits (Heli-Coil®, Microdot®, Keenserts®, etc.).

When assembling the engine, any parts that will be frictional contact must be prelubed to provide lubrication at initial start up. Any product specifically formulated for this purpose can be used, but engine oil is not recommended as a prelube.

When semipermanent (locked, but removable) installation of bolts or nuts is desired, threads should be cleaned and coated with Loctite® or other similar, commercial nonhardening sealant.

REPAIRING DAMAGED THREADS

▶ **See Figures 31, 32, 33, 34 and 35**

Several methods of repairing damaged threads are available. Heli-Coil® (shown here), Keenserts® and Microdot® are among the most widely used. All involve basically the same principle, drilling out stripped threads, tapping the hole and installing a prewound insert, making welding, plugging and oversize fasteners unnecessary.

Two types of thread repair inserts are usually supplied: a standard type for most Inch Coarse, Inch Fine, Metric Course and Metric Fine thread sizes and a spark lug type to fit most spark plug port sizes. Consult the individual manufacturer's catalog to determine exact applications. Typical thread repair kits will contain a selection of prewound threaded inserts, a tap (corresponding to the outside diameter threads of the insert) and an installation tool. Spark plug inserts usually differ because they require a tap equipped with pilot threads and a combined reamer/tap section. Most manufacturers also supply blister packed thread repair inserts separately in addition to a master kit containing a variety of taps and inserts plus installation tools.

Before effecting a repair to a threaded hole, remove any snapped, broken or damaged bolts or studs. Penetrating oil can be used to free frozen threads; the offending item can be removed with locking pliers or with a screw or stud extractor. After the hole is clear, the thread can be repaired, as follows:

Checking Engine Compression

A noticeable lack of engine power, excessive oil consumption and/or poor fuel mileage measured over an extended period are all indicators of internal engine war. Worn piston rings, scored or worn cylinder bores, blown head gaskets, sticking or burnt valves and worn valve seats are all possible culprits here. A check of each cylinder's compression will help you locate the problems.

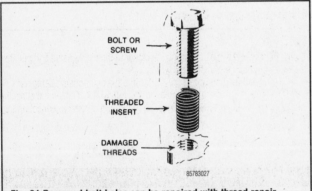

Fig. 31 Damaged bolt holes can be repaired with thread repair inserts

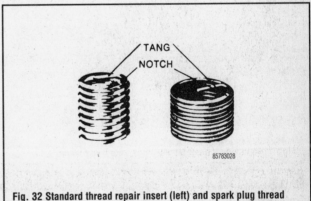

Fig. 32 Standard thread repair insert (left) and spark plug thread insert (right)

Fig. 33 Drill out the damaged threads with specified drill—drill completely through the hole or to the bottom of a blind hole

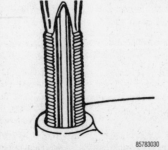

Fig. 34 With the tap supplied, tap the hole to receive the thread insert—keep the tap well oiled and back it out frequently to avoid clogging the threads

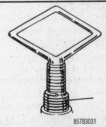

Fig. 35 Screw the threaded insert onto the installation tool until the tang engages the slot—screw the insert into the tapped hole until it is 1/4-1/2 turn below the top surface—after installation, break off the tang with a hammer and punch

As mentioned in the Tools and Equipment section of Section 1, a screw-in type compression gauge is more accurate that the type you simply hold against the spark plug hole, although it takes slightly longer to use. It's worth it to obtain a more accurate reading. Follow the procedures below for gasoline and diesel engine trucks.

GASOLINE ENGINES

▶ **See Figure 36**

1. Warm up the engine to normal operating temperature.
2. Remove all spark plugs.
3. Disconnect the high tension lead from the ignition coil.
4. On carbureted trucks, fully open the throttle either by operating the carburetor throttle linkage by hand or by having an assistant floor the accelerator pedal. On fuel injected trucks, disconnect the cold start valve and all injector connections.
5. Screw the compression gauge into the No. 1 spark plug hole until the fitting is snug.

➡ **Be careful not to crossthread the plug hole. On aluminum cylinder heads use extra care, as the threads in these heads are easily ruined.**

6. Ask an assistant to depress the accelerator pedal fully on both carbureted and fuel injected trucks. Then, while you read the compression gauge, ask the assistant to crank the engine two or three times in short bursts using the ignition switch.
7. Read the compression gauge at the end of each series of cranks, and record the highest of these readings. Repeat this procedure for each of the engine's cylinders. Compare the highest reading of each cylinder to the compression pressure specification in the Tune-Up Specifications chart in Section 2. The specs in this chart are maximum values.

A cylinders compression pressure is usually acceptable if it is not less than 80% of maximum. The difference between each cylinder should be no more than 12-14 pounds.

8. If a cylinder is unusually low, pour a tablespoon of clean engine oil into the cylinder through the spark plug hole and repeat the compression test. If the compression comes up after adding the oil, it appears that the cylinder's piston rings or bore are damaged or worn. If the pressure remains low, the valves may not be seating properly (a valve job is needed), or the head gasket may be blown near that cylinder. If compression in any two adjacent cylinders is low, and if the addition of oil doesn't help the compression, there is leakage past the head gasket. Oil and coolant water in the combustion chamber can result from this problem. There may be evidence of water droplets on the engine dipstick when a had gasket has blown.

DIESEL ENGINES

▶ **See Figure 37**

Checking cylinder compression on diesel engines is basically the same procedure as on gasoline engines except for the following:

1. A special compression gauge adapter suitable for diesel engines (because these engines have much greater compression pressures) must be used.
2. Remove the injector tubes and remove the injectors from each cylinder.

➡ **Don't forget to remove the washer underneath each injector; otherwise, it may get lost when the engine is cranked.**

3. When fitting the compression gauge adapter to the cylinder head, make sure the bleeder of the gauge (if equipped) is closed.
4. When reinstalling the injector assemblies, install new washers underneath each injector.

TCCS3801

Fig. 36 A screw-in type compression gauge is more accurate and easier to use without an assistant

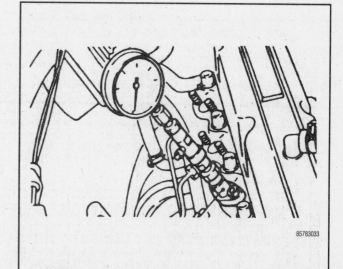

85783033

Fig. 37 Diesel engines require a special compression gauge adapter

GENERAL ENGINE SPECIFICATIONS

Year	Engine Type	Engine Displacement Cu. In. (cc)	Carburetor Type	Horsepower (@ rpm)	Torque @ rpm (ft. lbs.)	Bore × Stroke (in.)	Compression Ratio	Oil Pressure @ rpm (psi)
1986	22R	144.4 (2367)	2 bbl	96 @ 4800	129 @ 2800	3.62 × 3.50	9.3:1	36-71 @ 3000
	22R-E	144.4 (2367)	EFI	116 @ 4800	140 @ 2800	3.62 × 3.50	9.3:1	36-71 @ 3000
	22R-TE	144.4 (2367)	EFI①	135 @ 4800	173 @ 2800	3.62 × 3.50	7.5:1	36-71 @ 3000
	2F	257.9 (4200)	2 bbl	125 @ 3600	200 @ 1800	3.70 × 4.00	7.8:1	60 @ 2000
1987	22R	144.4 (2367)	2 bbl	103 @ 4800	133 @ 2800	3.62 × 3.50	9.3:1	36-71 @ 3000
	22R-E	144.4 (2367)	EFI	116 @ 4800	140 @ 2800	3.62 × 3.50	9.3:1	36-71 @ 3000
	22R-TE	144.4 (2367)	EFI①	135 @ 4800	173 @ 2800	3.62 × 3.50	7.5:1	36-71 @ 3000
	2F	257.9 (4200)	2 bbl	125 @ 3600	200 @ 1800	3.70 × 4.00	7.8:1	60 @ 2000
1988	22R	144.4 (2367)	2 bbl	103 @ 4800	133 @ 2800	3.62 × 3.50	9.3:1	36-71 @ 3000
	22R-E	144.4 (2367)	EFI	116 @ 4800	140 @ 2800	3.62 × 3.50	9.3:1	36-71 @ 3000
	22R-TE	144.4 (2367)	EFI①	135 @ 4800	173 @ 2800	3.62 × 3.50	7.5:1	36-71 @ 3000
	3VZ-E	180.0 (2950)	EFI	150 @ 4500	189 @ 3400	3.45 × 3.23	NA	36-71 @ 3000
	3F-E	241.3 (3955)	EFI	154 @ 4000	220 @ 3000	3.70 × 3.74	8.1:1	36-71 @ 4000

NA—Not available at time of publication
EFI—Electronic Fuel Injection
DFI—Diesel Fuel Injection
①—Turbocharged

85783CA1

GENERAL ENGINE SPECIFICATIONS

Year	Engine Type	Engine Displacement Cu. In. (cc)	Carburetor Type	Horsepower (@ rpm)	Torque @ rpm (ft. lbs.)	Bore × Stroke (in.)	Compression Ratio	Oil Pressure @ rpm (psi)
1970	8R-C	113.4 (1858)	2 bbl	108 @ 5500	113 @ 3800	3.38 × 3.15	9.0:1	57 @ 2500
	F	236.7 (3878)	2 bbl	135 @ 4000	213 @ 2000	3.54 × 4.00	7.8:1	60 @ 2000
1971	8R-C	113.4 (1858)	2 bbl	108 @ 5500	113 @ 3800	3.38 × 3.15	9.0:1	57 @ 2500
	F	236.7 (3878)	2 bbl	135 @ 4000	213 @ 2000	3.54 × 4.00	7.8:1	60 @ 2000
1972	18R-C	123.0 (1980)	2 bbl	97 @ 5500	106 @ 3600	3.48 × 3.15	8.5:1	54 @ 2500
	F	236.7 (3878)	2 bbl	135 @ 4000	213 @ 2000	3.54 × 4.00	7.8:1	60 @ 2000
1973	18R-C	123.0 (1980)	2 bbl	97 @ 5500	106 @ 3600	3.48 × 3.15	8.5:1	54 @ 2500
	F	236.7 (3878)	2 bbl	135 @ 4000	213 @ 2000	3.54 × 4.00	7.8:1	60 @ 2000
1974	18R-C	123.0 (1980)	2 bbl	97 @ 5500	106 @ 3600	3.48 × 3.15	8.5:1	54 @ 2500
	F	236.7 (3878)	2 bbl	135 @ 4000	213 @ 2000	3.54 × 4.00	7.8:1	60 @ 2000
1975	20R	133.6 (2189)	2 bbl	95 @ 4800	122 @ 2400	3.48 × 3.50	8.4:1	64 @ 2500
	2F	257.9 (4200)	2 bbl	125 @ 3600	200 @ 1800	3.70 × 4.00	7.8:1	60 @ 2000
1976	20R	133.6 (2189)	2 bbl	95 @ 4800	122 @ 2400	3.48 × 3.50	8.4:1	64 @ 2500
	2F	257.9 (4200)	2 bbl	125 @ 3600	200 @ 1800	3.70 × 4.00	7.8:1	60 @ 2000
1977	20R	133.6 (2189)	2 bbl	95 @ 4800	122 @ 2400	3.48 × 3.50	8.4:1	64 @ 2500
	2F	257.9 (4200)	2 bbl	125 @ 3600	200 @ 1800	3.70 × 4.00	7.8:1	60 @ 2000
1978	20R	133.6 (2189)	2 bbl	95 @ 4800	122 @ 2400	3.48 × 3.50	8.4:1	64 @ 2500
	2F	257.9 (4200)	2 bbl	125 @ 3600	200 @ 1800	3.70 × 4.00	7.8:1	60 @ 2000
1979	20R	133.6 (2189)	2 bbl	90 @ 4800	122 @ 2400	3.48 × 3.50	8.4:1	64 @ 2500
	2F	257.9 (4200)	2 bbl	125 @ 3600	200 @ 1800	3.70 × 4.00	7.8:1	60 @ 2000
1980	20R	133.6 (2189)	2 bbl	90 @ 4800	122 @ 2400	3.48 × 3.50	8.4:1	64 @ 2500
	2F	257.9 (4200)	2 bbl	125 @ 3600	200 @ 1800	3.70 × 4.00	7.8:1	60 @ 2000
1981	22R	144.4 (2367)	2 bbl	96 @ 4800	129 @ 2800	3.62 × 3.50	9.0:1	64 @ 2500
	2F	257.9 (4200)	2 bbl	125 @ 3600	200 @ 1800	3.70 × 4.00	7.8:1	60 @ 2000
	1L	133.5 (2188)	DFI	62 @ 4200	93 @ 2400	3.54 × 3.38	21.5:1	36-85 @ 3000
1982	22R	144.4 (2367)	2 bbl	96 @ 4800	129 @ 2800	3.62 × 3.50	9.0:1	64 @ 2500
	2F	257.9 (4200)	2 bbl	125 @ 3600	200 @ 1800	3.70 × 4.00	7.8:1	60 @ 2000
	2L	133.5 (2188)	DFI	62 @ 4200	93 @ 2400	3.54 × 3.38	21.5:1	36-85 @ 3000
1983	22R	144.4 (2367)	2 bbl	96 @ 4800	129 @ 2800	3.62 × 3.50	9.0:1	36-71 @ 3000
	2F	257.9 (4200)	2 bbl	125 @ 3600	200 @ 1800	3.70 × 4.00	7.8:1	60 @ 2000
	1L	133.5 (2188)	DFI	62 @ 4200	93 @ 2400	3.54 × 3.38	21.5:1	36-85 @ 3000
1984	22R	144.4 (2367)	2 bbl	96 @ 4800	129 @ 2800	3.62 × 3.50	9.0:1	36-71 @ 3000
	22R-E	144.4 (2367)	EFI	105 @ 4800	137 @ 2800	3.62 × 3.50	9.0:1	36-71 @ 3000
	2F	257.9 (4200)	2 bbl	125 @ 3600	200 @ 1800	3.70 × 4.00	7.8:1	60 @ 2000
	2L, 2L-T	149.3 (2477)	DFI	NA	NA	3.62 × 3.62	21.5:1	36-85 @ 3000
1985	22R	144.4 (2367)	2 bbl	96 @ 4800	129 @ 2800	3.62 × 3.50	9.0:1	36-71 @ 3000
	22R-E	144.4 (2367)	EFI	116 @ 4800	140 @ 2800	3.62 × 3.50	9.0:1	36-71 @ 3000
	2F	257.9 (4200)	2 bbl	125 @ 3600	200 @ 1800	3.70 × 4.00	7.8:1	60 @ 2000
	2L, 2L-T	149.3 (2477)	DFI	NA	NA	3.62 × 3.62	21.5:1	36-85 @ 3000

85783C01

VALVE SPECIFICATIONS

Year	Engine Type	Seat Angle (deg.)	Face Angle (deg.)	Spring Test Pressure (lbs.) Inner	Spring Test Pressure (lbs.) Outer	Spring Installed Height (in.) Inner	Spring Installed Height (in.) Outer	Stem-to-Guide Clearance (in.) ▲ Intake	Stem-to-Guide Clearance (in.) ▲ Exhaust	Stem Diameter (in.) Intake	Stem Diameter (in.) Exhaust
1981	22R	45	44.5	—	55.1	—	1.594	0.0008-0.0024	0.0012-0.0026	0.3138-0.3145	0.3136-0.3142
	2F	45	44.5	—	71.6	—	1.693	0.0012-0.0024	0.0016-0.0028	0.3140	0.3137
	1L	45	44.5	—	56	—	1.547	0.0012-0.0024	0.0016-0.0028	0.3339	0.3332
1982	22R	45	44.5	—	55.1	—	1.594	0.0008-0.0024	0.0012-0.0026	0.3138-0.3145	0.3136-0.3142
	2F	45	44.5	—	71.6	—	1.693	0.0012-0.0024	0.0016-0.0028	0.3140	0.3137
	1L	45	44.5	—	56	—	1.547	0.0012-0.0024	0.0016-0.0028	0.3339	0.3332
1983	22R	45	44.5	—	55.1	—	1.594	0.0008-0.0024	0.0012-0.0026	0.3138-0.3145	0.3136-0.3142
	2F	45	44.5	—	71.6	—	1.693	0.0012-0.0024	0.0016-0.0028	0.3140	0.3137
	1L	45	44.5	—	56	—	1.547	0.0008-0.0024	0.0016-0.0030	0.3339	0.3332
1984	22R	45	44.5	—	55.1	—	1.594	0.0010-0.0024	0.0012-0.0026	0.3138-0.3144	0.3136-0.3142
	2F	45	44.5	—	71.6	—	1.693	0.0012-0.0024	0.0016-0.0028	0.3140	0.3137
	2L, 2L-T	45	44.5	—	64.4	—	1.547	0.0008-0.0022	0.0008-0.0030	0.3336-0.3342	0.3328-0.3335
1985	22R	45	44.5	—	55.1	—	1.594	0.0010-0.0024	0.0012-0.0026	0.3138-0.3144	0.3136-0.3142
	2F	45	44.5	—	71.6	—	1.693	0.0012-0.0024	0.0016-0.0028	0.3140	0.3137
	2L, 2L-T	45	44.5	—	64.4	—	1.547	0.0008-0.0022	0.0016-0.0030	0.3336-0.3342	0.3328-0.3335
1986	22R	45	44.5	—	66.1	—	1.594	0.0010-0.0024	0.0012-0.0026	0.3138-0.3144	0.3136-0.3142
	2F	45	44.5	—	71.6	—	1.693	0.0012-0.0024	0.0016-0.0028	0.3140	0.3137
1987	22R	45	44.5	—	66.1	—	1.594	0.0010-0.0024	0.0012-0.0026	0.3138-0.3144	0.3136-0.3142
	2F	45	44.5	—	71.6	—	1.693	0.0012-0.0024	0.0016-0.0026	0.3140	0.3137
1988	22R	45	44.5	—	66.1	—	1.594	0.0010-0.0024	0.0012-0.0026	0.3138-0.3144	0.3136-0.3142
	3VZ-E	45	44.5	—	57	—	1.575	0.0010-0.0024	0.0012-0.0026	0.3138-0.3144	0.3134-0.3140
	3F-E	45	44.5	—	71.6	—	1.693	0.0010-0.0024	0.0014-0.0028	0.3138-0.3144	0.3136-0.3142

▲ Valve guides are removable

85783CA2

VALVE SPECIFICATIONS

Year	Engine Type	Seat Angle (deg.)	Face Angle (deg.)	Spring Test Pressure (lbs.) Inner	Spring Test Pressure (lbs.) Outer	Spring Installed Height (in.) Inner	Spring Installed Height (in.) Outer	Stem-to-Guide Clearance (in.) ▲ Intake	Stem-to-Guide Clearance (in.) ▲ Exhaust	Stem Diameter (in.) Intake	Stem Diameter (in.) Exhaust
1970	8R-C	45	45	15.2	50.6	1.480	1.640	0.0010-0.0022	0.0014-0.0030	0.3140	0.3137
	F	45	45	—	150	—	1.324	0.0010-0.0026	0.0014-0.0028	0.3141	0.3137
1971	8R-C	45	45	15.2	50.6	1.480	1.640	0.0010-0.0022	0.0014-0.0030	0.3140	0.3137
	F	45	45	—	150	—	1.324	0.0010-0.0026	0.0014-0.0028	0.3141	0.3137
1972	18R-C	45	45	15.2	50.6	1.480	1.640	0.0010-0.0022	0.0014-0.0028	0.3140	0.3137
	F	45	45	—	71.5	—	1.693	0.0010-0.0026	0.0014-0.0030	0.3141	0.3137
1973	18R-C	45	45	15.2	50.6	1.480	1.640	0.0010-0.0022	0.0014-0.0028	0.3140	0.3137
	F	45	45	—	71.5	—	1.693	0.0010-0.0026	0.0014-0.0030	0.3141	0.3137
1974	18R-C	45	45	15.2	50.6	1.480	1.640	0.0010-0.0022	0.0014-0.0030	0.3140	0.3137
	F	45	44.5	—	71.5	—	1.693	0.0010-0.0026	0.0014-0.0028	0.3141	0.3137
1975	20R	45	44.5	—	60	—	1.594	0.0006-0.0024	0.0012-0.0026	0.3141	0.3140
	2F	45	44.5	—	71.6	—	1.693	0.0012-0.0024	0.0016-0.0028	0.3140	0.3137
1976	20R	45	44.5	—	60	—	1.594	0.0006-0.0024	0.0012-0.0026	0.3141	0.3140
	2F	45	44.5	—	71.6	—	1.693	0.0016-0.0024	0.0016-0.0028	0.3140	0.3137
1977	20R	45	44.5	—	60	—	1.594	0.0006-0.0024	0.0012-0.0026	0.3141	0.3140
	2F	45	44.5	—	71.6	—	1.693	0.0012-0.0024	0.0016-0.0028	0.3140	0.3137
1978	20R	45	44.5	—	55.1	—	1.594	0.0008-0.0024	0.0012-0.0026	0.3138-0.3144	0.3136-0.3142
	2F	45	44.5	—	71.6	—	1.693	0.0012-0.0024	0.0016-0.0028	0.3140	0.3137
1979	20R	45	44.5	—	55.1	—	1.594	0.0008-0.0024	0.0012-0.0026	0.3138-0.3146	0.3136-0.3142
	2F	45	44.5	—	71.6	—	1.693	0.0012-0.0024	0.0016-0.0028	0.3140	0.3137
1980	20R	45	44.5	—	55.1	—	1.594	0.0008-0.0024	0.0012-0.0026	0.3138-0.3146	0.3136-0.3142
	2F	45	44.5	—	71.6	—	1.693	0.0012-0.0024	0.0016-0.0028	0.3140	0.3137

85783C02

CAMSHAFT SPECIFICATIONS
All measurements given in inches.

Year	Engine	Journal Diameter 1	2	3	4	5	6	7	Bearing Clearance	Lobe Lift Intake	Lobe Lift Exhaust	Camshaft End Play
1981	22R	1.2984-1.2992	1.2984-1.2992	1.2984-1.2992	1.2984-1.2992	—	—	—	0.0004-0.0020	—	—	0.0031-0.0071
	2F	1.8880-1.8888	1.8289-1.8297	1.7699-1.7707	1.7108-1.7116	—	—	—	0.0010-0.0030	—	—	0.0079-0.0103
1982	22R	1.2984-1.2992	1.2984-1.2992	1.2984-1.2992	1.2984-1.2992	—	—	—	0.0004-0.0020	—	—	0.0031-0.0071
	2F	1.8880-1.8888	1.8289-1.8297	1.7699-1.7707	1.7108-1.7116	—	—	—	0.0010-0.0030	—	—	0.0079-0.0103
1983	22R	1.2984-1.2992	1.2984-1.2992	1.2984-1.2992	1.2984-1.2992	—	—	—	0.0004-0.0020	—	—	0.0031-0.0071
	2F	1.8880-1.8888	1.8289-1.8297	1.7699-1.7707	1.7108-1.7116	—	—	—	0.0010-0.0030	—	—	0.0079-0.0103
1984	22R	1.2984-1.2992	1.2984-1.2992	1.2984-1.2992	1.2984-1.2992	—	—	—	0.0004-0.0020	—	—	0.0031-0.0071
	2F	1.8880-1.8888	1.8289-1.8297	1.7699-1.7707	1.7108-1.7116	—	—	—	0.0010-0.0030	—	—	0.0079-0.0103
1985	22R	1.2984-1.2992	1.2984-1.2992	1.2984-1.2992	1.2984-1.2992	—	—	—	0.0004-0.0020	—	—	0.0031-0.0071
	2F	1.8880-1.8888	1.8289-1.8297	1.7699-1.7707	1.7108-1.7116	—	—	—	0.0010-0.0030	—	—	0.0079-0.0103
1986	22R	1.2984-1.2992	1.2984-1.2992	1.2984-1.2992	1.2984-1.2992	—	—	—	0.0004-0.0020	—	—	0.0031-0.0071
	2F	1.8880-1.8888	1.8289-1.8297	1.7699-1.7707	1.7108-1.7116	—	—	—	0.0010-0.0030	—	—	0.0079-0.0103
1987	22R	1.2984-1.2992	1.2984-1.2992	1.2984-1.2992	1.2984-1.2992	—	—	—	0.0004-0.0020	—	—	0.0031-0.0071
	2F	1.8880-1.8888	1.8289-1.8297	1.7699-1.7707	1.7108-1.7116	—	—	—	0.0010-0.0030	—	—	0.0079-0.0103
1988	22R	1.2984-1.2992	1.2984-1.2992	1.2984-1.2992	1.2984-1.2992	—	—	—	0.0004-0.0020	—	—	0.0031-0.0071
	3VZ-E	1.3370-1.3376	1.3370-1.3376	1.3370-1.3376	1.3370-1.3376	—	—	—	0.0010-0.0026	—	—	0.0031-0.0075
	3F-E	1.8880-1.8888	1.8289-1.8297	1.7699-1.7707	1.7108-1.7116	—	—	—	0.0010-0.0030	—	—	0.0079-0.0114

85783CA3

CAMSHAFT SPECIFICATIONS
All measurements given in inches.

Year	Engine	Journal Diameter 1	2	3	4	5	6	7	Bearing Clearance	Lobe Lift Intake	Lobe Lift Exhaust	Camshaft End Play
1970	8R-C	1.3768-1.3778	1.3768-1.3778	1.3768-1.3778	1.3768-1.3778	—	—	—	0.0010-0.0020	0.4	0.4	0.0017-0.0066
	F	1.8880-1.8888	1.8289-1.8297	1.7699-1.7707	1.7108-1.7116	—	—	—	0.0010-0.0030	—	—	0.0079-0.0103
1971	8R-C	1.3768-1.3778	1.3768-1.3778	1.3768-1.3778	1.3768-1.3778	—	—	—	0.0010-0.0020	0.4	0.4	0.0017-0.0066
	F	1.8880-1.8888	1.8289-1.8297	1.7699-1.7707	1.7108-1.7116	—	—	—	0.0010-0.0030	—	—	0.0079-0.0103
1972	18R-C	1.3773-1.3782	1.3773-1.3782	1.3773-1.3782	1.3773-1.3782	—	—	—	0.0005-0.0014	0.3126-0.3205	0.3150-0.3228	0.0016-0.0067
	F	1.8880-1.8888	1.8289-1.8297	1.7699-1.7707	1.7108-1.7116	—	—	—	0.0010-0.0030	—	—	0.0079-0.0103
1973	18R-C	1.3773-1.3782	1.3773-1.3782	1.3773-1.3782	1.3773-1.3782	—	—	—	0.0005-0.0014	0.3126-0.3205	0.3150-0.3228	0.0016-0.0067
	F	1.8880-1.8888	1.8289-1.8297	1.7699-1.7707	1.7108-1.7116	—	—	—	0.0010-0.0030	—	—	0.0079-0.0103
1974	18R-C	1.3773-1.3782	1.3773-1.3782	1.3773-1.3782	1.3773-1.3782	—	—	—	0.0005-0.0014	0.3126-0.3205	0.3150-0.3228	0.0016-0.0067
	F	1.8880-1.8888	1.8289-1.8297	1.7699-1.7707	1.7108-1.7116	—	—	—	0.0010-0.0030	—	—	0.0079-0.0103
1975	20R	1.2984-1.2992	1.2984-1.2992	1.2984-1.2992	1.2984-1.2992	—	—	—	0.0004-0.0020	—	—	0.0031-0.0071
	2F	1.8880-1.8888	1.8289-1.8297	1.7699-1.7707	1.7108-1.7116	—	—	—	0.0010-0.0030	—	—	0.0079-0.0103
1976	20R	1.2984-1.2992	1.2984-1.2992	1.2984-1.2992	1.2984-1.2992	—	—	—	0.0004-0.0020	—	—	0.0031-0.0071
	2F	1.8880-1.8888	1.8289-1.8297	1.7699-1.7707	1.7108-1.7116	—	—	—	0.0010-0.0030	—	—	0.0079-0.0103
1977	20R	1.2984-1.2992	1.2984-1.2992	1.2984-1.2992	1.2984-1.2992	—	—	—	0.0004-0.0020	—	—	0.0031-0.0071
	2F	1.8880-1.8888	1.8289-1.8297	1.7699-1.7707	1.7108-1.7116	—	—	—	0.0010-0.0030	—	—	0.0079-0.0103
1978	20R	1.2984-1.2992	1.2984-1.2992	1.2984-1.2992	1.2984-1.2992	—	—	—	0.0004-0.0020	—	—	0.0031-0.0071
	2F	1.8880-1.8888	1.8289-1.8297	1.7699-1.7707	1.7108-1.7116	—	—	—	0.0010-0.0030	—	—	0.0079-0.0103
1979	20R	1.2984-1.2992	1.2984-1.2992	1.2984-1.2992	1.2984-1.2992	—	—	—	0.0004-0.0020	—	—	0.0031-0.0071
	2F	1.8880-1.8888	1.8289-1.8297	1.7699-1.7707	1.7108-1.7116	—	—	—	0.0010-0.0030	—	—	0.0079-0.0103
1980	20R	1.2984-1.2992	1.2984-1.2992	1.2984-1.2992	1.2984-1.2992	—	—	—	0.0004-0.0020	—	—	0.0031-0.0071
	2F	1.8880-1.8888	1.8289-1.8297	1.7699-1.7707	1.7108-1.7116	—	—	—	0.0010-0.0030	—	—	0.0079-0.0103

85783C03

CRANKSHAFT AND CONNECTING ROD SPECIFICATIONS
All measurements are given in inches.

Year	Engine Type	Main Brg. Journal Dia.	Crankshaft Main Brg. Oil Clearance	Crankshaft Shaft End-play	Crankshaft Thrust on No.	Connecting Rod Journal Diameter	Connecting Rod Oil Clearance	Connecting Rod Side Clearance
1981	22R	2.3613-2.3622	0.0010-0.0022	0.0008-0.0087	3	2.0862-2.0866	0.0010-0.0022	0.0063-0.0102
	2F	⊘	0.0008-0.0017	0.0024-0.0065	3	2.1252-2.1260	0.0012-0.0028	0.0031-0.0079
	2L	2.0858-2.0866	0.0012-0.0028	0.0016-0.0098	3	2.0858-2.0866	0.0012-0.0028	0.0063-0.0102
1982	22R	2.3613-2.3622	0.0010-0.0022	0.0008-0.0087	3	2.0862-2.0866	0.0010-0.0022	0.0063-0.0102
	2F	⊘	0.0008-0.0017	0.0024-0.0065	3	2.1252-2.1260	0.0012-0.0028	0.0031-0.0079
	1L	2.4402-2.4409	0.0012-0.0028	0.0016-0.0098	3	2.0858-2.0866	0.0012-0.0028	0.0063-0.0102
1983	22R	2.3613-2.3622	0.0010-0.0022	0.0008-0.0087	3	2.0862-2.0866	0.0010-0.0022	0.0063-0.0102
	2F	⊘	0.0008-0.0017	0.0024-0.0065	3	2.1252-2.1260	0.0012-0.0028	0.0031-0.0079
	1L	2.4402-2.4409	0.0012-0.0028	0.0016-0.0098	3	2.0858-2.0866	0.0010-0.0022	0.0063-0.0102
1984	22R	2.3616-2.3622	0.0010-0.0022	0.0008-0.0087	3	2.0862-2.0866	0.0010-0.0022	0.0063-0.0102
	2F	⊘	0.0008-0.0017	0.0024-0.0065	3	2.1252-2.1260	0.0012-0.0028	0.0031-0.0079
	2L	2.4403-2.4409	0.0013-0.0026	0.0016-0.0098	3	2.0858-2.0866	0.0012-0.0028	0.0031-0.0079
1985	22R	2.3616-2.3622	0.0010-0.0022	0.0008-0.0087	3	2.0862-2.0866	0.0010-0.0022	0.0063-0.0102
	2F	⊘	0.0008-0.0017	0.0024-0.0065	3	2.1252-2.1260	0.0012-0.0028	0.0031-0.0079
	2L	2.4403-2.4409	0.0013-0.0026	0.0008-0.0087	3	2.0858-2.0866	0.0010-0.0022	0.0063-0.0102
1986	22R	2.3616-2.3622	0.0010-0.0022	0.0008-0.0087	3	2.0862-2.0866	0.0012-0.0028	0.0031-0.0079
	2F	⊘	0.0008-0.0017	0.0024-0.0065	3	2.1252-2.1260	0.0010-0.0022	0.0063-0.0102
1987	22R	2.3616-2.3622	0.0010-0.0022	0.0008-0.0087	3	2.0862-2.0866	0.0012-0.0028	0.0031-0.0079
	2F	⊘	0.0008-0.0017	0.0024-0.0065	3	2.1252-2.1260	0.0010-0.0022	0.0063-0.0102
1988	22R	2.3616-2.3622	0.0010-0.0022	0.0008-0.0098	3	2.0862-2.0866	0.0012-0.0028	0.0031-0.0079
	3VZ-E	2.5195-2.5197	0.0009-0.0017	0.0008-0.0098	3	2.1648-2.1654	0.0009-0.0021	0.0059-0.0130
	3F-E	⊙	0.0008-0.0017	0.0006-0.0088	3	2.0861-2.0866	0.0008-0.0020	0.0063-0.0118

⊘ #1: 2.6367-2.6376
#2: 2.6957-2.6967
#3: 2.7548-2.7557
#4: 2.8139-3.8148

⊙ #1: 2.6366-2.6378
#2: 2.6957-2.6969
#3: 2.7547-2.7559
#4: 2.8138-2.8150

85783CA4

CRANKSHAFT AND CONNECTING ROD SPECIFICATIONS
All measurements are given in inches.

Year	Engine Type	Main Brg. Journal Dia.	Crankshaft Main Brg. Oil Clearance	Crankshaft Shaft End-play	Crankshaft Thrust on No.	Connecting Rod Journal Diameter	Connecting Rod Oil Clearance	Connecting Rod Side Clearance
1970	8R-C	2.3613-2.3622	0.0008-0.0020	0.0020-0.0100	3	2.0857-2.0866	0.0008-0.0020	0.0043-0.0097
	F	⊙	0.0012-0.0018	0.0024-0.0065	3	2.1252-2.1260	0.0008-0.0024	0.0040-0.0090
1971	8R-L	2.3613-2.3622	0.0008-0.0020	0.0020-0.0100	3	2.0857-2.0866	0.0008-0.0020	0.0043-0.0097
	F	⊙	0.0012-0.0018	0.0024-0.0065	3	2.1252-2.1260	0.0008-0.0024	0.0040-0.0090
1972	18R-C	2.3613-2.3622	0.0008-0.0020	0.0020-0.0080	3	2.0857-2.0866	0.0008-0.0020	0.0060-0.0100
	F	⊙	0.0014-0.0018	0.0024-0.0065	3	2.1252-2.1260	0.0008-0.0024	0.0040-0.0090
1973	18R-C	2.3613-2.3622	0.0008-0.0020	0.0020-0.0080	3	2.0857-2.0866	0.0010-0.0021	0.0060-0.0100
	F	⊙	0.0014-0.0018	0.0024-0.0065	3	2.1252-2.1260	0.0008-0.0024	0.0040-0.0090
1974	18R-C	2.3613-2.3622	0.0008-0.0020	0.0020-0.0080	3	2.0857-2.0866	0.0008-0.0021	0.0060-0.0100
	F	⊙	0.0014-0.0018	0.0024-0.0065	3	2.1252-2.1260	0.0008-0.0024	0.0040-0.0090
1975	20R	2.3614-2.3622	0.0010-0.0022	0.0007-0.0079	3	2.0862-2.0866	0.0010-0.0021	0.0063-0.0102
	2F	⊙	0.0008-0.0017	0.0024-0.0065	3	2.1252-2.1260	0.0012-0.0028	0.0031-0.0079
1976	20R	2.3614-2.3622	0.0010-0.0022	0.0007-0.0079	3	2.0862-2.0866	0.0010-0.0021	0.0063-0.0102
	2F	⊙	0.0008-0.0017	0.0024-0.0065	3	2.1252-2.1260	0.0012-0.0028	0.0031-0.0079
1977	20R	2.3614-2.3622	0.0010-0.0022	0.0007-0.0079	3	2.0862-2.0866	0.0010-0.0021	0.0063-0.0102
	2F	⊙	0.0008-0.0017	0.0024-0.0065	3	2.1252-2.1260	0.0012-0.0028	0.0031-0.0079
1978	20R	2.3614-2.3622	0.0010-0.0022	0.0007-0.0079	3	2.0862-2.0866	0.0010-0.0021	0.0063-0.0102
	2F	⊙	0.0008-0.0017	0.0024-0.0065	3	2.1252-2.1260	0.0012-0.0028	0.0031-0.0079
1979	20R	2.3614-2.3622	0.0010-0.0022	0.0007-0.0079	3	2.0862-2.0866	0.0010-0.0021	0.0063-0.0102
	2F	⊙	0.0008-0.0017	0.0024-0.0065	3	2.1252-2.1260	0.0012-0.0028	0.0031-0.0079
1980	20R	2.3614-2.3622	0.0010-0.0022	0.0007-0.0079	3	2.0862-2.0866	0.0010-0.0021	0.0063-0.0102
	2F	⊙	0.0008-0.0017	0.0024-0.0065	3	2.1252-2.1260	0.0012-0.0028	0.0031-0.0079

⊙ #1: 2.6366-2.6378
#2: 2.6957-2.6969
#3: 2.7547-2.7559
#4: 2.8138-2.8150

85783C04

PISTON AND RING SPECIFICATIONS
All measurements are given in inches.

Year	Engine Type	Piston Clearance 68°F	Ring Gap			Ring Side Clearance (Ring to Land)		
			Top Compression	Bottom Compression	Oil Control	Top Compression	Bottom Compression	Oil Control
1981	22R	0.0020-0.0028	0.009-0.015	0.007-0.017	0.008-0.032	0.0012-0.0028	0.0012-0.0028	SNUG
	2F	0.0012-0.0020	0.008-0.016	0.008-0.016	SNUG	0.0012-0.0028	0.0008-0.0024	SNUG
	1L	0.0014-0.0022	0.008-0.016	0.012-0.020	0.012-0.020	0.0024-0.0039	0.0016-0.0031	0.0012-0.0028
1982	22R	0.0020-0.0028	0.009-0.015	0.007-0.017	0.008-0.032	0.0012-0.0028	0.0012-0.0028	SNUG
	2F	0.0012-0.0020	0.008-0.016	0.008-0.016	SNUG	0.0012-0.0028	0.0008-0.0024	SNUG
	1L	0.0014-0.0022	0.008-0.016	0.012-0.020	0.012-0.020	0.0024-0.0039	0.0016-0.0031	0.0012-0.0028
1983	22R	0.0020-0.0028	0.009-0.015	0.007-0.017	0.008-0.032	0.0012-0.0028	0.0012-0.0028	SNUG
	2F	0.0012-0.0020	0.008-0.016	0.008-0.016	SNUG	0.0012-0.0028	0.0008-0.0024	SNUG
	1L	0.0014-0.0022	0.008-0.016	0.012-0.020	0.012-0.020	0.0024-0.0039	0.0016-0.0031	0.0012-0.0028
1984	22R	0.0020-0.0028	0.009-0.015	0.007-0.017	0.008-0.032	0.0012-0.0028	0.0012-0.0028	SNUG
	2F	0.0012-0.0020	0.008-0.016	0.008-0.016	SNUG	0.0012-0.0028	0.0008-0.0024	SNUG
	2L	0.0020-0.0028	0.014-0.024	0.008-0.019	0.001-0.003	0.0008-0.0026	0.0016-0.0031	SNUG
1985	22R	0.0012-[2]0.0020	0.009-0.015	0.007-0.017	0.008-0.032	0.0012-0.0028	0.0012-0.0028	SNUG
	2F	0.0012-0.0020	0.008-0.016	0.008-0.016	SNUG	0.0012-0.0028	0.0008-0.0024	SNUG
	2L	0.0020-0.0028	0.014-0.024	0.008-0.019	0.001-0.003	0.0008-0.0026	0.0016-0.0031	SNUG
1986	22R	0.0012-[2]0.0020	0.014-0.022	0.010-0.019	0.008-0.032	0.0012-0.0028	0.0012-0.0028	SNUG
	2F	0.0012-0.0020	0.008-0.016	0.008-0.016	SNUG	0.0012-0.0028	0.0008-0.0024	SNUG
1987	22R	0.0012-[2]0.0020	0.014-0.022	0.010-0.019	0.008-0.032	0.0012-0.0028	0.0012-0.0028	SNUG
	2F	0.0012-0.0020	0.008-0.016	0.008-0.016	SNUG	0.0012-0.0028	0.0008-0.0024	SNUG
1988	22R	0.0008-[3]0.0016	0.010-0.019	0.024-0.032	0.008-0.022	0.0012-0.0028	0.0012-0.0028	SNUG
	3VZ-E	0.0031-0.0039	0.009-0.013	0.015-0.019	0.006-0.016	0.0012-0.0028	0.0012-0.0028	SNUG
	3F-E	0.0011-0.0019	0.008-0.017	0.020-0.028	0.008-0.032	0.0012-0.0028	0.0020-0.0035	SNUG

[1] Limit: 0.008
[2] 22R-TE 0.0022-0.0030

85783CA5

PISTON AND RING SPECIFICATIONS
All measurements are given in inches.

Year	Engine Type	Piston Clearance 68°F	Ring Gap			Ring Side Clearance (Ring to Land)		
			Top Compression	Bottom Compression	Oil Control	Top Compression	Bottom Compression	Oil Control
1970	8R-C	0.0010-0.0020	0.004-0.012	0.004-0.012	0.004-0.012	0.0012-0.0028	0.0012-0.0028	0.0008-0.0028
	F	0.0012-0.0020	0.006-0.016	0.006-0.016	0.006-0.018	0.0016-0.0031	0.0016-0.0031	⊘
1971	8R-C	0.0010-0.0020	0.004-0.012	0.004-0.012	0.004-0.012	0.0012-0.0028	0.0012-0.0028	0.0008-0.0028
	F	0.0012-0.0020	0.006-0.016	0.006-0.016	0.006-0.018	0.0016-0.0031	0.0016-0.0031	⊘
1972	18R-C	0.0020-0.0030	0.004-0.012	0.004-0.012	0.004-0.012	0.0012-0.0028	0.0012-0.0028	0.0008-0.0028
	F	0.0012-0.0020	0.008-0.016	0.006-0.014	0.006-0.014	0.0012-0.0028	0.0008-0.0024	0.0008-0.0026
1973	18R-L	0.0020-0.0030	0.004-0.012	0.004-0.012	0.004-0.012	0.0012-0.0028	0.0012-0.0028	0.0008-0.0028
	F	0.0012-0.0020	0.008-0.016	0.006-0.014	0.006-0.014	0.0012-0.0028	0.0008-0.0024	0.0008-0.0026
1974	18R-C	0.0020-0.0030	0.004-0.012	0.004-0.012	0.004-0.012	0.0012-0.0028	0.0012-0.0028	0.0008-0.0028
	F	0.0012-0.0020	0.008-0.016	0.006-0.014	0.006-0.014	0.0012-0.0028	0.0008-0.0024	0.0008-0.0026
1975	20R	0.0012-0.0020	0.004-0.012	0.004-0.012	0.004-0.012	0.0012-0.0028	0.0012-0.0028	SNUG
	2F	0.0012-0.0020	0.008-0.016	0.008-0.016	SNUG	0.0012-0.0028	0.0012-0.0024	SNUG
1976	20R	0.0012-0.0020	0.004-0.012	0.004-0.012	0.004-0.012	0.0012-0.0028	0.0012-0.0028	SNUG
	2F	0.0012-0.0020	0.008-0.016	0.008-0.016	SNUG	0.0012-0.0028	0.0008-0.0024	SNUG
1977	20R	0.0012-0.0020	0.004-0.012	0.004-0.012	0.004-0.012	0.0012-0.0028	0.0012-0.0028	SNUG
	2F	0.0012-0.0020	0.008-0.016	0.008-0.016	SNUG	0.0012-0.0028	0.0008-0.0024	SNUG
1978	20R	0.0012-0.0020	0.004-0.012	0.004-0.012	0.004-0.012	0.0012-0.0028	0.0012-0.0028	SNUG
	2F	0.0012-0.0020	0.008-0.016	0.008-0.016	SNUG	0.0012-0.0028	0.0008-0.0024	SNUG
1979	20R	0.0012-0.0020	0.004-0.012	0.004-0.012	0.004-0.012	0.0012-0.0028	0.0012-0.0024	SNUG
	2F	0.0012-0.0020	0.008-0.016	0.008-0.016	SNUG	0.0012-0.0028	0.0008-0.0024	SNUG
1980	20R	0.0012-0.0020	0.004-0.012	0.004-0.012	0.004-0.012	0.0012-0.0028	0.0012-0.0028	SNUG
	2F	0.0012-0.0020	0.008-0.016	0.008-0.016	SNUG	0.0012-0.0028	0.0008-0.0024	SNUG

85783C05

TORQUE SPECIFICATIONS
(All readings in ft. lbs.)

Year	Engine Type	Cylinder Head Bolts	Rod Bearing Bolts	Main Bearing Bolts	Crankshaft Pulley Bolt	Flywheel to Crankshaft Bolts	Manifold	
							Intake	Exhaust
1988	22R	53-63	49-53	69-83	102-130	73-86	13-19	29-36
	3VZ-E	⑤	16-20	43-47	176-186	63-67	11-15	25-33
	3F-E	87-93	40-46	⑥	247-259	60-68	⑥	⑥

⑤ Intake and exhaust manifolds combined
⑥ Rear bearing: 76-94
2L: 25-33
2L-T: 34-42
Step 1: 27
Step 2: 33
Step 3: 90° turn
Step 4: 90° turn
19 mm bolt: 99
17 mm bolt: 85
14 mm bolt: 37
17 mm bolt: 51
Nut: 41

85783CA6

TORQUE SPECIFICATIONS
(All readings in ft. lbs.)

Year	Engine Type	Cylinder Head Bolts	Rod Bearing Bolts	Main Bearing Bolts	Crankshaft Pulley Bolt	Flywheel to Crankshaft Bolts	Manifold	
							Intake	Exhaust
1970	8R-C	75-85	42-48	72-80	43-51	42-49	20-25①	20-25①
	F	83-98	35-55	90-108②	116-145	43-51	14-22②	14-22②
1971	8R-C	75-85	42-48	72-80	43-51	42-49	20-25①	20-25①
	F	83-98	35-55	90-108②	116-145	43-51	14-22②	14-22②
1972	18R-C	72-82	39-48	69-83	43-51	51-58	30-35①	30-35①
	F	83-98	35-55	90-108②	116-145	43-51	14-22②	14-22②
1973	18R-C	72-82	39-48	69-83	43-51	51-58	30-35①	30-35①
	F	83-98	35-55	90-108②	116-145	43-51	14-22②	14-22②
1974	18R-C	72-82	39-48	69-83	43-51	51-58	30-35①	30-35①
	F	83-98	35-55	90-108②	116-145	43-51	14-22②	14-22②
1975	20R	52-63	39-48	69-83	80-94	62-69	10	29-36
	2F	83-98	35-55	90-108②	116-145	59-62	28-37①	28-37①
1976	20R	52-63	39-48	69-83	80-94	62-69	10	29-36
	2F	83-98	35-55	90-108②	116-145	59-62	28-37①	28-37①
1977	20R	52-63	39-48	69-83	80-94	62-69	10	29-36
	2F	83-98	35-55	90-108②	116-145	59-62	28-37①	28-37①
1978	20R	52-63	39-48	69-83	80-94	62-69	10	29-36
	2F	83-98	35-55	90-108②	116-145	59-62	28-37①	28-37①
1979	20R	52-63	39-48	69-83	80-94	62-69	10	29-36
	2F	83-98	35-55	90-108②	116-145	59-62	28-37①	28-37①
1980	20R	52-63	39-48	69-83	80-94	62-69	10	29-36
	2F	83-98	35-55	90-108②	116-145	59-62	28-37①	28-37①
1981	1L	84-90	37-43	71-81	69-75	84-90	8-11	11-15
	22R	53-63	40-47	69-83	120-130	73-86	13-19	29-36
1982	1L	84-90	37-43	71-81	69-75	84-90	8-11	11-15
	22R	53-63	40-47	69-83	120-130	73-86	13-19	29-36
	2F	83-98	35-55	90-108②	116-145	59-62	28-37①	28-37①
1983	1L	84-90	37-43	71-81	69-75	84-90	8-11	11-15
	22R	53-63	40-47	69-83	120-130	73-86	13-19	29-36
	2F	83-98	35-55	90-108②	116-145	59-62	28-37①	28-37①
1984	1L	84-90	37-43	71-81	69-75	84-90	8-11	11-15
	22R	53-63	40-47	69-83	120-130	73-86	13-19	29-36
	2F	83-98	35-55	90-108②	116-145	59-62	28-37①	28-37①
1985	2L	84-90	40-47	70-82	95-107	—	13-19	29-36
	22R	53-63	40-47	69-83	120-130	73-86	13-19	29-36
	2F	83-98	35-55	90-108②	116-145	59-62	28-37①	28-37①
1986	2L	84-90	40-47	70-82	95-107	73-86	13-19	29-36
	22R	53-63	40-47	69-83	120-130	73-86	13-19	29-36
	2F	83-98	35-55	90-108②	116-145	59-62	28-37①	28-37①
1987	2L	84-90	40-47	70-82	95-107	—	13-19	29-36
	22R	53-63	40-47	69-83	120-130	73-86	13-19	29-36
	2F	83-98	35-55	90-108②	116-145	59-62	28-37①	28-37①

85783CO6

Engine

REMOVAL & INSTALLATION

2WD Pick-Ups—1970–82

GASOLINE ENGINES

1. Drain the radiator, cooling system, transmission, and engine oil.
2. Disconnect the battery-to-starter cable at the positive battery terminal.
3. Scribe marks on the hood and its hinges to aid in alignment during installation, then remove the hood.

➡**Do not remove the supports from the hood.**

4. Remove the headlight bezel and the radiator grille.
5. Remove the fan shroud, the hood lock base and the base support.
6. Detach both the upper and lower hoses from the radiator. If equipped with an automatic transmission, disconnect the lines from the oil cooler. Remove the radiator.
7. Unfasten the clamps and remove the heater and bypass hoses from the engine. Remove the heater control cable from the water valve.
8. Remove the wiring from the coolant temperature and oil pressure sending units.
9. Remove the air cleaner from its bracket, complete with its attendant hoses.
10. Unfasten the accelerator torque rod from the carburetor. If equipped with an automatic transmission, remove the transmission linkage as well.
11. Remove the emission control system hoses and wiring, as necessary.
12. Remove the clutch hydraulic line support bracket.
13. Unfasten the high tension and primary wires from the coil.
14. Mark the spark plug cables and remove them from the distributor.
15. Detach the right hand front engine mount.
16. Remove the fuel line at the pump.
17. Detach the downpipe from the exhaust manifold.
18. Detach the left hand front engine mount.
19. Disconnect all the wiring harness multiconnectors.

Perform the following steps on models with manual transmission.

20. Remove the center console if so equipped.
21. Remove the shift lever boot(s).
22. Unfasten the four shift lever cap retaining screws. Remove the cap and withdraw the shift lever assembly.

Perform the following steps on models equipped with automatic transmission:

23. Remove the transmission selector linkage:
    a. On models equipped with a floor mounted selector, disconnect the control rod from the transmission.
    b. On column mounted gear selection models, remove the shifter rod.
24. Disconnect the neutral safety switch wiring connector.
25. Raise the rear of the vehicle with jacks and support it on jackstands.
26. Remove the retaining screws and remove the parking brake equalizer support bracket. Disconnect the cable which runs between the lever and the equalizer.
27. Remove the speedometer cable from the transmission. Disconnect the back-up wiring.
28. Detach the driveshaft from the rear of the transmission.

➡**If oil runs out of the transmission , an old U-joint yoke sleeve makes an excellent plug.**

29. Detach the clutch release cylinder assembly, complete with hydraulic lines. Do not disconnect the lines.
30. Unbolt the rear support member mounting insulators.
31. Support the transmission and detach the rear support member retaining bolts. Withdraw the support member from the truck.
32. Install lifting hooks on the engine lifting brackets. Attach a suitable hoist to the engine.
33. Remove the jack from under the transmission.
34. Raise the engine and move it toward the front of the truck. Use care to avoid damaging the components which remain on the truck.
35. Follow the removal steps on installation of the engine. Adjust all of the linkages as detailed in the appropriate section. Install the hood and adjust it. Replenish the fluid levels in the engine, radiator and transmission.

DIESEL ENGINE

1. Make accurate marks on the body to indicate the relationship between the hood supports and the body. Unbolt the hood support at the body and remove the hood.
2. Disconnect and remove both batteries from the vehicle.
3. Drain the cooling system and remove the radiator, shroud, and radiator hoses.
4. If equipped with A/C, remove the compressor drive belt, unbolt the compressor, then tie it out of the way. Do NOT disconnect the refrigerant lines from the compressor.
5. Remove the engine cooling fan, pulley, and drive belt.
6. Disconnect the two heater hoses from the left side of the engine and the vacuum reservoir hose from the rear of the alternator.
7. If equipped with A/C, disconnect the vacuum hose from the idle-up unit.
8. Disconnect the fuel hoses from the fuel pump return connection and the sediment inlet connection.
9. Tag and disconnect the wiring from the following:
    a. Alternator
    b. Thermo-switch
    c. Oil pressure switch
    d. No. 1 glow plug relay (terminal +B)
    e. Starter
10. Disconnect the wiring from the left fender and the injection pump (accelerator wire). Also mark and tie these wires out of the way.
11. Using Toyota special service tool #09305-20012 or its equivalent, remove the transmission lever from inside the vehicle.
12. Raise the vehicle and support it safely.
13. Drain the engine oil.
14. Remove the engine under cover and remove the backup light switch wire.
15. Remove the engine shock absorber.
16. Remove the propeller (drive) shaft from the vehicle. Mark the propeller shaft and the companion flange so that the shaft may be reinstalled in its original position.
17. Disconnect the speedometer cable from the transmission.
18. Disconnect the exhaust pipe clamp from the transmission housing and the exhaust pipe mounting nuts from the exhaust manifold.
19. Unbolt the clutch release cylinder and lay the cylinder alongside the frame.
20. Remove the engine mounting bolts from each side of the engine.
21. Place a jack under the transmission so that it just touches the transmission.
22. Unbolt the transmission mounting bracket from the transmission and the crossmember. Remove the bracket.
23. Attach the engine lifting equipment to the engine.
24. Check that all wiring and hoses air clear of the engine and transmission.
25. Carefully raise the engine and transmission assembly out of the engine compartment, being especially careful not to damage the air conditioning compressor, if so equipped.
26. Remove the starter, and with the help of an assistant, disconnect the transmission from the engine. Mount the engine securely in a workstand and service the engine as necessary, according to the appropriate sections of this book.
27. Follow the removal steps on installation of the engine. Adjust all of the linkages as detailed in the appropriate section. Install the hood and adjust it. Replenish the fluid levels in the engine, radiator and transmission.

4wd Pick-Ups—1970–82

❋❋ CAUTION

Be sure to support the rear of the engine with a jack to avoid damage to the front motor mounts while performing engine removal procedures.

1. Set the engine to top dead center according to the marks on the vibration damper and timing cover pointer.
2. Remove the transmission and transfer case according to the procedures found in the appropriate sections.

3. Make accurate marks on the body to indicate the relationship between the hood supports and the body. Unbolt the hood supports at the body and remove the hood.

4. Remove the battery and the air cleaner assembly. Mark the hoses from the air cleaner to simplify installation.

5. Drain the cooling system and remove the radiator hoses.

6. Remove the radiator fan shroud and disconnect the heater outlet hose at the radiator.

7. Remove the radiator.

8. If equipped with A/C, remove the compressor drive belt, unbolt the compressor and tie it out of the way. Do NOT disconnect the refrigerant lines.

9. Remove the water pump drive belt, pulley and cooling fan.

10. Disconnect the heater inlet hose, brake booster hose and emission control hoses. Move the hoses out of the way and tie if necessary. Mark the hose locations to simplify installation.

11. Disconnect the two fuel hoses from the pipes beneath the intake manifold.

12. Disconnect all wiring attached to the engine. Mark the wire locations to simplify installation.

13. Remove the wiring from the spark plugs, distributor and ignition coil. Be sure to mark the spark plug wire locations.

14. Disconnect the accelerator linkage at the carburetor.

15. Attach an engine hoist to the engine but do not raise the hoist.

16. Remove the two engine mount-to-frame bolts from each side of the engine.

17. Be sure that all wires and hoses are clear of the engine.

18. Carefully raise the engine out of the engine compartment, being especially careful not to damage the air conditioning condenser, if so equipped.

19. Securely mount the engine on a workstand.

20. Perform the necessary service(s) to the engine according to the appropriate sections of the book.

21. Follow the removal steps on installation of the engine. Adjust all of the linkages as detailed in the appropriate section. Install the hood and adjust it. Replenish the fluid levels in the engine, radiator and transmission.

Pick-Up—1983–88

22R, 22R-E AND 22R-3T ENGINES

1. Disconnect the negative battery cable.

2. Remove the engine undercover.

3. Disconnect the windshield washer hose and then remove the hood. Scribe matchmarks around the hinges for easy installation.

4. Drain the engine oil. Drain the engine coolant from the radiator and the cylinder block.

5. Drain the automatic transmission fluid on models so equipped.

6. Disconnect the air cleaner hose and then remove the air cleaner.

7. Remove the radiator and shroud as detailed later in this section. Remember to disconnect the No. 1 turbocharger water line on the 22R-TE.

8. Remove the coupling fan.

9. Disconnect the two heater hoses at the engine.

10. If equipped with an automatic transmission, disconnect the accelerator cable at the carburetor or the accelerator and throttle cables from their bracket.

11. For 22R engines, tag and disconnect the following wires:
   a. VSV wire at the EVAP canister
   b. VSV wire at the air conditioning compressor
   c. Vacuum switch wire
   d. HAC wire (ex. Calif.)
   e. Cold mixture heater wire
   f. Fuel cut solenoid wire
   g. Water temperature sender gauge wire
   h. EACV wire (Calif.)
   i. Starter wire
   j. Oil pressure switch wire.

12. For the 22R-E and 22R-TE engines, tag and disconnect the following components:
   a. No. 1 and No. 2 PCV hoses.
   b. Brake booster hose.
   c. Air control valve hoses.
   d. EVAP hose at the canister.
   e. Actuator hose on models with cruise control.
   f. Vacuum modulator hose at the EGR valve.

   g. Air valve hoses at the throttle body and chamber.
   h. Two water by-pass hoses at the throttle body.
   i. Air control valve hose at the actuator.
   j. Pressure regulator hose at the chamber.
   k. Cold start injector pipe.
   l. BVSV hose.
   m. Brake booster hose
   n. Main fuel line at the fuel inlet pipe
   o. Fuel return line at the fuel return pipe
   p. Charcoal canister hose.

13. For the 22-R engines, perform the following:
   a. Remove the drive belt.
   b. If equipped, remove the power steering pump from its bracket and disconnect the ground strap from the bracket.

14. For the 22R-E and 22R-TE engines, perform the following:
   a. Tag and disconnect the cold start injector wire and the throttle position sensor wire.
   b. Remove the EGR valve from the throttle chamber.
   c. Disconnect the throttle chamber at the stay. Remove the chamber-to-intake manifold mounting bolts and lift off the throttle chamber.
   d. Tag and disconnect the following wires:
   e. Cold start injector time switch wire
   f. Water temperature sensor wire
   g. On models with air conditioning: VSV and air conditioning compressor wires
   h. O$_2$ sensor wire (22R-TE only)
   i. OD temperature switch wire (models w/AT)
   j. Injector wires
   k. Knock sensor connector
   l. Air valve wire
   m. Oil pressure switch wire
   n. Starter wire.

15. If equipped with A/C, loosen the drive belt and remove the A/C compressor. Position it out of the way with the refrigerant lines still attached.

16. Disconnect the engine ground straps at the rear and right side of the engine.

17. On trucks with a manual transmission, remove the shift lever from inside the truck.

18. Remove the rear driveshaft.

19. On models with automatic transmission, disconnect the manual shift linkage at the neutral start switch. On 4wd models with automatic transmission, disconnect the transfer shift linkage.

20. Disconnect the speedometer cable. Be sure not to lose the felt dust protector and washers.

21. Remove the transfer case undercover (4wd only).

22. Remove the stabilizer bar (4wd only).

23. Remove the front driveshaft (4wd only).

24. Remove the No. 1 frame crossmember.

25. Disconnect the front exhaust pipe at the manifold and tail pipe and remove the exhaust pipe.

26. On models with manual transmission, remove the clutch release cylinder and its bracket from the transmission.

27. Remove the No. 1 front floor heat insulator and the brake tube heat insulator (4wd only).

28. On 2wd models, remove the four rear engine mount bolts, raise the transmission slightly with a floor jack and then remove the four support member mounting bolts.

29. On 4wd models, remove the four rear engine mount bolts, raise the transmission slightly with a floor jack and then remove the four bolts from the side member and remove the No. 2 frame crossmember.

30. Attach an engine hoist chain to the lifting brackets on the engine. Remove the engine mount nuts and bolts and slowly lift the engine/transmission out of the truck.

To install:

31. Slowly lower the engine assembly into the engine compartment.

32. Raise the transmission onto the crossmember with a floor jack.

33. Align the holes in the engine mounts and the frame, install the bolts and then remove the engine hoist chain.

34. On 2wd models, raise the transmission slightly and align the rear engine mount with the support member and tighten the bolts to 9 ft. lbs. (13 Nm).

Lower the transmission until it rests on the extension housing and then tighten the bracket mounting bolts to 19 ft. lbs. (25 Nm).

35. On 4wd models, Raise the transmission slightly and tighten the No. 2 frame crossmember-to-side frame bolts to 70 ft. lbs. (95 Nm). Lower the transmission and tighten the four rear engine mount bolts to 9 ft. lbs. (13 Nm).

36. Install the remaining components in the reverse of the removal procedure. Tighten the clutch release cylinder bracket bolts to 29 ft. lbs. (39 Nm) and the cylinder bolts to 9 ft. lbs. (13 Nm).

37. Refill the engine with oil and the radiator with coolant.

38. Install the engine undercover.

39. Install and adjust the hood.

40. Connect the battery cable, start the truck and road test it.

3VZ-E ENGINE

1. Disconnect the battery cables and remove the battery.

2. Remove the engine undercover.

3. Disconnect the windshield washer hose and then remove the hood. Scribe matchmarks around the hinges for easy installation.

4. Drain the engine oil. Drain the engine coolant from the radiator and the cylinder block.

5. Drain the automatic transmission fluid on models so equipped.

6. Disconnect the air cleaner hose and then remove the air cleaner.

7. Remove the radiator.

8. Remove all drive belts and then remove the fluid coupling and fan pulley.

9. Tag and disconnect the following wires and connectors:
   a. Left side and rear ground straps
   b. Alternator connector and wire
   c. Igniter connector
   d. Oil pressure switch connector
   e. ECU connectors
   f. VSV connectors
   g. Starter relay connector (manual transmission only)
   h. Solenoid resistor connector
   i. Check connector
   j. air conditioning compressor connector

10. Tag and disconnect the following hoses:
   a. Power steering hoses at the gas filter and air pipe
   b. Brake booster hose
   c. Cruise control vacuum hose (if equipped)
   d. Charcoal canister hose at the canister
   e. VSV vacuum hoses.

11. Disconnect the accelerator, throttle and cruise control cables where applicable.

12. Unbolt the power steering pump and position it out of the way with the hydraulic lines still connected.

13. Remove the air conditioning compressor if equipped.

14. Disconnect the clutch release cylinder hose (manual transmission only).

15. Disconnect the two heater hoses.

16. Disconnect and plug the fuel inlet and outlet lines.

17. Remove the shift levers (manual transmission only).

18. Remove the rear driveshaft.

19. Disconnect the manual shift linkage (automatic transmission only).

20. Disconnect the speedometer cable — don't lose the felt dust protector and washers.

21. Remove the transfer case undercover.

22. Remove the stabilizer bar.

23. Remove the front drive shaft.

24. Remove the front exhaust pipe.

25. Remove the No. 1 front floor heat insulator and the brake tube heat insulator.

26. Remove the four rear engine mount bolts, raise the transmission slightly with a floor jack and then remove the four bolts from the side member and remove the No. 2 frame crossmember.

27. Attach an engine hoist chain to the lifting brackets on the engine. Remove the engine mount nuts and bolts and slowly lift the engine/transmission out of the truck.

To install:

28. Slowly lower the engine assembly into the engine compartment.

29. Raise the transmission onto the crossmember with a floor jack.

30. Align the holes in the engine mounts and the frame, install the bolts and then remove the engine hoist chain.

31. Raise the transmission slightly and tighten the No. 2 frame crossmember-to-side frame bolts to 70 ft. lbs. (95 Nm). Lower the transmission and tighten the four rear engine mount bolts to 9 ft. lbs. (13 Nm).

32. Install the remaining components in the reverse of the removal procedure.

33. Install the air cleaner. Refill the engine with oil and the radiator with coolant.

34. Install the engine undercover. Install the battery.

35. Install and adjust the hood.

36. Install the battery, start the truck and road test it.

Land Cruiser

F AND 2F ENGINES

1. Scribe marks on the hood and hinges to aid in alignment during installation. Remove the hinge bolt from the hood and then remove the hood.

2. Drain the cooling system and engine oil.

3. Unfasten the radiator grille mounting bolts and remove the grille.

➡ **Remove the parking light assembly and wiring first, if necessary.**

4. Remove the hood latch support rod. Detach the hood latch assembly from the radiator upper bracket. Remove the bracket.

5. Disconnect the heater hose from the radiator.

6. Detach the upper radiator hose at the water outlet housing and the lower hose at water pump.

7. Remove the six bolts which secure the radiator and lift the radiator out of the vehicle.

8. Remove the heater hoses from the water valve and heater box. Disconnect the temperature control cable from the water valve.

9. Detach both the battery cables and remove the battery.

10. Remove the wires from the starter solenoid terminal.

11. Detach the fuel lines from the pump and remove the fuel filter assembly.

12. Disconnect the primary wire from the ignition coil.

13. Detach both of the intermediate rods from the shifter shafts (column shift models only).

14. Remove the air cleaner assembly, complete with hoses, from its bracket.

15. Remove the emission control system cables and hoses as necessary.

16. Disconnect the alternator multiconnector.

17. Disconnect the hand throttle, accelerator, and choke linkage from the carburetor.

18. On models equipped with vacuum assisted 4WD engagement, remove the control unit vacuum hose from its manifold fitting.

19. Disconnect the oil pressure and water temperature gauge sender's wiring.

20. Unfasten the downpipe from the exhaust manifold.

21. Detach the parking brake cable from the intermediate lever.

22. Unbolt the front driveshaft from the flange on the transfer case output shaft.

23. Remove both the left and right engine stone shields. Remove the transmission skidplate.

24. Remove the cotter pin and disconnect both the high- and low-range shifter link lever and the high/low shift rod.

25. Remove the high/low range shifter link lever and the high/low shift rod.

26. Disconnect the clutch release fork spring. Remove the clutch release cylinder from its mounting bracket at the rear of the engine.

27. Unfasten the clamp screws and withdraw the vacuum lines from the transfer case control unit vacuum chamber (only on models with vacuum assist 4WD engagement).

28. Remove the 4WD indicator switch assembly.

29. Unfasten the speedometer cable from the transmission.

30. Detach the gearshift rod and gear selector rod from the shift outer lever and the gear selector outer lever respectively.

31. Unbolt the rear engine mounts from the frame.

32. Perform Step 31 to the front engine mounts.

33. Install lifting hooks on the engine lift points and connect a hoist.

34. Lift the engine slightly and toward the front, so the engine/transmission assembly clears the front of the vehicle.

Follow the removal steps on installation of the engine. Adjust all of the linkages as detailed in the appropriate section. Install the hood and adjust it. Replenish the fluid levels in the engine, radiator and transmission. Install the hood and align the matchmarks.

3F-E ENGINES

1. Drain the engine coolant. Drain the engine oil.
2. Scribe matchmarks around the hood hinges and then remove the hood.
3. Remove the battery and its tray.
4. Disconnect the accelerator and throttle cables.
5. Remove the air intake hose, air flow meter and air cleaner assembly.
6. Remove the coolant reservoir tank.
7. Remove the radiator.
8. Tag and disconnect the following wires and connectors:
   a. Oil pressure connector
   b. High tension cord at the coil
   c. Neutral start switch and transfer connectors near the starter
   d. Front differential lock connector
   e. Starter wire and connector
   f. Starter ground strap
   g. O$_2$sensor connectors
   h. Alternator wire and connector
   i. Cooling fan connector
   j. Check connector.
9. Disconnect the following hoses:
   a. Heater hoses
   b. Fuel hoses
   c. Transfer hose
   d. Brake booster hose
   e. AI hoses
   f. Distributor hose
   g. Emission control hoses.
10. Remove the glove box, pull out the four connectors and then pull the EFI wiring harness from the cowl.
11. Unbolt the power steering pump and position it out of the way with the hoses still connected.
12. Do the same with the air conditioning compressor.
13. Raise the truck and remove the transfer case undercover.
14. Remove the front and rear driveshafts.
15. Disconnect the speedometer cable.
16. Disconnect the engine ground strap.
17. Disconnect the two vacuum hoses at the diaphragm cylinder underneath the transfer case.
18. Remove the clip and pin and then disconnect the shift rod at the transfer case. Remove the nut, disconnect the washers and the shift lever at the shift rod.
19. Disconnect the transmission control rod.
20. Disconnect the exhaust pipe at the manifold.
21. With a floor jack under the transmission, remove the eight bolts and two nuts that attach the frame crossmember and then remove the crossmember.
22. Attach an engine hoist chain to the lifting brackets on the engine. Remove the engine mount nuts and bolts and slowly lift the engine/transmission out of the truck.

To install:

23. Slowly lower the engine assembly into the engine compartment.
24. Raise the transmission onto the crossmember with a floor jack.
25. Align the holes in the engine mounts and the frame, install the bolts and then remove the engine hoist chain.
26. Raise the transmission slightly and tighten the frame crossmember-to-chassis bolts to 29 ft. lbs. (39 Nm). Tighten the two nuts to 43 ft. lbs. (59 Nm).
27. Install the exhaust pipe with a new gasket and tighten the nuts (new!) to 46 ft. lbs. (62 Nm).

28. Install the remaining components in the reverse of the removal procedure. Tighten the power steering pump pulley nut to 35 ft. lbs. (47 Nm).
29. Refill the engine with oil and the radiator with coolant.
30. Install the engine undercover. Install the battery.
31. Install and adjust the hood.
32. Install the battery, start the truck and road test it.

Cylinder Head Cover

REMOVAL & INSTALLATION

▶ See Figures 38, 39 and 40

1. Remove the air cleaner assembly.
2. Disconnect the PCV hose(s) from the cam cover.
3. Remove the nuts and washers. Lift the cover off the cylinder head. Cover the oil return hole in the head to prevent dirt or objects from falling in. Remove the gasket.
4. To install, replace the cover gasket if it shows any signs of damage, breaks or cracking. Tighten the nuts evenly, reconnect the PCV hose and install the air cleaner assembly.

Valve Rocker Shafts

REMOVAL & INSTALLATION

▶ See Figures 41, 42 and 43

Valve rocker shaft removal and installation is given as part of the various Cylinder Head Removal & Installation procedures.

Perform only the steps of the appropriate Cylinder Head Removal & Installation procedures necessary to remove and install the rocker shafts. All rocker shaft assemblies may require a pry bar to remove them from the head. The 3VZ-E engine does not utilize rocker arms or shafts. The valves are activated directly by the camshaft.

Rocker Arms

REMOVAL & INSTALLATION

▶ See Figures 44 thru 55

All Engines Except 3VZ-E

1. Remove the rocker shaft assemblies.
2. On the single rocker shaft engines (8R-C, 18R-C, F, 2F, 3F-E and diesels), remove the rocker shaft support attaching bolts (#2 in illustration) and the rocker shaft retaining screw (#3 in illustration). Slide the tension springs, rocker arms and rocker supports off of the shafts. Make sure you keep the parts in order as they were removed from the shaft—this is very important.
3. On the double rocker shaft engines (20R, 22R, 22R-E and 22R-TE), remove the rocker shaft assemblies. Remove the three retaining screws and slide the rocker supports, springs and rocker arms off of the shafts. Keep all parts in order; the shafts must be reassembled in the correct order.
4. Assembly is in the opposite order of removal; make sure all components are reassembled in their original positions. Adjust the valves.

Fig. 38 Mark and remove all necessary washers and brackets for cylinder head cover removal

Fig. 39 Removing the cylinder head cover

Fig. 40 Always replace the cylinder head cover gasket before installation

Fig. 41 Removing the rocker shaft assembly bolts—note location of bolts

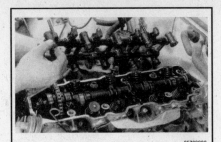

Fig. 42 Removing the rocker shaft assembly

Fig. 43 Installation of the rocker shaft assembly and bolts

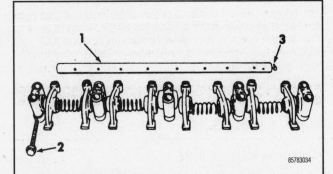

Fig. 44 Single rocker shaft (8R-C, 18R-C) assembly—note the support attaching bolts (#2) and shaft retaining screw (#3)

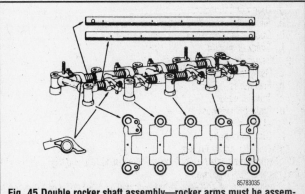

Fig. 45 Double rocker shaft assembly—rocker arms must be assembled in their original position-20R engine 22R similar

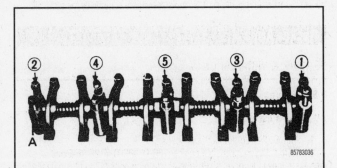

Fig. 46 8R-C and 18R-C rocker arm shaft removal sequence—pulling out of the rocker shaft bolts (A) will allow removal of the rocker supports

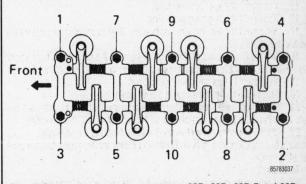

Fig. 47 Rocker arm loosening sequence—20R, 22R, 22R-E and 22R-TE engines

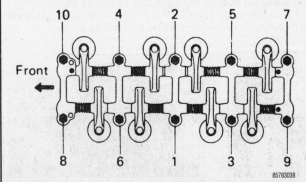

Fig. 48 Rocker arm torque sequence—20R, 22R, 22R-E and 22R-TE engines

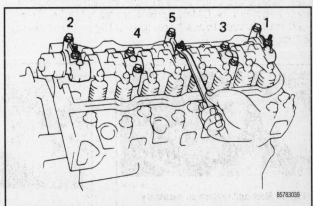

Fig. 49 Rocker arm loosening sequence—1L, 2L and 2L-T engines

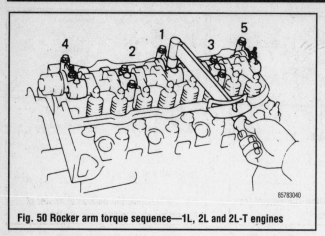

Fig. 50 Rocker arm torque sequence—1L, 2L and 2L-T engines

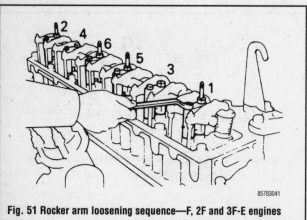

Fig. 51 Rocker arm loosening sequence—F, 2F and 3F-E engines

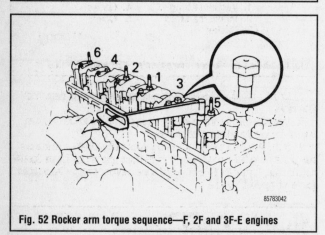

Fig. 52 Rocker arm torque sequence—F, 2F and 3F-E engines

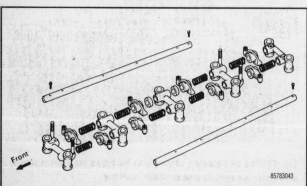

Fig. 53 Exploded view of the rocker assembly—20R, 22R, 22R-E and 22R-TE engines

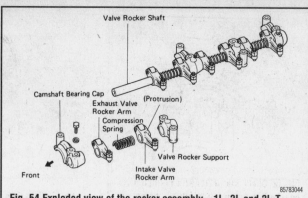

Fig. 54 Exploded view of the rocker assembly—1L, 2L and 2L-T engines

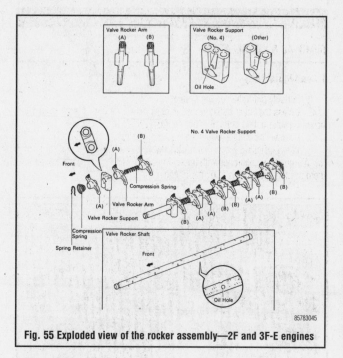

Fig. 55 Exploded view of the rocker assembly—2F and 3F-E engines

INSPECTION

▶ **See Figures 56, 57 and 58**

The oil clearance between the rocker arm and shaft is measured in two steps. Measure the outside diameter of the rocker shaft with a micrometer. Measure the inside diameter of the rocker arms with a dial indicator. The difference between the rocker arm inner diameter and the shaft outer diameter is the oil clearance. Clearance specs are as follows:

- 8R-C: 0.030–0.38mm
- 18R-C: 0.017–0.051mm
- 20R: 0.010–0.050mm
- 22R, 22R-E, 22R-TE: 0.010–0.050mm
- F, 2F, 3F-E: 0.010–0.050mm
- 1L, 2L, 2L-T: 0.018–0.056mm

If specifications are not within these ranges, replace either the rocker shaft or rocker arm. Clearance can also be checked by moving the rocker arm laterally on the shaft when assembled. There should be little or no movement.

While disassembled, check the cam follower end (the flat end that contacts the camshaft) of the rocker arm for excess wear. The surface should be smooth and shiny. If excess wear is evident, check also the lobe of the camshaft, it may also be worn.

Reassemble the rocker shaft assemblies in the exact opposite order or removal. Accelerated camshaft wear and/or sloppy valve action will result if rocker arms are mixed and end up operating against the wrong cam lobes.

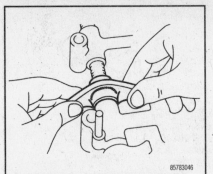

Fig. 56 Check the rocker arm-to-shaft wear by wiggling the arm laterally on the shaft; little or no movement should be felt

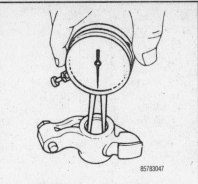

Fig. 57 Measure the inside diameter of the rocker with dial indicator

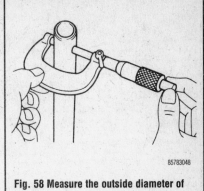

Fig. 58 Measure the outside diameter of the rocker shaft with a micrometer

Thermostat

REMOVAL & INSTALLATION

▶ **See Figure 59**

1. Partially drain the cooling system.
2. Unless the upper radiator hose is positioned over one of the thermostat housing (water outlet) bolts, it is not necessary to detach the hose.
3. Remove the bolts and remove the water outlet.
4. When installing a new thermostat always use a new gasket. Be sure that the thermostat is positioned with the spring down. The factory recommended thermostat temperature is 180° for all engines.

Fig. 59 Removing a typical thermostat

Intake Manifold

REMOVAL & INSTALLATION

20R and 22R Engines

▶ **See Figurets 60, 61 and 62**

1. Disconnect the battery.
2. Drain the cooling system.
3. Remove the air cleaner assembly, complete with hoses, from the carburetor.
4. Disconnect the vacuum lines from the EGR valve and carburetor. Mark them first to aid in the installation.
5. Remove the fuel lines, electrical leads, accelerator linkage, and water hose from the carburetor.
6. Remove the water by-pass hose from the manifold.

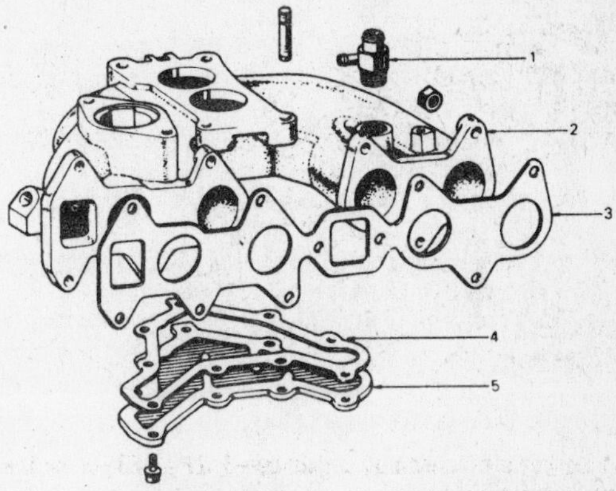

1. Vacuum fitting
2. Intake manifold
3. Gasket
4. Gasket
5. Cover

Fig. 60 20R intake manifold components—22R engine similar

7. Unbolt and remove the intake manifold, complete with carburetor and EGR valve.
8. Cover the cylinder head ports with clean shop cloths to keep anything from falling into the cylinder head or block.
9. Installation is the reverse of the removal procedure. Make sure to use a new gasket. Torque the mounting bolts to the figure given in the Torque Specifications chart. Tighten the bolts in several stages working from the inside bolts (center of manifold) outward.

Fig. 61 Mark all necessary connections for intake manifold removal; carburetor removed to expose intake manifold

Fig. 62 Removal of the intake manifold assembly is possible with carburetor still installed

22R-E and 22R-TE Engines

▶ **See Figure 63**

1. Disconnect the battery.
2. Drain the cooling system.
3. Disconnect the air intake hose from both the air cleaner assembly on one end and the air intake chamber on the other.
4. Tag and disconnect all vacuum lines attached to the intake chamber and manifold.
5. Tag and disconnect the wires to the cold start injector, throttle position sensor, and the water hoses from the throttle body.
6. Remove the EGR valve from the intake chamber.
7. Tag and disconnect the actuator cable, accelerator cable and AT throttle cable (if equipped) from the cable bracket on the intake chamber.
8. Unbolt the air intake chamber from the intake manifold and remove the chamber with the throttle body attached.
9. Disconnect the fuel hose from the fuel delivery pipe.
10. Tag and disconnect the air valve hose from the intake manifold.
11. Make sure all hoses, lines and wires are tagged for later installation and disconnected from the intake manifold. Unbolt the manifold from the intake manifold. Unbolt the manifold from the cylinder head, removing the delivery pipe and injection nozzle in unit with the manifold.
12. Cover the cylinder head ports with clean shop cloths to keep anything from falling into the cylinder head or block.
13. Installation is the reverse of the removal procedure. When installing the manifold, replace the gasket with a new one. Torque the mounting bolts to the figure given in the Torque Specifications chart. Tighten the bolts in several stages working from the inside (center of manifold mounting bolts) bolts outward.

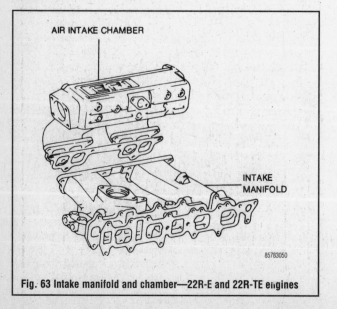

AIR INTAKE CHAMBER

INTAKE MANIFOLD

85783050

Fig. 63 Intake manifold and chamber—22R-E and 22R-TE engines

3VZ-E Engine

1. Disconnect the battery.
2. Drain the cooling system.
3. Disconnect the air intake hose from both the air cleaner assembly on one end and the air intake chamber on the other.
4. Tag and disconnect all vacuum lines attached to the intake chamber and manifold.
5. Disconnect the throttle position sensor connector at the air chamber. Disconnect the PCV hose at the union.
6. Disconnect the No.4 water by-pass hose at the manifold. Remove the No. 5 by-pass hose at the water by-pass pipe.
7. Disconnect the cold start injector and the vacuum hose at the fuel filter.
8. Remove the union bolt and two gaskets and then remove the cold start injector tube.
9. Disconnect the EGR gas temperature sensor and the EGR vacuum hoses from the air pipe and the vacuum modulator.
10. Remove the EGR valve.
11. Disconnect the No. 1 air hose at the reed valve.
12. Remove the air intake chamber and then remove the engine wire.
13. Remove the four union bolts and then remove the Nos. 2 and 3 fuel pipes.
14. Remove the No. 4 timing belt cover. Remove the No. 2 idler pulley and the No. 3 timing belt cover.
15. Remove the fuel delivery pipes with their injectors.
16. Remove the water by-pass outlet and then remove the intake manifold.
To install:
17. Install the intake manifold with new gaskets and tighten the mounting bolts to 29 ft. lbs. (39 Nm).
18. The remainder of installation is the reverse of the removal. Follow these tightening specifications:
   a. Water by-pass outlet bolts: 13 ft. lbs. (18 Nm)
   b. Timing belt cover bolts: 74 inch lbs. (8.3 Nm)
   c. Fuel pipe union bolts: 22 ft. lbs. (29 Nm)
   d. Air intake chamber nuts and bolts: 13 ft. lbs. (18 Nm)
19. Refill the engine with coolant and connect the battery cable.

Exhaust Manifold

REMOVAL & INSTALLATION

▶ **See Figures 64 thru 70**

20R, 22R, 22R-E, 22R-TE and 3VZ-E Engines

1. Remove the three exhaust pipe flange bolts (turbocharger flange bolts on the 22R-TE) and disconnect the exhaust pipe from the manifold.
2. Tag and disconnect the spark plug leads.
3. Position the spark plug wires out of the way. It may be best to tie them so they don't flop back in your way.
4. Remove the air cleaner tube from the heat stove on carbureted engines, and remove the outer part of the heat stove.

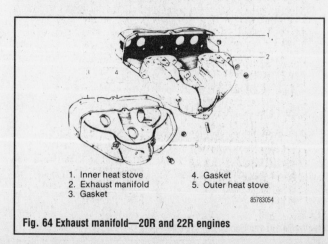

1. Inner heat stove
2. Exhaust manifold
3. Gasket
4. Gasket
5. Outer heat stove

85783054

Fig. 64 Exhaust manifold—20R and 22R engines

Fig. 65 Removing the exhaust manifold heat shield

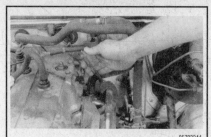

Fig. 66 Removing the exhaust manifold emission connections

Fig. 67 Removing the emission air pipes (inner mounting bolts)

Fig. 68 Removing the emission air pipes (outer mounting bolts)

Fig. 69 Removing the emission air pipe assembly

Fig. 70 Removing the exhaust manifold assembly—always replace all gaskets

5. Use a 14mm wrench to remove the manifold securing nuts.

6. Remove the manifold(s), complete with air injection tubes and the inner portion of the heat stove.

To install:

7. Separate the inner portion of the heat stove from the manifold.

8. When installing the manifold(s), tighten the retaining nuts to 29-36 ft. lbs., working from the inside out, and in several stages. Install the distributor and set the timing as previously outlined. Tighten the exhaust pipe flange nuts to 25–32 ft. lbs.

Combination Manifold

REMOVAL & INSTALLATION

✳✳ CAUTION

Do not perform this procedure on a warm engine. The exhaust and intake manifolds are connected and get very hot.

8R-C and 18R-C Engines

▶ See Figure 71

1. Remove the air cleaner assembly, complete with hoses, from its mounting bracket.

2. Remove the fuel line, vacuum lines, automatic choke stove hoses, PCV hose, and accelerator linkage from the carburetor.

3. Unfasten the carburetor securing nuts. Remove the torque rod support, carburetor, and heat insulator.

4. Use a jack to raise the front of the truck. Support the truck with jackstands.

✳✳ CAUTION

Be sure that the truck is securely supported.

5. Unfasten the bolts which attach the downpipe flange to the exhaust manifold.

6. In order to remove the manifold assembly, unfasten the manifold retaining bolts. On 1974 California engines, remove the EGR valve and tubes first.

✳✳ CAUTION

Remove and tighten the bolts in two or three stages, starting from the inside and working out.

7. When installing the manifolds, always use new gaskets. Tighten the manifold securing bolts to the figure shown in the Torque Specifications chart, in the reverse sequence of removal. Install the carburetor and air cleaner.

F, 2F and 3F-E Engines

▶ See Figures 71, 72 and 73

1. Remove the air cleaner assembly, complete with hoses.

2. Disconnect the accelerator and choke linkages from the carburetor, as well as the fuel and vacuum lines. Remove the hand throttle linkage.

3. Remove, or move aside, any of the emission control system components which are in the way.

4. Disconnect the oil filter lines and remove the oil filter assembly from the intake manifold. Unfasten the solenoid valve wire from the ignition coil terminal. Remove the EGR pipes from the exhaust gas cooler, if so equipped.

5. Unfasten the retaining bolts and remove the carburetor from the manifold.

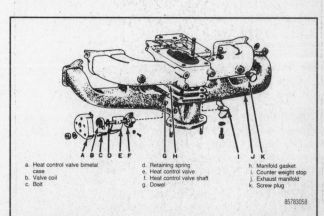

a. Heat control valve bimetal case
b. Valve coil
c. Bolt
d. Retaining spring
e. Heat control valve
f. Heat control valve shaft
g. Dowel
h. Manifold gasket
i. Counter weight stop
j. Exhaust manifold
k. Screw plug

Fig. 71 Combination manifold—F and 2F engines shown, 8R-C and 18R-C engines similar

6. Loosen the manifold retaining nuts, working from the inside out, in two or three stages.

7. Remove the intake/exhaust manifold assembly from the cylinder head as a complete unit.

8. When installing the manifolds, always use new gaskets. Tighten the bolts, working from the inside out.

➡**Tighten the bolts in two or three stages.**

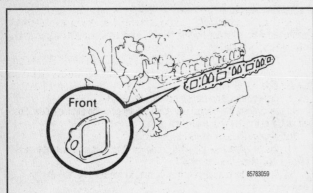

Fig. 72 Gasket installation on the combination manifold—3F-E engine

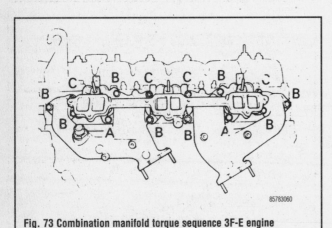

Fig. 73 Combination manifold torque sequence 3F-E engine

Diesel Manifolds

▶ **See Figures 74 and 75**

Removal of the intake manifold of the diesel engine requires removal of the air cleaner assembly, injection lines, and related hoses and brackets. If you are in doubt during the disconnection of any item, be sure to mark the item so that it may be properly reinstalled. Before installing the manifold, be sure to clean the cylinder head and manifold mating surfaces of the old gasket material, and use a new gasket when installing the manifold.

The exhaust manifold is retained to the cylinder head with eight fasteners. Disconnect the exhaust pipe from the manifold and remove these fasteners. Disconnect the exhaust pipe from the manifold and remove these fasteners to remove the exhaust manifold. On models with air conditioning, it may be necessary to remove the air conditioning compressor from the mounting bracket (without disconnecting the refrigerant lines) and tie the compressor out of the way. Also remove the compressor mounting bracket(s) if interference is encountered. Be sure that the manifold and cylinder head mating surfaces are clean, and install a new exhaust manifold gasket during manifold installation.

Refer to the torque specifications listed at the beginning of this section to determine the required tightening torque of the fasteners, working from the center of the manifold to the ends in several steps.

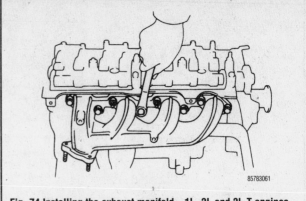

Fig. 74 Installing the exhaust manifold—1L, 2L and 2L-T engines

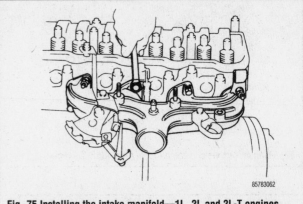

Fig. 75 Installing the intake manifold—1L, 2L and 2L-T engines

Turbocharger Assembly

REMOVAL & INSTALLATION

22R-TE

▶ **See Figures 76 and 77**

1. Disconnect the negative battery cable, then drain the coolant.
2. Detach the O_2 sensor wire clamp and connector.
3. Disconnect the Nos. 1 and 3 PCV hoses.
4. Disconnect the Nos. 1 and 2 turbocharger water hoses.
5. Loosen the clamp on the throttle body, remove the two nuts and lift off the air tube assembly.
6. Remove the No. 1 air cleaner hose assembly and the No. 2 air cleaner hose.
7. Remove the exhaust manifold and turbocharger heat insulators.
8. Disconnect the No. 3 turbocharger water hose.
9. Raise the truck and disconnect the exhaust pipe from the turbine outlet.
10. Remove the turbocharger bracket stay.
11. Disconnect the turbocharger oil pipe.
12. Remove the turbocharger and exhaust manifold as an assembly.
13. Remove the No. 2 turbocharger water pipe.
14. Remove the oil pipe.
15. Remove the No. 1 water pipe.
16. Remove the turbine outlet elbow with the O_2 sensor attached.
17. Disconnect the turbocharger from the manifold.

To install:

18. Pour approximately 20cc of new oil into the oil inlet and then turn the turbocharger impeller wheel so as to wet the bearing.
19. Using a new gasket, attach the turbocharger to the manifold and tighten the nuts to 29 ft. lbs. (39 Nm).

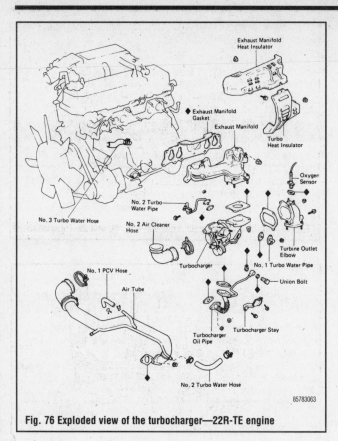

Fig. 76 Exploded view of the turbocharger—22R-TE engine

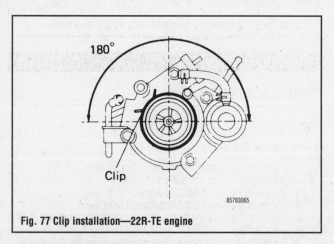

Fig. 77 Clip installation—22R-TE engine

20. Install the turbine outlet elbow and tighten the nuts to 19 ft. lbs. (25 Nm).

21. Install the No. 1 water pipe. Install the turbo oil pipe and tighten the nuts to 14 ft. lbs. (19 Nm).

22. Install the No. 2 water pipe and then mount the assembly to the cylinder head.

23. Install the oil pipe and tighten the union bolt to 20 ft. lbs. (27 Nm). Tighten the nuts to 14 ft. lbs. (19 Nm).

24. Install the turbocharger bracket stay.

25. Connect the exhaust pipe to the turbine outlet elbow and tighten the nuts to 32 ft. lbs. (43 Nm). Lower the truck.

26. Connect the No. 3 water hose and install the heat insulators.

27. Install the No. 2 air cleaner hose with the arrow facing the turbocharger and fasten the clip as shown.

28. Install the air tube assembly. Connect the O_2 sensor and clamp.

29. Refill the engine with coolant, start it and check for leaks.

2L-T

▶ **See Figures 78 and 79**

1. Disconnect the negative battery cable.

2. Drain the coolant.

3. Disconnect the vacuum hose for the air conditioning VSV at the idle-up actuator. Disconnect the vacuum hose at the intake pipe from the vacuum pump and HAC.

4. Disconnect the accelerator cable.

5. Disconnect the PCV hose.

6. Loosen the clamp and disconnect the No. 1 air cleaner hose. Loosen the clamp and remove the two bolts at the air cleaner pipe; remove the pipe along with he No. 2 air hose.

7. Disconnect and plug the heater hoses at the intake flange. Loosen the three clamps and two bolts and remove the air intake pipe. Remove the No. 1 air cleaner pipe.

8. Remove the compressor elbow and its gasket.

9. Disconnect the exhaust pipe from the flange at the turbine elbow. Position it out of the way and remove the gasket.

10. Remove the turbocharger heat insulator.

11. Disconnect and plug the No. 2 and No. 3 turbocharger water by-pass pipes. Position them out of the way.

12. Remove the two turbocharger oil pipe flange nuts. Remove the oil deflector.

13. Unscrew the four nuts and remove the turbocharger from the exhaust manifold.

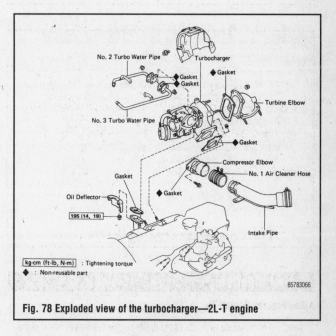

Fig. 78 Exploded view of the turbocharger—2L-T engine

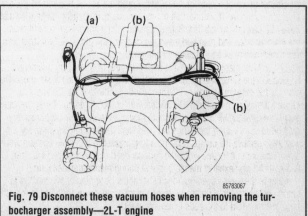

Fig. 79 Disconnect these vacuum hoses when removing the turbocharger assembly—2L-T engine

To install:

14. Pour approximately 20cc of new oil into the oil inlet and then turn the turbocharger impeller wheel so as to wet the bearing.

15. Using a new gasket, attach the turbocharger to the manifold and tighten the nuts to 38 ft. lbs. (52 Nm).

16. Install the turbine outlet elbow and tighten the nuts to 19 ft. lbs. (25 Nm).

17. Install the oil deflector and the oil pipe flange nuts. Tighten the nuts to 14 ft. lbs. (19 Nm).

18. Use new gaskets and install the No. 2 and No. 3 water by-pass pipes.

19. Install the turbocharger heat insulators.

20. Connect the exhaust pipe to the turbine elbow and tighten the nuts to 9 ft. lbs. (12 Nm).

21. Install the compressor elbow.

22. Install the air intake pipe.

23. Install the air cleaner pipe with the No. 2 air hose.

24. Connect the accelerator cable and the two vacuum hoses.

25. Fill the engine with coolant, connect the battery cable and road test the truck.

Radiator

REMOVAL & INSTALLATION

▶ **See Figures 80 thru 85**

1. Drain the cooling system.

> ✳✳ **CAUTION**
>
> **When draining the coolant, keep in mind that cats and dogs are attracted by the ethylene glycol antifreeze, and are quite likely to drink any that is left in an uncovered container or in puddles on the ground. This will prove fatal in sufficient quantity. Always drain the coolant into a sealable container. Coolant should be reused unless it is contaminated or several years old.**

2. Unfasten the clamps and remove the upper and lower radiator hoses. If equipped with an automatic transmission, remove the oil cooler lines. On models with the 22R-TE, disconnect the No. 1 turbocharger water line.

3. Detach the hood lock cable and remove the hood lock from the radiator upper support. On the Land Cruiser, remove the center grille support also

➡ It will be necessary to remove the grille in order to gain access to the hood lock/radiator support assembly.

4. Remove the fan shroud(s), if so equipped.

5. On models equipped with a coolant recovery system, disconnect the hose form the thermal expansion tank and remove the tank from its bracket.

6. Unbolt and remove the radiator upper support.

7. Unfasten the bolts and remove the radiator.

> ✳✳ **CAUTION**
>
> **Use care not to damage the radiator fins or the cooling fan.**

8. Installation is the reverse of the removal procedure. If equipped with an automatic transmission, remember to check the transmission fluid level.

9. Fill the radiator to the specified level and check for leaks.

Water Pump

REMOVAL & INSTALLATION

> ✳✳ **CAUTION**
>
> **When draining the coolant, keep in mind that cats and dogs are attracted by the ethylene glycol antifreeze, and are quite likely to drink any that is left in an uncovered container or in puddles on the ground. This will prove fatal in sufficient quantity. Always drain the coolant into a sealable container. Coolant should be reused unless it is contaminated or several years old.**

All Engines Except the 3VZ-E

▶ **See Figures 86 thru 91**

1. Drain the cooling system.

2. Unfasten the fan shroud securing bolts and remove the fan shroud, if so equipped.

3. Loosen the alternator adjusting link bolt and remove the drive belt.

4. Repeat Step 3 for the air and/or power steering pump drive belt, if so equipped.

5. Detach the by-pass hose from the water pump.

Fig. 80 Removing the fan assembly bolts—note position of holding tool

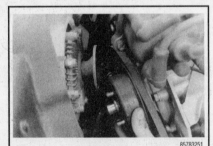

Fig. 81 Removing the fan

Fig. 82 Removing the fan from the vehicle

Fig. 83 Removing the fan pulley

Fig. 84 Removing the radiator mounting bolts

Fig. 85 Removing the radiator assembly— note hoses still attached

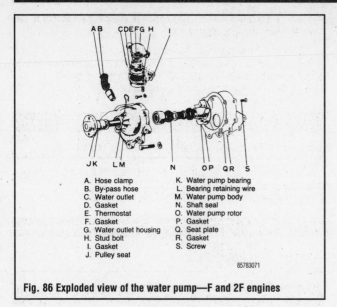

A. Hose clamp
B. By-pass hose
C. Water outlet
D. Gasket
E. Thermostat
F. Gasket
G. Water outlet housing
H. Stud bolt
I. Gasket
J. Pulley seat
K. Water pump bearing
L. Bearing retaining wire
M. Water pump body
N. Shaft seal
O. Water pump rotor
P. Gasket
Q. Seat plate
R. Gasket
S. Screw

Fig. 86 Exploded view of the water pump—F and 2F engines

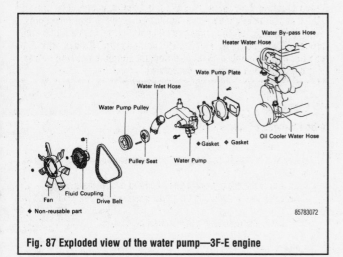

Fig. 87 Exploded view of the water pump—3F-E engine

6. Unfasten the water pump retaining bolts and nuts (note location and type of bolt—for correct installation) and remove the water pump and fan assembly, using care not to damage the radiator with the fan.

✳✳ CAUTION

If the fan is equipped with a fluid coupling, do not tip the fan/pump assembly on its side, as the fluid will run out.

To install:
7. Clean water pump mounting area. Install the water pump and tighten the mounting bolts (install correct bolts and nuts in the proper location) EVENLY in steps. Always use a new gasket between the pump body and its mounting.
8. Install the drive belt and adjust the tension.
9. Refill the cooling system, start the engine and check for leaks.

3VZ-E Engines

▶ See Figure 92

1. Drain the cooling system.
2. Remove the timing belt as detailed later in the section.
3. Remove the No. 1 idler pulley.
4. Remove the thermostat.
5. Remove the seven bolts and the tension spring bracket and then remove the water pump.

Fig. 88 Removing the water pump mounting bolts—4 cylinder engine (typical)

Fig. 89 Removing the water pump bolts—note bolt size and location

Fig. 90 Removing the water pump—4 cylinder engine (typical)

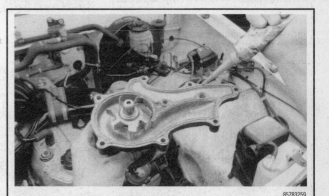

Fig. 91 Installing form-a-gasket sealer on the water pump

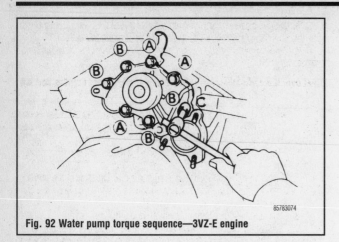

Fig. 92 Water pump torque sequence—3VZ-E engine

To install:

6. Apply sealer to the pump-to-block mating surface and then tighten the bolts marked **A** in the illustration to 13 ft. lbs. (18 Nm). Tighten those marked **B** to 14 ft. lbs. (20 Nm).

7. Installation of the remaining components is the reverse of the removal procedure.

8. Install the drive belt and adjust the tension. Refill the cooling system and check for leaks.

Cylinder Head

REMOVAL & INSTALLATION

8R-C and 18R-C Engines

▶ See Figures 93 and 94

✻ CAUTION

Do not perform this procedure on a warm engine.

1. Disconnect the battery and drain the cooling system.
2. Remove the air cleaner assembly from its bracket, complete with its attendant hoses.
3. Detach the accelerator cable from its support on the cylinder head cover and also from the carburetor throttle arm.
4. Remove the choke cable and fuel lines from the carburetor.
5. Remove the water hose bracket from the cylinder head cover.
6. Unfasten the water hose clamps and remove the hoses from the water pump and the water valve. Detach the heater temperature control cable from the water valve.
7. Disconnect the PCV line from the cylinder head cover.
8. Remove the vacuum lines from the distributor vacuum unit. Remove the lines which run from the vacuum switching valve to the various emission control system components on the cylinder head. Disconnect the EGR lines (1974 California only).
9. Remove the fuel and vacuum lines from the carburetor.
10. Remove the pipes from the automatic choke stove.
11. Tag and unfasten the wires from the spark plugs. Remove the spark plugs.
12. Remove the cylinder head cover retaining bolts, and withdraw the cover.

➡**Use a clean cloth, placed over the timing cover opening, to prevent anything from falling down into it.**

13. Remove the radiator upper hose from the cylinder head water outlet.
14. Remove the outlet elbow and thermostat.
15. Unfasten the downpipe clamp from the exhaust manifold. Remove the manifold from the head.
16. Remove the valve rocker assembly mounting bolts and the oil delivery pipes. Withdraw the valve rocker shaft assembly.

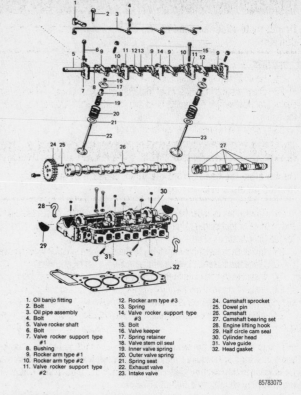

1. Oil banjo fitting	12. Rocker arm type #3	24. Camshaft sprocket
2. Bolt	13. Spring	25. Dowel pin
3. Oil pipe assembly	14. Valve rocker support type #3	26. Camshaft
4. Bolt	15. Bolt	27. Camshaft bearing set
5. Valve rocker shaft	16. Valve keeper	28. Engine lifting hook
6. Bolt	17. Spring retainer	29. Half circle cam seal
7. Valve rocker support type #1	18. Valve stem oil seal	30. Cylinder head
8. Bushing	19. Inner valve spring	31. Valve guide
9. Rocker arm type #1	20. Outer valve spring	32. Head gasket
10. Rocker arm type #2	21. Spring seat	
11. Valve rocker support type #2	22. Exhaust valve	
	23. Intake valve	

Fig. 93 Exploded view of the cylinder head assembly—8R-C and 18R-C engines

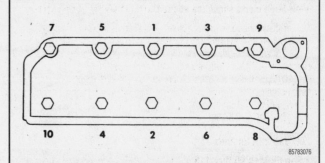

Fig. 94 Torque sequence for 8R-C and 18R-C cylinder head bolts— tighten to specified torque in three passes—loosen the bolts in the reverse of the order shown here, in two passes

✻ CAUTION

When removing the rocker shaft securing bolts, loosen them in two or three stages.

17. Remove the timing gear from the camshaft. Support it so that the chain does not fall down into the cover.
18. Remove the camshaft bearing caps and withdraw the camshaft. Remove the camshaft bearings.

➡**Temporarily assemble the bearings and caps to keep them with their mates. Be sure to keep the bearings in proper order.**

19. Remove the gear from the timing chain. Support the timing chain so that it does not fall into the cover.
20. Loosen the head bolts in two or three stages, in the sequence illustrated. Lift the head assembly off the block.

> ※※ **CAUTION**

Do not try to slide the head off the block as it is held in place by dowels.

To install:

21. Remove any water from the cylinder head bolt holes.
22. Clean the mating surfaces of the cylinder head and block. Use liquid sealer around the oil holes on the head and cylinder block. Do not get sealer in the holes.
23. Lower the cylinder head on to the block.

> ※※ **CAUTION**

Do not slide the head across the block because of the dowels located on the block.

24. Tighten the cylinder head bolts in the proper sequence (see the diagram) and in three or four stages. Tighten them to the specifications given in the Torque Specifications chart.
25. Install each lower bearing half into the seat from which it was removed.
26. Place the camshaft in the cylinder head.
27. Install each bearing into the cap from which it was removed.
28. Install the camshaft bearing caps on the head, in their numbered sequence, with the numbers facing forward. Tighten to 12–17 ft. lbs.
29. First, check the camshaft bearing clearance and end-play, using Plastigage®.

➡ **This is checked in the same manner that connecting rod and crankshaft bearings are checked. For the procedure see the appropriate sections later in this section. The oil clearance should be 0.025-0.050mm; the end-play should be 0.043-0.167mm.**

30. Crank the engine so that the No. 1 piston is at TDC of its compression stroke.
31. Align the mark on the timing chain with the dowel hole on the camshaft timing gear and the stamped mark on the camshaft.

➡ **All three marks should be aligned so that they are facing upward.**

32. Install the valve rocker assembly. Tighten its securing bolts to 12-17 ft. lbs., working from the center to the ends, and in two or three stages.
33. Attach the oil delivery pipe to the valve rocker assembly and camshaft bearing caps. Tighten their securing bolts to 11-16 ft. lbs.
34. Adjust the valve clearance as outlined in Section 2, to the following cold specifications:
- Intake — 0.18mm
- Exhaust — 0.33mm

20R and 22R Engines

▸ **See Figures 95 thru 115**

> ※※ **CAUTION**

Do not perform this operation on a warm engine.

1. Disconnect the battery.
2. Remove the three exhaust pipe flange nuts and separate the pipe from the manifold.

3. Drain the cooling system (both radiator and block). If the coolant is to be reused, place a large, clean container underneath the drains.
4. Remove the air cleaner assembly, complete with hoses, from the carburetor.

➡ **Cover the carburetor with a clean shop cloth so that nothing can fall into it.**

5. Mark all vacuum hoses to aid installation and disconnect them. Remove all linkages, fuel lines, etc., from the carburetor, cylinder head, and manifolds. Remove the wire supports.
6. Mark the spark plug leads and disconnect them from the plugs.
7. Matchmark the distributor housing and block. Disconnect the primary lead and remove the distributor. Installation will be easier if you leave the cap and leads in place.
8. Unfasten the four 14mm nuts which secure the cam cover.
9. Remove the rubber camshaft seals. Turn the crankshaft until the No. 1 piston is at TDC on its compression stroke. Match mark the timing sprocket to the cam chain, and remove the semi-circular lug. Using a 19mm wrench, remove the cam sprocket bolt. Slide the distributor drive gear and spacer off the cam and wire the cam sprocket in place.
10. Remove the timing chain cover 14mm bolt at the front of the head. This must be done before the head bolts are removed.
11. Remove the cylinder head bolts in the order shown below. Improper removal could cause head damage.
12. If necessary, remove the camshaft brackets, keeping them in order for installation. Remove any remaining components necessary for cylinder head removal.
13. Using pry bars applied evenly at the front and the rear of the valve rocker assembly, pry the assembly off its mounting dowels.
14. Lift the head off its dowels. Do NOT pry it off. Support the head on a workbench.
15. Drain the engine oil from the crankcase after the head has been removed, because the oil will become contaminated with coolant while the head is being removed.

To install:
16. Apply liquid sealer to the front corners of the block and install the head gasket.

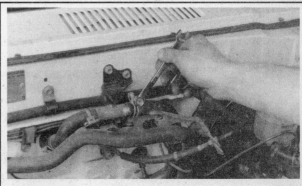

Fig. 95 Removing water hoses for cylinder head removal

Fig. 96 Remove all external brackets before removing the cylinder head assem-

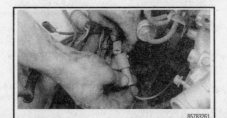

Fig. 97 Disconnect and tag all electrical connectors before removing the cylinder head assembly

Fig. 98 Remove the distributor assembly before removing the cylinder head assembly

Fig. 99 Remove the distributor and fuel pump drive gear assembly before removing the cylinder head assembly

Fig. 100 Remove the rear camshaft/cylinder head cover seal . . .

Fig. 101 . . . then remove the front seal

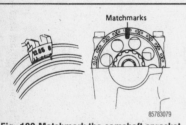

Fig. 102 Matchmark the camshaft sprocket to the camshaft chain—set No. 1 cylinder to TDC-20R, 22R, 22R-E and 22R-TE engines

Fig. 103 Wire timing chain and gear before removing the cylinder head assembly

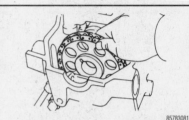

Fig. 104 Do not allow the camshaft chain to slip off the sprocket and fall into the lower end when removing the camshaft sprocket—20R, 22R, 22R-E and 22R-TE engines

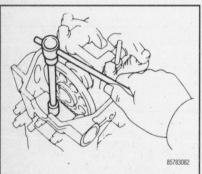

Fig. 105 Remove the front cover bolt before removing the cylinder head bolts—20R, 22R, 22R-E and 22R-TE engines

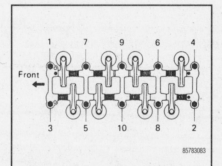

Fig. 106 Cylinder head bolt loosening sequence—20R, 22R, 22R-E and 22R-TE engines

Fig. 107 Removing the cylinder head assembly bolts in correct sequence—note location and length

Fig. 108 Removing the camshaft brackets in correct sequence—keep all parts in the order

Fig. 109 Remove all necessary components before removing the cylinder head

Fig. 110 Removing the cylinder head assembly

17. Lower the head over the locating dowels. Do not attempt to slide it into place.

18. Rotate the camshaft so that the sprocket aligning pin is at the top. Remove the wire and hold the cam sprocket. Manually rotate the engine so that the sprocket hole is also at the top. Wire the sprocket in place again.

19. Install the rocker arm assembly over its positioning dowels.

20. Tighten the cylinder head bolts evenly, in three stages and in the order shown, under Torque Sequences, to a specified torque of 52–63 ft. lbs.

21. Install the timing chain cover bolt and tighten it to 7–11 ft. lbs.

22. Remove the wire and fit the sprocket over the camshaft dowel. If the chain won't allow the sprocket to reach, rotate the crankshaft back and forth, while lifting up on the chain and sprocket.

23. Install the distributor drive gear and tighten the crankshaft bolt to 51–65 ft. lbs.

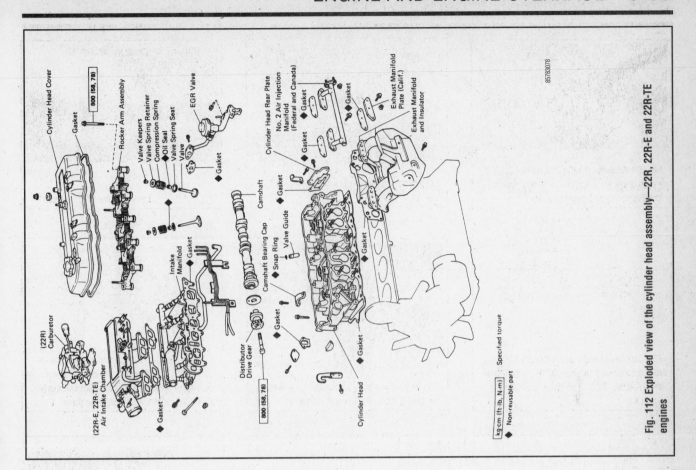

Fig. 112 Exploded view of the cylinder head assembly—22R, 22R-E and 22R-TE engines

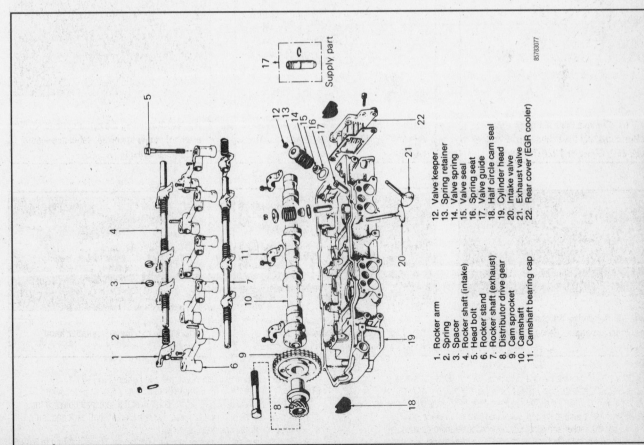

1. Rocker arm
2. Spring
3. Spacer
4. Rocker shaft (intake)
5. Head bolt
6. Rocker stand
7. Rocker shaft (exhaust)
8. Distributor drive gear
9. Cam sprocket
10. Camshaft
11. Camshaft bearing cap
12. Valve keeper
13. Spring retainer
14. Valve spring
15. Valve seal
16. Spring seat
17. Valve guide
18. Half circle cam seal
19. Cylinder head
20. Intake valve
21. Exhaust valve
22. Rear cover (EGR cooler)

Fig. 111 Exploded view of the cylinder head assembly—20R engine

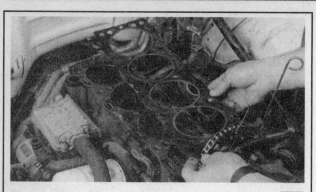

Fig. 113 Always replace the cylinder head gasket—install the new gasket in the correct position

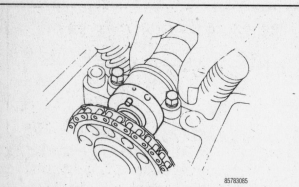

Fig. 114 Rotate the camshaft so that the pin is at top—20R, 22R, 22R-E and 22R-TE engines

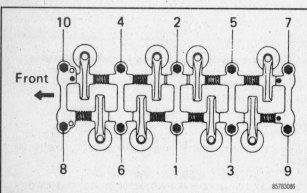

Fig. 115 Cylinder head bolt torque sequence—20R, 22R, 22R-E and 22R-TE engines

24. Set the No. 1 piston at TDC of its compression stroke and adjust the valves as outlined in Section 2.

25. After completing valve adjustment, rotate the crankshaft 352°, so that the 8° BTDC mark on the pulley aligns with the pointer.

26. Install the distributor.

27. Install the spark plugs and leads.

28. Make sure that the oil drain plug is installed. Fill the engine with oil after installing the rubber cam seals. Pour the oil over the distributor drive gear and the valve rockers.

29. Install the rocker cover and tighten the bolts to 8–11 ft. lbs.

30. Connect all the vacuum hoses and electrical leads which were removed during disassembly. Install the spark plug lead supports. Fill the cooling system. Install the air cleaner.

31. Tighten the exhaust pipe-to-manifold flange bolts to 25–33 ft. lbs.

32. Reconnect the battery. Start the engine and allow it to reach normal operating temperature. Check and adjust the timing and valve clearance. Adjust the idle speed and mixture. Road test the vehicle.

22R-E and 22R-TE Engines

❊❊ CAUTION

Never perform this operation on a hot engine.

1. Disconnect the negative battery cable.

2. Drain the coolant from the radiator and the cylinder block. Drain the engine oil.

3. Remove the turbocharger on the 22R-TE.

4. Disconnect and remove the air cleaner hose on the 22R-E.

5. Disconnect the oxygen sensor wire. Remove the three nuts attaching the manifold to the exhaust pipe and then separate the two.

6. Remove the oil dipstick.

7. Remove the distributor with the spark plug leads attached.

8. Disconnect the upper radiator hose and the two heater hoses where they attach to the engine and then position them out of the way.

9. Disconnect the actuator cable, the accelerator cable and the throttle cable for the automatic transmission at their bracket.

10. Tag and disconnect the following:
   a. Both PCV vacuum hoses
   b. Brake booster hose
   c. Actuator hose (if equipped with cruise control)
   d. Air control valve hoses and valve.

11. Tag and disconnect the EGR vacuum modulator hoses and then remove the modulator itself along with the bracket.

12. Tag and disconnect the following:
   a. Green and brown BVSV hoses
   b. Vacuum advance hoses
   c. The two air valve hoses; one at the throttle body, the other at the air chamber
   d. Air control valve hose (if equipped with air conditioning)
   e. Pressure regulator hose at the air chamber
   f. Cold start injector pipe and wire
   g. Throttle position sensor wire.

13. Remove the bolt holding the EGR valve to the air chamber. Disconnect the chamber from the stay. Remove the air chamber-to-intake manifold bolts and then lift off the chamber with the throttle body.

14. Disconnect the fuel return hose.

15. Tag and disconnect the following:
   a. Water temperature sender gauge wire
   b. Temperature sensor wire
   c. Start injection time switch wire
   d. Fuel injector wires.

16. Remove the pulsation damper. Remove the bolt holding the fuel hose to the delivery pipe and then disconnect and remove the fuel hose.

17. Disconnect the wire and hose and then remove the air valve from the intake manifold.

18. Disconnect the by-pass hose at the intake manifold on the 22R-E. On the 22R-TE, disconnect the oil cooler hose at the manifold.

19. If equipped with power steering, remove the pump and position it out of the way without disconnecting the hydraulic lines.

20. Remove the four nuts and then remove the cylinder head cover.

➡**Be sure to cover the oil return hole in the cylinder head with a clean rag to prevent anything form falling in.**

21. Remove the rubber camshaft seals. Turn the crankshaft until the No. 1 piston is at TDC of its compression stroke. Matchmark the timing sprocket to the timing chain and then remove the semi-circular plug. Using a 19mm wrench, remove the camshaft sprocket bolt. Slide the distributor drive gear and spacer off the camshaft and wire the cam sprocket in place.

22. Remove the timing chain cover bolt in front of the cylinder head.

➡**This must be done BEFORE the cylinder head bolts are removed.**

23. Remove the cylinder head bolts gradually, in two or three stages, in the order shown.

Removing the head bolts in the improper order could cause damage to the aluminum cylinder head.

24. Using pry bars applied evenly at the front and rear of the rocker arm assembly, pry the assembly off of its mounting dowels.

25. Lift the cylinder head off of its mounting dowels, DO NOT pry it off. Support the head on a workbench.

26. To install, follow Steps 15-31 of the 20R and 22R installation procedure and refer to the illustrations.

➡When installing the camshaft sprocket onto the camshaft, if the chain does not seem long enough, wiggle the chain back and forth slightly while pulling up on the chain and sprocket.

1L, 2L and 2L-T Engines

▶ **See Figures 116, 117, 118 and 119**

1. Disconnect the cables from both batteries.
2. Remove the air cleaner assembly.
3. Drain the cooling system and remove the radiator, shroud, and radiator hoses.
4. If the vehicle is equipped with A/C, remove the compressor drive belt and unbolt the compressor from its mounting brackets. Tie the compressor out of the way. Do not remove the refrigerant lines.
5. Remove the engine cooling fan, pulley, and drive belt.
6. Disconnect the heater hoses at the engine and move the hoses aside.
7. Disconnect the cables which are positioned above the valve cover and move the cables aside.
8. Remove the valve cover and upper front engine cover.
9. Disconnect and remove the glow plugs.
10. Disconnect the fuel injection lines at the injectors and the injection pump. Remove the lines.
11. Remove the fuel injectors. Arrange the injectors so that they may be reinstalled in their original locations.
12. Unbolt and remove the intake manifold assembly. Also remove the water outlet housing from the cylinder head.
13. Unbolt the exhaust manifold from the cylinder head. Secure the manifold in a position away from the cylinder head.
14. Disconnect the fuel feed line at the injection pump and plug the line.
15. Using a wrench on the center crankshaft pulley bolt, rotate the engine (clockwise only) until the TDC mark on the pulley is aligned with the pointer. Check that the valves on the number one cylinder are closed (rocker arms loose). If the valves are not closed, rotate the engine 360° and again align the TDC mark with the pointer.
16. Remove the crankshaft pulley using a puller.
17. Remove the timing belt cover from the front of the engine and the timing belt guide from the front of the crankshaft timing gear.
18. Remove the timing belt idler pulley. If the timing belt is to be reused, mark the belt and all timing gears to indicate their relationships. Remove the timing belt.
19. Remove the timing gear from the camshaft, using a puller.
20. Remove the camshaft oil seal retainer.
21. Gradually loosen the rocker shaft support nuts, working from the ends towards the center. Remove the rocker shaft and arms as an assembly.
22. Gradually remove the cylinder head bolts in the reverse order of the installation torque sequence.
23. Remove the cylinder head from the engine

To install:

24. Clean the mating surfaces of the cylinder block and head, and use a NEW head gasket during installation.
25. DO NOT rotate the engine while the cylinder head is removed.
26. Install the cylinder head, tighten the bolts in the order shown, in several stages, to the correct torque specification.
27. Torque the cylinder head bolts gradually, following the head bolt tightening sequence.
28. Align the timing marks according to the illustration accompanying the Timing Belt Removal & Installation procedure.
29. Install all remaining components in the reverse order the of removal procedure.
30. Replenish the cooling system with the proper type and quantity of coolant.
31. Check for leaks after the engine has been started.

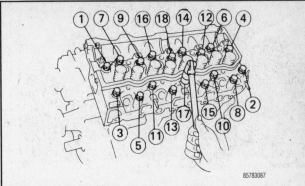

Fig. 116 Cylinder head bolt loosening sequence—1L,2L and 2L-T engines

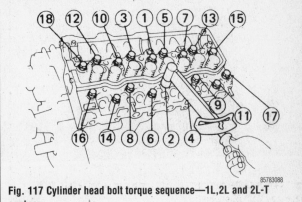

Fig. 117 Cylinder head bolt torque sequence—1L,2L and 2L-T engines

F and 2F Engines

▶ **See Figures 120, 121 and 122**

1. Disconnect the battery and drain the cooling system.
2. Remove the air cleaner assembly from its bracket, complete with its attendant hoses.
3. Detach the accelerator cable from its support on the cylinder head cover and also from the carburetor throttle arm.
4. Remove the choke cable and fuel lines from the carburetor.
5. Remove the water hose bracket from the cylinder head cover.
6. Unfasten the water hose clamps an remove the hoses from the water pump and the water valve. Detach the heater temperature control cable from the water valve.
7. Disconnect the PCV line from the cylinder head cover.
8. Disconnect the vacuum lines, which run from the vacuum switching valve, at the various components of the emission control system.
9. Drain the engine oil. Unfasten the oil lines from the oil filter and remove the filter assembly from the manifold.
10. Detach the vacuum valve solenoid wire from the coil.
11. Disconnect any remaining lines from the carburetor and remove the carburetor from the manifold.
12. Unfasten the alternator adjusting link and then remove the drive belt and the alternator.
13. Disconnect the distributor vacuum line from the distributor. Remove the wire from its supports on the head.
14. Disconnect the carburetor fuel line from the fuel pump. Remove the line.
15. Disconnect the spark plug and coil cables, after marking their respective locations.
16. Unfasten the primary wire from the distributor. Remove the distributor clamp bolts and withdraw the distributor.
17. Remove the oil gauge sending unit.
18. Remove the coil from its bracket on the cylinder head.
19. Remove the fuel pump.

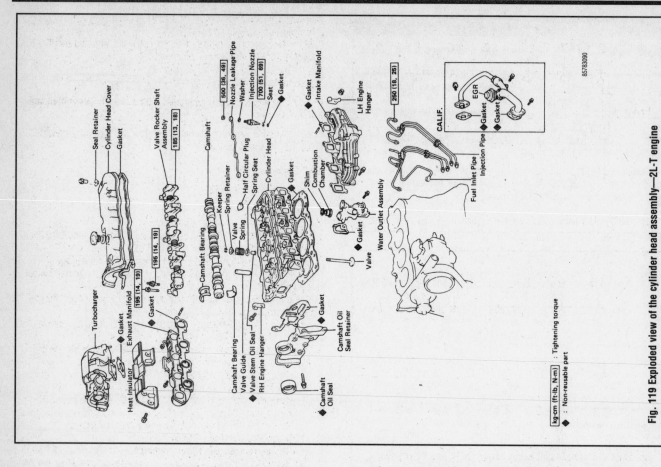

Fig. 119 Exploded view of the cylinder head assembly—2L-T engine

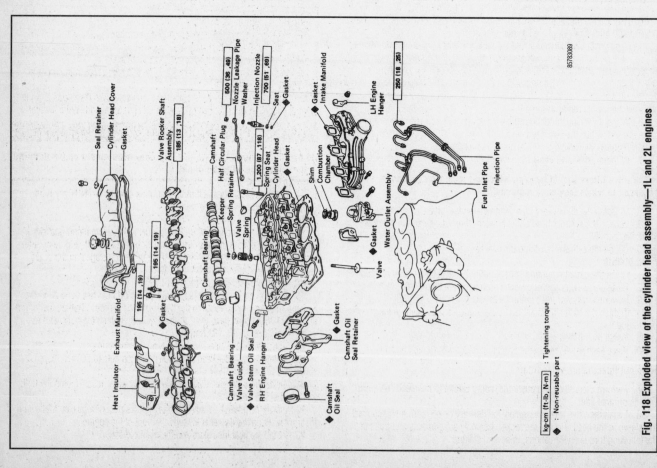

Fig. 118 Exploded view of the cylinder head assembly—1L and 2L engines

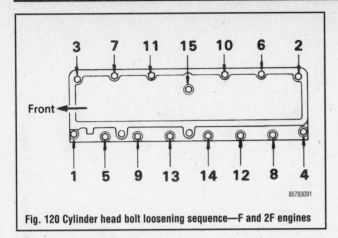

Fig. 120 Cylinder head bolt loosening sequence—F and 2F engines

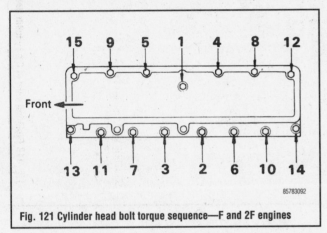

Fig. 121 Cylinder head bolt torque sequence—F and 2F engines

20. Remove the oil filter tube clamping bolt from the valve lifter (side) cover. Drive the oil filler tube out of the cylinder block

21. Remove the combination intake/exhaust manifold from the cylinder block.

22. Take off the cylinder head cover and its gasket.

23. Unfasten the oil delivery union, spring, and sleeve from the valve rocker shafts.

24. Unfasten the securing nuts and bolts from the valve rocker shaft supports. Withdraw the rocker assembly.

25. Withdraw the pushrods from their bores. Be sure to keep them in the same order in which they were removed.

26. Remove the valve lifter (side) cover and gasket.

27. Withdraw the valve lifters from the block.

➡The valve lifters should be kept, with their respective pushrods, in the sequence in which they were removed.

28. Unfasten the oil delivery union from the oil feel pipe.

29. Loosen the cylinder head bolts in two or three stages and in the order illustrated above.

30. Lift off the cylinder head and the gasket.

To install:

31. Clean the gasket mounting surfaces of both the cylinder head and block.

32. Place a new head gasket over the dowels on the block.

33. Lower the cylinder head on to the block.

34. Tighten the bolts, in stages, an in the sequence illustrated, to the specified torque.

35. Install the oil feed pipe.

36. Place each valve lifter in the original position from which it came.

➡Do not interchange valve lifters.

37. Perform Step 36 for the pushrods, being careful to mate each pushrod with its original lifter.

38. Install the valve rocker assembly, oil delivery union, spring and connecting sleeve in the head. Tighten the rocker assembly support nuts and bolts to the following torque specifications, in several stages:

- 10mm nuts and bolts: 24–30 ft. lbs.
- 8mm bolts: 14–22 ft. lbs.

39. Adjust the valves, as outlines above, to the following cold specifications (each piston TDC of its compression stroke):

- Intake: 0.20mm
- Exhaust: 0.36mm

➡Adjust the valve clearance again after the engine is assembled and warmed up.

40. The rest of the cylinder head installation is performed in the reverse order of the removal procedure.

3F-E Engines

♦ **See Figures 123 and 124**

1. Drain the coolant.
2. Disconnect the negative battery cable.
3. Scribe matchmarks around the hood hinges and then remove the hood.
4. Disconnect the accelerator and throttle cables.
5. Remove the air intake hose, air flow meter and air cleaner cap.
6. Unbolt the power steering pump and position it out of the way without disconnecting the hydraulic lines.
7. Unbolt the air conditioning compressor and position it out of the way without disconnecting the refrigerant lines.
8. Remove the power steering pump and air conditioning compressor brackets.
9. Disconnect the high tension cords from the spark plugs and the coil.
10. Disconnect and remove the heater water (oil cooler) pipe.
11. Disconnect the upper radiator hose.
12. Disconnect and plug the fuel lines.
13. Raise the vehicle and disconnect the exhaust pipe at the manifold.
14. Remove the air pump.
15. Remove the fuel delivery pipe along with the fuel injectors.
16. Remove the air injection manifold.
17. Remove the intake and exhaust manifolds.
18. Disconnect the water by-pass hose at the water outlet and then remove the outlet.
19. Remove the spark plugs.
20. Remove the cylinder head cover and its gasket.
21. Loosen the eight bolts and four nuts that attach the rocker shaft assembly in several stages and then remove the rocker shaft.
22. Remove the twelve pushrods — be sure they are kept in the order in which they were removed!
23. Loosen the cylinder head bolts in several stages, in the opposite order of the tightening sequence. Remove the air pump bracket and engine hanger.

✳✳ CAUTION

Removing the head bolts in the improper order could cause damage to the aluminum cylinder head.

24. Lift the cylinder head off of its mounting dowels, DO NOT pry it off. Support the head on a workbench.

To install:

25. Install the cylinder head on the cylinder block using a new gasket.

26. Lightly coat the threads of the cylinder head bolts with engine oil and then install them into the head. Tighten them in several stages, in the order shown.

27. Install the pushrods in the order that they were removed.

28. Position the rocker shaft assembly on the cylinder head and align the rocker arm adjusting screws with the heads of the pushrods. Tighten the mounting bolts with a 12mm head to 17 ft. lbs. (24 Nm); tighten the bolts with a 14mm head to 25 ft. lbs. (33 Nm).

29. Adjust the valve clearance and install the spark plugs.

30. Install the cylinder head and tighten the cap nuts to 78 inch lbs. (8.8 Nm).

31. Install the water outlet and connect the by-pass hose. Tighten the bolts to 18 ft. lbs. (25 Nm).

32. Install the intake and exhaust manifolds using a new gasket. Make sure the front mark on the gasket is towards the front of the engine.

33. Install the heat insulators and the manifold stay.

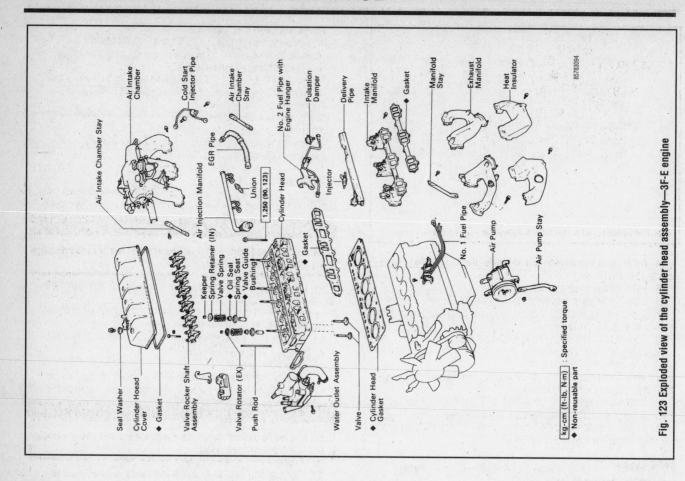

85783094

Air Intake Chamber Stay
Air Intake Chamber
Cold Start Injector Pipe
Air Intake Chamber Stay
Air Injection Manifold
EGR Pipe
No. 2 Fuel Pipe with Engine Hanger
Pulsation Damper
Delivery Pipe
Intake Manifold
Gasket
Manifold Stay
Exhaust Manifold
Heat Insulator
Cylinder Head
Injector
Union
1,250 (90, 123)
Air Injection Manifold (IN)
Keeper
Spring Retainer
Valve Spring
Oil Seal
Spring Seat
Valve Guide Bushing
Gasket
No. 1 Fuel Pipe
Air Pump
Air Pump Stay
Seal Washer
Cylinder Head Cover
Gasket
Valve Rocker Shaft Assembly
Valve Rotator (EX)
Push Rod
Water Outlet Assembly
Valve
Cylinder Head Gasket

kg-cm (ft.-lb, N.m) : Specified torque
◆ Non-reusable part

Fig. 123 Exploded view of the cylinder head assembly—3F-E engine

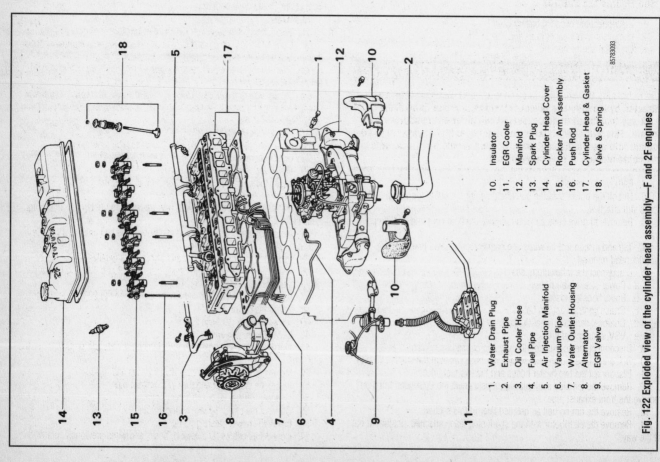

85783093

1. Water Drain Plug	10. Insulator
2. Exhaust Pipe	11. EGR Cooler
3. Oil Cooler Hose	12. Manifold
4. Fuel Pipe	13. Spark Plug
5. Air Injection Manifold	14. Cylinder Head Cover
6. Vacuum Pipe	15. Rocker Arm Assembly
7. Water Outlet Housing	16. Push Rod
8. Alternator	17. Cylinder Head & Gasket
9. EGR Valve	18. Valve & Spring

Fig. 122 Exploded view of the cylinder head assembly—F and 2F engines

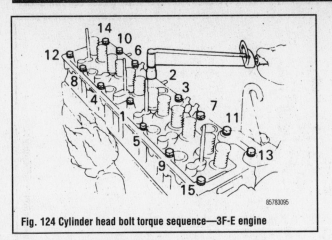

Fig. 124 Cylinder head bolt torque sequence—3F-E engine

34. Install the air injection manifold and tighten the union nuts and clamp bolts to 15 ft. lbs. (21 Nm).

35. Install the fuel injector/delivery pipe assembly.

36. Install the air pump and connect the air hose.

37. Connect the exhaust pipe to the manifold. Use a new gasket and tighten the bolts to 46 ft. lbs. (62 Nm).

38. Connect the fuel lines and the upper radiator hose.

39. Install the heater water pipe.

40. Connect the high tension cords.

41. Install the air conditioning compressor and the power steering pump. Remember to adjust the belt tension later.

42. Install the air intake hose, the air flow meter and the air cleaner cap.

43. Connect and adjust the accelerator and throttle cables.

44. Connect the battery cable, fill the engine with coolant, start the engine and check for any leaks. Road test the vehicle.

3VZ-E Engine

▶ **See Figures 125 thru 133**

1. Disconnect the negative battery cable.
2. Remove the air cleaner hose and case.
3. Drain the engine coolant.

✳✳ CAUTION

When draining the coolant, keep in mind that cats and dogs are attracted by the ethylene glycol antifreeze, and are quite likely to drink any that is left in an uncovered container or in puddles on the ground. This will prove fatal in sufficient quantity. Always drain the coolant into a sealable container. Coolant should be reused unless it is contaminated or several years old.

4. Remove the radiator.

5. Unbolt the power steering pump and position it out of the way with the hoses still attached.

6. Remove all drive belts and then remove the fluid coupling and fan pulley.

7. Tag and disconnect all wires and connectors that will interfere with cylinder head removal.

8. Disconnect the following hoses:
   a. Power steering air hoses
   b. Brake booster hose
   c. Cruise control vacuum hose
   d. Charcoal canister has at the canister
   e. VSV vacuum hose.

9. Disconnect the accelerator, throttle and cruise control cables.

10. Disconnect the clutch release cylinder hose (manual transmission only).

11. Disconnect the two heater hoses and the two fuel lines.

12. Remove the left side scuff plate and disconnect the O_2 sensor and then remove the front exhaust pipe.

13. Remove the timing belt as detailed later in this section.

14. Remove the distributor with the spark plug leads attached; position it out of the way.

15. Remove the air intake chamber.

16. Disconnect the connectors and then remove the engine wire.

17. Remove the Nos. 2 and 3 fuel pipes.

18. Remove the No. 4 timing belt cover.

19. Remove the No. 2 idler pulley and the No. 3 timing belt cover.

20. Disconnect the hose and remove the water by-pass outlet.

21. Remove the intake manifold.

22. Remove the exhaust crossover pipe.

Right side:

23. Remove the reed valve with the No. 1 air injection manifold.

24. Remove the water by-pass pipe mounting bolt.

25. Remove the cylinder head cover.

26. Remove the camshaft.

27. Loosen the cylinder head bolts in several stages, in the opposite order of the tightening sequence. Remove the air pump bracket and engine hanger.

✳✳ CAUTION

Removing the head bolts in the improper order could cause damage to the aluminum cylinder head.

28. Lift the cylinder head off of its mounting dowels, DO NOT pry it off. Support the head on a workbench.

Left side:

29. Remove the alternator.

30. Remove the oil dipstick guide tube.

31. Remove the cylinder head cover.

32. Remove the camshaft.

33. Loosen the cylinder head bolts in several stages, in the opposite order of the tightening sequence. Remove the air pump bracket and engine hanger.

✳✳ CAUTION

Removing the head bolts in the improper order could cause damage to the aluminum cylinder head.

34. Lift the cylinder head off of its mounting dowels, DO NOT pry it off. Support the head on a workbench.

To install:

35. Install the cylinder head on the cylinder block using a new gasket.

36. Lightly coat the threads of the cylinder head bolts with engine oil and then install them into the head. Tighten them in several stages, in the order shown. After the initial tightening, mark the front side the top of the bolt with paint. Tighten the bolts an additional 90° (¼ turn) and check that the mark is now facing the side of the head. Tighten the bolts an additional 90° and check that the mark is now facing the rear of the head. Install the bolt (A) and tighten it to 27 ft. lbs. (37 Nm).

37. Install the camshaft.

38. Install the alternator and the water by-pass pipe mounting bolt.

39. Install the reed valve with the No. 1 injection manifold.

40. Install the oil dipstick tube.

41. Install the crossover pipe and tighten it to 29 ft. lbs. (39 Nm).

42. Connect the O_2 sensor wire.

43. Install the intake manifold with new gaskets and tighten the mounting bolts to 29 ft. lbs. (39 Nm).

44. Install the water by-pass outlet and tighten the two bolts to 13 ft. lbs. (18 Nm).

45. Install the fuel delivery pipes and injectors as detailed in Section 5.

46. Install the No. 2 idler pulley. Install the Nos. 3 and 4 timing belt covers and tighten the bolts to 74 inch lbs. (8.3 Nm).

47. Install the fuel pipes and tighten the union bolts to 22 ft. lbs. (29 Nm).

48. Install the timing belt.

49. Install the cylinder head covers.

50. Install the engine wire.

51. Install the air intake chamber and tighten the nuts and bolts to 13 ft. lbs. (18 Nm).

52. Install the EGR valve and connect all hoses and lines.

53. Install the distributor and the front exhaust pipe.

54. Connect the fuel lines and heater hoses.

55. Connect the clutch release cylinder hose.

56. Install the power steering pump.

57. Connect all cables (and adjust), hoses and wires previously removed.

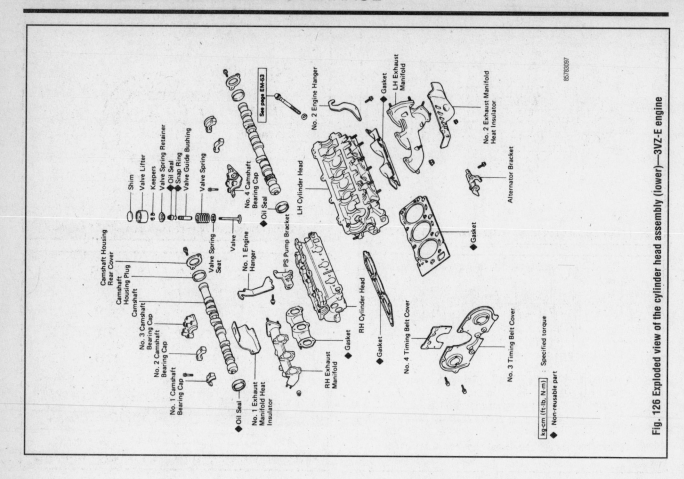

Fig. 126 Exploded view of the cylinder head assembly (lower)—3VZ-E engine

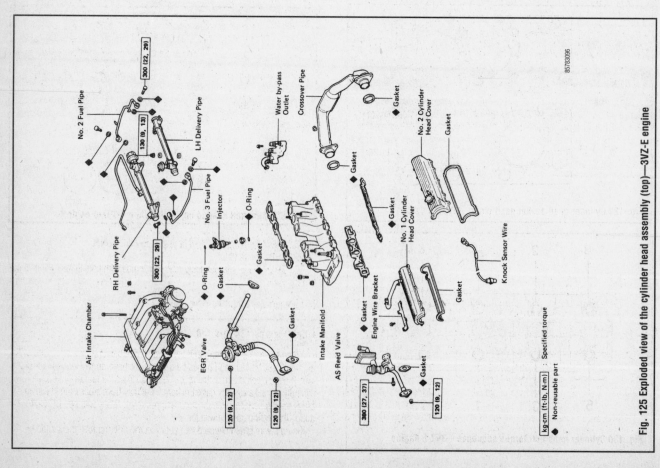

Fig. 125 Exploded view of the cylinder head assembly (top)—3VZ-E engine

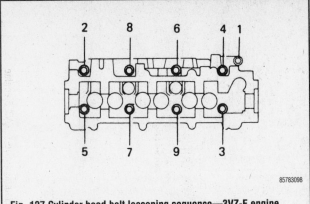

Fig. 127 Cylinder head bolt loosening sequence—3VZ-E engine

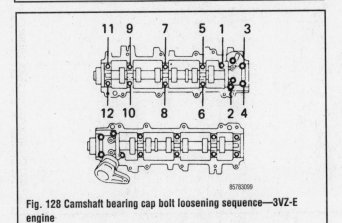

Fig. 128 Camshaft bearing cap bolt loosening sequence—3VZ-E engine

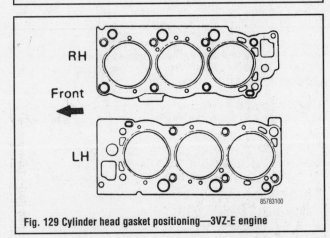

Fig. 129 Cylinder head gasket positioning—3VZ-E engine

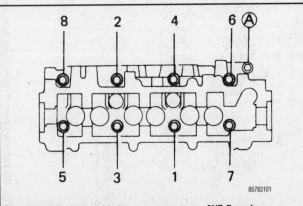

Fig. 130 Cylinder head bolt torque sequence—3VZ-E engine

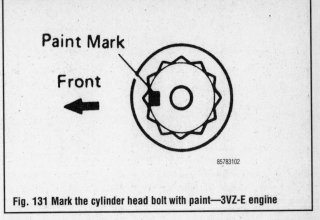

Fig. 131 Mark the cylinder head bolt with paint—3VZ-E engine

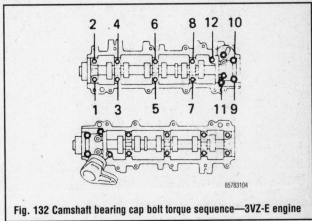

Fig. 132 Camshaft bearing cap bolt torque sequence—3VZ-E engine

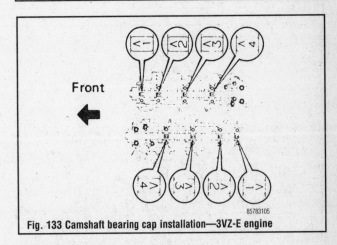

Fig. 133 Camshaft bearing cap installation—3VZ-E engine

58. Install the fan pulley, fluid coupling and drive belts.
59. Install the radiator.
60. Install the air cleaner hose, refill the engine with coolant and connect the battery cable.

CLEANING AND INSPECTION

▶ See Figures 134 thru 140

When the rocker assembly and valve train have been removed from the cylinder head (see Valves and Springs below), set the head on two wooden blocks on the bench, combustion chamber side up. Using a scraper or putty knife, carefully scrape away any gasket material that may have stuck to the head-to-block mating surface when the head was removed. Make sure you DO NOT gouge the mating surface with the tool.

Using a wire brush chucked into your electric drill, remove the carbon in

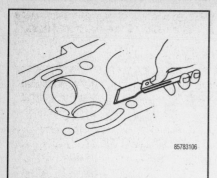

Fig. 134 Do not scratch the cylinder head mating surface when removing the old gasket material

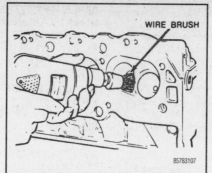

Fig. 135 Removing combustion chamber carbon—make sure it is removed and not merely burnished

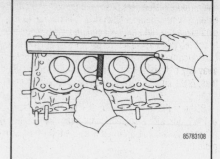

Fig. 136 Check the cylinder head mating surface straightness with a precision straight-edge and a feeler gauge

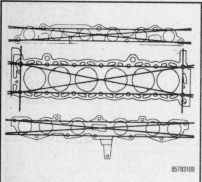

Fig. 137 Check the mating surface widthwise, lengthwise and diagonally

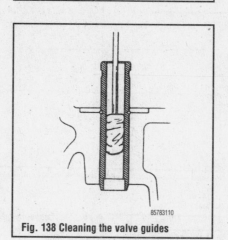

Fig. 138 Cleaning the valve guides

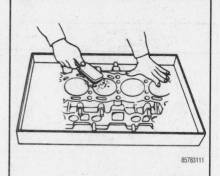

Fig. 139 Wire brush the top of the cylinder head block

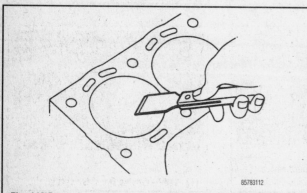

Fig. 140 Removing carbon from the piston tops—do not scratch the pistons

each combustion chamber. Make sure the brush is actually removing the carbon and not merely burnishing it.

Clean all the valve guides using a valve guide brush (available at most auto parts or auto tool shops) and solvent. A fine-bristled rifle bore cleaning brush also works here.

Inspect the threads of each spark plug hole by screwing a plug into each, making sure it screws down completely. Heli-coil® any plug hole that is damaged.

✳✳ CAUTION

DO NOT hot tank the cylinder head! The head material on most engines is aluminum, which is ruined if subjected to the hot tank solution. Some of the early 8R-C and 18R-C engines were equipped with cast iron heads, which can be hot-tanked (a service performed by most machine shops which immerses the head in a hot, caustic solution for cleaning). **To be sure your engine's cylinder head is aluminum, check around its perimeter with a magnet. Your engine has an iron head if the magnet sticks.**

➡Before hot-tanking any overhead cam head, check with the machine shop doing the work. Some cam bearings are easily damaged by the hot tank solution.

Finally, go over the entire head with a clean shop rag soaked in solvent to remove any grit, old gasket particles, etc. Blow out the bolt holes, coolant galleys, intake and exhaust ports, valve guides and plug holes with compressed air.

RESURFACING

While the head is removed, check the head-to-block mating surface for straightness. If the engine has overheated and blown a head gasket, this must be done as a matter of course. A warped mating surface must be resurfaced (milled); this is done on a milling machine and is quite similar to planing a piece of wood.

Using a precision steel straightedge and a blade-type feeler gauge, check the surface of the head across its length, width and diagonal length as shown in the illustrations. Also check the intake and exhaust manifold mating surfaces and cam cover (all) mating surfaces. If warpage exceed 0.076mm in a 152mm span, or 0.15mm over the total length, the head must be milled. If warpage is highly excessive, the head must be replaced. Again, consult the machine shop operator on head milling limitations.

CYLINDER BLOCK CLEANING

While the cylinder head is removed, the top of the cylinder block and pistons should also be cleaned. Before you begin, rotate the crankshaft until one or more pistons are flush with the top of the block (on the four cylinder engines, you will either have Nos. 1 and 4 up, or Nos. 2 and 3 up). Carefully stuff clean rags into the cylinders in which the pistons are down. This will help keep grit and carbon chips out during cleaning. Using care not to gouge or scratch the block-to-head mating surface and the piston top(s), clean away any old gasket material with a wire brush and/or scraper. On the piston tops, make sure you are actually removing the carbon and not merely burnishing it.

Remove the rags from the down cylinders after you have wiped the top of the block with a solvent soaked rag. Rotate the crankshaft until the other pistons come up flush with the top of the block, and clean those pistons.

➡Because you have rotated the crankshaft, you will have to re-time the engine following the procedure listed under the Timing Chain/Timing Belt removal. Make sure you wipe out each cylinder thoroughly with a solvent-soaked rag, to remove all traces of grit, before the head is reassembled to the block.

Valves and Springs

ADJUSTMENT (AFTER ENGINE SERVICE)

The valves on all engines covered here, except the 3VZ-E, must be adjusted following any valve train disassembly. Follow the procedure listed in Section 2 for valve adjustment.

REMOVAL & INSTALLATION

▶ **See Figures 141 thru 148**

A valve spring compressor is needed to remove the valves and springs; these are available at most auto parts and auto tool shops. A small magnet is very helpful for removing the keepers and spring seats.

Set the head on its side on the bench. Install the spring compressor so that the fixed side of the tool is flat against the valve head in the combustion chamber, and the screw side is against the retainer. Slowly turn the screw in towards the head,

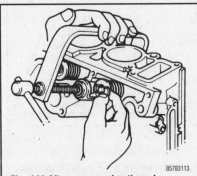

Fig. 141 After compressing the valve spring, be careful removing the keepers— they are easily fumbled

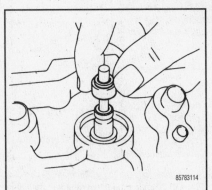

Fig. 142 Always install new valve stem seals

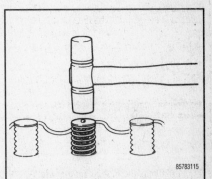

Fig. 143 Lightly tap each assemble valve stem to ensure correct fit of the keepers, retainer and seals

Fig. 144 Special tool to remove the valve spring—you also need tool to hold valve up

Fig. 145 Removing the keepers with a magnet

Fig. 146 Removing the valve spring

Fig. 147 Removing the valve seal

Fig. 148 Installing the valve seal

compressing the spring. As the spring compresses, the keepers will be revealed; pick them off of the valve stem with the magnet as they are easily fumbled and lost. When the keepers are removed, back the screw out and remove the retainers and springs. Remove the compressor and pull the valves out of the head from the other side. Remove the valve seals by hand and remove the spring seats with the magnet.

Since it is very important that each valve and its spring, retainer, spring seat and keepers is reassembled in its original location, you must keep these parts in order. The best way to do this to cut either eight (four cylinder) or twelve (six cylinder) holes in a piece of heavy cardboard or wood. Label each hole with the cylinder number and either **IN** or **EX,** corresponding to the location of each valve in the head. As you remove each valve, insert it into the holder, and assemble the seats, springs, keepers and retainers to the stem on the labeled side of the holder. This way each valve and its attending parts are kept together, and can be put back into the head in their proper locations.

After lapping each valve into its seat (see Valve Lapping below), oil each valve stem, and install each valve into the head in the reverse order of removal, so that all parts except the keepers are assembled on the stem. Always use new valve stem seals. Install the spring compressor, and compress the retainer and spring until the keeper groove on the valve stem is fully revealed. Coat the groove with a wipe of grease (to hold the keepers until the retainer is released) and install both keepers, wide end up. Slowly back the screw of the compressor out until the spring retainer covers the keepers. Remove the tool. Lightly tap the end of each valve stem with a rubber hammer to ensure proper fit of the retainers and keepers.

INSPECTION

▶ **See Figures 149, 150, 151, 152 and 153**

Before the valves can be properly inspected, the stem, lower end of the stem and the entire valve face and head must be cleaned. An old valve works well for chipping carbon from the valve head, and a wire brush, gasket scraper or putty knife can be used for cleaning the valve face and the area between the face and lower stem. Do not scratch the valve face during cleaning. Clean the entire stem with a rag soaked in thinners to remove all varnish and gum.

Thorough inspection of the valves requires the use of a micrometer, and a dial indicator is needed to measure the inside diameter of the valve guides. If there instruments are not available to you, the valves and head can be taken to a reputable machine ship for inspection. Refer to the Valve Specifications chart for valve stem and stem-to-guide specifications.

If the above instruments are at your disposal, measure the diameter of each valve stem at the locations illustrated. Jot these measurements down. Using the dial indicator, measure the inside diameter of the valve guides at their bottom, top and midpoint 90° apart. Jot these measurements down also. Subtract the valve stem measurement from the valve guide inside measurement; if the clearance exceed that listed in the specifications chart under Stem-to-Guide Clearance, replace the valve(s). Stem-to-guide clearance can also be checked at a machine shop, where a dial indicator would be used.

Check the top of each valve stem for pitting and unusual wear due to improper rocker adjustment, etc. The stem tip can be ground flat if it is worn, but no more than 0.50mm can be removed; if this limit must be exceeded to make the tip flat and square, then the valve must be replaced. If the valve stem tips are ground, make sure you fix the valve securely into a jig designed for this purpose, so the tip contacts the grinding wheel squarely at exactly 90°. Most machine shops that handle automotive work are equipped for this job.

REFACING

Valve refining should only be handled by a reputable machine shop, as the experience and equipment needed to do the job are beyond that of the average owner/mechanic. During the course of a normal valve job, refining is necessary when simply lapping the valves into their seats will not correct the seat and face wear. When the valves are reground (resurfaced), the valve seats must also be recta, again requiring special equipment and experience.

VALVE LAPPING

▶ **See Figure 154**

The valves must be lapped into their seats after resurfacing, to ensure proper sealing. Even if the valves have not been refaced, they should be lapped into the head before reassembly.

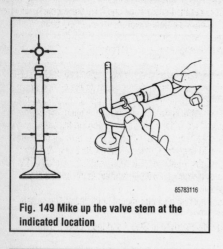

Fig. 149 Mike up the valve stem at the indicated location

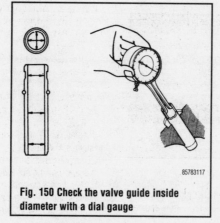

Fig. 150 Check the valve guide inside diameter with a dial gauge

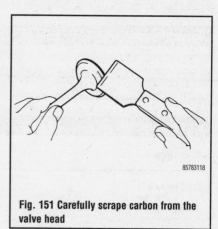

Fig. 151 Carefully scrape carbon from the valve head

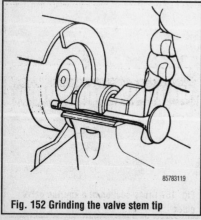

Fig. 152 Grinding the valve stem tip

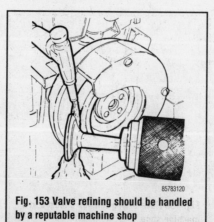

Fig. 153 Valve refining should be handled by a reputable machine shop

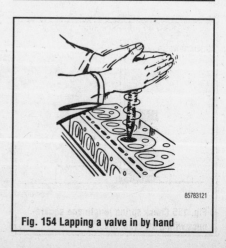

Fig. 154 Lapping a valve in by hand

Set the cylinder head on the workbench, combustion chamber side up. Rest the head on wooden blocks on either end, so there are two or three inches between the tops of the valve guides and the bench.

1. Lightly lube the valve stem with clean engine oil. Coat the valve seat completely with valve grinding compound. Use just enough compound that the full width and circumference of the seat are covered.

2. Install the valve in its proper location in the head. Attach the suction cup end of the valve lapping tool to the valve head. It usually helps to put a small amount of saliva into the suction cup to aid it sticking to the valve.

3. Rotate the tool between the palms, changing position and lifting the tool often to prevent grooving. Lap the valve in until a smooth, evenly polished seat and valve face are evident.

4. Remove the valve from the head. Wipe away all traces of grinding compound from the valve face and seat. Wipe out the port with a solvent soaked rag, and swab out the valve guide with a piece of solvent soaked rag to make sure there are no traces of compound grit inside the guide. This cleaning is important.

5. Proceed through the remaining valves, one at a time. Make sure the valve faces, seats, cylinder ports and valve guides are clean before reassembling the valve train.

Valve Springs

INSPECTION

▶ See Figures 155 and 156

Valve spring squareness, length and tension should be checked while the valve train is disassembled. Place each valve spring on a flat surface next to a steel square. Measure the length of the spring, and rotate it against the edge of the square to measure distortion. If spring length varies (by comparison) by more than 1.6mm or if distortion exceeds 1.6mm, replace the spring.

Spring tension must be checked on a spring tester. Springs used on most Toyota engines should be within one pound of each other when tested at their specified installed heights.

Valve Seats

The valve seats in the engines covered in this guide are all non-replaceable, and must be recut when service is required. Seat recutting requires a special tool and experience, and should be handled at a reputable machine shop. Seat concentricity should also be checked by a machinist.

Valve Guides

INSPECTION

▶ See Figure 157

Valve guides should be cleaned as outlined earlier, and checked when valve stem diameter and stem-to-guide clearance is checked. Generally, if the engine is using oil through the guides (assuming the valve seals are OK) and the valve stem diameter is within specification, it is the guides that are worn and need replacing.

Valve guides which are not excessively worn or distorted may, in some cases, be knurled rather than replaced. Knurling is a process in which metal inside the valve guide bore is displaced and raised (forming a very fine cross-hatch pattern), thereby reducing clearance. Knurling also provides for excellent oil control. The possibility of knurling rather than replacing the guides should be discussed with a machinist.

REMOVAL & INSTALLATION

Valve guide replacement on all Toyota engines requires breaking off the top end of the guides, heating the cylinder head to almost 200°F, then driving the rest of the guide out of the head with a hammer and drift. Unless you and your family don't mind baking an oily cylinder head in the oven (and probably smelling it in the house for months), take the head to a machine shop and have a machinist replace the guides.

Oil Pan

REMOVAL & INSTALLATION

▶ See Figures 158 thru 168

Pick-Ups and 4Runner

1. Raise the hood and leave it open for the duration of this repair.
2. Drain the engine oil.
3. Raise the front end of the truck and support it on jackstands.
4. Remove the steering relay rod and the tie rods from the idler arm, pitman arm, and steering knuckles as outlined in Section 8.
5. Remove the engine stiffening plates.
6. Remove the splash pans from under the engine.
7. Position a floor jack under the transmission and raise the engine/transmission assembly slightly. Remove the front motor mount attaching bolts.
8. Remove the front motor mount attaching bolts.
9. Remove the oil pan bolts and remove the oil pan.

To install:

10. Use a razor blade and scrape the cylinder block and oil pan mating surfaces clean of any old sealing material. Apply gasket sealer to the oil pan when installing a new gasket. On 1985-88 models with a four cylinder engine, apply 5mm bead of gasket sealer; on models with the six cylinder engine, use 3mm bead. The parts should be installed within 5 minutes of applying the sealer.

11. The oil pan bolts should be tightened to 3–5 ft. lbs.—8R-C and 18R-C engines; 33–70 inch lbs.—20R engines; 9 ft. lbs.—22R, 22R-E and 22R-TE engines; 6 ft. lbs. (bolt), 13 ft. lbs. (nut)—1L, 2L, 2L-T; and, 52 inch lbs.—3V-ZE engines. Tighten the bolts in a circular pattern, starting in the middle of the pan and working out towards the ends.

12. Lower the engine and tighten the motor mount bolts. Install the splash shields and stiffening plates.

13. Install any steering arms removed in Step 4 and then lower the truck;

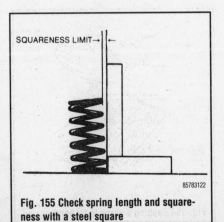

Fig. 155 Check spring length and square-ness with a steel square

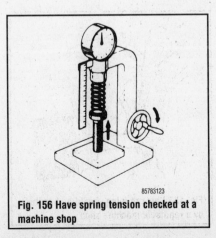

Fig. 156 Have spring tension checked at a machine shop

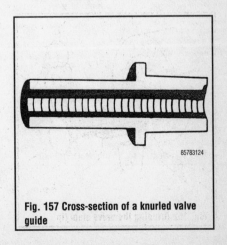

Fig. 157 Cross-section of a knurled valve guide

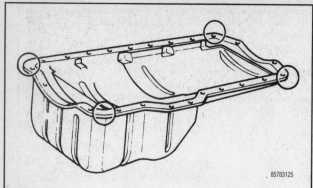

Fig. 158 Apply sealer to the corners of the oil pan gasket—20R engines

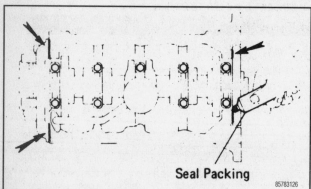

Fig. 159 Sealant application points—22R, 22R-E and 22R-TE engines

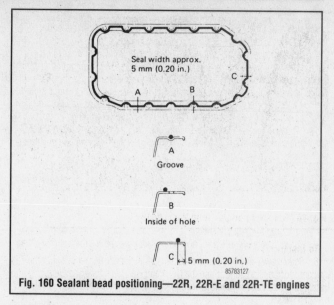

Fig. 160 Sealant bead positioning—22R, 22R-E and 22R-TE engines

tighten all suspension components and the motor mounts to their final torque with the vehicle resting on the ground.

14. Fill the engine with oil, road test the truck and check for leaks.

Land Cruiser

1. Remove the engine skid plates.
2. Remove the flywheel side cover and skid plate.
3. Disconnect the front driveshaft from the engine.
4. Drain the engine oil.
5. Remove the bolts which secure the oil pan. Remove the pan and its gasket.

Fig. 161 Removing all necessary steering components for oil pan removal

Fig. 162 Removing crossmember retaining bolts for oil pan removal

Fig. 163 Removing crossmember for oil pan removal

Fig. 164 Removing oil pan retaining bolts

Fig. 165 Removing oil pan—note position of scraper tool

Fig. 166 Removing oil pan

Fig. 167 Removing oil pan from the vehicle

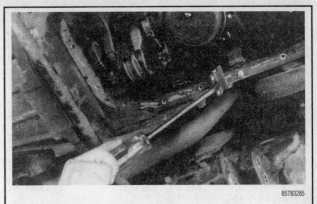

Fig. 168 Cleaning the oil pan-to-engine mounting area

To install:

6. Scrape away any old gasket material and then apply gasket sealer to the cylinder block mating surface and the No. 1 and No. 4 main bearing caps. Install the oil pan and tighten the bolts to 69 inch lbs. (7.8 Nm). Always use a new pan gasket.

7. Connect the driveshaft, skid plate and flywheel side cover.

8. Lower the vehicle, fill the engine with oil and check for any leaks.

Oil Pump

REMOVAL & INSTALLATION

8R-C and 18R-C Engines

♦ See Figure 169

1. Remove the oil pan.
2. Unbolt the oil pump attaching bolts and remove the entire assembly.
3. Installation requires no special procedures. Simply position the pump and reinstall the attaching bolts. Replace the oil pan.
4. Fill the engine with clean engine oil.

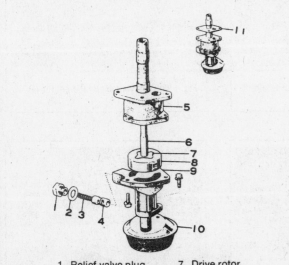

1. Relief valve plug
2. Gasket
3. Relief valve spring
4. Relief valve
5. Pump body
6. Pump shaft
7. Drive rotor
8. Driven rotor
9. Pump cover
10. Strainer
11. Gasket

Fig. 169 Exploded view of the oil pump-8R-C and 18R-C engines

20R, 22R, 22R-E and 22R-TE Engines

♦ See Figures 170 thru 175

1. Drain the oil, and remove the oil pan and the oil strainer and pick-up tube.
2. Remove the drive belts from the crankshaft pulley.
3. Remove the crankshaft bolt, and remove the pulley with a gear puller, as outlined in the timing chain cover section.
4. Remove the five bolts from the oil pump and remove the oil pump assembly.

Inspect the drive spline, driven gear, pump body, and timing chain cover for excessive wear or damage. If necessary, replace the gears or pump body or cover. Unbolt the relief valve (the vertical bolt on the pump body) when attached to the engine) and check the pistons, oil passages, and sliding surfaces for burrs or scoring. Inspect the crankshaft front oil seal and replace if worn or damaged.

When installing, use a new O-ring if necessary. Apply a sealer to the upper bolt and install the five bolts. Install the crankshaft pulley as outlined in the timing cover section, and use a new gasket on the oil strainer and oil pan. Be sure to apply sealer to the corners of the oil pan gasket before installing the pan.

3VZ-E Engines

♦ See Figures 176 and 177

1. Remove the engine under cover.
2. Drain the oil and then remove the timing belt as detailed later in this section.
3. Remove the crankshaft timing pulley.
4. Raise the engine slightly and remove the oil pan.
5. Remove the oil strainer. Insert a drift between the cylinder block and the oil pan baffle plate, cut off the sealer and remove the baffle plate.

➡ When removing the baffle plate with the drift, do not damage the baffle plate flange.

6. Remove the oil pump and O-ring.
To install:
7. Apply sealer to the oil pump mating surface running the bead on the inside of the bolts holes. Position a **new** O-ring in the groove in the cylinder block and install the pump so that the spline teeth of the drive gear engage the large teeth on the crankshaft. Tighten the mounting bolts to 14 ft. lbs. (20 Nm).
8. Remove any old sealer and install the baffle plate with new sealer.
9. Install the oil strainer and tighten the bolts to 61 inch lbs. (7 Nm).
10. Install the oil pan, crankshaft pulley and the timing belt.
11. Install the undercovers.
12. Fill the engine with oil and check for leaks.

1L, 2L and 2L-T Engines

♦ See Figure 178

1. Disconnect the cables which are positioned above the valve cover and move the cable aside. Remove the valve cover.
2. Disconnect the cables from both batteries.

Fig. 170 Removing the crankshaft pulley bolt

Fig. 171 Installing special tool to remove the crankshaft pulley

Fig. 172 Removing the crankshaft pulley

Fig. 173 Removing the oil pump assembly—4cylinder engine (typical)

Fig. 174 Removing the oil pump gear

Fig. 175 Removing the oil pump assembly gasket

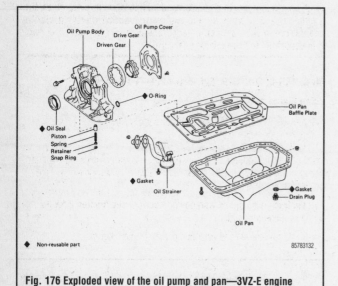

Fig. 176 Exploded view of the oil pump and pan—3VZ-E engine

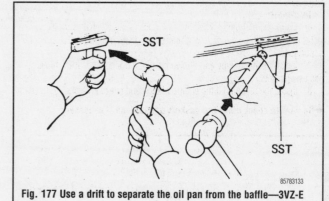

Fig. 177 Use a drift to separate the oil pan from the baffle—3VZ-E engine

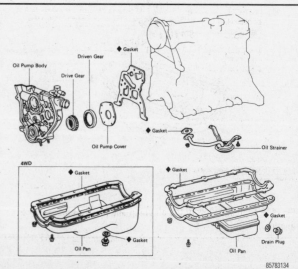

Fig. 178 Exploded view of the oil pump and pan—1L, 2l and 2L-T engines

3. Using a wrench on the center crankshaft pulley bolt, rotate the engine (clockwise only) until the TDC mark on the pulley is aligned with the pointer. Check that the valves of the number one cylinder are closed (rocker arms loose). If the valves are not closed, rotate the engine 360° and again align the TDC mark with the pointer.

4. Remove the following components as previously outlined:
   a. Oil pan and pump strainer assembly
   b. Timing cover and belt.

5. Disconnect the wiring from the alternator. Remove the alternator and the mounting brackets.

6. If equipped with air conditioning, unbolt the air conditioning compressor and tie it out of the way (without disconnecting the refrigerant hoses). Also remove the compressor brackets.

7. Remove the fuel injection pump.

8. Remove the crankshaft timing gear, using a puller.

9. Unbolt and remove the water pump.

10. Unbolt and remove the timing case assembly.

11. Remove the oil pump cover plate from the rear of the timing case

assembly to gain access to the oil pump. Clearances are checked in the same manner as the pump used in the 20R, 22R and 22R-E engines.

12. Remove the pump gears and check the gears and timing case gear surfaces for damage or excessive wear.

To install:

13. Install the gears with the triangular markings of each gear facing the pump plate side of the timing case.

14. Install the pump cover plate.

15. When installing the pump, note that all gasket surfaces must be cleaned, and that damaged gaskets must be replaced.

16. Be sure to follow the specific procedures concerning timing belt installation and fuel injection pump installation, as outlined previously and in the Diesel Fuel System section.

F, 2F and 3F-E Engines

▶ **See Figures 179 and 180**

1. Remove the oil pan as previously outlined.

2. Remove the oil strainer and unfasten the union nuts on the oil pump pipe.

3. Remove the lock wire and the oil pump retaining bolt and pipe from the engine.

4. Remove the oil pump cover and inspect the following parts for nicks, scoring, grooving, etc.:

   a. pump cover

   b. drive and driven gears

   c. pump body

5. Replace either the damaged parts or the complete pump if damage is excessive.

To install:

6. Install the oil pump so that the slot in the oil pump shaft is in alignment with the protrusion on the governor shaft of the distributor. Tighten the mounting bolts to 13 ft. lbs. (18 Nm).

7. Install the outlet pipe and tighten the union bolt to 33 ft. lbs. (44 Nm); use new gaskets.

8. Install the oil pan, fill the engine with oil and check for leaks.

➡ **Be sure to check all of the gaskets and replace if necessary.**

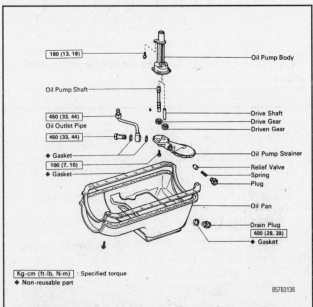

Fig. 179 Exploded view of the oil pump and pan assembly—3F-E engine

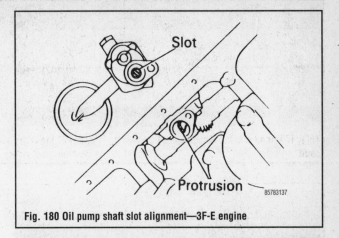

Fig. 180 Oil pump shaft slot alignment—3F-E engine

Timing Chain/Timing Belt/Timing Gear Cover

REMOVAL & INSTALLATION

✷✷ CAUTION

When draining the coolant, keep in mind that cats and dogs are attracted by the ethylene glycol antifreeze, and are quite likely to drink any that is left in an uncovered container or in puddles on the ground. This will prove fatal in sufficient quantity. Always drain the coolant into a sealable container. Coolant should be reused unless it is contaminated or several years old.

8R-C, 18R-C, 20R, 22R, 22R-E and 22R-TE Engines

▶ **See Figure 181**

1. Remove the cylinder head as detailed previously.

2. Remove the radiator.

3. Remove the alternator. Remove the oil pan.

4. On engines equipped with air pumps, unfasten the adjusting link bolts and the drive belt. Remove the hoses from the pump; remove the pump and bracket from the engine.

➡ **If the truck is equipped with power steering, see Section 8 for its pump removal procedure.**

5. Remove the fan and water pump as a complete assembly.

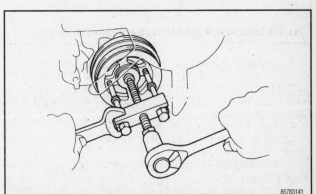

Fig. 181 Front cover removal—18R-C, 20R, 22R, 22R-E and 22R-TE engines

To prevent the fluid from running out of the fan coupling, do not tip the assembly over on its side.

6. Unfasten the crankshaft pulley securing bolt and remove the pulley with a gear puller.

Do not remove the 10mm bolt from its hole, if installed, as it is used for balancing.

7. Remove the water by-pass pipe.
8. Remove the fan belt adjusting bar.
9. Disconnect and remove the heater water outlet pipe. On the 22R-TE, remove the No. 3 turbocharger water pipe.
10. Remove the bolts securing the timing chain cover. Withdraw the cover.

To install:

11. Install the cover and tighten the 8mm bolts to 9 ft. lbs. (13 Nm). Tighten the 10mm bolts to 29 ft. lbs. (39 Nm). Apply sealer to the gaskets for both the timing chain cover and the oil pan.
12. Install the fan belt adjusting bar and tighten it to 9 ft. lbs. (13 Nm).
13. Install the heater water outlet pipe and the No. 3 turbo water hose. Install the water by-pass pipe.
14. Install the crankshaft pulley and tighten the bolt to the proper torque.
15. Install the water pump and fluid coupling. Install the air conditioning compressor and then adjust the tension on all drive belts.
16. Install the oil pan. Install the radiator and then install the cylinder head.
17. Refill the engine with oil and coolant. Road test the truck and check for any leaks.

1L, 2L and 2L-T Engines

1. Disconnect the cables from both batteries.
2. Remove the air cleaner assembly.
3. Drain the cooling system and remove the radiator, shroud, and radiator hoses.
4. If the vehicle is equipped with air conditioning, remove the compressor drive belt and unbolt the compressor from its mounting brackets. Tie the compressor out of the way. Do not remove the refrigerant lines.
5. Remove the engine cooling fan, pulley, and drive belt.
6. Disconnect the heater hoses at the engine and move the hoses aside.
7. Disconnect the cables which are positioned above the valve cover and move the cables aside.
8. Remove the valve cover and upper front engine cover.
9. Using a wrench on the center crankshaft pulley bolt, rotate the engine (clockwise only) until the TDC mark on the pulley is aligned with the pointer. Check that the valves on the number one cylinder are closed (rocker arms loose). If the valves are not closed, rotate the engine 360° and again align the TDC mark with the pointer.
10. Remove the crankshaft pulley using a puller.
11. Remove the timing belt cover from the front of the engine and the timing belt guide from the front of the crankshaft timing gear.
12. Follow or refer to only the necessary steps of the Cylinder Head Installation procedure. Torque the timing belt cover fasteners to 3-5 ft. lbs., and the crankshaft pulley center bolt to 69-75 ft. lbs.

F and 2F Engines

1. Drain the cooling system and the crankcase.
2. Disconnect the battery.
3. Remove the air cleaner assembly, complete with hoses, from its bracket.
4. Remove the hood latch as well as its brace and support.
5. Remove the headlight bezels and grille assembly.
6. Unfasten the upper and lower radiator hose clamps and remove both of the hoses from the engine.
7. Unfasten the radiator securing bolts and remove the radiator.

➡ **Take off the shroud first, if so equipped.**

8. Loosen the drive belt adjusting link and remove the drive belt. Unfasten

the alternator multi-connector, withdraw the retaining bolts, and remove the alternator.
9. Perform Step 8 to the air injection pump, if so equipped. Disconnect the hoses from the pump before removing it.
10. Remove the fan and water pump as an assembly.
11. Remove the crankshaft pulley with a gear puller.
12. Remove the gravel shield from underneath the engine.
13. Remove the front driveshaft.
14. Remove the front oil pan bolts, to gain access to the bottom of the timing chain cover.

➡ **It may be necessary to insert a thin knife between the pan and the gasket in order to break the pan loose. Use care not to damage the gasket.**

15. Remove the timing chain cover.

To install:

16. Install the timing gear cover and then install the front driveshaft and gravel shield.
17. Press the crankshaft pulley onto the shaft and then install the fan and water pump as an assembly.
18. Install the air injection pump and the alternator. Adjust the drive belts.
19. Install the radiator and shroud. Reconnect the heater hoses.
20. Install the headlight bezels and the grille. Replace the hood latch and its support.
21. Install the air cleaner and connect the battery. Refill the engine with coolant and check for leaks.

3F-E Engines

1. Disconnect the negative battery cable and drain the coolant.
2. Disconnect the accelerator and throttle cables.
3. Remove the air intake hose, air flow meter and air cleaner as an assembly.
4. Loosen the power steering pump drive pulley nut.
5. Remove the fluid coupling with the fan and water pump pulley.
6. Remove the power steering pump and the air conditioning compressor. Remove their brackets. Remove the power steering pump idler pulley and its bracket.
7. Remove the cylinder head cover. Remove the rocker shaft assembly.
8. Remove (mark for correct installation) the distributor.
9. Remove the pushrod cover and then remove the valve lifters. Be certain that they are kept in order.
10. Loosen the six bolts and then slide the power steering pump pulley off the crankshaft.
11. Using Special Tool 09213-58011 and a 46mm socket wrench, remove the crankshaft pulley bolt. Remove the pulley.
12. Remove the oil cooler pipe and its hose.
13. Remove the timing gear cover and gasket.

To install:

14. Install the timing gear cover and gasket.
15. There are three sizes of timing gear cover bolts. Apply adhesive to the two larger bolts. Install a new gasket and then position the cover. Finger tighten all bolts. Align the crankshaft pulley set key with the groove of the pulley; gently tap the pulley onto the crankshaft. Tighten the larger cover bolts to 18 ft. lbs. (25 Nm). Tighten smaller bolts to 43 inch lbs. (5 Nm). Tighten the pulley bolt to 253 ft. lbs. (343 Nm).
16. Position the power steering pulley on the crankshaft and tighten the six bolts to 13 ft. lbs. (18 Nm).
17. Insert the valve lifters into their bores and install the pushrod cover. Tighten the bolts to 35 inch lbs. (4 Nm). Make sure the valve lifters are installed in the same bore from which they came.
18. Install the rocker shaft assembly, the cylinder head cover and the distributor.
19. Install the water pump pulley, fluid coupling and fan.
20. Install the power steering pump idler pulley and bracket. Install the power steering pump and air conditioning compressor. Adjust the drive belts.
21. Install the air cleaner assembly and then connect and adjust the accelerator and throttle cables.
22. Fill the engine with coolant and connect the battery cable. Start the engine and check for leaks. Check the ignition timing.

3VZ-E Engine

▶ **See Figures 182, 183 and 184**

1. Disconnect the negative battery cable and drain the coolant.
2. Remove the radiator and shroud.
3. Remove the power steering belt and pump. .
4. Remove the spark plugs.
5. Disconnect the Nos. 2 and 3 air hoses at the air pipe.
6. Disconnect the No. 1 water by-pass hose at the air pipe and then remove the water outlet.
7. Remove the air conditioning belt. Remove the alternator drive belt, fluid coupling, guide and fan pulley.
8. Disconnect the high tension cords and their clamps at the No. 2 (upper) timing belt cover and then remove the cover and its three gaskets.
9. Rotate the crankshaft pulley until the groove on its lip is aligned with the **0** on the No. 1 (lower) timing belt cover, this should set the No. 1 cylinder at TDC of its compression stroke. The matchmarks on the camshaft timing pulleys must be in alignment with those on the No. 3 (upper rear) timing cover. If not, rotate the engine 360° (one complete revolution).
10. Remove the crankshaft pulley using a puller.
11. Remove the fan pulley bracket and then remove the No. 1 timing belt cover.

To install:

12. Install the No. 1 cover with the two gaskets and tighten the bolts to 48 inch lbs. (5.4 Nm).
13. Install the fan pulley bracket and tighten it to 30 ft. lbs. (41 Nm).
14. Install the No. 2 cover and tighten the bolts 48 inch lbs. (5.4 Nm).
15. Position the crankshaft pulley so the groove in the pulley is aligned with the woodruff key in the crankshaft. Tighten the bolt to 181 ft. lbs. (245 Nm).
16. Install the fan pulley, guide, fluid coupling and alternator drive belt. Adjust the belt tension.
17. Install the power steering pump and belt. Install the air conditioning belt. Adjust the belt tension.
18. Install the water outlet and connect the by-pass hose. Connect the Nos. 2 and 3 air hoses.
19. Install the spark plugs. Install the radiator, fill with coolant and road test the vehicle. Check for leaks and check the ignition timing.

TIMING COVER OIL SEAL REPLACEMENT

▶ **See Figures 185, 186, 187 and 188**

8R-C, 18R-C, F, 2F and 3F-E Engines

1. Remove the timing chain cover, as previously detailed in the appropriate section.

2. Inspect the oil seal for signs of wear, leakage, or damage.
3. If worn, pry the old oil seal out, using a suitable pry bar. Remove it toward the front of the cover.

➡ **Once the oil seal has been removed, it must be replaced with a new one.**

4. Use a socket, pipe, or block of wood and a hammer to drift the oil seal into place. Work from the front of the cover.

※※ CAUTION

Be extremely careful not to damage the seal or else it will leak.

5. Install the timing chain cover as previously outlined.

20R, 22R, 22R-E and 22R-TE Engines

➡ **When repairing the oil pump, the oil pan and strainer should be removed and cleaned.**

1. Remove the fan shroud and fan assembly.
2. Remove all drive belts.
3. Remove the crankshaft pulley.
4. Unbolt the oil pump from the front cover and remove.
5. Using a suitable pry bar, remove the old oil seal from the pump.
6. Lightly oil the new seal, and using an old socket or block of wood and hammer, carefully drive the new seal into place, working from the front of the pump.

1L, 2L, 2L-T and 3VZ-E Engines

➡ **The following procedure covers front oil seal and oil pump seal removal with the front timing belt case removed from the block. It is possible to remove the seal with the case installed, but a special service tool is required.**

1. Remove the timing belt covers, timing belt assembly and lower timing pulleys from the engine.
2. Remove the timing belt case (the rear section of the timing belt cover) from the cylinder block.
3. Using a small pry bar, remove the front oil seal and the pump drive oil seal. Do not gouge the case.
4. Apply a multi-purpose grease to the lips of the new oil seals. Carefully install the new seals using an old socket or oil seal tool.

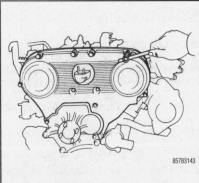

Fig. 182 Remove the No. 2 timing belt cover—3VZ-E engine

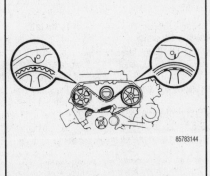

Fig. 183 Matchmark alignment on the camshaft timing pulleys—3VZ-E engine

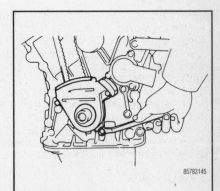

Fig. 184 Remove the No. 1 timing belt cover—3VZ-E engine

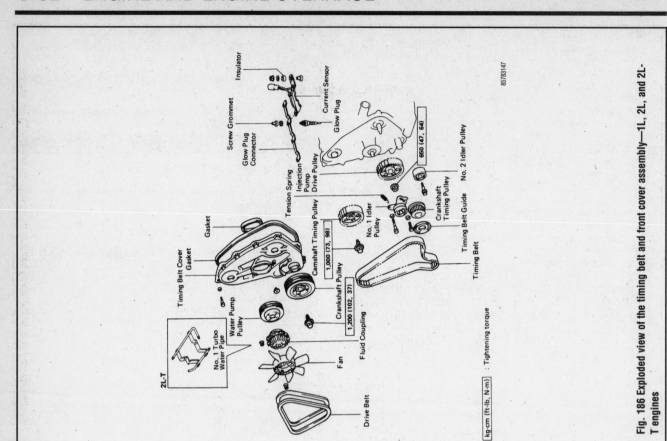

Fig. 186 Exploded view of the timing belt and front cover assembly—1L, 2L, and 2L-T engines

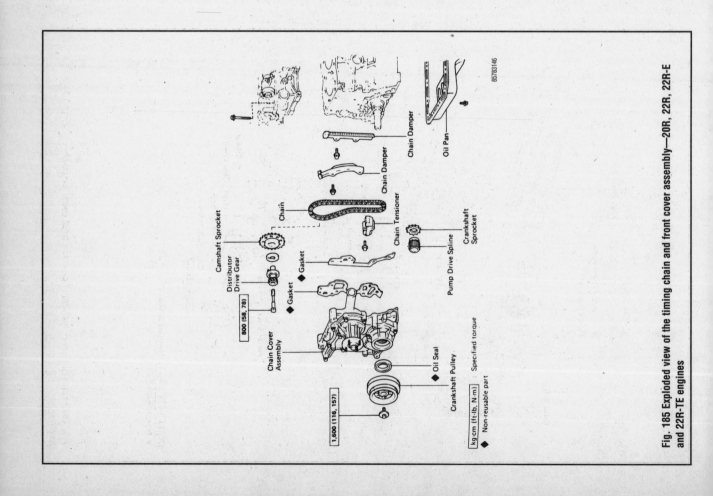

Fig. 185 Exploded view of the timing chain and front cover assembly—20R, 22R, 22R-E and 22R-TE engines

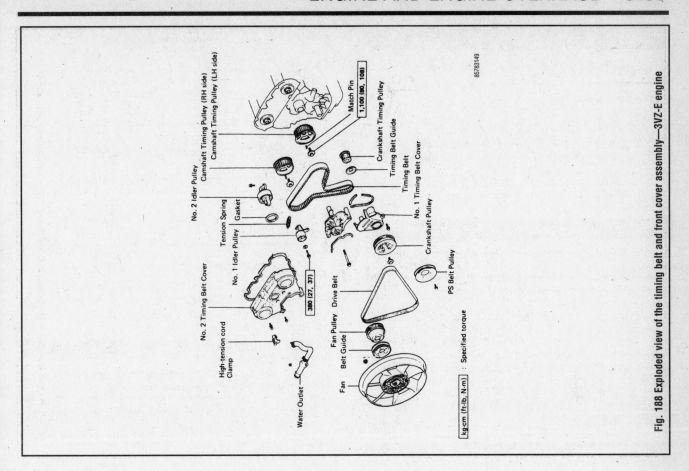

85783149

Match Pin

1,100 (80, 108)

Camshaft Timing Pulley (RH side)

Camshaft Timing Pulley (LH side)

Crankshaft Timing Pulley

Crankshaft Belt Guide

Timing Belt Cover

No. 2 Idler Pulley

Timing Belt

No. 1 Timing Belt Cover

Tension Spring

Gasket

Crankshaft Pulley

No. 1 Idler Pulley

No. 2 Timing Belt Cover

380 (27, 37)

PS Belt Pulley

High-tension cord Clamp

Fan Pulley

Drive Belt

Belt Guide

Water Outlet

Fan

kg·cm (ft-lb, N·m) : Specified torque

Fig. 188 Exploded view of the timing belt and front cover assembly—3VZ-E engine

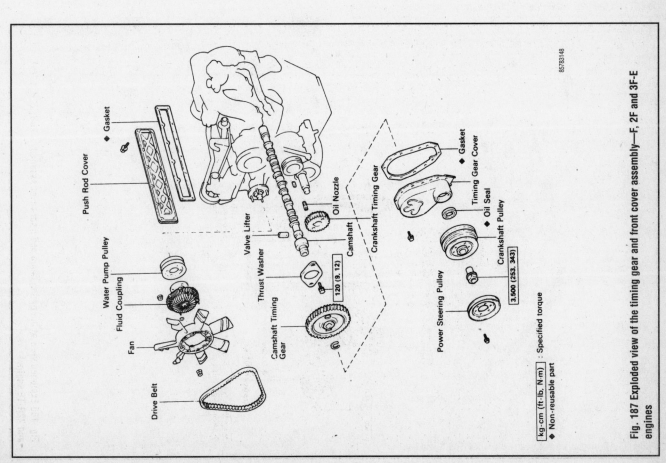

85783148

Gasket

Push Rod Cover

Oil Nozzle

Gasket

Timing Gear Cover

Water Pump Pulley

Valve Lifter

Camshaft

Oil Seal

Crankshaft Timing Gear

Fluid Coupling

Thrust Washer

120 (9, 12)

Crankshaft Pulley

Fan

Camshaft Timing Gear

3,500 (253, 343)

Power Steering Pulley

Drive Belt

kg·cm (ft-lb, N·m) : Specified torque

◆ Non-reusable part

Fig. 187 Exploded view of the timing gear and front cover assembly—F, 2F and 3F-E engines

Timing Chain and Tensioner

REMOVAL & INSTALLATION

◊ **See Figures 189 and 190**

8R-C and 18R-C Engines

1. Remove the cylinder head and timing chain cover as previously detailed.
2. Remove the timing chain (front) together with the camshaft drive sprocket.
3. Remove the crankshaft sprocket and oil pump jack shaft, complete with the pump jack shaft, complete with the pump drive chain (rear). Remove the chain vibration damper.

✳✳ CAUTION

Both timing chains are identical; tag them for proper identification during installation.

4. Inspect the chains and sprockets for wear or damage. Clean the chains with solvent.
5. Use a vernier caliper to measure the amount of stretch of both chains. Measure any 17 links while pulling the chain which is being measured taut.
6. Repeat Step 5 at two other places on each chain. Replace either of the chains if any of the 17 link measurements exceed 147mm or if the difference between the minimum and maximum readings is more than 0.20mm, on any one chain.
7. Remove the plunger and spring from one of the chain tensioners. Inspect all of the parts of the tensioner for wear of damage. Fill it with oil and assemble it if it is not defective.
8. Repeat Step 7 for the other tensioner.

✳✳ CAUTION

Do not mix the parts of the two chain tensioners together.

To install:
9. Position the No. 1 piston at TDC by having the crankshaft keyway point straight up (perpendicular to) toward the cylinder head.

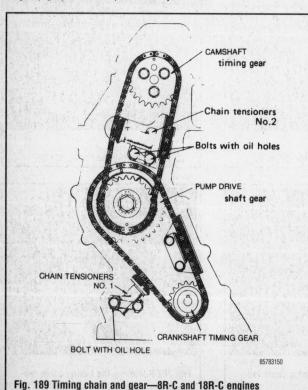

Fig. 189 Timing chain and gear—8R-C and 18R-C engines

Fig. 190 Timing chain stretch measurement—8R-C and 18R-C engines

10. Align the oil pump jack shaft, with its keyway pointing straight up as well.
11. Align the marks on the timing sprocket and the oil pump drive sprocket with each of the marks on the chain.
12. Install the chain and sprocket assembly over the keyways, while retaining alignment of the chain/sprocket timing marks.

✳✳ CAUTION

Use care not to disengage the welch plug at the rear of the oil pump driveshaft by forcing the sprocket over its keyway.

13. Install the oil pump drive chain vibration damper.
14. Install the gasket for the timing chain cover.

➡ **Use liquid sealer on the gasket before installation.**

15. Install both of the chain tensioners in their respective places, being careful not to mix them up. Tighten their securing bolts to 12–17 ft. lbs.

✳✳ CAUTION

Use care when installing the chain tensioner bolts; they have oil holes tapped in them.

16. Fit the camshaft drive sprocket over the keyway on the oil pump driveshaft. Tighten its securing nut to 58–72 ft. lbs.
17. Install the camshaft drive chain over the camshaft drive sprocket. Align the mating marks on the chain and sprocket.
18. Apply tension to the chain by tying it to the chain tensioner. This will prevent it from falling back into the timing chain cover once it is installed.
19. Install the timing chain cover and cylinder head as previously outlined.

20R, 22R, 22R-E and 22R-TE Engines

◊ **See Figures 191 thru 206**

1. Remove the cylinder head and timing chain cover as previously outlined.
2. Separate the chain from the damper, and remove the chain, complete with the camshaft sprocket.
3. Remove the crankshaft sprocket and the oil pump drive with a puller.
4. Inspect the chain for wear or damage. Replace it if necessary.
5. Inspect the chain tensioner for wear. If it measures less than 11mm, replace it.
6. Check the dampers for wear. If their measurements are below the following specifications, replace them:
   • Upper damper: 5.0mm
   • Lower damper: 4.5mm
To install:
7. Rotate the crankshaft until its key is at TDC. Slide the sprocket in place over the key.
8. Place the chain over the sprocket so that its single bright link aligns with the mark on the camshaft sprocket.
9. Install the cam sprocket so that the timing mark falls between the two bright links on the chain.

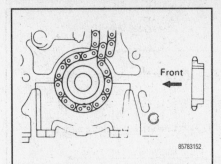

Fig. 191 Timing chain-to-crankshaft alignment—20R, 22R, 22R-E and 22R-TE engines

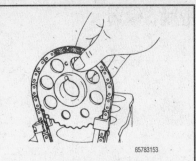

Fig. 192 Timing chain-to-camshaft alignment—20R, 22R, 22R-E and 22R-TE engines

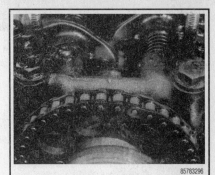

Fig. 193 Timing mark locations—22R engine

Fig. 194 Removing the distributor and fuel pump drive gear assembly retaining bolt

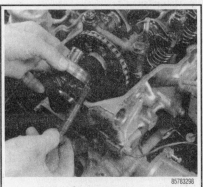

Fig. 195 Removing the distributor and fuel pump drive gear assembly

Fig. 196 Removing the timing cover front bolt

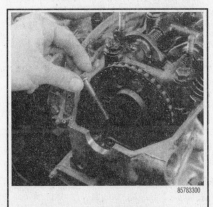

Fig. 197 Timing cover front bolt

Fig. 198 Removing the drive spline

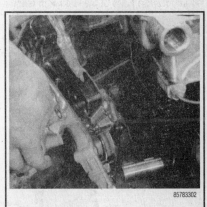

Fig. 199 Removing the timing cover

Fig. 200 Timing chain tied-to-sprocket

Fig. 201 Removing the timing chain tensioner mounting bolts

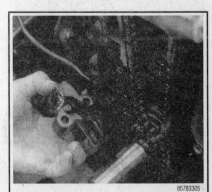

Fig. 202 Removing the timing chain tensioner assembly

Fig. 203 Removing the timing chain damper

Fig. 204 Inspecting the timing chain tensioner assembly for wear

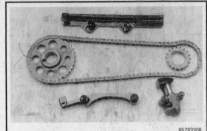

Fig. 205 View of the timing chain and related parts

Fig. 206 Cleaning the timing chain cover

10. Fit the oil pump drive spline over the crankshaft key.

11. Install the timing cover gasket on the front of the block.

12. Rotate the camshaft sprocket counterclockwise to remove the slack from the chain.

13. Install the timing chain cover and cylinder head as previously outlined.

Timing Belt

REMOVAL & INSTALLATION

1L, 2L and 2L-T Engines

▶ See Figures 207 and 208

The diesel timing belt may be removed by following Steps 1–8, then 15–18 of the Cylinder Head Removal & Installation procedure. To install the belt.

1. Temporarily install the idler pulley and check that the pulley bracket can be moved to the left and right by hand.

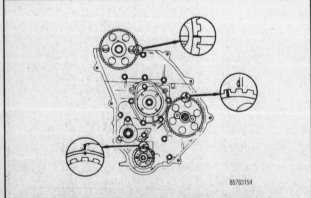

Fig. 207 Preliminary timing gear positioning–1L, 2L and 2L-T

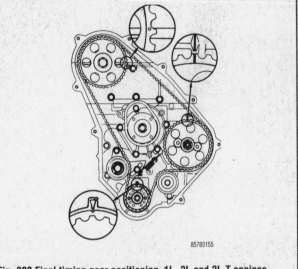

Fig. 208 Final timing gear positioning–1L, 2L and 2L-T engines

2. Align each timing gear according to the accompanying illustration. Note that the injection pump gear is positioned in a slightly retarded manner.

3. Install the timing belt without altering the position of any timing gear.

4. Install the idler pulley spring.

5. Temporarily install the crankshaft timing gear center bolt and turn the crankshaft timing gear center bolt and turn the crankshaft exactly two revolutions (clockwise). As you turn the crankshaft, you should notice movement of the idler pulley bracket.

6. Each timing gear should now align as shown in the accompanying illustration. Note that the injection pump gear marking should now be aligned with the corresponding diamond mark on the engine.

7. Tighten the idler pulley bolts to 1–15 ft. lbs.

8. Install the crankshaft belt drive pulley. Dip the pulley retaining bolt in engine oil, install the bolt and tighten to 69–75 ft. lbs. WITHOUT turning the engine.

9. Assemble the remaining engine components as detailed in their appropriate sections.

3VZ-E Engine

▶ See Figures 209, 210, 211, 212 and 213

1. Remove the timing belt covers as previously detailed.

2. Draw a directional arrow on the timing belt and matchmark the belt to each of the pulleys. Remove the timing belt guide and then remove the tension spring.

3. Loosen the idler pulley bolt and shift it left as far as it will go. Tighten the set bolt and relieve the tension on the timing belt. Remove the belt.

4. Remove the crankshaft and camshaft sprocket timing pulleys. Remove the idler pulley.

To install:

5. Align the groove in the crankshaft pulley with the key on the crankshaft and press the pulley onto the shaft.

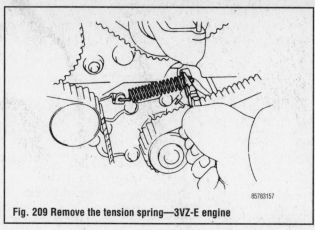

Fig. 209 Remove the tension spring—3VZ-E engine

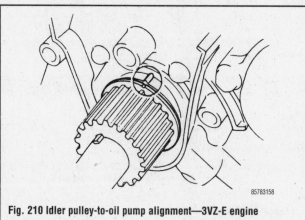

Fig. 210 Idler pulley-to-oil pump alignment—3VZ-E engine

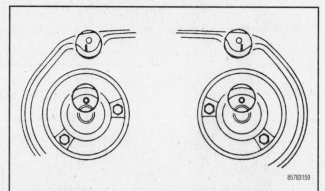

Fig. 211 Match hole alignment on the camshaft pulleys—3VZ-E engine

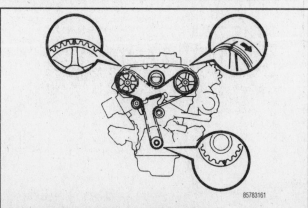

Fig. 212 Timing belt alignment—3VZ-E engine

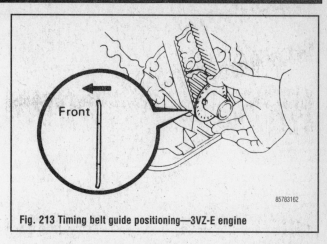

Fig. 213 Timing belt guide positioning—3VZ-E engine

6. Install the idler pulley. Align the groove on the pulley with the cavity of the oil pump and then force it to the left as far as it will go. Temporarily tighten it to 27 ft. lbs. (37 Nm).

7. Position the camshaft pulleys on the camshafts so the match holes in each pulley are in alignment with those on the No. 3 (upper rear) timing cover. Align the pulley matchmark with the one on the cover.

➡**Do not install the match pin. Check that the bolt head is not touching the pulley.**

8. Install the timing belt around the timing pulleys. If reusing the old belt, make sure the arrow and matchmarks all line up with those made earlier on the pulleys.

9. Move the idler pulley to the right as far as it will go. Install the tension spring and then loosen the pulley bolt until the pulley moves lightly with the tension spring force.

10. Check the valve timing and belt tension by turning the crankshaft two complete revolutions clockwise. Check that each pulley aligns with its timing marks. Retighten the idler pulley bolt to 27 ft. lbs. (37 Nm).

11. Remove the camshaft timing pulley bolts and align the match pin hole with the match pin hole in the camshaft. Install the pin and bolt and tighten to 80 ft. lbs. (108 Nm).

12. Remove the crankshaft timing pulley bolt and position the belt guide over the crankshaft pulley so the cupped side is out.

13. Install the timing covers as detailed previously.

Timing Gears

REMOVAL & INSTALLATION

F, 2F and 3F-E Engines

◗ **See Figures 214, 215 and 216**

➡**This procedure contains camshaft removal and installation**

1. Perform the cylinder head and timing cover removal procedures, as previously outlined.

2. Slip the oil slinger off the crankshaft.

3. Remove the camshaft thrust plate retaining bolts by working through the holes provided in the camshaft timing gear.

4. Remove the camshaft timing gear (with the camshaft attached) through the front of the cylinder block. Support the camshaft while removing it, so as not to damage its bearings or lobes.

➡**The timing gear is a press-fit and cannot be removed without removing the camshaft.**

5. Inspect the crankshaft timing gear. Replace it if it has worn or damaged teeth.

6. To remove it, remove the sliding key from the crankshaft. Withdraw the timing gear with a gear puller.

To install:

7. Use a large piece of pipe to press the timing gear onto the crankshaft. Lightly and evenly tap the end of the pipe until the gear is in its original position.

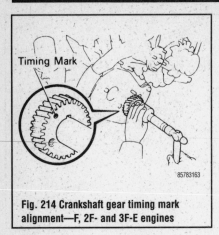

Fig. 214 Crankshaft gear timing mark alignment—F, 2F- and 3F-E engines

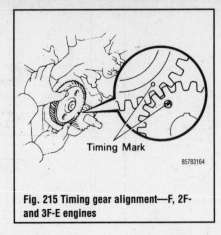

Fig. 215 Timing gear alignment—F, 2F- and 3F-E engines

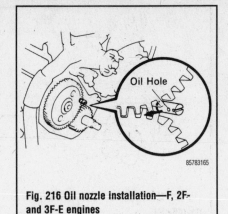

Fig. 216 Oil nozzle installation—F, 2F- and 3F-E engines

8. Apply a coat of engine oil to the camshaft journals and bearings.
9. Insert the camshaft into the block.

➡**Use care not to damage the camshaft lobes, bearings, or journals.**

10. Align the mating marks on each of the gears as illustrated.
11. Slip the camshaft into position. Tighten the camshaft thrust plate bolts to 9 ft. lbs. (12 Nm).
12. Check the gear backlash with a feeler gauge, inserted between the crankshaft and the camshaft timing gears. The backlash should be no more than 0.05-0.13mm. If it exceeds this, replace one or both of the gears, as required.
13. Check the gear runout with a dial indicator. Runout, for both gears, should not exceed 0.15mm. If it does, replace the gear.
14. Install the oil nozzle, if it was removed, by screwing it in place with a screwdriver and punching it in two places, to secure it.

➡**Be sure that the oil hole in the nozzle is pointed toward the timing gear before securing it.**

15. Install the oil slinger on the crankshaft.
16. Install the timing gear cover and cylinder head as outlined above.

Timing Gears/Pulleys And Sprockets

REMOVAL & INSTALLATION

All Except F, 2F and 3F-E Engines

To remove the sprockets or pulleys on all engines, first follow the timing chain or belt removal procedures, then follow below.
1. Remove the retaining bolt(s) for the drive sprocket you wish to remove. Do not use the timing chain or belt as a means of holding the sprocket; use a spanner that is made for the job.
2. Gently pry the sprocket or pulley off the shaft. If the sprocket or pulley is stubborn, use a gear puller. Never hammer on the sprocket or the camshaft!

3. Remove the sprocket or pulley and be careful not to lose the key if equipped.
4. On the engines with timing positioning pins, make sure the pins are properly aligned.

Camshaft And Bearings

REMOVAL & INSTALLATION

▶ **See Figures 217 thru 222**

➡**To service the camshaft on the F, 2F and 3F-E Engines, please refer to the previous Timing Gear Removal & Installation procedure.**

All Except F, 2F and 3F-E Engines

1. Perform the Cylinder Head Removal procedure (for your engine) far enough to gain access to the camshaft bearing cap bolts. If you are going to remove the head anyway, remove the cam after removing the cylinder head.
2. Prior to removing the camshaft, measure its end-play with a feeler gauge. The end-play limit is 0.25mm for gasoline engines and 0.3mm for diesels. If the end-play is beyond this, replace the head.
3. Use a 12mm wrench to remove the bearing cap bolts. Remove the caps. Keep them in order, or mark them.
4. Measure the bearing oil clearance by placing a piece of Plastigage® on each journal. Replace the caps and tighten their bolts to 13–16 ft. lbs. (18–22 Nm)
5. Remove the caps and measure each piece of Plastigage®. If the clearance is greater than 0.1mm, replace the head and cam.
6. Lift the camshaft out of the head.

To install:

7. Coat all of the camshaft bearing journals with engine oil.
8. Lay the camshaft in the head.

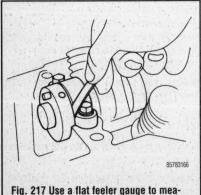

Fig. 217 Use a flat feeler gauge to measure the camshaft end-play

Fig. 218 Use a piece of Plastigage® to measure the camshaft bearing oil clearance

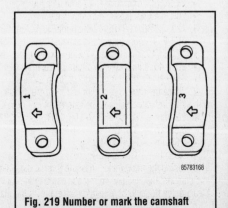

Fig. 219 Number or mark the camshaft bearing caps for latter installation

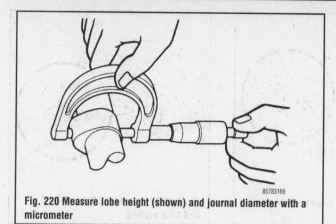

Fig. 220 Measure lobe height (shown) and journal diameter with a micrometer

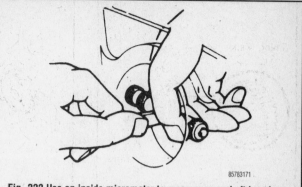

Fig. 222 Use an inside micrometer to measure camshaft housing bore diameter

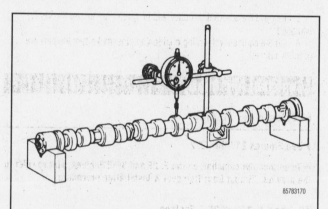

Fig. 221 Camshaft run-out must be measured with dial indicator

9. Install the bearing caps in numerical order with their arrows pointing forward (toward the front of the engine).

10. Install the cap bolts and tighten them to 13–16 ft. lbs.

11. Complete the cylinder head installation procedure as previously outlined.

CAMSHAFT INSPECTION

A dial indicator, micrometer and inside micrometer are all needed to properly measure the camshaft and camshaft housing. If these instruments are available to you, proceed; if they are not available, have the parts checked at a reputable machine shop. Camshaft specifications are included in a table in this section.

1. Using the micrometer, measure the height of each cam lobe. If a lobe height is less than the minimum specified, the lobe is worn and the cam must be replaced. Minimum intake and exhaust lobe heights are as follows:

- 8R-C: 43.7mm Intake; 43.8mm Exhaust
- 18R-C: 43.7mm Intake; 43.8mm Exhaust
- 20R: 42.6mm Intake; 42.7mm Exhaust
- 22R, 22R-E, 22R-TE: 42.6mm Intake; 42.7mm Exhaust
- 3VZ-E: 47.9mm Intake and Exhaust
- 1L, 2L: 46.8mm Intake; 47.2mm Exhaust
- 2L-T: 46.3mm Intake; 47.2mm Exhaust
- F, 2F, 3F-E: 38.4mm Intake; 38.3mm Exhaust

2. Place the cam in V-blocks and measure its run-out at the center journal with a dial indicator. Replace the cam if run-out exceeds:

- 0.20mm — 8R-C, 18R-C, 20R, 22R, 22R-E, 22R-TE
- 0.06mm — 3VZ-E
- 0.30mm — F, 2F, 3F-E
- 0.05mm — 1L, 2L, 2L-T

3. Using the micrometer, measure journal diameter, jot down the readings and compare the readings with those listed in the Camshaft Specifications chart. Measure the housing bore inside diameter with the inside micrometer, and jot the measurements down. Subtract the journal diameter measurement from the housing bore measurement. If the clearance is greater than the maximum listed under Bearing Clearance in the chart, replace the camshaft and/or the housing.

Pistons and Connecting Rods

REMOVAL & INSTALLATION

♦ See Figures 223 thru 234

➡Before removing the piston assemblies, connecting rod bearing clearance and side clearance should be checked. Refer to the Connecting Rod Inspection procedure in this section.

1. Remove the cylinder head as outlined in the appropriate preceding section.

2. Remove the oil pan and pump.

3. Position a cylinder ridge reamer into the top of the cylinder bore. Keeping the tool square, ream the ridges from the top of the bore. Clean out the ridge material with a solvent-soaked rag, or blow it out with compressed air.

4. Remove the oil strainer if it is in the way. Unbolt the connecting rod caps, after match marking each cap to its connecting rod.

5. Place pieces of rubber hose over the rod bolts, to protect the cylinder walls and crank journals from scratches. Push the connecting rod and piston up and out of the cylinder from the bottom using a wooden hammer handle.

✳✳ CAUTION

Use care not to scratch the crank journals or the cylinder walls.

6. Mark each connecting rod with the number of the cylinder from which it was removed. Number stamps are available at most hardware or auto supply stores.

To install:

7. Apply a light coating of engine oil to the pistons, rings, and outer ends of the wrist pins.

8. Examine the piston to ensure that it has been assembled with its parts positioned correctly. (See the illustrations.) Be sure that the ring gaps are not pointed toward the thrust face of the piston and that they do not overlap.

9. Place pieces of rubber hose over the connecting rod bolts, to keep the threads from damaging the crank journal and cylinder bore. Install the pistons, using a ring compressor, into the cylinder bore. Be sure that the appropriate marks on the piston are facing the front of the cylinder.

➡It is important that the pistons, rods, bearing, etc., be returned to the same cylinder bore from which they were removed.

10. Install the connecting rod bearing caps and tighten them to the torque figures given in the Torque Specifications chart.

➡Be sure that the mating marks on the connecting rods and rod bearing caps are aligned.

11. The rest of the removal procedure is performed in the reverse order of installation.

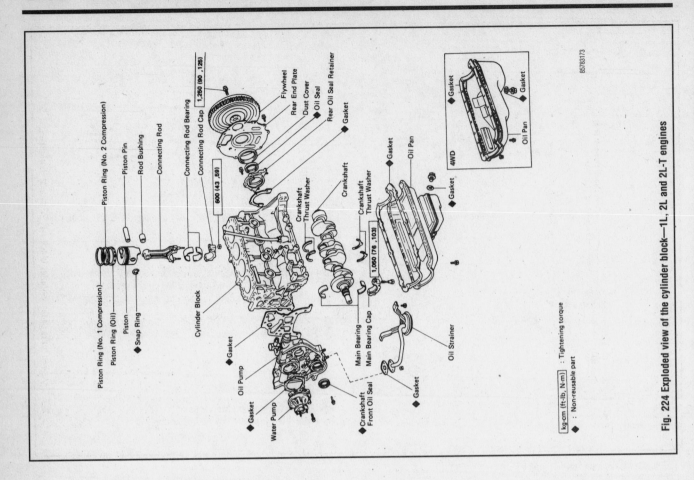

Fig. 224 Exploded view of the cylinder block—1L, 2L and 2L-T engines

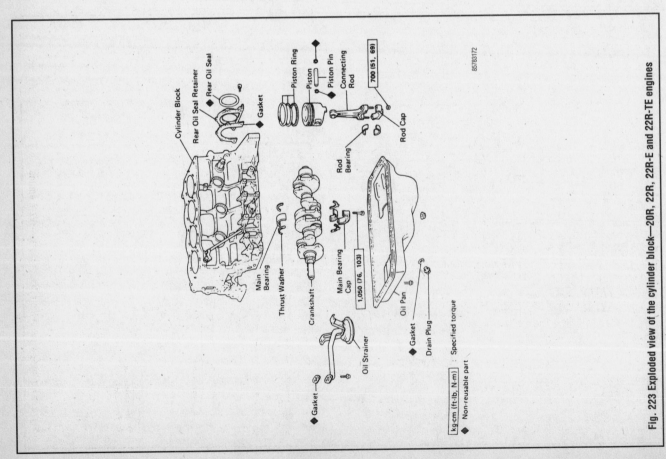

Fig. 223 Exploded view of the cylinder block—20R, 22R, 22R-E and 22R-TE engines

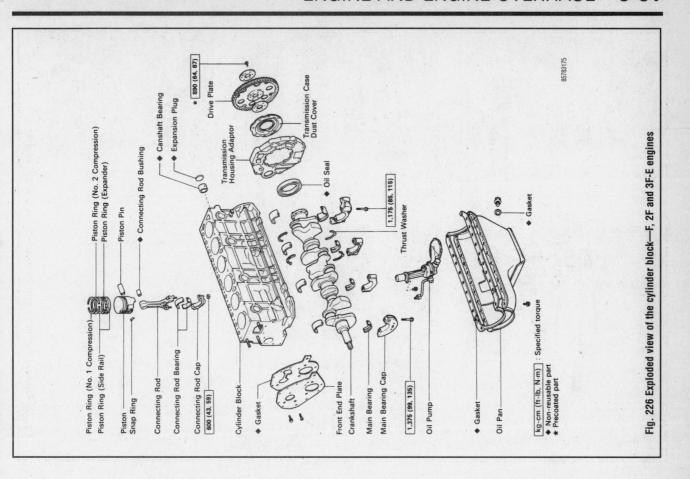

Fig. 226 Exploded view of the cylinder block—F, 2F and 3F-E engines

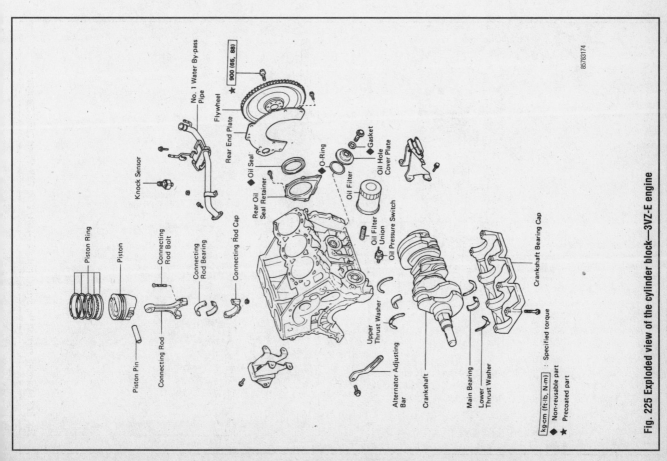

Fig. 225 Exploded view of the cylinder block—3VZ-E engine

Fig. 227 Removing the main bearing cap bolts

Fig. 228 Removing the main bearing cap

Fig. 229 Removing the connecting rod cap nuts

Fig. 230 Removing the connecting rod cap

Fig. 231 Removing the piston assembly— cylinder head must be removed

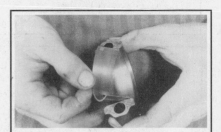

Fig. 232 Removing the bearing from the cap

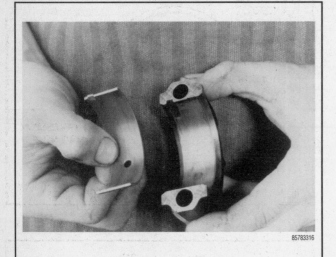

Fig. 233 View of bearing insert and cap

PISTON AND CONNECTING ROD IDENTIFICATION

▶ **See Figures 235 thru 244**

The pistons are marked with a notch in the piston head. When installed in the engine, the notch markings must be facing towards the front of the engine.

The connecting rods should be installed in the engine with the forged marks on the bearing caps and on the bottom of the rod facing toward the front of the engine also.

➡**It is advisable to number the pistons, connecting rods and bearing caps in some manner so that they can be reinstalled in the same cylinder, facing the same direction, from which they were removed.**

The piston rings must be installed with their gaps in the same position as shown in the illustrations below.

Fig. 234 Clean the oil pump strainer before installing the oil pan

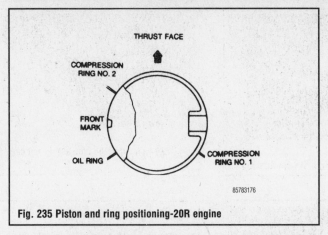

Fig. 235 Piston and ring positioning-20R engine

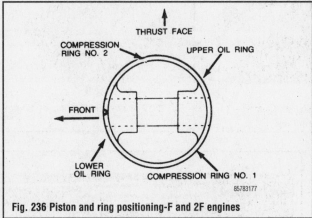

Fig. 236 Piston and ring positioning-F and 2F engines

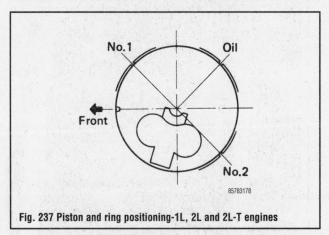

Fig. 237 Piston and ring positioning-1L, 2L and 2L-T engines

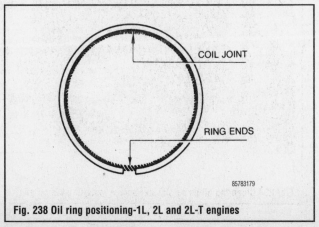

Fig. 238 Oil ring positioning-1L, 2L and 2L-T engines

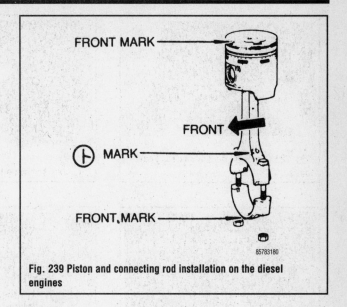

Fig. 239 Piston and connecting rod installation on the diesel engines

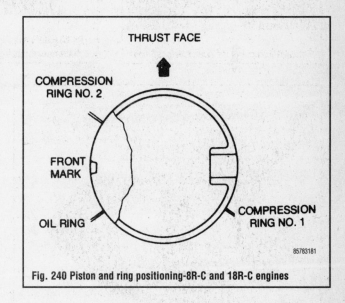

Fig. 240 Piston and ring positioning-8R-C and 18R-C engines

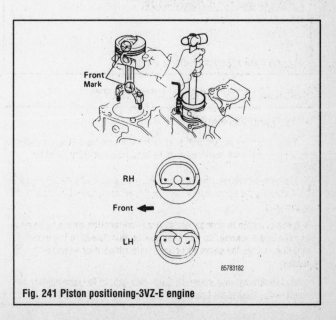

Fig. 241 Piston positioning-3VZ-E engine

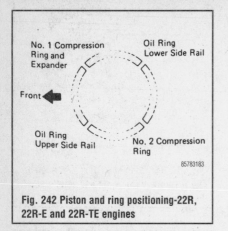

Fig. 242 Piston and ring positioning-22R, 22R-E and 22R-TE engines

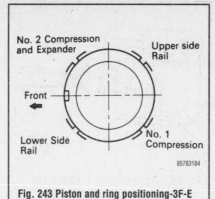

Fig. 243 Piston and ring positioning-3F-E engine

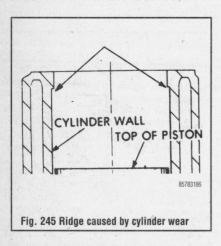

Fig. 244 Piston and ring positioning-3VZ-E engine

PISTON RING REPLACEMENT

◆ **See Figures 245 thru 250**

➡ **The cylinder walls must be de-glazed (honed) when the piston rings are replaced. De-glazing ensures proper ring seating and oil retention.**

Using a piston ring expander, remove the rings one by one. Always remove and replace the rings of each piston before going on to the next. This helps avoid mixing up the rings. When the rings have been removed from each piston, perform the end gap and piston inspection and cleaning procedure below. The rings are marked on one side, the mark denoting the up side for installation.

Install the rings using the ring expander, starting with the top compression ring and working down. Make sure the marks are facing up on each ring. Position the rings so that the ring and gaps are set as in the illustrations. Never align the end gaps!

WRIST PIN REMOVAL & INSTALLATION

◆ **See Figures 251 thru 259**

Wrist pin and/or connecting rod small-end bushing wear can be checked by rocking the piston at a right angle to the wrist pin by hand. If more than very slight movement is felt, the pin and/or rod busing must be replaced.

The pistons on the engines covered here must be heated in hot water to expand them before the wrist pins can be removed and installed. The four cylinder pistons must be heated to 176°F (80°C), and all six cylinder pistons must be heated to 140°F (60°C). This job can be performed at a machine shop if the idea of boiling pistons in the kitchen doesn't appeal to you. If you decide to do it, however, remember that each piston, pin and connecting rod assembly is a matched set and must be kept together until reassembly.

1. Using needlenose or snapring pliers, remove the snaprings from the piston.

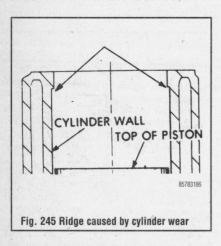

Fig. 245 Ridge caused by cylinder wear

Fig. 246 Removing the ridge with ridge reamer

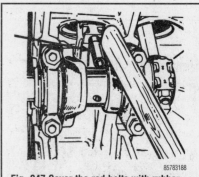

Fig. 247 Cover the rod bolts with rubber tubing before removing the piston and rod assemblies

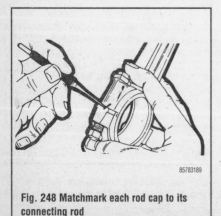

Fig. 248 Matchmark each rod cap to its connecting rod

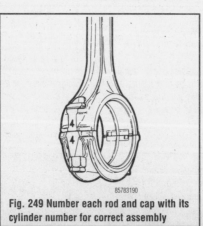

Fig. 249 Number each rod and cap with its cylinder number for correct assembly

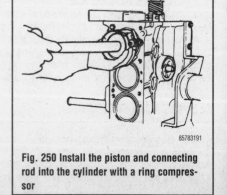

Fig. 250 Install the piston and connecting rod into the cylinder with a ring compressor

Fig. 251 Remove and install the piston rings with a ring expander

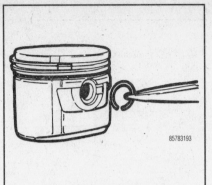

Fig. 252 Use needlenose or snapring pliers to remove the piston pin snaprings

Fig. 253 Rock the piston at a right angle to the wrist pin to check pin and small end bushing wear

Fig. 254 When fully heated, the wrist pin should be able to be pushed out by hand

Fig. 255 Clean the ring grooves with this tool or the edge of an old ring

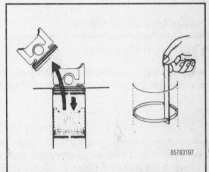

Fig. 256 To check ring end gap, push the ring to the bottom of its travel and check gap with feeler gauge

Fig. 257 Checking the piston ring-to-ring groove side clearance using the ring and a feeler gauge

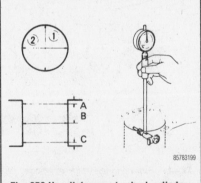

Fig. 258 Use dial gauge to check cylinder bore and piston clearance

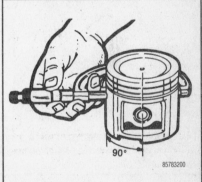

Fig. 259 Check piston diameter at these points

2. Heat the piston(s) in hot water (as noted above depending on engine).

3. Using a plastic-faced hammer and driver, lightly tap the wrist pin out of the piston. Remove the piston from the connecting rod.

4. Assembly is in the opposite order of disassembly. The piston must again be heated to install the wrist pin and rod; it should be able to be pushed into place with your thumb when heated. When assembling, make sure the marks on the piston and connecting rod are aligned on the same side as shown.

CLEANING AND INSPECTION

Clean the piston after removing the rings, by first scraping any carbon from the piston top. Do not scratch the piston in any way during cleaning. Use a broken piston ring or ring cleaning tool to clean out the ring grooves. Clean the entire piston with solvent and a brush (NOT a wire brush).

Once the piston is thoroughly cleaned, insert the side of a good piston ring (both No. 1 and No. 2 compression on each piston) into its respective groove. Using a feeler gauge, measure the clearance between the ring and its groove. If clearance is greater than the maximum listed under Ring Side Clearance in the Piston and Ring chart, replace the ring(s) and if necessary, the piston.

To check ring end-gap, insert a compression ring into the cylinder. Lightly oil the cylinder bore and push the ring down into the cylinder with a piston, to the bottom of its travel. Measure the ring end-gap with a feeler gauge. If the gap is not within specification, replace the ring; DO NOT file the ring ends.

CYLINDER BORE INSPECTION

Place a rag over the crankshaft journals. Wipe out each cylinder with a clean, solvent-soaked rag. Visually inspect the cylinder bores for roughness, scoring or scuffing; also check the bores by feel. Measure the cylinder bore diameter with an inside micrometer, or a telescope gauge and micrometer. Measure the bore at points parallel and perpendicular to the engine centerline at the top (below the ridge) and bottom of the bore. Subtract the bottom measurements from the top to determine cylinder taper.

Measure the piston diameter with a micrometer; since this micrometer may not be part of your tool kit as it is necessarily large, you have to have the pistons miked at a machine shop. Take the measurements at right angles to the wrist pin center line, about an inch down the piston skirt from the top. Compare this measurement to the bore diameter of each cylinder. The difference is the piston clearance. If the clearance is greater than that specified in the Piston and Ring Specifications chart, have the cylinders honed or rebored and replace the pistons with an oversize set. Piston clearance can also be checked by inverting a piston into a oiled cylinder, and sliding in a feeler gauge between the two.

CONNECTING ROD INSPECTION AND BEARING REPLACEMENT

♦ See Figures 260, 261 and 262

Connecting rod side clearance and big-end bearing inspection and replacement should be performed while the rods are still installed in the engine. Determine the clearance between the connecting rod sides and the crankshaft using a feeler gauge. If clearance is below the minimum tolerance, check with a machinist about machining the rod to provide adequate clearance. If clearance is excessive, substitute an unworn rod and recheck; if clearance is still outside specifications, the crankshaft must be welded and reground, or replaced.

To check connecting rod big-end bearing clearances, remove the rod bearing caps one at a time. Using a clean, dry shop rag, thoroughly clean all oil from the crank journal and bearing insert in the cap.

➡ The Plastigage® gauging material you will be using to check clearances which is soluble in oil; therefore any oil on the journal or bearing could result in an incorrect reading.

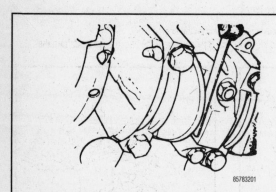

Fig. 260 Checking connecting rod side clearance—make sure feeler gauge is between shoulder of the crankshaft journal and side of rod

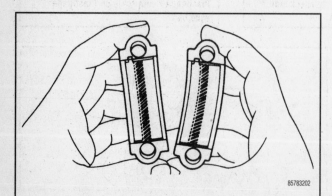

Fig. 261 Inspect the rod bearings for scuffing and other wear—also checking the crankshaft journal

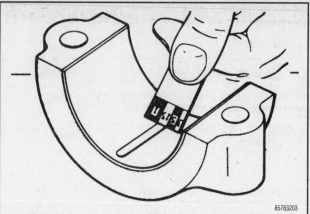

Fig. 262 Measure Plastigage® width by using scale on the envelope

Lay a strip of Plastigage® along the full length of the bearing insert (along the crank journal if the engine is out of the truck and inverted). Reinstall the cap and torque to specifications listed in the Torque Specifications chart.

Remove the rod cap and determine the bearing clearance by comparing the width of the now flattened Plastigage® to the scale on the Plastigage® envelope. Journal taper is determined by comparing the width of the Plastigage® strip near its ends. Rotate the crankshaft 90° and retest, to determine journal eccentricity.

➡ Do not rotate the crankshaft with the Plastigage® installed.

If the bearing insert and crank journal appear intact and are within tolerances, no further service is required and the bearing caps can be reinstalled (remove Plastigage® before installation). If clearances are not within tolerances, the bearing inserts in both the connecting rod and rod cap must be replaced with undersize inserts, and/or the crankshaft must be reground. To install the bearing insert halves, press them into the bearing caps and connecting rods. Make sure the tab in each insert fits into the notch in each rod and cap. Lube the face of each insert with engine oil prior to installing each rod into the engine.

The connecting rods can be further inspected when they are removed form the engine and separated from their pistons. Rod alignment (straightness and squareness) must be checked by a machinist, as the rod must be set in a special fixture. Many machine shops also perform a Magnafluxing service, which is a process that shows up any tiny cracks that you may be unable to see.

Rear Main Oil Seal

REPLACEMENT

➡ This procedure is a general service procedure—modify repair steps if necessary.

1. Remove the transmission as detailed in Section 7.
2. Remove the clutch cover assembly and flywheel or flexplate. See Section 7 also.
3. Remove the oil seal retaining plate, complete with the oil seal.
4. Use a small pry bar to pry the old seal from the retaining plate. Be careful not to damage the plate.
5. Install the new seal, carefully, by using a block of wood to drift it into place.

❋❋ CAUTION

Do not damage the seal; a leak will result.

6. Lubricate the lips of the seal with multi-purpose grease. Install retaining plate.
7. Install the clutch assembly and flywheel or flexplate.

Crankshaft and Main Bearings

REMOVAL & INSTALLATION

▶ **See Figures 263, 264 and 265**

➡ **Before removing the crankshaft, check main bearing clearances as described under Main Bearing Clearance Check below.**

1. Remove the piston and connecting rod assemblies following the procedure in this section.

2. Check crankshaft thrust clearance (end play) before removing the crank from the block. Using a pry bar, pry the crankshaft the extent of its travel forward, and measure thrust clearance at the center main bearing (No. 4 bearing on 6 cylinder engines, No. 3 on 4 cylinder engines) with a feeler gauge. Pry the crankshaft the extent of its rearward travel, and measure the other side of the bearing. If clearance is greater than that specified, the thrust washers must be replaced (see main bearing installation, below).

3. Using a punch, mark the corresponding main bearing caps and saddles according to position: one punch on the front main cap and saddle, two on the second, three on the third, etc. This ensures correct reassembly.

4. Remove the main bearing caps after they have been marked.

5. Remove the crankshaft form the block.

6. Follow the crankshaft inspection, main bearing clearance checking and replacement procedures below before reinstalling the crankshaft.

INSPECTION

Crankshaft inspection and servicing should be handled exclusively by a reputable machinist, as most of the necessary procedures require a dial indicator and fixing jig, a large micrometer, and machine tools such as a crankshaft grinder. While at the machine shop, the crankshaft should be thoroughly cleaned (especially the oil passages). Magnafluxed (to check for cracks) and the following checks made: main journal diameter, crank pin (connecting rod journal) diameter, taper and out-of-round, and run-out. Wear, beyond specification limits, in any of these areas means the crankshaft must be reground or replaced.

MAIN BEARING CLEARANCE CHECK

Checking main bearing clearances is done in the same manner as checking connecting rod big-end clearances.

1. With the crankshaft installed, remove the main bearing cap. Clean all oil form the bearing insert in the cap and from the crankshaft journal, as the Plastigage® material is oil-soluble.

2. Lay a strip of Plastigage® along the full width of the bearing cap (or along the width of the crank journal if the engine is out of the truck and inverted).

3. Install the bearing cap and torque to specification.

➡ **Do not rotate the crankshaft with the Plastigage® installed.**

4. Remove the bearing cap and determine bearing clearance by comparing the width of the now-flattened Plastigage® with the scale on the Plastigage® envelope. Journal taper is determined by comparing the width of the Plastigage® strip near its ends. Rotate the crankshaft 90° and retest, to determine journal eccentricity.

5. Repeat the above for the remaining bearings. If the bearing journal and insert appear in good shape (with not unusual wear visible) and are within tolerances, no further main bearing service is required. If unusual wear is evident and/or the clearances are outside specifications, the bearings must be replaced and the cause of their wear found.

MAIN BEARING REPLACEMENT

▶ **See Figures 266 thru 272**

Main bearings can be replaced with the crankshaft both in the engine (with the engine still in the truck) and out of the engine (with the engine on a work stand or bench). Both procedures are covered here. The main bearings must be replaced if the crankshaft has been reground; the replacement bearing being available in various undersize increments from most auto parts jobbers or your local Toyota dealer.

Engine Out of Truck

1. Remove the crankshaft from the engine block.

2. Remove the main bearing inserts from the bearing caps and from the

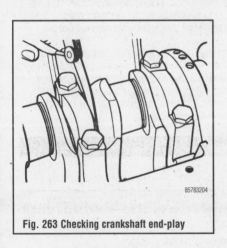

Fig. 263 Checking crankshaft end-play

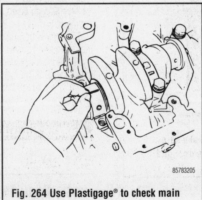
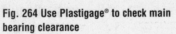

Fig. 264 Use Plastigage® to check main bearing clearance

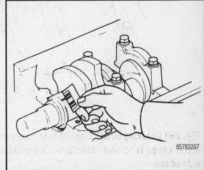

Fig. 265 Compare width of now flattened Plastigage® with scale on Plastigage® envelope

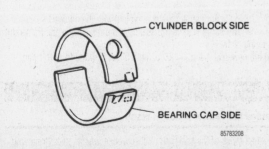

CYLINDER BLOCK SIDE

BEARING CAP SIDE

Fig. 266 Bearing insert halves must be installed with oil notches and holes properly positioned

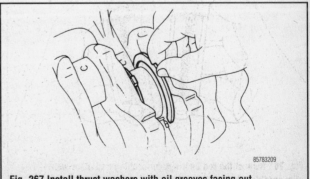

Fig. 267 Install thrust washers with oil grooves facing out

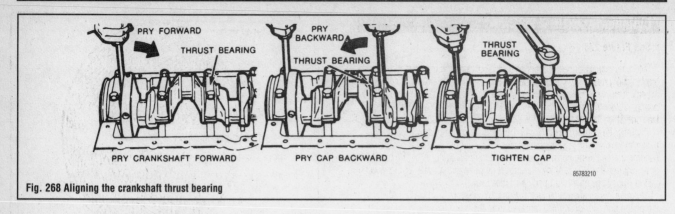

Fig. 268 Aligning the crankshaft thrust bearing

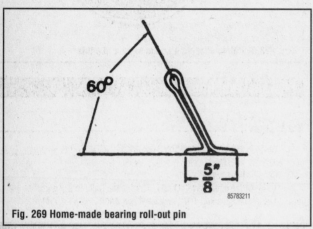

Fig. 269 Home-made bearing roll-out pin

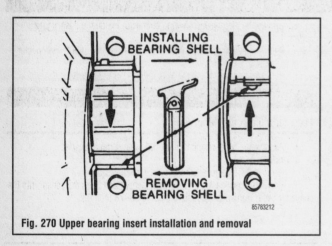

Fig. 270 Upper bearing insert installation and removal

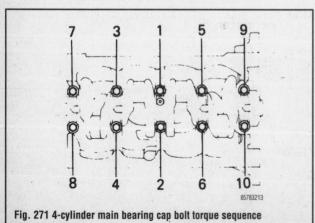

Fig. 271 4-cylinder main bearing cap bolt torque sequence

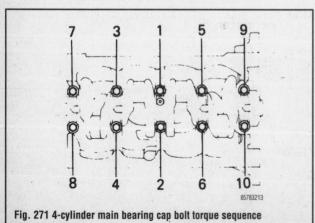

Fig. 272 6-cylinder main bearing cap bolt torque sequence

main bearing saddles. Remove the thrust washers from the No. 3 (4 cylinder) or No. 4 (6 cylinder) crank journal.

3. Thoroughly clean the saddles, bearing caps, and crankshaft.

4. Make sure the crankshaft has been fully checked and is ready for reassembly. Place the upper main bearings in the block saddles so that the oil grooves and/or oil holes are correctly aligned with their corresponding grooves or holes in the saddles.

5. Install the thrust washers on the center main bearing, with the oil grooves facing out.

6. Lubricate the faces of all bearings with clean engine oil, and place the crankshaft in the block.

7. Install the main bearing caps in numbered order with the arrows or any other orientation marks facing forward. Torque all bolts except the center cap bolts in sequence in two or three passes to the specified torque. Rotate the crankshaft after each pass to ensure even tightness.

8. Align the thrust bearing by prying the crankshaft the extent of its axial travel several times with a pry bar. On last movement hold the crankshaft toward the front of the engine and torque the thrust bearing cap to specifications. Measure the crankshaft thrust clearance (end play) as previously described in this section. If clearance is outside specifications (too sloppy), install a new set of oversize thrust washers and check clearance again.

Engine And Crankshaft Installed

1. Remove the main bearing caps and keep them in order.

2. Make a bearing roll-out pin from a cotter pin as shown.

3. Carefully roll out the old inserts from the upper side of the crankshaft journal, noting the positions of the oil grooves and/or oil holes so the new inserts can be correctly installed.

4. Roll each new insert into its saddle after lightly oiling the crankshaft-side face of each. Make sure the notches and/or oil holes are correctly positioned.

5. Replace the bearing inserts in the caps with new inserts. Oil the face of each, and install the caps in numbered order with the arrows or other orientation marks facing forward. Torque the bolts to the specified torque in two or three passes in the sequence shown.

Cylinder Block

♦ See Figure 273

Most inspection and service work on the cylinder block should be handled by a machinist or professional engine rebuilding shop. Included in this work are bearing alignment checks, line boring, deck resurfacing, hot-tanking and cylinder honing or boring. A block that has been checked and properly serviced will last much longer than one which has not had the proper attention when the opportunity was there for it.

Cylinder de-glazing (honing) can, however, be performed by the owner/mechanic who is careful and takes his or her time. The cylinder bores become glazed during normal operation as the rings continually ride up and down against them. This shiny glaze must be removed in order for a new set of piston rings to be able to properly seat themselves.

Cylinder hones are available at most auto tool stores and parts jobbers. With the piston and rod assemblies removed from the block, cover the crankshaft completely with a rag or cover to keep grit from the hone and cylinder material off of it. Chuck a hone into a variable speed power drill (preferable here to a constant speed drill), and insert it into the cylinder.

➡ Make sure the drill and hone are kept square to the cylinder bore throughout the entire honing operation.

Start the hone and move it up and down in the cylinder at a rate which will produce approximately a 60° cross-hatch pattern. DO NOT extend the hone below the cylinder bore! After developing the pattern, remove the hone and recheck piston fit. Wash the cylinders with a detergent and water solution to remove the hone and cylinder grit. Wipe the bores out several times with a clean rag soaked in clean engine oil. Remove the cover from the crankshaft, and check closely to see that no grit has found its way onto the crankshaft.

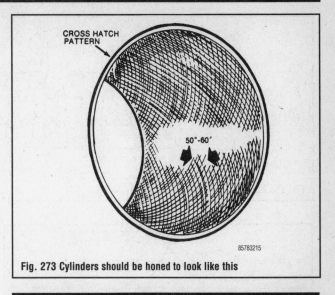

Fig. 273 Cylinders should be honed to look like this

Flywheel and Ring Gear

REMOVAL & INSTALLATION

1. Remove the transmission, if the engine is installed in the truck.
2. Remove the clutch assembly, if equipped.
3. Remove the flywheel.
4. To install, use new flywheel bolts. Torque the bolts in a criss-cross pattern to the torque specified in the chart in this section.

EXHAUST SYSTEM

※※ CAUTION

When working on the exhaust system, ALWAYS wear protective goggles! NEVER work on a hot exhaust system.

Catalytic Converter

REMOVAL & INSTALLATION

♦ See Figures 274, 275 and 276

1980–84

1. Raise and support the truck on jackstands.
2. Remove the heat shield if equipped.

3. Unplug the thermosensor wiring connector inside the passenger compartment.
4. Remove the wiring grommet from the floor pan and pull the connector from the interior.
5. Remove the four bolts at the front and rear of the converter.

※※ CAUTION

Make sure the converter is cool!

6. Remove the rubber hanger rings and remove the converter.
To install:
7. Remove the thermosensor from the converter case.
8. Position a new gasket on the thermosensor and push the sensor into the converter case. Tighten the mounting bolts to 53–78 inch lbs.

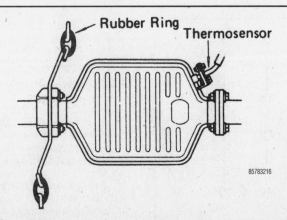

Fig. 274 Converter mounting—1980–84

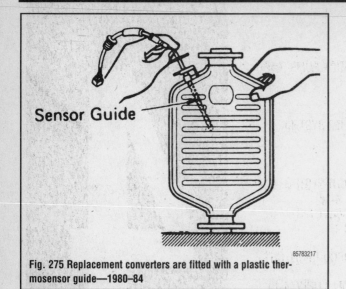

Fig. 275 Replacement converters are fitted with a plastic thermosensor guide—1980–84

➡Replacement converters are fitted with a plastic thermosensor guide. Insert the thermosensor into this guide.

9. Using new gaskets, connect the converter to the exhaust pipes. Tighten the bolts to 26–36 ft. lbs.

10. Stretch the rubber rings over the hangers and then plug in the thermosensor connector.

➡After installation, make sure that the sensor wire is not bent or interfering with other components.

1985–88

1. Raise and support the truck on jackstands.
2. Remove the heat shield if equipped.
3. Remove the four bolts at the front and rear of the converter.

✳✳ CAUTION

Make sure the converter is cool!

4. Remove the converter and gaskets.
5. Using new gaskets, connect the converter to the exhaust pipes. Tighten the bolts to 26–36 ft. lbs.

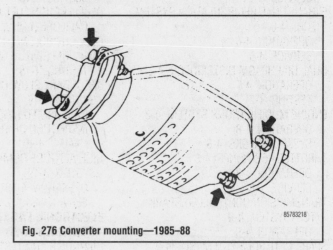

Fig. 276 Converter mounting—1985–88

4

DRIVEABILITY AND EMISSIONS CONTROLS

EMISSION CONTROLS

There are three sources of automotive pollutants; crankcase fumes, exhaust gases, and gasoline evaporation. The pollutants formed from these substances fall into three categories: unburned hydrocarbons (HC), carbon monoxide (C), and oxides of nitrogen (NOx). The equipment used to limit these pollutants is called emission control equipment.

Due to varying state, federal, and provincial regulations, specific emission control equipment have been devised for each. The U.S. emission equipment is divided into two categories: California and 49 State (Federal). In this section, the term "California" applies only to trucks originally built to be sold in California. California emissions equipment is generally not shared with equipment installed on trucks built to be sold in the other 49 States. Models built to be sold in Canada also have specific emissions equipment, although in most years 49 State and Canadian equipment is the same.

The following abbreviations are used in this section:
- AAP: Auxiliary Acceleration Pump
- ABV: Air By-Pass Valve
- AI: Air Injection
- ASV: Air Switching Valve
- BVSV: Bi-Metal Vacuum Switching Valve
- C: Carbon
- CB: Choke Breaker
- CCo: Catalytic Converter
- CO: Carbon Monoxide
- CO2: Carbon Dioxide
- DP: Dashpot
- EACV: Electronic Air Control Valve
- EGR: Exhaust Gas Recirculation
- EVAP: Fuel Evaporative Emission Control
- H: Hydrogen
- HAC: High Altitude Compensation
- HAI: Hot Air Intake
- HC: Hydrocarbon
- HIC: Hot Idle Compensation
- H2O: Water
- MC: Mixture Control
- N: Nitrogen
- NOx: Nitrogen Oxides
- PCV: Positive Crankcase Ventilation
- SC: Spark Control
- TP: Throttle Positioner
- TVSV: Thermostatic Vacuum Transmitting Valve
- VCV: Vacuum Control Valve
- VSV: Vacuum Switching Valve
- VTV: Vacuum Transmitting Valve

Positive Crankcase Ventilation (PCV) System

OPERATION

▶ See Figure 1

A closed, positive crankcase ventilation system is employed on all Toyota trucks. This system cycles incompletely burned fuel which works its way past the piston rings back into the intake manifold for reburning with the air/fuel mixture. The oil filler cap is sealed and the air is drawn from the top of the crankcase into the intake manifold through a valve with a variable orifice.

This valve (commonly known as the PCV valve) regulates the flow of air into the manifold according to the amount of manifold vacuum. When the throttle plates are open fairly wide, the valve opens to maximize the flow. However, at idle speed, when manifold vacuum is at a maximum, the PCV valve throttles the flow in order not to unnecessarily affect the small volume of mixture passing into the engine.

During most driving conditions, manifold vacuum is high and all of the vapor from the crankcase, plus a small amount of excess air, is drawn into the manifold via the PCV valve. However, at full throttle, the increase in the volume of blow-by and the decrease in manifold vacuum make the flow via the PCV valve inadequate. Under these conditions, excess vapors are drawn into the air cleaner and pass into the engine.

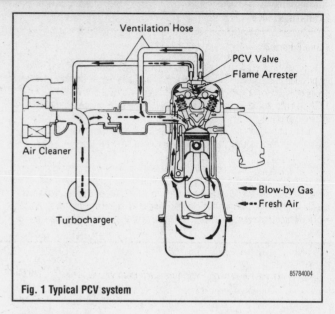

Fig. 1 Typical PCV system

TESTING

▶ See Figure 2

Check the PCV system hoses and connections, to ensure that there are no leaks; then replace or tighten, as necessary.

To check the valve, remove it and blow through both of its ends. When blowing form the side which goes toward the intake manifold, very little air should pass through it. When blowing from the crankcase (valve cover) side, air should pass through freely.

Replace the valve with a new one, if the valve fails to function as outlined.

➡**Do not attempt to clean or adjust the valve; replace it with a new one.**

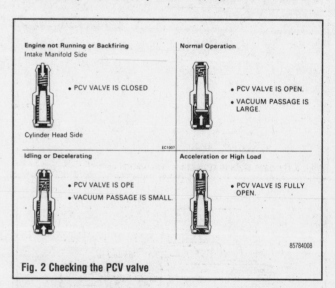

Fig. 2 Checking the PCV valve

REMOVAL & INSTALLATION

1. Remove the PCV valve from the cylinder head cover on all engines. Remove the hose from the valve.
2. Remove the valve from the manifold-to-crankcase hose.
3. Check the valve for proper operation and then insert it into the manifold-to-crankcase line.
4. Insert the other end of the PCV valve into the cylinder head cover.

Evaporative Emission Control System

OPERATION

▶ **See Figure 3**

To prevent hydrocarbon emissions from entering the atmosphere due to the evaporation of fuel in the tank and carburetor, Toyota Pick-Up trucks are equipped with evaporative emission control (EEC) systems. Between 1970 and 1971 the case storage system was used. Later models use the charcoal canister storage system.

The major components of the case storage system are a vacuum switching valve, a fuel vapor storage case, an air filter, a thermal expansion tank, and a special fuel tank.

When the vehicle is stopped or the engine is running at low speed, the vacuum switching valve is closed; fuel vapor travels only as far as the case where it is stored. At cruising speed the vacuum switching valve opens and the stored vapors are drawn into the intake manifold along with fresh air drawn through the air filter.

The charcoal storage system functions in a similar manner except that the vapors are stored in a canister filled with activated charcoal. The air filter is an integral part of the charcoal canister. This system employs:

1. A sealed fuel filler cap with a safety valve.
2. An activated charcoal canister with check valves.
3. A vacuum control valve (VCV)—Land Cruiser.
4. A vacuum switching valve (VSV)—carbureted trucks only.
5. A thermostatic vacuum switching valve (TVSV)—1980-82 only.
6. A bi-metal vacuum switching valve (BVSV)—Pick-Ups (3VZ-E only) and 1988 Land Cruiser.
7. An outer vent control valve.

SERVICE

Checking the Filler Cap

▶ **See Figures 4 and 5**

Check that the filler cap seals effectively. Remove the filler cap and pull the safety valve (check valve on later models) outward to check for smooth operation. Replace the filler cap if the seal (gasket) is defective or if it is not operating properly.

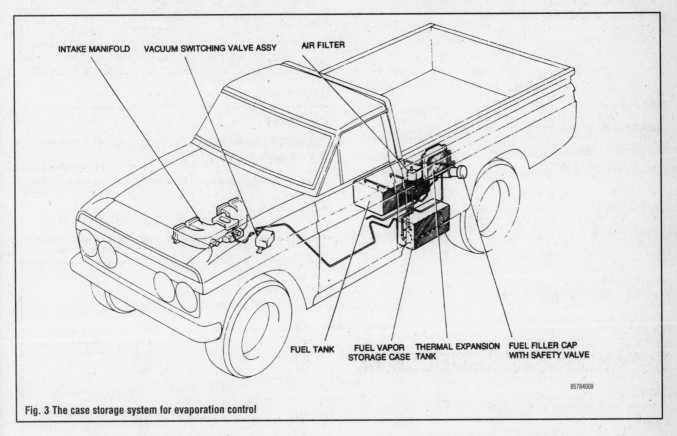

INTAKE MANIFOLD   VACUUM SWITCHING VALVE ASSY   AIR FILTER

FUEL TANK   FUEL VAPOR STORAGE CASE   THERMAL EXPANSION TANK   FUEL FILLER CAP WITH SAFETY VALVE

85784009

Fig. 3 The case storage system for evaporation control

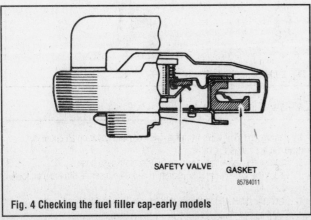

SAFETY VALVE   GASKET

85784011

Fig. 4 Checking the fuel filler cap-early models

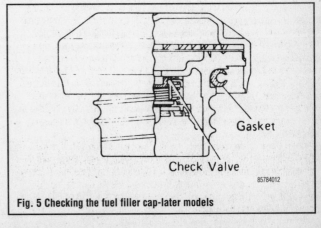

Gasket

Check Valve

85784012

Fig. 5 Checking the fuel filler cap-later models

Checking the Charcoal Canister and Check Valves

Remove the charcoal canister from the engine compartment and visually inspect it for cracks or other damage.

Check for stuck check valves. All Pick-Ups from 1970-78 have one check valve in the line between the fuel tank and the charcoal canister. It is located in the rear area. To check:

1. Remove the check valve from the line.

➡ Mark which end goes toward the fuel tank and which end goes toward the charcoal canister.

2. Blow into the fuel tank end. A slight resistance should be felt at first.
3. Blow through the other end. No resistance should be felt at all.
4. If your results differ from those above, the check valve will require replacement.

1970-87 Land Cruisers have one check valve located in the canister.

1979-88 Pick-Ups with a carburetor and 1988 Land Cruisers have two check valves, both are located in the charcoal canister.

1983-88 Pick-Ups with fuel injection have three check valves in the canister.

To check:

5. Using low pressure compressed air, blow into the tank pipe. The air should flow from the other pipes without resistance.
6. If the air flow is incorrect, the check valve will require replacement

Before installing the canister, clean the filter. Blow compressed air into the purge pipe while keeping the other blocked with your fingers.

➡ Do not attempt to wash the charcoal canister. While cleaning the canister, under no circumstances should any activated charcoal be removed.

Checking the VCV

LAND CRUISER ONLY

▶ See Figures 6 and 7

1. Locate the VCV by the intake air chamber and remove all the vacuum lines.

2. Apply vacuum to pipe **S**, blow air into pipe **Y** and check that air comes out of pipe **Z**.
3. Stop the vacuum and blow air into pipe **Y** again and check that air does not come out of pipe **Z**.
4. If the valve is not operating properly, it will require replacement.

Checking the VSV

CARBURETED TRUCKS ONLY

▶ See Figures 8 and 9

1. Disconnect the VSV electrical connector.
2. Connect the VSV terminals to the battery terminals.
3. Blow into the pipe and check that the valve is open.
4. Disconnect the positive battery terminal.
5. Blow into the pipe and check that the valve is closed.
6. If the valve is not operating properly it will require replacement.

Checking the TVSV

1980–82 ONLY

▶ See Figures 10 and 11

1. Locate the TVSV on the intake manifold and remove all vacuum lines.
2. Blow into the middle pipe and check that the air comes out of the top pipe.
3. Warm up the engine until it reaches normal operating temperature and then blow into the middle pipe again. The air should come out of the bottom pipe.
4. If the valve is not operating properly it will require replacement.

Checking the BVSV

PICK-UP WITH 3VZ-E ENGINE

▶ See Figures 12 and 13

1. Drain the engine coolant and remove the BVSV from the water outlet on the engine block.

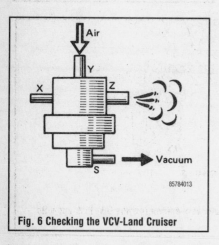

Fig. 6 Checking the VCV-Land Cruiser

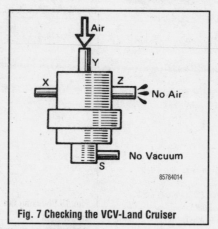

Fig. 7 Checking the VCV-Land Cruiser

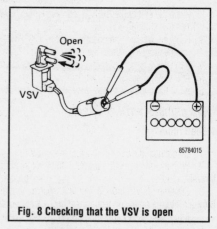

Fig. 8 Checking that the VSV is open

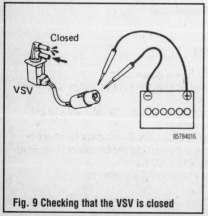

Fig. 9 Checking that the VSV is closed

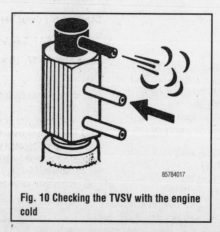

Fig. 10 Checking the TVSV with the engine cold

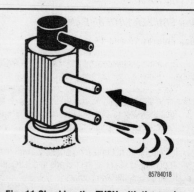

Fig. 11 Checking the TVSV with the engine warm

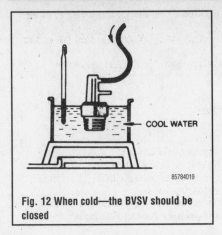

Fig. 12 When cold—the BVSV should be closed

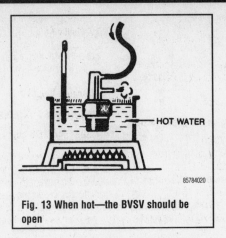

Fig. 13 When hot—the BVSV should be open

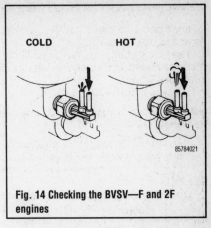

Fig. 14 Checking the BVSV—F and 2F engines

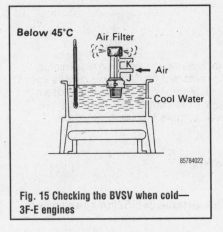

Fig. 15 Checking the BVSV when cold—3F-E engines

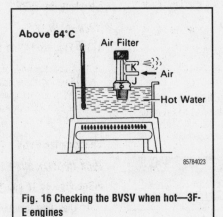

Fig. 16 Checking the BVSV when hot—3F-E engines

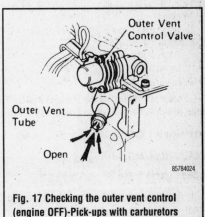

Fig. 17 Checking the outer vent control (engine OFF)-Pick-ups with carburetors

2. Place the end of the BVSV in cool water and blow into the top connection. The valve should be closed.

3. Heat the water to a temperature above 129°F (54°C) and again blow into the top connection. This time, the valve should be open.

4. If the valve is not operating properly it will require replacement.

5. Apply liquid sealer to the threads and reinstall the BVSV.

6. Refill the engine with coolant.

LAND CRUISER WITH 2F ENGINE

▶ See Figure 14

1. Disconnect the vacuum lines at the BVSV.

2. With the engine cold, blow air into the outer connection and check that the valve closes.

3. Start the engine and run it until it reaches normal operating temperature. Blow air into the outer connection and check that the valve opens.

4. If the valve is not operating properly it will require replacement.

5. Replace the vacuum lines.

LAND CRUISER WITH 3F-E ENGINE

▶ See Figures 15 and 16

1. Drain the engine coolant and remove the BVSV from the water outlet on the engine block.

2. Place the end of the BVSV in cool water and blow into the bottom connection. The air should come out of the air filter on top of the valve.

3. Heat the water to a temperature above 147°F (64°C) and again blow into the bottom connection. This time, the air should come out of the upper pipe and not the filter.

4. If the valve is not operating properly it will require replacement.

5. Apply liquid sealer to the threads and reinstall the BVSV.

6. Refill the engine with coolant.

Fig. 18 Checking the outer vent control (engine ON)-Pick-ups with carburetors

Checking the Outer Vent Control Valve

CARBURETED PICK-UP

▶ See Figures 17, 18 and 19

1. Disconnect the outer vent hose at the carburetor.

2. Blow air into the outer vent pipe and check that the control valve is open.

3. Start the engine.

4. With the engine running at idle, blow air into the outer vent pipe and check that the control valve is closed.

5. Unplug the control valve electrical connector and check the resistance between the positive (+) terminal in the connector and the solenoid body. Resistance should be 63-73ω at 68°F (20°C).

6. Replace the outer vent control valve if it fails either test.

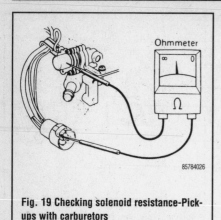

Fig. 19 Checking solenoid resistance-Pickups with carburetors

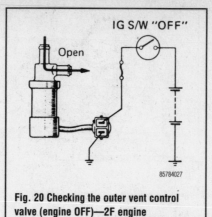

Fig. 20 Checking the outer vent control valve (engine OFF)—2F engine

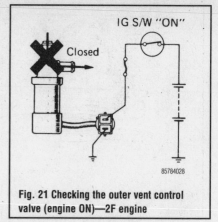

Fig. 21 Checking the outer vent control valve (engine ON)—2F engine

LAND CRUISER WITH 2F ENGINE

▶ See Figures 20 and 21

1. Remove the vacuum lines from the valve
2. With the ignition switch **OFF**, blow into the top pipe on the valve. The valve should be open.
3. With the ignition switch **ON**, blow into the top pipe again, the valve should now be closed.
4. If the valve is not working properly, first check the fuse and all the wiring connections. If they are all correct, the valve will require replacement.

Exhaust Gas Recirculation System (EGR)

OPERATION

▶ See Figures 22, 23 and 24

Oxides of nitrogen can only be formed under conditions of high pressure and high temperature. Elimination of one of these conditions reduces their production. A reduction of peak combustion temperature is accomplished by exhaust gas recirculation into the carburetor.

1974 California models, and all 1975 and later models (1988) are equipped with an EGR system. 1974 18R-C engines have a tube running from the exhaust manifold to the EGR valve, and a tube from the valve to the carburetor above the throttle plates. 1975-80 20R engines and 2F engines are similar, with the addition of an exhaust gas cooler cast into rear of the cylinder head. 1974-76 systems use a thermo switch, computer speed sensor, EGR valve and a vacuum switching valve (VSV). In addition, 1974 18R-C engines have a temperature switch at the carburetor flange. When the speed sensor and thermo switch are both within their operating ranges, the computer turns the VSV on, which in turn, opens the EGR valve, allowing a proportion of the exhaust gases to re-enter the engine through the carburetor. 1977 and later years, EGR systems eliminates all but the EGR valve, and add a TVSV (thermostatic VSV). At coolant temperatures above 50°F, the TSVS opens allowing engine vacuum to open the EGR valve. This permits a recirculation of exhaust gases.

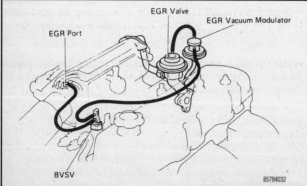

Fig. 22 Typical EGR system component layout and vacuum diagram

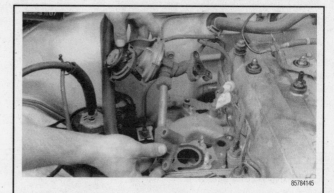

Fig. 23 EGR valve and related hardware

Fig. 24 Removing the EGR valve

SERVICE

▶ See Figures 25, 26 and 27

EGR Valve Check

1974–78

1. Allow the engine to warm up and remove the top from the air cleaner.

➡**Do not remove the entire air cleaner assembly.**

2. Disconnect the hose (white tape coded), which runs from the vacuum switching valve to the EGR valve, at its EGR valve end.
3. Remove the intake manifold hose (red coded) from the vacuum switching valve and connect it to the EGR valve. When the engine is at idle, a "hollow" sound should be heard coming from the air cleaner.
4. Disconnect the hose from the EGR valve; the hollow sound should disappear.

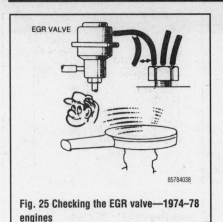

Fig. 25 Checking the EGR valve—1974–78 engines

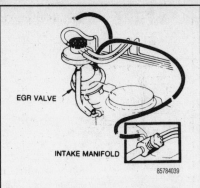

Fig. 26 The engine should stall when vacuum is applied directly to the EGR valve

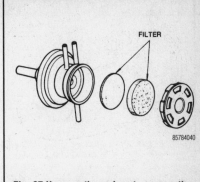

Fig. 27 Unscrew the endcap to remove the vacuum modulator filter

5. If the sound doesn't vary, the EGR valve is defective and must be replaced.

6. Reconnect the vacuum hoses as they were originally found. Install the top of the air cleaner.

1979–88

1. Start the engine.
2. Disconnect the vacuum hose leading from the EGR valve.
3. Disconnect the hose coming from the intake manifold and connect it to the empty pipe on the EGR valve.
4. When applying vacuum directly to the EGR valve, the engine should stall, if not, the EGR valve will probably require replacement.

EGR Valve Thermo-Sensor

1. Disconnect the electrical lead which runs to the EGR valve thermo-sensor.
2. Remove the thermo-sensor from the side of the EGR valve.
3. Heat the thermo-sensor in a pan of water to the following temperature: 260°F.
4. Connect an ohmmeter, in series with a 10 ohms; resistor, between the thermo-sensor terminal and case.
5. With the ohmmeter set on the kilo-ohms; scale, the following reading should be obtained: 2.55 kilo-ohms.
6. Replace the thermo-sensor if the ohmmeter readings vary considerably from those specified.
7. To install the thermo-sensor on the EGR valve, tighten it to 15–21 ft. lbs.

✳✳ CAUTION

Do not tighten the thermo-sensor with an impact wrench.

Checking the EGR Vacuum Modulator

1. Tag and disconnect all hoses leading form the vacuum modulator.
2. Remove the vacuum modulator.
3. Unscrew the vented top plate and remove the filter.
4. Check the filter for any contamination or other damage.
5. Clean the filter using compressed air.
6. Installation is in the reverse order of removal.

EGR Warning Light (1975 Only)

1975 trucks have an EWGR warning light on the instrument panel above the windshield wiper switch. The light remains on until the switch is reset. The switch should not be reset until all required maintenance on the EGR and other emission systems has been performed. To reset the switch:

1. Remove the lockscrew from the switch cover. This screw requires a tool with two prongs.
2. Remove the cover. Reset the switch by moving it to the position opposite its present position.
3. Replace the cover and lockscrew, and check to see that the light turns on when the ignition switch is turned to the Start position.

Dual Diaphragm Distributor

OPERATION

▸ See Figure 28

Carbureted Models Only

Some Toyota half-ton Pick-Ups with an 8R-C engine are equipped with a dual diaphragm distributor unit. This distributor has a retard diaphragm as well as an advance diaphragm.

Retarding the timing helps to reduce exhaust emissions as well as compensating for the lack of engine braking caused by the activation of the throttle positioner.

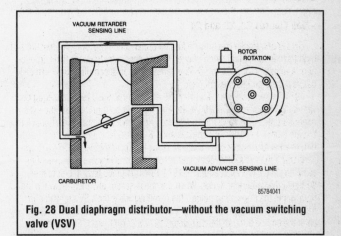

Fig. 28 Dual diaphragm distributor—without the vacuum switching valve (VSV)

TESTING

➡ Check all the vacuum hoses for leaks, kinks, or improper connections before making any test, and install replacements where necessary.

1. Connect the timing light to the engine. Check the ignition timing.

➡ Before proceeding with the test, disconnect any spark control devices, distributor vacuum valves, etc. If these are left connected, inaccurate results may be obtained.

2. Remove the retard hose from the distributor and plug it. As the engine speed increases, the timing should advance. If it does not, the vacuum unit is faulty and should be replaced.
3. Check the ignition timing with the engine running at idle speed. Connect the retard hose to the vacuum unit; the timing should instantly be retarded 4–10°. If this does not occur, the retard diaphragm has a leak and the vacuum unit must be replaced.

Engine Modifications System

OPERATION

Toyota uses an assortment of engine modifications to regulate exhaust emissions. Most of these devices fall into the category of engine vacuum controls. There are three principal components used on the engine modifications system, as well as a number of smaller parts. The three major components are: a speed sensor; a computer (speed marker); and a vacuum switching valve.

The vacuum switching valve and computer circuit operates most of the emission control components. Depending upon year and engine usage, the vacuum switching valve and computer may operate the pure control for the evaporative emission control system; the transmission controlled spark (TCS) or speed controlled spark (SCS); the dual-diaphragm distributor, the throttle positioner systems, the EGR system, the catalyst protection system, etc.

The functions of the evaporative emission control system, the throttle positioner, and the dual-diaphragm distributor are described in detail in the preceding sections. However, a word is necessary about the functions of the TCS and SCS systems before discussing operation of the vacuum switching valve/computer circuit.

The major difference between the transmission controlled spark and speed controlled spark systems is the manner in which system operation is determined. Toyota TCS systems use a mechanical switch to determine which gear is selected; SCS systems use a speed sensor built into the speedometer cable.

Below a predetermined speed, or any gear other than Fourth, the vacuum advance unit on the distributor is rendered inoperative or the timing retarded. By changing the distributor advance curve in this manner, it is possible to reduce emissions of oxides of nitrogen (NOx).

➡**Some engines are equipped with a thermo-sensor so the TCS or SCS system only operates when the coolant temperature is 140-212°F.**

Aside from determining the preceding conditions, the vacuum switching valve computer circuit operates other devices in the emission control system (EGR, catalytic converter, etc.).

The computer acts as a speed marker; at certain speeds it sends a signal to the vacuum switching valve which acts as a gate, opening and closing the emission control system vacuum circuits.

The vacuum switching valve on some 1971 engines is a simple affair; a single solenoid operates a valve which uncovers certain vacuum ports at the same time others are covered.

The valve used on all 1972 and later and some 1971 engines contains several solenoid and valve assemblies so that different combinations of opened and closed vacuum ports are possible. This allows greater flexibility of operation for the emission control system.

SYSTEM CHECKS

Due to the complexity of the components involved, about the only engine modification system checks which can be made, are the following:
1. Examine the vacuum lines to ensure that they are not clogged, pinched, or loose.
2. Check the electrical connections for tightness and corrosion.
3. Be sure that the vacuum sources for the vacuum switching valve are not plugged.
4. On models equipped with speed controlled spark, a broken speedometer cable could also render the system inoperative.

Beyond these checks, servicing the engine modifications system is best left to an authorized service facility.

➡**A faulty vacuum switching valve or computer could cause more than one of the emission control systems to fail. Therefore, if several systems are out, these two units (and the speedometer cable) would be the first things to check.**

Throttle Positioner

OPERATION

Carbureted Models Only

◢ **See Figures 29 and 30**

On carbureted Toyotas with an engine modification system, a throttle positioner is included to reduce exhaust emissions during deceleration. The positioner prevents the throttle from closing completely. Vacuum is reduced under the throttle valve which, in turn, acts on the retard chamber of the distributor vacuum unit. This compensates for the loss of engine braking caused by the partially opened throttle.

➡**For a description of the operation of the dual-diaphragm distributor, see Dual-Diaphragm Distributor.**

Once the vehicle drops below a predetermined speed, the vacuum switching valve provides vacuum to the throttle positioner diaphragm; the throttle positioner retracts allowing the throttle valve to close completely. The distributor also is returned to normal operation.

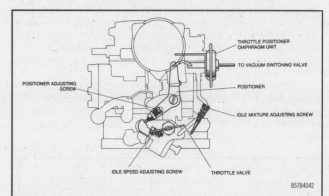

Fig. 29 Components of the throttle positioner—8R-C engine, other models similar

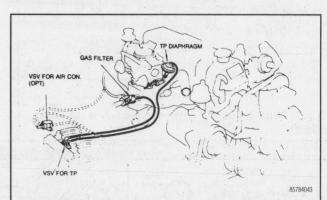

Fig. 30 Throttle positioner system component layout and vacuum diagram—22R engine

SERVICE

1. Start the engine and allow it to reach normal operating temperature.
2. Adjust the idle speed.

➡**Leave the tachometer connected after completing the idle adjustments, as it will be needed in Step 5.**

3. Detach the vacuum line from the positioner diaphragm unit and plug the line up.

4. Accelerate the engine slightly to set the throttle positioner in place.

5. Check the engine speed with a tachometer when the throttle positioner is set.

6. If necessary, adjust the engine speed, with the throttle positioner adjusting screw.

7. Connect the vacuum hose to the positioner diaphragm.

8. The throttle lever should be freed from the positioner as soon as the vacuum hose is connected. Engine idle should return to normal.

9. If the throttle positioner fails to function properly, check its linkage, and vacuum diaphragm. If there are no defects in either of these, the fault probably lies in the vacuum switching valve or the speed marker unit.

➡**Due to the complexity of these two components, and also because they require special test equipment, their service is best left to an authorized facility.**

Transmission Controlled Spark (TCS) System

OPERATION

The TCS system alters the distributor advance curve under certain operating conditions, thereby reducing emissions of oxide of nitrogen (NOx).

When the system is operational, the computer closes the vacuum switching valve (VSV) ground circuit. The valve in the VSV closes the passage between the distributor advance side and the carburetor advancer port. In this manner, advance of the engine timing is stopped.

The computer receives its messages from the speed sensor unit and the thermal sensor which only operates when the coolant temperature is between 140–210°F. 1975 and 1976 trucks use a TVSV (thermostatic vacuum switching valve) in addition to the VSV, computer, and speed sensor, to provide normal vacuum advance at engine temperatures below 122°F.

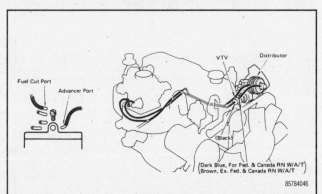

Fig. 31 Typical spark control system component layout and vacuum diagram

Spark Control System (SC)

OPERATION

Carbureted Models Only

▶ **See Figure 31**

The spark control system is sued to reduce the NOx and HC emissions. The system serves to delay the vacuum advance for a given time, while also lowering the maximum combustion temperature.

SERVICE

▶ **See Figures 32, 33, 34 and 35**

1979—Federal and Canada

1. Connect a vacuum gauge to the line leading from the distributor advance diaphragm.

2. Start the engine.

3. Check that the vacuum reading changes quickly when the throttle valve is opened and closed. If it does not change, check the TVSV.

4. Run the engine until it reaches normal operating temperature and then pinch the line between the TVSV and the advance port.

5. Rev the engine to 2000 rpm and release the hose.

6. The reading on the vacuum gauge should be at least 4 in. Hg within 2–4 seconds after releasing the hose.

7. With the engine speed maintained at 2000 rpm, check to see that the vacuum gauge indicates zero vacuum when the hose is disconnected from the advancer port. If it does not, check the TVSV.

8. Remove the TVSV and place its end in cool water. When blowing into one pipe, a large flow of air should be felt at the other one. Test both pipes in the same manner.

9. Heat the water to a temperature above 129°F (54°C). Blow into the vertical pipe. Air flow from the horizontal pipe should be good.

10. Blow into the horizontal pipe. Air flow from the vertical pipe should be minimal.

11. If the valve is not operating properly it will require replacement.

1979—California

1. Perform Steps 1–3 of the "1979—Federal and Canada" procedure.

2. Run the engine until it reaches normal operating temperature and then pinch the line between the TVSV and the spark control port.

3. Maintain the engine speed at 2000 rpm; the vacuum gauge should indicate at least 4 in. Hg within 2-4 seconds.

4. Release the hose. The gauge should indicate less that 4 in. Hg. If the preceding tests were positive, the procedure is finished. If not, inspect the TVSV and the VTV.

5. With the engine cold, blow into the pipe on the outside end of the TVSV.

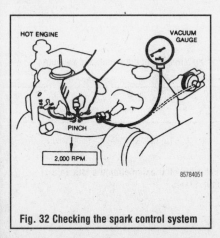

Fig. 32 Checking the spark control system

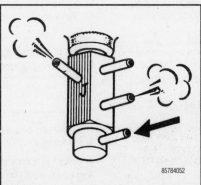

Fig. 33 Checking the TVSV with the engine cold

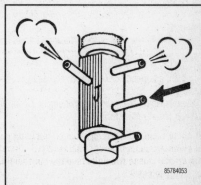

Fig. 34 Checking the TVSV with the engine hot

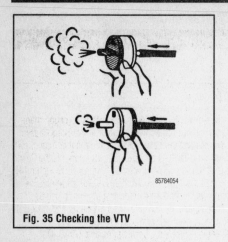

Fig. 35 Checking the VTV

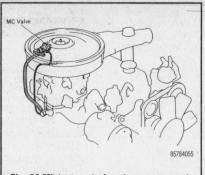

Fig. 36 Mixture control system component layout and vacuum diagram—1984–88 engines

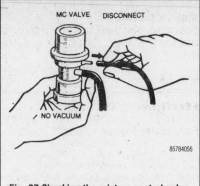

Fig. 37 Checking the mixture control valve through 1980 year

The air should come out of the middle pipe and the one on the side. No air should be felt coming out of the pipe on the inside end of the valve.

6. Run the engine until it reaches normal operating temperature and then blow into the middle pipe. The air should come out of the pipe on the side and the one on the inside end. No air should be felt coming from the pipe on the outside end of the valve. Replace the valve if it is not operating properly.

7. Remove the VTV and blow into the light colored side. The air should flow freely out of the other side.

8. Blow into the dark side of the valve. The flow of air coming out of the other side should be minimal. Replace the valve if it is not operating properly.

1980–81 with Carbureted Engine

1. Perform Steps 1–7 of the "1979—Federal and Canada" procedure.

➡ **When performing Steps 1–7, remember that there is no TVSV, only a VTV.**

2. Remove the VTV and blow into each side. Air should flow without resistance from the dark side to the light side WITH resistance from the light side to the dark side.

1982–84—California

1. Start the engine and connect a vacuum gauge to the hose leading from the inside half of the distributor diaphragm. The vacuum gauge should indicate high vacuum.

2. Run the engine until it reaches normal operating temperature. The gauge should indicate low vacuum. If the preceding tests were positive, the procedure is finished. If not, inspect the check valve and the BVSV.

3. Remove the check valve. When air is blown into the white pipe, the valve should be open. When air is blown into the black pipe, the valve should be closed.

4. Check the BVSV.

Mixture Control System (MC)

OPERATION

Carbureted Models Only

▶ **See Figure 36**

The mixture control system is used on carbureted models with manual transmissions in order to reduce HC and CO emissions under sudden deceleration. When the throttle is suddenly closed, the vacuum created opens the valve and allows fresh air to pass into the intake manifold.

SERVICE

▶ **See Figures 37 and 38**

1. Start the engine.
2. Disconnect the vacuum sensing hose (top) from the MC valve.

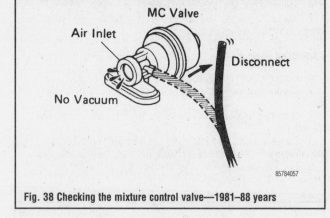

Fig. 38 Checking the mixture control valve—1981–88 years

3. Place your hand over the air inlet of the valve and check that no suction can be felt.

4. Reconnect the vacuum sensing hose. Suction should be felt momentarily.

➡ **At this time the engine will idle roughly or stall out altogether. This is normal.**

5. If the valve is not operating properly is will require replacement.

Dash Pot (DP) System

OPERATION

▶ **See Figure 39**

The dash pot (DP) system is used on all fuel injected models with manual transmissions and all 1985–87 carbureted models with automatic transmis-

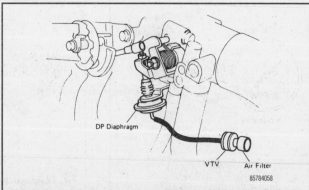

Fig. 39 Typical dashpot system component layout and vacuum diagram

sions. The system is used primarily to reduce HC and CO emissions upon deceleration. When decelerating, the dash pot opens the throttle slightly more than when at idle. This causes a more efficient burn of the air/fuel mixture.

SERVICE

▶ **See Figures 40, 41, 42 and 43**

Fuel Injected Engines

1. Run the engine until it reaches normal operating temperature.
2. Check the idle speed and ignition timing. Adjust if necessary.
3. Remove the cap and filter from the dash pot on the 3VZ-E.
4. Run the engine at 2500 rpm and pinch the vacuum hose between the dash pot and the VTV. On the 3VZ-E, plug the VTV hole.
5. Release the throttle and check that the dash pot holds the engine speed at 2000 rpm.
6. Adjust the dash pot to the proper speed (if necessary).
7. Release the pinched vacuum hose and check that the engine returns to idle speed within 1 second.

Carbureted Engines

1. Run the engine until it reaches normal operating temperature.
2. Check and adjust the idle speed and ignition timing as previously detailed.
3. Open the throttle valve until the throttle lever separates from the end of the dash pot.
4. Gradually release the throttle valve and check that the dash pot set speed is 3,000 rpm when the throttle lever contacts the end of the dash pot.
5. To adjust the set speed, loosen the locknut and rotate the dash pot.

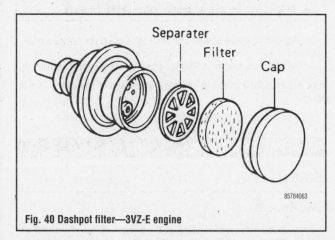

Fig. 40 Dashpot filter—3VZ-E engine

Air Injection System

OPERATION

▶ **See Figures 44 and 45**

On 1975-81 engines, a belt-drive air pump supplies air to an injection manifold which has nozzles in each exhaust port. Injection of air at this point causes combustion of unburned hydrocarbons in the exhaust manifold rather than allowing them to escape into the atmosphere. An anti-backfire valve controls the flow of air from the pump to prevent backfiring which results from an overly rich mixture under closed throttle conditions. There are two types of anti-backfire valve used: 1971 models use "gulp" valves; 1972-84 models "air by-pass" valves.

A check valve prevents hot exhaust gas backflow into the pump and hoses, in case of a pump failure, or when the anti-backfire valve is not working.

In addition all 1975-82 engines have an air switching valve (ASV). On engines without catalytic converters, the ASV is used to stop air injection under a constant heavy engine load condition.

On 1975-81 engines with catalytic converters, the ASV is also used to protect the catalyst from overheating, by blocking the injected air necessary for the operation of the converter.

On all 1975-82 engines, the pump relief valve is build into the ASV.

On 1982 and later carbureted engines, the air injection system incorporates a "feedback" loop. An oxygen sensor threaded into the exhaust manifold monitors the oxygen concentration in the exhaust gas, and indirectly signals the air pump to divert compressed air to either the exhaust ports or the air cleaner, depending on the oxygen levels in the exhaust. On 1983 and later engines, an EACV (electronic air control valve) serves as gate keeper for the air flow according to engine temperature. The EACV takes the place of the ASV on earlier engines. Thus, the feedback system constantly readjusts itself in order to reduce hydrocarbon, carbon monoxide and nitrogen oxides in the exhaust. If the catalytic converter overheats during operation, a converter-mounted sensor will temporarily shut the air injection system off.

REMOVAL & INSTALLATION

Air Pump

1. Disconnect the air hoses from the pump.
2. Loosen the bolt on the adjusting link and remove the drive belt.
3. Remove the mounting bolts and withdraw the pump.

➡ **Do not pry on the pump housing, it may be distorted.**

4. Installation is in the reverse order of removal. Adjust the drive belt tension after installation. Belt deflection should be ½–¾ in. with 22 lbs. pressure.

Air Injection Manifold

1. Remove the check valve, as previously outlined.
2. Loosen the air injection manifold attachment nuts and withdraw the manifold.

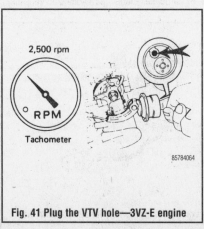

Fig. 41 Plug the VTV hole—3VZ-E engine

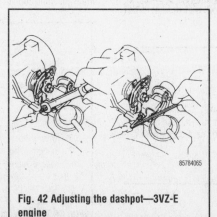

Fig. 42 Adjusting the dashpot—3VZ-E engine

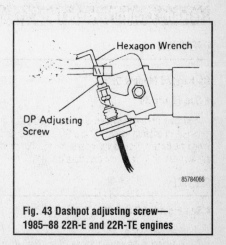

Fig. 43 Dashpot adjusting screw— 1985–88 22R-E and 22R-TE engines

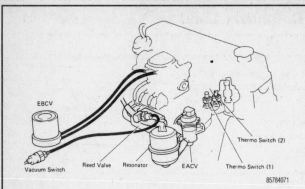

Fig. 44 Typical air suction with feedback control system component layout and vacuum diagram

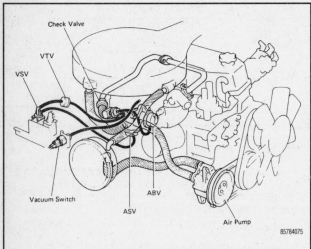

Fig. 45 Typical air injection system component layout and vacuum diagram

➡On 20R engines, it will first be necessary to remove the exhaust manifold.

3. Installation is in the reverse order of removal.

Air Injection Nozzles

1. Remove the air injection manifold as previously outlined.
2. Remove the cylinder head, as detailed in Section 3.
3. Place a new nozzle on the cylinder head.
4. Install the air injection manifold over it.
5. Install the cylinder head on the engine block.

SERVICE

Air Pump

➡Do not hammer, pry, or bend the pump housing while tightening the drive belt or testing the pump.

BELT TENSION AND AIR LEAKS

1. Before proceeding with the tests, check the pump drive belt tension to ensure that it is within specifications.
2. Turn the pump by hand. If it has seized, the belt will slip, making a noise. Disregard any chirping, squealing, or rolling sounds from inside the pump; these are normal when it is turned by hand.
3. Check the hoses and connections for leaks. Hissing or a blast of air is indicative of a leak. Soapy water, applied lightly around the area in question, is a good method for detecting leaks.

AIR OUTPUT

1. Disconnect the air supply hose at the anti-backfire valve.
2. Connect a vacuum gauge, using a suitable adapter, to the air supply hose.

➡**If there are two hoses, plug the second one.**

3. With the engine at normal operating temperature, increase the idle speed and watch the vacuum gauge.
4. The air flow from the pump should be steady and fall between 2 and 6 psi. If it is unsteady or falls below this, the pump is defective and must be replaced.

PUMP NOISE DIAGNOSIS

▶ **See Figure 46**

The air pump is normally noisy; as engine speed increases, the noise of the pump will rise in pitch. The rolling sound the pump bearing make is normal. But if this sound becomes objectionable at certain speeds, the pump is defective and will have to be replaced.

A continual hissing sound from the air pump pressure relief valve at idle, indicates a defective valve. Replace the relief valve.

If the pump rear bearing fails, a continual knocking sound will be heard. Since the rear bearing is not separately replaceable, the pump will have to be replaced as an assembly.

Anti-backfire Valve Tests

There are two different types of anti-backfire valve used with air injection systems. A by-pass valve is used in 1972–81 engines, while 1971 engines use a gulp type of anti-backfire valve. Test procedures for both types are given below.

GULP VALVE

1. Detach the air supply hose which runs between the pump and the gulp valve.
2. Connect a tachometer and run the engine to 1500–2000 rpm.
3. Allow the throttle to snap shut. This should produce a loud sucking sound from the gulp valve.
4. Repeat this operation several times. If no sound is present, the valve is not working or else the vacuum connections are loose.
5. Check the vacuum connections. If they are secure, replace the gulp valve.

BY-PASS VALVE

1. Detach the hose, which runs from the by-pass valve to the check valve, at the by-pass valve hose connection.
2. Connect a tachometer to the engine. With the engine running at normal idle speed check to see that air is flowing from the by-pass valve hose connection.
3. Speed up the engine so that it is running at 1500–2000 rpm. Allow the throttle to snap shut. The flow of air from the by-pass valve at the check valve hose connection should stop momentarily and air should then flow from the exhaust port on the valve body or the silencer assembly.
4. Repeat Step 3 several times. If the flow of air is not diverted into the atmosphere from the valve exhaust port or if it fails to stop flowing from the hose connection, check the vacuum lines and connections. If these are tight, the valve is defective and requires replacement.
5. A leaking diaphragm will cause the air to flow out both the hose connection and the exhaust port at the same time. If this happens, replace the valve.

Check Valve Test

▶ **See Figure 47**

1975–78

1. Before starting the test, check all of the hoses and connections for leaks.
2. Detach the air supply hose from the check valve.
3. Insert a suitable probe into the check valve and depress the plate. Release it; the plate should return to its original position against the valve seat. If binding is evident, replace the valve.
4. With the engine running at normal operating temperature, gradually increase its speed to 1500 rpm. Check for exhaust gas leakage. If any is present, replace the valve assembly.

➡**Vibration and flutter of the check valve at idle speed is a normal condition and does not mean that the valve should be replaced.**

Air Injection System Diagnosis Chart

Problem	Cause	Cure
1. Noisy drive belt	1a Loose belt 1b Seized pump	1a Tighten belt 1b Replace
2. Noisy pump	2a Leaking hose 2b Loose hose 2c Hose contacting other parts 2d Diverter or check valve failure 2e Pump mounting loose 2g Defective pump	2a Trace and fix leak 2b Tighten hose clamp 2c Reposition hose 2d Replace 2e Tighten securing bolts 2g Replace
3. No air supply	3a Loose belt 3b Leak in hose or at fitting 3c Defective antibackfire valve 3d Defective check valve 3e Defective pump 3f Defective ASV	3a Tighten belt 3b Trace and fix leak 3c Replace 3d Replace 3e Replace 3f Replace
4. Exhaust backfire	4a Vacuum or air leaks 4b Defective antibackfire valve 4c Sticking choke 4d Choke setting rich	4a Trace and fix leak 4b Replace 4c Service choke 4d Adjust choke

85784079

Fig. 46 Air Injection System Diagnosis Chart

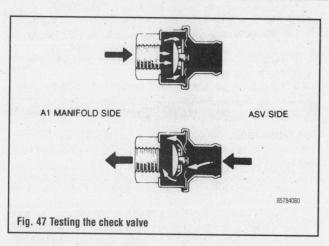

A1 MANIFOLD SIDE   ASV SIDE

85784080

Fig. 47 Testing the check valve

1979–84

1. Remove the check valve from the air injection manifold.
2. Blow into the manifold side (large side) and check that the valve is closed.
3. Blow into the ASV side (small side) and check that the valve is open.
4. If the valve is not operating properly it will probably require replacement.

Air Switching Valve (ASV) Tests

1. Start the engine and allow it to reach normal operating temperature and speed.
2. At curb idle, the air from the by-pass valve should be discharged through the hose which runs to the ASV.
3. When the vacuum line to the ASV is disconnected, the air from the by-pass valve should be diverted out through the ASV-to-air cleaner hose. Reconnect the vacuum line.
4. Disconnect the ASV-to-check valve hose and connect a pressure gauge to it.
5. Increase the engine speed. The relief valve should open when the pressure gauge registers 2.7–6.5 psi.
6. If the ASV fails any of the above tests, replace it. Reconnect all hoses.

Vacuum Delay Valve Test

The vacuum delay valve is located in the line which runs from the intake manifold to the vacuum surge tank. To check it, proceed as follows:
1. Remove the vacuum delay valve from the vacuum line. Be sure to not which end points toward the intake manifold.
2. When air is blown in from the ASV (surge tank) side, it should pass through the valve freely.
3. When air is blown in from the intake manifold side, a resistance should be felt.
4. Replace the valve if it fails either of the above tests.
5. Install the valve in the vacuum line, being careful not to install it backward.

EACV Test

1983 AND LATER

The EACV should be checked with the engine in three stages: cold, idling warm, and running at 2000 rpm at normal operating temperature.
1. Start the engine from cold and check that air is discharged from the air by-pass hose.
2. Warm the engine up to between 64°F and 109°F (after about two minutes worth of running). Idle the engine, and check that air is not discharging from the by-pass hose.
3. Run the engine up to 2000 rpm after the thermostat has opened fully (normal operating temperature). Check that air is being discharged intermittently (in staggered impulses) from the hose.

Catalytic Converter

OPERATION

The catalytic converter is a muffler-like container built into the exhaust system to aid in the reduction of exhaust emissions. The catalyst element consists of individual pellets coated with a noble metal such as platinum, palladium, rhodium or a combination. When the exhaust gases come into contact with the catalyst, a chemical reaction occurs which will reduce the pollutants into harmless substances like water and carbon dioxide.

There are essentially two types of catalytic converters: an oxidizing type and a three-way type. Both are used on the late model Toyotas. The oxidizing catalyst requires the addition of oxygen to spur the catalyst into reducing the engine's HC and CO emissions into H_2O and CO_2.

An air injection system is used to supply air to the exhaust system to aid in the reaction. A thermo-sensor, inserted into the converter, shuts off the air supply if the temperature of the catalyst becomes excessive.

The same sensor circuit will also cause an instrument panel warning light labeled **EXH TEMP** to come on when the catalyst temperature gets too high.

➡**It is normal for the light to come on temporarily if the truck is being driven downhill for long periods of time (such as descending a mountain).**

The light will come on and stay on if the air injection system is malfunctioning of if the engine is misfiring.

The oxidizing catalytic converter, while effectively reducing HC and CO emissions, does little, if anything, in the way of reducing NOx emissions. Thus, the three-way catalytic converter.

The three-way converter, unlike the oxidizing type, is capable of reducing HC, CO and NOx emissions; all at the same time. In theory, it seems impossible to reduce all three pollutants in one system since the reduction of HC and CO requires the addition of oxygen, while the reduction of NOx calls for the removal of oxygen. In actuality, the three-way system really can reduce all three pollutants, but only if the amount of oxygen in the exhaust system is precisely controlled. Due to this precise oxygen control requirement, the three-way converter system is used only in later trucks equipped with an oxygen sensing system.

PRECAUTIONS

1. Use only unleaded fuel.
2. Avoid prolonged idling; the engine should run no longer than 20 min. at curb idle and no longer than 10 min. at fast idle.
3. Don't disconnect any of the spark plug leads while the engine is running.
4. Make engine compression checks as quickly as possible.

CATALYST TESTING

At the present time there is no known way to reliably test catalytic converter operation in the field. The only reliable test is a 12 hour and 40 min. "soak" test (CVA) which must be done in a laboratory.

An infrared HC/CO tester is not sensitive enough to measure the higher tail pipe emissions from a failing converter. Thus, a bad converter may allow enough emissions to escape so that the truck is no longer is compliance with Federal or state standards, but will still not cause the needle on a tester to move off zero.

The chemical reactions which occur inside a catalytic converter generate a great deal of heat. Most converter problems can be traced to fuel or ignition system problems which cause unusually high emissions. As a result of the increased intensity of the chemical reactions, the converter literally burns itself up.

A completely failed converter might cause a tester to show a slight reading. As a result, it is occasionally possible to detect one of these.

As long as you avoid severe overheating and the use of leaded fuels it is reasonably safe to assume that the converter is working properly. If you are in doubt, take the truck to a diagnostic center that has a tester.

THERMO-SENSOR TESTING

▶ **See Figure 48**

The procedure for testing the thermo sensor is included in the Fuel Injection in Section 5. When checking resistance with the ohmmeter, consult the chart and remember that sensor resistance varies with coolant temperature as shown.

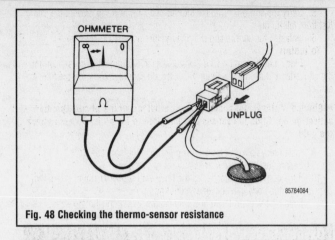

Fig. 48 Checking the thermo-sensor resistance

WARNING LIGHT CHECKS

➡**The warning light will come on when the ignition switch is turned to the Start position, as a means of checking its operation.**

1. If the warning light illuminates and remains on, check the components of the air injection system. If these are not defective, check the ignition system for faulty leads, plugs, points or igniter.
2. If no problems can be found in Step 1, check the warning light wiring for short or open circuits.
3. If nothing can be found in Steps 1 or 2, check the operation of the emission control system vacuum switching valve or the computer, either by substitution of a new unit, or by taking the truck to a service facility which has Toyota's diagnostic emission control system checker.

REMOVAL & INSTALLATION

▶ **See Figure 49**

✳✳ CAUTION

Do not perform this operation on a hot (or even warm) engine. Catalyst temperatures may go as high as 1700°F, so that any contact with the catalyst could cause severe burns.

1. Disconnect the lead from the converter thermo-sensor.
2. Remove the wiring shield.
3. Unfasten the pipe clamp, securing bolts at either end of the converter. Remove the clamps.
4. Push the tail pipe rearward and remove the converter, complete with thermo-sensor.

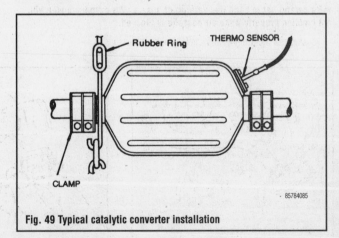

Fig. 49 Typical catalytic converter installation

5. Carry the converter with the thermo-sensor upward to prevent the catalyst from falling out.

6. Unfasten the screws and take out the thermo-sensor and gasket.

To install:

7. Place a new gasket on the thermo-sensor. Push the thermo-sensor into the converter and secure it with its two bolts. Be careful not to drop the thermo-sensor.

➡**Service replacement converters are provided with a plastic thermo-sensor guide. Slide the sensor into the glide to install it. Do not remove the guide.**

8. Install new gaskets on the converter mounting flanges.

9. Secure the converter with its mounting clamps.

10. If the converter is attached to the body with rubber O-rings, install the O-rings over the body and converter mounting hooks.

11. Install the wire protector and connect the lead to the thermo-sensor.

Oxygen Sensor System

OPERATION

The three-way catalytic converter, which is capable of reducing HC, CO and NOx into CO_2, H_2O, O_2 and N_2 can only function as long as the air/fuel mixture is kept within a critically precise range. The oxygen sensor system is what keeps the oxygen range in control.

Basically, the oxygen sensor system works like this: As soon as the engine warms up, the computer begins to work. The oxygen sensor, located in the exhaust manifold, senses the oxygen content of the exhaust gases. The amount of oxygen in the exhaust varies according to the air/fuel mixture. The O_2 sensor produces a small voltage that varies depending on the amount of oxygen in the exhaust at the time. This voltage is picked up by the computer. The computer works together with the fuel distributor and together they will vary the amount of fuel which is delivered to the engine at any given time.

If the amount of oxygen in the exhaust system is low, which indicates a rich mixture, the sensor voltage will be high. The higher the voltage signal sent to the computer, the more it will reduce the amount of fuel supplied to the engine. The amount of fuel is reduced until the amount of oxygen in the exhaust system increases, indicating a lean mixture. When the mixture is lean, the sensor will send a low voltage signal to the computer. The computer will then increase the quantity of fuel until the sensor voltage increases again and then the cycle will start all over.

OXYGEN SENSOR REPLACEMENT

▶ **See Figure 50**

1. Disconnect the negative battery cable.

2. Unplug the wiring connector leading from the O_2 sensor.

➡**Be careful not to bend the waterproof hose as the oxygen sensor will not function properly if the air passage is blocked.**

3. Unscrew the two nuts and carefully pull out the sensor.

4. Installation is in the reverse order of removal. Please note the following:
- Always use a new gasket.
- Tighten the nuts to 13–16 ft. lbs.

OXYGEN SENSOR WARNING LIGHT

▶ **See Figures 51 and 52**

All models are equipped with an oxygen sensor warning light on the instrument panel. The light may go on when the truck is started, then it should go out. If the light stays on, check your odometer. The light is hooked up to an elapsed mileage counter which goes off every 30,000 miles. This is your signal that it is time to replace the oxygen sensor and have the entire system checked out. After replacement of the sensor, the elapsed mileage counter must be reset. To reset:

1. Locate the counter. It can be found under the left side of the instrument panel, on the brake pedal bracket. On some Land Cruiser models, the counter is located under the hood near the firewall area.

2. Unscrew the mounting bolt, disconnect the wiring connector and remove the counter.

3. Remove the bolt on top of the counter.

4. Lift off the counter cover and push the reset switch.

➡**The warning light on the instrument panel must go out at this time.**

5. Installation is in the reverse order of removal.

Automatic Hot Air Intake System (HAI)

OPERATION

Carbureted Models Only

▶ **See Figures 53, 54 and 55**

This system allows hot air from the exhaust manifold to be routed to the carburetor in cold weather. Instead of cold air being sucked into the air cleaner all the time, a thermo valve in the air cleaner housing closes when the temperature inside the air cleaner falls below a certain point. When the thermo valve is closed, a diaphragm on the air cleaner neck is activated and it opens the air control valve. This prevents cold outside air from entering the air cleaner, but allows the hotter air from around the exhaust manifold to flow in. Not only does this system improve driveability, but it prevents carburetor icing in extremely cold weather.

SERVICE

Checking the HAI System

▶ **See Figure 56**

1. Visually inspect all hoses and connections for cracks, leaks or other damage.

2. Remove the air cleaner top.

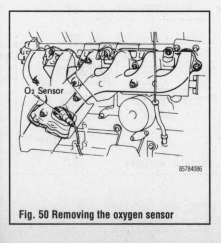

Fig. 50 Removing the oxygen sensor

Fig. 51 Remove the counter cover

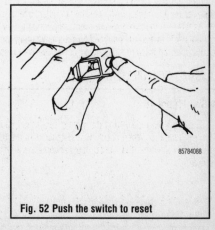

Fig. 52 Push the switch to reset

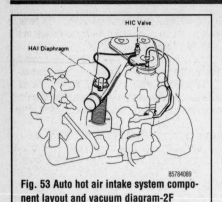

Fig. 53 Auto hot air intake system component layout and vacuum diagram-2F engine

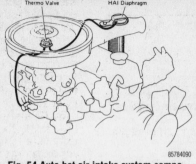

Fig. 54 Auto hot air intake system component layout and vacuum diagram—1984 22R engine

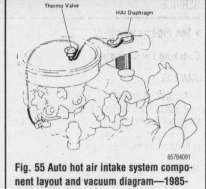

Fig. 55 Auto hot air intake system component layout and vacuum diagram—1985-88 22R engine

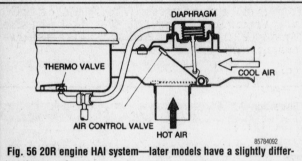

Fig. 56 20R engine HAI system—later models have a slightly different thermo valve

3. Cool the thermo valve by blowing compressed air on it.

4. With the engine idling and the thermo valve closed (cool), check to see if the air control valve in the neck of the air cleaner is open and allowing hot air to enter the air cleaner.

5. Install the top of the air cleaner and run the engine until it reaches normal operating temperature.

6. Check that the air control valve is now closed and only cool air is being allowed to enter the air cleaner.

Automatic Choke System

OPERATION

Carbureted Models Only

The purpose of the automatic choke is to temporarily richen the air/fuel mixture to the engine by closing the choke valve when the engine is cold. By shutting the choke valve you are effectively choking the engine by reducing the amount of air which is allowed to enter the carburetor. This then enables the air/fuel mixture to be ignited sooner (faster).

SERVICE

Checking the Automatic Choke System

▶ **See Figure 57**

1. Check the choke housing its hoses for any leaks, cracks or other damage.
2. Check that the middle mark on the thermostatic case is aligned with the mark on the coil housing.

➡**Loosen only the three screws around the outside edge of the case. Do not loosen the bolt at the center of the case because it will allow coolant to come out.**

3. Remove the top of the air cleaner.
4. With the engine cold and turned off, press down on the gas pedal and release it. The small valve in the center of the carburetor bore should be almost completely closed.
5. Run the engine until it reaches normal operating temperature and then check that the choke valve has opened up.
6. Reinstall the top of the air cleaner.

Choke Breaker System (CB)

OPERATION

▶ **See Figures 58 and 59**

Canada

The choke breaker system is used to monitor the automatic choke system. To prevent too rich a mixture when the choke is closed, the choke breaker forces the choke valve open slightly.

USA

This system performs the same function that the previous one does except that it goes one step further and forces the choke valve to open up even further after the engine has warmed up.

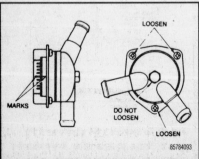

Fig. 57 A close-up view of the choke housing

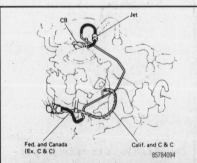

Fig. 58 Choke breaker system components layout and vacuum diagram—1984-88

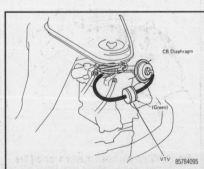

Fig. 59 Choke breaker system components layout and vacuum diagram—2F engine

SERVICE

▶ **See Figures 60 and 61**

Checking the CB System

CANADA

1. Start the engine.
2. Disconnect the hose from the choke breaker diaphragm and check that the choke linkage returns to its previous position.
3. Reconnect the hose to the diaphragm and check that the choke linkage is pulled back by the diaphragm.

USA

1. Carefully note the position of the choke breaker linkage rod.
2. Disconnect the vacuum hose between the choke breaker diaphragm and the 3-way connector at the diaphragm side.
3. Start the engine and check that the choke breaker linkage moves from its former position.
4. Reconnect the vacuum hose to the diaphragm. The linkage should move even further than it was.
5. Check the VSV and the TVSV as detailed in the "Evaporative Emission Control" section.

Auxiliary Acceleration Pump (AAP) System

OPERATION

Carbureted Models Only

▶ **See Figure 62**

To reduce emissions, carburetor air/fuel mixtures are calibrated to be as lean as possible. Although a lean mixture will burn readily at hotter temperatures, it is reluctant to ignite when cold, not because of the mixture as such, but because fuel vaporizes less readily when cold. Thus, increasing the amount of fuel in a cold air/fuel mixture increased the amount of vaporized fuel available.

The problem of a poor air/vaporized fuel mixture in a cold engine is accentuated when accelerating. Although the carburetor is equipped with an acceleration pump for normal accelerating engine demands, its capacity is insufficient for a cold engine. The auxiliary acceleration pump (AAP) is designed to send additional fuel into the acceleration nozzle in the carburetor independent of the regular acceleration pump.

The AAP itself is an integral part of the carburetor. It consists of two check valves controlled be springs, and a diaphragm controlled by both a spring and engine vacuum obtained from the intake manifold. At constant speeds, intake manifold vacuum draws the AAP DIAPHRAGM BACK, ENLARGING THE AAP CHAMBER AND THUS ALLOWING GASOLINE TO ENTER. When the engine is accelerated, intake manifold vacuum drops, allowing the AAP DIAPHRAGM TO BE PUSHED BACK BY THE SPRING. The resultant reduction in chamber volume forces the gasoline out through the other check valve, into the acceleration nozzle. Thus, the engine gets a needed squirt of gasoline.

AAP operation is governed by the same TVSV described in the AI section earlier. At cold coolant temperatures, the TSVS allows intake manifold vacuum to reach the AAP diaphragm. At approximately 122°F, the TSVS closes off the passage to vacuum, thus shutting off the AAP.

SERVICE

Inspection

▶ **See Figure 63**

The vacuum hose should be checked for leaks, kinks, or improper connection.

1. With the engine cold (below 75°F) and idling (front wheels blocked, parking brake on, transmission in neutral) remove the air cleaner cap and look into the carburetor. At the instant the vacuum hose is removed from the AAP, gasoline should squirt from the nozzle.
2. If it does not, check for vacuum in the hose. If present, the AAP diaphragm may be defective, the nozzle may be blocked, the check valves may be stuck, or gasoline may not be flowing into the chamber.
3. If there is no vacuum in the line, either the line has an air leak or the TSVS is defective.
4. After warming the engine to operating temperature, perform the same test as in Step 1. If gasoline spurts out, the TSVS is defective.

Fast Idle Cam Breaker System (FICB)

OPERATION

Carbureted Models Only

After the engine has warmed up, this vacuum operated system forces the fast idle cam to move to the third step, which in turn lowers the engine speed.

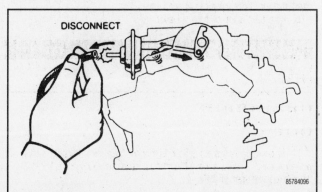

Fig. 60 When the vacuum hose is pulled from the diaphragm, the choke linkage should move

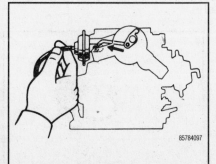

Fig. 61 When the hose is reconnected the linkage should return to its original position

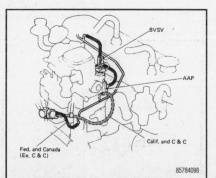

Fig. 62 Auxiliary acceleration pump system component layout and vacuum diagram—1984–88 22R engine

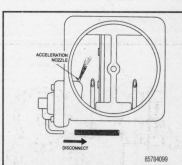

Fig. 63 To test the AAP, disconnect the vacuum hose while looking down into the carburetor for a squirt of gas from the acceleration nozzle

SERVICE

Checking the FICB System

▶ **See Figures 64, 65 and 66**

1. Disconnect the vacuum hose from the fast idle cam breaker diaphragm.
2. While holding the throttle valve slightly open, pull up the fast idle cam linkage and then release the throttle. This will set the fast idle cam.
3. Start the engine but do not touch the gas pedal.
4. Reconnect the hose. The fast idle cam should be released to the third step and the engine speed should thereby be lowered.
5. Apply vacuum to the FICB diaphragm and check that the linkage moves. If it does not, replace the diaphragm.
6. Check the VSV and the TVSV as detailed earlier in the "Evaporative Emission Control" section.

Deceleration Fuel Cut System

CALIFORNIA ONLY

▶ **See Figures 67 and 68**

This system cuts off part of the fuel in the slow circuit of the carburetor to prevent overheating and afterburning of the exhaust system.

1. Connect a tachometer to the engine.
2. Start the engine and check that it runs normally.
3. Pinch the vacuum hose to the vacuum switch.
4. Gradually increase the engine speed to 3000 rpm. Check that the engine misfires slightly between 2400 and 3000 rpm.

✳✳ CAUTION

Perform this procedure quickly to avoid overheating the catalytic converter.

5. Release the hose and gradually increase the engine speed to 3000 rpm. Check that the engine operation is normal.
6. With the engine at idle unplug the solenoid valve. Check that the engine misfires or stalls.
7. If a problem is found check the switch and solenoid. If everything is normal connect the vacuum line and wiring.

Fuel Cut Solenoid Valve and Vacuum Switch

TESTING

Carbureted Models Only

1. Remove the solenoid.
2. Test that the solenoid is operating properly. This can be done by connecting two wires to the battery terminals, one negative, one positive. By attaching these wires to the switch you will hear it click. The click indicates it is operating properly.
3. Check the O-ring for damage.
4. Reinstall the solenoid, if no problem is found.
5. Use an ohmmeter to check that there is continuity between the switch terminal and the body.
6. Start the engine.
7. Check now for no continuity between the switch terminal and the body.

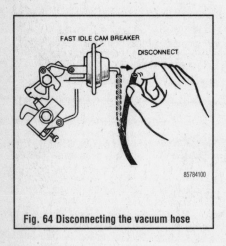

Fig. 64 Disconnecting the vacuum hose

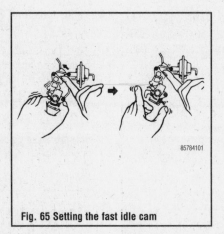

Fig. 65 Setting the fast idle cam

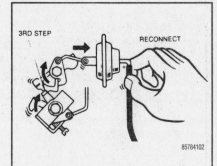

Fig. 66 When the vacuum hose is reconnected the fast idle cam should move to the 3rd step

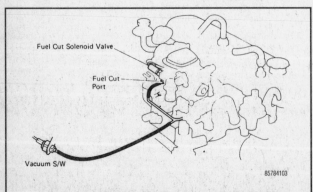

Fig. 67 Deceleration fuel cut system component layout and vacuum diagram—1984–88 22R engine

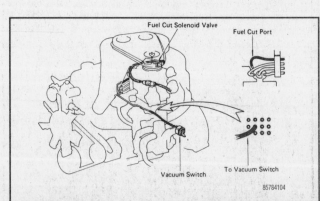

Fig. 68 Deceleration fuel cut system component layout and vacuum diagram—2F engine

Secondary Slow Circuit Fuel Cut System

CARBURETED MODELS ONLY

This system cuts off part of the fuel in the secondary slow circuit of the carburetor to prevent dieseling.

INSPECTION OF THE FUEL CUT VALVE

1. Fully open and close the throttle valve.
2. Measure the stroke. It should be 1.5-2.0mm.
3. If adjustment is necessary bend the lever.

➡The stroke should be set to the above specifications before the secondary throttle valve opens. (Before kick up).

High Altitude Compensation (HAC) System

OPERATION

▶ **See Figures 69 and 70**

Carbureted Models Only

At high altitudes, air/fuel mixtures become richer, due to the thinner air available. The High Altitude Compensation (HAC) system installed on 1977-88 trucks sold in federally designated areas insures a proper air/fuel mix by supplying additional air to the low and/or high speed circuits at high altitude (above 4000 feet) to minimize HC and CO emissions. The system also advances the ignition timing to improve driveability at high altitudes.

The HAC system consists of an HAC valve, a dual diaphragm distributor, and a check valve.

HIGH ALTITUDE OPERATION

Low atmospheric pressure allows the bellows in the HAC valve to expand and close port A. Intake manifold vacuum acts on the diaphragm in the HAC valve through the check valve, opening the passages between the carburetor and the atmosphere via the HAC valve. These open passages allow air to flow into the low and/or high speed circuits in the carburetor. As a result, the air/fuel mixture becomes leaner.

The intake manifold vacuum also acts on the sub-diaphragm in the distributor. This vacuum in maintained by the check valve, except in the following instance: a vacuum in the main diaphragm of the distributor rises above 127mm of mercury (Hg), the vacuum advance will revert to normal.

LOW ALTITUDE OPERATION

High atmospheric pressure, entering through the bottom of the HAC valve acts on the bellows and opens port A. Since the intake manifold vacuum does not act on the diaphragm in the HAC valve, the air passage from the carburetor to the atmosphere is closed by the diaphragm. This prevents a lean mixture at lower altitudes.

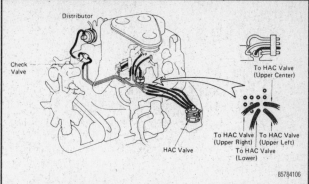

Fig. 70 High altitude compensation system component layout vacuum diagram—2F engine

The intake manifold vacuum also cannot act on the distributor sub-diaphragm, so the distributor advance in normal.

SERVICE

▶ **See Figures 71, 72, 73 and 74**

Inspection

➡Before checking the HAC system at altitudes near 4000 feet, determine the position of the HAC valve. This can be done by blowing into any one of the three ports on top of the HAC valve when the engine is idling. If the passage is open, the valve is in the high altitude position. If it is closed, the valve is in the low altitude position. When the position is determined, proceed with the appropriate high altitude or low altitude inspection.

INSPECTION AT HIGH ALTITUDE

1. Check all vacuum hoses for leaks, breaks, kinks, or improper connections.
2. Visually inspect the HAC filter and replace it if clogged. It is located at the bottom of the HAC valve.
3. Start the engine and check the ignition timing. If it is about 13° BTDC, go on with the procedure. If it is only slightly out of adjustment, adjust the timing. If the hose between the HAC valve and the three way connector is pinched, does the ignition timing become about 13° BTDC? If so, the HAC valve should be replaced. If not, the check valve must be inspected. It should be possible to blow air through it from the HAC side, and not from the intake manifold side. If faulty, replace. If not, the distributor vacuum advance is faulty and must be repaired or replaced.
4. If the hose between the white side of the check valve and the three way connector is pinched, the ignition timing should stay at 13° BTDC for a minute or more. If not, replace the HAC valve.
5. If the hose is disconnected from the black side of the check valve and the

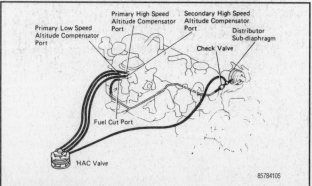

Fig. 69 High altitude compensation system component layout vacuum diagram—1984–88 22R engine

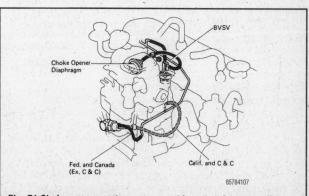

Fig. 71 Choke opener system component layout and vacuum diagram—1984–88 22R engine

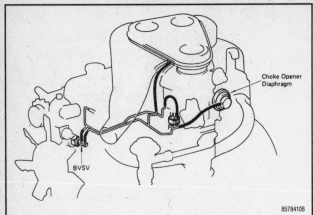

Fig. 72 Choke opener system component layout and vacuum diagram—2F engine

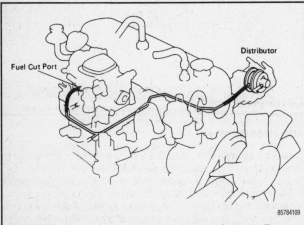

Fig. 73 Idle advance system component layout and vacuum diagram—1984–88 22R engine

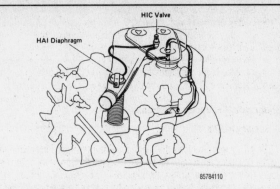

Fig. 74 Hot idle compensation system component layout and vacuum diagram—2F engine

hose end blocked, the ignition timing should stay at 13° BTDC for one minute or more. If not, replace the check valve.

6. Disconnect the two HAC hoses from the carburetor. If air is blown into each hose, it should flow into the carburetor. If not, the carburetor air passages are blocked.

7. If the air does flow into the carburetor, reconnect the hoses. The HAC system is operating correctly.

INSPECTION AT LOW ALTITUDE

1. Check all hoses for leaks, breaks, kinks, and improper connections.
2. Inspect the HAC filter, located in the bottom of the HAC valve, and replace it if clogged.
3. Start the engine and disconnect the two HAC hoses from the carburetor.
4. If air is blown into each hose, it should not flow into the HAC valve. If it does, replace the valve.
5. Reconnect the two hoses. Check the ignition timing according to the procedures outlined in Section 2. The transmission should be in Neutral. If the timing is correct, the HAC system is okay. It should be:
   - 8° BTDC @ 800 rpm with manual transmission
   - 8° BTDC @ 850 rpm with automatic transmission
6. If the timing is incorrect, disconnect the vacuum hose from the distributor sub-diaphragm. If the timing does not change, adjust the ignition timing. If the timing changes, replace the HAC valve.

ELECTRONIC ENGINE CONTROLS

Diagnosis and Testing

SERVICE PRECAUTIONS

- Do not operate the fuel pump when the fuel lines are empty.
- Do not reuse fuel hose clamps.
- Make sure all EFI harness connectors are fastened securely. A poor connection can cause an extremely high surge voltage and result in damage to integrated circuits.
- Keep the EFI harness at least 4 in. away from adjacent harnesses to prevent system malfunction due to external electronic noise.
- Keep all EFI parts and harnesses dry during service.
- Before attempting to remove any parts, turn **OFF** the ignition switch and disconnect the battery ground cable.
- Always use a 12 volt battery as a power source.
- Do not attempt to disconnect the battery cables with the engine running.
- Do not rev up the engine immediately after starting or just prior to shutdown.
- Do not attempt to disassemble the EFI control unit under any circumstances.
- If installing a 2-way or CB radio, mobile phone or other radio equipment, keep the antenna as far as possible away from the electronic control unit. Keep the antenna feeder line at least 8 in. away from the EFI harness and do not run them parallel for a long distance. Be sure to ground the radio to the vehicle body.

- Handle the air flow meter carefully to avoid damage.
- Do not disassemble the air flow meter or clean the meter with any type of detergent.
- Before connecting or disconnecting control unit ECU harness connectors, make sure the ignition switch is **OFF** or the negative battery cable is disconnected.
- When performing ECU input/output signal diagnosis, remove the waterproofing rubber plug, if equipped, from the connectors to make it easier to insert tester probes into the connector. Always reinstall it after testing.
- When connecting or disconnecting pin connectors from the ECU, take care not to bend or break any pin terminals. Check that there are no bends or breaks on ECU pin terminals before attempting any connections.
- Before replacing any ECU, perform the ECU input/output signal diagnosis to make sure the ECU is functioning properly.
- When measuring supply voltage of ECU-controlled components with a circuit tester, keep the tester probes separated from each other and from accidental grounding. If the tester probes accidentally make contact with each other during measurement, a short circuit will result and damage the ECU.

DIAGNOSTIC CODES

Diagnosis codes are held in memory and may be displayed by grounding the proper terminals at the diagnostic connector or check connector. The system should be interrogated for stored codes before any disconnection of the battery cables; once disconnected, the stored codes will be lost. Certain conditions must be met before the codes will be transmitted from the ECU. The initial conditions are:

- Engine at normal operating temperature
- Battery voltage 11 volts or above
- Throttle fully closed (IDL points engaged)
- Transmission in **N**
- All accessories and electrical loads **OFF**

If any of the initial conditions are not met, the ECU will note a problem and display a switch condition code when the diagnostic circuit is grounded.

Diagnostic Connector Locations

▶ See Figure 75

On all equipped vehicles the check connector (near the ignition coil) or diagnostic connector are located under the hood in the engine area on the shock tower (passenger side) or near the junction or relay block (driver's side). A small plastic cap covers the check connector terminals and hinged plastic cap covers the diagnostic connector. Each terminal is mark inside the diagnostic cap cover for proper identification.

Reading Stored Codes

1. Check that the initial conditions are met.
2. Turn the ignition switch **ON** but do not start the engine.
3. At the diagnostic connector or check connector, use a jumper wire to connect terminals T and E$_1$.
4. Observe the CHECK ENGINE warning lamp on the dashboard; read the code(s) based on the number and rate of flashes.
5. If the system is operating normally, with no codes stored, the warning lamp will flash on/off in a constant, unchanging pattern. This is the System Normal signal; the ECU is acknowledging the request for codes but has nothing to report.
6. If malfunction codes are stored, the light will blink every ½-second. The first number of blinks will indicate the first digit of a 2-digit code. After a 1½ second pause, the second digit will be transmitted. If there is more than one code stored, they will be separated by a 2½-second pause. After all stored codes have been transmitted, the cycle will begin again after a 4½ second pause. The codes will continuously transmit until the jumper wire is disconnected. Even when transmission has stopped, the codes remain in memory until the memory is cleared.

➡ If more than one code is stored, the codes will be transmitted in numerical order from lowest to highest. The order of the codes does not indicate the order of fault occurrence.

7. Record the codes as they are received.
8. Disconnect the diagnostic jumper; switch the ignition **OFF**.

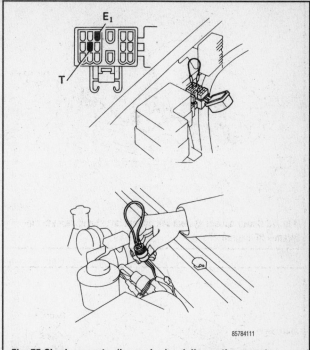

Fig. 75 Check connector (lower view) and diagnostic connector (upper view)

Clearing Stored Codes

Stored codes will remain in memory until cleared. The correct method of clearing codes is to turn the ignition switch **OFF**, then remove the EFI 15A fuse for at least 30 seconds. The time required will be longer in cold weather. Disconnecting the negative battery cable will also clear the memory but is not recommended due to other on-board memories being cleared as well. Once the system power is restored, re-check for stored codes. Only the System Normal indication should be present. If any other code is stored, the clearing procedure must be repeated or the old code will be stored with any new ones.

After repairs, it is recommended to clear the memory before test driving the vehicle. Upon returning from the drive, interrogate the memory; if the original code is again present, the repair was unsuccessful.

TROUBLE CODES

Year — 1984
Model — Pick-Up
Engine — 2.4L (144 cid) EFI 4 cyl
Engine Code — 22R-E

ECM TROUBLE CODES

Code	Explanation
1	Normal operation
2	Open or shorted air flow meter circuit — defective air flow meter or Electronic Fuel Injection (EFI) computer
3	Open or shorted air flow meter circuit — defective air flow meter or Electronic Fuel Injection (EFI) computer
4	Open Water Thermo Sensor (THW) circuit — defective Water Thermo Sensor (THW) or Electronic Fuel Injection (EFI) computer
5	Open oxygen sensor circuit — lean indication — defective oxygen sensor or Electronic Fuel Injection (EFI) computer
6	No ignition signal — defective ignition system circuit, distributor, ignition coil and igniter or Electronic Fuel Injection (EFI) computer
7	Defective Throttle Position Sensor (TPS) circuit, Throttle Position Sensor (TPS) or Electronic Fuel Injection (EFI) computer

85784112

Fig. 76 ECM TROUBLE CODES—1984 Pick-up with 22R-E engine

Year—1986
Model—Pick-Up
Engine—2.4L (144 cid) EFI 4 cyl
Engine Code—22R-TE

ECM TROUBLE CODES

Code	Explanation
1	Normal operation
2	Open or shorted air flow meter circuit – defective air flow meter or Electronic Control Unit (ECU)
3	No signal from igniter 4 times in succession – defective igniter or main relay circuit, igniter or Electronic Control Unit (ECU)
4	Open or shorted Water Thermo Sensor (THW) circuit – defective Water Thermo Sensor (THW) or Electronic Control Unit (ECU)
5	Open or shorted oxygen sensor circuit – lean or rich indication – defective oxygen sensor or Electronic Control Unit (ECU)
6	No engine revolution sensor (Ne) signal to Electronic Control Unit (ECU) or Ne value being over 1000 rpm in spite of no Ne signal to ECU – defective igniter circuit, igniter, distributor or Electronic Control Unit (ECU)
7	Open or shorted Throttle Position Sensor (TPS) circuit – defective Throttle Position Sensor (TPS) or Electronic Control Unit (ECU)
8	Open or shorted intake air thermo sensor circuit – defective intake air thermo sensor circuit or Electronic Control Unit (ECU)
10	No starter switch signal to Electronic Control Unit (ECU) with vehicle speed at 0 and engine speed over 800 rpm – defective speed sensor circuit, main relay circuit, igniter switch-to-starter circuit, igniter switch or Electronic Control Unit (ECU)
11	Throttle switch (IDL) point in the Throttle Position Sensor (TPS) is OFF during diagnostic check – defective Throttle Position Sensor (TPS) or Electronic Control Unit (ECU)
12	Knock control sensor signal has not reached judgement level in succession – defective knock control sensor circuit, knock control sensor or Electronic Control Unit (ECU)
13	Knock CPU faulty – defective Electronic Control Unit (ECU)
14	The turbocharger pressure is abnormal – defective turbocharger, air flow meter or Electronic Control Unit (ECU)

85784118

Fig. 79 ECM TROUBLE CODES—1986 Pick-up and 4Runner with 22R-TE engine.

Year—1987
Model—Pick-Up, 4Runner
Body VIN—N
Engine—2.4L (2366cc)   Cylinders—4
Fuel System—Feedback Carburetor/Electronic Fuel Injection
Engine Identifier—22R, 22R-E, 22R-TE   VIN—R
Automatic Transmission Identifier—A340H

ENGINE CODES

Code	Explanation
1	Normal – appears when no other codes are detected
2	Air flow meter signal – VC open, E2 open, VS-E2 shorted, or VC-VS shorted
3	Igniter signal (IGf) – missing 4 times in succession
4	Water temperature sensor signal – open/short
5	Oxygen sensor signal – sufficient feedback but oxygen sensor signal unchanged
6	RPM NE signal (crank angle pulse) to ECU – missing while engine cranking or NE value over 1000 rpm in spite of missing NE signal
7	Throttle position sensor signal – open/short
8	Intake air temperature sensor signal – open/short
10	Starter signal to ECU – missing when vehicle stopped and engine running over 800 rpm
11	Switch signal – neutral start switch ON (22R-E) or IDL point in throttle position sensor is OFF during diagnostic check
12	Knock sensor signal – has not reached judgment level in succession
13	Knock control part (ECU) – faulty ECU
14	Turbocharger pressure – abnormal (air flow meter may also exhibit abnormalities)

Codes listed are for the 22R-E and 22R-TE engines only, the 22R engine does not use engine codes.

85784120

Fig. 80 ECM TROUBLE CODES—1987 Pick-up and 4Runner with 22R, 22R-E and 22R-TE engines

---

Year—1985
Model—4Runner
Engine—2.4L (144 cid) EFI 4 cyl
Engine Code—22R-TE

ECM TROUBLE CODES

Code	Explanation
1	Normal operation
2	Open or shorted air flow meter circuit – defective air flow meter or Electronic Control Unit (ECU)
3	No signal from igniter 4 times in succession – defective igniter or main relay circuit, igniter or Electronic Control Unit (ECU)
4	Open or shorted Water Thermo Sensor (THW) circuit – defective Water Thermo Sensor (THW) or Electronic Control Unit (ECU)
5	Open or shorted oxygen sensor circuit – lean or rich indication – defective oxygen sensor or Electronic Control Unit (ECU)
6	No engine revolution sensor (Ne) signal to Electronic Control Unit (ECU) or Ne value being over 1000 rpm in spite of no Ne signal to ECU – defective igniter circuit, igniter, distributor or Electronic Control Unit (ECU)
7	Open or shorted Throttle Position Sensor (TPS) circuit – defective Throttle Position Sensor (TPS) or Electronic Control Unit (ECU)
8	Open or shorted intake air thermo sensor circuit – defective intake air thermo sensor circuit or Electronic Control Unit (ECU)
10	No starter switch signal to Electronic Control Unit (ECU) with vehicle speed at 0 and engine speed over 800 rpm – defective speed sensor circuit, main relay circuit, igniter switch-to-starter circuit, igniter switch or Electronic Control Unit (ECU)
11	Short circuit in check connector terminal T with the air conditioning switch ON or throttle switch (IDL) point OFF – defective air conditioner switch, Throttle Position Sensor (TPS) circuit, Throttle Position Sensor (TPS) or Electronic Control Unit (ECU)
12	Knock control sensor signal has not reached judgement level in succession – defective knock control sensor circuit, knock control sensor or Electronic Control Unit (ECU)
13	Knock CPU faulty

85784116

Fig. 77 ECM TROUBLE CODES—1985 Pick-up and 4Runner with 22R-E and 22R-TE engines

---

Year—1986
Model—Pick-Up / 4Runner
Engine—2.4L (144 cid) EFI 4 cyl
Engine Code—22R-E

ECM TROUBLE CODES

Code	Explanation
1	Normal operation
2	Open or shorted air flow meter circuit – defective air flow meter or Electronic Control Unit (ECU)
3	No signal from igniter 4 times in succession – defective igniter or main relay circuit, igniter or Electronic Control Unit (ECU)
4	Open or shorted Water Thermo Sensor (THW) circuit – defective Water Thermo Sensor (THW) or Electronic Control Unit (ECU)
5	Open or shorted oxygen sensor circuit – lean or rich indication – defective oxygen sensor or Electronic Control Unit (ECU)
6	No engine revolution sensor (Ne) signal to Electronic Control Unit (ECU) or Ne value being over 1000 rpm in spite of no Ne signal to ECU – defective igniter circuit, igniter, distributor or Electronic Control Unit (ECU)
7	Open or shorted Throttle Position Sensor (TPS) circuit – defective Throttle Position Sensor (TPS) or Electronic Control Unit (ECU)
8	Open or shorted intake air thermo sensor circuit – defective intake air thermo sensor circuit or Electronic Control Unit (ECU)
10	No starter switch signal to Electronic Control Unit (ECU) with vehicle speed at 0 and engine speed over 800 rpm – defective speed sensor circuit, main relay circuit, igniter switch-to-starter circuit, igniter switch or Electronic Control Unit (ECU)
11	Throttle switch (IDL) point in the Throttle Position Sensor (TPS) circuit, Throttle Position Sensor (TPS) or Electronic Control Unit (ECU)
12	Knock control sensor signal has not reached judgement level in succession – defective knock control sensor circuit, knock control sensor or Electronic Control Unit (ECU)
13	Knock CPU faulty – defective Electronic Control Unit (ECU)

85784117

Fig. 78 ECM TROUBLE CODES—1986 Pick-up and 4Runner with 22R-E engine

Year—1988
Model—Pick-Up, 4Runner VZN Series
Body VIN—N
Engine—3.0L (2959cc) **Cylinders**—6
Fuel System—Electronic Fuel Injection
Engine Identifier—3VZ-E **VIN**—V
Automatic Transmission Identifier—A340H

ENGINE CODES

Code	Explanation
--	Constant blinking of indicator light: No faults detected
11	Momentary interruption in ECU power supply
12	RPM NE or G signal to ECU—missing within 2 seconds after engine is cranked
13	RPM NE signal to ECU—missing when engine speed is above 1000 rpm
14	Igniter signal (IGF) to ECU—missing 6-8 times in succession
21	Oxygen sensor—detection of sensor/signal deterioration or open/short in sensor heater signal
22	Water temperature sensor signal (THW)—open/short
24	Intake air temperature sensor signal (THA)—open/short
25	Air-fuel ratio LEAN malfunction—feedback compensation or adaptive control value feedback frequency is abnormally high. Open circuit in oxygen sensor signal.
26	Air-fuel ratio RICH malfunction—feedback compensation or adaptive control value feedback frequency is abnormally high. Open circuit in oxygen sensor signal.
31	Air flow meter signal—VC circuit open/VC–E2 shorted when idle contacts are closed
32	Air flow meter signal—E2 circuit open/VC–VS shorted
41	Throttle position sensor signal (VTA)—open/short
42	Vehicle speed sensor—SPD signal missing for 8 seconds when engine speed is between 1500–4000 rpm and coolant temperature is above 176°F(80°C) except with engine racing
43	Starter signal (STA) to ECU—missing until engine speed reaches 800 rpm with vehicle stopped
51	Switch signal—A/C switch ON, Neutral start switch OFF, Idle switch OFF during diagnostic check
52	Knock sensor signal—open/short
53	Knock control signal in ECU—faulty knock control program
71	EGR system malfunction—EGR gas temperature below limit during EGR operation or open EGR gas temperature circuit (California only)

Fig. 82 ECM TROUBLE CODES—1988 Pick-up and 4Runner with 3VZ-E engine

85784122

Year—1988
Model—Land Cruiser
Body VIN—J
Engine—4.0L (3956cc) **Cylinders**—6
Fuel System—Electronic Fuel Injection
Engine Identifier—3F-E **VIN**—F

ENGINE CODES

Code	Explanation
--	Constant blinking of indicator light: No faults detected
11	Momentary interruption in ECU power supply
12	RPM NE or G signal to ECU—missing within 2 seconds after engine is cranked
13	RPM NE signal to ECU—missing when engine speed is above 1000 rpm
14	Igniter signal (IGf) to ECU—missing 6-8 times in succession
21	Oxygen sensor—detection of sensor/signal deterioration or open/short in sensor heater signal
22	Water temperature sensor signal—open/short
24	Intake air temperature sensor signal—open/short
25	Air-fuel ratio LEAN malfunction—feedback value at upper limit for a certain period, or feedback frequency is abnormally high during feedback condition
26	Air-fuel ratio RICH malfunction—feedback value at lower limit for a certain period, or feedback frequency is abnormally high during feedback condition
28	No. 2 oxygen sensor signal/heater signal—SAME AS CODE No. 21
31	Air flow meter signal—VC circuit open/VS–E2 shorted when idle contacts are closed
32	Air flow meter signal—E2 circuit open/VC–VS shorted
35	Altitude compensation (HAC) sensor signal—open/short
41	Throttle position sensor signal—open/short
42	Vehicle speed sensor—SPD signal missing for 8 seconds when engine speed is between 1500–5000 rpm and coolant temperature is below 176°F(80°C) except with engine racing
43	Starter signal (STA) to ECU—missing until engine speed reaches 800 rpm with vehicle stopped
51	IDL, NSW, or A/C signal to ECU—missing with check terminals E1 and TE1 shorted
71	EGR system malfunction—EGR gas temperature below limit during EGR operation (California only)

Fig. 83 ECM TROUBLE CODES—1988 Land Cruiser with 3F-E engine

85784123

Year—1988
Model—Pick-Up, 4Runner
Body VIN—N
Engine—2.4L (2366cc) **Cylinders**—4
Fuel System—Feedback Carburetor/Electronic Fuel Injection
Engine Identifier—22R, 22R-E, 22R-TE **VIN**—R
Automatic Transmission Identifier—A340H

ENGINE CODES (22R-E)

Code	Explanation
--	Constant blinking of indicator light: No faults detected
12	RPM NE signal to ECU—missing within 2 seconds after engine is cranked
13	RPM NE signal to ECU—missing when engine speed is above 1500 rpm
14	Igniter signal (IGf) to ECU—missing 4-5 times in succession
21	Oxygen sensor—detection of sensor/signal deterioration or open/short in sensor heater signal
22	Water temperature sensor signal—open/short
24	Intake air temperature sensor signal—open/short
25	Air-fuel ratio LEAN malfunction—feedback value continues at upper limit or oxygen sensor signal continues at the lower limit, for a certain period of time during feedback condition.
26	Air-fuel ratio RICH malfunction—feedback value continues at lower limit or oxygen sensor signal continues at the upper limit, for a certain period of time during feedback condition.
31	Air flow meter signal—short between VC-VB, VC-E2, or VS-VC or open circuit between VC-E2
35	HAC sensor circuit—open/short
41	Throttle position sensor signal—open/short
42	Vehicle speed sensor—SPD signal missing for 5 seconds when engine speed is above 2500 rpm
43	Starter signal (STA) to ECU—missing until engine speed reaches 800 rpm with vehicle stopped
51	Switch signal—IDL, NSW, or A/C signal to ECU missing with check terminals E1 and T shorted
52	Knock sensor signal—open/short
53	Knock control in ECU—faulty
71	EGR system malfunction—EGR gas temperature below limit during EGR operation

Codes listed above are for the 22R-E engine only, the 22R engine does not use engine codes.

ENGINE CODES (22R-TE)

Code	Explanation
1	Normal—appears when no other codes are detected
2	Air flow meter signal—VC-E2 open or VC-VB, VC-E2, or VS-VC shorted
3	Igniter signal (IGf)—missing 4-5 times in succession
4	Water temperature sensor signal—open/short
5	Oxygen sensor signal—open/short
6	RPM NE signal to ECU—missing when engine speed is over 1500 rpm
7	Throttle position sensor signal—open/short
8	Intake air temperature sensor signal—open/short
10	Starter "STA" signal to ECU—missing until engine speed reaches 800 rpm with vehicle stopped
11	Switch signal—A/C switch ON, Neutral start switch OFF, Idle switch OFF during diagnostic check
12	Knock sensor signal—open/short
13	Knock control signal—faulty knock control ECU
14	Turbocharger pressure—fuel cut-off due to high boost has occurred

Codes listed above are for the 22R-TE engine only, the 22R engine does not use engine codes.

Fig. 81 ECM TROUBLE CODES—1988 Pick-up and 4Runner with 22R, 22R-E and 22R-TE engines

85784121

VACUUM DIAGRAMS

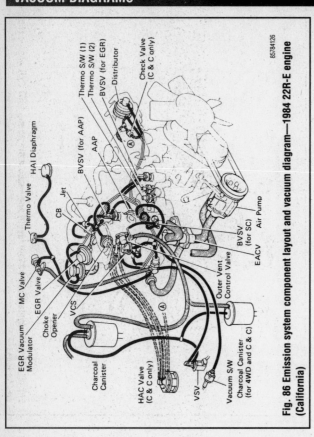

Fig. 86 Emission system component layout and vacuum diagram—1984 22R-E engine (California)

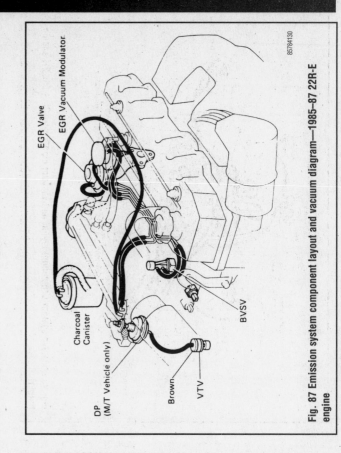

Fig. 87 Emission system component layout and vacuum diagram—1985–87 22R-E engine

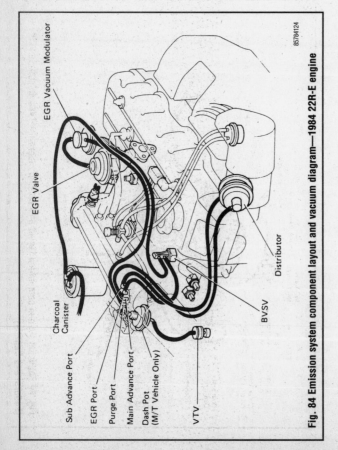

Fig. 84 Emission system component layout and vacuum diagram—1984 22R-E engine

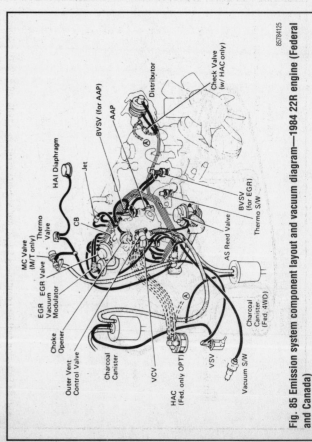

Fig. 85 Emission system component layout and vacuum diagram—1984 22R engine (Federal and Canada)

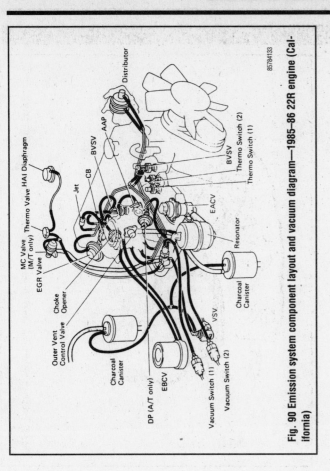

Fig. 90 Emission system component layout and vacuum diagram—1985-86 22R engine (California)

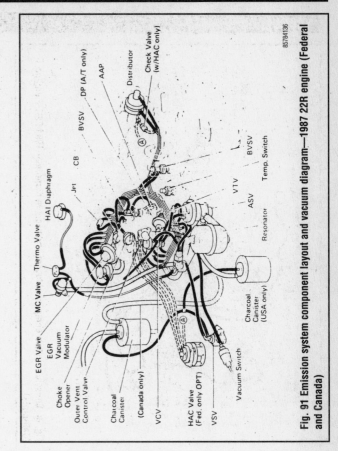

Fig. 91 Emission system component layout and vacuum diagram—1987 22R engine (Federal and Canada)

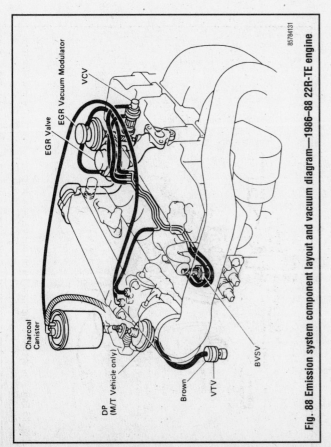

Fig. 88 Emission system component layout and vacuum diagram—1986-88 22R-TE engine

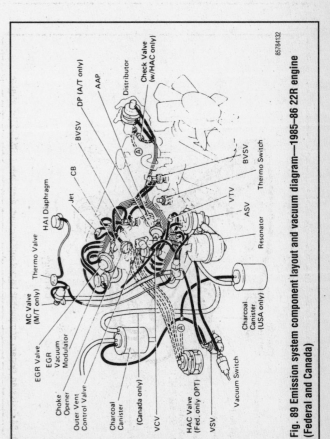

Fig. 89 Emission system component layout and vacuum diagram—1985-86 22R engine (Federal and Canada)

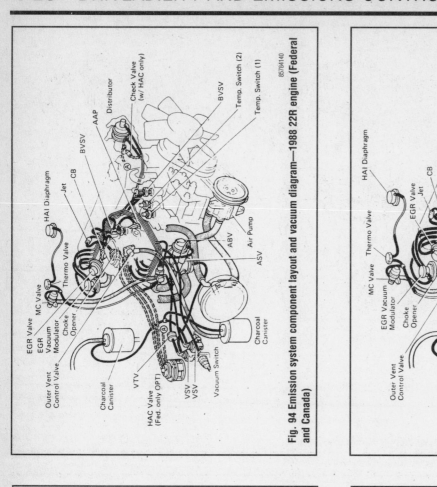

Fig. 94 Emission system component layout and vacuum diagram—1988 22R engine (Federal and Canada)

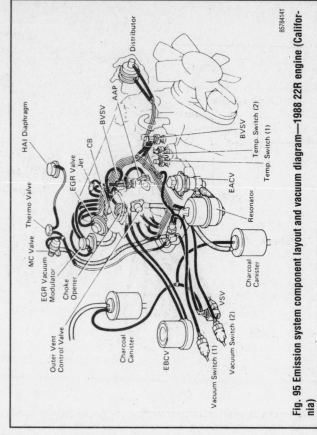

Fig. 95 Emission system component layout and vacuum diagram—1988 22R engine (California)

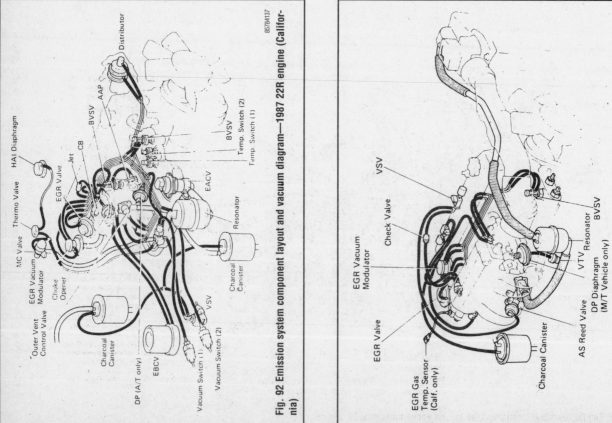

Fig. 92 Emission system component layout and vacuum diagram—1987 22R engine (California)

Fig. 93 Emission system component layout and vacuum diagram—1988 22R-E engine

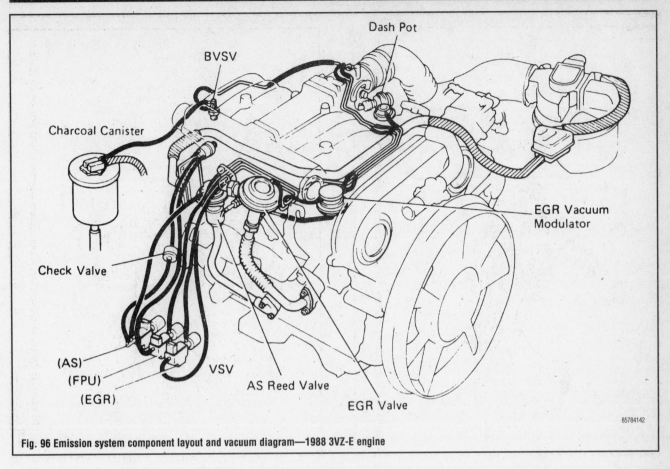

Fig. 96 Emission system component layout and vacuum diagram—1988 3VZ-E engine

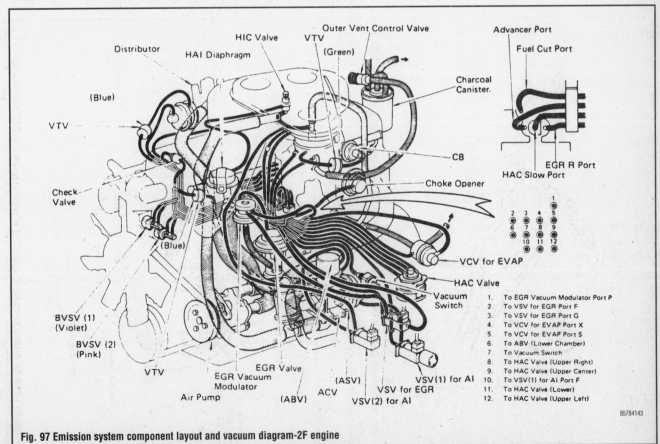

Fig. 97 Emission system component layout and vacuum diagram-2F engine

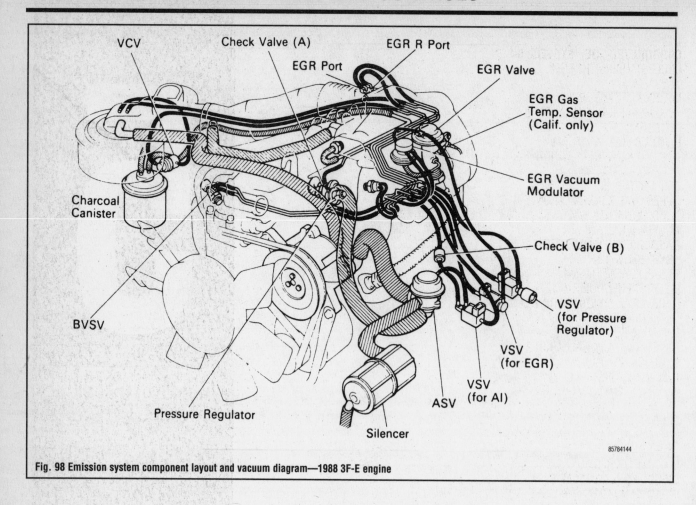

Fig. 98 Emission system component layout and vacuum diagram—1988 3F-E engine

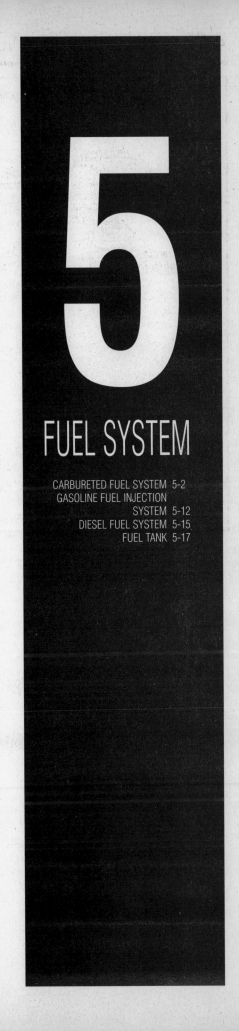

5

FUEL SYSTEM

CARBURETED FUEL SYSTEM

Understanding the Fuel System

An automotive fuel system consists of everything between the fuel tank and the carburetor or fuel injection unit. This includes the tank itself, all the lines, one or more fuel filters, a fuel pump (mechanical or electric), and the carburetor or fuel injection unit.

With the exception of the carburetor or fuel injection unit, the fuel system is quite simple in operation. Fuel is drawn from the tank through the fuel line by the fuel pump, which forces it to the fuel filter, and from there to the carburetor where it is distributed to the cylinders.

Mechanical Fuel Pump

All 1970–74 and 1980–88 Pick-Ups and all 1970–87 Land Cruisers are equipped with a mechanically operated fuel pump of diaphragm construction (some 1980–88 models use two different types of pump). A separate fuel filter is incorporated into the fuel line (see Section 1 for its required service). On 1970–74 Pick-Ups and all Land Cruisers, the fuel pump is located on the right side of the engine block. On 1980–88 models, it is located on the right side of the cylinder head.

REMOVAL & INSTALLATION

1970–74 Pick-Ups and 1970–87 Land Cruisers

▶ See Figure 1

1. Disconnect the negative battery cable.
2. Disconnect and plug both of the fuel lines from the fuel pump.
3. Unscrew and remove the two fuel pump mounting bolts.
4. Withdraw the fuel pump assembly from the engine block.
5. Installation is the reverse of the removal procedure. Make sure to use a new gasket when installing the fuel pump.
6. Start the engine and check the pump for any leaks.

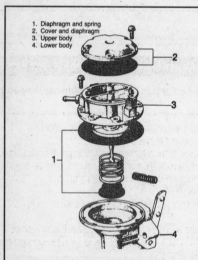

1. Diaphragm and spring
2. Cover and diaphragm
3. Upper body
4. Lower body

85785001

Fig. 1 Exploded view of the mechanical fuel pump—2F engine shown, 8R-C and 18R-C similar

1980–88 Pick-Ups

▶ See Figures 2 thru 7

1. Disconnect the negative battery cable.
2. Drain the radiator coolant.
3. Disconnect the upper radiator hose and wire it out of the way.
4. Disconnect and plug the three fuel lines from the fuel pump.
5. Unscrew the two fuel pump retaining bolts and remove the fuel pump and gasket.

To install:
6. Position a new gasket, then install the pump into the block and tighten the two mounting screws.
7. The remainder of installation is the reverse of the removal procedure.
8. Fill the system with coolant.
9. Connect the negative battery cable, then start the engine and check for any leaks.

TESTING

Fuel pumps should always be tested on the vehicle. The larger line between the pump and tank is the suction side of the system and the smaller line,

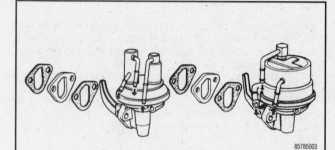

85785003

Fig. 2 Exploded view of the mechanical fuel pump—20R (1980) and 22R engines

85785053

Fig. 3 Removing the fuel lines from the fuel pump

85785054

Fig. 4 Removing the fuel pump mounting (left) bolt

Fig. 5 Removing the fuel pump mounting (right) bolt

Fig. 6 Removing the fuel pump

Fig. 7 View of the fuel pump assembly— always replace the gasket when installing

between the pump and carburetor or fuel injection pump is the pressure side. A leak in the pressure side would be apparent because of dripping fuel. A leak in the suction side is usually only apparent because of a reduced volume of fuel delivered to the pressure side.

1. Tighten any loose line connections and look for any kinks or restrictions.
2. Disconnect the fuel line at the carburetor or fuel pump. Disconnect the distributor-to-coil primary wire. Place a container at the end of the fuel line and crank the engine a few revolutions. If little or no fuel flows from the line, either the fuel pump is inoperative or the line is plugged. Blow through the lines with compressed air and try the test again. Reconnect the line.
3. If fuel flows in good volume, check the fuel pump pressure to be sure.
4. Attach a pressure gauge to the pressure side of the fuel line. On trucks equipped with a vapor return system, squeeze off the return hose.
5. Run the engine at idle and note the reading on the gauge. Stop the engine and compare the reading with the specifications listed in the "Tune-Up Specifications" chart, located in Section 2 of this manual. If the pump is operating properly, the pressure will be as specified and will be constant at idle speed. If pressure varies sporadically or is too high or low, the pump should be replaced.
6. Remove the pressure gauge.

The following flow test can also be performed:
7. Disconnect the fuel line from the carburetor or the fuel pump. Run the fuel line into a suitable measuring container.
8. Run the engine at idle until there is one pint of fuel in the container. One pint should be pumped in 30 seconds or less.
9. If the flow is below minimum, check for a restriction in the line.

The only way to check fuel pump pressure is by connecting an accurate pressure gauge to the fuel line at the carburetor level. Never replace a fuel pump without performing this simple test. If the engine seems to be starving out, check the ignition system first. Also check for a plugged fuel filter or a restricted fuel line before replacing the pump.

Electric Fuel Pump

▶ **See Figure 8**

All 1975–79 Pick-Ups are equipped with an electric fuel pump. The pump is located inside the fuel tank.

REMOVAL & INSTALLATION

1. Disconnect the negative battery cable.
2. Remove the trim panel from inside the trunk.
3. Remove the screws which secure the pump access plate to the fuel tank.
4. Withdraw the plate, gasket and pump assembly as one unit.

To install:
5. Disconnect all leads and hoses from the fuel pump.
6. Connect all leads and hoses to the fuel pump and then position the pump/plate assembly.

➡**Always use a new gasket when installing the fuel pump.**

7. Install the fuel pump access plate and the trim panel.
8. Connect the battery cable.
9. Start the engine and check for any leaks.

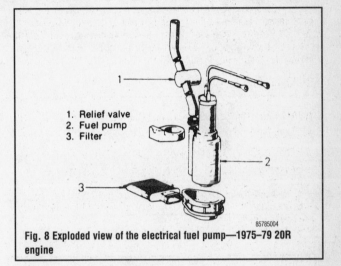

1. Relief valve
2. Fuel pump
3. Filter

Fig. 8 Exploded view of the electrical fuel pump—1975–79 20R engine

TESTING

⁕⁕ CAUTION

Do not operate the fuel pump unless it is immersed in gasoline and connected to its resistor.

1. Disconnect the lead from the oil pressure warning light sender.
2. Unfasten the line from the outlet side of the fuel filter.
3. Connect a pressure gauge to the filter outlet with a length of rubber hose.
4. Turn the ignition switch to the "ON" position, but do not start the engine.
5. Check the pressure gauge reading against the figure given in the "Tune-Up Specifications" chart in Section 2.
6. Check for a clogged filter or pinched lines if the pressure is not up to specification.
7. If there is nothing wrong with the filter or lines, replace the fuel pump.
8. Turn the ignition OFF and reconnect the fuel line to the filter. Connect the lead to the oil pressure sender also.

Carburetor

▶ **See Figures 9, 10, 11, 12 and 13**

The carburetors used on Toyota models are conventional 2 bbl, downdraft types similar to domestic carburetors. The main circuits are: primary, for normal operational requirements; secondary, to supply high speed fuel needs; float, to supply fuel to the primary and secondary circuits; accelerator, to supply fuel for quick and safe acceleration; choke, for reliable starting in cold weather; and power valve, for fuel economy. Although slight differences in appearance may be noted, these carburetors are basically alike. Of course, different jets and settings are demanded by the different engines to which they are fitted.

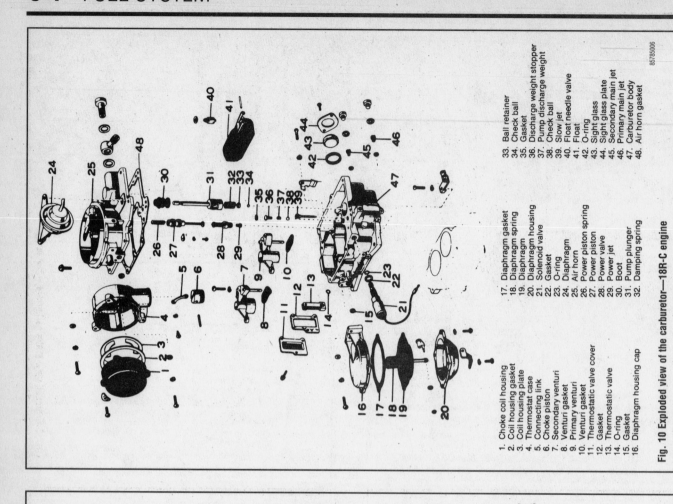

1. Choke coil housing
2. Coil housing gasket
3. Coil housing plate
4. Thermostat case
5. Connecting link
6. Choke piston
7. Secondary venturi
8. Venturi gasket
9. Primary venturi
10. Venturi gasket
11. Thermostatic valve cover
12. Gasket
13. Thermostatic valve
14. O-ring
15. Gasket
16. Diaphragm housing cap

17. Diaphragm gasket
18. Diaphragm spring
19. Diaphragm
20. Diaphragm housing
21. Solenoid valve
22. Gasket
23. O-ring
24. Diaphragm
25. Air horn
26. Power piston spring
27. Power piston
28. Power valve
29. Power jet
30. Boot
31. Pump plunger
32. Damping spring

33. Ball retainer
34. Check ball
35. Gasket
36. Discharge weight stopper
37. Pump discharge weight
38. Check ball
39. Slow jet
40. Float needle valve
41. Float
42. O-ring
43. Sight glass
44. Sight glass plate
45. Secondary main jet
46. Primary main jet
47. Carburetor body
48. Air horn gasket

Fig. 10 Exploded view of the carburetor—18R-C engine

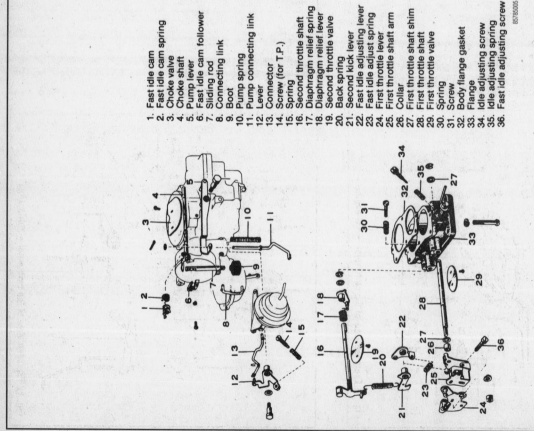

1. Fast idle cam
2. Fast idle cam spring
3. Choke valve
4. Choke shaft
5. Pump lever
6. Fast idle cam follower
7. Sliding rod
8. Connecting link
9. Boot
10. Pump spring
11. Pump connecting link
12. Lever
13. Connector
14. Screw (for T.P.)
15. Spring
16. Second throttle shaft
17. Diaphragm relief spring
18. Diaphragm relief lever
19. Second throttle valve
20. Back spring
21. Second kick lever
22. Fast idle adjusting lever
23. Fast idle adjust spring
24. First throttle lever
25. First throttle shaft arm
26. Collar
27. First throttle shaft shim
28. First throttle shaft
29. First throttle valve
30. Spring
31. Screw
32. Body flange gasket
33. Flange
34. Idle adjusting screw
35. Idle adjusting spring
36. Fast idle adjusting screw

Fig. 9 Exploded view of the carburetor—18R-C engine

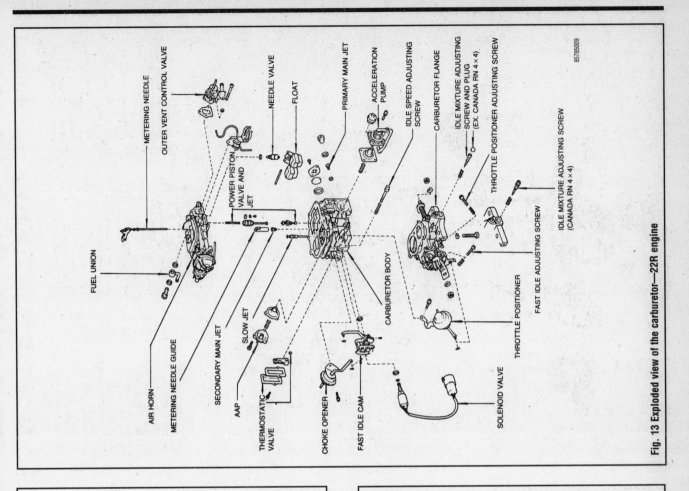

Fig. 13 Exploded view of the carburetor—22R engine

Labels: METERING NEEDLE, OUTER VENT CONTROL VALVE, NEEDLE VALVE, FLOAT, PRIMARY MAIN JET, ACCELERATION PUMP, IDLE SPEED ADJUSTING SCREW, CARBURETOR FLANGE, IDLE MIXTURE ADJUSTING SCREW AND PLUG (EX. CANADA RN 4 × 4), THROTTLE POSITIONER ADJUSTING SCREW, IDLE MIXTURE ADJUSTING SCREW (CANADA RN 4 × 4), POWER PISTON VALVE AND JET, CARBURETOR BODY, FAST IDLE ADJUSTING SCREW, THROTTLE POSITIONER, FUEL UNION, SECONDARY MAIN JET, SLOW JET, AAP, THERMOSTATIC VALVE, CHOKE OPENER, FAST IDLE CAM, SOLENOID VALVE, AIR HORN, METERING NEEDLE GUIDE

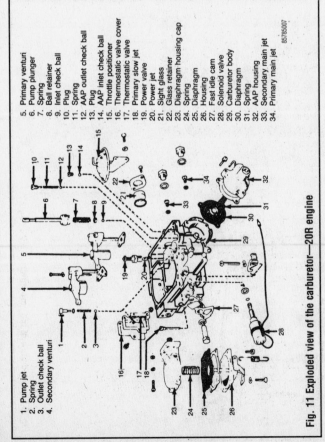

1. Pump jet
2. Spring
3. Outlet check ball
4. Secondary venturi
5. Primary venturi
6. Pump plunger
7. Spring
8. Ball retainer
9. Inlet check ball
10. Plug
11. Spring
12. AAP outlet check ball
13. Plug
14. AAP inlet check ball
15. Throttle positioner
16. Thermostatic valve cover
17. Thermostatic valve
18. Primary slow jet
19. Power valve
20. Power jet
21. Sight glass
22. Glass retainer
23. Diaphragm housing cap
24. Spring
25. Diaphragm
26. Housing
27. Fast idle cam
28. Solenoid valve
29. Carburetor body
30. Diaphragm
31. Spring
32. AAP housing
33. Secondary main jet
34. Primary main jet

Fig. 11 Exploded view of the carburetor—20R engine

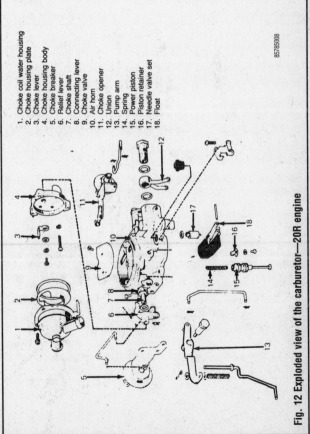

1. Choke coil water housing
2. Choke housing plate
3. Choke lever
4. Choke housing body
5. Choke breaker
6. Relief lever
7. Choke shaft
8. Connecting lever
9. Choke valve
10. Air horn
11. Choke opener
12. Union
13. Pump arm
14. Spring
15. Power piston
16. Piston retainer
17. Needle valve set
18. Float

Fig. 12 Exploded view of the carburetor—20R engine

REMOVAL & INSTALLATION

▶ **See Figures 14 thru 29**

1. Disconnect the negative battery cable.
2. Loosen the radiator drain plug and drain the coolant into a suitable container.
3. Unscrew the mounting screws and remove the air filter housing. Disconnect all hoses and lines leading from the air cleaner.
4. Tag and disconnect all fuel, vacuum, coolant and electrical lines or hoses leading from the carburetor.

5. Disconnect the accelerator linkage from the carburetor. On cars equipped with an automatic transmission, disconnect the throttle cable linkage running from the transmission.
6. Remove the four carburetor mounting bolts and lift off the carburetor and its gasket.

➡ **Cover the manifold opening with a clean rag to prevent anything from falling into the engine.**

7. Install the carburetor (with a new gasket), tighten the mounting bolts EVENLY in steps and reconnect all linkage.
8. Start the engine and check for any leaks. Check the float level.

Fig. 14 Removing the fuel line from the carburetor

Fig. 15 Side view of the carburetor

Fig. 16 Mark all hoses for correct installation before removing the carburetor

Fig. 17 Removing the carburetor front mounting bolts

Fig. 18 Removing the carburetor back mounting bolts

Fig. 19 Removing the carburetor front mounting bolts

Fig. 20 View of the carburetor front mounting bolts

Fig. 21 Removing all external brackets for carburetor removal

Fig. 22 Removing the carburetor assembly

Fig. 23 Removing the carburetor mounting gasket (insulator)

Fig. 24 Clean the carburetor mounting gasket (insulator) before installing the carburetor

Fig. 25 Adjust the idle speed after installing the carburetor

Fig. 26 Removing the pin for gas pedal linkage

Fig. 27 Removing the housing for gas pedal linkage

Fig. 28 Removing the clip for gas pedal linkage

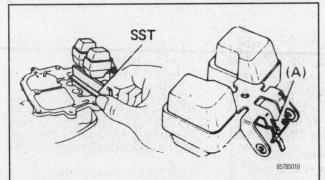

Fig. 29 Removing the wheel assembly pin for gas pedal linkage

ADJUSTMENTS

Float Level Adjustment

EXCEPT F AND 2F ENGINES

▶ See Figures 30 and 31

Float level adjustments are unnecessary on models equipped with a carburetor sight glass, if the fuel level falls within the lines when the engine is running.

There are two float level adjustments which may be made on Toyota carburetors. One is with the air horn inverted, so that the float is in a fully raised position; the other is with the air horn in an upright position, so that the float falls to the bottom of its travel.

The float level is either measured with a special carburetor float level gauge, which comes with a rebuilding kit, or with a standard wire gauge.

1. Turn the air horn upside down and let the float hang down by its own weight.

2. Using a special float gauge (available at your local dealer), check the

Fig. 30 Bend tab A to adjust the float in the raised position—22R engine

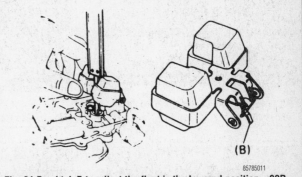

Fig. 31 Bend tab B to adjust the float in the lowered position—22R engine

clearance between the tip of the float and the flat surface of the air horn. The clearance should be:

  a. 8R-C: 9.4mm
  b. 18R-C: 5.0mm
  c. 20R:
  • 1975–77 — 5.0mm
  • 1978–80 — 7.0mm
  d. 22R:
  • 1981 — 9.8mm
  • 1982 — 10.5mm
  • 1982–88 — 9.8mm

➡**This measurement should be made without the gasket on the air horn.**

3. If the float clearance is not within specifications, adjust it by bending the upper (center) float tab.

4. Lift up the float and check the clearance between the needle valve plunger and the float lip. Clearance on the 8R-C and 18R-C engines may be checked with a special float gauge or with a standard wire feeler gauge. 20R and 22R engines must only use the special float gauge. The clearance should be 48mm on all engines.

5. If the clearance is not within specifications, adjust it by bending the lower float tabs (2).

F AND 2F ENGINES

1. Remove the carburetor air horn. Invert the air horn and allow the float to hang towards the air horn.

2. With the air horn gasket removed, measure the distance between the float and the air horn, at the end of the float opposite the needle valve. The distance should be 7.5mm. If adjustment is necessary, remove the float and bend the tab which is centered between the hinge pivot points. After the adjustment is completed, reinstall the float and recheck the setting.

3. Lift upward on the float and measure the distance between the needle valve push pin and the lip of the float. The distance should be 1.1mm. If adjustment is necessary, remove the float and bend the tabs located just inside of the hinge points. After the adjustment is completed, reinstall the float and recheck the setting.

Fast Idle Adjustment—Carburetor Off Truck

8R-C AND 18R-C

With the carburetor inverted and the choke fully closed, measure the distance from the primary throttle plate to the throttle bore using a wire gauge. It should measure 0.74mm on 8R-C carburetors, 1.0mm on 18R-Cs. Adjust the clearance to specifications by turning the fast idle adjustment screw.

1975–79 20R, F AND 2F ENGINES

1. Remove the carburetor as previously outlined.
2. Close the choke valve completely and invert the carburetor.
3. Using a wire type feeler gauge, check the clearance between the upper half of the primary throttle blade and the throttle bore. The clearance should be 0.047 for 20R engines; 0.051 for F and 2F engines. If necessary, adjust the clearance by turning the fast idle screw.
4. Install the carburetor as previously outlined.

1980 20R AND 1981–88 22R ENGINES

◗ See Figure 32

➡A special blade angle tool must be obtained to properly make this adjustment.

1. Remove the carburetor as previously outlined.
2. Close the choke valve completely and set the throttle shaft lever to the first seep of the fast idle cam.
3. Attach the blade angle tool to the primary throttle blade. Adjust the primary throttle blade angle to 23° from horizontal by turning the fast idle screw.
4. Remove the angle tool from the carburetor and install the carburetor as previously outlined.

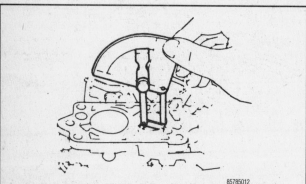

Fig. 32 Fast idle adjustment with the carburetor off the vehicle—22R engine

Fast Idle Adjustment—Carburetor On Truck

1975–79 20R ENGINE

1. Start the engine and allow it to reach normal operating temperature.
2. Stop the engine and disconnect the vacuum hose from the EGR valve. Connect a tachometer to the engine as previously outlined.
3. Open the throttle valve slightly and close the choke plate, which will set the fast idle cam.
4. Disconnect the vacuum hose(s) from the distributor vacuum unit. Plug the vacuum hose end(s).
5. Without touching the accelerator pedal, start the engine and read the tachometer. If necessary, adjust the fast idle speed to 2400 rpm by turning the fast idle screw.
6. Reconnect the vacuum hoses to both the EGR valve and the distributor vacuum unit. Disconnect the tachometer from the engine.

1980 20R AND 1981–88 22R ENGINES

1. Start the engine and allow it to reach normal operating temperature.
2. Stop the engine and connect a tachometer to the engine as previously outlined.
3. Remove the air cleaner assembly.

4. Disconnect the vacuum hose at the fast idle cam breaker (if so equipped) and plug the hose end.
5. Disconnect the vacuum hose(s) from the distributor vacuum unit.
6. Disconnect the vacuum hose from the EGR valve.
7. Open the throttle valve slightly and fully pull up on the fast idle linkage. Release the throttle.
8. Without touching the accelerator pedal, start the engine and read the tachometer. If necessary, adjust the fast idle speed by turning the fast idle screw. 20R and 1981-83 22R: 2400 rpm; 1984-86: 2600 rpm; 1987-88: 3000 rpm.
9. Reconnect the vacuum hoses, disconnect the tachometer and reinstall the air cleaner.

F AND 2F ENGINES

1. Start the engine and allow it to reach normal operating temperature.
2. Stop the engine and connect a tachometer to the engine as previously outlined.
3. Remove the air cleaner assembly.
4. Disconnect the vacuum hoses from both the EGR valve and the distributor vacuum unit.
5. Pull the dash mounted choke control knob fully outward.
6. Open the choke plate and prevent it from closing using a screwdriver. Do not jam the screwdriver into place.
7. Start the engine and read the tachometer. If necessary, adjust the fast idle speed to 1800 rpm by turning the fast idle screw.
8. Remove the screwdriver from the choke. Disconnect the tachometer and reconnect the vacuum hoses.
9. Install the air cleaner assembly.

Unloader Adjustment

◗ See Figure 33

The unloader adjustment is made with the primary throttle valve fully open. With the valve open, check the choke valve angle with a special gauge supplied in the rebuilding kit or with a gauge of the proper angle fabricated out of cardboard. The angle of the choke valve opening should be:

- 8R-C: 51°
- 18R-C: 47°
- 20R: 50°
- 22R: 45° (50° for 1983)

All angles, should be measured from the horizontal plane created by a closed choke valve.

To adjust the angle, bend the fast idle lever until the proper measurement is achieved.

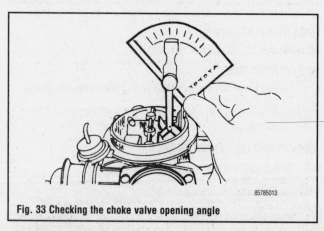

Fig. 33 Checking the choke valve opening angle

ON VEHICLE—1975–88

➡Disconnect the EGR valve vacuum line on 20R engines.

1. Perform the idle speed/mixture adjustments as outlined in Section 2. Leave the tachometer connected.
2. Remove the top of the air cleaner.
3. Open the throttle valve slightly and close the choke valve. Next, hold the choke valve with your finger and close the throttle valve. The choke valve is now fully closed.

4. Without depressing the accelerator pedal, start the engine.

5. Check to see that the engine fast idle speed is as noted previously.

6. If the reading on the tachometer is not within specifications, adjust the fast idle speed by turning the fast idle screw.

7. Disconnect the tachometer, install the air cleaner cover, and connect the EGR valve vacuum line if it was disconnected.

Reloader Adjustment

▶ See Figure 34

A reloader is used on the 8R-C engine to prevent the throttle valve from opening during automatic choke operation.

1. When the choke valve is opened 45° from the closed position, the reloader lever should disengage from its stop.

➥**Angle, "A", in the illustration, should be 20° when measured with a gauge.**

2. To adjust, bend the portion of the linkage where angle "|`A" was measured.

3. When the primary throttle valve is fully opened, with the reloader in operating position, the clearance between the secondary throttle valve edge and bore should be 0.35–0.76mm. Measure the clearance with a wire gauge and bend the reloader tab to adjust it.

4. Fully open the choke valve by hand; the reloader lever should be disengaged from its stop by the weight on its link.

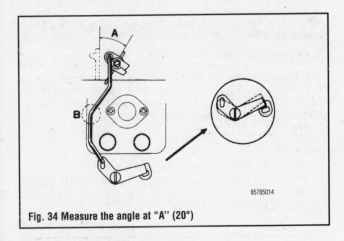

Fig. 34 Measure the angle at "A" (20°)

Choke Breaker Adjustment

▶ See Figures 35, 36, 37 and 38

1975–79 20R ENGINES

1. Push the rod which comes out of the upper (choke breaker) diaphragm so that the choke valve opens.

2. Measure the choke valve opening angle. It should be 40°.

3. Adjust the angle, if necessary, by bending the relief lever link.

1980 20R AND 1981–88 22R ENGINES

1. Apply vacuum to the larger of the two diaphragms.

2. Check that the angle of the choke plate is 38°, measured from the horizontal plane. Angle on 1983-88 engines is 42°.

3. If the angle is incorrect, adjust it by bending the choke breaker link.

4. Apply vacuum to both of the diaphragms and check the choke plate angle again. It should be approximately 60° (measured from the horizontal plane as before).

5. If the angle is not within specifications, the choke breaker will require replacement.

Initial Idle Mixture Screw Adjustment

When assembling the carburetor, turn the idle mixture screw the number of turns specified below. After the carburetor is installed, perform the appropriate idle speed/mixture adjustment as detailed in Section 2.

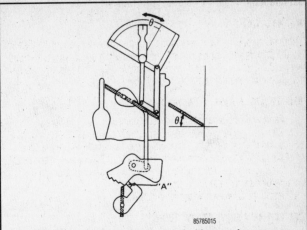

Fig. 35 The choke angle can be measured with an angle gauge, as shown here, or with a piece of cardboard cut to the proper angle— on the 20R, blend the fast idle lever at "A" to adjust the unloader angle

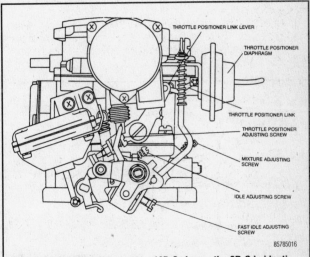

Fig. 36 Carburetor adjustments—18R-C shown, the 8R-C is identical, except that the idle speed screw is opposite the fast idle screw

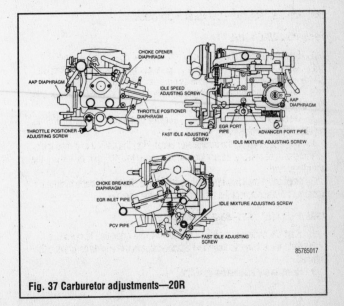

Fig. 37 Carburetor adjustments—20R

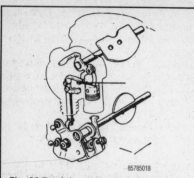

Fig. 38 Bend the choke shaft tab to adjust the unloader angle on 8R-C and 18R-C carburetors

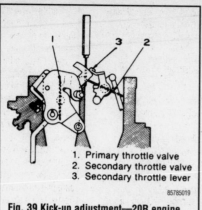

1. Primary throttle valve
2. Secondary throttle valve
3. Secondary throttle lever

Fig. 39 Kick-up adjustment—20R engine

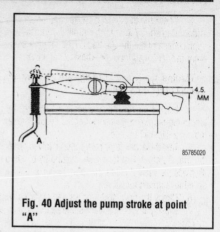

Fig. 40 Adjust the pump stroke at point "A"

8R-C: 2 turns from seating.
18R-C: 2½ turns from fully closed.
20R:
- 1975–79—1¾ turns from fully closed
- 1980 Federal—2½ turns from fully closed
- 1980 California—1⅓ turns from fully closed
22R:
- 1982—2½ turns from fully closed
- 1983–88—4 turns from fully closed
F:1¾ turns from fully closed
2F: 1¾ turns from fully closed.

Kick-Up Adjustment

18R-C AND 20R

♦ See Figure 39

1. Open the primary throttle valve. On 18R-C engines, the valve should be open 64° from bore; on 20R engines, the valve should be open all the way.
2. The secondary throttle valve-to-bore clearance should be 0.20mm. If not, adjust the clearance by bending the secondary throttle lever.

F AND 2F ENGINES

➡A special blade angle gauge is needed for this adjustment.

1. Remove the carburetor as previously outlined.
2. Attach the blade angle gauge to the secondary throttle blade.
3. Open the primary throttle blade fully and read the blade angle gauge. The secondary throttle blade should open slightly to an angle of 28° (except California) or 25° (California). If adjustment is necessary, bend the secondary throttle lever as required to attain the proper angle.
4. Detach the blade angle gauge and install the carburetor as previously outlined.

Throttle Positioner Adjustment

1. Apply vacuum to the throttle positioner diaphragm.
2. The throttle valve opening angle should be 16.5° from the horizontal plane. If not, adjust it by turning the adjusting screw.

Pump Stroke Adjustment

♦ See Figure 40

Check that the length of the pump stroke (length that the pump lever travels) is 4.0mm. If it is not, it can be adjusted by bending the connecting link.

Accelerator Pump Adjustment

18R-C, 20R AND 2F

Adjust the amount of pump stroke to 4.5mm on 18R-C and 1975–79 20R carburetors by bending the pump rod at point "A". The 1980 20R adjustment should be 4.0mm. The 2F is 9.5mm.

Automatic Choke Inspection and Adjustment

➡Steps 1–4 must be performed with the engine cold and turned OFF.

1. Remove the air cleaner lid.
2. Depress the accelerator pedal. The choke plate should close. If the choke plate closes, proceed to Step 5.
3. If the choke plate does not close, loosen the three screws around the thermostat case.

❋ CAUTION

Do not loosen the center housing screw, coolant leakage will occur.

4. Rotate the case just until the choke plate closes and tighten the case screws.
5. Start the engine and allow it to reach normal operating temperature. If the choke plate opens fully, the choke adjustment is correct. If it does not, loosen the three case screws and rotate the case until the choke is fully open. Tighten the case screws.

OVERHAUL

Efficient carburetion depends greatly on careful cleaning and inspection during overhaul, since dirt, gum, water, or varnish in or on the carburetor parts are often responsible for poor performance.

Overhaul your carburetor in a clean, dust-free area. Carefully disassemble the carburetor, referring often to the exploded views. Keep all similar and look-alike parts segregated during disassembly and cleaning to avoid accidental interchange during assembly. Make a note of all jet sizes.

When the carburetor is disassembled, wash all parts (except diaphragms, electric choke units, pump plunger, and any other plastic, leather, fiber, or rubber parts) in clean carburetor solvent. Do not leave parts in the solvent any longer than is necessary to sufficiently loosen the deposits. Excessive cleaning may remove the special finish from the float bowl and choke valve bodies, leaving these parts unfit for service. Rinse all parts in clean solvent and blow them dry with compressed air. Wipe clean all cork, plastic, leather, and fiber parts with a clean, lint-free cloth.

➡Carburetor solvent is available in various-sized solvent cans, which are designed with a removable small parts basket in the top. The carburetor choke chamber and body, and all small parts can be soaked in this can until clean. These solvent cans are available at most auto parts stores, and are quite handy for soaking other small engine parts.

Blow out all passages and jets with compressed air and be sure that there are not restrictions or blockages. Never use wire or similar tools to clean jets, fuel passages, or air bleeds. Clean all jets and valves separately to avoid accidental interchange.

Check all parts for wear or damage. If wear or damage is found, replace the defective parts. Especially check the following:

1. Check the float needle and seat for wear. If wear is found, replace the complete assembly.
2. Check the float hinge pin for wear and the float(s) for dents or distortion. Replace the float if fuel has leaked into it.

3. Check the throttle and choke shaft bores for wear or an out-of-round condition. Damage or wear to the throttle arm, shaft, or shaft bore will often require replacement of the throttle body. These parts require a close tolerance of fit; wear may allow air leakage, which could affect starting and idling.

➡**Throttle shafts and bushings are not included in overhaul kits. They can be purchased separately.**

4. Inspect the idle mixture adjusting needles for burrs or grooves. Any such condition requires replacement of the needle, since you will not be able to obtain a satisfactory idle.

5. Test the accelerator pump check valves. They should pass air one way but not the other. Test for proper seating by blowing and sucking on the valve. Replace the valve if necessary. If the valve is satisfactory, wash the valve again to remove breath moisture.

6. Check the bowl cover for warped surfaces with a straight edge.

7. Closely inspect the valves and seats for wear and damage, replacing as necessary.

8. After the carburetor is assembled, check the choke valve for freedom of operation.

Carburetor overhaul kits are recommended for each overhaul. These kits contain all gaskets and new parts to replace those that deteriorate most rapidly. Failure to replace all parts supplied with the kit (especially gaskets) can result in poor performance and a leaky carburetor later.

Most carburetor manufacturers supply overhaul kits in at least one of three basic types: minor repair; major repair; and gasket kits. Basically, they contain the following, and are available at most auto parts jobbers and Toyota dealers:

• **Minor Repair Kits**—All gaskets, float, needle valve, volume control screw, all diaphragms, and spring for the pump diaphragm.

• **Major Repair Kits**—All jets and gaskets, diaphragms, float, needle valve, volume control screw, pump ball valve, main jet carrier and float.

• **Gasket Kits**—All gaskets.

After cleaning and checking all components, reassemble the carburetor, using new parts and referring to the exploded view. When reassembling, make sure that all screws and jets are tight in their seats, but do not overtighten as the tips will be distorted. Tighten all screws gradually in rotation. Do not tighten needle valves into their seats; uneven jetting will result. Always use new gaskets. Be sure to adjust the float level when reassembling.

CARBURETOR SPECIFICATIONS

Year	Engine	Float Level Adjustment (in.)	Fast Idle Adjustment	Choke Unloader (deg.)	Choke Reloader (in.)	Choke Breaker (deg.)	Kick Up Adjustment	Accelerator Pump Adjustment (in.)
1970	8R-C	0.37	0.029 in.	51	0.014–0.030	—	—	—
	F	0.295①	—	50	—	38	28°②	0.374
1971	8R-C	0.37	0.029 in.	51	0.014–0.030	—	—	—
	F	0.295①	—	50	—	38	28°②	0.374
1972	18R-C	0.20	0.040 in.	47	—	—	0.008 in.	0.177
	F	0.295①	—	50	—	38	28°②	0.374
1973	18R-C	0.20	0.040 in.	47	—	—	0.008 in.	0.177
	F	0.295①	—	50	—	38	28°②	0.374
1974	18R-C	0.20	0.040 in.	47	—	—	0.008 in.	0.177
	F	0.295①	—	50	—	38	28°②	0.374
1975	20R	0.197	0.047 in.	50	—	40	0.008 in.	0.177
	2F	0.295①	—	50	—	38	28°②	0.374
1976	20R	0.197	0.047 in.	50	—	40	0.008 in.	0.177
	2F	0.295①	—	50	—	38	28°②	0.374
1977	20R	0.197	0.047 in.	50	—	40	0.008 in.	0.177
	2F	0.295①	—	50	—	38	28°②	0.374
1978	20R	0.276	0.047 in.	50	—	40	0.008 in.	0.177
	2F	0.295①	—	50	—	38	28°②	0.374
1979	20R	0.28	0.047 in.	50	—	38	0.008 in.	0.177
	2F	0.295①	—	50	—	38	28°②	0.374
1980	20R	0.28	0.047 in.	50	—	38	0.008 in.	0.154
	2F	0.236①	0.051 in.	50	—	45	25°	0.374
1981	22R	0.413③	24°	45④	—	38	—	—
	2F	0.236①	0.051 in.	50	—	45	25°	0.374
1982	22R	0.413③	24°	45④	—	38	—	—
	2F	0.236①	0.051 in.	50	—	45	25°	0.374
1983	22R	0.386③	22°	45④	—	38–42	—	—
	2F	0.236①	0.051 in.	50	—	45	25°	0.374
1984	22R	0.386③	22°	45④	—	38–42	—	—
	2F	0.236①	0.051 in.	50	—	45	25°	0.374
1985	22R	0.386③	22°	45④	—	38–42	—	—
	2F	0.236①	0.051 in.	50	—	45	25°	0.374
1986	22R	0.386③	23°	45	—	42	—	—
	2F	0.236①	0.051 in.	50	—	45	25°	0.374
1987	22R	0.386③	23°	45	—	42	—	—
	2F	0.236①	0.051 in.	50	—	45	25°	0.374
1988	22R	0.386③	23°	45	—	42	—	—

① Raised; float lowered: 0.043 in.
② California: 25°
③ Raised position; lowered position: 1.89 in.
④ Canada: 50°

85785021

Carburetor Specifications (cont.)

Year	Engine	Float Level Adjustment (in.)	Fast Idle Adjustment	Choke Unloader (deg.)	Choke Reloader (in.)	Choke Breaker (deg.)	Kick Up Adjustment	Accelerator Pump Adjustment (in.)
1984	22R	0.386 ③	22°	45 ④	—	38–42	—	—
	2F	0.236 ①	0.051 in.	50	—	45	25°	0.374
1985	22R	0.386 ③	22°	45 ④	—	38–42	—	—
	2F	0.236 ①	0.051 in.	50	—	45	25°	0.374
1986	22R	0.386 ③	23°	45	—	42	—	—
	2F	0.236 ①	0.051 in.	50	—	45	25°	0.374
1987	22R	0.386 ③	23°	45	—	42	—	—
	2F	0.236 ①	0.051 in.	50	—	45	25°	0.374
1988	22R	0.386 ③	23°	45	—	42	—	—

① Raised; float lowered: 0.043 in.
② California: 25°
③ Raised position; lowered position: 1.89 in.
④ Canada: 50°

85785C21

GASOLINE FUEL INJECTION SYSTEM

Troubleshooting

Engine troubles are not usually caused by the EFI system. When troubleshooting, always check first the condition of all other related systems.

Many times the most frequent cause of problems is a bad contact in a wiring connector, so always make sure that the connections are secure. When inspecting the connector, pay particular attention to the following:

1. Check to see that the terminals are not bent.
2. Check to see that the connector is pushed in all the way and locked.
3. Check that there is no change in signal when the connector is tapped or wiggled.

Actual troubleshooting of the EFI system and the EFI computer is a complex process which requires the use of a few expensive and hard to find tools. Other than checking the operation of the main components individually, we suggest that you leave any further troubleshooting to an authorized service facility.

➡ **The worst enemy of any fuel injection system is water or moisture. The best (i.e., cheapest and simplest) insurance for your truck's injection system is to change the fuel filter as frequently as the maintenance schedule recommends. When you follow the filter change interval strictly, many possible expensive injection system problems are eliminated.**

Electric Fuel Pump

All fuel injected trucks are equipped with an electric fuel pump. The fuel pump on the 1984 Pick-Up is attached to the front side of the fuel tank. The pump on 1985-88 models is located inside the fuel tank.

REMOVAL & INSTALLATION

1984 Pick-Up

1. Disconnect the negative battery cable.
2. Unplug the fuel pump wiring connector.
3. Unscrew the four bolts and remove the service hole cover.
4. Disconnect and plug the fuel pump inlet hose.
5. Remove the bolt at the fuel pump bracket.
6. Raise the rear of the truck and support it with jack stands.
7. Remove the fuel pipe bracket. Slowly loosen and then disconnect the fuel pump outlet hose.
8. Unscrew the two remaining fuel pump bracket bolts and then remove the pump.
9. Installation is the reverse of the removal procedure. Start the engine and check for any leaks.

1985–88 Pick-Up and 1988 Land Cruiser

♦ **See Figure 41**

1. Drain the fuel from the tank and then remove the fuel tank.
2. Remove the seven bolts and then pull the fuel pump bracket up and out of the fuel tank.
3. Remove the two nuts and then tag and disconnect the wires at the fuel pump.
4. Pull the fuel pump out of the lower side of the bracket. Disconnect the pump from the fuel hose.
5. Remove the rubber cushion and the clip. Disconnect the fuel pump filter from the pump.

To install:

6. Install the fuel pump filter to the pump.
7. Insert the outlet port of the fuel pump into the fuel hose.
8. Install the rubber cushion to the lower side of the fuel pump.
9. Push the lower side of the fuel pump (and the rubber cushion) into the pump bracket.
10. Using a new gasket, position the bracket on the fuel tank and then install and tighten the seven mounting bolts to 30 inch lbs. (3.4 Nm).
11. Install the fuel tank.
12. Start the truck and check for any loose connections or leaks.

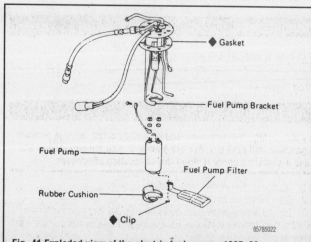

Fig. 41 Exploded view of the electric fuel pump—1985–88

85785022

TESTING

▶ See Figures 42 and 43

1. Turn the ignition switch to the "ON" position, but don't start the engine.
2. Remove the rubber cap from the fuel pump check connector and short terminals **FP** and **+B**.
3. Check that there is pressure in the hose to the cold start injector.

➡ At this time you should be able to hear the fuel return noise from the pressure regulator.

4. If no pressure can be felt in the line, check the fuses and all other related electrical connections. If everything is all right, the fuel pump will probably require replacement.
5. Remove the service wire, reinstall the rubber cap and turn off the ignition switch.

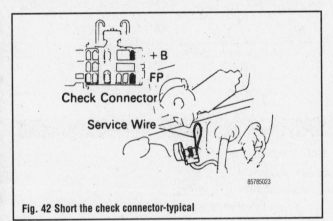

Fig. 42 Short the check connector-typical

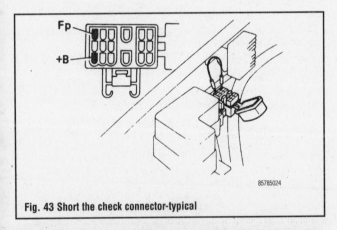

Fig. 43 Short the check connector-typical

Throttle Body

REMOVAL & INSTALLATION

▶ See Figure 44

✳✳ CAUTION

Any time a high fuel pressure line is disconnected, a large amount of gasoline will spill out. Always slowly loosen the connection and place a container under it. Plug the connection afterwards.

1. Disconnect the negative battery cable.
2. Drain the engine coolant.
3. Tag and disconnect all lines, hoses or wires that lead from the throttle body. Position them out of the way. Remove the air intake connector and the air cleaner hose.
4. Unscrew the mounting bolts and remove the throttle body and gasket.

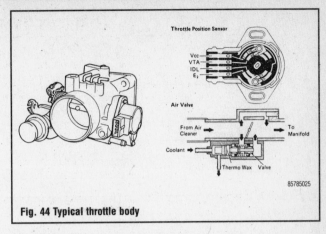

Fig. 44 Typical throttle body

To install:

5. Install the throttle body using a new gasket and tighten the mounting bolts to 9–13 ft. lbs. (12–18 Nm).
6. Connect the air cleaner hose and the air intake connector.
7. Reconnect all lines, hoses and wires.
8. Fill the engine with coolant and connect the battery cable.

CHECKING

1. Check that the throttle linkage moves smoothly.
2. Start the engine and remove the hose from the vacuum port.
3. With your finger, check that there is no vacuum at idle and that there is vacuum at anything other than idle.
4. Unplug the electrical connector from the throttle position sensor.
5. Insert a flat feeler gauge between the throttle stop screw and the stop lever.
6. Using an ohmmeter, check the continuity between each terminal on the sensor.
7. Check the dash pot as detailed previously in this section and also in Section 2.

Fuel Injectors

There is one fuel injector for each cylinder. They spray fuel into the intake port, in front of the intake valve. When the injector is energized, the coil pulls the plunger up, opening the needle valve and allowing the fuel to pass through the injector. Opening of the injectors is controlled by the EFI computer. The injectors operate at low pressure and are open for only a fraction of a second at a time.

REMOVAL & INSTALLATION

▶ See Figures 45 thru 50

1. Disconnect the negative battery cable.
2. Place a suitable container under the intake manifold to catch any dripping fuel.
3. Remove the air intake chamber as detailed in "Cylinder Head Removal & Installation" in Section 3 of this manual. Throttle body also must be removed on 22R-E.
4. On all engines, tag and disconnect all hoses and wires which interfere with injector removal.
5. Unplug the wiring connectors from the tops of the fuel injectors and remove the two plastic clamps that hold the wiring harness to the fuel delivery pipe.
6. Unscrew the four mounting bolts and remove the delivery pipe with the injectors attached. Do not remove the injector cover.
7. Pull the injectors out of the delivery pipe.
   To install:
8. Insert new insulators into the injector holes on the intake manifold.
9. Install the grommet and a new O-ring to the delivery pipe end of each injector.
10. Apply a thin coat of gasoline to the O-ring on each injector and then press them into the delivery pipe.

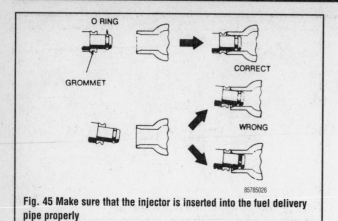

Fig. 45 Make sure that the injector is inserted into the fuel delivery pipe properly

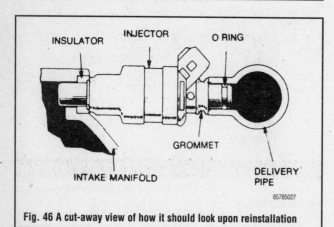

Fig. 46 A cut-away view of how it should look upon reinstallation

11. Install the injectors together with the delivery pipe in the intake manifold. Tighten the mounting bolts to 11–15 ft. lbs.

12. Clip the wiring harness into the delivery pipe and then connect the wiring connectors to the top of each injector.

13. Reconnect all hoses and wires.

14. Install the throttle body and air intake chamber.

15. Connect the battery cable.

16. Start the engine and check for any fuel leaks.

TESTING

♦ See Figure 51

We recommend that any checking or testing of the injectors, other than that included below, be left to an authorized service facility.

Injector operation can be checked with the injectors installed in the engine. A sound scope is needed here (a stethoscope-like device you can usually rent from tool rental shops; they are also available new from most auto tool and parts jobbers).

With the engine running or cranking, check each injector for normal operating noise (a buzzing or humming), which changes in proportion to engine rpm. If a sound scope is not available to you, check injector operation by touching each injector with your finger. It should be buzzing. If no sound or an unusual sound is heard, check the wiring connector, or have the injector checked professionally.

Measure injector resistance by unplugging the wiring connector from the injector, and connecting an ohmmeter. Check the continuity at both terminals; resistance should be:
- 1984-87 22R-E and 22R-TE: 1.5–3.0 ohms.
- 1988 22R-E: 1.0–2.5 ohms.
- 1988 22R-TE: 1.1–2.0 ohms.
- 1988 3V-ZE: 1.1–2.2 ohms.
- 1988 3F-E: 13.8 ohms.

Fig. 47 Do not remove the cover after each injector is removed

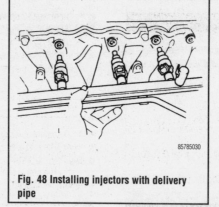

Fig. 48 Installing injectors with delivery pipe

Fig. 49 When installing, make sure the injectors rotate smoothly; if not, check the O-rings

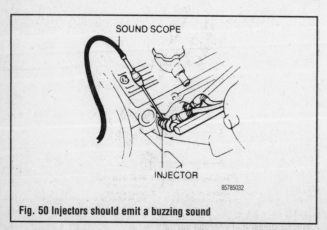

Fig. 50 Injectors should emit a buzzing sound

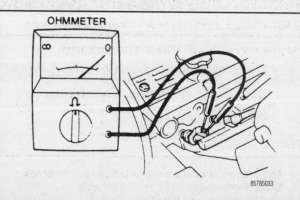

Fig. 51 Measuring injector resistance across both terminals

Cold Start Injector

During cold engine starting, the cold start injector is used to supply additional fuel to the intake manifold to aid in initial start-up. The opening and closing of the injector is determined by the Start Injector Time Switch. When the engine coolant temperature falls below a certain point, the switch is tripped and then opens the cold start injector. As the engine coolant warms up, the switch will eventually close the injector.

REMOVAL & INSTALLATION

▶ **See Figure 52**

1. Disconnect the negative battery cable.
2. Remove the cold start injector union bolt(s) on the delivery pipe.

➡ **Before removing the union bolt, place a suitable container under it to catch any escaping fuel.**

3. Disconnect the wiring connector at the injector.
4. Unscrew the two mounting bolts and then remove the cold start injector from the air intake chamber.
5. Installation is the reverse of the removal procedure. Always use a new gasket when reinstalling the injector.
6. Start the engine and check for any leaks.

TESTING

1. Unplug the wiring connector and remove the cold start injector from the air intake chamber.

➡ **Do not disconnect the fuel line.**

2. Using Special Tool 09843-30011, connect one end to the injector and the other to the battery.

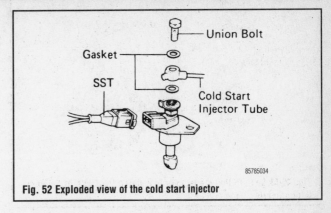

Fig. 52 Exploded view of the cold start injector

3. Remove the rubber cap from the Fuel Pump Check terminal and short both terminals with a wire.
4. Hold the injector over a suitable container and then turn the ignition switch to the "ON" position. Do not start the engine.
5. Check that the fuel splash pattern is even and V-shaped.
6. Disconnect the test probes from the battery and check that the fuel does not leak from the injector tip any more than one drop per minute.
7. Remove the Special Tool and reinstall the cold start injector.
8. Check the resistance of the injector. It should be 2–4 ohms.
9. If the cold start injector did not operate properly in any of these tests, it will require replacement.

EFI Computer

The EFI computer is located below the glove box in the right side kick panel. Removal and/or inspection of this unit should be left to an authorized service facility.

DIESEL FUEL SYSTEM

Injector Nozzles and Lines

REMOVAL

▶ **See Figures 53, 54, 55, 56 and 57**

1. Remove the air cleaner pipe on the 2L-T.
2. Remove the air intake pipe on the 2L-T.
3. Remove the clamps, loosen the union nuts and then remove the injection lines.
4. Remove the leakage pipe from the injectors and note the location of each sealing washer.
5. Remove the nozzle(s) from the cylinder head, noting the positions of the nozzle seats and seat gaskets.

❄❄ CAUTION

DO NOT allow dirt to enter the engine through the nozzle holes.

➡ **Remove accumulations of carbon from the nozzle hoses.**

6. Keep the injectors in order so that they may be installed in their original positions.
7. If the engine exhibited any type of severe miss, excessive smoking, or drastic decrease in power, it is best to have the nozzles professionally tested for opening pressure, leakage, and spray pattern.

CLEANING

1. Remove the nozzle holder retaining nut from the nozzle holder body.
2. Disassemble the injector.
3. Wash the nozzles in clean diesel fuel.
4. Remove carbon from the nozzle needle tip with a small, wooden stick. Do not use any metallic object to clean the nozzle tip.

5. Remove carbon from the exterior of the nozzle body with a brass bristled brush. Don't use a brush having regular, steel bristles.
6. Inspect all parts for damage and/or corrosion. If either of these conditions exist, the entire injector assembly must be replaced.
7. Assemble the injector. Torque the nozzle holder retaining nut to 44–57 ft. lbs.

INSTALLATION

1. Install the injector assembly, noting that:
   a. The nozzle seat is installed between the injector and the seat gasket, and
   b. The nozzle seat must be positioned with the concave side of the seat toward the injector.

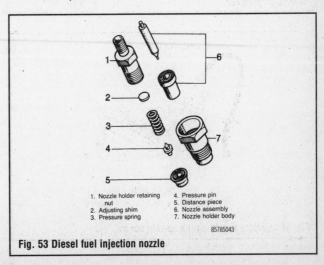

1. Nozzle holder retaining nut
2. Adjusting shim
3. Pressure spring
4. Pressure pin
5. Distance piece
6. Nozzle assembly
7. Nozzle holder body

Fig. 53 Diesel fuel injection nozzle

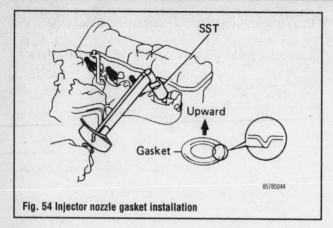

Fig. 54 Injector nozzle gasket installation

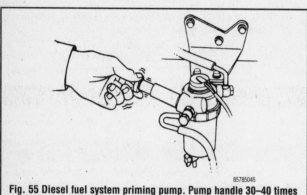

Fig. 55 Diesel fuel system priming pump. Pump handle 30–40 times after any fuel system work to purge air from the system

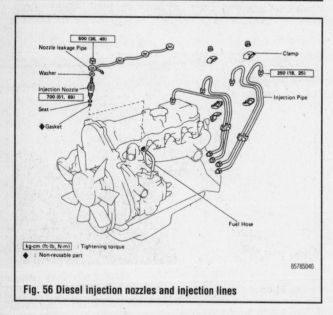

Fig. 56 Diesel injection nozzles and injection lines

2. Position a wrench on the hex of the nozzle body (not the nozzle retaining nut) and torque to 51–65 ft. lbs.

3. Install the leakage pipe and tighten the nuts to 36 ft. lbs. (49 Nm). Connect the fuel hose to the leakage pipe.

4. Assemble the remaining lines to the injectors. Torque the injection pipe union nuts to 15–21 ft. lbs.

➡**After any service is performed to the diesel fuel system, pump the priming handle on the fuel sedimenter assembly 30–40 times to purge air from the system.**

5. Install the air cleaner and air intake pipes on the 2L-T.

6. Start the engine and check for any leaks.

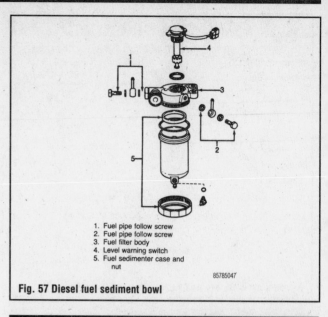

1. Fuel pipe follow screw
2. Fuel pipe follow screw
3. Fuel filter body
4. Level warning switch
5. Fuel sedimenter case and nut

Fig. 57 Diesel fuel sediment bowl

Injection Pump

REMOVAL & INSTALLATION

▶ **See Figures 58 and 59**

1. Disconnect the cables which are positioned above the valve cover and move the cables aside. Remove the valve cover.

2. Disconnect the cables from both batteries.

3. Using a wrench on the center crankshaft pulley bolt, rotate the engine (clockwise only) until the TDC mark on the pulley is aligned with the pointer. Check that the valves of the number one cylinder are closed (rocker arms loose). If the valves are not closed, rotate the engine 360° and again align the TDC mark with the pointer.

4. Disconnect the fuel injection lines at the injection pump and the injectors. Remove the injection lines.

5. Disconnect the fuel feed line at the injection pump and plug the line.

6. Remove the engine cooling fan, belts, and water pump pulley.

7. Remove the crankshaft pulley, using an appropriate puller.

8. Remove the timing belt cover.

9. Using a piece of chalk or crayon, mark the relationships between each of the timing gears and the timing belt.

10. Remove the timing belt idler pulley, then remove the timing belt.

11. Remove the injection pump drive gear, using an appropriate puller.

12. Note the factory made alignment mark next to the outer pump fastener. This mark signifies the required relationship between the pump and the timing case assembly. Align this mark during installation.

13. Unbolt and remove the injection pump.

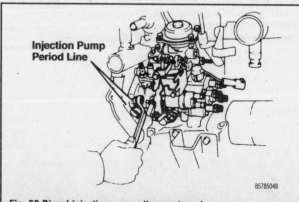

Injection Pump Period Line

Fig. 58 Diesel injection pump alignment marks

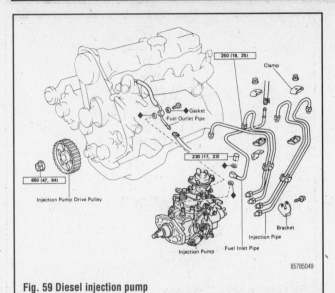

Fig. 59 Diesel injection pump

DO NOT disassemble the injection pump; only factory authorized repair centers have the facilities to do so. No adjustments are possible.

To install:

14. Align the injection pump lines on the injection pump and oil pump body. Install the injection pump and tighten the mounting nuts to 15 ft. lbs. (21 Nm).

15. Install the pump stay and tighten the bolts to 13 ft. lbs. (18 Nm).

16. Install the injection pump pulley and the timing belt.

17. Install the fuel inlet and outlet pipes with new gaskets and tighten the union nut to 17 ft. lbs. (23 Nm).

18. Install the injection pipes as previously detailed.

19. Connect the accelerator link on the 2L-T.

20. Connect all remaining lines and hoses and then fill the engine with coolant.

21. Connect the battery cable, start the engine and check for leaks.

22. Check the injection timing.

FUEL TANK

Removal & Installation

▶ **See Figures 60, 61, 62 and 63**

1. Remove the negative battery cable.
2. Jack up the vehicle and support it with jack stands.
3. Remove the drain plug and drain any remaining fuel into a suitable container.

➡It is best to run the tank as low on fuel as possible before removing it.

4. Disconnect the plug from the sending unit. Remove the gravel shield if equipped.

5. Disconnect the three fuel lines. Plug the outlet line to prevent fuel from leaking.

6. Disconnect the filler neck and vent line.

7. Remove the fuel tank protector.

8. Remove the six bolts from the tank and carefully lower the tank.

9. Install the fuel tank. Tighten the six tank bolts to 11–16 ft. lbs. This procedure similar for all models.

Fig. 60 Removing the fuel filter from the retaining clip

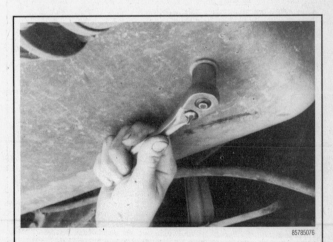

Fig. 61 Drain plug location on the fuel tank assembly

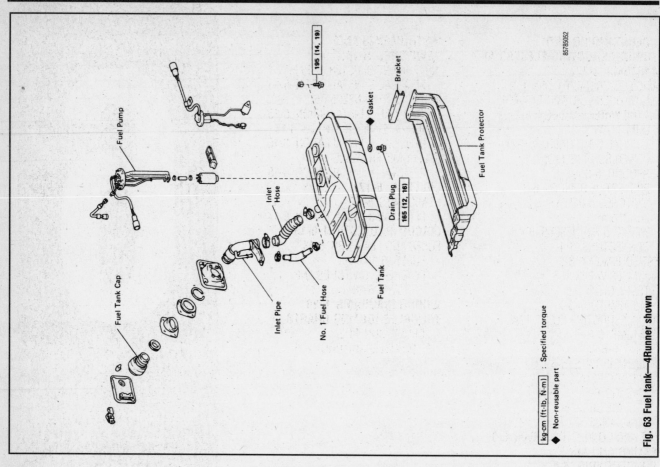

Fig. 63 Fuel tank—4Runner shown

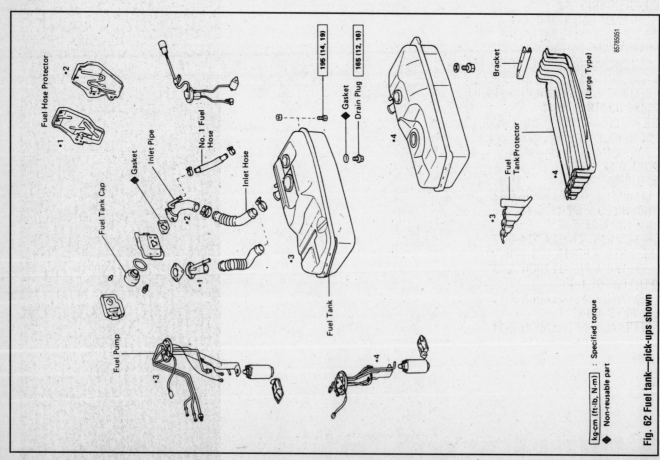

Fig. 62 Fuel tank—pick-ups shown

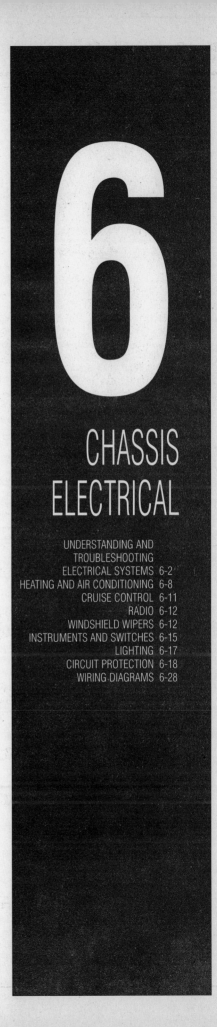

6

CHASSIS ELECTRICAL

UNDERSTANDING AND TROUBLESHOOTING ELECTRICAL SYSTEMS

Basic Electrical Theory

▶ See Figure 1

For any 12 volt, negative ground, electrical system to operate, the electricity must travel in a complete circuit. This simply means that current (power) from the positive (+) terminal of the battery must eventually return to the negative (-) terminal of the battery. Along the way, this current will travel through wires, fuses, switches and components. If, for any reason, the flow of current through the circuit is interrupted, the component fed by that circuit will cease to function properly.

Perhaps the easiest way to visualize a circuit is to think of connecting a light bulb (with two wires attached to it) to the battery—one wire attached to the negative (-) terminal of the battery and the other wire to the positive (+) terminal. With the two wires touching the battery terminals, the circuit would be complete and the light bulb would illuminate. Electricity would follow a path from the battery to the bulb and back to the battery. It's easy to see that with longer wires on our light bulb, it could be mounted anywhere. Further, one wire could be fitted with a switch so that the light could be turned on and off.

The normal automotive circuit differs from this simple example in two ways. First, instead of having a return wire from the bulb to the battery, the current travels through the frame of the vehicle. Since the negative (-) battery cable is attached to the frame (made of electrically conductive metal), the frame of the vehicle can serve as a ground wire to complete the circuit. Secondly, most automotive circuits contain multiple components which receive power from a single circuit. This lessens the amount of wire needed to power components on the vehicle.

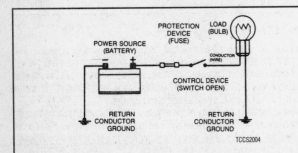

Fig. 1 This example illustrates a simple circuit. When the switch is closed, power from the positive (+) battery terminal flows through the fuse and the switch, and then to the light bulb. The light illuminates and the circuit is completed through the ground wire back to the negative (-) battery terminal. In reality, the two ground points shown in the illustration are attached to the metal frame of the vehicle, which completes the circuit back to the battery

HOW DOES ELECTRICITY WORK: THE WATER ANALOGY

Electricity is the flow of electrons—the subatomic particles that constitute the outer shell of an atom. Electrons spin in an orbit around the center core of an atom. The center core is comprised of protons (positive charge) and neutrons (neutral charge). Electrons have a negative charge and balance out the positive charge of the protons. When an outside force causes the number of electrons to unbalance the charge of the protons, the electrons will split off the atom and look for another atom to balance out. If this imbalance is kept up, electrons will continue to move and an electrical flow will exist.

Many people have been taught electrical theory using an analogy with water. In a comparison with water flowing through a pipe, the electrons would be the water and the wire is the pipe.

The flow of electricity can be measured much like the flow of water through a pipe. The unit of measurement used is amperes, frequently abbreviated as amps (a). You can compare amperage to the volume of water flowing through a pipe. When connected to a circuit, an ammeter will measure the actual amount of current flowing through the circuit. When relatively few electrons flow through a circuit, the amperage is low. When many electrons flow, the amperage is high.

Water pressure is measured in units such as pounds per square inch (psi);

The electrical pressure is measured in units called volts (v). When a voltmeter is connected to a circuit, it is measuring the electrical pressure.

The actual flow of electricity depends not only on voltage and amperage, but also on the resistance of the circuit. The higher the resistance, the higher the force necessary to push the current through the circuit. The standard unit for measuring resistance is an ohm. Resistance in a circuit varies depending on the amount and type of components used in the circuit. The main factors which determine resistance are:

• Material—some materials have more resistance than others. Those with high resistance are said to be insulators. Rubber materials (or rubber-like plastics) are some of the most common insulators used in vehicles as they have a very high resistance to electricity. Very low resistance materials are said to be conductors. Copper wire is among the best conductors. Silver is actually a superior conductor to copper and is used in some relay contacts, but its high cost prohibits its use as common wiring. Most automotive wiring is made of copper.

• Size—the larger the wire size being used, the less resistance the wire will have. This is why components which use large amounts of electricity usually have large wires supplying current to them.

• Length—for a given thickness of wire, the longer the wire, the greater the resistance. The shorter the wire, the less the resistance. When determining the proper wire for a circuit, both size and length must be considered to design a circuit that can handle the current needs of the component.

• Temperature—with many materials, the higher the temperature, the greater the resistance (positive temperature coefficient). Some materials exhibit the opposite trait of lower resistance with higher temperatures (negative temperature coefficient). These principles are used in many of the sensors on the engine.

OHM'S LAW

There is a direct relationship between current, voltage and resistance. The relationship between current, voltage and resistance can be summed up by a statement known as Ohm's law.

Voltage (E) is equal to amperage (I) times resistance (R): $E = I \times R$

Other forms of the formula are $R = E/I$ and $I = E/R$

In each of these formulas, E is the voltage in volts, I is the current in amps and R is the resistance in ohms. The basic point to remember is that as the resistance of a circuit goes up, the amount of current that flows in the circuit will go down, if voltage remains the same.

The amount of work that the electricity can perform is expressed as power. The unit of power is the watt (w). The relationship between power, voltage and current is expressed as:

Power (w) is equal to amperage (I) times voltage (E): $W = I \times E$

This is only true for direct current (DC) circuits; The alternating current formula is a tad different, but since the electrical circuits in most vehicles are DC type, we need not get into AC circuit theory.

Electrical Components

POWER SOURCE

Power is supplied to the vehicle by two devices: The battery and the alternator. The battery supplies electrical power during starting or during periods when the current demand of the vehicle's electrical system exceeds the output capacity of the alternator. The alternator supplies electrical current when the engine is running. Just not does the alternator supply the current needs of the vehicle, but it recharges the battery.

The Battery

In most modern vehicles, the battery is a lead/acid electrochemical device consisting of six 2 volt subsections (cells) connected in series, so that the unit is capable of producing approximately 12 volts of electrical pressure. Each subsection consists of a series of positive and negative plates held a short distance apart in a solution of sulfuric acid and water.

The two types of plates are of dissimilar metals. This sets up a chemical reaction, and it is this reaction which produces current flow from the battery when its positive and negative terminals are connected to an electrical load .

The power removed from the battery is replaced by the alternator, restoring the battery to its original chemical state.

The Alternator

On some vehicles there isn't an alternator, but a generator. The difference is that an alternator supplies alternating current which is then changed to direct current for use on the vehicle, while a generator produces direct current. Alternators tend to be more efficient and that is why they are used.

Alternators and generators are devices that consist of coils of wires wound together making big electromagnets. One group of coils spins within another set and the interaction of the magnetic fields causes a current to flow. This current is then drawn off the coils and fed into the vehicles electrical system.

GROUND

Two types of grounds are used in automotive electric circuits. Direct ground components are grounded to the frame through their mounting points. All other components use some sort of ground wire which is attached to the frame or chassis of the vehicle. The electrical current runs through the chassis of the vehicle and returns to the battery through the ground (-) cable; if you look, you'll see that the battery ground cable connects between the battery and the frame or chassis of the vehicle.

➡️**It should be noted that a good percentage of electrical problems can be traced to bad grounds.**

PROTECTIVE DEVICES

▶ **See Figure 2**

It is possible for large surges of current to pass through the electrical system of your vehicle. If this surge of current were to reach the load in the circuit, the surge could burn it out or severely damage it. It can also overload the wiring, causing the harness to get hot and melt the insulation. To prevent this, fuses, circuit breakers and/or fusible links are connected into the supply wires of the electrical system. These items are nothing more than a built-in weak spot in the system. When an abnormal amount of current flows through the system, these protective devices work as follows to protect the circuit:

• Fuse—when an excessive electrical current passes through a fuse, the fuse "blows" (the conductor melts) and opens the circuit, preventing the passage of current.

• Circuit Breaker—a circuit breaker is basically a self-repairing fuse. It will open the circuit in the same fashion as a fuse, but when the surge subsides, the circuit breaker can be reset and does not need replacement.

• Fusible Link—a fusible link (fuse link or main link) is a short length of special, high temperature insulated wire that acts as a fuse. When an excessive electrical current passes through a fusible link, the thin gauge wire inside the link melts, creating an intentional open to protect the circuit. To repair the circuit, the link must be replaced. Some newer type fusible links are housed in plug-in modules, which are simply replaced like a fuse, while older type fusible links must be cut and spliced if they melt. Since this link is very early in the electrical path, it's the first place to look if nothing on the vehicle works, yet the battery seems to be charged and is properly connected.

✷✷ CAUTION

Always replace fuses, circuit breakers and fusible links with identically rated components. Under no circumstances should a component of higher or lower amperage rating be substituted.

SWITCHES & RELAYS

▶ **See Figures 3 and 4**

Switches are used in electrical circuits to control the passage of current. The most common use is to open and close circuits between the battery and the various electric devices in the system. Switches are rated according to the amount of amperage they can handle. If a sufficient amperage rated switch is not used in a circuit, the switch could overload and cause damage.

Some electrical components which require a large amount of current to operate use a special switch called a relay. Since these circuits carry a large amount of current, the thickness of the wire in the circuit is also greater. If this large wire were connected from the load to the control switch, the switch would have to carry the high amperage load and the fairing or dash would be twice as large to accommodate the increased size of the wiring harness. To prevent these problems, a relay is used.

Relays are composed of a coil and a set of contacts. When the coil has a current passed though it, a magnetic field is formed and this field causes the contacts to move together, completing the circuit. Most relays are normally open, prevent-

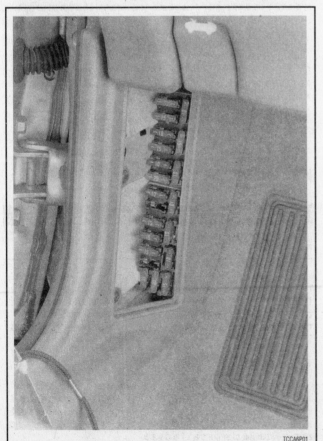

TCCA6P01

Fig. 2 Most vehicles use one or more fuse panels. This one is located on the driver's side kick panel

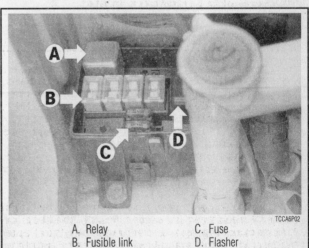

A. Relay	C. Fuse
B. Fusible link	D. Flasher

TCCA6P02

Fig. 3 The underhood fuse and relay panel usually contains fuses, relays, flashers and fusible links

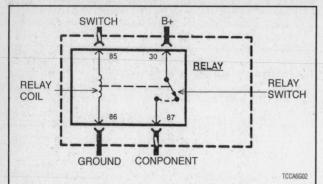

Fig. 4 Relays are composed of a coil and a switch. These two components are linked together so that when one operates, the other operates at the same time. The large wires in the circuit are connected from the battery to one side of the relay switch (B+) and from the opposite side of the relay switch to the load (component). Smaller wires are connected from the relay coil to the control switch for the circuit and from the opposite side of the relay coil to ground

ing current from passing through the circuit, but they can take any electrical form depending on the job they are intended to do. Relays can be considered "remote control switches." They allow a smaller current to operate devices that require higher amperages. When a small current operates the coil, a larger current is allowed to pass by the contacts. Some common circuits which may use relays are the horn, headlights, starter, electric fuel pump and other high draw circuits.

LOAD

Every electrical circuit must include a "load" (something to use the electricity coming from the source). Without this load, the battery would attempt to deliver its entire power supply from one pole to another. This is called a "short circuit." All this electricity would take a short cut to ground and cause a great amount of damage to other components in the circuit by developing a tremendous amount of heat. This condition could develop sufficient heat to melt the insulation on all the surrounding wires and reduce a multiple wire cable to a lump of plastic and copper.

WIRING & HARNESSES

The average vehicle contains meters and meters of wiring, with hundreds of individual connections. To protect the many wires from damage and to keep them from becoming a confusing tangle, they are organized into bundles, enclosed in plastic or taped together and called wiring harnesses. Different harnesses serve different parts of the vehicle. Individual wires are color coded to help trace them through a harness where sections are hidden from view.

Automotive wiring or circuit conductors can be either single strand wire, multi-strand wire or printed circuitry. Single strand wire has a solid metal core and is usually used inside such components as alternators, motors, relays and other devices. Multi-strand wire has a core made of many small strands of wire twisted together into a single conductor. Most of the wiring in an automotive electrical system is made up of multi-strand wire, either as a single conductor or grouped together in a harness. All wiring is color coded on the insulator, either as a solid color or as a colored wire with an identification stripe. A printed circuit is a thin film of copper or other conductor that is printed on an insulator backing. Occasionally, a printed circuit is sandwiched between two sheets of plastic for more protection and flexibility. A complete printed circuit, consisting of conductors, insulating material and connectors for lamps or other components is called a printed circuit board. Printed circuitry is used in place of individual wires or harnesses in places where space is limited, such as behind instrument panels.

Since automotive electrical systems are very sensitive to changes in resistance, the selection of properly sized wires is critical when systems are repaired. A loose or corroded connection or a replacement wire that is too small for the circuit will add extra resistance and an additional voltage drop to the circuit.

The wire gauge number is an expression of the cross-section area of the conductor. Vehicles from countries that use the metric system will typically describe the wire size as its cross-sectional area in square millimeters. In this method, the larger the wire, the greater the number. Another common system for

expressing wire size is the American Wire Gauge (AWG) system. As gauge number increases, area decreases and the wire becomes smaller. An 18 gauge wire is smaller than a 4 gauge wire. A wire with a higher gauge number will carry less current than a wire with a lower gauge number. Gauge wire size refers to the size of the strands of the conductor, not the size of the complete wire with insulator. It is possible, therefore, to have two wires of the same gauge with different diameters because one may have thicker insulation than the other.

It is essential to understand how a circuit works before trying to figure out why it doesn't. An electrical schematic shows the electrical current paths when a circuit is operating properly. Schematics break the entire electrical system down into individual circuits. In a schematic, usually no attempt is made to represent wiring and components as they physically appear on the vehicle; switches and other components are shown as simply as possible. Face views of harness connectors show the cavity or terminal locations in all multi-pin connectors to help locate test points.

CONNECTORS

▶ See Figures 5 and 6

Three types of connectors are commonly used in automotive applications—weatherproof, molded and hard shell.
• Weatherproof—these connectors are most commonly used where the connector is exposed to the elements. Terminals are protected against moisture and dirt by sealing rings which provide a weathertight seal. All repairs require the use of a special terminal and the tool required to service it. Unlike standard blade type terminals, these weatherproof terminals cannot be straightened once they are bent. Make certain that the connectors are properly seated and all of the sealing rings are in place when connecting leads.

Fig. 5 Hard shell (left) and weatherproof (right) connectors have replaceable terminals

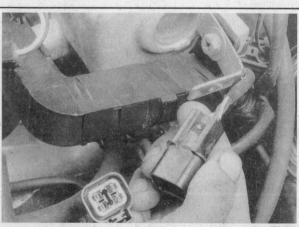

Fig. 6 Weatherproof connectors are most commonly used in the engine compartment or where the connector is exposed to the elements

• Molded—these connectors require complete replacement of the connector if found to be defective. This means splicing a new connector assembly into the harness. All splices should be soldered to insure proper contact. Use care when probing the connections or replacing terminals in them, as it is possible to create a short circuit between opposite terminals. If this happens to the wrong terminal pair, it is possible to damage certain components. Always use jumper wires between connectors for circuit checking and NEVER probe through weatherproof seals.

• Hard Shell—unlike molded connectors, the terminal contacts in hard-shell connectors can be replaced. Replacement usually involves the use of a special terminal removal tool that depresses the locking tangs (barbs) on the connector terminal and allows the connector to be removed from the rear of the shell. The connector shell should be replaced if it shows any evidence of burning, melting, cracks, or breaks. Replace individual terminals that are burnt, corroded, distorted or loose.

Test Equipment

Pinpointing the exact cause of trouble in an electrical circuit is most times accomplished by the use of special test equipment. The following describes different types of commonly used test equipment and briefly explains how to use them in diagnosis. In addition to the information covered below, the tool manufacturer's instructions booklet (provided with the tester) should be read and clearly understood before attempting any test procedures.

JUMPER WIRES

❊❊ CAUTION

Never use jumper wires made from a thinner gauge wire than the circuit being tested. If the jumper wire is of too small a gauge, it may overheat and possibly melt. Never use jumpers to bypass high resistance loads in a circuit. Bypassing resistances, in effect, creates a short circuit. This may, in turn, cause damage and fire. Jumper wires should only be used to bypass lengths of wire or to simulate switches.

Jumper wires are simple, yet extremely valuable, pieces of test equipment. They are basically test wires which are used to bypass sections of a circuit. Although jumper wires can be purchased, they are usually fabricated from lengths of standard automotive wire and whatever type of connector (alligator clip, spade connector or pin connector) that is required for the particular application being tested. In cramped, hard-to-reach areas, it is advisable to have insulated boots over the jumper wire terminals in order to prevent accidental grounding. It is also advisable to include a standard automotive fuse in any jumper wire. This is commonly referred to as a "fused jumper". By inserting an in-line fuse holder between a set of test leads, a fused jumper wire can be used for bypassing open circuits. Use a 5 amp fuse to provide protection against voltage spikes.

Jumper wires are used primarily to locate open electrical circuits, on either the ground (-) side of the circuit or on the power (+) side. If an electrical component fails to operate, connect the jumper wire between the component and a good ground. If the component operates only with the jumper installed, the ground circuit is open. If the ground circuit is good, but the component does not operate, the circuit between the power feed and component may be open. By moving the jumper wire successively back from the component toward the power source, you can isolate the area of the circuit where the open is located. When the component stops functioning, or the power is cut off, the open is in the segment of wire between the jumper and the point previously tested.

You can sometimes connect the jumper wire directly from the battery to the "hot" terminal of the component, but first make sure the component uses 12 volts in operation. Some electrical components, such as fuel injectors or sensors, are designed to operate on about 4 to 5 volts, and running 12 volts directly to these components will cause damage.

TEST LIGHTS

▶ See Figure 7

The test light is used to check circuits and components while electrical current is flowing through them. It is used for voltage and ground tests. To use a 12 volt test light, connect the ground clip to a good ground and probe wherever

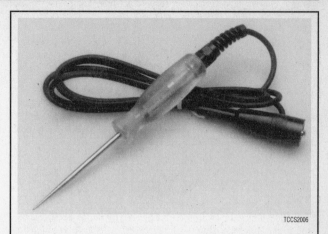

TCCS2006

Fig. 7 A 12 volt test light is used to detect the presence of voltage in a circuit

necessary with the pick. The test light will illuminate when voltage is detected. This does not necessarily mean that 12 volts (or any particular amount of voltage) is present; it only means that some voltage is present. It is advisable before using the test light to touch its ground clip and probe across the battery posts or terminals to make sure the light is operating properly.

❊❊ WARNING

Do not use a test light to probe electronic ignition, spark plug or coil wires. Never use a pick-type test light to probe wiring on computer controlled systems unless specifically instructed to do so. Any wire insulation that is pierced by the test light probe should be taped and sealed with silicone after testing.

Like the jumper wire, the 12 volt test light is used to isolate opens in circuits. But, whereas the jumper wire is used to bypass the open to operate the load, the 12 volt test light is used to locate the presence of voltage in a circuit. If the test light illuminates, there is power up to that point in the circuit; if the test light does not illuminate, there is an open circuit (no power). Move the test light in successive steps back toward the power source until the light in the handle illuminates. The open is between the probe and a point which was previously probed.

The self-powered test light is similar in design to the 12 volt test light, but contains a 1.5 volt penlight battery in the handle. It is most often used in place of a multimeter to check for open or short circuits when power is isolated from the circuit (continuity test).

The battery in a self-powered test light does not provide much current. A weak battery may not provide enough power to illuminate the test light even when a complete circuit is made (especially if there is high resistance in the circuit). Always make sure that the test battery is strong. To check the battery, briefly touch the ground clip to the probe; if the light glows brightly, the battery is strong enough for testing.

➡**A self-powered test light should not be used on any computer controlled system or component. The small amount of electricity transmitted by the test light is enough to damage many electronic automotive components.**

MULTIMETERS

Multimeters are an extremely useful tool for troubleshooting electrical problems. They can be purchased in either analog or digital form and have a price range to suit any budget. A multimeter is a voltmeter, ammeter and ohmmeter (along with other features) combined into one instrument. It is often used when testing solid state circuits because of its high input impedance (usually 10 megaohms or more). A brief description of the multimeter main test functions follows:

• Voltmeter—the voltmeter is used to measure voltage at any point in a circuit, or to measure the voltage drop across any part of a circuit. Voltmeters usually have various scales and a selector switch to allow the reading of different voltage ranges. The voltmeter has a positive and a negative lead. To avoid damage to the meter, always connect the negative lead to the negative (-) side of the circuit (to ground or nearest the ground side of the circuit) and connect the positive lead to the positive (+) side of the circuit (to the power source or the nearest power source). Note that the negative voltmeter lead will always be black and that the positive voltmeter will always be some color other than black (usually red).

• Ohmmeter—the ohmmeter is designed to read resistance (measured in ohms) in a circuit or component. Most ohmmeters will have a selector switch which permits the measurement of different ranges of resistance (usually the selector switch allows the multiplication of the meter reading by 10, 100, 1,000 and 10,000). Some ohmmeters are "auto-ranging" which means the meter itself will determine which scale to use. Since the meters are powered by an internal battery, the ohmmeter can be used like a self-powered test light. When the ohmmeter is connected, current from the ohmmeter flows the circuit or component being tested. Since the ohmmeter's internal resistance and voltage are known values, the amount of current flow through the meter depends on the resistance of the circuit or component being tested. The ohmmeter can also be used to perform a continuity test for suspected open circuits. In using the meter for making continuity checks, do not be concerned with the actual resistance readings. Zero resistance, or any ohm reading, indicates continuity in the circuit. Infinite resistance indicates an opening in the circuit. A high resistance reading where there should be none indicates a problem in the circuit. Checks for short circuits are made in the same manner as checks for open circuits, except that the circuit must be isolated from both power and normal ground. Infinite resistance indicates no continuity, while zero resistance indicates a dead short.

❋❋ WARNING

Never use an ohmmeter to check the resistance of a component or wire while there is voltage applied to the circuit.

• Ammeter—an ammeter measures the amount of current flowing through a circuit in units called amperes or amps. At normal operating voltage, most circuits have a characteristic amount of amperes, called "current draw" which can be measured using an ammeter. By referring to a specified current draw rating, then measuring the amperes and comparing the two values, one can determine what is happening within the circuit to aid in diagnosis. An open circuit, for example, will not allow any current to flow, so the ammeter reading will be zero. A damaged component or circuit will have an increased current draw, so the reading will be high. The ammeter is always connected in series with the circuit being tested. All of the current that normally flows through the circuit must also flow through the ammeter; if there is any other path for the current to follow, the ammeter reading will not be accurate. The ammeter itself has very little resistance to current flow and, therefore, will not affect the circuit, but it will measure current draw only when the circuit is closed and electricity is flowing. Excessive current draw can blow fuses and drain the battery, while a reduced current draw can cause motors to run slowly, lights to dim and other components to not operate properly.

Troubleshooting Electrical Systems

When diagnosing a specific problem, organized troubleshooting is a must. The complexity of a modern automotive vehicle demands that you approach any problem in a logical, organized manner. There are certain troubleshooting techniques, however, which are standard:

• Establish when the problem occurs. Does the problem appear only under certain conditions? Were there any noises, odors or other unusual symptoms? Isolate the problem area. To do this, make some simple tests and observations, then eliminate the systems that are working properly. Check for obvious problems, such as broken wires and loose or dirty connections. Always check the obvious before assuming something complicated is the cause.

• Test for problems systematically to determine the cause once the problem area is isolated. Are all the components functioning properly? Is there power going to electrical switches and motors? Performing careful, systematic checks will often turn up most causes on the first inspection, without wasting time checking components that have little or no relationship to the problem.

• Test all repairs after the work is done to make sure that the problem is fixed. Some causes can be traced to more than one component, so a careful verification of repair work is important in order to pick up additional malfunctions that may cause a problem to reappear or a different problem to arise. A blown fuse, for example, is a simple problem that may require more than another fuse to repair. If you don't look for a problem that caused a fuse to blow, a shorted wire (for example) may go undetected.

Experience has shown that most problems tend to be the result of a fairly simple and obvious cause, such as loose or corroded connectors, bad grounds or damaged wire insulation which causes a short. This makes careful visual inspection of components during testing essential to quick and accurate troubleshooting.

Testing

OPEN CIRCUITS

▶ **See Figure 8**

This test already assumes the existence of an open in the circuit and it is used to help locate the open portion.

1. Isolate the circuit from power and ground.
2. Connect the self-powered test light or ohmmeter ground clip to the ground side of the circuit and probe sections of the circuit sequentially.
3. If the light is out or there is infinite resistance, the open is between the probe and the circuit ground.
4. If the light is on or the meter shows continuity, the open is between the probe and the end of the circuit toward the power source.

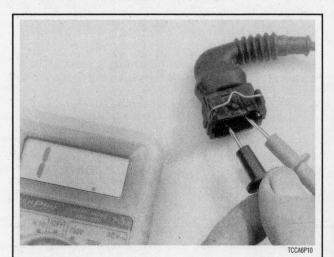

TCCA6P10

Fig. 8 The infinite reading on this multimeter indicates that the circuit is open

SHORT CIRCUITS

➡**Never use a self-powered test light to perform checks for opens or shorts when power is applied to the circuit under test. The test light can be damaged by outside power.**

1. Isolate the circuit from power and ground.
2. Connect the self-powered test light or ohmmeter ground clip to a good ground and probe any easy-to-reach point in the circuit.
3. If the light comes on or there is continuity, there is a short somewhere in the circuit.
4. To isolate the short, probe a test point at either end of the isolated circuit (the light should be on or the meter should indicate continuity).
5. Leave the test light probe engaged and sequentially open connectors or switches, remove parts, etc. until the light goes out or continuity is broken.
6. When the light goes out, the short is between the last two circuit components which were opened.

VOLTAGE

This test determines voltage available from the battery and should be the first step in any electrical troubleshooting procedure after visual inspection. Many electrical problems, especially on computer controlled systems, can be caused by a low state of charge in the battery. Excessive corrosion at the battery cable terminals can cause poor contact that will prevent proper charging and full battery current flow.

1. Set the voltmeter selector switch to the 20V position.

2. Connect the multimeter negative lead to the battery's negative (-) post or terminal and the positive lead to the battery's positive (+) post or terminal.

3. Turn the ignition switch **ON** to provide a load.

4. A well charged battery should register over 12 volts. If the meter reads below 11.5 volts, the battery power may be insufficient to operate the electrical system properly.

VOLTAGE DROP

▶ **See Figure 9**

When current flows through a load, the voltage beyond the load drops. This voltage drop is due to the resistance created by the load and also by small resistances created by corrosion at the connectors and damaged insulation on the wires. The maximum allowable voltage drop under load is critical, especially if there is more than one load in the circuit, since all voltage drops are cumulative.

1. Set the voltmeter selector switch to the 20 volt position.

2. Connect the multimeter negative lead to a good ground.

3. Operate the circuit and check the voltage prior to the first component (load).

4. There should be little or no voltage drop in the circuit prior to the first component. If a voltage drop exists, the wire or connectors in the circuit are suspect.

5. While operating the first component in the circuit, probe the ground side of the component with the positive meter lead and observe the voltage readings. A small voltage drop should be noticed. This voltage drop is caused by the resistance of the component.

6. Repeat the test for each component (load) down the circuit.

7. If a large voltage drop is noticed, the preceding component, wire or connector is suspect.

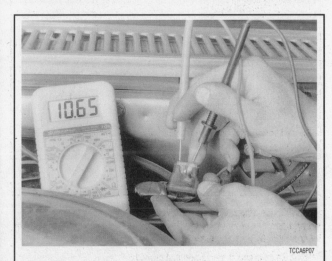

TCCA6P07

Fig. 9 This voltage drop test revealed high resistance (low voltage) in the circuit

RESISTANCE

▶ **See Figures 10 and 11**

✳✳ WARNING

Never use an ohmmeter with power applied to the circuit. The ohmmeter is designed to operate on its own power supply. The normal 12 volt electrical system voltage could damage the meter!

1. Isolate the circuit from the vehicle's power source.

2. Ensure that the ignition key is **OFF** when disconnecting any components or the battery.

TCCA6P08

Fig. 10 Checking the resistance of a coolant temperature sensor with an ohmmeter. Reading is 1.04 kilohms

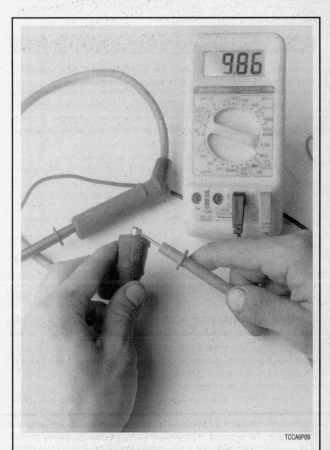

TCCA6P09

Fig. 11 Spark plug wires can be checked for excessive resistance using an ohmmeter

3. Where necessary, also isolate at least one side of the circuit to be checked, in order to avoid reading parallel resistances. Parallel circuit resistances will always give a lower reading than the actual resistance of either of the branches.

4. Connect the meter leads to both sides of the circuit (wire or component) and read the actual measured ohms on the meter scale. Make sure the selector switch is set to the proper ohm scale for the circuit being tested, to avoid misreading the ohmmeter test value.

Wire and Connector Repair

Almost anyone can replace damaged wires, as long as the proper tools and parts are available. Wire and terminals are available to fit almost any need. Even the specialized weatherproof, molded and hard shell connectors are now available from aftermarket suppliers.

Be sure the ends of all the wires are fitted with the proper terminal hardware and connectors. Wrapping a wire around a stud is never a permanent solution and will only cause trouble later. Replace wires one at a time to avoid confusion. Always route wires exactly the same as the factory.

➡**If connector repair is necessary, only attempt it if you have the proper tools. Weatherproof and hard shell connectors require special tools to release the pins inside the connector. Attempting to repair these connectors with conventional hand tools will damage them.**

HEATING AND AIR CONDITIONING

➡**On models equipped with A/C, the heater and air conditioner are completely separate units. The heater removal procedure is the same as outlined here. However, be certain when working under the dashboard that only the heater hoses are disconnected. The A/C hoses are under pressure. If disconnected, the escaping refrigerant will freeze any surface with which it comes in contact, including your skin and eyes. Refer all air conditioning work to a qualified mechanic.**

Heater Unit/Heater Core

➡**The heater unit, blower motor and heater core are all removed as a unit except where noted. Heater core and blower motor removal procedures are detailed within these Heater Unit/Heater Core procedures.**

REMOVAL & INSTALLATION

◆ See Figures 12 thru 33

1970–78 Pick-Ups

The heater core and blower motor are assembled into one unit which is centrally located in the passenger compartment. To effect repairs on either the core or blower motor, remove the entire assembly from the truck and separate the components with the unit removed.

1. Drain the cooling system completely.
2. Remove the package tray from under the dashboard.
3. Unfasten the hose clamps holding the heater hoses to the core.

➡**Hold a shallow pan under the hoses so that any water left in them will not run on the floor of the truck.**

4. Remove the defroster hoses from the heater case.
5. Disconnect the heater control cables from the heater case.

6. Remove the fresh air intake duct.
7. Remove the electrical connector feeding the heater blower motor.
8. There are four bolts holding the assembly to the inside of the cowl. Remove the bolts and withdraw the heater assembly from the passenger compartment.
9. To remove the blower motor, tap the fan retaining nut slightly and then remove the nut from the shaft. Withdraw the fan. Remove the blower motor-to-heater case attaching screws and remove the motor.
10. To remove the core, remove the heater control panel and heater lower case cover as a unit. The core may then be taken out of the heater case.
11. Upon reassembly of the unit be sure to tighten all clamps to prevent leaks. Fill the cooling system with the correct mixture of coolant. With the heater off, run the engine to operating temperature. Open the heater control valve and see if the system is functioning properly.

1979 and Later Pick-Ups and 4Runners

Heater removal is basically the same with the following exceptions:
1. Remove the glove box from the dashboard.
2. Remove the heater controls from the dashboard.
3. Remove the 3 bolt holding the unit in place.
4. To remove the blower motor, remove the 3 screws on the blower motor housing and remove the motor.

1971–79 Land Cruiser

FRONT CORE

1. Turn off the water valve.
2. Detach both hoses from the heater core.
3. Unfasten the air duct clamp.
4. Detach the defroster hoses from the heater box.
5. Unfasten its attachment bolts and withdraw the core.

Fig. 12 View of the heater fan assembly

Fig. 13 Removing the heater fan assembly

Fig. 14 Removing the glove box assembly

Fig. 15 Removing the heater control cable

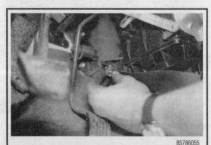
Fig. 16 Removing the heater unit assembly mounting screw

Fig. 17 View of the heater control cable

Fig. 18 Removing the heater duct

Fig. 19 Removing the heater unit lower brace

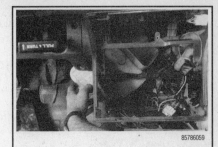

Fig. 20 Removing the center heater duct

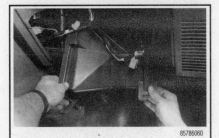

Fig. 21 Removing the heater duct work

Fig. 22 Removing the heater unit mounting bolt (lower)

Fig. 23 Removing the heater unit mounting bolt (upper)

Fig. 24 Removing the heater unit assembly

Fig. 25 Removing the heater unit from the vehicle

Fig. 26 View of the heater unit assembly

Fig. 27 Removing the heater core tube clamp from heater unit assembly

Fig. 28 Removing the heater core from heater unit assembly

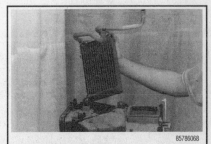

Fig. 29 Removing the heater core from heater unit assembly

Fig. 30 Installing the heater core tube clamp to heater unit assembly

Fig. 31 Installing the heater unit to the vehicle

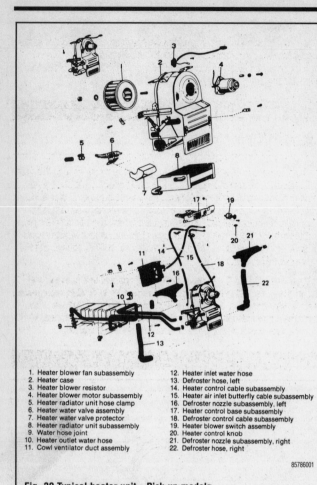

1. Heater blower fan subassembly
2. Heater case
3. Heater blower resistor
4. Heater blower motor subassembly
5. Heater radiator unit hose clamp
6. Heater water valve assembly
7. Heater water valve protector
8. Heater radiator unit subassembly
9. Water hose joint
10. Heater outlet water hose
11. Cowl ventilator duct assembly
12. Heater inlet water hose
13. Defroster hose, left
14. Heater control cable subassembly
15. Heater air inlet butterfly cable subassembly
16. Defroster nozzle subassembly, left
17. Heater control base subassembly
18. Defroster control cable subassembly
19. Heater blower switch assembly
20. Heater control knob
21. Defroster nozzle subassembly, right
22. Defroster hose, right

85786001

Fig. 32 Typical heater unit—Pick-up models

6. Installation is the reverse of the removal procedure.
7. Turn the water valve on, check the coolant level and check for any leaks.

1980 and Later Land Cruiser

FRONT CORE

➡The entire heater unit must be removed to gain access to the heater core. This procedure requires almost complete disassembly of the instrument panel and lowering of the steering column. If you decide to perform this operation, note the following points before proceeding.

1. Be sure to tag any wiring which must be disconnected so that it may be correctly installed.
2. As fasteners are removed, arrange them so that they may be installed in their original locations.
3. Do not force any parts to remove them; if a part cannot easily be removed, remove any additional fasteners which may have been initially overlooked.
4. When disconnecting coolant hoses, be careful not to damage the heater core tubes. Place a drain pan under the coolant hose connections before disconnecting the hoses.
5. Disconnect the negative battery cable at the battery.
6. Remove the glove box and the glove box door.
7. Remove the lower heater ducts.
8. Remove the large heater duct from the passenger side of the heater unit.
9. Remove the ductwork from behind the instrument panel.
10. If equipped, remove the radio.

1. Glove compartment
2. Duct
3. Duct
4. Duct
5. Safety pad
6. Hood release lever
7. Throttle cable
8. Fuse block setting screw
9. Rheostat connector
10. Steering column mounting nut
11. Center duct
12. Lower instrument panel
13. Heater unit

85786002

Fig. 33 Typical heater unit—Land Cruiser models

11. Detach the wiring connector from the right side inner portion of the glove opening.
12. Remove the instrument panel pad (8 fasteners).
13. Remove the hood release lever.
14. Disconnect the hand throttle control cable.
15. Remove the retaining screw from the left side of the fuse block.
16. Remove the steering column-to-instrument panel attaching nuts and carefully lower the steering column. Tag and disconnect the wiring as necessary in order to lower the column assembly.
17. Detach the electrical connector from the rheostat located to the left of the steering column opening.
18. Remove the center duel outlet duct which is attached to the upper portion of the heater unit.
19. Remove the lower instrument panel. The fasteners are located in the following places:

   a. Left side of the instrument panel: two at the left side end and two at the left lower end.
   b. Above the steering column: two.
   c. To the right of the steering column opening: two.
   d. Left upper corner of the glove box opening: two.
   e. Left lower corner of the glove box opening: one.
   f. Right side of the instrument panel: two at the right side end and two at the right lower end.

20. Tag and disconnect the hoses from the heater unit.
21. Remove the heater unit-to-firewall fasteners and remove the heater unit.
22. Remove the heater core pipe clamps from the heater unit. Also remove the heater core retaining clamp.
23. Withdraw the heater core from the heater unit.

To install:

24. Upon reassembly of the unit and installation in the vehicle, be sure to install all necessary parts in the reverse order of removal.
25. Install heater hoses to heater unit. Install new clamps where necessary.
26. Torque the steering column-to-instrument panel fasteners to 14–15 ft. lbs.
27. Replenish the cooling system and check for leaks.

REAR CORE

1. Shut the water valve.
2. Detach both of the hoses from the rear heater core.
3. Detach the wiring from the rear heater.
4. Unfasten the bolts and lift out the core.
5. Installation is the reverse of the removal procedure.

Heater Blower Motor

➥To service the blower motor of Pick-Up models, refer to the previous Heater Unit/Heater Core Removal & Installation procedures.

REMOVAL & INSTALLATION

Land Cruiser

1971–79

1. Loosen the air duct clamping screws and remove the ducts.
2. Remove the air duct screen.
3. Unfasten the mounting bolts and remove the blower motor complete with fan.
4. Installation is the reverse of the removal procedure.
5. Check the coolant system level, run the motor and check for proper operation.

1980 AND LATER

1. Detach the electrical connector from the blower motor.
2. Disconnect the flexible tube from the side of the blower motor.
3. Remove the blower motor fasteners and lower the blower motor out of the air inlet duct.

To install:

4. Install the motor into the inlet duct. Be sure to position the motor so that the flexible tube can be attached to the motor and connect it.
5. Connect the electrical lead, check the coolant level, run the heater and check for any leaks.

Air Conditioning Components

REMOVAL & INSTALLATION

Repair or service of air conditioning components is not covered by this manual, because of the risk of personal injury or death, and because of the legal ramifications of servicing these components without the proper EPA certification and experience. Cost, personal injury or death, environmental damage, and legal considerations (such as the fact that it is a federal crime to vent refrigerant into the atmosphere), dictate that the A/C components on your vehicle should be serviced only by a Motor Vehicle Air Conditioning (MVAC) trained, and EPA certified automotive technician.

➥If your vehicle's A/C system uses R-12 refrigerant and is in need of recharging, the A/C system can be converted over to R-134a refrigerant (less environmentally harmful and expensive). Refer to Section 1 for additional information on R-12 to R-134a conversions, and for additional considerations dealing with your vehicle's A/C system.

CRUISE CONTROL

General Description

The cruise control, which is a speed control system, maintains a desired speed of the vehicle under normal driving conditions. The cruise control ECM controls all cruise control functions. The use of the speed control is not recommended when driving conditions do not permit maintaining a constant speed, such as in heavy traffic or on roads that are winding, icy, snow covered or slippery.

CONTROL CABLE FREE-PLAY ADJUSTMENT

▶ See Figure 34

Measure the cable stroke to where the throttle valve begins to open. This distance should be within 0.39 in. (10mm) with a slight amount of free-play. If free-play is not as specified, adjust control cable free-play.

85786005

Fig. 34 Actuator cable adjustment

CRUISE CONTROL TROUBLESHOOTING

Problem	Possible Cause
Will not hold proper speed	Incorrect cable adjustment
	Binding throttle linkage
	Leaking vacuum servo diaphragm
	Leaking vacuum tank
	Faulty vacuum or vent valve
	Faulty stepper motor
	Faulty transducer
	Faulty speed sensor
	Faulty cruise control module
Cruise intermittently cuts out	Clutch or brake switch adjustment too tight
	Short or open in the cruise control circuit
	Faulty transducer
	Faulty cruise control module
Vehicle surges	Kinked speedometer cable or casing
	Binding throttle linkage
	Faulty speed sensor
	Faulty cruise control module
Cruise control inoperative	Blown fuse
	Short or open in the cruise control circuit
	Faulty brake or clutch switch
	Leaking vacuum circuit
	Faulty cruise control switch
	Faulty stepper motor
	Faulty transducer
	Faulty speed sensor
	Faulty cruise control module

Note: Use this chart as a guide. Not all systems will use the components listed.

TCCA6C01

RADIO

✳✳ CAUTION

Never operate the radio without a speaker; severe damage to the output transistors will result. If the speaker must be replaced, use a speaker of the correct impedance (ohms) or else the output transistors will be damaged and require replacement.

Radio

REMOVAL & INSTALLATION

1970–78

1. Remove the knobs from the radio.
2. Remove the nuts from the radio control shafts.
3. Detach the antenna lead from the jack on the radio case.
4. Detach the power and speaker leads.
5. Remove the radio support nuts and bolts, then remove the radio from beneath the dashboard.
6. Installation is the reverse of the removal procedure.

1979 And Later

1. Disconnect the negative battery cable from the battery.
2. Remove the steering column upper and lower covers.
3. Remove the five screws holding the instrument cluster trim panel and remove trim panel.
4. Remove the knobs from the radio and remove the securing nuts from the control shafts.
5. Remove the heater/air conditioner knobs from their control arms. Do not remove the blower fan control knob.
6. Remove the two screws holding the heater control dash light. Remove the ashtray and remove all of the screws holding the center dash facade onto the dash.
7. Pull the facade out and carefully disconnect the cigarette lighter and the blower fan control at their plugs.
8. Unscrew any remaining screws holding the radio and pull it out part way. Disconnect the power source, speaker coupling and antenna from the radio and remove through the dash.

To install:

9. Install the radio into the dash slightly. Connect the power source, speaker coupling and antenna to the radio and insert it fully into the dash.
10. Install the remaining components in the reverse order of removal.
11. Connect the negative battery cable and check for proper radio operation.

WINDSHIELD WIPERS

Blade and Arm

REMOVAL & INSTALLATION

▶ **See Figures 35, 36, 37, 38 and 39**

➡ **Wiper blade element replacement is covered in Section 1.**

1. To remove the wiper blades, lift up on the spring release tab on the wiper blade-to-wiper arm connector.
2. Pull the blade assembly off the wiper arm.

3. There are two types of replacements for Toyotas:

  a. Pre-1973: replace the entire wiper blade as an assembly. Simply snap the replacement into place on the arm.

  b. Post-1973: press the old wiper blade insert down, away from the blade assembly, to free it from the retaining clips on the blade ends. Slide the insert out of the blade. Slide the new insert into the blade assembly and bend the insert upward slightly to engage the retaining clips.

4. To replace a wiper arm, unscrew the acorn nut which secures it to the pivot and carefully pull the arm upward and off the pivot. Install the arm by reversing this procedure.

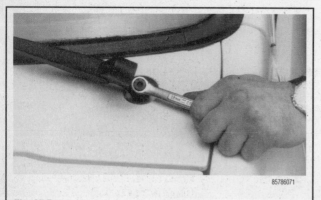

Fig. 35 Removing the wiper arm retaining nut

Fig. 36 Removing the wiper arm

Fig. 37 Removing the wiper arm from the vehicle

Fig. 38 Removing the wiper element

Fig. 39 Installation of the wiper arm to the vehicle

➡Later models are equipped with a cover over the acorn nut. To expose the nut, lift the wiper arm and the cover at the same time; this will afford access to the nut.

Windshield Wiper Motor

REMOVAL & INSTALLATION

▶ **See Figures 40, 41 and 42**

Pick-Up and 4Runner

1. Disconnect the wiring from the wiper motor and unbolt it from the fire wall.
2. On 1970–78 models, remove the arm nut and crank arm from the wiper motor. On 1979 and later models, pry the wiper link from the crank arm.
3. Remove the motor.
4. Installation is the reverse of the removal procedure.

Land Cruiser

EXCEPT 1980 AND LATER STATION WAGON

1. Detach the wiper link from the motor with a screwdriver.
2. Unfasten the two bracket bolts at the rear of the motor.
3. Disconnect the wiper motor wiring.
4. Unfasten the wiper motor screws and withdraw the motor.
5. Installation is the reverse of the removal procedure.

1980 AND LATER STATION WAGON

➡On these models, the wiper motor is removed with the linkage assembly.

1. Remove the wiper arm retaining nuts and remove the wiper arm and blade assemblies.
2. Remove both wiper arm pivot covers.
3. Remove the pivot-to-cowl attaching screws.
4. Remove the two service hole covers from the cowl area of the engine compartment.
5. Disconnect the wiring from the wiper motor.
6. From the engine compartment, remove the wiper motor plate-to-cowl retaining screws.
7. Withdraw the wiper motor and linkage from the cowl panel as an assembly.

8. Pry the linkage off of the wiper motor and linkage from the cowl panel as an assembly.
9. Pry the linkage off of the wiper motor and disconnect the linkage from the motor.
10. Installation is the reverse of the removal procedure.

Wiper Linkage

REMOVAL & INSTALLATION

▶ **See Figures 43 thru 54**

Pick-Up and 4Runner

1. Remove the wiper motor.
2. Remove the wiper arms by removing their retaining nuts and working them off their shafts.
3. Remove the nuts and spacers holding the wiper shafts and push the shafts down into the body cavity. Pull the linkage out of the cavity through the wiper motor hole.

To install:
4. Insert the wiper linkage through the hole and install the nuts and spacers.
5. Press the wiper arm onto their shafts and install the retaining nuts, then install the wiper motor.

2 Door Land Cruiser

1. Remove the wiper arm assemblies.
2. Remove the end plate from the pivot housing.
3. Remove the wiper motor complete with the linkage cable.
4. Separate the wiper motor and transmission.

To install:
5. Remove the linkage cable.
6. Install the linkage cable and connect the wiper motor to the transmission.
7. Install the motor with the linkage attached, install the end plate into the pivot housing and press on the wiper arms.

Land Cruiser Station Wagon

1. Remove the wiper motor.
2. Remove the wiper arm assemblies.
3. Remove the instrument cluster, as detailed below.

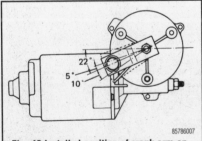

Fig. 40 Installed position of crank arm on wiper motor

Fig. 41 Removing the windshield wiper motor electrical connection

Fig. 42 Removing the windshield wiper motor electrical connection

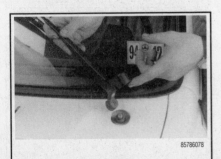

Fig. 43 Removing the wiper arm nut

Fig. 44 Removing the wiper arm

Fig. 45 Removing the wiper motor assembly retaining bolts

Fig. 46 Removing the wiper motor assembly

85786081

Fig. 47 Removing the wiper motor cowl panel retaining screws

85786082

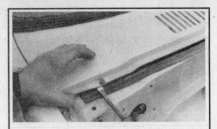

Fig. 48 Removing the wiper motor cowl panel

85786083

Fig. 49 Removing the wiper motor cowl panel

85786084

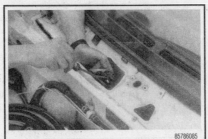

Fig. 50 Removing the wiper linkage connection

85786085

Fig. 51 Removing the wiper linkage-to-vehicle connection

85786086

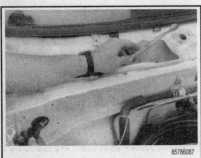

Fig. 52 Removing the wiper linkage

85786087

Fig. 53 View of the wiper linkage

85786088

Fig. 54 Removing the wiper linkage

85786089

4. Loosen the throttle cable to improve access to the wiper linkage.
5. Remove the linkage attachment bolts and withdraw the linkage.

Rear Wiper

REMOVAL & INSTALLATION

4Runner

▶ **See Figure 55**

1. Disconnect the negative battery cable.
2. Pop up the acorn nut cover, remove the nut and pull off the rear wiper.
3. Remove the pivot nut.
4. Inside, above the tailgate, pop out the 4 clips and remove the wiper motor cover.
5. Disconnect the electrical lead and the washer hose, remove the 3 mounting bolts and lift out the wiper motor.
6. Installation is the reverse of the removal procedure. Tighten the pivot nut to 8 ft. lbs. (11 Nm).

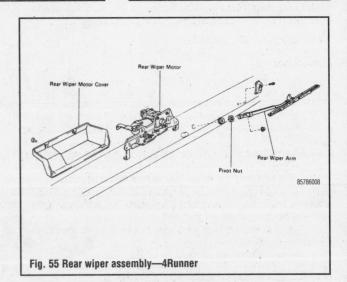

Rear Wiper Motor Cover

Rear Wiper Motor

Rear Wiper Arm

Pivot Nut

85786008

Fig. 55 Rear wiper assembly—4Runner

INSTRUMENTS AND SWITCHES

Instrument Cluster

REMOVAL & INSTALLATION

Pick-Up

1970–78

1. Loosen the steering column clamp bolts at the base of the instrument panel. This will allow the steering column to drop slightly.
2. Remove the three retaining screws on the instrument group and pull out gently on the hood of the cluster.
3. Disconnect the speedometer cable and the wiring connector and withdraw the cluster.
4. Installation is the reverse of the removal procedure.

1980 AND LATER

1. Disconnect the negative battery cable.
2. Remove the upper and lower steering column covers.
3. Remove the five screws holding the instrument trim panel and remove the panel.
4. Disconnect the speedometer cable from the back of the speedometer.
5. Remove the four screws holding the instrument panel in place and pull the panel forward. Unplug the two connectors from the back of the panel and remove the panel.
6. Installation is the reverse of the removal procedure.

Land Cruiser

1971–83

1. Disconnect the speedometer cable.
2. Remove the instrument panel attaching screws.
3. Loosen the steering column clamp by removing the attaching bolts.
4. Pull out the instrument panel and the speedometer, disconnect the wiring connectors, and remove the panel.
5. Installation is the reverse of the removal procedure.

Instrument Panel

REMOVAL & INSTALLATION

▶ **See Figures 56, 57, 58 and 59**

Land Cruiser

1984–87

1. Disconnect the negative battery cable.
2. Remove the steering wheel and the steering column cover.
3. Disconnect the throttle cable from the pedal and retainer. Remove the set nut and cable.
4. Loosen the set screw on the choke knob and remove the knob. Remove the choke cable set nut and pull out the cable.
5. Remove the hood lock release lever. Remove the fuel lid opener.
6. Disconnect the speedometer cable and the instrument leads and then remove the 5 instrument cluster mounting screws and lift out the cluster finish panel with the combination meter attached.
7. Unplug all electrical leads, remove the 9 mounting screws and lift out the cluster center panel.
8. Remove the heater control panel.
9. Remove the radio.
10. Remove the assist handle from the instrument panel.
11. Loosen the 3 mbunting screws and the glove box door. Remove the glove box light and switch. Remove the door lock striker and remove the glove box.

12. Remove the speaker from the safety pad.
13. Remove both side defroster nozzles.
14. Remove the 4 nuts and 2 clips and lift out the safety pad.
15. Remove the fuse box.
16. Push the heater control panel into the instrument panel, disconnect any connectors, remove the 15 bolts and lift out the instrument panel.

1988

1. Disconnect the negative battery cable.
2. Remove the steering wheel and the steering column cover.
3. Remove the No. 2 side air duct nozzle and the No. 3 air duct.
4. Disconnect the throttle cable from the pedal and retainer. Remove the set nut and cable.
5. Remove the hood lock release lever. Remove the fuel lid opener.
6. Disconnect all electrical leads and remove the ash tray. Remove the 5 mounting screws and 2 clips and lift out the cluster center panel.
7. Detach the speedometer cable and the instrument leads and then remove the 7 instrument cluster mounting screws and lift out the cluster finish panel with the combination meter attached.
8. Remove the radio.
9. Loosen the 3 mounting screws and the glove box door. Remove the glove box light and switch. Remove the door lock striker and remove the glove box.
10. Remove the EFI computer.
11. Remove the No. 1, No. 3 and No. 4 side air ducts.
12. Remove the lower side defroster nozzle set screw and disconnect the hose.
13. Remove the 4 screws, 4 nuts and 2 clips and lift the safety pad out toward the rear.
14. Remove the heater control panel and the No. 2 air duct.
15. Remove the mirror control switch, rheostat and the 4wd control connectors.
16. Remove the fuse box.
17. Remove the 2 upper side mounting bolts on the steering column.
18. Loosen the 15 mounting bolts and remove the instrument panel toward the rear.
19. Installation is the reverse of the removal procedure.
20. Check operation of all related items in the instrument panel assembly.

Windshield Wiper Switch

REMOVAL & INSTALLATION

1. Disconnect the negative battery cable.
2. Pry out the horn pad and remove the steering wheel.
3. Remove the terminals from the connector.
4. Slide the switch assembly off the steering column.
5. Installation is the reverse of the removal procedure.

Speedometer Cable

REMOVAL & INSTALLATION

1. Remove the instrument cluster and disconnect the cable at the speedometer.
2. Disconnect the other end of the speedometer cable at the transmission extension housing and pull the cable from its jacket at the transmission end. If you are replacing the cable because it is broken, don't forget to remove both pieces of broken cable.
   To install:
3. Lubricate the new cable with graphite speedometer cable lubricant, and feed it into the cable jacket from the lower end.
4. Connect the cable to the transmission, then to the speedometer. Plug the electrical connector into the instrument cluster, and replace the cluster. Road test for proper operation.

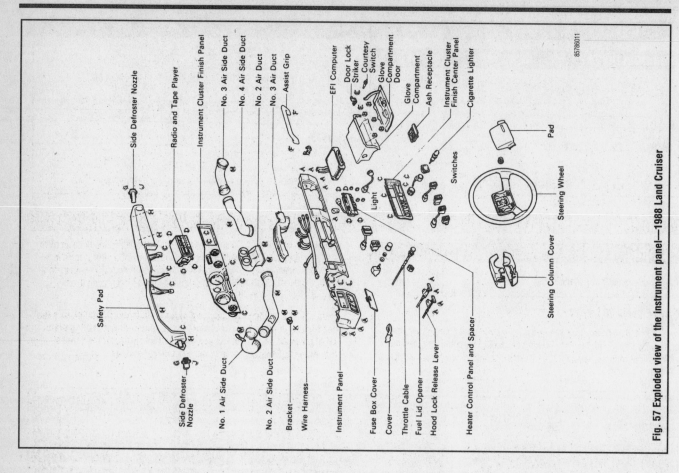

Side Defroster Nozzle
Radio and Tape Player
Instrument Cluster Finish Panel
No. 3 Air Side Duct
No. 4 Air Side Duct
No. 2 Air Duct
No. 3 Air Duct
Assist Grip
EFI Computer
Door Lock Striker
Courtesy Switch
Glove Compartment Door
Glove Compartment
Ash Receptacle
Instrument Cluster Finish Center Panel
Cigarette Lighter
Pad
Switches
Steering Wheel
Steering Column Cover

Safety Pad
Side Defroster Nozzle
No. 1 Air Side Duct
No. 2 Air Side Duct
Bracket
Wire Harness
Instrument Panel
Fuse Box Cover
Cover
Throttle Cable
Fuel Lid Opener
Hood Lock Release Lever
Heater Control Panel and Spacer
Light

Fig. 57 Exploded view of the instrument panel—1988 Land Cruiser

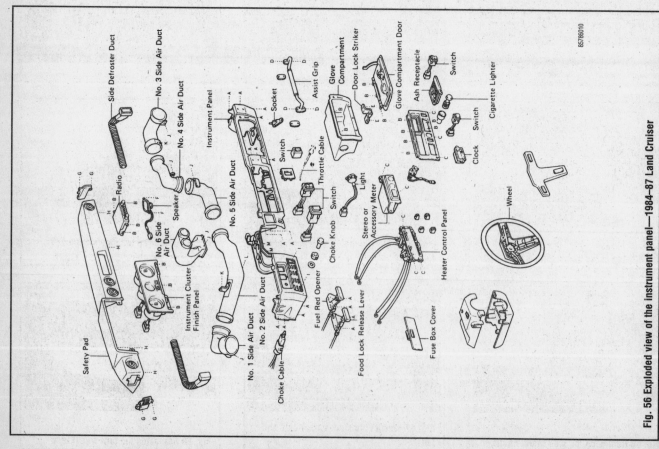

Side Defroster Duct
No. 3 Side Air Duct
No. 4 Side Air Duct
Instrument Panel
Socket
Assist Grip
Glove Compartment
Door Lock Striker
Glove Compartment Door
Ash Receptacle
Switch
Cigarette Lighter
Switch
Clock
Switch
Throttle Cable
Switch
Light
Stereo or Accessory Meter
Choke Knob
Wheel
Radio
Speaker
No. 6 Side Air Duct
No. 5 Side Air Duct

Safety Pad
Instrument Cluster Finish Panel
No. 1 Side Air Duct
No. 2 Side Air Duct
Choke Cable
Fuel Red Opener
Food Lock Release Lever
Fuse Box Cover
Heater Control Panel

Fig. 56 Exploded view of the instrument panel—1984–87 Land Cruiser

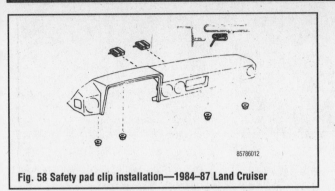

Fig. 58 Safety pad clip installation—1984–87 Land Cruiser

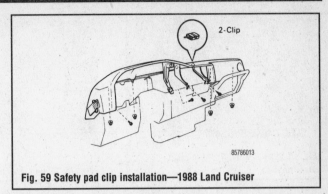

Fig. 59 Safety pad clip installation—1988 Land Cruiser

LIGHTING

Headlights

REMOVAL & INSTALLATION

▶ **See Figures 60 thru 76**

1. On 1970–72 models, remove the three trim cover retaining screws, and remove the cover. On later models, the half of the grille covering the affected unit must be removed. There are seven retaining screws on 1973–74 trucks, and six screws 1975 and later (one is hidden behind the grille emblem).

2. Loosen the three headlight ring retaining screws, but do not remove them. Turn the retaining ring clockwise and pull out the headlight with the ring.

3. Unplug the electrical connector from the rear of the headlight, and remove the headlight from the ring.

➡**Do not interchange the inner and outer headlights. Do not disturb the headlight aiming screws located on the retaining ring mounting plate. All other bulbs on the vehicle are replaced by removing the screws retaining the lens and twisting out the defective bulb.**

Fig. 60 Removing the headlight retaining screws

Fig. 61 Removing the headlight retaining screws

Fig. 62 Removing the headlight retaining bezel

Fig. 63 Removing the headlight

Fig. 64 Removing the side marker light signal lens assembly

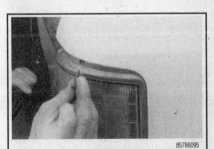

Fig. 65 Removing the side marker light signal lens assembly retaining screw

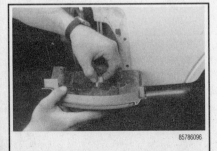

Fig. 66 Removing the side marker bulb

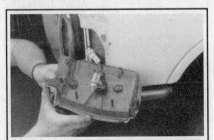

Fig. 67 View of the side marker bulb and lens

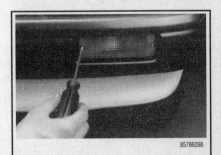

Fig. 68 Removing the turn signal lens

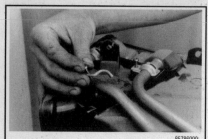

Fig. 69 View of the turn signal light assembly

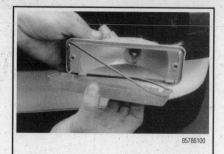

Fig. 70 View of the turn signal lens gasket

Fig. 71 Removing the turn signal bulb

Fig. 72 Removing the rear light lens retaining screws

Fig. 73 View of the rear light assembly

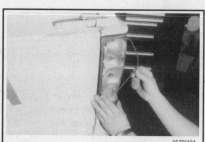

Fig. 74 Removing the rear light assembly gasket

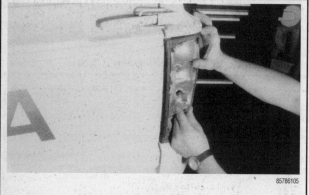

Fig. 75 Removing the rear light bulb

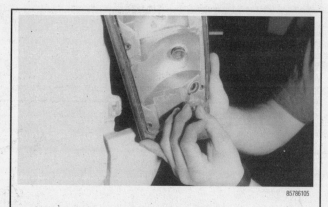

Fig. 76 Removing the rear side marker light

CIRCUIT PROTECTION

Fuses and Flashers

FUSES

▶ **See Figures 77, 78 and 79**

The fuse block is located on the inner fender will on 1970–72 trucks, and below the left side of the instrument panel on 1973–88 trucks. In addition, the radio is protected by a separate fuse located in the wire between the radio and the fuse block.

If a fuse should blow, turn off the ignition switch and also the circuit involved. Replace the fuse with one of the same amperage rating, and turn on the switches. If the new fuse immediately blows out, the circuit should be tested for shorts, broken insulation, or loose connections.

➡**Do not use fuses of a higher amperage than recommended.**

FLASHERS, SWITCHES AND RELAYS

▶ **See Figures 80 thru 97**

The headlight control relay (1973–88 only) is located next to the fuse block under the left side of the instrument panel.

The turn signal flasher is installed on the center portion of the back side of the instrument panel. The hazard warning flasher is wired into the turn signal flasher, and so has no flasher unit of its own.

The turn signal flasher and hazard warning flasher are separate units on 1970–72 trucks. They are located on the inner fender of the engine compartment, next to the fuse block.

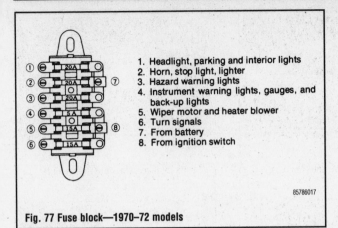

1. Headlight, parking and interior lights
2. Horn, stop light, lighter
3. Hazard warning lights
4. Instrument warning lights, gauges, and back-up lights
5. Wiper motor and heater blower
6. Turn signals
7. From battery
8. From ignition switch

Fig. 77 Fuse block—1970–72 models

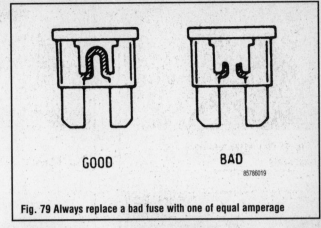

GOOD   BAD

Fig. 79 Always replace a bad fuse with one of equal amperage

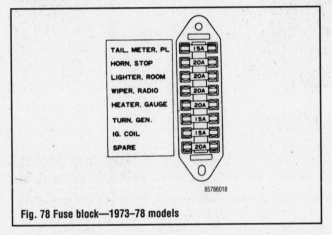

TAIL, METER, PL   15A
HORN, STOP   20A
LIGHTER, ROOM   20A
WIPER, RADIO   20A
HEATER, GAUGE   20A
TURN, GEN.   15A
IG. COIL   15A
SPARE   20A

Fig. 78 Fuse block—1973–78 models

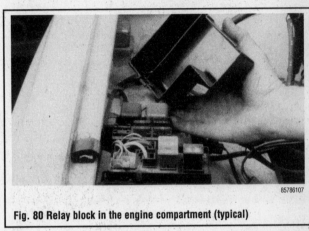

Fig. 80 Relay block in the engine compartment (typical)

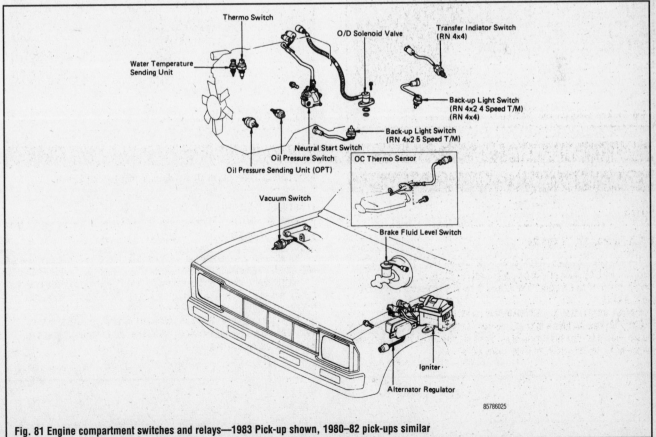

Fig. 81 Engine compartment switches and relays—1983 Pick-up shown, 1980–82 pick-ups similar

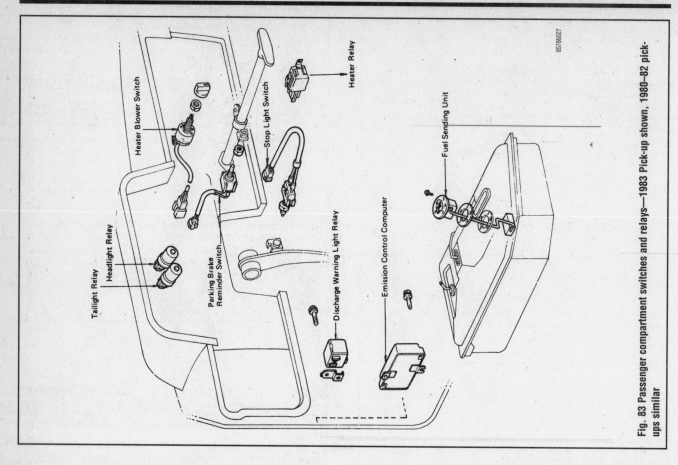

Heater Relay

Fuel Sending Unit

Heater Blower Switch

Stop Light Switch

Tailight Relay

Headlight Relay

Parking Brake Reminder Switch

Discharge Warning Light Relay

Emission Control Computer

Fig. 83 Passenger compartment switches and relays—1983 Pick-up shown, 1980-82 pick-ups similar

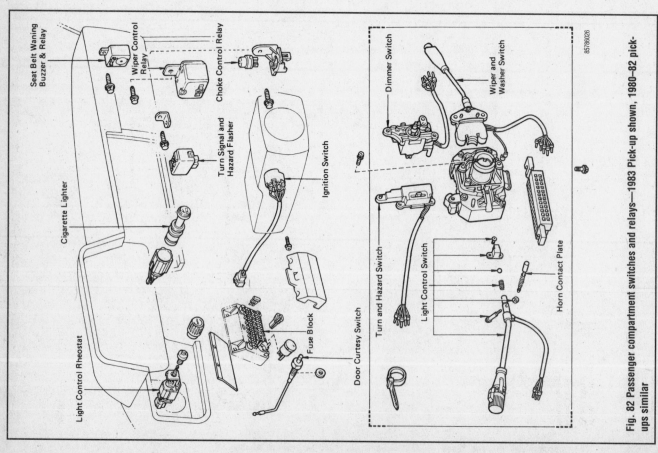

Seat Belt Warning Buzzer & Relay

Wiper Control Relay

Choke Control Relay

Dimmer Switch

Wiper and Washer Switch

Cigarette Lighter

Turn Signal and Hazard Flasher

Ignition Switch

Turn and Hazard Switch

Light Control Switch

Horn Contact Plate

Light Control Rheostat

Fuse Block

Door Curtesy Switch

Fig. 82 Passenger compartment switches and relays—1983 Pick-up shown, 1980-82 pick-ups similar

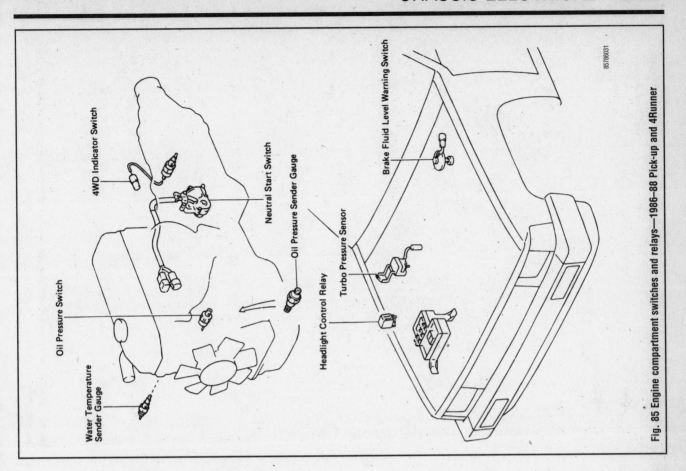

Fig. 85 Engine compartment switches and relays—1986–88 Pick-up and 4Runner

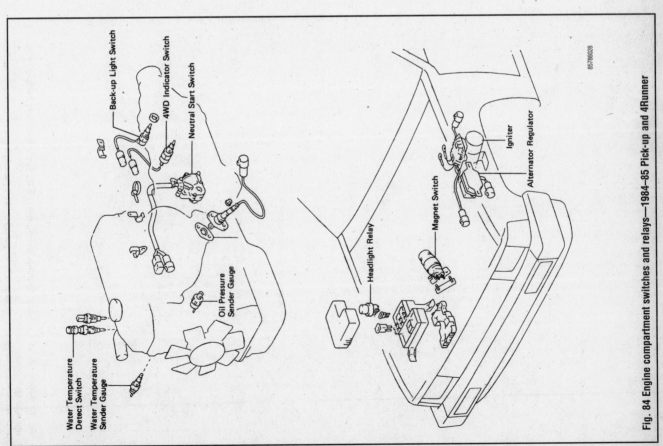

Fig. 84 Engine compartment switches and relays—1984–85 Pick-up and 4Runner

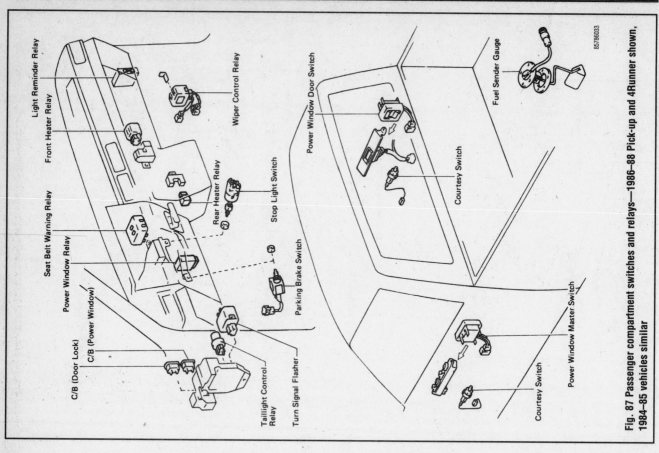

Fig. 87 Passenger compartment switches and relays—1986–88 Pick-up and 4Runner shown, 1984–85 vehicles similar

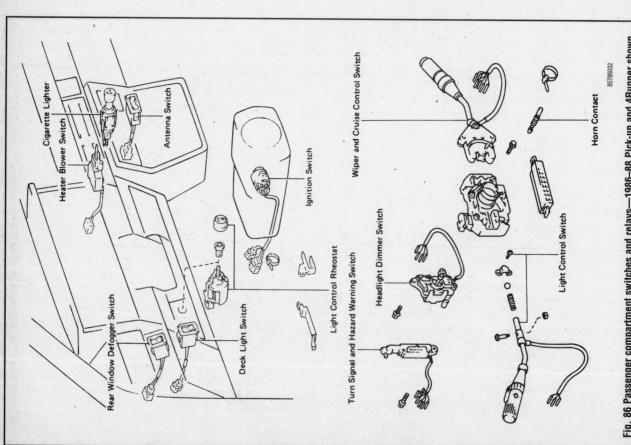

Fig. 86 Passenger compartment switches and relays—1986–88 Pick-up and 4Runner shown, 1984–85 vehicles similar

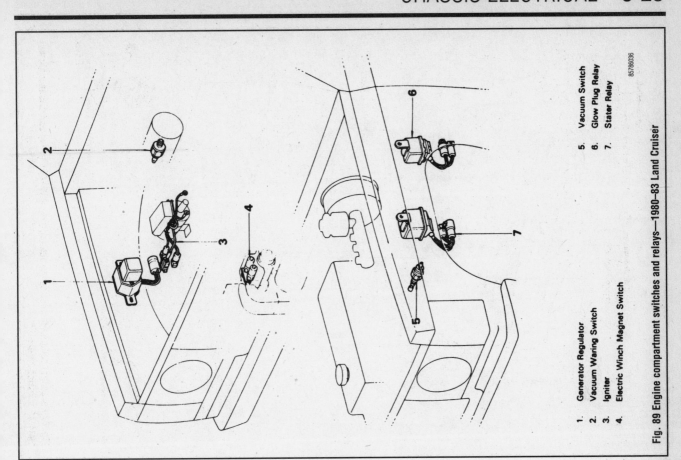

85786036

1. Generator Regulator
2. Vacuum Waring Switch
3. Igniter
4. Electric Winch Magnet Switch

5. Vacuum Switch
6. Glow Plug Relay
7. Stater Relay

Fig. 89 Engine compartment switches and relays—1980-83 Land Cruiser

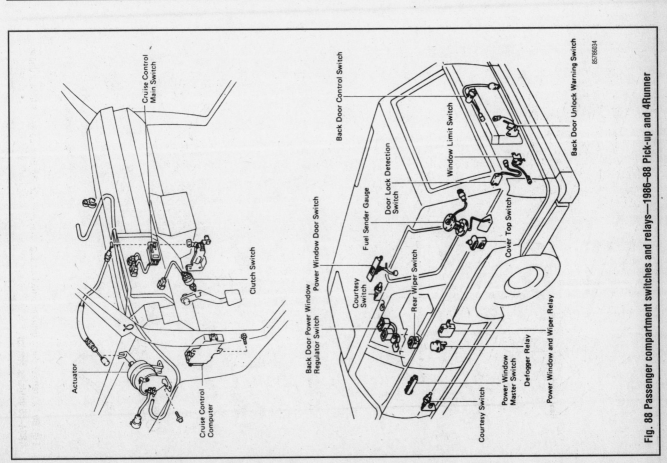

85786034

Fig. 88 Passenger compartment switches and relays—1986-88 Pick-up and 4Runner

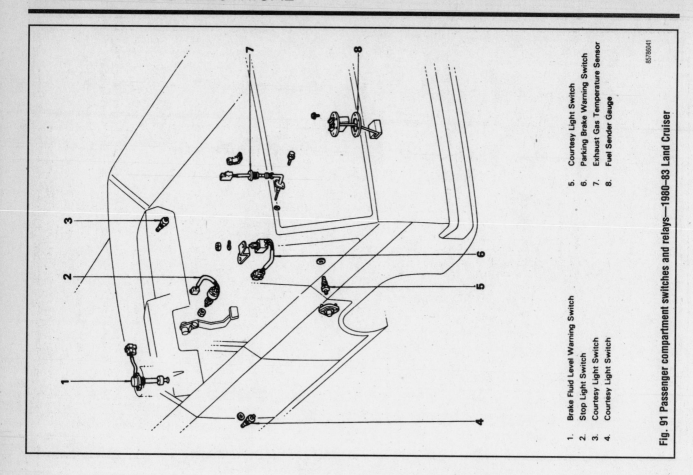

85786041

1. Brake Fluid Level Warning Switch
2. Stop Light Switch
3. Courtesy Light Switch
4. Courtesy Light Switch
5. Courtesy Light Switch
6. Parking Brake Warning Switch
7. Exhaust Gas Temperature Sensor
8. Fuel Sender Gauge

Fig. 91 Passenger compartment switches and relays—1980-83 Land Cruiser

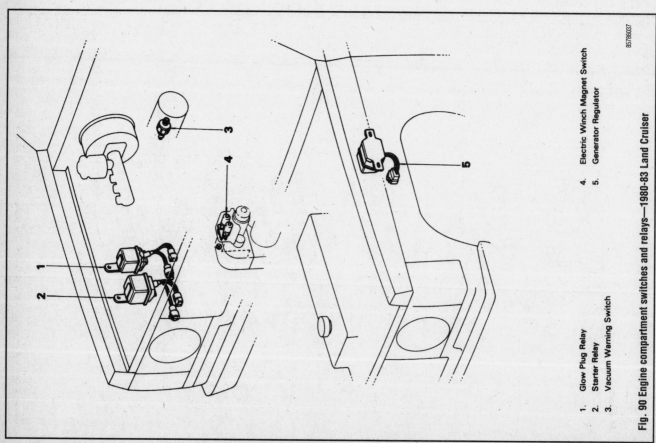

85786037

1. Glow Plug Relay
2. Starter Relay
3. Vacuum Warning Switch
4. Electric Winch Magnet Switch
5. Generator Regulator

Fig. 90 Engine compartment switches and relays—1980-83 Land Cruiser

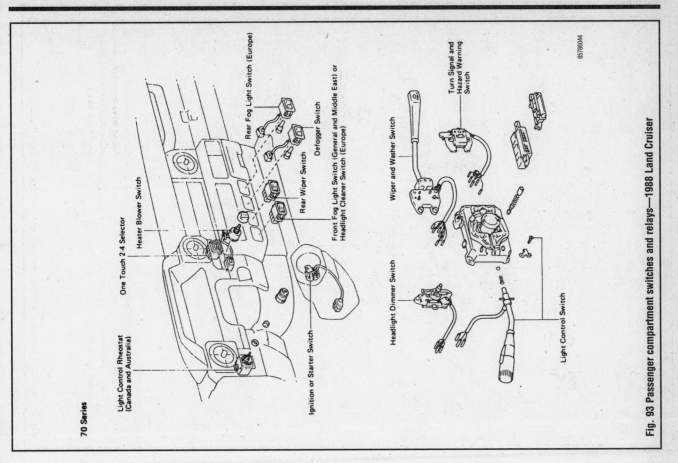

70 Series

Light Control Rheostat (Canada and Australia)

One Touch 2-4 Selector

Heater Blower Switch

Rear Fog Light Switch (Europe)

Defogger Switch

Rear Wiper Switch

Front Fog Light Switch (General and Middle East) or Headlight Cleaner Switch (Europe)

Ignition or Starter Switch

Wiper and Washer Switch

Turn Signal and Hazard Warning Switch

Headlight Dimmer Switch

Light Control Switch

Fig. 93 Passenger compartment switches and relays—1988 Land Cruiser

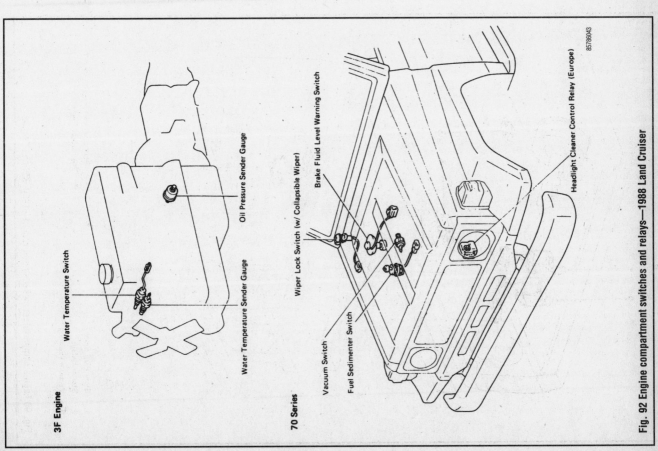

3F Engine

Water Temperature Switch

Oil Pressure Sender Gauge

Water Temperature Sender Gauge

70 Series

Wiper Lock Switch (w/ Collapsible Wiper)

Brake Fluid Level Warning Switch

Vacuum Switch

Fuel Sedimenter Switch

Headlight Cleaner Control Relay (Europe)

Fig. 92 Engine compartment switches and relays—1988 Land Cruiser

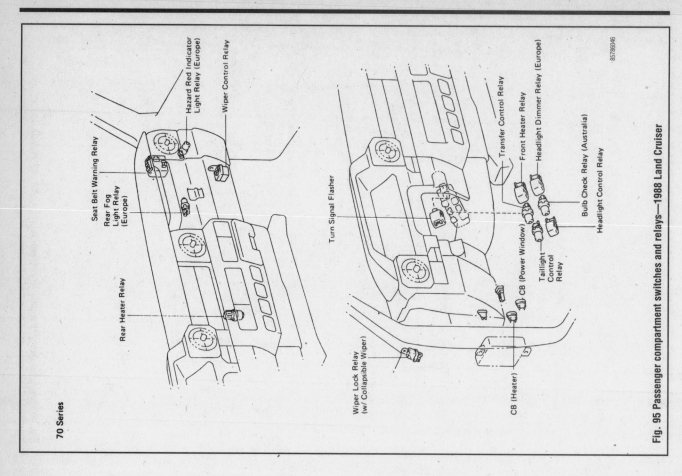

70 Series

Seat Belt Warning Relay

Rear Fog Light Relay (Europe)

Hazard Red Indicator Light Relay (Europe)

Wiper Control Relay

Rear Heater Relay

Turn Signal Flasher

Transfer Control Relay

Front Heater Relay

Headlight Dimmer Relay (Europe)

Bulb Check Relay (Australia)

Headlight Control Relay

Taillight Control Relay

CB (Power Window)

Wiper Lock Relay (w/ Collapsible Wiper)

CB (Heater)

Fig. 95 Passenger compartment switches and relays—1988 Land Cruiser

85786046

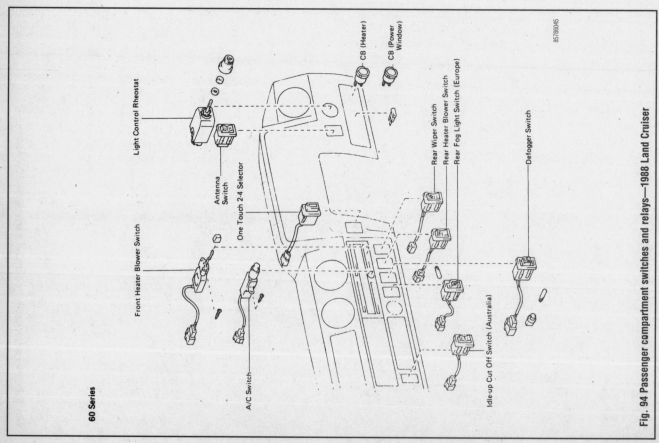

60 Series

Light Control Rheostat

Front Heater Blower Switch

Antenna Switch

One Touch 2-4 Selector

A/C Switch

CB (Heater)

CB (Power Window)

Rear Wiper Switch

Rear Heater Blower Switch

Rear Fog Light Switch (Europe)

Defogger Switch

Idle-up Cut Off Switch (Australia)

Fig. 94 Passenger compartment switches and relays—1988 Land Cruiser

85786045

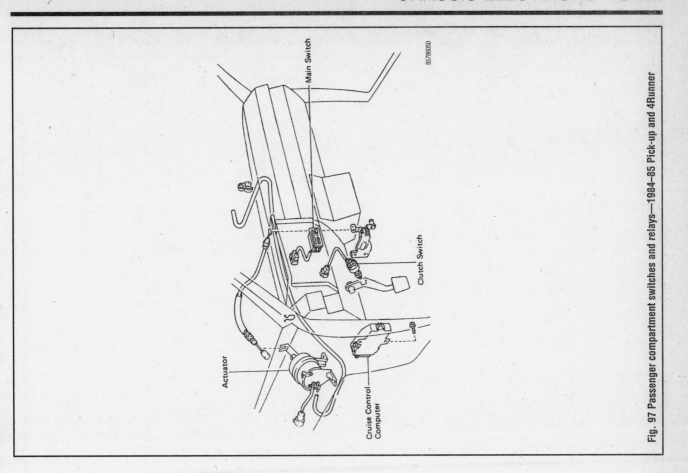

Fig. 97 Passenger compartment switches and relays—1984–85 Pick-up and 4Runner

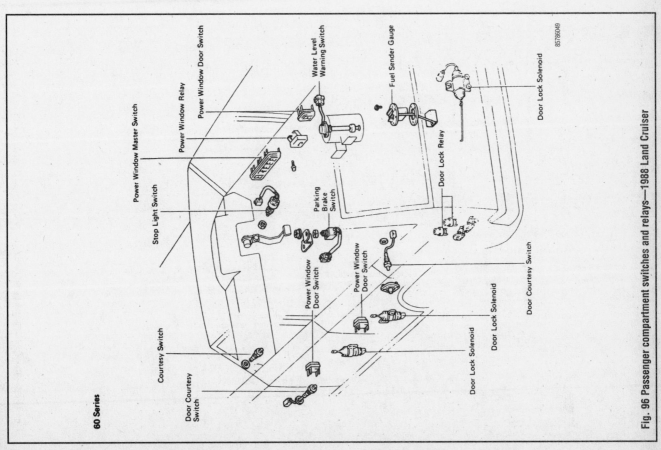

Fig. 96 Passenger compartment switches and relays—1988 Land Cruiser

WIRING DIAGRAMS

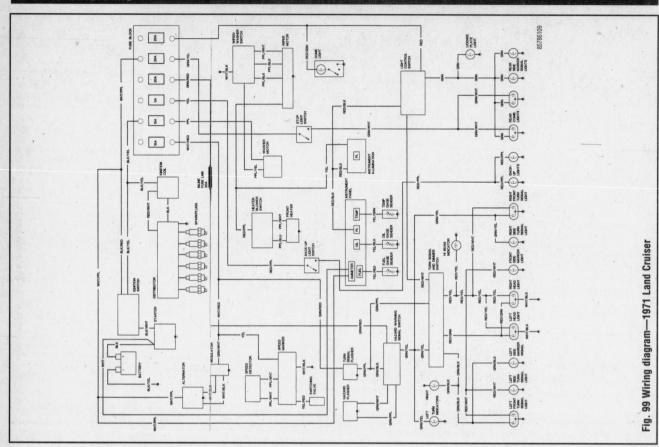

Fig. 99 Wiring diagram—1971 Land Cruiser

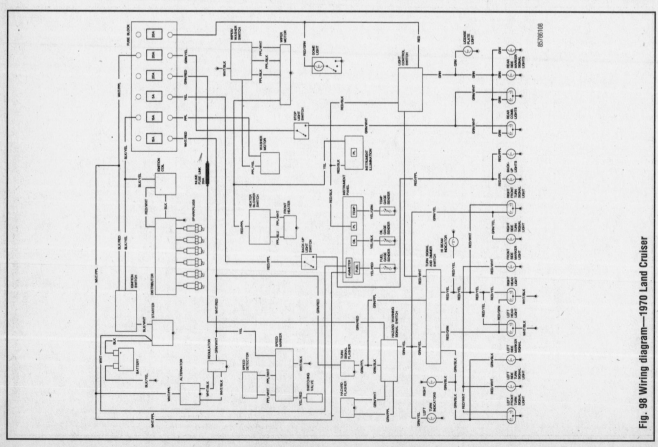

Fig. 98 Wiring diagram—1970 Land Cruiser

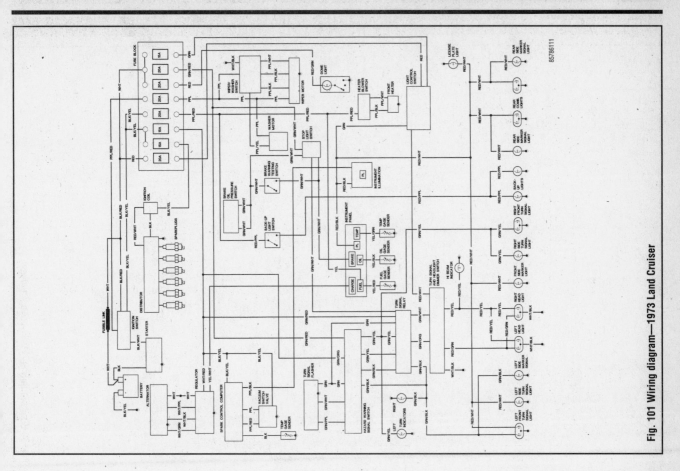

Fig. 101 Wiring diagram—1973 Land Cruiser

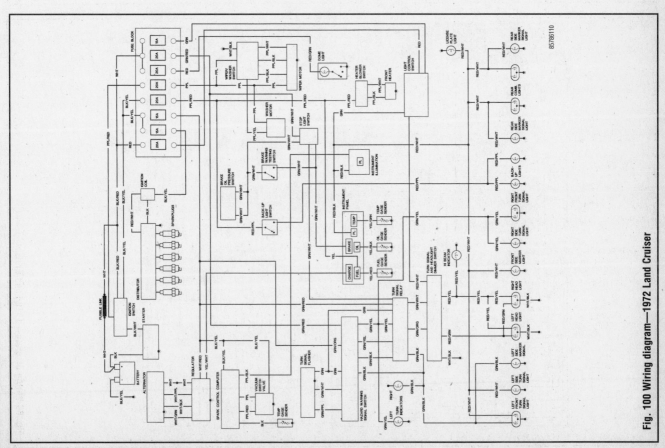

Fig. 100 Wiring diagram—1972 Land Cruiser

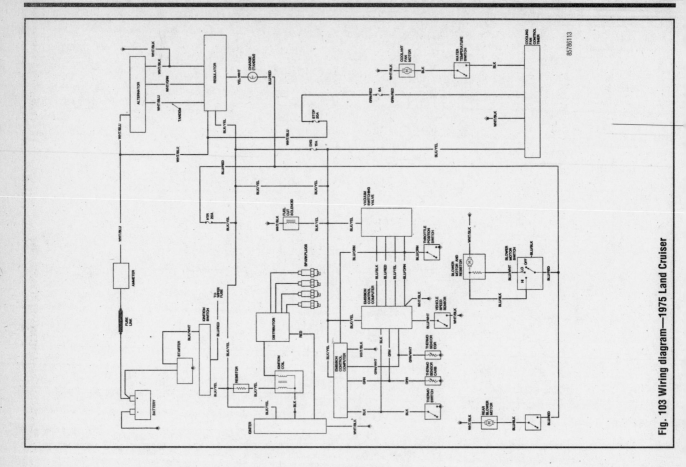

Fig. 103 Wiring diagram—1975 Land Cruiser

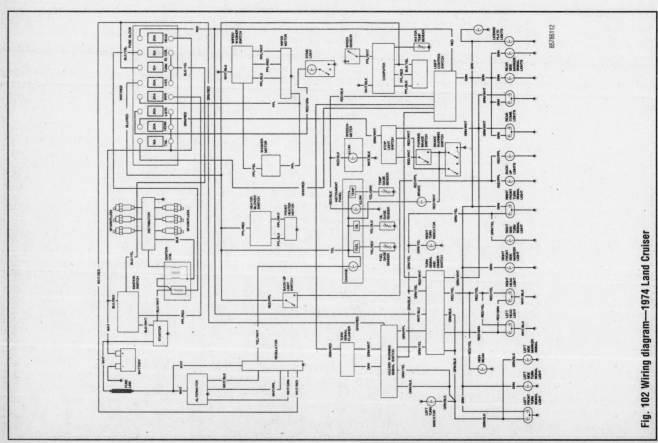

Fig. 102 Wiring diagram—1974 Land Cruiser

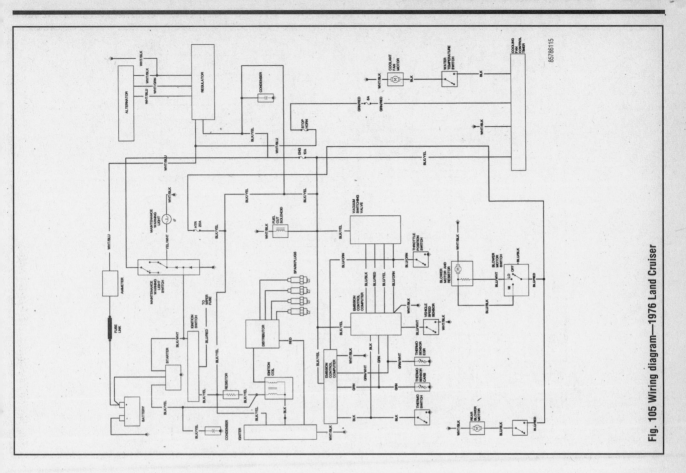

Fig. 105 Wiring diagram—1976 Land Cruiser

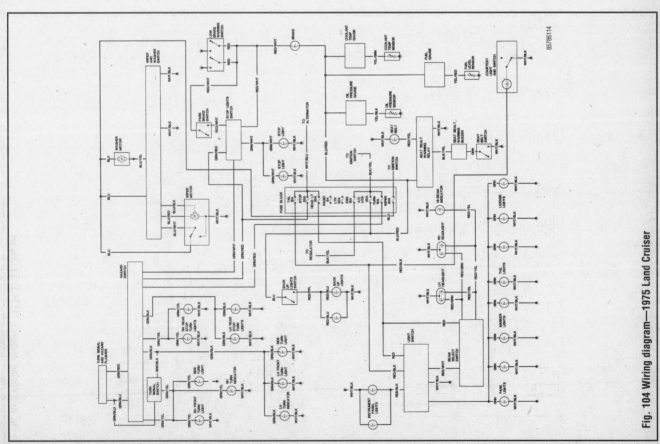

Fig. 104 Wiring diagram—1975 Land Cruiser

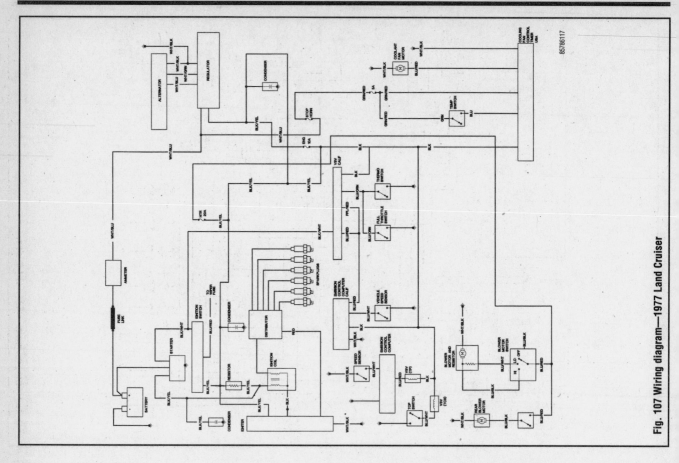

Fig. 107 Wiring diagram—1977 Land Cruiser

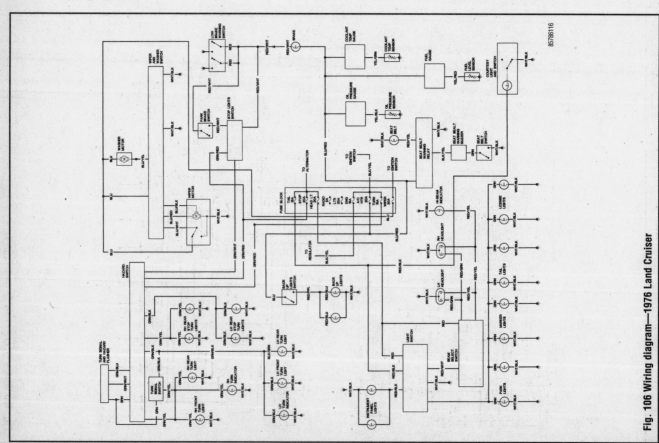

Fig. 106 Wiring diagram—1976 Land Cruiser

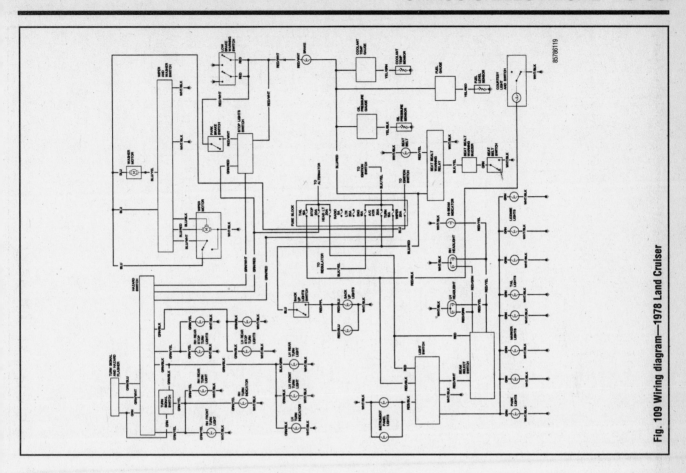

Fig. 109 Wiring diagram—1978 Land Cruiser

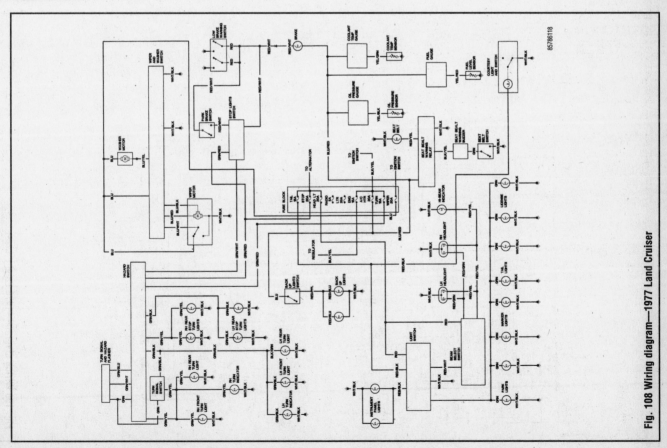

Fig. 108 Wiring diagram—1977 Land Cruiser

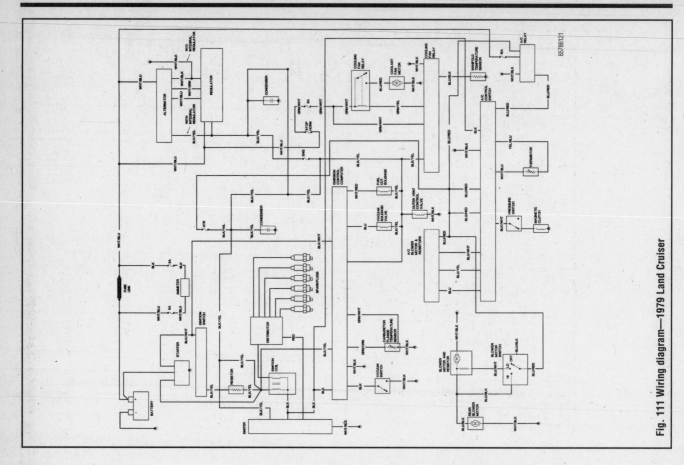

Fig. 111 Wiring diagram—1979 Land Cruiser

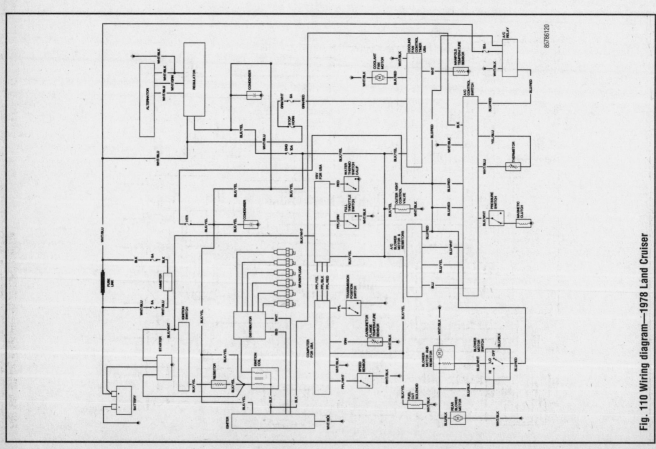

Fig. 110 Wiring diagram—1978 Land Cruiser

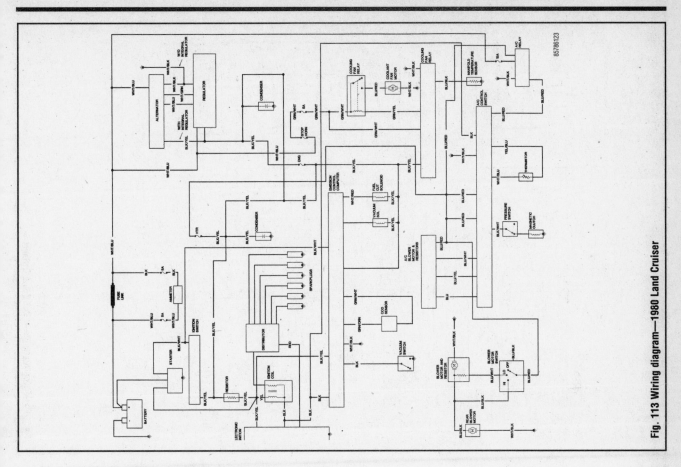

Fig. 113 Wiring diagram—1980 Land Cruiser

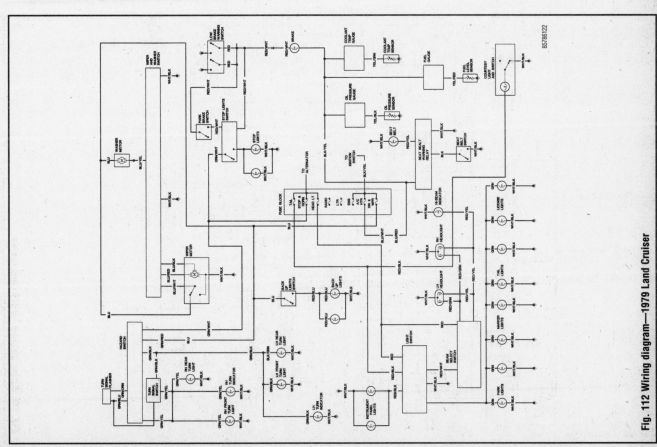

Fig. 112 Wiring diagram—1979 Land Cruiser

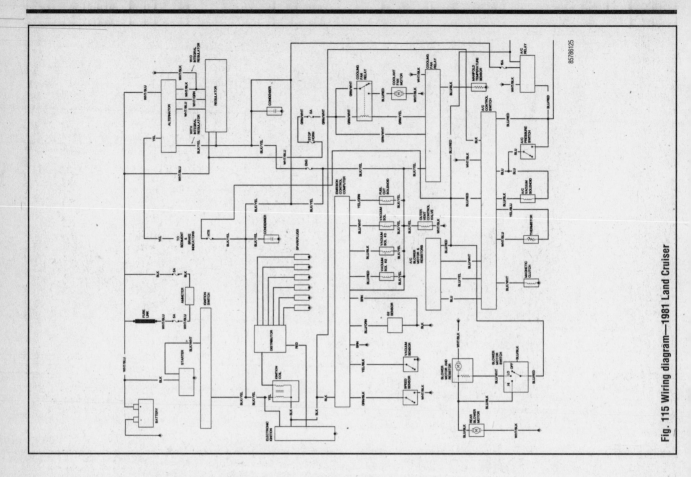

Fig. 115 Wiring diagram—1981 Land Cruiser

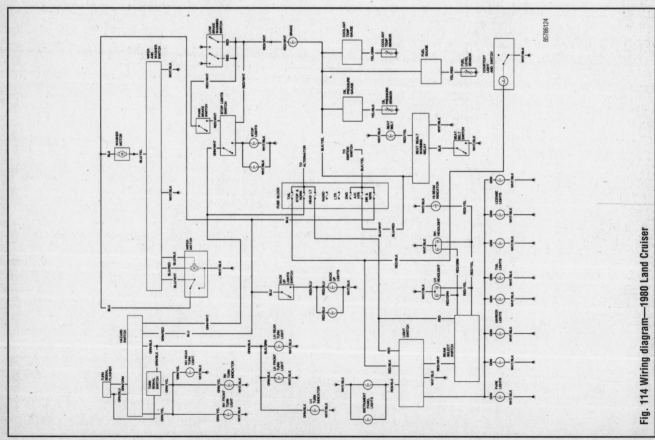

Fig. 114 Wiring diagram—1980 Land Cruiser

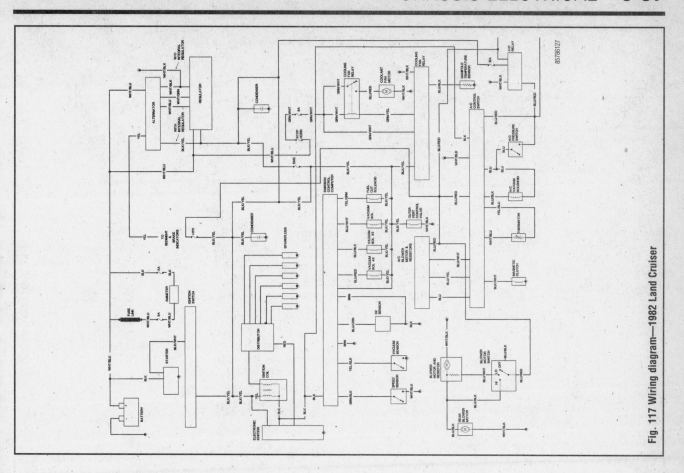

Fig. 117 Wiring diagram—1982 Land Cruiser

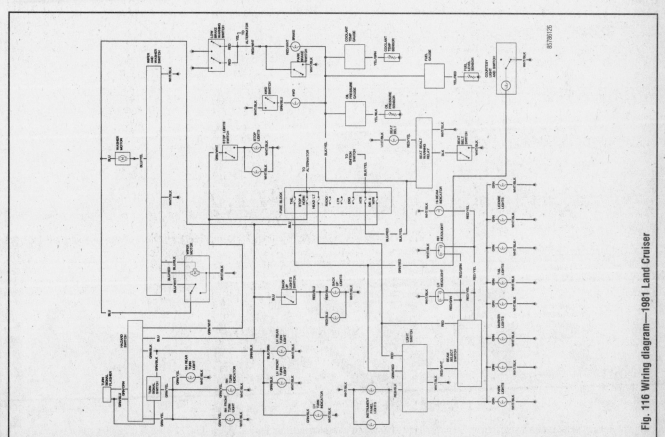

Fig. 116 Wiring diagram—1981 Land Cruiser

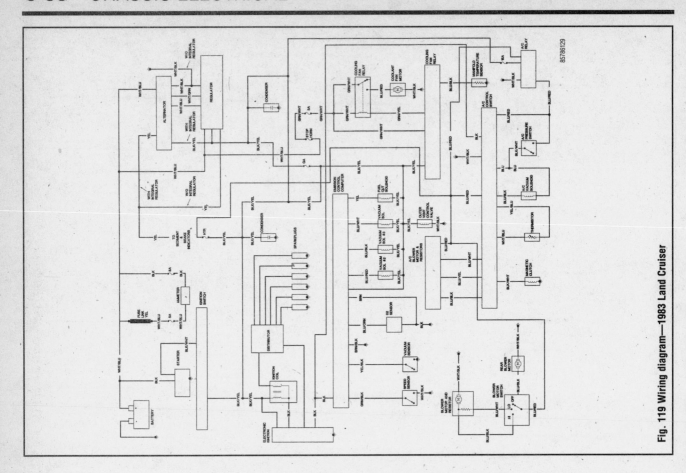

Fig. 119 Wiring diagram—1983 Land Cruiser

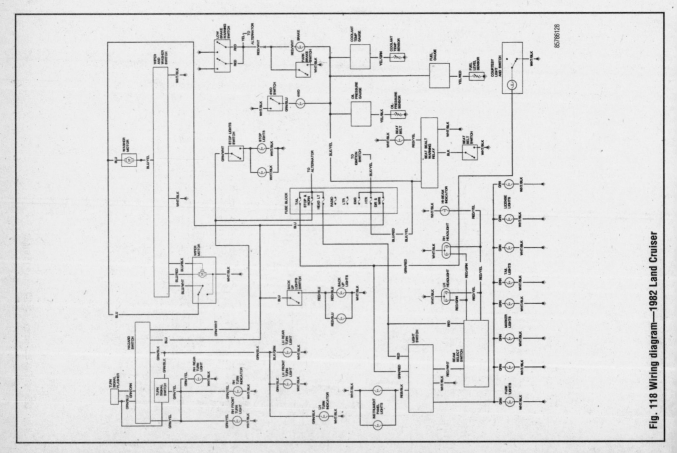

Fig. 118 Wiring diagram—1982 Land Cruiser

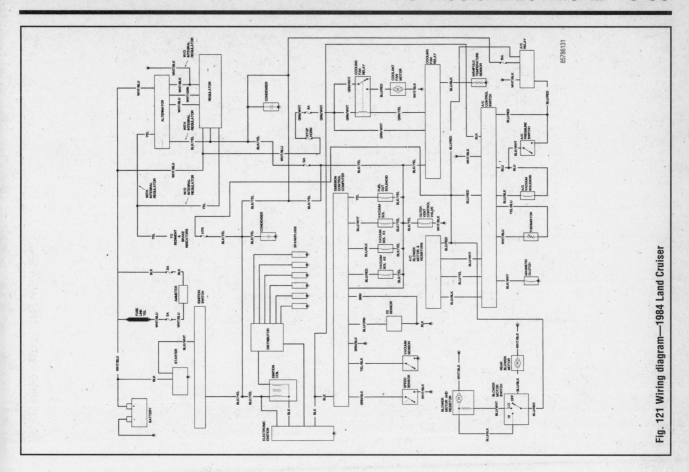

Fig. 121 Wiring diagram—1984 Land Cruiser

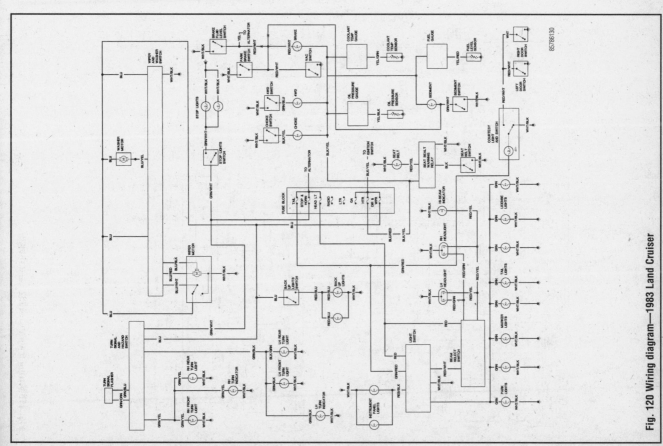

Fig. 120 Wiring diagram—1983 Land Cruiser

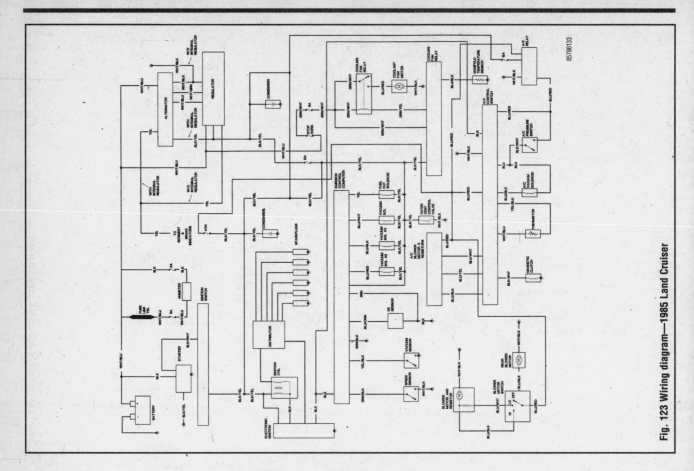

Fig. 123 Wiring diagram—1985 Land Cruiser

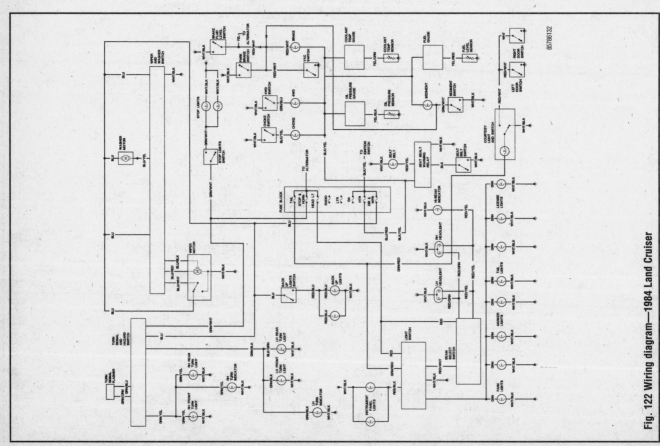

Fig. 122 Wiring diagram—1984 Land Cruiser

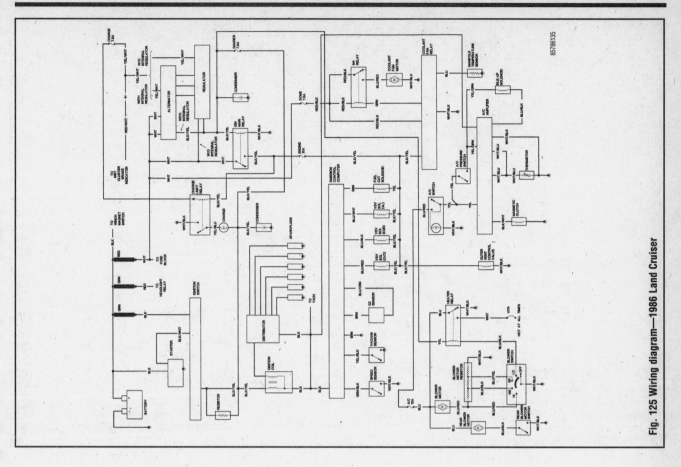

Fig. 125 Wiring diagram—1986 Land Cruiser

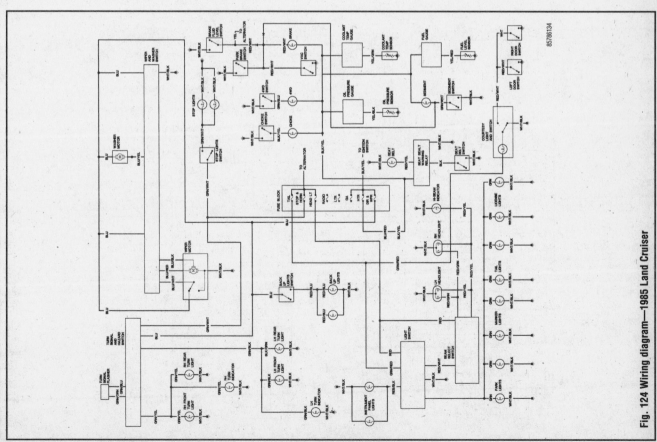

Fig. 124 Wiring diagram—1985 Land Cruiser

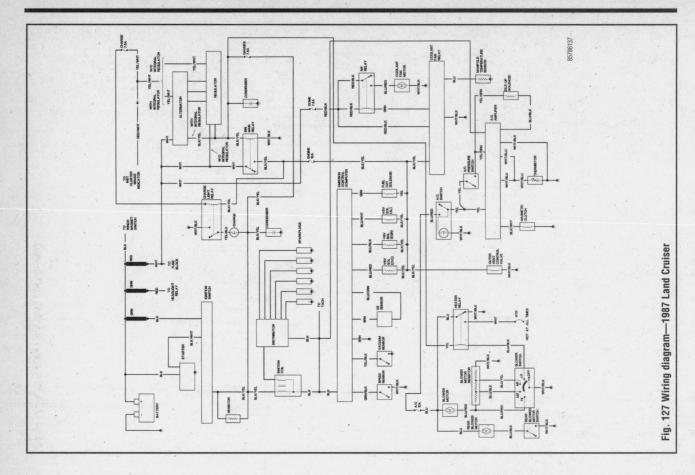

Fig. 127 Wiring diagram—1987 Land Cruiser

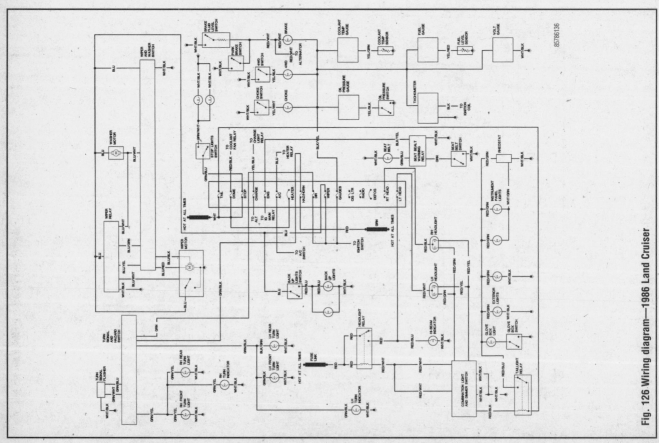

Fig. 126 Wiring diagram—1986 Land Cruiser

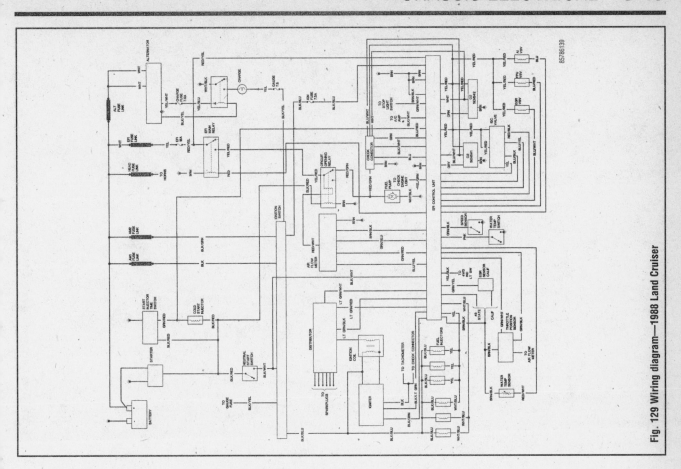

Fig. 129 Wiring diagram—1988 Land Cruiser

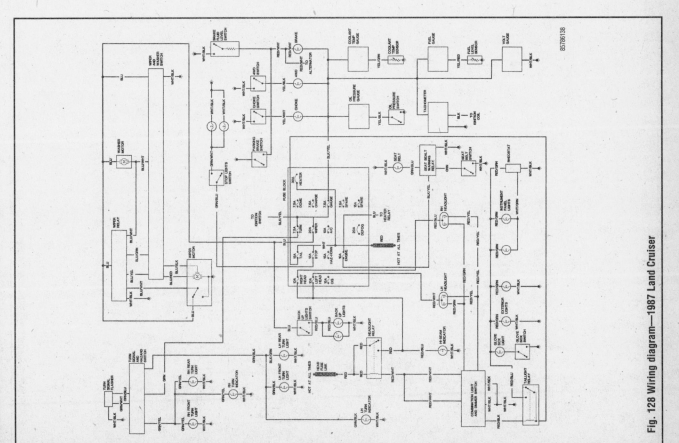

Fig. 128 Wiring diagram—1987 Land Cruiser

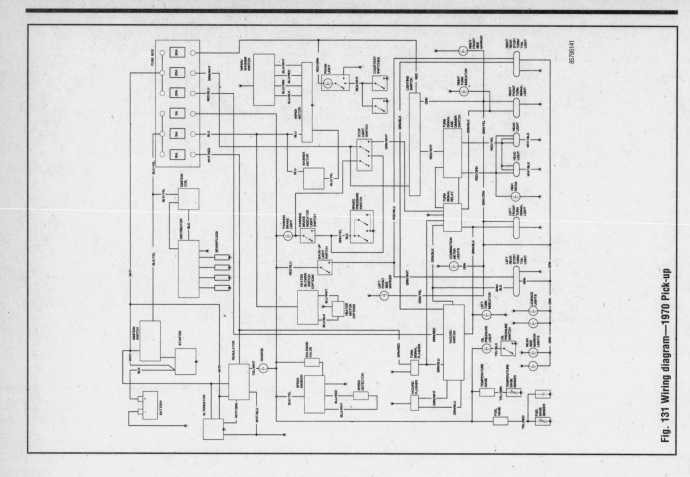

Fig. 131 Wiring diagram—1970 Pick-up

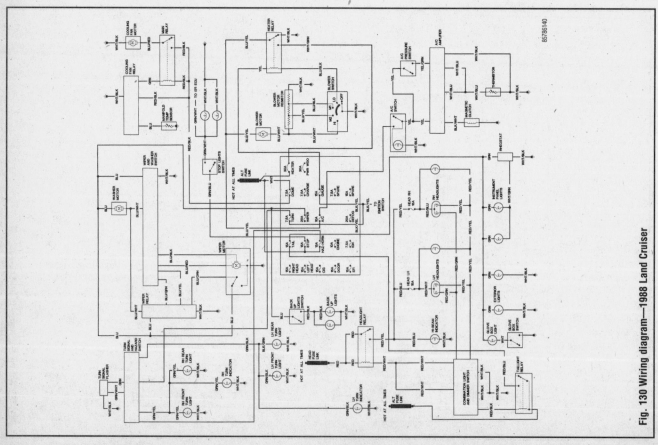

Fig. 130 Wiring diagram—1988 Land Cruiser

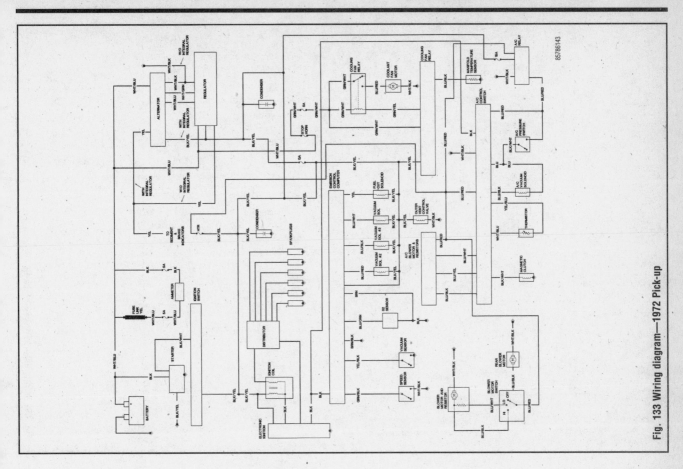

Fig. 133 Wiring diagram—1972 Pick-up

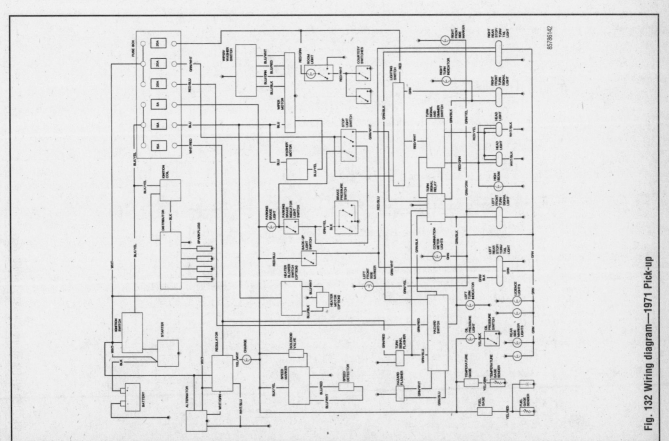

Fig. 132 Wiring diagram—1971 Pick-up

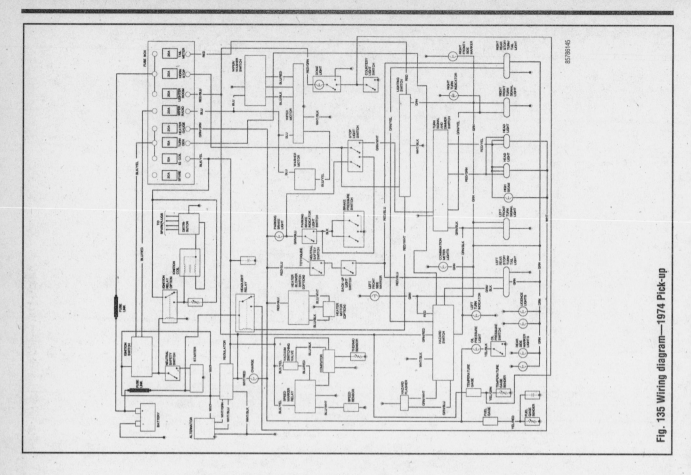

Fig. 135 Wiring diagram—1974 Pick-up

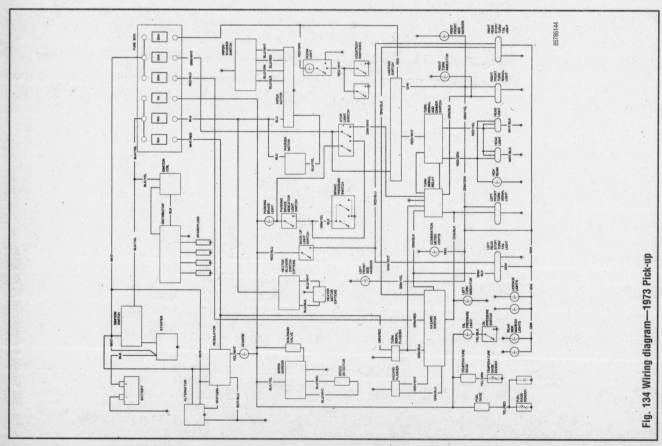

Fig. 134 Wiring diagram—1973 Pick-up

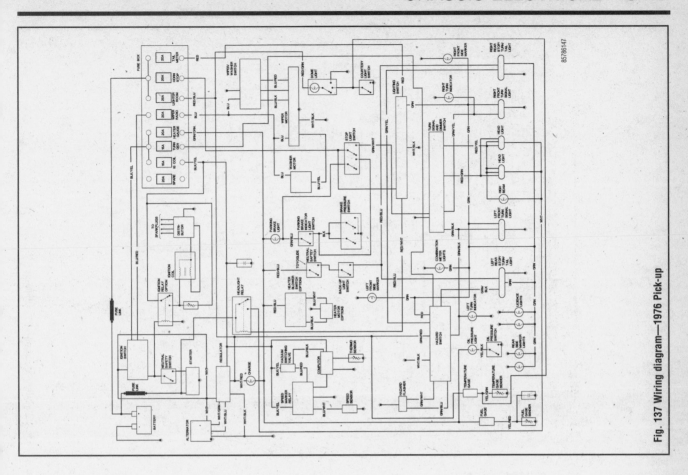

Fig. 137 Wiring diagram—1976 Pick-up

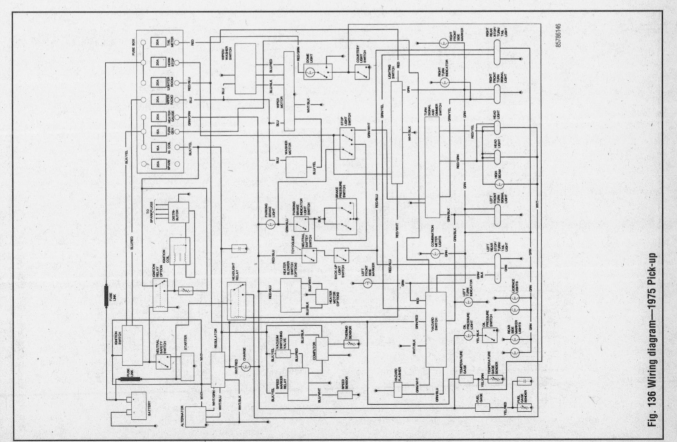

Fig. 136 Wiring diagram—1975 Pick-up

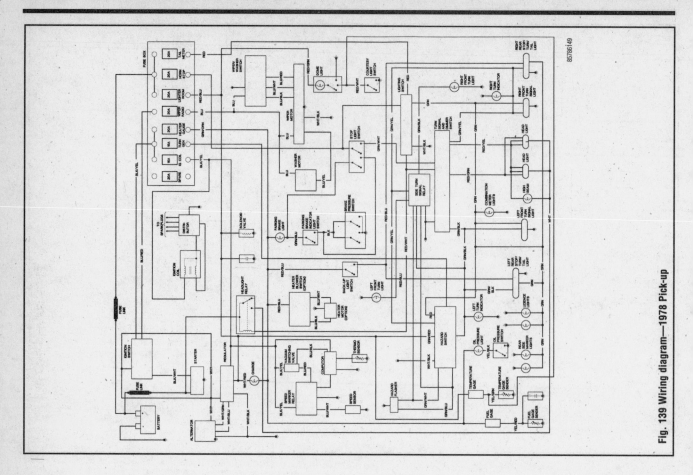

Fig. 139 Wiring diagram—1978 Pick-up

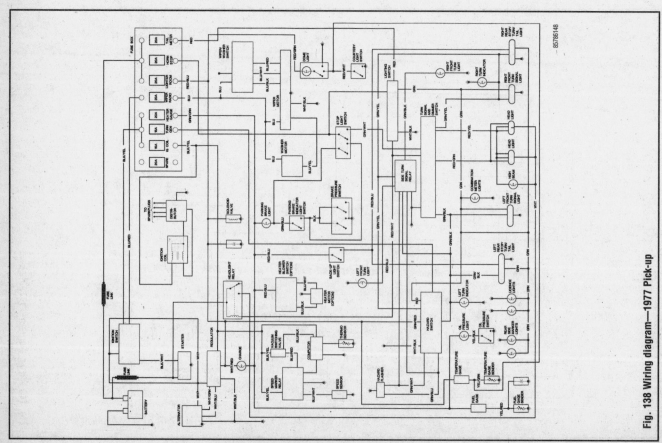

Fig. 138 Wiring diagram—1977 Pick-up

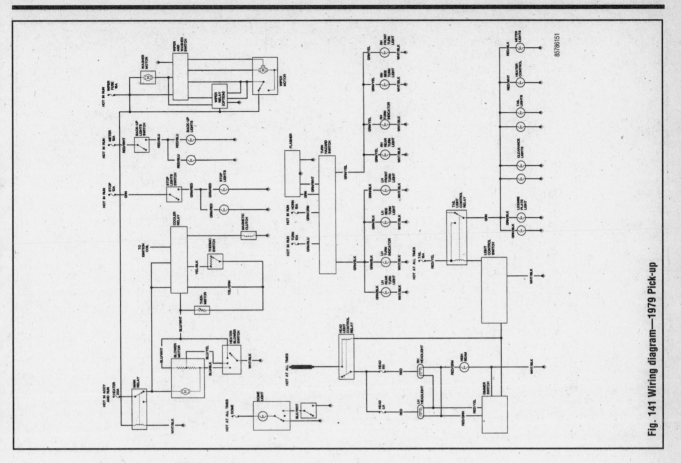

Fig. 141 Wiring diagram—1979 Pick-up

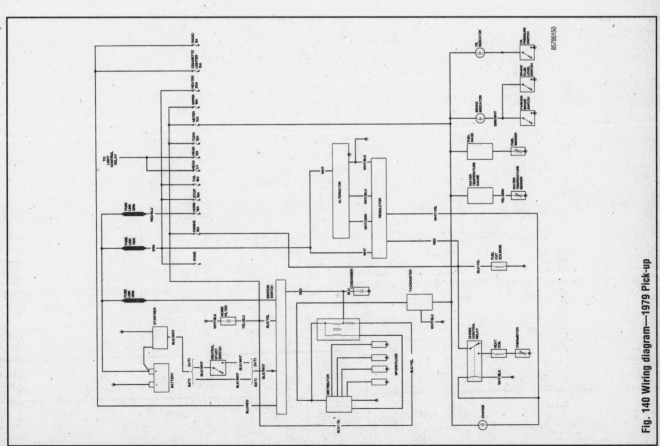

Fig. 140 Wiring diagram—1979 Pick-up

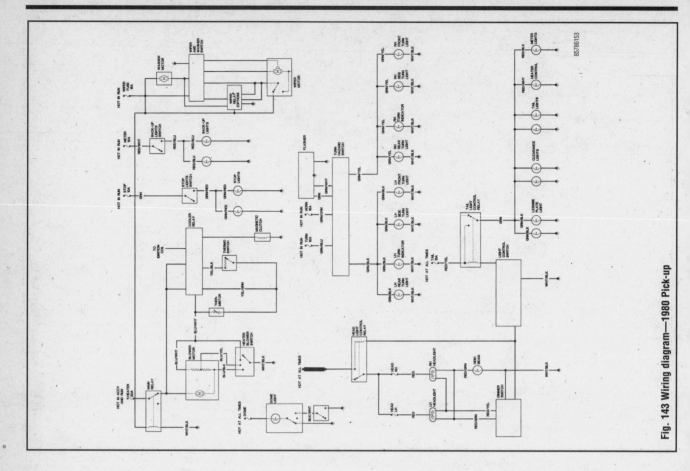

Fig. 143 Wiring diagram—1980 Pick-up

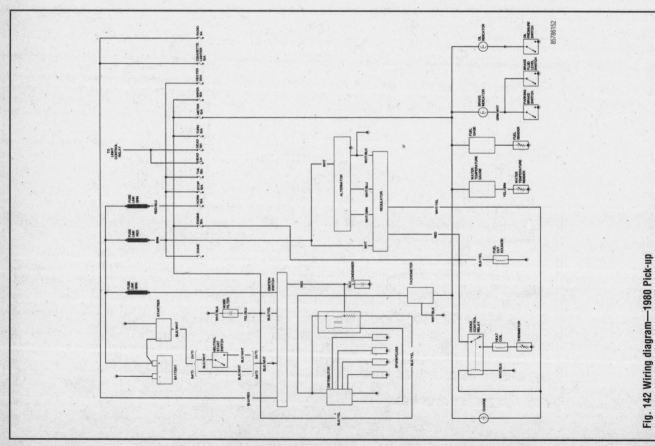

Fig. 142 Wiring diagram—1980 Pick-up

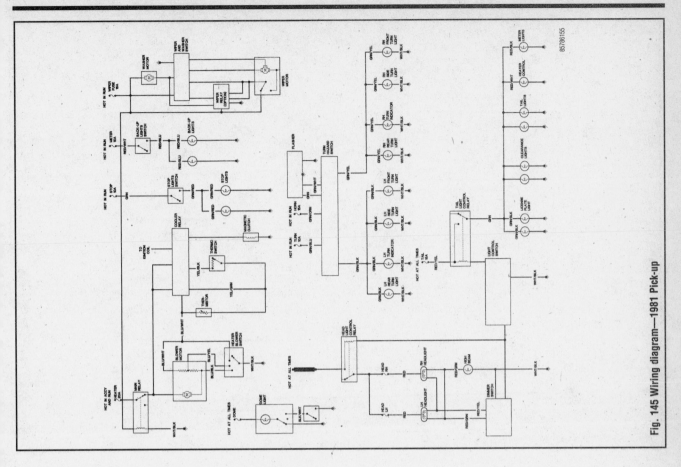

Fig. 145 Wiring diagram—1981 Pick-up

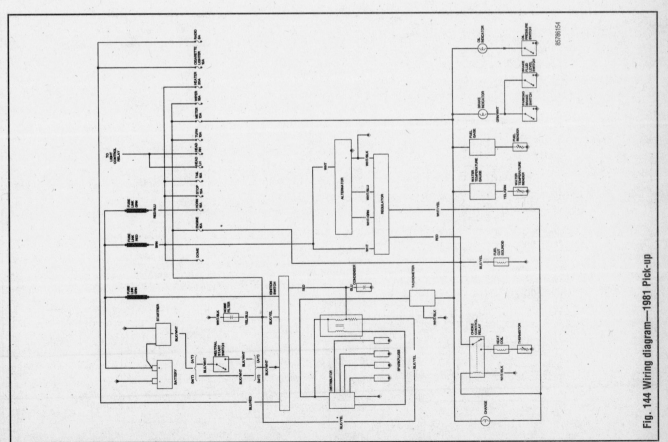

Fig. 144 Wiring diagram—1981 Pick-up

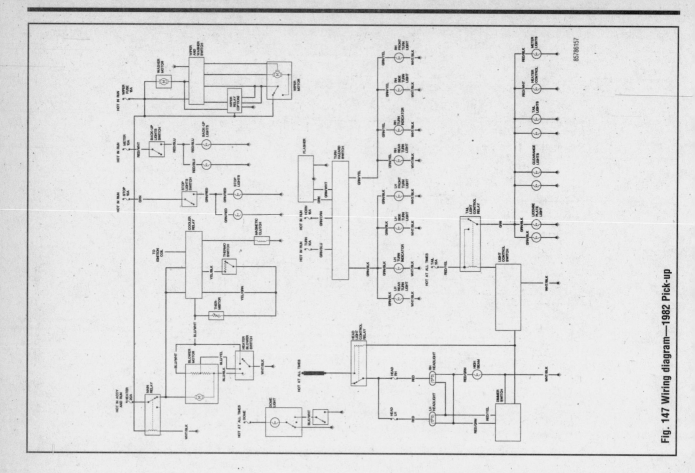

Fig. 147 Wiring diagram—1982 Pick-up

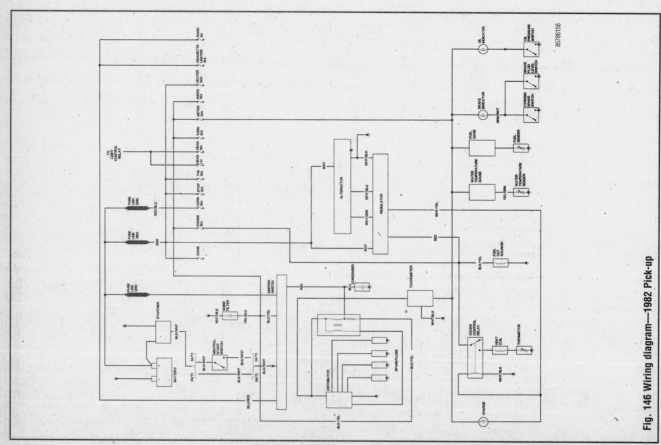

Fig. 146 Wiring diagram—1982 Pick-up

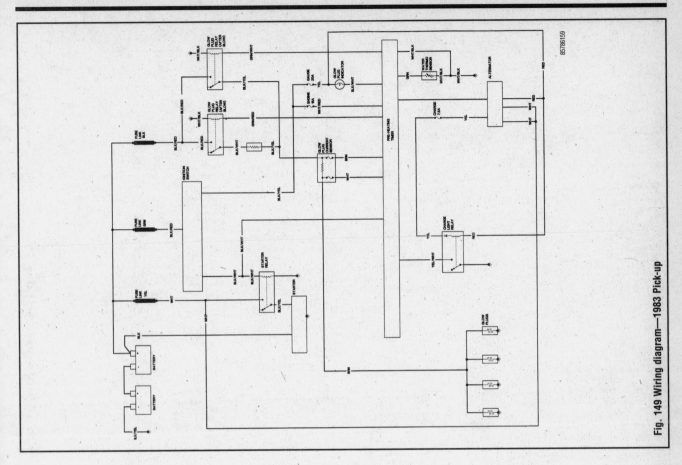

Fig. 149 Wiring diagram—1983 Pick-up

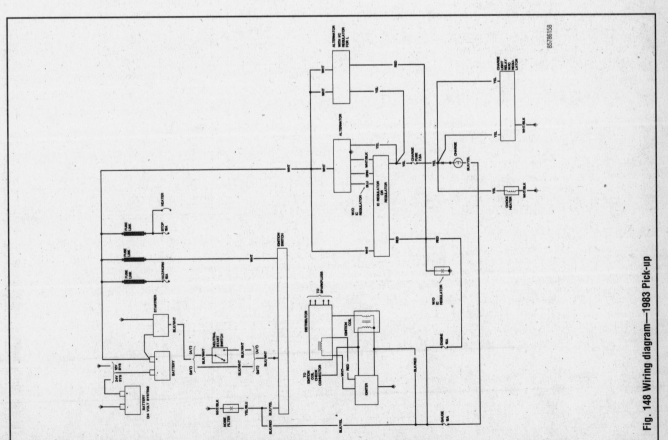

Fig. 148 Wiring diagram—1983 Pick-up

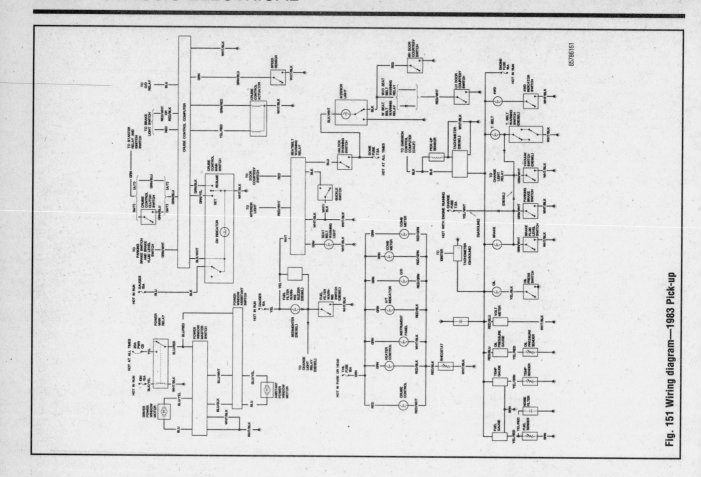

Fig. 151 Wiring diagram—1983 Pick-up

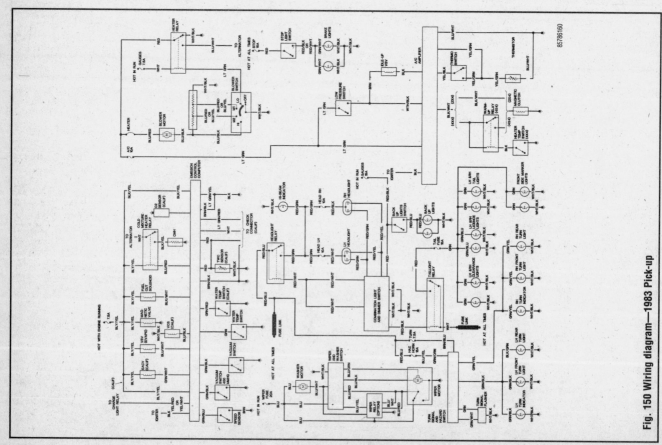

Fig. 150 Wiring diagram—1983 Pick-up

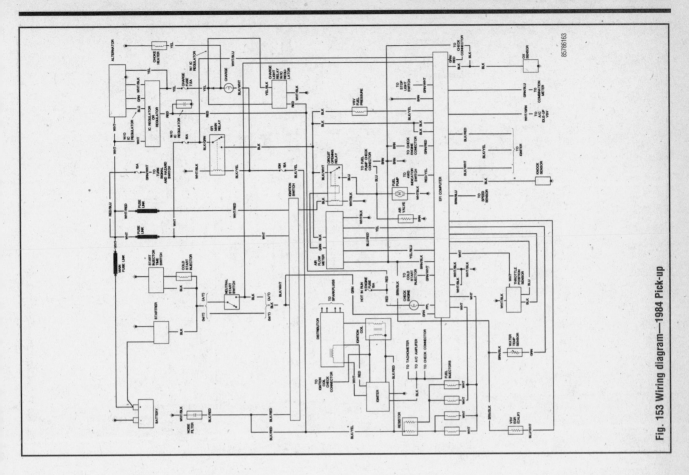

Fig. 153 Wiring diagram—1984 Pick-up

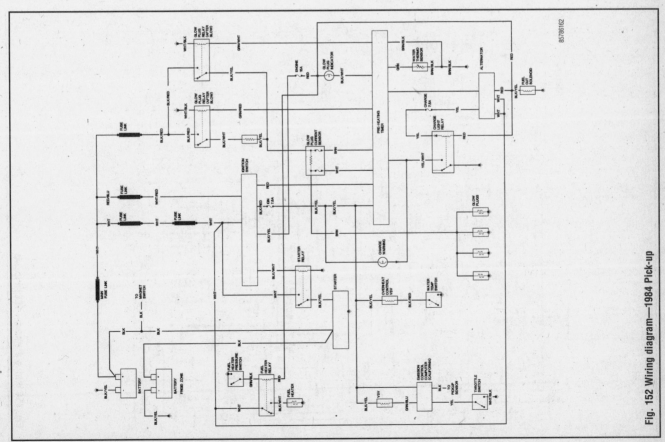

Fig. 152 Wiring diagram—1984 Pick-up

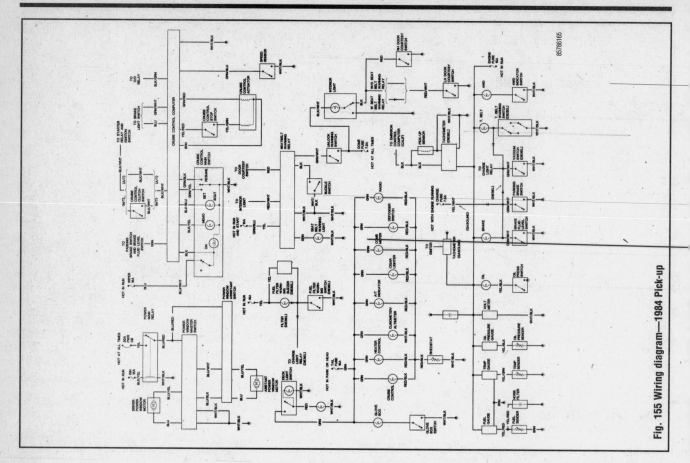

Fig. 155 Wiring diagram—1984 Pick-up

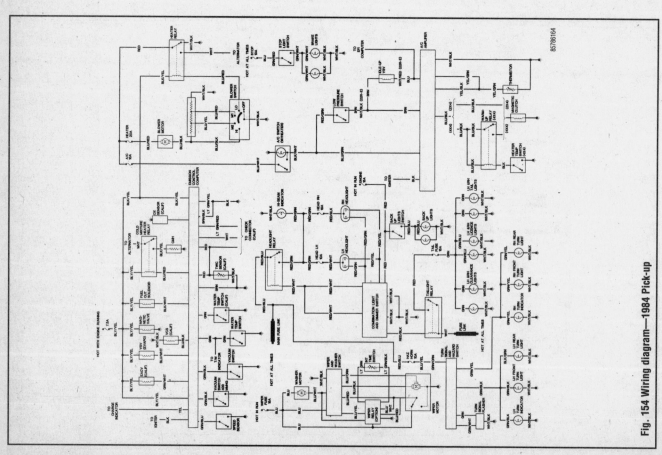

Fig. 154 Wiring diagram—1984 Pick-up

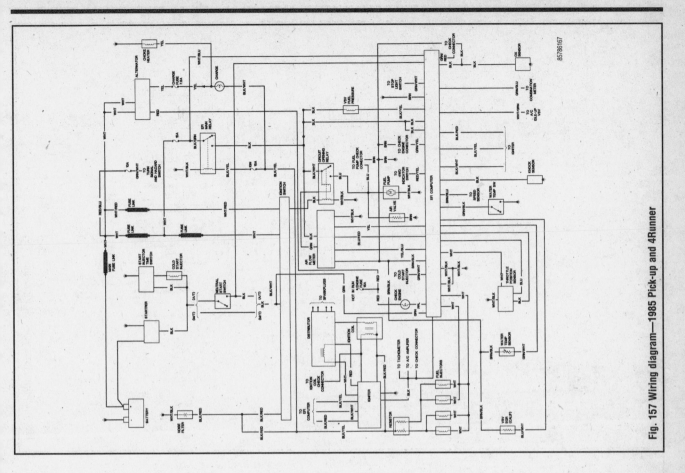

Fig. 157 Wiring diagram—1985 Pick-up and 4Runner

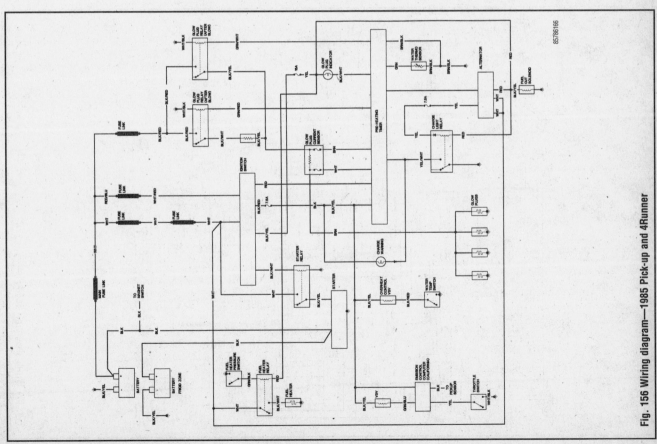

Fig. 156 Wiring diagram—1985 Pick-up and 4Runner

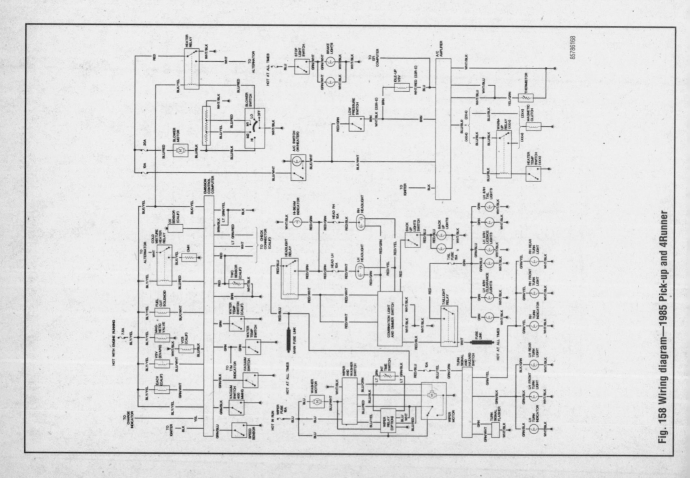

Fig. 159 Wiring diagram—1985 Pick-up and 4Runner

Fig. 158 Wiring diagram—1985 Pick-up and 4Runner

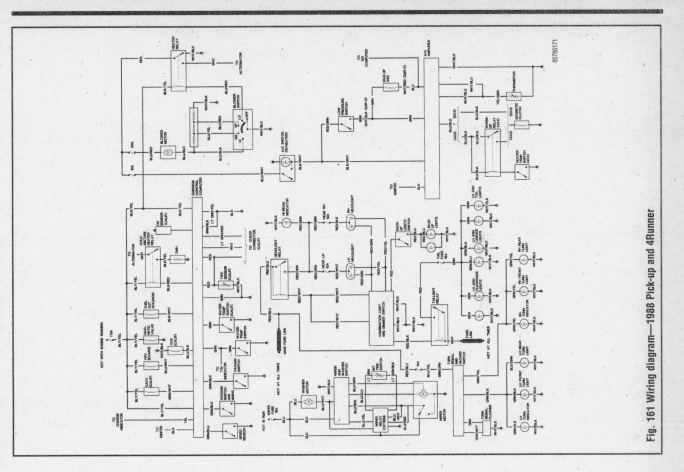

Fig. 161 Wiring diagram—1988 Pick-up and 4Runner

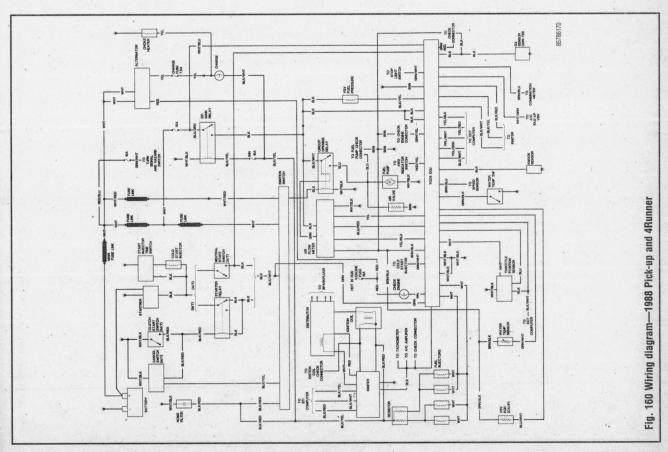

Fig. 160 Wiring diagram—1988 Pick-up and 4Runner

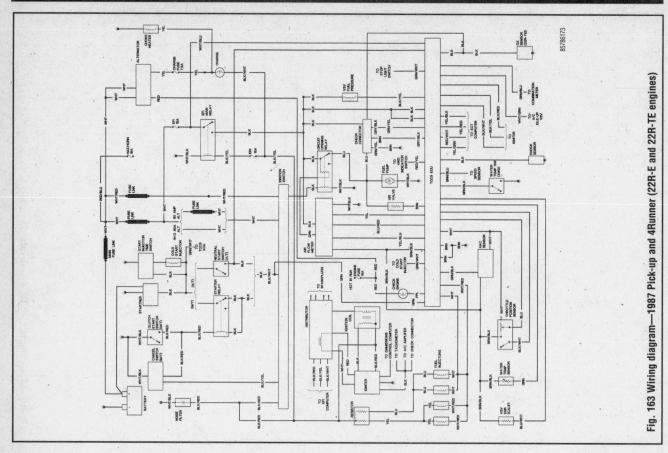

Fig. 163 Wiring diagram—1987 Pick-up and 4Runner (22R-E and 22R-TE engines)

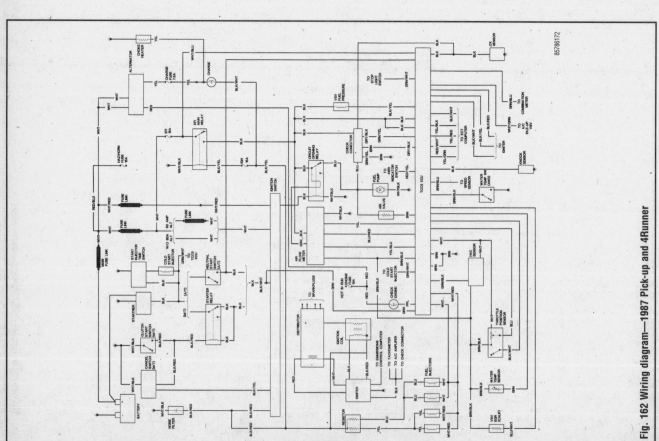

Fig. 162 Wiring diagram—1987 Pick-up and 4Runner

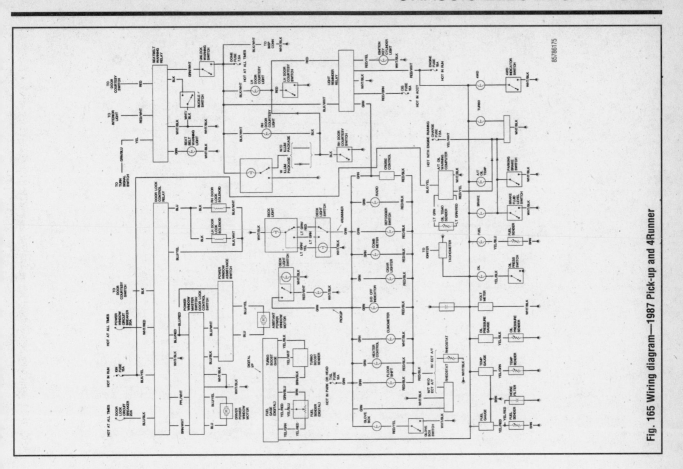

Fig. 165 Wiring diagram—1987 Pick-up and 4Runner

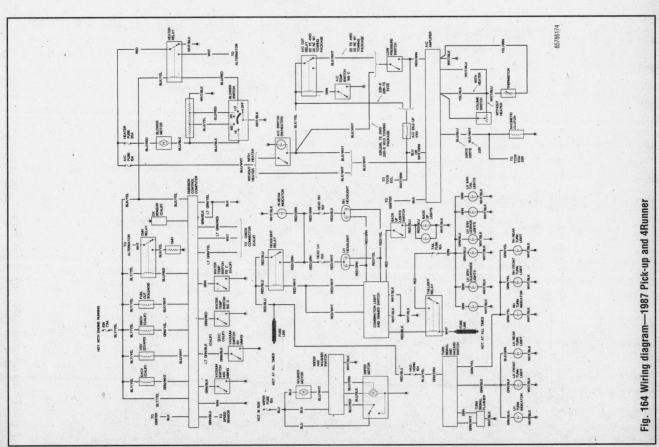

Fig. 164 Wiring diagram—1987 Pick-up and 4Runner

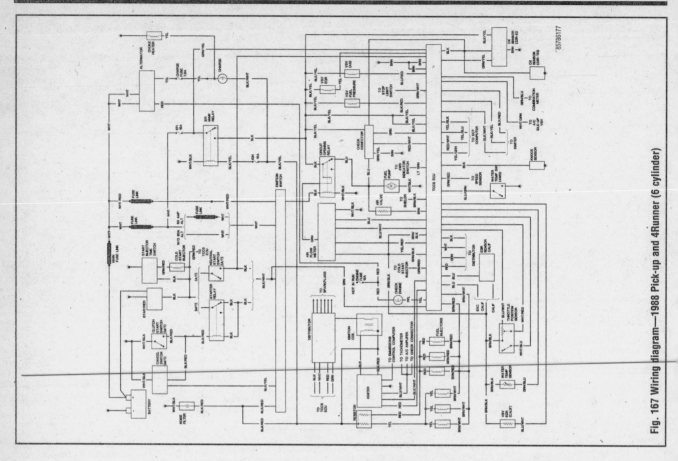

Fig. 167 Wiring diagram—1988 Pick-up and 4Runner (6 cylinder)

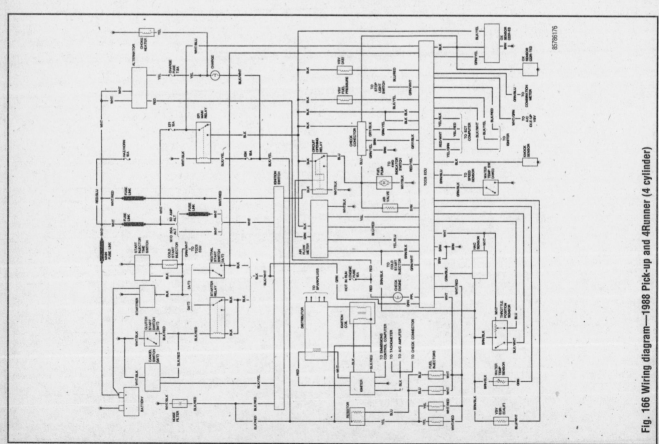

Fig. 166 Wiring diagram—1988 Pick-up and 4Runner (4 cylinder)

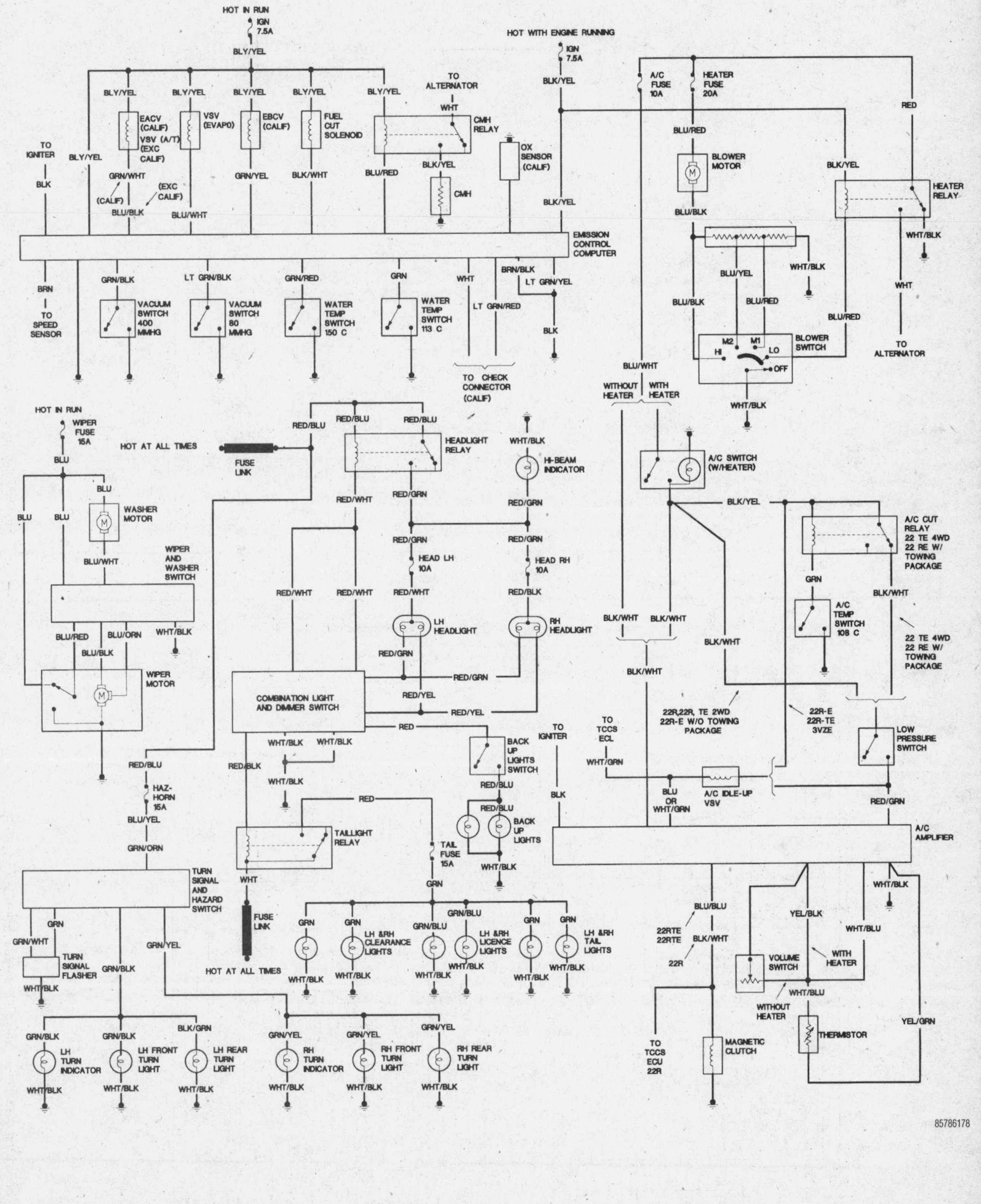

Fig. 168 Wiring diagram—1988 Pick-up and 4Runner

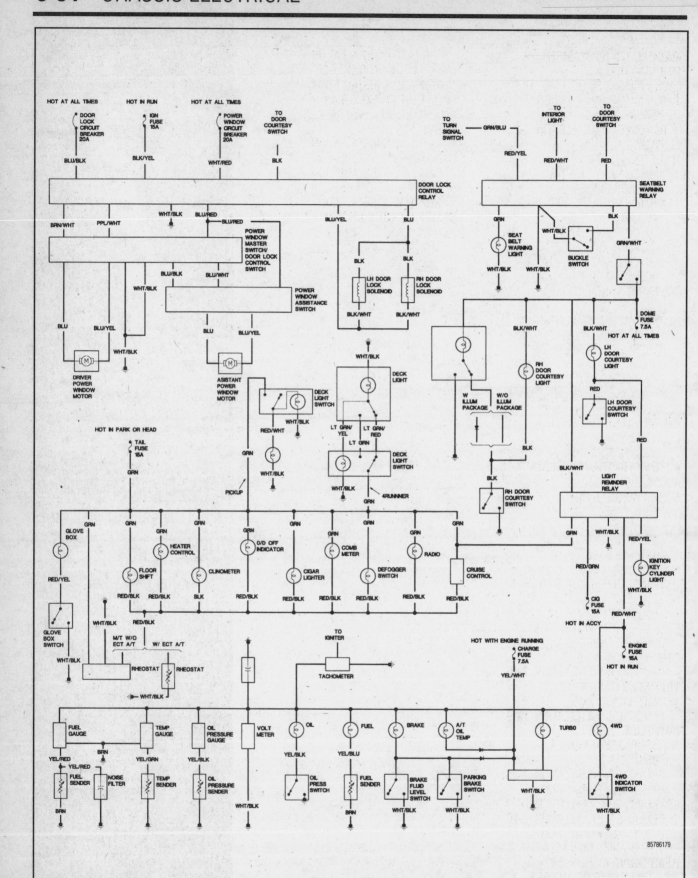

Fig. 169 Wiring diagram—1988 Pick-up and 4Runner

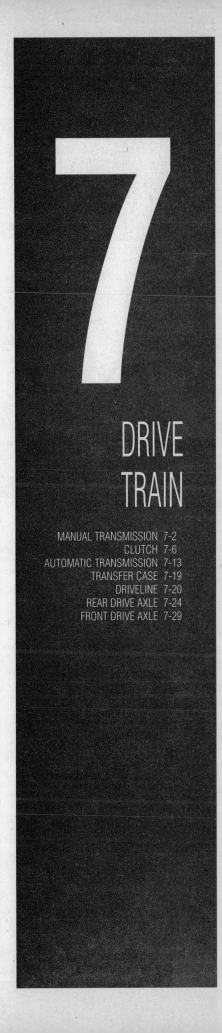

7

DRIVE
TRAIN

MANUAL TRANSMISSION

Adjustments

Most models utilize a floor-mounted shifter and an internally-mounted shift linkage. On some older models, the linkage is contained in a side cover which is bolted on to the transmission case, but the majority of all trucks have the linkage mounted inside the top of the transmission case itself.

No external adjustments are either necessary or possible.

Back-Up Light Switch

REMOVAL & INSTALLATION

1. Position the shift lever in neutral.
2. Raise the truck and support it on safety stands.
3. Disconnect the electrical connector at the switch.
4. Unscrew the back-up light switch from the extension housing.

To install:

5. Screw the new switch into the housing and tighten it to 60 inch lbs.
6. Connect the wire and lower the truck.

Transmission

REMOVAL & INSTALLATION

▶ See Figures 1 thru 22

❋❋ CAUTION

The clutch driven disc contains asbestos, which has been determined to be a cancer causing agent. Never clean clutch surfaces with compressed air! Avoid inhaling any dust from any clutch surface! When cleaning clutch surfaces, use a commercially available brake cleaning fluid.

Pick-Up—2WD

1970–88

1. Disconnect the negative battery cable.
2. Remove the console box or floor mat, and remove the shift lever boot retainer. Raise the boot and remove the shift lever assembly.
3. Drain the coolant from the engine and disconnect the upper radiator hose.
4. On 1970–74 models, there is a bracket which supports the flexible line from the clutch master cylinder to the slave cylinder. Unbolt the bracket from the engine.

➡**Do not separate the tubes. Just remove the bracket.**

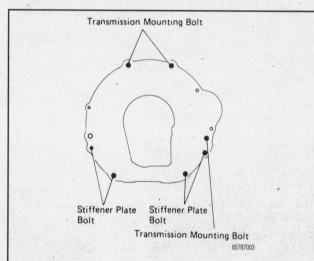

Fig. 1 Transmission mounting bolts—1985–88 2WD and 4WD Pick-up and 4Runner

Fig. 2 Removing the floor shifter retaining plate

Fig. 3 Removing the floor shifter assembly

Fig. 4 Removing the driveshaft—match-mark before removal

Fig. 5 Removing the driveshaft from the flange

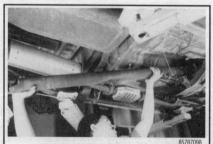

Fig. 6 Removing the driveshaft from the vehicle

Fig. 7 Removing the driveshaft—plug transmission opening

5. For 1970–84 vehicles, disconnect the accelerator torque rod, which runs from the gas pedal to the carburetor, at the firewall.

6. Remove the upper starter mounting nut on 1970–74 and 1980–82 models.

7. Raise the truck and support it on safety stands.

8. Drain the fluid from the transmission into a suitable container.

9. On 1970–74 models, remove the starter lower mounting bolt and the starter wiring, and remove the starter. On 1975–79 models, disconnect the starter wiring, remove the mounting nut and bolt, and remove the starter.

10. On 1970–79 vehicles, perform the following:

a. Remove the clamp holding the clutch slave cylinder in position.

➡ **Do not disconnect the hydraulic line from the cylinder.**

b. Disconnect the exhaust pipe from the manifold flange, and remove the pipe clamp closest to the manifold. On 1975–79 models, also remove the heat insulator, transmission mounting bolts, and bracket on that side.

c. Disconnect the clutch slave cylinder-to-clutch fork link at the clutch fork.

d. Remove the parking brake cable from the lever. It is not necessary to remove the entire equalizer assembly, as it will drop out of the way when the frame crossmember is removed.

11. For 1985–88 vehicles, remove the exhaust pipe clamp and exhaust pipe.

12. For 1980–84 vehicles, perform the following:

a. Remove the clutch release cylinder mounting bolts and position the cylinder out of the way.

b. Remove the lower starter mounting bolt, disconnect the wiring and remove the starter.

13. Disconnect the speedometer cable.

14. Disconnect the back-up light wiring.

15. Matchmark the driveshaft flange and the transmission flange, then unbolt the driveshaft and move it out of the way. Plug the transmission output shaft opening to prevent oil leakage.

16. For 1970–79 vehicles, perform the following:

a. Support the transmission on a jack and remove the rear engine support/frame crossmember.

b. Loosen but do not remove the clutch housing-to-engine block bolts. Drop the transmission down slightly and then remove the bolts completely. The transmission must be drawn to the rear of the truck while lowering so that it will clear the clutch assembly.

17. For 1980–88 vehicles, perform the following:

a. If not already done, disconnect the exhaust pipe clamp at the extension housing.

b. For 1983–88 vehicles, remove the exhaust pipe bracket and stiffener plate, remove the clamp and exhaust pipe and the insulator plate.

c. Remove the 4 rear engine mount bolts at the extension housing. Position a block of wood on a floor jack and raise the engine slightly. Remove the 4 rear mount-to-support member bolts and remove the rear engine mount.

d. For 1985–88 vehicles, tape a piece of wood about 50mm thick to the front crossmember, then lower the transmission.

e. Remove any remaining transmission housing bolts.

f. With a floor jack under the transmission case, pull it toward the rear and slowly lower it until it can be removed from the truck. On models using the R150 transmission, turn the transmission about 45° clockwise and slide it to the rear, lower the front, then remove it from the truck.

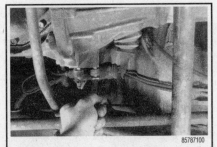
Fig. 8 Removing the clutch release cylinder mounting bolts

Fig. 9 Removing the clutch release cylinder—with line attached

Fig. 10 Removing the clutch release cylinder

Fig. 11 Removing the speedometer cable

Fig. 12 Removing the suspension parts—before transmission removal

Fig. 13 Removing all necessary brackets—before transmission removal

Fig. 14 Unplug all necessary electrical connections

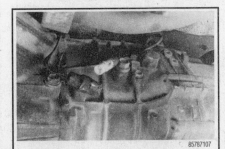
Fig. 15 Removing all necessary electrical connections—before transmission removal

Fig. 16 Removing the transmission mount bolts

To install:

18. Before installing the transmission, apply a thin coating of multipurpose grease on the input shaft end and splines, the clutch release bearing, and the clutch diaphragm spring contact surfaces.

19. For 1970–79 vehicles, perform the following:

➡**To prevent the oil pan from striking the suspension on 1970–74 models, and to prevent the EGR valve from striking the firewall on 1975–79 models, place a wood block under the oil pan and support it with a jack.**

a. When installing the transmission, it is necessary to use an alignment tool to center the clutch disc. These are available at auto parts stores.

b. After aligning the clutch, insert the transmission input shaft, being certain that its splines are properly meshed with those on the clutch. Use a jack to support the transmission while aligning the mounting bolts of the clutch housing. Tighten the clutch housing-to-engine block bolts to 36–51 ft. lbs.

c. After installing all the components removed earlier, adjust the parking brake if necessary and the clutch release fork end play to 2-3$FR1/2mm. Apply gear oil to the shift lever ball, and the multipurpose grease to the shift lever bushing. Be certain that the driveshaft matchmarks are aligned. Fill the engine cooling system and check the level of transmission oil before road testing the truck.

➡**If the clutch master cylinder hydraulic system has been separated at one of its connections, the system will have to be bled.**

20. For 1980–84 vehicles, perform the following:

a. Position the transmission case so the input shaft splines align with the clutch disc and push it fully into position. Install the 2 upper mounting bolts.

b. Position the rear engine mount in the support member and tighten the bolts to 26–36 ft. lbs.

c. Lower the transmission until it rests on the rear mount. Install the 4 bolts and tighten them to 14–22 ft. lbs.

d. Install the remaining transmission housing bolts.

21. For 1985–88 vehicles, perform the following:

a. Position the transmission case so the input shaft splines align with the clutch disc and push it fully into position. Install the 2 upper mounting bolts.

b. Install the transmission housing and stiffener plate bolts. Tighten the transmission bolts to 53 ft. lbs. (72 Nm) and the stiffener plate bolts to 27 ft. lbs. (37 Nm).

c. Install the rear engine mount and bracket. Tighten the bolts to 19 ft. lbs. (25 Nm).

d. Raise the engine slightly and position the rear engine mount in the support member and tighten the bolts to 32 ft. lbs. (43 Nm).

e. Lower the transmission until it rests on the rear mount. Install the 4 bolts and tighten them to 9 ft. lbs. (13 Nm).

f. Remove the piece of wood from the front crossmember.

g. Install the exhaust pipe, bracket and clamp. Tighten the pipe bolts to 46 ft. lbs. (62 Nm). Tighten the upper pipe bracket bolts to 27 ft. lbs. (37 Nm) and the lower one to 51 ft. lbs. (69 Nm).

22. The remainder of installation is the reverse of the removal procedure.

23. Refill the transmission and radiator. Connect the battery cable and road test the truck.

Pick-Up and 4Runner—4WD

▶ **See Figure 1**

➡**The manual transmission on 4WD Toyota trucks is removed with the transfer case attached.**

➡**A special service tool, Toyota #09305-20012 or its equivalent, is needed to remove the transmission shift lever.**

1. Disconnect the battery cables at the battery.

2. Remove the shift lever handles. Remove the front floor mat or carpet along with both shift lever boots to gain access to the shift levers.

3. Using a special shift lever removal tool mentioned previously, remove the transmission shift lever.

4. Using needle nose pliers, remove the transfer case shift lever retainer, then remove the shift lever.

5. Raise the vehicle and support is securely with jackstands.

➡**Because of space limitations, it may be necessary to raise both the front and rear of the vehicle. If this is done, place jackstands under both axles as follows: On the outside of the U-bolts at the front axle; on the inside of the U-bolts at the rear axle.**

6. Drain the lubricant from both the transmission and the transfer case.

7. Chalk matchmarks on the driveshaft flanges and the differential pinion flanges to indicate their relationships. These marks must be aligned during installation.

8. Remove the four bolts from each end of the front driveshaft and remove the driveshaft assembly.

➡**Do not disassemble the front driveshaft to remove it.**

Fig. 17 Removing the transmission mount

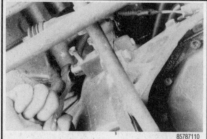
Fig. 18 Removing transmission mounting bolts

Fig. 19 Removing transmission mounting gusset bolts

Fig. 20 Removing transmission mounting bolts

Fig. 21 Removing transmission from the engine assembly

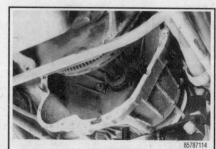
Fig. 22 View of the splines on transmission input shaft

9. Chalk matchmarks on the rear driveshaft and the slip yoke to indicate their relationships. These marks must be aligned during installation.

10. Remove the four bolts from the rearward flange of the rear driveshaft. Lower the driveshaft out of the vehicle. Remove the four bolts from the slip yoke flange then remove the flange and yoke assembly.

11. Unbolt the clutch release cylinder and tie it out of the way.

➡ **It is not necessary to disconnect the hydraulic line from the clutch release cylinder.**

12. Disconnect the positive battery cable at the starter motor switch.

13. Disconnect the remaining wire at the starter.

14. Remove the two starter retaining bolts and lower the starter out of vehicle.

15. Disconnect the speedometer cable at the transfer case and tie it out of the way.

16. Disconnect the exhaust pipe clamp at the transmission housing.

17. Disconnect the wiring for the back-up lamp switch and the 4WD indictor switch.

18. For 1970–79 vehicles, perform the following:

a. Remove the crossmember-to-transfer case adapter mounting bolts. Using a jack, raise the transmission and transfer case assembly SLIGHTLY off of the crossmember, just enough to take the weight off of the crossmember.

b. Remove the crossmember-to-frame attaching bolts and remove the crossmember.

c. Place a support under the engine with a wooden block between the support and the engine.

✳✳ CAUTION

The wooden block and support should be no more than about 6mm away from the engine so that when the engine is lowered, damage will not occur to any underhood components. If possible, shims and support so that the wooden block touches the engine.

d. Lower the jack until the engine rests on the support.

➡ **For the next step, it is recommended that you have an assistant help you guide the transmission and transfer case assembly out of the vehicle.**

e. Remove the transmission-to-engine attaching bolts and draw the transmission and transfer case assembly rearward and down away from the engine.

f. To separate the transmission and transfer case, stand the transmission on its front face with the tailshaft pointing upward. Remove the transfer case-to-adapter mounting bolts and lift the transfer case off of the transmission assembly.

19. For 1980–84 vehicles, perform the following:

a. Remove the 4 rear engine mount-to-support member bolts.

b. Using a floor jack, raise the transmission enough to remove any weight from the rear support member.

c. Remove the 8 bolts and lift out the rear support member.

d. Remove any remaining transmission housing bolts.

e. Position a support stand under the engine and lower the engine until it just rests on the support. Remove the transmission/transfer case assembly down and to the rear.

20. For 1985–88 vehicles, perform the following:

a. Unbolt the clutch release cylinder and tie it out of the way.

➡ **It is not necessary to disconnect the hydraulic line from the clutch release cylinder.**

b. Disconnect the exhaust pipe clamp at the transmission housing. Remove the exhaust pipe.

c. Remove the 4 rear engine mount-to-support member bolts.

d. Using a floor jack, raise the transmission enough to remove any weight from the rear support member.

e. Remove the 4 bolts from the side frame and remove the No. 2 crossmember.

f. Position a piece of wood between the oil pan and front axle. Lower the transmission/transfer case assembly.

g. Remove the exhaust pipe bracket and stiffener plate bolts.

h. Remove any remaining transmission housing bolts.

i. Position a support stand under the engine and lower the engine until it just rests on the support. Remove the transmission/transfer case assembly down and to the rear.

To install:

21. Installation is the reverse of the removal procedure.

22. For 1980–84 vehicles, tighten the following components to specifications:

a. Position the transmission/transfer case assembly and tighten the mounting bolts to 37–57 ft. lbs.

b. While supporting the transmission with a floor jack, install the rear support member and tighten the mounting bolts to 55–75 ft. lbs.

c. Remove the engine support and lower the jack. Install the rear mount-to-support member bolts and tighten them to 8–11 ft. lbs.

23. For 1985–88 vehicles, perform the following:

a. Position the transmission/transfer case assembly and tighten the mounting bolts to 53 ft. lbs. (72 Nm). Tighten the stiffener plate bolts to 27 ft. lbs. (37 Nm).

b. Raise the transmission slightly and install the No. 2 crossmember bolts. Tighten to 70 ft. lbs. (95 Nm).

c. Lower the transmission and install the rear engine mount. Tighten the bolts to 9 ft. lbs. (13 Nm).

d. Remove the piece of wood from the axle.

24. Install the exhaust pipe to the manifold. Install the pipe bracket and tighten the upper bolt to 27 ft. lbs. (37 Nm). Tighten the lower bolt to 51 ft. lbs. (69 Nm).

25. Fill the transmission and transfer cases with lubricant and lower the vehicle. Check all fluid levels, adjustments and road test the vehicle for proper operation.

Land Cruiser

1970–79

➡ **Steps 2–4 pertain to 2 door models.**

1. Disconnect the battery cables at the battery.

2. Remove the front seats, seat tracks, and the console box, if so equipped.

3. Remove the heater pipe clamp which is located on the transmission tunnel to the right of the transfer case shift lever.

4. If the fuel tank is mounted beneath the passenger seat, drain the fuel, remove the fuel tank cover, disconnect the lines, etc., and remove the fuel tank.

5. Remove the shift lever knobs and the shift lever boots.

6. Using Toyota special service tool #09305-60010 or its equivalent, remove the transmission shift lever.

7. Remove the transmission tunnel cover.

8. Raise the vehicle and support it safely with jackstands.

9. Drain the lubricant from both the transmission and the transfer case.

10. Remove the undercover located beneath the front driveshaft.

11. Chalk matchmarks on the driveshaft flanges and the differential pinion flanges to indicate their relationships. These marks must be aligned during installation.

12. Unbolt the driveshaft flanges and remove both the front and rear driveshafts.

13. Disconnect the speedometer cable from the transfer case and tie it out of the way.

14. Disconnect the parking brake cable at the parking brake lever. Leave the cable attached at the drum end; the cable will be removed with the transmission and transfer case assembly.

15. If the vehicle is equipped with a vacuum 4WD engagement system, mark and disconnect the following items at the transfer case:
• Wiring for the indicator
• Wiring for the transfer switch
• Vacuum hoses

16. Disconnect the wiring for the back-up lamp switch. Unbolt the back-up lamp wiring harness clamp from the transfer case, if so equipped.

17. On column shift models, disconnect the shift linkage at the transmission.

18. Remove the Power Take-Off (PTO) lever, if so equipped.

19. Remove the crossmember-to-transfer case adapter mounting bolts. Using a jack, raise the transmission and transfer case assembly SLIGHTLY off of the crossmember, just enough to take the weight off of the crossmember.

20. Remove the crossmember-to-frame attaching bolts and remove the crossmember.

21. Place a support under the engine with a wooden block between the support and the engine.

✳✳ CAUTION

The wooden block and support should be no more than about 6mm away from the engine so that when the engine is lowered, damage will not occur to any underhood components. If possible, shims and support so that the wooden block touches the engine.

22. Lower the jack until the engine rests on the support.

➡ **For the next step, it is recommended that you have an assistant help you guide the transmission and transfer case assembly out of the vehicle.**

23. Remove the transmission-to-engine attaching bolts and draw the transmission and transfer case assembly rearward and down away from the engine.

24. To separate the transmission from the transfer case:
    a. Remove the 4WD engagement lever guide.
    b. Remove the 4WD lever and rod as an assembly.
    c. Remove the back-up lamp switch.
    d. If the vehicle is equipped with a PTO, remove the PTO unit from the transmission. If the vehicle does not have a PTO, remove the cover from the left side of the transfer case.
    e. Remove the rear transfer case cover (six bolts) from the transfer case. Remove the shaft nut located behind the cover.

➡ **This nut is staked at the factory. To remove it, you must tap the staked portions outward to clear the shaft. Restake the nut after installation.**

    f. Remove the 5 transfer case-to-transmission bolts.

➡ **Two of these bolts are located inside the left side of the transfer case, where the PTO or cover was previously removed.**

    g. Using a puller assembled to the transfer case and the transmission output shaft, separate the transfer case from the transmission.

25. Installation is the reverse of the removal procedure. Check all fluid levels and adjustments, roadtest the vehicle for proper operation.

1980–88

1. Disconnect the battery cables at the battery.
2. Remove the entrance scuff plates from the floor of the interior.
3. Remove both side trim panels from beneath the instrument panel.
4. Remove the center heater duct.
5. Remove the floor mat or carpet.
6. Remove the handles from both shift levers.

7. Remove the transmission tunnel cover along with the shift lever boots.

8. Disconnect the wiring from both the back-up lamp switch and the 4WD indicator (if so equipped).

9. Using Toyota SST #09305-55010 or its equivalent, remove the transmission shift lever.

10. Raise the vehicle and support it safely with jackstands.

11. Remove the transfer case skid plate.

12. Disconnect the speedometer cable at the transfer case and tie it out of the way.

13. Chalk matchmarks on the driveshaft flanges and the differential pinion flanges to indicate their relationships. These marks must be aligned during installation.

14. Remove the mounting bolts from the driveshaft flanges and remove the driveshaft assemblies.

15. Disconnect the starter wire. Remove the starter mounting bolts and remove the starter from the vehicle.

16. Unbolt the clutch release cylinder and move it out of the way.

➡ **It is not necessary to disconnect the hydraulic line from the release cylinder.**

17. Drain the lubricant from both the transmission and the transfer case.

18. Remove the tachometer sensor, if so equipped.

19. Support the transmission on a jack and remove the rear engine support/frame crossmember.

20. Loosen but do not remove the clutch housing-to-engine block bolts. Drop the transmission down slightly and then remove the bolts completely. The transmission must be drawn to the rear of the truck while lowering so that it will clear the clutch assembly.

To install:

21. Before installing the transmission, apply a thin coating of multipurpose grease on the input shaft end and splines, the clutch release bearing, and the clutch diaphragm spring contact surfaces.

When installing the transmission, it is necessary to use an alignment tool to center the clutch disc. These are available at auto parts stores.

After aligning the clutch, insert the transmission input shaft, being certain that its splines are properly meshed with those on the clutch. Use a jack to support the transmission while aligning the mounting bolts of the clutch housing. Tighten the clutch housing-to-engine block bolts to 36–51 ft. lbs.

After installing all the components removed earlier, adjust the parking brake if necessary and the clutch release fork end play. Apply gear oil to the shift lever ball, and the multipurpose grease to the shift lever bushing. Be certain that the driveshaft matchmarks are aligned. Fill the engine cooling system and check the level of transmission oil before road testing the truck.

➡ **If the clutch master cylinder hydraulic system has been separated at one of its connections, the system will have to be bled.**

CLUTCH

Adjustments

▶ **See Figures 23, 24, 25 and 26**

CLUTCH PEDAL HEIGHT ADJUSTMENT

The pedal height measurement is gauged from the angle section of the floorboard to the center of the clutch pedal pad. Refer to the accompanying specification chart to determine the recommended pedal height.

If necessary, adjust the pedal height by loosening the locknut and turning the pedal stop bolt which is located above the pedal toward the driver's seat. Tighten the locknut after the adjustment.

CLUTCH PEDAL PUSHROD PLAY ADJUSTMENT

The pedal pushrod play is the distance between the clutch master cylinder piston and the pedal pushrod located above the pedal towards the firewall. Since it is nearly impossible to measure this distance at the source, it must be measured at the pedal pad, preferably with a dial indicator gauge. Refer to the accompanying specification chart to determine the recommended play.

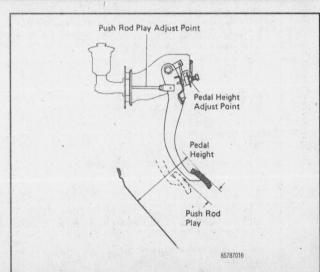

Fig. 23 Clutch pedal adjustment points—Pick-up and 4Runner

Clutch Adjustment Specifications
(All measurements in inches)

Year	Model	Pedal Height	Pedal Rush Rod Play	Pedal Free-Play	Fork Tip Play
1970	Pick-Up	6.0–6.4	0.02–0.20	0.20–0.60	0.079–0.118
	Land Cruiser	①	0.02–0.12	—	0.120–0.160
	Land Cruiser Wagon	②	0.02–0.20	—	0.120–0.160
1971	Pick-Up	6.0–6.4	0.02–0.20	0.20–0.60	0.079–0.118
	Land Cruiser	①	0.02–0.12	—	0.120–0.160
	Land Cruiser Wagon	②	0.02–0.20	—	0.120–0.160
1972	Pick-Up	6.0–6.4	0.02–0.20	0.20–0.60	0.079–0.118
	Land Cruiser	①	0.02–0.12	—	0.120–0.160
	Land Cruiser Wagon	②	0.02–0.20	—	0.120–0.160
1973	Pick-Up	6.0–6.4	0.02–0.20	0.20–0.60	0.079–0.118
	Land Cruiser	①	0.02–0.12	—	0.120–0.160
	Land Cruiser Wagon	②	0.02–0.20	—	0.120–0.160
1974	Pick-Up	6.0–6.4	0.02–0.20	0.20–0.60	0.079–0.118
	Land Cruiser	①	0.02–0.12	—	0.120–0.160
	Land Cruiser Wagon	②	0.02–0.20	—	0.120–0.160
1975	Pick-Up	6.0–6.4	0.02–0.20	0.20–0.60	0.079–0.118
	Land Cruiser	①	0.02–0.12	—	0.120–0.160
	Land Cruiser Wagon	②	0.02–0.20	—	0.120–0.160
1976	Pick-Up	6.0–6.4	0.02–0.20	0.20–0.60	0.079–0.118
	Land Cruiser	①	0.02–0.12	—	0.120–0.160
	Land Cruiser Wagon	②	0.02–0.20	—	0.120–0.160
1977	Pick-Up	6.0–6.4	0.02–0.20	0.20–0.60	0.079–0.118
	Land Cruiser	①	0.02–0.12	—	0.120–0.160
	Land Cruiser Wagon	②	0.02–0.20	—	0.120–0.160
1978	Pick-Up	6.0–6.4	0.02–0.20	0.20–0.60	0.079–0.118
	Land Cruiser	①	0.02–0.12	—	0.120–0.160
	Land Cruiser Wagon	②	0.02–0.20	—	0.120–0.160
1979	Pick-Up	6.0–6.4	0.02–0.20	0.20–0.60	0.079–0.118
	Land Cruiser	①	0.02–0.12	—	0.120–0.160
	Land Cruiser Wagon	②	0.02–0.20	—	0.120–0.160

8578TC01

Clutch Adjustment Specifications
(All measurements in inches)

Year	Model	Pedal Height	Pedal Rush Rod Play	Pedal Free-Play	Fork Tip Play
1980	Pick-Up	5.98–6.38	0.039–0.197	③	0.079–0.118
	Land Cruiser	8.5	0.04–0.20	—	0.160–0.197
	Land Cruiser Wagon	7.7	0.04–0.20	—	0.160–0.197
1981	Pick-Up	5.98–6.38	0.039–0.197	0.20–0.59	—
	Land Cruiser	8.5	0.04–0.20	—	0.160–0.197
	Land Cruiser Wagon	7.7	0.04–0.20	—	0.160–0.197
1982	Pick-Up	5.98–6.38	0.039–0.197	0.20–0.59	—
	Land Cruiser	8.5	0.04–0.20	—	0.160–0.197
	Land Cruiser Wagon	7.7	0.04–0.20	—	0.160–0.197
1983	Pick-Up	④	0.039–0.197	0.20–0.59	—
	Land Cruiser	8.5	0.04–0.20	—	0.160–0.197
	Land Cruiser Wagon	7.7	0.04–0.20	—	0.160–0.197
1984	Pick-Up	5.94	0.039–0.197	0.20–0.59	—
	Land Cruiser	7.13	0.039–0.197	0.51–0.91	—
1985	Pick-Up & 4 Runner	5.67	0.039–0.197	0.20–0.59	—
	Land Cruiser	7.13	0.039–0.197	0.51–0.91	—
1986	Pick-Up & 4 Runner	5.67	0.039–0.197	0.20–0.59	—
	Land Cruiser	7.13	0.039–0.197	0.51–0.91	—
1987	Pick-Up & 4 Runner	6.20	0.039–0.197	0.20–0.59	—
	Land Cruiser	7.13	0.039–0.197	0.51–0.91	—
1988	Pick-Up & 4 Runner	6.20	0.039–0.197	0.20–0.59	—
	Land Cruiser	7.13	0.039–0.197	0.51–0.91	—

① w/power brakes: 8.5
   w/o power brakes: 7.9
② w/power brakes: 7.3
   w/o power brakes: 6.8
③ 2 wd: 0.20–0.59
   4 wd: 0.98–1.77
④ Gas: 5.98–6.38
   Diesel: 6.38–6.79

8578TC1A

If necessary, adjust the pedal play by loosening the pedal pushrod locknut and turning the pushrod. Tighten the locknut after the adjustment.

CLUTCH FORK TIP PLAY ADJUSTMENT

1970–80

The fork tip play is the total amount of travel evident at the outer end of the clutch release fork where the fork comes in contact with the release cylinder pushrod. Refer to the accompanying specification chart to determine the recommended fork tip play.

The fork tip play is adjusted by loosening the release cylinder pushrod locknut and effectively increasing or decreasing the pushrod length as required.

➡**Some models do not have adjustable release cylinder pushrods. These models are identified by having no adjustment nuts on the pushrod.**

CLUTCH PEDAL FREE-PLAY ADJUSTMENT

The free-play measurement is the total travel of the clutch pedal from the fully released position to where resistance is felt as the pedal is pushed down-

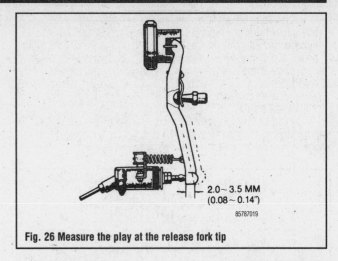

Fig. 26 Measure the play at the release fork tip

ward. Refer to the accompanying specification chart to determine the recommended pedal free-play.

If the clutch pedal free-play is incorrect, perform the previous clutch adjustments then bleed the system according to the procedure which follows. If a pedal free-play dimension is not listed for your model, perform the previous clutch adjustments and disregard the pedal free-play measurement.

Driven Disc and Pressure Plate

REMOVAL & INSTALLATION

◆ **See Figures 27 thru 53**

> ❊❊ **CAUTION**
>
> **The clutch driven disc contains asbestos, which has been determined to be a cancer causing agent. Never clean clutch surfaces with compressed air! Avoid inhaling any dust from any clutch surface! When cleaning clutch surfaces, use a commercially available brake cleaning fluid.**

1. Remove the transmission.
2. Stamp or chalk matchmarks on the clutch cover and flywheel, indicating their relationship.
3. Loosen the clutch cover-to-flywheel retaining bolts one turn at a time. The pressure on the clutch disc must be released GRADUALLY.
4. Remove the clutch cover-to-flywheel bolts. Remove the clutch cover and the clutch disc.
5. If the clutch release bearing is to be replaced, do so at this time as follows:
   a. Remove the bearing retaining clip(s) and remove the bearing and hub.
   b. Remove the release fork and the boot.

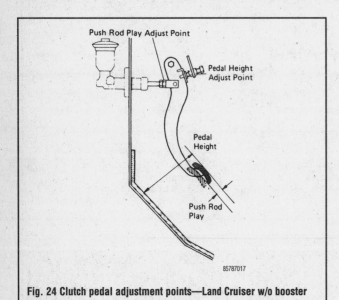

Fig. 24 Clutch pedal adjustment points—Land Cruiser w/o booster

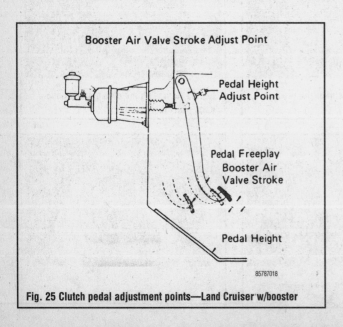

Fig. 25 Clutch pedal adjustment points—Land Cruiser w/booster

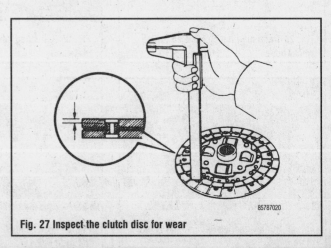

Fig. 27 Inspect the clutch disc for wear

c. The bearing is press fitted to the hub. In some cases, the bearing is available with the hub from automotive suppliers. If this is not the case with your model, contact a machine shop and have the bearing replaced using a hydraulic press. Using other means to replace the bearing could result in personal injury.

d. Clean all parts and lightly grease the input shaft splines and all of the contact points.

e. Install the bearing/hub assembly, fork, boot, and retaining clip(s) in their original locations.

6. Inspect the flywheel surface for cracks, heat scoring (blue marks), and warpage. If oil is present on the flywheel surface, this indicates that either the engine rear oil seal or the transmission front oil seal is leaking. If necessary,

refer to the appropriate section for seal replacement. If in doubt concerning the condition of the flywheel, consult an automotive machine shop.

To install:

7. Before installing any new parts, make sure that they are clean. During installation, do not get grease or oil on any of the components, as this will shorten clutch life considerably.

8. Position the clutch disc against the flywheel. On Pick-Ups, the short side of the splined section faces the flywheel. On Land Cruisers, the long side of the splined section faces the flywheel.

9. Install the clutch cover over the disc and install the bolts loosely. Align the matchmarks made during Step 2. If a new or rebuilt clutch cover

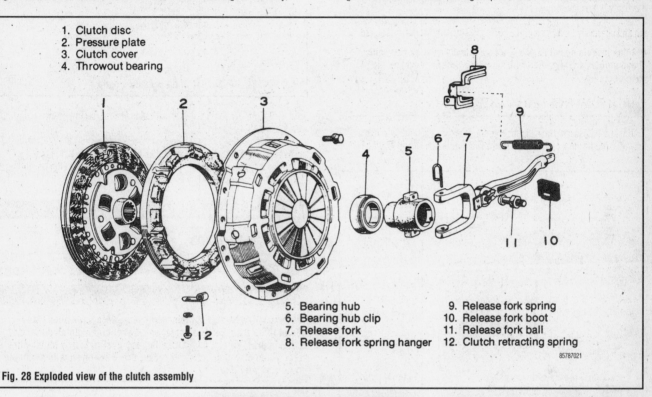

1. Clutch disc
2. Pressure plate
3. Clutch cover
4. Throwout bearing

5. Bearing hub
6. Bearing hub clip
7. Release fork
8. Release fork spring hanger

9. Release fork spring
10. Release fork boot
11. Release fork ball
12. Clutch retracting spring

85787021

Fig. 28 Exploded view of the clutch assembly

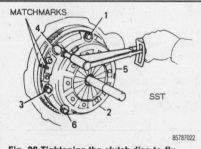

Fig. 29 Tightening the clutch disc-to-fly-wheel bolts

Fig. 30 Removing the clutch and pressure plate bolts

Fig. 31 Removing the clutch and pressure plate assembly

Fig. 32 Removing the clutch and pressure plate

Fig. 33 Removing the flywheel bolts—lock the flywheel

Fig. 34 Removing the flywheel

Fig. 35 Check the flywheel bolts—add locking agent to bolts upon installation

Fig. 36 Cleaning the flywheel—after installation

Fig. 37 Checking the flywheel for wear

Fig. 38 Checking the pressure plate for wear

Fig. 39 Install special tool to align the clutch assembly

Fig. 40 Clutch plate installed with tool

Fig. 41 Clutch plate and pressure plate installed with special tool

Fig. 42 Install locking agent to clutch assembly bolts

Fig. 43 Install the clutch assembly bolts and tighten in steps

Fig. 44 Install the clutch assembly bolts and tighten in steps with torque wrench

Fig. 45 Install grease on the clutch release fork ball

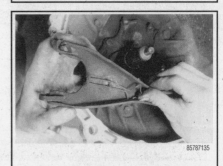

Fig. 46 View of the clutch release fork

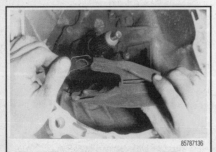

Fig. 47 View of the clutch release fork bearing clips

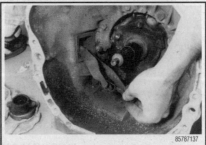

Fig. 48 Removing the clutch release fork bearing clips

Fig. 49 Grease the throwout bearing assembly

Fig. 50 Grease the throwout bearing assembly

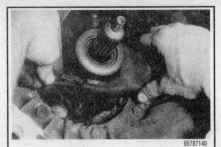

Fig. 51 Installing the clutch release fork bearing clip

Fig. 52 View of the clutch release fork assembly—installed

Fig. 53 View of special tool, used to install the clutch and pressure plate assembly

assembly is installed, use the matchmark on the old cover assembly as a reference.

10. Align the clutch disc with the flywheel using a clutch aligning tool, which is available in most auto stores at a reasonable price.

11. With the clutch aligning tool installed, tighten the clutch cover bolts gradually in a star pattern, as is done with lug nuts. Finally tighten the bolts to 14 ft. lbs. (19 Nm).

12. Install the transmission.

Clutch Master Cylinder

REMOVAL & INSTALLATION

1. Disconnect the master cylinder pushrod from the clutch pedal.
2. Remove the hydraulic line from the master cylinder being careful not to damage the compression fitting.
3. Remove the two bolts holding the master cylinder to the engine compartment.

✳✳ CAUTION

Brake fluid dissolves paint. Do not allow it to drip onto the body when removing the master cylinder.

4. Install the master cylinder. Partially tighten the hydraulic line and then tighten the cylinder mounting bolts.
5. Connect the pushrod to the clutch pedal.
6. Adjust the clutch pedal and bleed the system.

OVERHAUL

▸ See Figure 54

1. Disassemble the master cylinder by unscrewing the clutch pedal clevis from the pushrod. Also remove the locknut.

2. Pull off the rubber boot to expose an internal snapring. Remove the snapring and withdraw the piston and compression spring.

3. Take a clean rag and wipe out the inside of the cylinder. Inspect the inside of the cylinder for scoring and deposits. Use crocus cloth or a small hone to refinish the inside of the cylinder. If light honing will not remove score marks replace the cylinder.

➡**Be careful not to remove too much from the cylinder walls as the cups will not be able to seal the cylinder if the diameter is enlarged excessively.**

4. Wash all metal parts in solvent.

5. Further disassembly should be avoided unless the reservoir is leaking. If the reservoir needs to be replaced, remove the cap and remove the master cylinder reservoir bolt located at the bottom of the reservoir. Tighten the bolt upon reassembly.

6. With new parts from the rebuilding kit assemble the master cylinder. Coat the cylinder wall with brake fluid so that the edges of the new cups will not be damaged. Coat the piston with lithium soap based glycol grease.

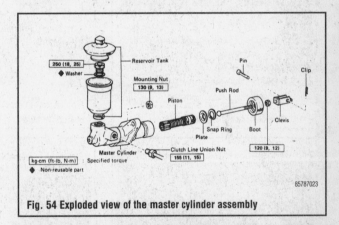

Fig. 54 Exploded view of the master cylinder assembly

Clutch Release Cylinder

REMOVAL & INSTALLATION

1. Jack up the front of the truck and support it on jackstands.
2. Remove the tension spring on the clutch fork.
3. Remove the hydraulic line from the release cylinder. Be careful not to damage the fitting.
4. Turn the release cylinder pushrod in sufficiently to gain clearance from the fork.
5. Remove the mounting bolts and withdraw the cylinder.
To install:
6. Install the hydraulic line from the master cylinder.
7. Position the cylinder on the clutch housing and install the clamp and retaining screws.
8. Adjust the fork tip clearance as previously outlined.

➡**The system must be bled after the cylinder is reinstalled.**

OVERHAUL

♦ **See Figure 55**

1. Remove the pushrod, rubber boot, piston and cups from the cylinder.
2. Clean the inside of the cylinder with a rag and inspect for scoring. If there is no serious damage, hone the cylinder just enough to remove deposits. Replace the cylinder if light honing does not remove the score marks. Wash all the parts in brake fluid before assembly.
3. Coat the new rubber parts in brake fluid and reassemble. Coat the piston with lithium soap based glycol grease.

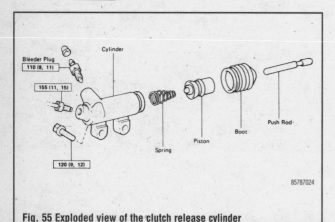

Fig. 55 Exploded view of the clutch release cylinder

Hydraulic System Bleeding

♦ **See Figure 56**

➥ **This procedure may be utilized when either the clutch master or release cylinder has been removed or if any of the hydraulic lines have been disturbed.**

❋ CAUTION

Do not spill brake fluid on the body of the vehicle as it will destroy the paint.

1. Fill the master cylinder reservoir with brake fluid.
2. Remove the cap and loosen the bleeder screw on the clutch release cylinder. Cover the hole with your finger.
3. Have an assistant pump the clutch pedal several times. Take your finger off the hole while the pedal is being depressed so that the air in the system can be released. Put your finger back on the hole and release the pedal.
4. After fluid pressure can be felt (with your finger) tighten the bleeder screw.
5. Put a short length of hose over the bleeder screw and place the other end into a jar half full of clean brake fluid.

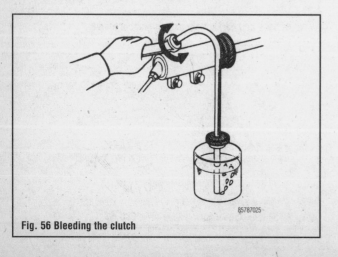

Fig. 56 Bleeding the clutch

6. Depress the clutch pedal and loosen the bleeder screw. Allow the fluid to flow into the jar.
7. Tighten the plug and then release the clutch pedal.
8. Repeat Steps 6-7 until no air bubbles are visible in the bleeder tube.
9. When there are no more air bubbles in the system, tighten the plug fully with the pedal depressed. Replace the plastic cap.
10. Fill the master cylinder to the correct level with brake fluid.
11. Check the system for leaks.

Clutch Booster

REMOVAL & INSTALLATION

Land Cruiser Only

♦ **See Figures 57 and 58**

1. Remove the master cylinder.
2. Disconnect the vacuum hose at the booster.
3. Remove the clutch pipe. Remove the vacuum pipe clamp bolts.
4. Remove the clip and disconnect the clevis at the clutch pedal.
5. Remove the 3 bolts and lift out the clutch booster.

To install:

6. Adjust the length of the clutch booster pushrod. Set SST #09737-00010 on the master cylinder and lower the pin until its tip rests on the piston. Take the tool off the master cylinder, turn it upside down and set it on the booster. Pull the pushrod out until it just touches the pin head. There should be no clearance.
7. Install the booster to the firewall and connect the clevis to the clutch pedal.
8. Install the master cylinder.
9. Connect the union line and vacuum hose.
10. Adjust the clutch pedal and bleed the system.

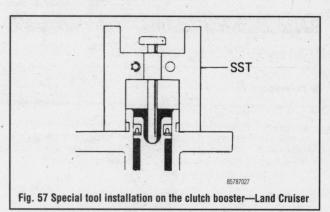

Fig. 57 Special tool installation on the clutch booster—Land Cruiser

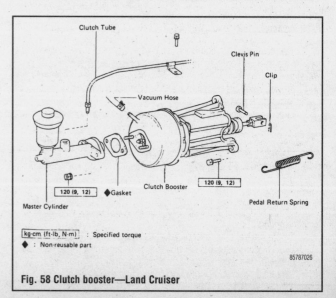

Fig. 58 Clutch booster—Land Cruiser

AUTOMATIC TRANSMISSION

Application

The A-30 Toyoglide transmission is used in all 1970–77 models. The A-30 is a fully automatic three speed transmission using a combination of multiple disc clutches and front and rear bands to accomplish gear ratio changes. Internal adjustments necessary on this transmission include only the front and rear bands.

The A-40 transmission is used in 1978–79 models. The A-40 is also a fully automatic three speed, but it does not use bands for gear changes, thus internal adjustments are not possible.

In 1980, the A-40 was replaced by the A-43 three speed, which is used through the current model year. Internal adjustments are not required on this transmission.

The A-43D is a fully automatic four speed transmission first offered as an option on 1981 models and is available through the current model year. The A340E and A340H are also fully automatic transmissions with the difference being that they are controlled electronically by computer, where conventional transmissions are controlled by oil pressure. These transmissions became available in 1986 and are still used in 1988. The fourth speed of this transmission is an overdrive ratio, which offers improved gasoline mileage by lowering the engine rpm at highway speeds. The hydraulic circuit of the overdrive mode on the A43D is electrically controlled. The main electrical components include the following:

1. A dash mounted overdrive control switch.
2. A dash mounted **OVERDRIVE-OFF** indicator lamp.
3. A transmission mounted solenoid.
4. An engine mounted thermo switch which prevents overdrive engagement until the engine coolant temperature reaches 131°F.

The 1984–88 Land Cruiser is equipped with an A440F transmission which is similar to the A-43D.

Adjustments

FRONT BAND

A-30 Transmission

1. Remove the pan as previously outlined.
2. Pry the band engagement lever toward the band with a screwdriver.
3. The gap between the end of the piston rod and the engagement bolt should be 3mm.
4. Turn the engagement bolt until the proper clearance is obtained.
5. Install the pan and refill the transmission.

REAR BAND

A-30 Transmission

The rear band adjusting bolt is located on the outside of the transmission case so that it is not necessary to remove the pan in order to perform the adjustment.

1. Loosen the adjust bolt locknut and turn the screw all the way in.
2. Back off the adjusting screw one full turn.
3. Lock the adjustment by tightening the adjusting screw locknut.

SHIFT LINKAGE

▶ **See Figures 59, 60 and 61**

1970–79

1. Check all of the shift linkage bushings for wear. Replace any that are excessively worn.
2. Set the manual valve lever on the transmission in the Neutral position.
3. Lock the connecting rod swivel with the locknut so that the pointer, selector, and manual valve lever are all in the Neutral position.
4. Check the operation by moving the selector through all the gears.

1980–83

1. Loosen the adjustment nut on the transmission connecting rod.
2. Push the manual lever of the transmission fully forward.
3. Move the manual lever back three notches, which is the **N** position.
4. Set the gearshift selector lever in its **N** position.
5. Apply a slight amount of forward pressure on the selector lever (towards the reverse position) and tighten the connecting rod adjustment nut.

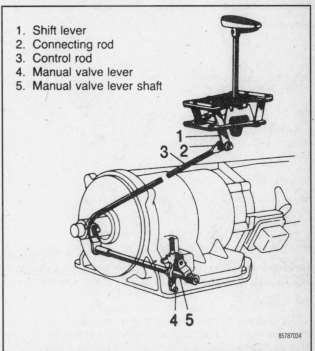

1. Shift lever
2. Connecting rod
3. Control rod
4. Manual valve lever
5. Manual valve lever shaft

Fig. 59 1979 and earlier automatic transmission floor shift—adjustment is made at point 2

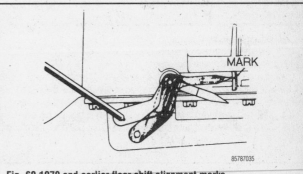

Fig. 60 1979 and earlier floor shift alignment marks

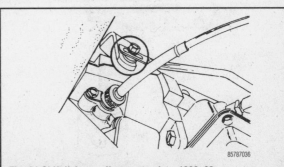

Fig. 61 Shift linkage adjustment point—1980–83

1984–88

1. Loosen the adjustment nut on the transmission shift linkage.
2. Push the manual lever of the transmission fully rearward (forward on the Land Cruiser).
3. Move the manual lever back two notches, which is the **N** position.
4. Set the gearshift selector lever in its **N** position.
5. Apply a slight amount of forward pressure on the selector lever (towards the **R** position) and tighten the shift linkage adjustment nut.

THROTTLE CABLE

▶ **See Figures 62, 63 and 64**

1970–77

When the carburetor throttle is wide open, the throttle linkage pointer should line up with the mark stamped on the transmission case. To adjust:
1. Loosen the locknuts on either end of the linkage adjusting turnbuckle located midway between the carburetor and the transmission.
2. Detach the throttle linkage connecting rod from the carburetor.
3. Align the pointer on the throttle valve lever with the mark stamped on the transmission case.
4. Rotate the turnbuckle so that the end of the throttle linkage rod and the carburetor throttle lever are aligned.

➡ **The throttle valve of the carburetor must be fully open during this adjustment.**

5. Tighten the turnbuckle locknuts and connect the throttle rod to the carburetor.
6. Open the throttle valve and check to see that the pointer and the mark are aligned on the transmission.
7. Road test the truck. If the transmission keeps shifting rapidly back and forth between gears at certain speeds or if it fails to downshift properly when going up hills, repeat the throttle linkage adjustment.

1978–88

PICK-UP AND 4RUNNER

1. Remove the air cleaner assembly.
2. Push the accelerator to the floor and check that the throttle opens fully. If not, adjust the accelerator link so that it does.
3. Push back the rubber boot from the throttle cable which runs down to the transmission. Loosen the throttle cable adjustment nuts so that the cable housing can be adjusted.
4. Fully open the carburetor throttle by having an assistant press the accelerator all the way to the floor.
5. Adjust the cable housing so that, with the throttle wide open, the distance between the end of the rubber boot and the cable stopper is 52mm for 1978; and 0-1mm for 1979-88.
6. Tighten the nuts and double check the adjustment. Install the rubber boot and the air cleaner.

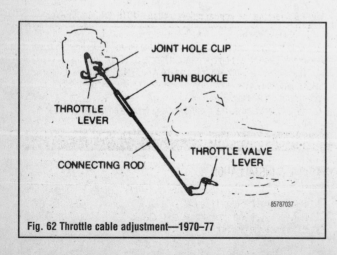

Fig. 62 Throttle cable adjustment—1970–77

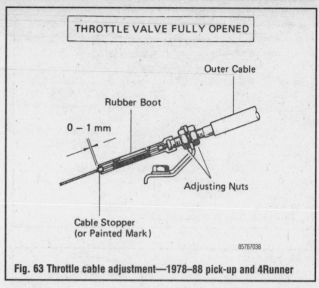

Fig. 63 Throttle cable adjustment—1978–88 pick-up and 4Runner

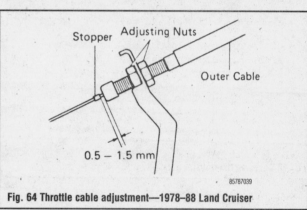

Fig. 64 Throttle cable adjustment—1978–88 Land Cruiser

LAND CRUISER

1. Remove the air cleaner assembly.
2. Push the accelerator to the floor and check that the throttle opens fully. If not, adjust the accelerator link so that it does.
3. Push back the rubber boot from the throttle cable which runs down to the transmission. Loosen the throttle cable adjustment nuts so that the cable housing can be adjusted.
4. Adjust the cable housing so that, with the throttle fully closed, the distance between the end of the rubber boot and the cable stopper is 0.50-1.5mm.
5. Tighten the nuts and double check the adjustment. Install the rubber boot and the air cleaner.

TRANSFER LINKAGE

A340E and A340H

▶ **See Figure 65**

1. Shift the transfer lever to the **H2** position.
2. Disconnect the No. 1 transfer linkage from the cross shaft.
3. Position the transfer indicator switch to the **H2** position.
4. Connect the No. 1 transfer linkage to the cross shaft.

TRANSFER POSITION SWITCH

A340E and A340H

▶ **See Figure 66**

1. Loosen the transfer position switch bolt and set the shift position to the **L4** position.
2. Disconnect the electrical connector.

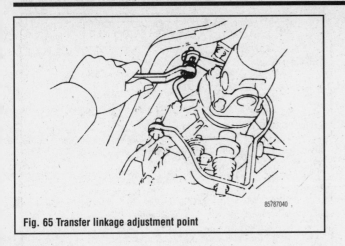
Fig. 65 Transfer linkage adjustment point

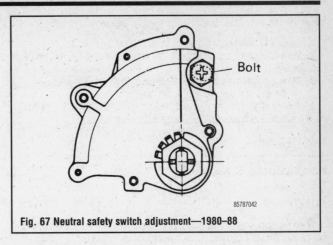
Fig. 67 Neutral safety switch adjustment—1980–88

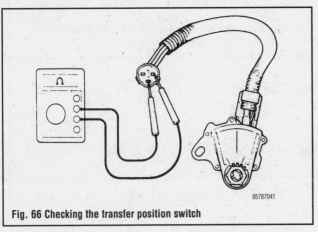
Fig. 66 Checking the transfer position switch

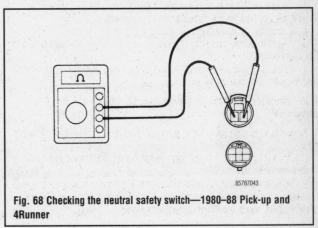
Fig. 68 Checking the neutral safety switch—1980–88 Pick-up and 4Runner

3. Connect an ohmmeter between the terminals and adjust the switch so there is continuity.

4. Connect the electrical lead and tighten the switch bolt to 48 inch lbs. (5.4 Nm).

5. Check the idle speed.

Neutral Safety Switch

The neutral safety switch prevents the vehicle from starting unless the gearshift selector is in either the **P** or **N** positions. If the vehicle will start in any other positions, adjustment of the switch is required.

ADJUSTMENT

♦ See Figures 67, 68 and 69

1970–79

1. Remove the screws which hold the center console in place.
2. Remove the electrical connector and remove the console from the vehicle.
3. Loosen the switch securing bolts.
4. Set the selector in the Drive position.
5. Move the switch so that the arm just contacts the control shaft lever.
6. Tighten the switch retaining bolts.
7. Check the operation of the switch; the truck should start only in Neutral or in Park. The back-up lamps should only operate in the Reverse position.
8. If the switch cannot be adjusted so that it functions properly, replace it with a new one.
9. Reinstall the console.

1980–88

1. Loosen the neutral start switch bolt.
2. Place the gearshift selector lever in the **N** position.

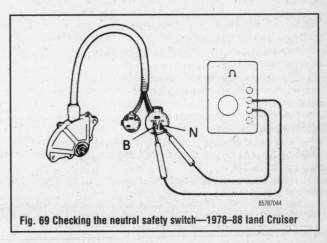
Fig. 69 Checking the neutral safety switch—1978–88 land Cruiser

3. Align the shaft groove of the switch with the neutral Basic line. Hold the switch in this position and tighten the switch bolts to 35–60 inch lbs.

4. There is also a continuity check on the A340E, A340H and A440F transmissions. Disconnect the electrical connector and connect an ohmmeter between the two terminals.

5. Adjust the switch so that there is continuity between terminals **N** and **B**.

Back-Up Light Switch

REMOVAL & INSTALLATION

1. Position the shift lever in neutral.
2. Raise the truck and support it on safety stands.
3. Disconnect the electrical connector at the switch.

4. Unscrew the back-up light switch from the extension housing.

5. Installation is the reverse of the removal procedure Tighten the switch to 60 inch lbs.

Transmission

REMOVAL & INSTALLATION

A-30 and A-40

1. Disconnect the battery cables at the battery.
2. Disconnect the transmission throttle linkage at the carburetor.
3. Raise the vehicle and support it with jackstands.
4. Drain the transmission fluid.
5. Disconnect the wiring from the starter.
6. Unbolt the starter and lower it out of the vehicle.
7. Disconnect the exhaust pipe from the exhaust manifold. Remove the exhaust clamp from the exhaust pipe.
8. Disconnect the linkage from the drivers side of the transmission.
9. Disconnect the speedometer cable and tie it out of the way.
10. Disconnect the parking brake cable from the parking brake control lever.
11. Chalk matchmarks on the rear driveshaft flange and the differential pinion flange. These marks must be aligned during installation.
12. Unbolt the rear driveshaft flange. If the vehicle has a two piece driveshaft, remove the center bearing bracket-to-frame bolts. Remove the driveshaft from the vehicle.
13. Support the transmission using a jack with a wooden block placed between the jack and the transmission pan. Do not raise the transmission, just raise the jack until the wooden block touches the transmission pan.
14. Place a support under the engine with a wooden block between the support and the engine.

✳✳ CAUTION

The wooden block and support should be no more than about 25mm away from the engine so that when the engine is lowered, damage will not occur to any underhood components.

15. Remove the transmission mount-to-crossmember bolts.
16. Raise the transmission SLIGHTLY, just enough to take the weight of the transmission off of the crossmember. Remove the crossmember-to-frame mounting bolts and remove the crossmember from the vehicle.
17. Slowly lower the transmission until the engine rests on the support placed during Step 14.
18. Disconnect the two fluid cooler lines at the transmission. Plug the lines and the holes in the transmission to prevent the entry of dirt.

➡**Before performing Step 19, place a drain pan under the torque converter area of the transmission. Fluid leakage will occur as the transmission is uncoupled.**

19. Remove the transmission-to-engine mounting bolts. Carefully pull the transmission to the rear and after the transmission uncouples from the engine, lower the transmission out of the vehicle.
20. Remove the torque converter from the flywheel.

➡**Prior to installation of the transmission, Toyota recommends to check the torque converter and flywheel run-out dimensions. If either of these run-out limits are beyond the maximum allowable limits, excessive wear of the front transmission seal will occur.**

21. Mount the torque converter on the flywheel and torque the converter bolts to 11–16 ft. lbs.
22. Mount the dial indicator so that the indicator probe touches the outer surface of the converter extension sleeve (90° to the converter centerline).
23. Adjust the dial indicator to zero.
24. Slowly rotate the converter and read the dial indicator. The indicator needle should not deviate more than the following amounts:
• 1970–80 transmissions: 0.20mm
• 1981 and later transmissions: 0.30mm
25. Remove the torque converter from the flywheel.

26. Mount the dial indicator so that the indicator probe touches the flywheel drive plate (converter mounting) surface.
27. Zero the indicator needle and slowly rotate the flywheel. The indicator needle should not deviate more than the following amounts:
• A-30 transmissions: 0.13mm
• A-40 transmissions: 0.30mm
To install:
28. Apply a coat of multipurpose grease to the torque converter stub shaft and the pilot hole of the flywheel.
29. Assemble the torque converter into the transmission, so that its output shaft and the transmission input shaft are aligned. Rotate the torque converter until the dowel pin is at the bottom.
30. Install a guide pin into the bottom bolt hole next to the dowel pin. Align the flywheel and the torque converter.
31. Tighten the torque converter bolts to 11–16 ft. lbs. Rotate the crankshaft half a turn to reach all the bolts, and tighten them evenly.
32. Bolt the transmission to the engine. Tighten the bolts to 37–51 ft. lbs.
33. Install the remaining components in the reverse of the removal procedure.
34. Fill the transmission with the specified type fluid. If the torque converter was completely drained, the transmission will need about 7 quarts of fluid.
35. Connect the battery cables. Road test and check for leaks.

A-43, A-43D and A340E

1. Disconnect the battery cables at the battery.
2. Remove the air cleaner assembly.
3. Disconnect the transmission throttle cable at the carburetor.
4. Raise the vehicle and support it safely with jackstands.
5. Disconnect the wiring connectors (near the starter) for the neutral start switch and the back-up light switch. Also, on A-43D and A340E transmission equipped models, disconnect the solenoid switch wiring at the same location.
6. Disconnect the starter wiring at the starter. Unbolt the starter and remove it from the vehicle.
7. Drain the transmission fluid.
8. Chalk matchmarks on the rear driveshaft flange and the differential pinion flange. These marks must be aligned during installation.
9. Unbolt the rear driveshaft flange. If the vehicle has a two piece driveshaft, remove the center bearing bracket-to-frame bolts. Remove the driveshaft from the vehicle.
10. Disconnect the speedometer cable from the transmission and tie it out of the way.
11. Disconnect the shift linkage at the transmission.
12. Disconnect the exhaust pipe clamp at the bell housing and remove the oil filler tube.
13. Disconnect the transmission oil cooler lines at the transmission.
14. Support the transmission using a jack with a wooden block placed between the jack and the transmission pan. Do not raise the transmission, just raise the jack until the wooden block touches the transmission pan.
15. Place a wooden block (or blocks) between the engine oil pan and the front frame crossmember.

✳✳ CAUTION

The wooden block(s) should be no more than about 6mm away from the engine so that when the engine is lowered, damage will not occur to any underhood components.

16. Remove the transmission mount-to-crossmember bolts.
17. Raise the transmission SLIGHTLY, just enough to take the weight of the transmission off of the crossmember. Remove the crossmember-to-frame mounting bolts and remove the crossmember from the vehicle.
18. Slowly lower the transmission until the engine rests on the wooden block placed during Step 15.
19. Remove the engine undercover in order to gain access to the engine crankshaft pulley.
20. Remove the two rubber plugs from the service holes located at the rear of the engine in order to gain access to the torque converter bolts.
21. Rotate the crankshaft as necessary to remove the torque converter bolt (6). Access to these bolts is through the service holes mentioned in Step 20.
22. Obtain a bolt of the same dimensions as the torque converter bolts. Cut the head off of the bolt and hacksaw a screwdriver slot in the bolt opposite the threaded end.

➡**This modified bolt is used as a guide pin. Two guide pins are needed to properly install the transmission.**

23. Thread the guide pin into one of the torque converter bolt holes. The guide pin will help keep the converter with the transmission.

24. Remove the transmission-to-engine mounting bolts.

25. Carefully move the transmission rearward by prying on the guide pin through the service hole.

➡**As soon as the transmission is away from the engine about 3mm, feed wire through the front of the transmission and secure the wire in order to keep the converter attached to the transmission. Also, try to keep the nose of the transmission pointed upward SLIGHTLY to help keep the converter in place.**

26. Pull the transmission rearward and lower it out of the vehicle.

➡**Do not allow the attached cables to catch on any components during removal.**

27. With the transmission out of the vehicle, remove the torque converter as follows:
   a. Place a drain pan under the front of the transmission
   b. Pull the converter straight off of the transmission and allow the fluid to drain.

➡**Prior to installation of the transmission, Toyota recommends to check the torque converter and flywheel run-out dimensions. If either of these run-out limits are beyond the maximum allowable limits, excessive wear of the front transmission seal will occur.**

28. Mount the torque converter on the flywheel and torque the converter bolts to 11–16 ft. lbs.

29. Mount the dial indicator so that the indicator probe touches the outer surface of the converter extension sleeve (90° to the converter centerline).

30. Adjust the dial indicator to zero.

31. Slowly rotate the converter and read the dial indicator. The indicator needle should not deviate more than 0.30mm.

32. Remove the torque converter from the flywheel.

33. Mount the dial indicator so that the indicator probe touches the flywheel ring gear just inside of the gear teeth (surface faces the rear of the vehicle).

34. Zero the indicator needle and slowly rotate the flywheel. The indicator needle should not deviate more than 0.20mm.

To install:

35. Apply a coat of multi-purpose grease to the torque converter stub shaft and the corresponding pilot hole in the flywheel.

36. Install the torque converter into the front of the transmission. Push inward on the torque converter while rotating it to completely couple the torque converter to the transmission.

37. To make sure that the converter is properly installed, measure the distance between the torque converter mounting lugs and the front mounting face of the transmission. The proper distance is 2.5mm.

38. Install the guide pins into two opposite mounting lugs of the torque converter.

39. Raise the transmission to the engine and align the transmission with the engine alignment dowels. Also, position the converter guide pins into the mounting holes of the flywheel.

40. Install and tighten the transmission-to-engine mounting bolts. Torque the bolts to 37–57 ft. lbs.

41. Remove the converter guide pins and install the converter mounting bolts. Rotate the crankshaft as necessary to gain access to the guide pins and bolts through the service holes.

42. Evenly tighten the converter mounting bolts to 11–15 ft. lbs. Install the rubber plugs into the access holes.

43. Install the engine undercover.

44. Raise the transmission slightly and remove the wood block(s) from beneath the engine oil pan.

45. Install the transmission crossmember. Torque the crossmember-to-frame bolts to 26–36 ft. lbs.

46. Lower the transmission onto the crossmember and install the transmission mounting bolts. Torque the bolts to 14–22 ft. lbs.

47. Install the remaining components in the reverse of the removal procedure.

48. Fill the transmission with the specified type of fluid. If the torque converter was completely drained, the transmission will need about 7 quarts of fluid.

49. Road test the vehicle and check for leaks.

A340H

◆ **See Figures 70, 71, 72, 73 and 74**

1. Disconnect the negative battery cable.

2. Disconnect the air intake connector.

3. Loosen the adjusting nuts and disconnect the throttle cable housing at the bracket. Disconnect the cable at the linkage and then disconnect it from the rear of the engine.

4. Underneath the air intake chamber there are 5 connectors, disconnect them.

5. Remove the upper starter mounting bolt.

6. Raise the truck, support it on safety stands and drain the transmission fluid.

7. Remove the driveshafts.

8. Remove the 2 bolts, bracket and pipe clamp and then disconnect the exhaust pipe at the tail pipe.

9. Disconnect and plug the 2 oil cooler lines at the transmission case.

10. Pull out the cotter pin and disconnect the manual shift linkage at the neutral safety switch.

11. Pull out the cotter pins and then disconnect the No. 1 and No. 2 transfer shift linkages at the cross shaft over the transmission case. Remove the cross shaft.

12. Disconnect the speedometer cable.

13. On models with the 22R-TE, disconnect the 2 oil cooler lines at the transfer case.

14. Using a transmission jack, or a floor jack and a block of wood, raise the transmission just enough to remove pressure on the rear support member.

15. Position a piece of wood between the cowl and the rear of the cylinder head, remove the 8 bolts and lift out the rear support member.

16. Remove the engine under cover.

17. Remove the 6 torque converter mounting bolts.

➡**Rotate the crankshaft in order to gain access to the torque converter mounting bolts.**

18. Insert a guide pin (just cut off the head of an old bolt!) into one of the torque converter bolt holes.

19. Remove the starter and then remove the transmission housing mounting bolts.

20. Using the guide pin to keep the transmission and torque converter together, pry on the end of the pin to get the transmission assembly moving rearward. Be careful!

21. With a large drip pan under the assembly, pull off the converter. Remove the filler tube from the side of the transmission case.

➡**Prior to installation of the transmission, Toyota recommends to check the torque converter and flywheel run-out dimensions. If either of these run-out limits are beyond the maximum allowable limits, excessive wear of the front transmission seal will occur.**

22. Mount the torque converter on the flywheel and torque the converter bolts to 30 ft. lbs.

23. Mount the dial indicator so that the indicator probe touches the outer surface of the converter extension sleeve (90° to the converter centerline).

24. Adjust the dial indicator to zero.

25. Slowly rotate the converter and read the dial indicator. The indicator needle should not deviate more than 0.30mm.

26. Remove the torque converter from the flywheel.

27. Mount the dial indicator so that the indicator probe touches the flywheel ring gear just inside of the gear teeth (surface faces the rear of the vehicle).

28. Zero the indicator needle and slowly rotate the flywheel. The indicator needle should not deviate more than 0.20mm.

To install:

29. Use a new O-ring and press the filler tube into the transmission case.

30. Coat the pilot hole in the crankshaft and the center hub of the converter with grease.

31. Install the torque converter into the transmission case. Using calipers and a straight edge, make sure the distance from the installed surface of the converter to the transmission housing lip is 26mm.

➡**Be sure the converter is filled with ATF DEXRON®II**

32. Install a guide pin in the converter and align it with one of the drive plate holes. Align the 2 sleeves on the cylinder block with the converter housing and temporarily install a bolt.

✸✸ CAUTION

Never tilt the transmission forward during installation as the converter will fall out!

If all holes are aligned, install the starter and then all remaining transmission housing bolts. Tighten to 47 ft. lbs. (64 Nm).

33. Remove the guide pin and install the 6 converter bolts. Tighten the bolts evenly to 20 ft. lbs. (27 Nm) on models with 4 cylinder engines and to 30 ft. lbs. (41 Nm) on those with the V6.

34. Install the engine under cover.

35. Install the rear support member and tighten the 8 bolts to 58 ft. lbs. (78 Nm).

36. Install the remaining components in the reverse of the removal procedure.

37. Connect the air intake connector and the negative battery cable. Fill the transmission with fluid and road test the truck. Check for any leaks.

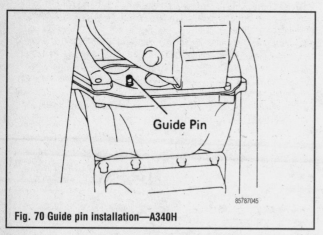

Fig. 70 Guide pin installation—A340H

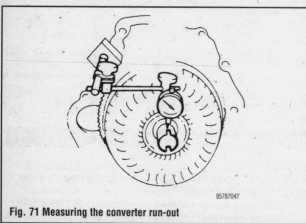

Fig. 71 Measuring the converter run-out

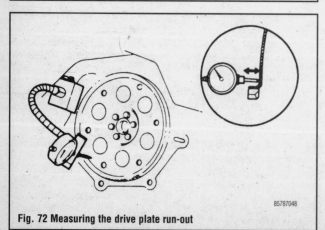

Fig. 72 Measuring the drive plate run-out

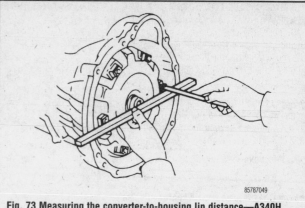

Fig. 73 Measuring the converter-to-housing lip distance—A340H

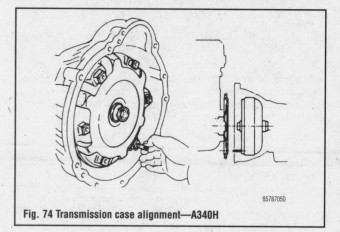

Fig. 74 Transmission case alignment—A340H

A440F

▶ See Figures 75 and 76

1. Disconnect the negative battery cable.

2. Drain the coolant from the radiator and disconnect the upper radiator hose.

3. Loosen the throttle cable adjusting nuts and disconnect the cable housing from the bracket. Disconnect the cable from the linkage.

4. Disconnect the connectors located near the starter.

5. Unscrew the transfer case shift lever knob and then remove the rubber boot.

6. Raise the vehicle and support it on safety stands. Drain the transmission fluid.

7. Remove the under covers from the transmission and transfer cases.

8. Pull out the cotter pin and disconnect the shift rod at the transfer case. Remove the nut and washers and then remove the shift lever with the control rod attached.

9. Disconnect the transmission control rod from the control shaft lever.

10. On models with a mechanical winch, remove the button in the PTO shift lever. Lift out the spring and then loosen the 2 Allen screws to remove the shifter knob. Remove the shift lever boot.

11. Disconnect the shifter rod at the PTO under the truck. Remove the bolt and then remove the shift lever with the rod still attached.

12. On models with a mechanical winch, remove the engine under cover. Matchmark the yoke and flange on the PTO driveshaft, remove the bolts and then remove the PTO driveshaft.

13. Disconnect the speedometer cable. Disconnect the 2 vacuum hoses at the transmission.

14. Disconnect and plug the 2 oil cooler lines at the transmission.

15. Disconnect the electrical leads, remove the mounting bolts and remove the starter. Pull out the filler tube.

16. Remove the plug in the end plate and then remove the 6 torque converter mounting bolts.

➡ **The crankshaft will have to be rotated to gain access to all the converter bolts.**

17. Support the transmission with a floor jack and a block of wood. Remove the 8 bolts and 2 nuts and lift out the frame crossmember.

18. Disconnect the front exhaust pipe at the tail pipe and exhaust manifold and remove it.

19. Position another floor jack under the engine and lower the rear of the transmission slightly. Remove the transmission-to-cylinder block mounting bolts and slowly lower the transmission to the rear.

20. With a large pan under the transmission assembly, pull out the torque converter.

➡**Prior to installation of the transmission, Toyota recommends to check the torque converter and flywheel run-out dimensions. If either of these run-out limits are beyond the maximum allowable limits, excessive wear of the front transmission seal will occur.**

21. Mount the torque converter on the flywheel and torque the converter bolts to 30 ft. lbs.

22. Mount the dial indicator so that the indicator probe touches the outer surface of the converter extension sleeve (90° to the converter centerline).

23. Adjust the dial indicator to zero.

24. Slowly rotate the converter and read the dial indicator. The indicator needle should not deviate more than 0.30mm.

25. Remove the torque converter from the flywheel.

26. Mount the dial indicator so that the indicator probe touches the flywheel ring gear just inside of the gear teeth (surface faces the rear of the vehicle).

27. Zero the indicator needle and slowly rotate the flywheel. The indicator needle should not deviate more than 0.20mm.

To install:

28. Coat the pilot hole in the crankshaft and the center hub of the converter with grease.

29. Install the torque converter into the transmission case. Using calipers and a straight edge, make sure the distance from the installed surface of the converter to the transmission housing lip is 16.6mm.

➡**Be sure the converter is filled with ATF DEXRON®II**

30. Install a guide pin (cut off the head of an old bolt!) in the torque converter. Align the pin with one of the holes in the drive plate and then align the 2 sleeves on the cylinder block with the converter housing. Install one bolt to hold the assembly and then install all 9 mounting bolts. Tighten the 8mm bolts to 13 ft. lbs. (18 Nm); the 10mm bolts to 27 ft. lbs. (37 Nm); and the 12mm bolts to 53 ft. lbs. (72 Nm).

31. Use a new gasket and connect the front pipe to the manifold. Tighten the new nuts to 46 ft. lbs. (62 Nm). Use a new gasket and connect it to the tail pipe. Tighten the nuts to 29 ft. lbs. (39 Nm). Install the exhaust pipe clamp.

32. Install the frame crossmember and tighten the 8 bolts to 29 ft. lbs. (39 Nm). Tighten the 2 nuts to 43 ft. lbs. (59 Nm). Remove the jacks from the transmission and engine.

33. Pull out the guide pin and install the 6 converter bolts by hand. Tighten the bolts evenly to 21 ft. lbs. (28 Nm). Install the plug in the end plate.

34. Fit a new O-ring to the filler tube and press it into the transmission. Install the bleeder hose.

35. Install the remaining components in the reverse of the removal procedure. Tighten the oil cooler line union nuts to 25 ft. lbs. Tighten the PTO driveshaft nuts to 14 ft. lbs. (20 Nm).

36. Fill the engine with coolant, reconnect the leads at the starter and then connect and adjust the throttle cable.

37. Connect the negative battery cable, fill the transmission with fluid and road test the truck. Check for any leaks.

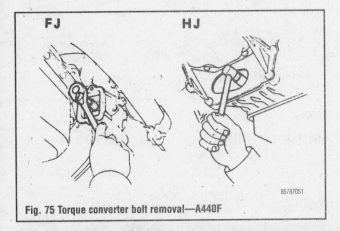

Fig. 75 Torque converter bolt removal—A440F

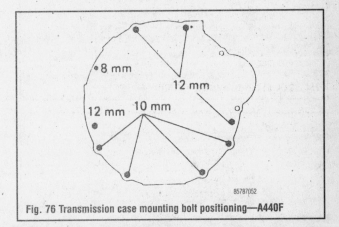

Fig. 76 Transmission case mounting bolt positioning—A440F

TRANSFER CASE

Transfer Case

REMOVAL & INSTALLATION

◆ See Figure 77

➡**The transfer case is removed as an assembly with the transmission.**

1. Remove the transmission assembly.
2. Remove the rear engines mount from the case.
3. Remove the upper driveshaft dust cover.
4. Remove the transfer adapter rear mounting bolts and then pull the transfer case straight up and remove it.

✳ CAUTION

Be careful not to damage the adapter rear oil seal during removal.

5. Move the 2 shift forks into the **HIGH-FOUR** position.
6. Coat the adapter oil seal with grease and position a new gasket on the transfer case adapter.

7. Install the transfer case to the transmission. Tighten the bolts to 29 ft. lbs. (39 Nm). The longer bolts (43mm) are used at the dust cover, the shorter ones (39mm) are used in all other locations.

8. Install the rear engine mount and tighten the bolts to 19 ft. lbs. (25 Nm).

9. Install the transmission assembly.

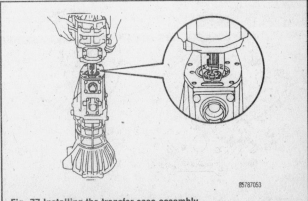

Fig. 77 Installing the transfer case assembly

DRIVELINE

Front Driveshaft and U-Joints

REMOVAL & INSTALLATION

4WD Models Only

1. Jack up the front of the truck and support with jackstands.
2. Paint a mating mark on the two halves of the rear universal joint flange.
3. Remove the bolts which hold the rear flange to the front of the transfer case.
4. Paint a mating mark on the two halves of the front universal joint flange.
5. Remove the bolts which hold the front flange to the front differential.
6. Remove the front driveshaft.
   To install:
7. Position the driveshaft so that the paint marks made previously line up.
8. Install the flange bolts and tighten to 29-43 ft. lbs. on 1970-83 Pick-Ups; 54 ft. lbs. (74 Nm) on 1984-88 Pick-Ups and 4Runner; and 65 ft. lbs. (88 Nm) on the Land Cruiser.
9. Lower the vehicle and road test it.

U-JOINT OVERHAUL

1. Matchmark the yoke and the driveshaft.
2. Remove the snaprings from the bearings.
3. Position the yoke on vise jaws. Using a bearing remover and a hammer, gently tap the remover until the bearing is driven out of the yoke about 25mm.
4. Place the tool in the vise and drive the yoke away from the tool until the bearing is removed.
5. Repeat Steps 3 and 4 for the other bearings.
6. Check for worn or damaged parts. Inspect the bearing journal surfaces for wear.
   To assemble:
7. Install the bearing cups, seals, and O-rings in the spider.
8. Grease the spider and the bearings.
9. Position the spider in the yoke.
10. Start the bearings in the yoke and then press them into place, using a vise.
11. Repeat Step 4 for the other bearings.
12. If the axial play of the spider is greater than 0.05mm, select snaprings which will provide the correct play. Be sure that the snaprings are the same size on both sides or driveshaft noise and vibration will result.
13. Check the U-joint assembly for smooth operation.

Rear Driveshaft and U-Joints

REMOVAL & INSTALLATION

▶ **See Figures 78 thru 88**

2WD Pick-Up—1970–88

ONE-PIECE DRIVESHAFT

1. Jack up the rear of the truck and support the rear axle housing with jackstands.
2. Paint a mating mark on the two halves of the rear universal joint flange.
3. Remove the bolts which hold the rear flange together.
4. Remove the splined end of the driveshaft from the transmission.

➡**If you don't want to lose a lot of gear oil, plug the end of the transmission with a rag.**

5. Remove the driveshaft from under the truck.
   To install:
6. Apply multipurpose grease to the splined end of the shaft.
7. Insert the driveshaft sleeve into the transmission.

➡**Be careful not to damage the extension housing grease seal.**

8. Align the mating marks on the rear flange and replace the bolts. Tighten to 22–36 ft. lbs. on 1970–83 models and 54 ft. lbs. (74 Nm) on 1984–88 models.
9. Remove the jackstands and lower the vehicle.

TWO-PIECE DRIVESHAFT W/CENTER BEARING

1. Jack up the rear of the truck and support the rear axle housing on jackstands.
2. Before you begin to disassemble the driveshaft components, you must first paint accurate alignment marks on the mating . Do this on the rear universal joint flange, the center flange, and on the transmission flange.
3. Remove the bolts attaching the rear universal joint flange to the drive pinion flange.
4. Drop the rear section of the shaft slightly and pull the unit out of the center bearing sleeve yoke.
5. Remove the center bearing support from the crossmember.
6. Separate the transmission output flange and remove the front half of the driveshaft together with the center bearing assembly.
   To install:
7. Connect the output flange of the transmission to the flange on the front half of the shaft.
8. Install the center bearing support to the crossmember, but do not fully tighten the bolts.
9. Install the rear section of the shaft making sure that all mating marks are aligned.
10. Tighten all flange bolts to 22–36 ft. lbs.

4WD Pick-Up—1970–83

1. Jack the truck off the ground and place support stands under both the front and rear axles.
2. Matchmark all driveshaft flanges BEFORE removing the bolts.
3. Unbolt the driveshaft rear flange from the rear pinion flange.
4. Unbolt the driveshaft front flange from the rear transfer case flange and remove the driveshaft.
5. Position the driveshaft so that the paint marks made previously line up.
6. Install the flange bolts and tighten to 29–43 ft. lbs.
7. Lower the vehicle and road test it.

➡**For 4WD long bed Pick-Ups, see above for rear driveshaft removal and installation.**

4WD Pick-Up and 4Runner—1984–88

1. Raise the vehicle and support it with jackstands.
2. Matchmark all driveshaft flanges BEFORE removing any bolts.
3. Disconnect the driveshaft flange at the companion flange on the differential.
4. Remove the center bearing from the frame crossmember.
5. Disconnect the front flange at the companion flange on the rear of the transfer case and remove the driveshaft.
6. Separate the front portion of the shaft at the intermediate shaft flange.
7. Disconnect the rear of the driveshaft at the center bearing flange.
8. Using a hammer and chisel, loosen the staked portion of the center bearing nut and then remove the nut. Matchmark the flange to the intermediate shaft and then pull the bearing off the shaft.
   To install:
9. Install the center bearing on the intermediate shaft and tighten the nut to 134 ft. lbs. (181 Nm), loosen the nut and then retighten it to 51 ft. lbs. (69 Nm). Stake the nut.
10. Connect the front portion of the driveshaft to the intermediate shaft and the rear portion to the center flange. Make sure the marks all line up and then tighten the bolts to 54 ft. lbs. (74 Nm).
11. Connect the rear flange to the differential flange and tighten the bolts to 54 ft. lbs. (74 Nm).
12. Connect the front flange to the transfer case flange and tighten the bolts to 54 ft. lbs. (74 Nm).
13. Mount the center bearing on the crossmember and tighten the mounting bolts to 27 ft. lbs. (36 Nm).
14. Lower the vehicle and give it a road test.

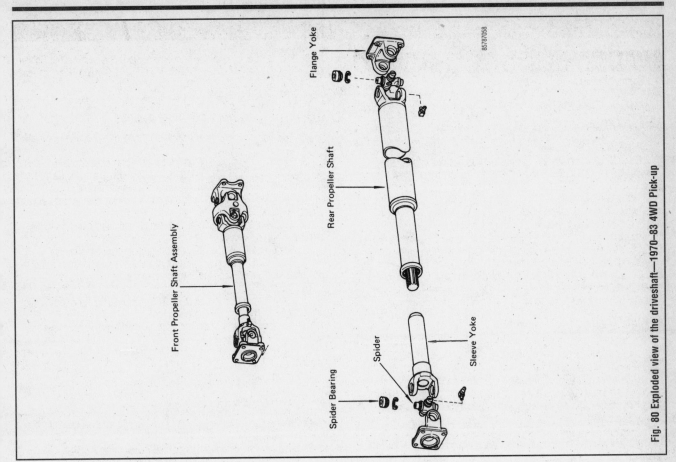

85787058

Flange Yoke

Rear Propeller Shaft

Spider

Sleeve Yoke

Spider Bearing

Fig. 80 Exploded view of the driveshaft—1970–83 4WD Pick-up

Front Propeller Shaft Assembly

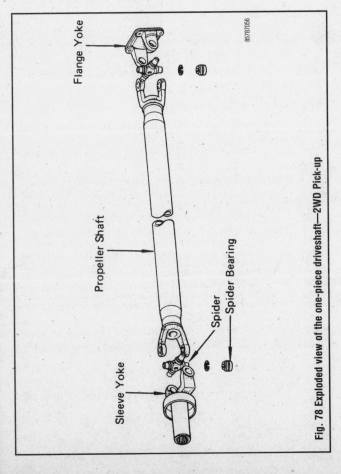

85787056

Flange Yoke

Propeller Shaft

Spider

Spider Bearing

Sleeve Yoke

Fig. 78 Exploded view of the one-piece driveshaft—2WD Pick-up

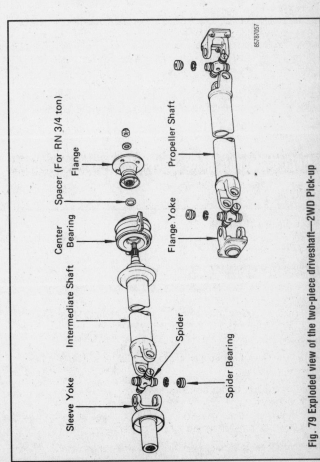

85787057

Spacer (For RN 3/4 ton)

Flange

Center Bearing

Intermediate Shaft

Sleeve Yoke

Spider

Spider Bearing

Propeller Shaft

Flange Yoke

Fig. 79 Exploded view of the two-piece driveshaft—2WD Pick-up

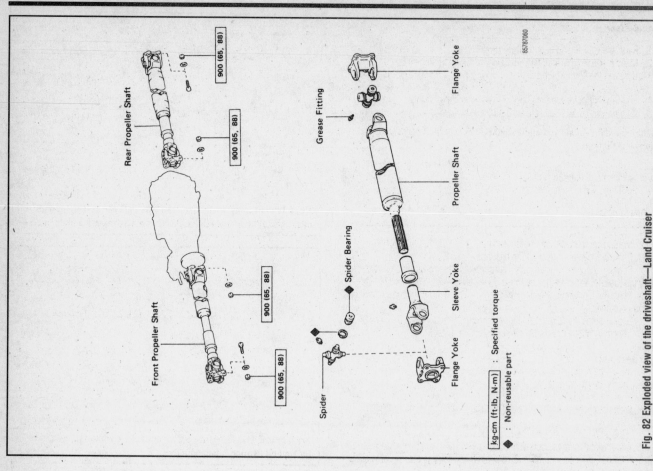

Fig. 82 Exploded view of the driveshaft—Land Cruiser

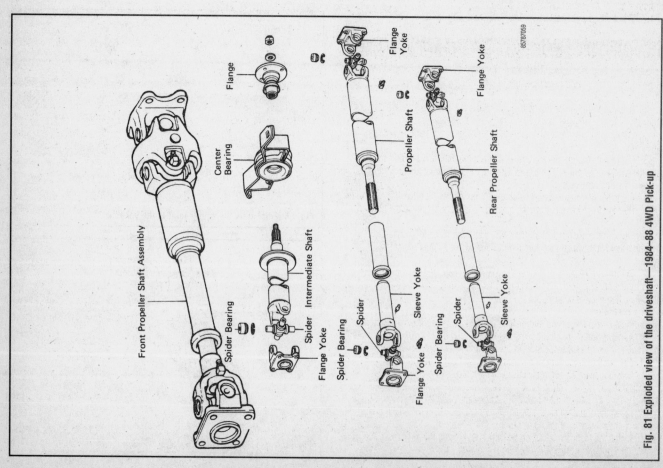

Fig. 81 Exploded view of the driveshaft—1984–88 4WD Pick-up

Land Cruiser

1. Raise the vehicle and support it with jackstands.
2. Matchmark all driveshaft flanges BEFORE removing the bolts.
3. Unfasten the bolts which secure the universal joint flange to the differential pinion flange.
4. Perform Step 2 for the U-joint-to-transfer case flange bolts.
5. Withdraw the driveshaft from beneath the vehicle.

➡️**Lubricate the U-joints and sliding joints with multipurpose grease before installation.**

6. Position the driveshaft so that all paint marks line up and then tighten the flange bolts to 65 ft. lbs. (88 Nm).
7. Lower the vehicle and road test it.

U-JOINT OVERHAUL

1. Matchmark the yoke and the driveshaft.
2. Remove the snaprings from the bearings.
3. Position the yoke on vise jaws. Using a bearing remover and a hammer, gently tap the remover until the bearing is driven out of the yoke about 25mm.
4. Place the tool in the vise and drive the yoke away from the tool until the bearing is removed.
5. Repeat Steps 3 and 4 for the other bearings.
6. Check for worn or damaged parts. Inspect the bearing journal surfaces for wear.

To assemble:

7. Install the bearing cups, seals, and O-rings in the spider.
8. Grease the spider and the bearings.
9. Position the spider in the yoke.
10. Start the bearings in the yoke and then press them into place, using a vise.
11. Repeat Step 4 for the other bearings.
12. If the axial play of the spider is greater than 0.05mm, select snaprings which will provide the correct play. Be sure that the snaprings are the same size on both sides or driveshaft noise and vibration will result.
13. Check the U-joint assembly for smooth operation.

Center Bearing Replacement

The center support bearing is a sealed unit which requires no periodic maintenance. The following procedure should be used if it should become necessary to replace the bearing.

1. Remove the intermediate driveshaft and the center support bearing assembly.
2. Paint mating marks on the universal joint flange and the intermediate driveshaft.
3. Remove the cotter pin and castle nut from the intermediate driveshaft (on later models, the nut will be staked). Remove the universal joint flange from the driveshaft using a press.
4. Remove the center support bearing assembly from the driveshaft.
5. Remove the two bolts from the bearing housing and remove the housing.
6. Remove the dust deflectors (type #2) from both sides of the bearing cushion. Remove the dust deflectors type #3 and #4 from either side of the bearing.
7. Remove the snaprings from each side of the bearing. This is easy to do if you have a snapring tool which fits the holes in the ring, and very difficult otherwise. Remove the bearing.

To assemble:

8. Install the new bearing into the cushion and fit a snapring on each side.
9. Apply a coat of multipurpose grease to the dust deflectors type #3 and #4, and put them in their respective places on each side of the bearing. Type #4, which has a slightly larger diameter, goes on the rear of the bearing.
10. Press the type #2 dust deflector onto each side of the cushion. The water drain holes in the deflectors should be in the same position on each side of the cushion. The water drain holes should face the bottom of the housing.
11. Press the support bearing assembly firmly onto the intermediate driveshaft, with the #3 type seal facing front.
12. Match the mating marks painted earlier, and install the universal joint flange to the driveshaft. Tighten the castle nut to about 130 ft. lbs., and use a

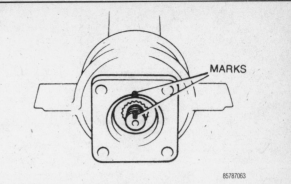

Fig. 83 After removing the retaining nut, slide the center support bearing and the flange off the intermediate shaft—note matchmarks

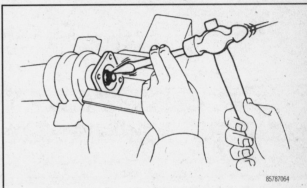

Fig. 84 Once installed—use a hammer and punch to stake the center support bearing retaining nut

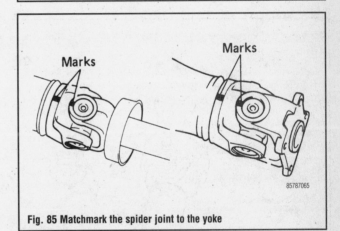

Fig. 85 Matchmark the spider joint to the yoke

Fig. 86 Removing the spider bearing

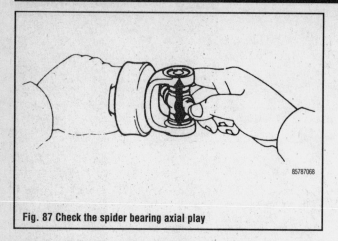

Fig. 87 Check the spider bearing axial play

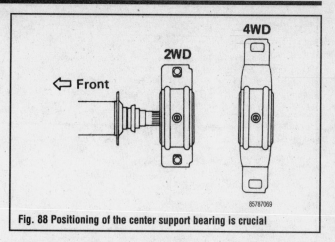

Fig. 88 Positioning of the center support bearing is crucial

new cotter pin to lock it in place. Tighten the nut to align the holes for the cotter pin, but do not loosen it. It is okay to tighten it up to 150 lbs. On later models, install the center bearing on the intermediate shaft and tighten the nut to 134 ft. lbs. (181 Nm), loosen the nut and then retighten it to 51 ft. lbs. (69 Nm). Stake the nut.

➥ Check to see if the center support bearing assembly will rotate smoothly around the driveshaft.

13. When reinstalling the driveshaft, be certain to match up the marks on both the front transmission flange and the flange on the sleeve yoke of the rear driveshaft.

REAR DRIVE AXLE

Axleshaft, Bearing and Seal

REMOVAL & INSTALLATION

Pick-Ups and 4Runner

♦ See Figures 89 thru 101

SINGLE TIRE

1. Loosen the lug nuts on the wheel, then raise the truck and support it on jackstands.
2. Drain the axle housing.
3. Remove the lug nuts and remove the wheel.
4. Remove the brake drum securing screw and remove the drum.
5. Remove the brake springs and the retracting spring clamp bolt. Remove the lower springs and shoe strut. Remove the brake shoes, screws, and the parking brake lever. Disengage the parking brake cable from the lever and the backing plate.

6. Plug the master cylinder reservoir inlet to prevent the fluid from running out. Disconnect the brake line from the wheel cylinder, being careful not to damage the fitting. Plug the brake line.
7. Remove the four nuts retaining the brake backing plate to the axle housing.
8. Remove the snapring and then press the axle shaft out of the backing plate and slide the assembly out of the housing.
9. Remove the oil seal and press out the axle bearing.

To install:

10. Press a new bearing into the brake backing plate and replace the oil seal.
11. Install a new O-ring into the axle housing.
12. Install the axle shaft and brake backing plate assembly into the axle housing. Be careful not to damage the oil seal with the axle splines. Rotate the axle back and forth until the shaft splines mesh with the differential gear splines.
13. Install the brake backing plate nuts and tighten to 44-58 ft. lbs. Install a new snapring.
14. Install the brake shoes and lever assembly. Connect the parking brake cable and the brake shoe springs.

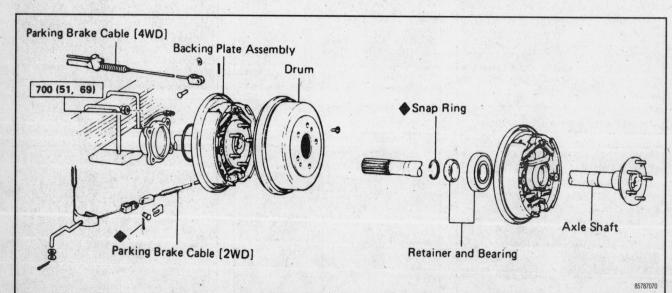

Fig. 89 Exploded view of the rear axle (single tire)—Pick-up and 4Runner

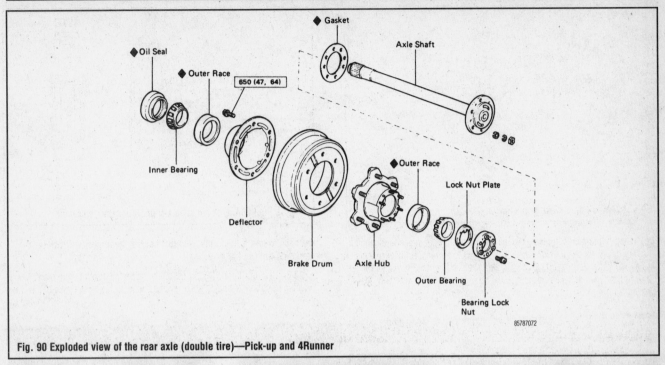

Fig. 90 Exploded view of the rear axle (double tire)—Pick-up and 4Runner

Fig. 91 Removing the parking brake cable assembly retaining bolt

Fig. 92 Removing the parking brake cable assembly

Fig. 93 Removing the brake backing plate—rear axle assembly removal

Fig. 94 Removing the rear axle assembly

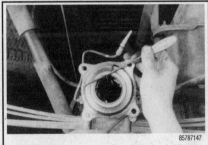

Fig. 95 Removing the rear axle-to-backing plate gasket

Fig. 96 Removing the rear axle seal

Fig. 97 Installing the rear axle seal—note position of wood tool

Fig. 98 Removing the rear axle bearing assembly snapring with special tool

Fig. 99 Removing the rear axle bearing assembly snapring

Fig. 100 Removing the rear axle bearing

15. After installing the brake drum, bleed the brakes and adjust the brake shoe clearance.

16. Refill the axle housing with lubricant.

Land Cruiser

SEMI-FLOATING TYPE

▶ See Figures 101 and 102

1. Remove the hub cap and loosen the wheel nuts.
2. Raise the rear axle housing with a jack and support the rear of the vehicle with jackstands.
3. Drain the oil from the differential.
4. Remove the wheel nuts and take off the wheels.
5. Remove the brake drum and related parts.
6. Remove the cover from the back of the differential housing.
7. Remove the pin from the differential pinion shaft.
8. Withdraw the pinion shaft and its spacer from the case.
9. Use a mallet to tap the rear shaft toward the differential, to aid in the removal of the axle shaft C-lock.
10. Remove the C-lock.

11. Withdraw the axle shaft from the housing.
12. Repeat the removal procedure for the opposite side.
13. To remove oil seal and bearing, use a bearing puller and remove the axle bearing and oil seal together. To replace, use a metal tube to drive bearing and seal into seat.
14. After installing the axle shaft, C-lock, spacer and pinion shaft, measure the clearance between the axle shaft and the pinion shaft spacer with a feeler gauge. The clearance should fall between 0.06–0.46mm (1971-83) and no more than 5mm (1984–88). If the clearance is not within specifications, use one of the following spacers to adjust it.

1971–83 models
- 29.77–29.80mm
- 30.18–30.20mm
- 30.58–30.60mm

1984–88 models
- 29.00mm
- 29.39mm
- 29.80mm
- 30.20mm
- 30.60mm

15. Remember to fill the axle with lubricant.

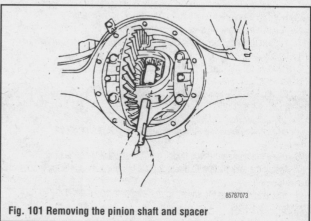

Fig. 101 Removing the pinion shaft and spacer

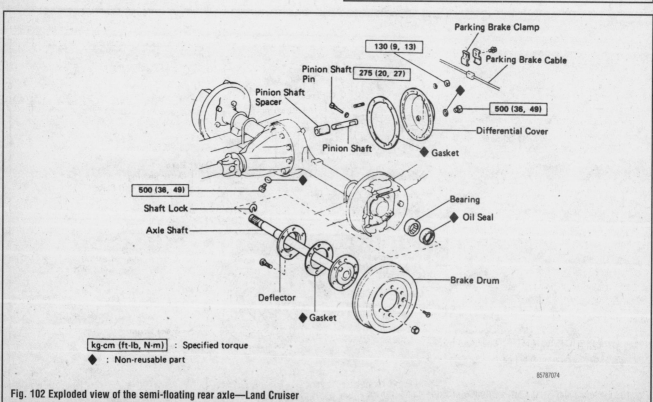

Fig. 102 Exploded view of the semi-floating rear axle—Land Cruiser

FULL FLOATING TYPE

♦ **See Figure 103**

1. Remove the nuts from the rear axle shaft plate.
2. Remove the cone washers from the mounting studs by tapping the slits of the washers with a tapered punch.
3. Install bolts into the two unused holes of the axle shaft plate.
4. Tighten the bolts to draw the axle shaft assembly out of the housing.
5. Install the axle using a new gasket and torque the axle shaft cone nuts to 25 ft. lbs. (33 Nm).

Rear Axle Hub

REMOVAL & INSTALLATION

Land Cruiser

FULL FLOATING TYPE

♦ **See Figures 104, 105, 106 and 107**

1. Raise the vehicle and support it safely with jackstands.
2. Remove the rear wheels.
3. Remove the rear axle shaft as previously outlined.
4. Loosen the lock screws and remove the adjusting nut from inside the hub using Toyota special tool #09509-25011 or its equivalent.
5. Remove the hub from the axle housing. Inspect all parts for damage or excessive wear. If the seal needs to be replaced, pry the seal out of the hub with an appropriate tool. The seal is installed by tapping it into the hub until it is firmly seated. If the bearing race(s) needs replacement, drive the race(s) from the hub using a brass drift. Use the brass drift to install the race(s). Drive the new race(s) into the hub until firmly seated.

To install:

6. Place the hub on the axle housing and install the outer bearing.
7. Install the lock plate with the lock plate tab positioned into the groove of the axle housing.
8. Install and tighten the adjusting nut with the special tool used during removal.

Fig. 104 Removing the rear axle hub and bearing—Land Cruiser w/full-floating rear axle

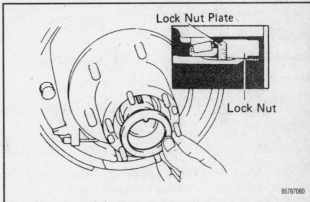

Fig. 105 Lock plate installation—Land Cruiser w/full-floating rear axle

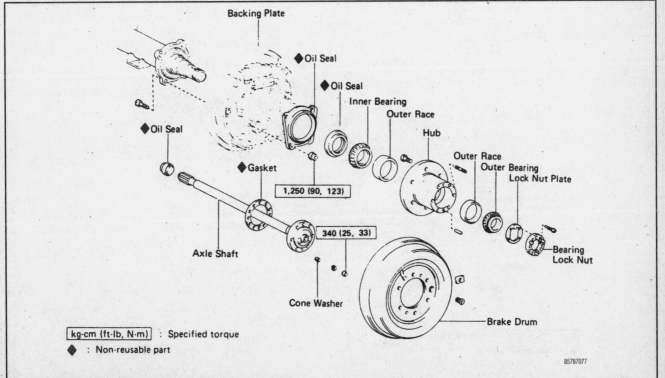

Fig. 103 Exploded view of the full-floating rear axle—Land Cruiser

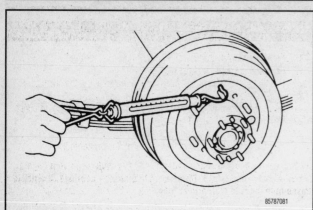

Fig. 106 Checking the bearing preload—Land Cruiser w/full-floating rear axle

Fig. 107 Lock screw installation—Land Cruiser w/full-floating rear axle

9. Torque the nut to 43 ft. lbs. (59 Nm). Rotate the hub a few times and retorque the adjusting nut to 43 ft. lbs. (59 Nm).

10. Loosen the adjusting nut until the hub can be turned by hand.

11. Tighten the nut a small amount and check the amount of pressure required to rotate the hub using a spring tension gauge.

12. The recommended rotational torque is 5.7–12.6 lbs. (1984–88: 0.9–7.3 lbs.). Tighten or loosen the adjusting nut as required to obtain this reading.

13. Align one of the axle housing slots with one of the adjusting nut slots. Install the lock screws into the holes of the adjusting nut which are at right angles to the aligned slots. Torque the lock screws to 35–60 inch lbs.

14. Recheck the rational torque and install the axle shaft using a new gasket.

15. Install the wheels and lower the vehicle.

Differential Carrier

REMOVAL & INSTALLATION

♦ See Figure 108

1. Raise the rear of the truck and support it on safety stands.
2. Remove the drain plug and drain the differential oil.
3. Remove the rear axle shaft.
4. Disconnect the driveshaft at the differential.
5. Remove the mounting bolts and lift out the differential carrier assembly.

To install:

6. Install a new gasket and position the carrier assembly into the axle housing. Tighten the mounting bolts to 19 ft. lbs. (25 Nm) on the Pick-Up and 4Runner and 34 ft. lbs. (47 Nm) on the Land Cruiser.

7. Connect the driveshaft to the companion flange on the differential.

8. Install the rear axle shafts.

9. Lower the truck and fill the differential with gear oil. Drive the truck and check for any leaks.

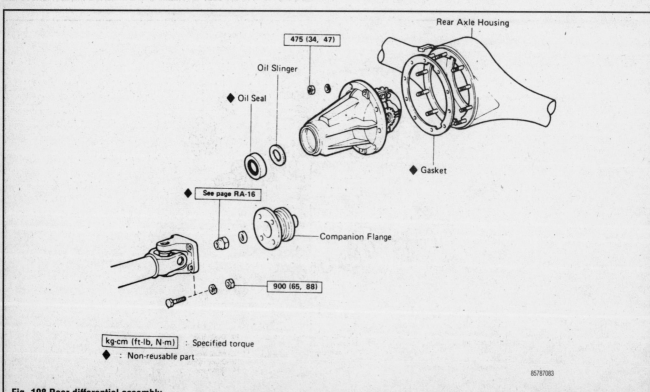

Fig. 108 Rear differential assembly

FRONT DRIVE AXLE

Axleshaft, Hub, Bearing and Seal

REMOVAL & INSTALLATION

1970–85 Pick-Up and 4Runner—4WD

▶ **See Figures 109, 110 and 111**

1. Set the control handle in the free position.
2. Remove the bolts in the hub and remove the hub and gasket.
3. Remove the nuts, spring washers, and cone washers.

➡**Cone washers can be removed by using a tapered punch.**

4. Remove hub body and gasket.
5. Remove snapring from free wheel hub body.
6. Remove hub ring, spacer and inner hub.
7. Remove compression spring, follower, tension spring, and clutch.
8. Remove snapring, free wheel hub cover ball and spring, seal, and control handle.

➡**Check inner hub and free wheel hub ring oil clearance. Clearance should be 0.30mm.**

9. Disconnect the brake line and the two bolts holding the brake caliper.
10. Remove the dust cap and snapring.
11. Remove the cone washers with a tapered punch.
12. Remove the flange by installing two bolts in the special holes for flange removal. Tighten these bolts until the flange comes loose. Remove the bolts by loosening them and remove the flange.
13. Remove the locknut, washer, and adjusting nut. Pull the rotor assembly off the spindle. The outer and inner bearings and seal will come apart as a unit.
14. Set the rotor on two blocks of wood. Using a drift pin drive the seal out. The inner bearing will drop out at this time. Using this pin drive the front and rear race from the rotor.
15. Place the rotor in a vice and remove the front axle hub.
16. Inspect the rotor, spindle and hub for damage.

17. Remove the dust seal, gasket, and dust cover.
18. Remove the spindle and gasket.
19. Position the flat part of the outer shaft up and pull out the shaft.
20. Remove the oil seal retainer.
21. Remove the cone type washers from the drag link with a tapered punch.
22. Remove the drag link and tie rod.
23. Remove the bottom bearing cap and shim.
24. Remove the upper and lower bearings with the proper tool.

➡**The steering knuckle bearing remover is available from your Toyota dealer. Part #09606-60010. Remember to mark the bearings in order to reassemble them in their proper place:**

25. Remove the upper and lower races with a brass drift pin.
26. Remove the steering knuckle and inspect for damage or wear.
27. Place the inner shaft in a vice. Using a drift pin drive the outer shaft apart and remove six ball bearings.

➡**Tilt the inner race and cage. Take the balls out one at a time.**

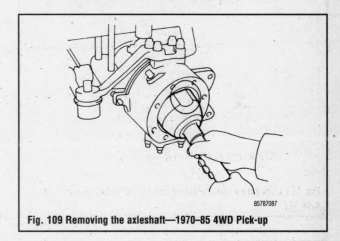

Fig. 109 Removing the axleshaft—1970–85 4WD Pick-up

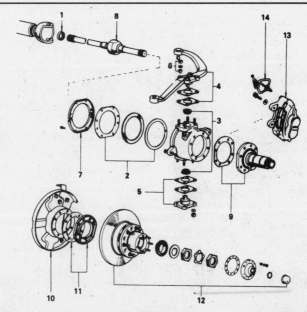

1. Oil seal	6. Nut, washer dowel	10. Dust cover
2. Oil seal set	7. Oil seal retainer	11. Dust seal and gasket
3. Bearings	8. Front axle shaft	12. Front axle hub with disc
4. Steering knuckle	9. Knuckle spindle and	13. Brake caliper
5. Bearing cup and shim	gasket	14. Brake line

Fig. 110 Exploded view of the front axle hub assembly—1970–85 4WD pick-up and 1970–88 Land Cruiser

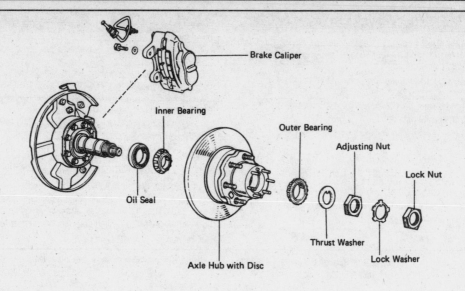

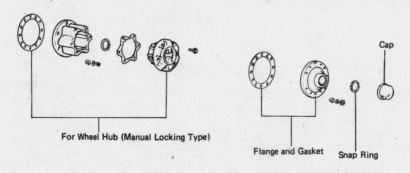

For Wheel Hub (Manual Locking Type)

Flange and Gasket   Snap Ring

FREEWHEEL HUB (Automatic Locking Type)

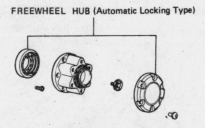

Fig. 111 Exploded view of the front axleshaft, hub, bearing and seal—1970–85 4WD pick-up

28. Remove the cage and race from the shaft.

→**Turn the large opening in the cage against the protruding portion of the shaft, pull the race and cage out.**

29. Remove the inner race from the cage through the large opening.

30. Remove the inner oil seal. Thoroughly wash and inspect all parts for wear or damage.

31. On installation:
   a. Replace all oil and grease seals.
   b. Pack the hub interior, inner and outer bearings with a multipurpose grease.

1986–88 Pick-Up and 4Runner—4WD

▶ **See Figures 112 and 113**

1. Raise the front of the vehicle and support on safety stands. Remove the wheel.

2. Remove the free-wheeling or automatic locking hub.

3. Disconnect and plug the brake line at the disc and wire it out of the way.

4. Remove the brake caliper.

5. Pop off the axle nut lock washer and remove the nut and washer. Remove the adjusting nut. Remove the axle hub/brake disc as an assembly along with the outer wheel bearing.

6. Pry out the oil seal and remove the inner bearing from the hub.

7. Loosen the 6 axle shaft-to-differential housing nuts.

→**This may require that a friend steps on the brake pedal.**

8. Remove the snapring and spacer from the end of the axle shaft.

9. Separate the inboard axle shaft flange from the side gear shaft and then remove the shaft down and through the steering knuckle.

To install:

10. Coat the outboard end of the axle shaft with molybdenum disulfide lithium based grease.

11. Insert the outboard end of the shaft into the steering knuckle and then install it to the differential. Handtighten the bolts.

✳✳ CAUTION

Do not damage the axle shaft boots.

12. Install the spacer and a new snapring.

13. Depress the brake pedal and tighten the inner mounting nuts to 61 ft. lbs. (83 Nm).

14. Pack the inner axle bearing with grease and press it into the hub. Coat a new oil seal with grease and press it into the hub.

15. Position the axle hub/brake disc assembly on the steering knuckle and press in the outer bearing.

16. Tighten the bearing adjusting nut to 43 ft. lbs. (59 Nm) and spin the hub a few times. Loosen the nut and then retighten it to 18 ft. lbs. (25 Nm).

17. Use a tension gauge and check that the bearing preload is 6,4–12.6 lbs.

18. Install a new locknut and washer and tighten to 58 ft. lbs. (78 Nm). Check that the bearing has no axial play. Secure the locknut by bending one of the washer teeth inward and another outward.

19. Install the free-wheeling or automatic hub.

20. Install the brake caliper and line. Install the wheel, lower the vehicle and bleed the brakes. Road test the truck.

Land Cruiser

1. Raise and support the vehicle securely and remove the wheel assembly.

2. Plug the brake master cylinder reservoir to prevent brake fluid leakage from the disconnected brake flexible hose.

3. Remove the outer axle shaft flange cap, and then remove the shaft snapring on the outer shaft.

4. Remove the bolts retaining the outer axle shaft flange onto the front axle hub, and then, screw service bolts into the shaft flange alternately, and remove the shaft flange with its gasket.

5. Remove the brake drum set screws and remove the brake drum. If equipped with disc brakes, remove the caliper and disc.

6. Straighten the lockwasher, and remove the front wheel bearing adjusting nuts with front wheel adjusting nut wrench or similar tool.

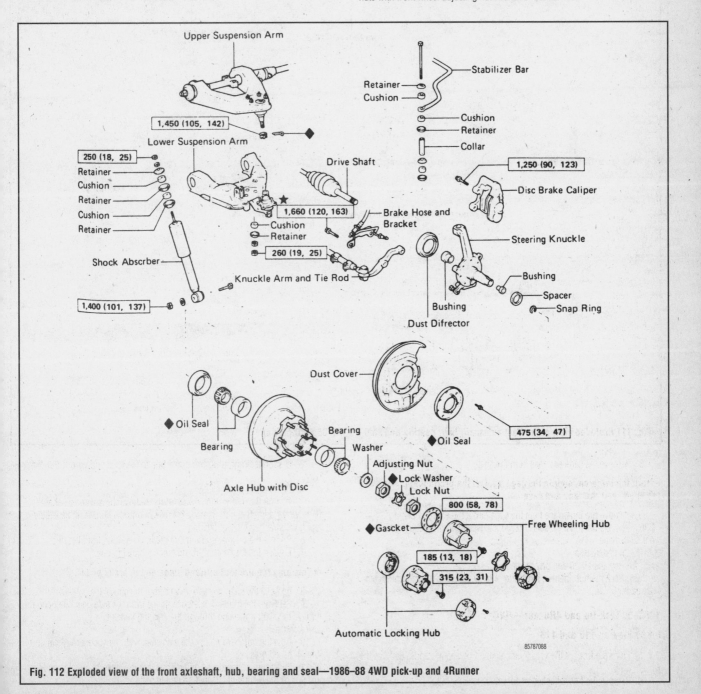

Fig. 112 Exploded view of the front axleshaft, hub, bearing and seal—1986–88 4WD pick-up and 4Runner

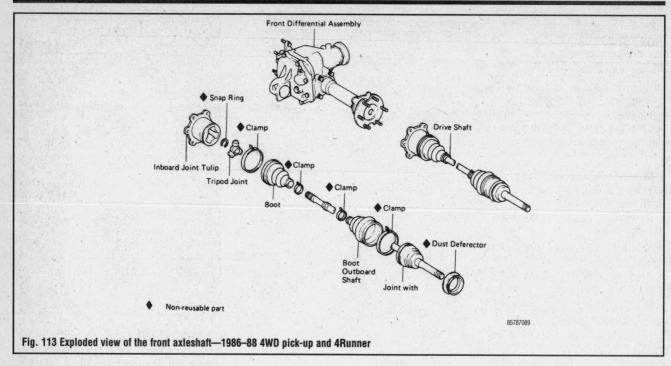

Front Differential Assembly

◆ Snap Ring

◆ Clamp

Inboard Joint Tulip

Tripod Joint

Boot

◆ Clamp

◆ Clamp

◆ Clamp

Drive Shaft

◆ Dust Deferector

Boot
Outboard
Shaft

Joint with

◆ Non-reusable part

85787089

Fig. 113 Exploded view of the front axleshaft—1986–88 4WD pick-up and 4Runner

7. Remove the front axle hub together with its claw washer, bearings, and oil seal.

8. Remove the clip and disconnect the brake flexible hose from the brake tube.

9. Cut and remove the lock wire and remove the bolts retaining the brake backing plate onto the steering knuckle. Remove the brake backing plate together with the brake shoes, tension spring, and the wheel cylinder still assembled to the backing plate.

10. Tap the steering knuckle spindle lightly with a soft mallet, and remove the spindle with its gasket.

➡**When removing the steering knuckle spindle on a vehicle equipped with the ball joint type axle shaft joint, be prepared for the disconnection of the outer axle shaft from the joint. The joint ball will fall from the joint. Try to cushion its fall or catch it if you can.**

11. On those models equipped with the ball type axle shaft joint, slide the inner front axle shaft out of the axle housing. On those models equipped with the Birfield constant velocity joint type of axle joint, remove the entire axle shaft assembly from the axle housing.

12. Remove bushing from inside of knuckle spindle with a bearing puller. Install new bushing using a metal tube as a seating tool.

13. Remove axle housing oil seal with a bearing puller. To install, use a metal tube as a seating tool.

14. Install the axle shaft in the reverse order of removal. On those models equipped with the ball joint type axle joint, install the inner axle with its proper spacer in position until the splines are fully meshed with the differential side gear splines. Next, fill the steering knuckle three quarters full with grease and place the joint ball on the inner shaft end. Install the outer shaft and the front axle shaft spacer into the steering knuckle spindle and install the spindle with its gasket onto the steering knuckle.

15. On those models equipped with the Birfield constant velocity joint axle joint, install the axle into the housing and rotate the axle shaft until its splines mesh with the splines in the differential. Fill the steering knuckle housing three quarters full with grease and install the steering knuckle spindle.

16. Adjust the wheel bearing preload.

Locking Hubs

REMOVAL & INSTALLATION

1. Set the hub control handle to the FREE position.

2. Remove the hub bolts which retain the front cover and handle assembly and remove the assembly.

3. Remove the snapring from the axle shaft using snapring pliers.

4. Remove the hub body mounting nuts.

5. Remove the cone washers from the hub body mounting studs by tapping on the washer slits with a tapered punch.

6. Remove the hub body from the axle hub.

To install:

7. Install the hub with a new gasket and tighten the mounting nuts to 23 ft. lbs. (31 Nm).

8. Install the bolt and washer and tighten it to 13 ft. lbs. (18 Nm).

9. Coat the inner hub splines with grease.

10. Make sure the control handle on the cover is still at FREE (if not automatic), position a new gasket in the cover and install the cover so that the pawl-tabs are lines up with the non-toothed portions of the hub body. Tighten the mounting nuts to 7 ft. lbs. (10 Nm).

Differential

REMOVAL & INSTALLATION

1. Raise the front of the truck and support it on safety stands.

2. Remove the drain plug and drain the differential oil.

3. Remove the axle shaft.

4. Disconnect the driveshaft at the differential.

5. Remove the mounting bolts and lift out the differential carrier assembly. On 1986-88 models, there are a bolt and nut at the front and 2 bolts at the rear.

To install:

6. On all models except the 1986–88 Pick-Up and 4Runner, install a new gasket and position the carrier assembly into the axle housing. Tighten the mounting bolts to 19 ft. lbs. (25 Nm) on the Pick-Up and 4Runner and 34 ft. lbs. (47 Nm) on the Land Cruiser. On the 1986–88 models, tighten the rear bolts to 123 ft. lbs. (167 Nm) and the front bolt to 108 ft. lbs. (147 Nm).

7. Connect the driveshaft to the companion flange on the differential.

8. Install the axle shafts.

9. Lower the truck and fill the differential with gear oil. Drive the truck and check for any leaks.

8

SUSPENSION AND STEERING

FRONT SUSPENSION

Coil Springs

REMOVAL & INSTALLATION

▶ See Figures 1 thru 9

1970–78 Pick-Up—2WD

❋❋ WARNING

The coil springs are retained under considerable pressure. They can exert enough force when released to cause serious injury. Exercise extreme caution when disassembling the strut for coil spring removal.

1. Remove the hub cap and loosen the lug nuts.
2. Raise the front of the truck and support the front suspension crossmember with jackstands.
3. Remove the lug nuts and the wheel.
4. Remove the stabilizer bar connecting bolts and remove the bracket parts, being careful to note their removal sequence in order to aid in installation.
5. Remove the tie rod cotter pin and nut. Use a puller to remove the end of the tie rod from the knuckle arm.
6. Remove the shock absorber. Detach the brake hose.
7. Raise the lower control arm using a jack, so that the arm is free of the steering knuckle.
8. Loosen the ball joint attachment nut and remove the ball joint.
9. Slowly lower the jack underneath the control arm.

❋❋ CAUTION

If the jack is lowered too quickly, the spring could suddenly release, causing damage and/or injury.

10. Remove the coil spring and its insulator from beneath the truck.
To install:
11. Inspect the coil spring, its insulator, and bumper for cracks, wear or damage. Replace parts as necessary.
12. A coil spring compressor should be used to install the spring, rather than the method for removing it.

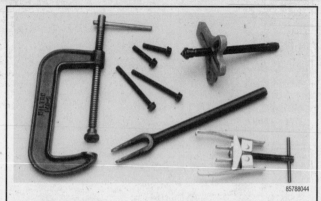

Fig. 2 View of special tools for front end and steering work

Fig. 3 Removing the front shock absorber top mounting bolt

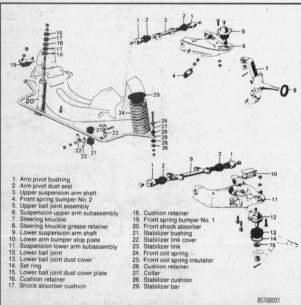

1. Arm pivot bushing
2. Arm pivot dust seal
3. Upper suspension arm shaft
4. Front spring bumper No. 2
5. Upper ball joint assembly
6. Suspension upper arm subassembly
7. Steering knuckle
8. Steering knuckle grease retainer
9. Lower suspension arm shaft
10. Lower arm bumper stop plate
11. Suspension lower arm subassembly
12. Lower ball joint
13. Lower ball joint dust cover
14. Set ring
15. Lower ball joint dust cover plate
16. Cushion retainer
17. Shock absorber cushion
18. Cushion retainer
19. Front spring bumper No. 1
20. Front shock absorber
21. Stabilizer bushing
22. Stabilizer link cover
23. Stabilizer link
24. Front coil spring
25. Front coil spring insulator
26. Cushion retainer
27. Collar
28. Stabilizer cushion
29. Stabilizer bar

Fig. 1 Exploded view of the coil spring front suspension—1970–78 2WD Pick-Up

Fig. 4 Removing the front shock absorber lower mounting bolt

Fig. 5 Removing the rear shock absorber lower mounting bolt

Fig. 6 View of the rear shock absorber top mounting bolt

Fig. 7 Removing the steering stop rubber caps

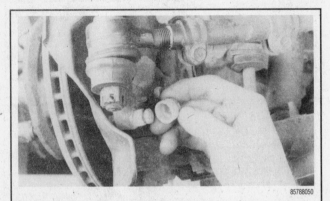

Fig. 8 View of the steering stop rubber caps

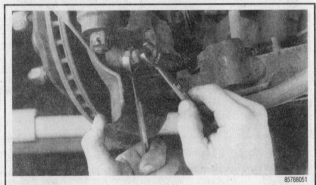

Fig. 9 Adjusting the steering stop bolt—should not be necessary under normal conditions

13. Tighten the suspension components to the following specifications:
Lower control arm:
- 1970–75: 51–65 ft. lbs.
- 1976–78: 33–43 ft. lbs.
Ball joint: 87–123 ft. lbs.

Leaf Springs

REMOVAL & INSTALLATION

1970–85 Pick-Up—4WD

▶ See Figures 10 and 11

1. Raise the front of vehicle and place support stands under the chassis frame.

➡Do not place supports under front axle housing.

2. Remove wheel.
3. Remove the bolt from the bottom of the shock absorber and raise shock up out of the way.

4. If removing driver's side front leaf spring, remove the cotter pin from the end of the steering drag link at the axle housing. Unscrew the slotted bolt in the end of the drag link and remove the bolt, spring holder, spring, and outer socket holder. Remove drag link from steering knuckle arm.

➡Be careful not to lose inner socket holder.

5. Remove stabilizer bar bolt and spacer and washer assembly.
6. Disconnect the brake line at the holder behind the brake assembly. Drive out the shim holding the brake line to the holder and withdraw the brake line. Plug the end of brake line to prevent fluid loss.
7. Position a jack under the front axle housing and raise it just enough to put pressure on the leaf spring. Remove the 4 nuts holding the 2 U-bolts to the axle housing and remove the U-bolts. Remove the lower spring seat and spring bumper.
8. Lower the jack enough to take the pressure off the leaf spring, but so it still supports the axle housing.
9. Remove the hanger pin and shackle pin mounting nuts and then remove the 2 pins. Carefully pry the spring from its holders.

➡It may be necessary to lower the jack under the axle housing to remove spring.

To install:

10. Insert the bushings into the frame and each end of the leaf. Position the spring, install the hanger pin and tighten the bolt to 9 ft. lbs. (13 Nm).
11. Finger tighten the hanger pin nut and install the shackle pin. Install the plate and finger tighten the nuts.
12. Install the spring bumper and U-bolts onto the leaf. Install the spring seat and nuts. Tighten the nuts to 90 ft. lbs. (123 Nm).

➡When tightening the U-bolts, the exposed length of each bolt below the nut should be the same for all 4 threaded ends.

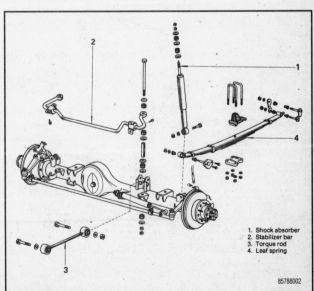

1. Shock absorber
2. Stabilizer bar
3. Torque rod
4. Leaf spring

Fig. 10 Exploded view of the leaf spring front suspension—1970–85 4WD Pick-Up

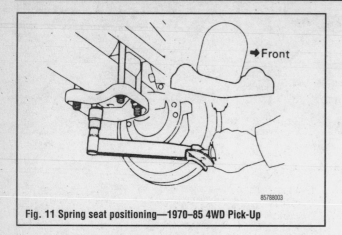

Fig. 11 Spring seat positioning—1970–85 4WD Pick-Up

13. Connect the drag link to the steering knuckle arm.
14. Connect the stabilizer bar and tighten the nuts to 19 ft. lbs. (25 Nm).
15. Install the shock absorber.
16. Lower the truck and bounce it a few times to stabilize the suspension.
17. Tighten the hanger pin nut to 67 ft. lbs. (91 Nm). Tighten the shackle pin nut to 67 ft. lbs. (91 Nm).

Land Cruiser

♦ See Figures 12 and 13

1. Remove the wheels and then raise the front of the truck and support it on safety stands.
2. Position a floor jack under the differential housing and lower it until there is no tension on the leaf springs.
3. Remove the shock absorber.
4. Remove the U-bolt mounting nuts, pull the spring set away and remove the U-bolts.
5. Remove the hanger and shackle pin mounting nuts. Remove the pins and then lift out the leaf spring.

➡It may be necessary to lower the jack under the axle housing to remove spring.

To install:

6. Insert the bushings into the frame and each end of the leaf. Position the spring, install the hanger pin and tighten the bolt to 9 ft. lbs. (13 Nm).
7. Finger tighten the hanger pin nut and install the shackle pin. Install the plate and finger tighten the nuts.
8. Insert the head of the center leaf spring bolt into the hole in the axle housing bracket and then install the U-bolts onto the leaf. Install the spring seat and nuts. Tighten the nuts to 90 ft. lbs. (123 Nm).

Fig. 13 Leaf spring positioning—Land Cruiser

➡When tightening the U-bolts, the exposed length of each bolt below the nut should be the same for all 4 threaded ends.

9. Install the shock absorber.
10. Lower the truck and bounce it a few times to stabilize the suspension.
11. Tighten the hanger pin nut to 67 ft. lbs. (91 Nm). Tighten the shackle pin nut to 67 ft. lbs. (91 Nm).

Torsion Bars

REMOVAL & INSTALLATION

1979–88 Pick-Up—2WD

♦ See Figures 14 thru 29

✳✳ CAUTION

Great care must be taken to make sure springs are not mixed after removal, it is strongly suggested that before removal, each spring be marked with paint, showing the front and rear of spring and from which side of the truck it was taken. If springs are installed backward or on the wrong sides of the truck, they could fracture. If replacing springs, it is not necessary to mark them.

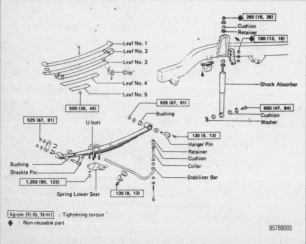

Fig. 12 Exploded view of the leaf spring front suspension—Land Cruiser

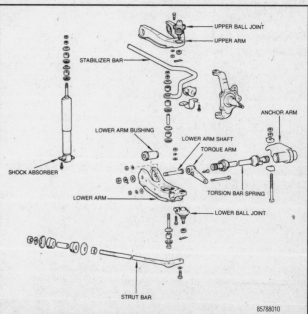

Fig. 14 Exploded view of the torsion bar front suspension—1979–88 2WD Pick-Up and 1986–88 4WD Pick-Up and 4Runner

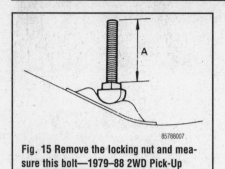

Fig. 15 Remove the locking nut and measure this bolt—1979–88 2WD Pick-Up

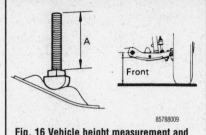

Fig. 16 Vehicle height measurement and adjustment—1979–88 2WD Pick-Up

Fig. 17 View of the torsion bar assembly—marked for correct installation

Fig. 18 View of the torsion bar boot

Fig. 19 Removing the rear torsion bar boot

Fig. 20 Removing the front torsion bar boot

Fig. 21 Measuring the torsion bar bolt—note bolt removed from holder for clear view

Fig. 22 Removing the torsion bar bolt and nut

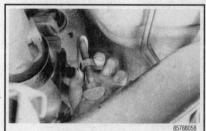

Fig. 23 View of the torsion bar bolt assembly

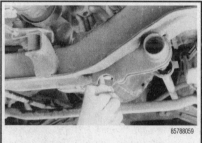

Fig. 24 Removing the torsion bar bolt

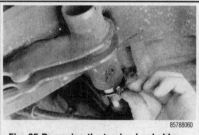

Fig. 25 Removing the torsion bar holder bolt

Fig. 26 Removing the torsion bar from the holder

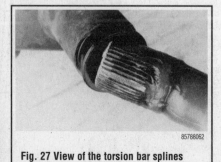

Fig. 27 View of the torsion bar splines

Fig. 28 View of the torsion bar marked R—right side installation

Fig. 29 Installing the torsion bar into the holder. Note the torsion bar splines and cutout on the holder

1. Raise the truck and support the frame on stands.
2. Slide the boot from the rear of torsion bar spring housing and onto spring.
3. Follow the same procedure on the front of the spring.

➡**Be sure to make a mark showing front of spring from back of spring.**

4. On the rear torsion bar spring holder, there is a long bolt that passes through the arm of the holder and up through the frame crossmember. REMOVE THE LOCKING NUT ONLY, FROM THE BOLT.
5. Using a small ruler, measure the length from the bottom of the retaining nut to the threaded tip of the bolt and record this measurement.

➡**Be sure to complete Step 5 accurately.**

6. Position a floor jack under the rear torsion bar spring holder arm and jack up the arm to remove the spring pressure from the long bolt. Loosen the adjusting nut until there is no tension on the torsion bar.
7. Slowly lower the jack.
8. Remove the long bolt and its spacer and remove rear holder. You should be able to pull the torsion bar out of the front and rear holders.
9. Inspect all parts for wear, damage or cracks. Check the boot for rips and wear. Inspect the splined ends of the torsion bar spring and the splined holes in the rear holder and the front torque arm for damage. Replace as necessary. On the rear end of the torsion bar springs, there are markings to show which is right and which is the left bar. Do not confuse them!

To install:

10. Coat the splined ends of the torsion bar with multipurpose grease.
11. If fitting old torsion bars:
   a. Align the toothless portion and install the anchor arm to the torsion bar spring.
   b. Slide the front of the bar into the opening on the torque arm, making sure you line up the marks you made earlier on the torsion bar spring and the torque arm.
   c. Repeat the above step with the rear spring holder and replace the long bolt and its spacers.
   d. Place a pipe that will fit in the notch on the rear holder arm an a jack and jack up the arm.
   e. Tighten the adjusting nut so that it is the same length it was before removal.

➡**Do not replace the locknut yet.**

12. When installing a new torsion bar spring:
   a. Slide the front of the torsion bar into the opening on the torque arm.
   b. Fit the rear holder in place and install the rear of the torsion bar into it so that when the long bolt and spacers are installed, the distance from the top of the upper spacer to the tip of the threaded end of the bolt is 18-25mm.

➡**Make sure the bolt and bottom spacer are snugly in the holder arm while measuring.**

   c. When the correct measurement is achieved, fit a pipe or round bar in the notch or rear holder arm. Jack up arm on pipe.
   d. Replace the adjusting nut and tighten until the distance from the bottom of the nut to the top of the threaded end of the bolt is 71–89mm.

➡**Do not install the locknut yet.**

13. Apply multipurpose grease to the boot lips and refit the boots over splines.
14. Replace the wheel and lower the truck.
15. With the wheels on the ground, measure the distance from the ground to the center of the lower arm shaft (See Chart). Adjust vehicle height with the adjusting nut on the rear spring holder.

➡**If, after achieving the correct vehicle height, the distance from the bottom of the adjusting nut to the top of the threaded end of the long bolt is more than 97mm, change the position of the rear spring holder arm spline and reassemble.**

16. Replace the locknut on the long bolt. Tighten it to 61 ft. lbs. (83 Nm).

➡**Make sure the adjusting nut does not move when tightening the locknut.**

1986–88 Pick-Up and 4Runner—4WD

▶ See Figures 30, 31, 32 and 33

✳✳ CAUTION

Great care must be taken to make sure springs are not mixed after removal, it is strongly suggested that before removal, each spring be marked with paint, showing the front and rear of spring and from which side of the truck it was taken. If springs are installed backward or on the wrong sides of the truck, they could fracture. If replacing springs, it is not necessary to mark them.

1. Raise the truck and support the frame on stands.
2. Slide the boot from the rear of torsion bar spring housing and onto spring.
3. Follow the same procedure on the front of the spring.
4. Paint matchmarks on the torsion bar spring, anchor arm and torque arm.
5. On the rear torsion bar spring holder, there is a long bolt that passes through the arm of the holder and up through the frame crossmember, using a small ruler, measure the length from the bottom of the retaining nut to the threaded tip of the bolt and record this measurement.

➡**Be sure to complete Step 5 accurately.**

6. Loosen the adjusting nut and remove the anchor arm and torsion bar spring.
7. Inspect all parts for wear, damage or cracks. Check the boot for rips and wear. Inspect the splined ends of the torsion bar spring and the splined holes in the rear holder and the front torque arm for damage. Replace as necessary. On the rear end of the torsion bar springs, there are markings to show which is right and which is the left bar. Do not confuse them!

To install the existing spring:

8. Coat the splined ends of the torsion bar with multipurpose grease.
9. Align the matchmarks and install the torsion bar spring to the torque arm.
10. Align the matchmarks and install the anchor arm to the torsion bar spring.
11. Tighten the adjusting nut so that the bolt protrusion measured previously is equal to that of the new adjustment.

To install a new torsion bar spring:

12. Install the 2 bolts to the torsion bar spring.
13. Lightly coat the spring end splines with grease and then install the anchor arm to the small end of the spring temporarily. Paint matchmarks on the spring and arm.

➡**There is one spline on the spring that is larger than the others. When connecting the spring to the arm, turn the arm slowly until you can feel the larger spline match up with the slot in the arm.**

14. Remove the anchor arm from the spring and install the spring into the torque arm.

➡**There is on spline on the spring that is larger than the others. When connecting the spring to the arm, turn the arm slowly until you can feel the larger spline match up with the slot in the arm.**

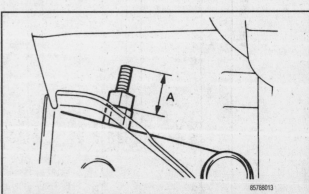

Fig. 30 Measure the height of this bolt for installation—1986–88 4WD Pick-Up and 4Runner

Vehicle Height

Yr.	Model	Pay Load	Tire Size	Front Height in. (Unloaded)
1979-80	RN32L	½ Ton	185 SR 14-4PR	9.827
	RN42L		7.00-14-6PR	10.291
			E78-14(B)	10.016
			ER78-14(B)	9.866
	RN42L-KH	¾ Ton	7.50-14-6PR	10.961
	RN421-3W C & C	¾ Ton	7.50-14-6PR	10.961
1981-83	RN34	½ Ton	7.00-14-6PR	10.291
	RN44		E78-14(B)	10.016
			ER78-14(B)	9.866
			205/70 SR 14	9.512
	RN44L-KH	¾ Ton	7.50-14-6PR	10.961
	RN44L-3W C & C	¾ Ton	7.50-14-6PR	10.961
1984	Short Bed (Std)		7.00-14-6PR	10.59
			ER78-14	10.04
	Long Bed (Std)		7.00-14-6PR	10.75
			ER78-14	10.20
	Long Bed (Soft Ride)		ER78-14	10.20
	Extra Cab (Soft Ride)		ER78-14	9.80
	Extra Cab (Std)		ER78-14	9.80
	¾ Ton		7.50-14-6PR.	10.71
	C & C		7.50-14-6PR	10.83
	SR-5 (Short)		P195/75R 14	9.76
			205/70 R 14	10.00
			ER78-14	10.00
	SR-5 (Long)		P195/75 R 14	9.96
			205/70 SR 14	10.20
			ER 78-14	10.12
	Extra Cab SR5 (Long Bed)		P195/75 R 14	9.80
			205/70 SR 14	10.04
			ER78-14	9.96

Fig. 31 Vehicle height chart

Vehicle Height (cont.)

Yr.	Model	Pay Load	Tire Size	Front Height in. (Unloaded)
1985	Short Bed (Std)		7.00-14-6 PR	10.63
	Long Bed (Std)		7.00-14-6 PR	10.83
	Long Bed (Soft Ride)		P195/75 R 14	10.24
	Extra Cab (Soft Ride)		P195/75 R 14	9.84
	Extra Cab (Std)		P195/75 R 14	9.84
	1 Ton		185 R 14-LT8PR	10.31
	C & C		185 R 14-LT8PR	10.20
	Short Bed (SR-5)		P195/75 R 14	9.80
			205/70 SR 14	10.04
	Long Bed (SR-5)		P195/75 R 14	9.96
			205/70 SR 14	10.20
	Extra Cab SDR-5 (Long Bed)		P195/75 R 14	9.84
			205/70 SR 14	10.08
	(Diesel) Short Bed (Std)		7.00-14-6PR	10.59
	Long Bed (Soft Ride)		P195/75 R 14	9.96
	Extra Cab (Soft Ride)		P195/75 R 14	9.80
	Extra Cab (Std)		P195/75 R 14	9.80
1986	Short Bed (Std)		7.00-14-6PR	10.59
	Long Bed (Std)		7.00-14-6PR	10.83
	Long Bed (Soft Ride)		P195/75 R 14	10.83
	Extra Cab (Soft Ride)		P195/75 R 14	9.84
	Extra Cab (Std)		P195/75 R 14	9.84
	1 Ton		185 R 14-LT8PR	10.31
	C & C		185 R 14-LT8PR	10.28
	Short Bed (SR-5)		P195/75 R 14	9.88
	Long Bed (SR-5)		P195/75 R 14	9.96
			205/70 SR 14	10.20
	Extra Cab SR-5 (Long Bed)		P195/75 R 14	10.04
			205/70 SR 14	10.28
	(Diesel) Short Bed (Std)		7.00-14-6PR	10.59
	Long Bed (Soft Ride)		P195/75 R 14	9.96
	Extra Cab (Soft Ride)		P195/75 R 14	9.80
	Extra Cab (Std)		P195/75 R 14	9.80

Fig. 32 Vehicle height chart, cont.

Vehicle Height (cont.)

Yr.	Model	Pay Load	Tire Size	Front Height in. (Unloaded)
1987–88	½ Ton (Short)		7.00-14-6PR	10.59
			P195/75 R 14	9.88
	½ Ton (Long)		7.00-14-6PR	10.75
			P195/75 R 14	10.04
			205/70 SR 14	10.28
	½ Ton (Extra Long)		P195/75 R 14	10.04
	1 Ton		185 R 14LT-8PR	10.31
	C&C Long SRW		185 R 14LT-8PR	10.31
	Long DRW		185 R 14LT-6PR	10.28
	Super Long DRW		185 R 14LT-6PR	10.35

8578811B

Fig. 33 Vehicle height chart, cont.

15. Align the matchmarks and install the anchor arm to the spring. Tighten the adjusting nut so that the exposed thread on the bolt is no greater than 87mm.

All models:

16. Install the locknut and wheels, lower the truck and bounce it several times to set the suspension.

17. Measure the ground clearance and adjust with the adjusting nut. Tighten the locknut to 61 ft. lbs. (83 Nm).

Shock Absorber

TESTING

The function of the shock absorber is to dampen harsh spring movement and provide a means of controlling the motion of the wheels so that the bumps encountered by the wheels are not totally transmitted to the body of the truck and, therefore, to you and your passengers. As the wheel moves up and down, the shock absorber shortens and lengthens, thereby imposing a restraint on excessive movement by its hydraulic action.

A good way to see if your shock absorbers are working properly is to push on one corner of the truck until it is moving up and down for almost the full suspension travel, then release it and watch its recovery. If the truck bounces slightly about one more time and then comes to a rest, you can be fairly certain that the shock is OK. If the truck continues to bounce excessively, the shocks will probably require replacement.

REMOVAL & INSTALLATION

1. Remove the hubcap and loosen the lug nuts.
2. Raise front of the truck and support it with safety stands.
3. Remove the lug nuts and the wheel.
4. Unfasten the double nuts at the top end of the shock absorber. Remove the cushions and cushion retainers.
5. On 2WD models, remove the 2 bolts which secure the lower end of the shock absorber to the lower control arm. On 4WD models, remove the lower thru-bolt.
6. Remove the shock absorber.

To install:

7. Install the shock absorber and tighten the lower mounting nuts/bolt to 13 ft. lbs. (18 Nm)—2WD; 101 ft. lbs. (137 Nm)—4WD Pick-Up and 4Runner; 47 ft. lbs. (64 Nm)—Land Cruiser. Tighten the upper mounting nut to 18 ft. lbs. (25 Nm).

8. Install the wheels and lower the truck.

Ball Joints

INSPECTION

To check the lower ball joint for wear, jack up the lower suspension arm, after removing all excess play from the other suspension parts (wheel bearings, tie rods, etc.). The bottom of the tire should not move more than 5mm when the tire is pushed and pulled inward and outward. The tire should not move more than 2.3mm up and down. If the play is greater than these figures, replace the ball joint. The upper ball joint should be replaced if a distinct looseness is felt when turning the ball joint stud with the steering knuckle removed.

REMOVAL & INSTALLATION

1970–78 Pick-Up—2WD

1. Raise the front of the truck and remove the wheel and tire.
2. Support the front suspension crossmember with jackstands.
3. Position a floor jack under the lower control arm and raise the control arm until the spring bumper is off the frame.
4. Disconnect the flexible brake hose.
5. Disconnect the tie rod end from the steering knuckle using a puller.
6. Using a suitable puller remove the ball joint from the steering knuckle.
7. Remove the ball joint from the lower arm.
8. From this position the upper ball joint may also be removed in a similar manner. Removal and installation will be easier if the lower is removed first.

To install:

9. Install the new ball joints and reassemble the steering components. Due to the fact that the shock absorber is not removed in this procedure the coil spring may be positioned with the jack and no compressor is necessary.

➡ **Be sure to grease the new ball joints before using the vehicle.**

10. Tighten the upper ball joint nuts to 15–22 ft. lbs., the lower to 22–29 ft. lbs. Tighten the steering knuckle to upper joint to 65–94 ft. lbs.; the knuckle to the lower joint to 87–123 ft. lbs. Bleed the brakes before driving the truck.

1979–88 Pick-Up—2WD, 1986–88 Pick-Up and 4Runner—4WD

▶ **See Figures 34, 35, 36, 37 and 38**

1. Raise the vehicle and support it with jackstands.
2. Remove the front wheel.
3. Support the lower control arm with a floor jack and remove the steering knuckle.

Fig. 34 View of the upper ball joint assembly

Fig. 35 Removing the upper ball joint cotter pin

Fig. 36 Removing the upper ball joint nut

Fig. 37 Removing the upper ball joint with special tool

Fig. 38 Removing the lower ball joint mounting bolts

4. Loosen the mounting bolts and remove the lower ball joint from the lower control arm. On 4WD models, remove the cotter pin and then remove the mounting nut.

5. Reach up and unbolt the upper ball joint from the upper control arm.

To install:

6. Install the upper ball joint and tighten the bolts to 20 ft. lbs. (26 Nm) on 2WD models; 25 ft. lbs. 33 Nm) on 4WD models.

7. On 2WD models, install the lower ball joint and tighten the bolts to 51 ft. lbs. (69 Nm). On 4WD models, install the lower ball joint, tighten the nut to 105 ft. lbs. (142 Nm) and install a new cotter pin.

8. Install the steering knuckle. Install the wheels and lower the truck.

➡Be sure to grease the ball joints before moving the vehicle.

Strut Bar

REMOVAL & INSTALLATION

1979–88 Pick-Up—2WD

▶ See Figures 39, 40, 41, 42 and 43

1. Remove the wheels, raise the truck and support it on safety stands.
2. Paint matchmarks on the strut bar and retaining nut.
3. Remove the retaining nut from the front of the bar.
4. Remove the nuts holding the bar to the lower control arm and lift out the strut bar.

To install:

5. Position the bar and install the front nut so that the matchmarks line up.
6. Slide the washer and bushing onto the bar and install it to the bracket at the rear.
7. Install the collar, bushing and washer to the other side and then connect the rear of the bar to the control arm. Tighten the mounting nut to 70 ft. lbs. (95 Nm).
8. Lower the truck and bounce it several times to set the suspension.
9. Tighten the front nut to 90 ft. lbs. (123 Nm) and check the alignment.

Fig. 39 View of the strut bar mounting bolts

Fig. 40 Remove the strut bar mounting bolts

Fig. 41 Removing the strut bar nut

Fig. 42 Removing the strut bar from the vehicle

Fig. 43 View of the strut bar and related hardware

Stabilizer Bar

REMOVAL & INSTALLATION

1979–88 Pick-Up—2WD

1. Raise the truck and support it on safety stands. Remove the wheels.
2. Remove one torsion bar spring.
3. Remove the nuts and cushions at both sides of the stabilizer bar where it attaches to the control arms.
4. Remove the 2 bushings and brackets where the bar mounts to the frame member. Remove the stabilizer bar.

To install:

5. Position the stabilizer bar and install the 2 center bushings and brackets to the frame. Finger tighten the bolts.
6. Connect the bar to the control arms on each side. Use new nuts and tighten to 9 ft. lbs. (13 Nm).
7. Tighten the center bracket bolts to 9 ft. lbs. (13 Nm) and install the torsion bar.
8. Install the wheels and lower the truck.

1970–85 Pick-Up—4WD and 1971–88 Land Cruiser

1. Raise the truck and support it on safety stands. Remove the wheels.
2. Remove the nuts and cushions at both sides of the stabilizer bar where it attaches to the front axle housing.
3. Remove the 2 bushings and brackets where the bar mounts to the frame member. Remove the stabilizer bar.

To install:

4. Position the stabilizer bar and install the 2 center bushings and brackets to the frame. Finger tighten the bolts.
5. Connect the bar to the axle housing on each side. Use new nuts and tighten to 19 ft. lbs. (25 Nm) on the Pick-Up and 13 ft. lbs. (18 Nm) on the Land Cruiser.

6. Tighten the center bracket bolts to 9 ft. lbs. (13 Nm) and install the torsion bar.
7. Install the wheels and lower the truck.

1986–88 Pick-Up and 4Runner—4WD

1. Raise the truck and support it on safety stands. Remove the wheels.
2. Remove the nuts, cushions and retainers at both sides of the stabilizer bar where it attaches to the lower control arm.
3. Remove the 2 bushings and brackets where the bar mounts to the frame member. Remove the stabilizer bar.

To install:

4. Position the stabilizer bar and install the 2 center bushings and brackets to the frame. Finger tighten the bolts.
5. Connect the bar to the control arm on each side. Use new nuts and tighten to 19 ft. lbs. (25 Nm).
6. Tighten the center bracket bolts to 9 ft. lbs. (13 Nm) and install the torsion bar.
7. Install the wheels and lower the truck.

Torque Rod

REMOVAL & INSTALLATION

1970–85 Pick-Up—4WD

1. Raise the truck and support it on safety stands. Remove the wheels.
2. Disconnect the torque rod at the axle housing.
3. Disconnect the torque rod at the frame. Remove the rod.

To install:

4. Install the torque rod with the mounting bolts fingertight.
5. Install the wheels and lower the truck. Bounce the truck several times to set the suspension and then tighten the mounting bolts to 105 ft. lbs. (142 Nm).

Upper Control Arm

REMOVAL & INSTALLATION

▶ See Figure 44

1970–88 Pick-Up—2WD

1. Raise and support the truck under the frame.
2. Remove the wheel. Remove the brake caliper on models with disc brakes.
3. Raise the lower control arm with a floor jack.
4. Remove the nut from the upper ball joint stud.
5. Separate the ball joint from the steering knuckle.
6. Unbolt and remove the upper arm at the 2 bolts holding the inner shaft to the frame, taking note of the number, size and position of the aligning shims.

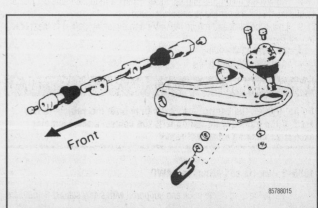

Fig. 44 Exploded view of upper control arm-typical

To install:

7. Install the upper arm with the adjusting shims in the same position and the same number as they were before removal. Tighten the bolts to 72 ft. lbs. (98 Nm).

8. Install the upper ball joint to the arm and tighten the bolts to 20 ft. lbs. (26 Nm). Raise the jack under the lower arm enough to connect the ball joint to the steering knuckle. Tighten the mounting nut to 80 ft. lbs. (108 Nm) and install a new cotter pin.

9. Install the caliper and wheels. Lower the truck and bounce it several times to set the suspension. Tighten the upper control arm shaft bolts to 93 ft, lbs. (126 Nm).

1986-88 Pick-Up and 4Runner—4WD

1. Raise the truck and support it on safety stands. Remove the wheels.
2. Remove the torsion bar spring.
3. Remove the cotter pin and nut and press the upper ball joint out of the steering knuckle.
4. Remove the upper shock absorber mounting nut.
5. Disconnect the intermediate shaft from the steering gear housing. Remove the 2 nuts and bolt and lift out the upper arm.

To install:

6. Install the upper arm and tighten the mounting bolts to 111 ft. lbs. (150 Nm).

7. Connect the intermediate shaft to the steering gear housing.
8. Install a new upper shock absorber nut.
9. Connect the upper ball joint to the steering knuckle and tighten the nut to 105 ft. lbs. (142 Nm). Install a new cotter pin.
10. Install the torsion bar spring and check the alignment.

Lower Control Arm

REMOVAL & INSTALLATION

1970-88 Pick-Up—2WD

1. Raise the truck and support it on safety stands. Remove the wheels.
2. On 1970–78 models, remove the coil spring. On 1979–88 models, remove the torsion bar spring.
3. Remove the stabilizer bar and the strut bar from the lower arm.
4. On 1979–88 models, remove the shock absorber.
5. Unbolt and remove lower ball joint.

➡️If the lower ball joint is not to be replaced, simply unbolt it from the lower control arm. It is not necessary to separate the ball joint from the steering knuckle.

6. On 1970–78 models, unbolt and remove the lower control arm at the 4 bolts mounting the lower control arm on the frame. On 1979–88 models, unbolt and remove the nut from the lower arm shaft. Remove the nut from the lower arm shaft. Remove the spring torque arm from the other side.

7. Remove the lower control arm.

To install:

8. Tighten the bolt(s) holding the lower control arm to the frame but do not torque them until the vehicle is on level ground.

9. Lower the truck and torque the lower arm mounting bolt(s) to the following values:
   - 1970–78: 33–43 ft. lbs.
   - 1979–88: 145–217 ft. lbs.

✳✳ CAUTION

Do not tighten the control arm bolts fully until the vehicle is lowered. If the bolts are tightened with the control arm(s) hanging, excessive bushing wear will result.

1986-8 Pick-Up and 4Runner—4WD

1. Raise the front of the truck and support it with safety stands. Remove the wheels.
2. Remove the shock absorber.

3. Disconnect the stabilizer bar at the lower arm.
4. Disconnect the lower ball joint from the control arm.
5. Paint matchmarks on the front and rear adjusting cams, remove them and lift out the control arm.

To install:

6. Install the lower arm and adjusting cams to the frame. Temporarily tighten the nuts.

7. Connect the ball joint to the arm. Tighten the nut to 105 ft. lbs. (142 Nm) and install a new cotter pin.

8. Connect the stabilizer bar and tighten the nuts to 19 ft. lbs. (25 Nm).
9. Install the shock absorber.
10. Install the wheels and lower the truck. Bounce the truck several times to set the suspension.

11. Align the matchmarks on the adjusting cams and tighten the nuts to 203 ft. lbs. (275 Nm).
12. Check the alignment.

Steering Knuckle And Spindle

REMOVAL & INSTALLATION

1970-78 Pick-Up—2WD

➡️It will be necessary to obtain a spring compressor for installation.

1. Raise the front of the vehicle and support on stands.
2. Remove wheel.
3. If vehicle has front disc brakes, remove brake caliper.
4. Remove axle hub dust cap. Remove cotter key, lock, front nut and front nut washer from axle hub. Remove front bearing and remove brake disc or drum.
5. On drum brakes, remove brake line and plug.
6. Remove cotter keys and 4 bolts holding the brake backing plate and brake shoes on drum and the rotor dust cover on disk brakes. Remove the plate or cover.
7. Remove steering link from back of knuckle.
8. Support the lower arm with a jack and raise to put pressure on spring.

✳✳ CAUTION

Be careful not to unbalance vehicle support stands when jacking up lower arm.

9. Remove cotter key and large lower ball joint nut and separate the ball joint from the steering knuckle with a gear puller.
10. Repeat Step 9 on upper ball joint.

➡️Do not let the steering knuckle fall after removing upper ball joint.

11. Use a spring compressor when reassembling. Observe the following torques:
   - Large nut on upper ball joint: 66–94 ft. lbs.
   - Large nut on lower ball joint: 87–123 ft. lbs.
   - Rotor dust cover or drum backing plate to steering knuckle: 66–99 ft. lbs.
12. Bleed the brake system and refill the master cylinder.

1979-88 Pick-Up—2WD

▶ See Figure 45

1. Raise the front of the truck and support with safety stands. Remove the wheels.
2. Remove the front axle hub. Remove the brake caliper.
3. Remove the 2 cotter pins and bolts and remove the dust cover.
4. Disconnect the knuckle arm from the steering knuckle.
5. Position a floor jack under the lower control arm and remove the 2 cotter pins and nuts attaching the knuckle to the ball joints.
6. Press the upper and lower ball joints out of the steering knuckle.
7. Remove the steering knuckle.

To install:

8. Install the steering knuckle into the 2 ball joints and tighten the upper nut to 80 ft. lbs. (108 Nm). Tighten the lower nut to 105 ft. lbs. (142 Nm). Install new cotter pins.

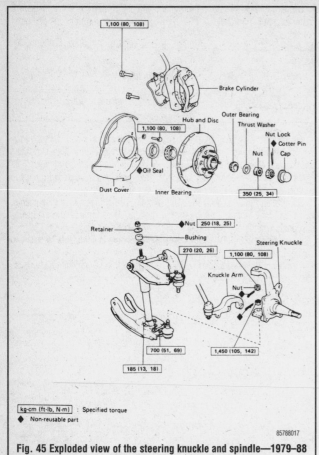

Fig. 45 Exploded view of the steering knuckle and spindle—1979–88 2WD Pick-Up

9. Install the knuckle arm and dust cover. Tighten the bolts to 80 ft. lbs. (108 Nm) and secure them with new cotter pins.

10. Install the front axle hub and brake caliper.

11. Install the wheels, lower the truck and check the alignment.

1970–85 Pick-Up—4WD

Steering knuckle and spindle removal and installation procedures for these models are detailed under "Axleshaft, Hub, Bearing and Seal" located in Section 7 of this manual.

1986–88 Pick-Up and 4Runner—4WD

▶ **See Figure 46**

1. Raise the front of the truck and support it on safety stands. Remove the wheels.

2. Remove the brake caliper. Remove the front axle hub.

3. Remove the dust cover and oil seal.

4. Disconnect the knuckle arm at the steering knuckle.

5. Disconnect the shock absorber at the lower control arm.

6. Disconnect the stabilizer bar at the lower control arm.

7. Remove the snapring and spacer from the end of the knuckle spindle.

8. Remove the cotter pin and nut from the upper ball joint and disconnect it from the knuckle.

9. Remove the 4 bolts and disconnect the lower ball joint from the knuckle.

10. Press down on the lower control arm and lift out the steering knuckle.

To install:

11. Coat the splines of the axleshaft with grease, press down on the lower control arm and slide the knuckle over the axleshaft and into position.

12. Connect the lower ball joint to the knuckle and tighten the 4 bolts to 43 ft. lbs. (58 Nm).

13. Connect the upper ball joint to the knuckle and tighten the nut to 105 ft. lbs. (142 Nm). Install a new cotter pin.

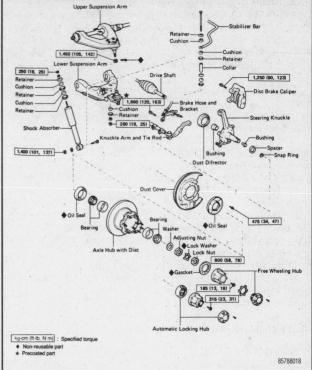

Fig. 46 Exploded view of the steering knuckle and spindle—1986–88 4WD Pick-Up and 4Runner

14. Install the spacer and snapring to the end of the axleshaft.

15. Connect the stabilizer bar and the shock absorber to the lower arm.

16. Connect the knuckle arm to the steering knuckle and tighten the bolt to 120 ft. lbs. (163 Nm).

17. Install the dust cover with a new oil seal and tighten the bolt to 34 ft. lbs. (47 Nm).

18. Install the front axle hub and brake caliper.

19. Install the wheels, lower the truck and bleed the brakes.

Land Cruiser

1. Complete front axleshaft removal procedures in drive axle section, above.

2. Unbolt and remove the tie rod from the knuckle arm with a gear puller.

3. Remove the oil seal retainer at the back of the steering knuckle.

4. Remove the 4 nuts on the top steering knuckle cap along with the cone washers. See section on axleshaft removal for procedures in removing cone washers.

5. Remove the 4 nuts on the bottom steering knuckle cap along with cone washers.

6. Using a small drift and hammer, tap the knuckle bearing caps out from inside the steering knuckle.

➡ **Do not tap on the bearings! Do not mix or lose the upper and lower bearing cap shims.**

7. To test the knuckle bearing preload, attach a spring scale to the end hole in the steering knuckle at a right angle to the arm. The force required to move the knuckle from side to side should be 4–5 lbs. If the preload is not correct, adjust by replacing shims.

Front Axle Hub and Bearing

REMOVAL & INSTALLATION

2WD Pick-Up

1. Raise the front of the truck and support with safety stands. Remove the wheels.

2. Remove the brake caliper and suspend it with wire, out of the way. Remove the caliper torque plate.

3. Remove the axle end cap and then remove the cotter pin, nut lock and nut.

4. Pull the hub/disc assembly off the spindle with the outer bearing. Don't let the bearing fall out!

5. Pry the inner oil seal out and remove the inner bearing from the hub.

To install:

6. Clean the bearings and outer races and inspect them for wear or cracks.

7. Using a brass drift and a hammer, drive out the bearing outer race. Press a new one into position.

8. Pack the bearings with grease until it oozes out the other side. Coat the inside of the hub and cap with grease.

9. Position the inner bearing into the hub, coat the oil seal with grease and press it into the hub.

10. Press the hub assembly onto the spindle and install the outer bearing and thrust washer.

11. Install the hub nut and tighten it to 25 ft. lbs. (34 Nm). Turn the hub a few times to seat the bearings and then loosen the nut until there is 0.5–1.0mm axial play. Using a spring tension gauge, check that the preload is 1.3–4.0 lbs.

12. Install the locknut, new cotter pin and hub grease cap.

13. Install the brake torque plate to the knuckle and tighten the bolts to 80 ft. lbs. (108 Nm). Install the brake caliper and tighten the bolts to 65 ft. lbs. (88 Nm).

14. Install the wheels and lower the truck.

4WD Pick-Up, 4Runner and Land Cruiser

Hub and bearing removal and installation procedures for these models are detailed in the "Front Drive Axle" in Section 7 of this manual.

Front End Alignment

➡ **See Figures 47, 48 and 49**

Alignment should only be performed after it has been verified that all parts of the steering and suspension systems are in good operating condition. The truck must be empty. The tires must be cold and inflated to the correct pressure and the test surface must be level and horizontal.

Because special, elaborate equipment is required for proper front end alignment, it is recommended that the truck be taken to a reputable alignment

CASTER

Caster is the tilt of the front steering axis either forward or backward away from the front of the vehicle.

Caster on 1970–85 4WD Pick-Ups and all Land Cruisers is not adjustable. If caster is out of specification on these models, check for worn or damaged suspension parts.

Caster on 1986–88 4WD Pick-Ups and 4Runners is adjustable by means of cam bolts on the lower control arms.

Caster on all 2WD models is adjustable by adding or subtracting shims at the upper control arm shaft

CAMBER

Camber is the slope of the front wheels from the vertical when viewed from the front of the vehicle. When the wheels tile outward at the top, the camber is positive (+). When the wheels tile inward at the top, the camber is negative (–). The amount of positive and negative camber is measured in degrees from the vertical and the measurement is called camber angle.

Camber on 1970–85 4WD Pick-Ups and all Land Cruisers is not adjustable. If camber is out of specification on these models, check for worn or damaged suspension parts.

Camber on 1986–88 4WD Pick-Ups and 4Runners is adjustable by means of cam bolts on the lower control arms.

Camber on all 2WD models is adjustable by adding or subtracting shims at the upper control arm shaft

TOE

Toe is the amount measured in a fraction of an inch, that the front wheels are closer together at one end than the other. Toe-in means that the front wheels are closer together at the front of the tire than at the rear; toe-out means that the rear of the tires are closer together than the front.

Although it is recommended that this adjustment be made by your dealer or a qualified shop, you can make it yourself if you make very careful measurement. The wheels must be dead straight ahead. The truck must have a full tank of gas, all fluids must be at their proper levels, all other suspension and steering adjustments must be correct and the tires must be properly inflated to their cold specification.

1. Toe can be determined by measuring the distance between the centers of the tire treads, at the front of the tire and the rear. If the tread pattern of your truck's tires makes this impossible, you can measure between the edges of the wheel rims, but be sure to move the truck and measure in a few places to avoid errors caused by bent rims or wheel runout.

2. If the measurement is not within specifications loosen the retaining clamp locknuts on the adjustable tie rods.

3. Turn the left and right tie rods EQUAL amounts until the measurements are within specifications.

4. Tighten the lock bolts and then recheck the measurements. Check to see that the steering wheel is still in the proper position. If not, remove it and reposition it as detailed later in this section.

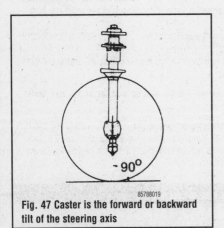

Fig. 47 Caster is the forward or backward tilt of the steering axis

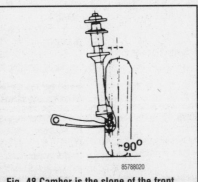

Fig. 48 Camber is the slope of the front wheels when viewed from the front of the truck

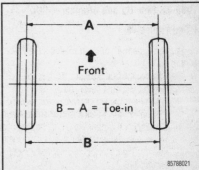

Fig. 49 When the front of the tires are closer together than the rear of the tires, you have toe-in

Wheel Alignment Specifications

Year	Model	Caster Range (deg)	Caster Preferred Setting (deg)	Camber Range (deg)	Camber Preferred Setting (deg)		Toe-in (in.)
1970	Pick-Up	—	⅓N	—	1P	¼	—
1971	Pick-Up	—	⅓N	—	1P	¼	—
	Land Cruiser	½P–1½P	1P	½P–1½P	1P	0.12–0.21	9½
1972	Pick-Up	1¼N–¼P	½N	¼P–1¾P	1P	3/16	7¼
	Land Cruiser	½P–1½P	1P	½P–1½P	1P	0.12–0.21	9½
1973	Pick-Up	1¼N–¼P	½N	¼P–1¾P	1P	3/16	7¼
	Land Cruiser	½P–1½P	1P	½P–1½P	1P	0.12–0.21	9½
1974	Pick-Up	1¼N–¼P	½N	¼P–1¾P	1P	3/16	7¼
	Land Cruiser	½P–1½P	1P	½P–1½P	1P	0.12–0.21	9½
1975	Pick-Up	0–1P	½P	½P–1½P	1P	0.24	—
	Land Cruiser	½P–1½P	1P	½P–1½P	1P	0.12–0.21	9½
1976	Pick-Up	0–1P	½P	½P–1½P	1P	0.24	—
	Land Cruiser	½P–1½P	1P	½P–1½P	1P	0.12–0.21	9½
1977	Pick-Up	0–1P	½P	½P–1½P	1P	0.24	—
	Land Cruiser	½P–1½P	1P	½P–1½P	1P	0.12–0.21	9½
1978	Pick-Up	0–1P	½P	½P–1½P	1P	0.24	—
	Land Cruiser	½P–1½P	1P	½P–1½P	1P	0.12–0.21	9½
1979	Pick-Up (2 wd)	½N–½P	0	½N–½P	0	①	7
	(4 wd)	—	3½P	—	1P	①	—
	Land Cruiser	½P–1½P	1P	½P–1½P	1P	②	9½
1980	Pick-Up (2 wd)	½N–½P	0	½N–½P	0	①	7
	(4 wd)	—	3½P	—	1P	①	—
	Land Cruiser	½P–1½P	1P	½P–1½P	1P	②	9½
1981	Pick-Up (2 wd)	½N–½P	0	½N–½P	0	①	7
	(4 wd)	—	3½P	—	1P	①	—
	Land Cruiser	½P–1½P	1P	½P–1½P	1P	②	9½
1982	Pick-Up (2 wd)	½N–½P	0	½N–½P	0	①	7
	(4 wd)	—	3½P	—	1P	①	—
	Land Cruiser	½P–1½P	1P	½P–1½P	1P	②	9½

85788C01

Wheel Alignment Specifications (cont.)

Year	Model	Caster Range (deg)	Caster Preferred Setting (deg)	Camber Range (deg)	Camber Preferred Setting (deg)		Toe-in (in.)
1983	Pick-Up (2 wd Short)	¼P–1¾P	1P	½N–½P	1P	①	7⅙
	(2 wd Long)	¼N–1¼P	½P	0–1P	½P	①	7⅙
	(4 wd)	2¾P–4¼P	3½P	¼P–1¾P	¾P	③	9½
	Land Cruiser	½P–1½P	1P	½P–1½P	1P	②	9½
1984	Pick-Up (2 wd Short)	¼P–1¾P	1P	½N–½P	1P	①	7⅙
	(2 wd Long)	¼N–1¼P	½P	0–1P	½P	①	7⅙
	(4 wd)	2¾P–4¼P	3½P	¼P–1¾P	¾P	③	9½
	Land Cruiser	½P–1½P	1P	½P–1½P	1P	②	9½
1985	Pick-Up (2 wd Short)	1/12N–5/12P	⅔P	¼N–1¼P	½P	③	10
	(2 wd Long)	5/12P–1 11/12P	1⅙P	¼N–1¼P	½P	0.08–0.16	10
	(4 wd)	1¼P–2¼P	1¾P	¼P–1¾P	¾P	③	12
	Land Cruiser	¼P–1¾P	1P	¼P–1¾P	1P	③	9½
1986	Pick-Up (2 wd Short)	1/12N–1 5/12P	⅔P	¼N–1¼P	½P	③	10
	(2 wd Long)	5/12P–1 11/12P	1⅙P	¼N–1¼P	½P	④	10
	(4 wd)	¾P–2¼P	1½P	1/12N–1 5/12P	⅔P	③	12
	Land Cruiser	¼P–1¾P	1P	¼P–1¾P	1P	③	9½
1987	Pick-Up (2 wd Short)	1/12N–1 5/12P	⅔P	¼N–1¼P	½P	③	10
	(2 wd Long)	5/12P–1 11/12P	1⅙P	¼N–1¼P	½P	④	10
	(4 wd)	¾P–2¼P	1½P	1/12N–1 5/12P	⅔P	③	12
	Land Cruiser	¼P–1¾P	1P	¼P–1¾P	1P	③	9½
1988	Pick-Up (2 wd Short)	1/12N–1 5/12P	⅔P	¼N–1¼P	½P	③	10
	(2 wd Long)	5/12P–1 11/12P	1⅙P	¼N–1¼P	½P	④	10
	(4 wd)	¾P–2¼P	1½P	1/12N–1 5/12P	⅔P	③	12
	Land Cruiser	¼P–1¾P	1P	¼P–1¾P	1P	③	9½

① Bias: 0.16–0.24
Radial: 0.04–0.12
② Bias: 0.10–0.20
Radial: 0.04 out 0.04 in.
③ Bias: 0.12–0.20
Radial: 0–0.08
④ Bias: 0.20–0.28
Radial: 0.08–0.16

85788C1A

REAR SUSPENSION

Leaf Springs

REMOVAL & INSTALLATION

▶ **See Figures 50 and 51**

1. Loosen the rear wheel lug nuts.
2. Raise the rear of the vehicle. Support the frame and rear axle housing with stands.
3. Remove the lug nuts and the wheel.
4. Remove the cotter pin, nut, and washer from the lower end of the shock absorber.
5. On the Land Cruiser, perform the following:
   a. Remove the cotter pins and nuts from the lower end of the stabilizer link.
   b. Detach the link from the axle housing.
6. Detach the shock absorber from the spring seat pivot pin.
7. Remove the parking brake cable clamp (except Land Cruiser).

➡**Remove the parking brake equalizer, if necessary.**

8. Unfasten the U-bolt nuts and remove the spring seat assemblies.
9. Adjust the height of the rear axle housing so that the weight of the rear axle is removed from the rear springs.
10. Unfasten the spring shackle retaining nuts. Withdraw the spring shackle inner plate. Carefully pry out the spring shackle with a bar.
11. Remove the spring bracket pin from the front end of the spring hanger and remove the rubber bushing.
12. Remove the spring.

✳✳ CAUTION

Use care not to damage the hydraulic brake line or the parking brake cable.

To install:
13. Install the rubber bushing in the eye of the spring.
14. Align the eye of the spring with the spring hanger bracket and drive the pin through the bracket holes and rubber bushings.

➡**Use soapy water as lubricant, if necessary, to aid in pin installation. Never use oil or grease.**

15. Finger-tighten the spring hanger nuts and/or bolts.
16. Install the rubber bushing in the spring eye at the opposite end of the spring.

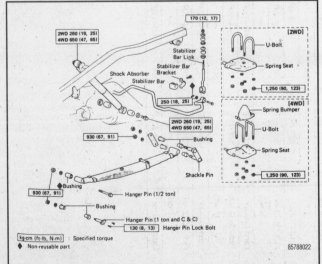

Fig. 50 Exploded view of the rear suspension—Pick-Up and 4Runner

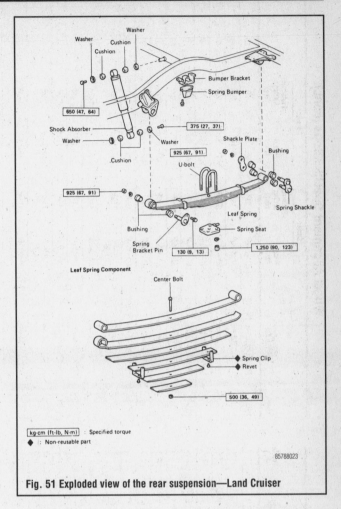

Fig. 51 Exploded view of the rear suspension—Land Cruiser

17. Raise the free end of the spring. Install the spring shackle through the bushing and the bracket.
18. Install the shackle inner plate and finger-tighten the retaining nuts.
19. Center the bolt head in the hole which is provided in the spring seat on the axle housing.
20. Fit the U-bolts over the axle housing. Install the lower spring seat. Install the spring bumper on later 4WD models.
21. Tighten the U-bolt nuts to 90 ft. lbs. (123 Nm).

➡**Some models have 2 sets of nuts, while others have a nut and lock-washer. Be sure that the exposed thread of the U-bolt is the same length on all U-bolt ends.**

22. Install the parking brake cable clamp. Install the equalizer, if it was removed.
23. Pick-Up, 4Runner and Land Cruiser:
   a. Raise the rear axle with the jack so that the stands no longer support the frame.
   b. Tighten the hanger pin and shackle nuts.
   c. Install the shock absorber bushings and washers. Tighten, and install the cotter pins.
   d. Install the stabilizer link and hand tighten its retaining nuts (Land Cruiser).
   e. Install the wheels, remove the stands, and lower the vehicle to the ground.
24. Bounce the truck several times to set the suspension and then tighten the shock absorber bolt. Tighten the hanger pin and shackle pin to 67 ft. lbs. (91 Nm).

Shock Absorbers

REMOVAL & INSTALLATION

1. Jack up the rear of the vehicle.
2. Support the rear axle housing with jackstands.
3. Unfasten the upper shock absorber retaining nuts and/or bolts from the upper frame member.
4. Depending upon the type of rear spring used, either disconnect the lower end of the shock absorber from the spring seat, or the rear axle housing, by removing its cotter pins, nuts and/or bolts.
5. Remove the shock absorber. Inspect the shock for wear, leaks, or other signs of damage.
   To install:
6. Install the shock absorber and tighten the bolts to 19 ft. lbs. (25 Nm) on 2WD models; 47 ft. lbs. (64 Nm) on 4WD Pick-Ups and 4Runners. On the Land Cruiser, tighten the upper bolt to 47 ft. lbs. (64 Nm) and the lower bolt to 27 ft. lbs. (37 Nm).

STEERING

Steering Wheel

REMOVAL & INSTALLATION

▶ See Figures 52, 53, 54, 55 and 56

Three Spoke

✲✲ CAUTION

Do not attempt to remove or install the steering wheel by hammering on it. Damage to the energy absorbing steering column could result.

1. Position the wheels in the straight ahead position.
2. Disconnect the horn and turn signal connectors at the bottom of the steering column shroud.
3. Loosen the trim pad retaining screws from the back of the steering wheel.
4. Lift the trim pad and horn button assembly from the wheel.
5. Remove the steering wheel hub retaining nut.
6. Scribe matchmarks on the hub and the steering shaft to aid in proper installation.
7. Grasp the steering wheel with both hands and firmly pull it off the column.

➡**If the wheel cannot be pulled off with your hands, use a steering wheel puller.**

8. Tighten the steering wheel hub retaining nut to 15–22 ft. lbs.

Four Spoke

✲✲ CAUTION

Do not attempt to remove or install the steering wheel by hammering on it. Damage to the energy absorbing steering column could result.

1. Position the wheels in the straight ahead position.
2. Disconnect the horn and turn signal connectors at the bottom of the steering column shroud.
3. Remove the plastic center insert on the steering wheel pad. Some models will require a small prybar to pry the insert out. On other models, remove the wheel pad screws on the back of the wheel and pull the pad off.
4. Remove the steering wheel retaining nut.
5. Scribe matchmarks on the hub and the steering shaft to aid in proper installation.
6. Grasp the steering wheel with both hands and firmly pull if off the shaft.

Stabilizer Bar

REMOVAL & INSTALLATION

1. Raise the truck and support it with safety stands.
2. Disconnect the stabilizer bar link at the body. Remove the retainer and cushion from the link.
3. Disconnect the stabilizer bar bracket and cushion from the axle housing.
4. Remove the stabilizer bar.
   To install:
5. Position the stabilizer bar at the axle housing and install the bracket and cushion. Tighten the mounting bolts to 8 ft. lbs. (11 Nm).
6. Install the link to the body with the retainers and cushion. Tighten the mounting bolts to 12 ft. lbs. (17 Nm).
7. Lower the truck.

➡**If the wheel cannot be pulled off with your hands, use a steering wheel puller.**

7. Tighten the steering wheel retaining nut to 22–28 ft. lbs.

Two Spoke

✲✲ CAUTION

Do not attempt to remove or install the steering wheel by hammering on it. Damage to the energy absorbing steering column could result.

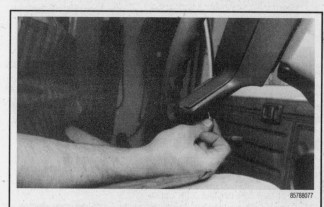

Fig. 52 Removing the horn pad screws

Fig. 53 Removing the horn assembly screws

Fig. 54 Mark the steering wheel before removal

Fig. 55 Removing the steering wheel with puller type tool

Fig. 56 Installing the steering wheel—always torque the retaining nut

1. Position the front wheels in the straight ahead position.
2. Disconnect the horn and turn signal connectors at the bottom of the steering column shroud.
3. Carefully pry off the steering wheel center pad. Some models utilize a mounting screw at the bottom of the pad. Remove the screw and pull the pad out.
4. Remove the steering wheel center nut.
5. Scribe matchmarks on the hub and the steering shaft to aid in proper installation.
6. Using a steering wheel puller, remove the wheel.
7. Torque the retaining nut to 22–28 ft. lbs.

Combination Switch

→On some earlier models, the combination switch may only be the turn signal switch. Removal and installation procedures are the same for both.

REMOVAL & INSTALLATION

1. Disconnect the negative battery cable.
2. Unscrew the two retaining bolts and remove the steering column garnish.
3. Remove the upper and lower steering column covers.
4. Remove the steering wheel as detailed previously.
5. Trace the switch wiring harness to the multi-connector. Push in the lock levers and pull apart the connector.
6. Unscrew the 4 mounting screws and remove the switch.
7. Installation is the reverse of the removal procedure.

Ignition Lock/Switch

REMOVAL & INSTALLATION

▶ **See Figure 57**

1. Disconnect the negative battery cable.
2. Unscrew the retaining screws and remove the upper and lower steering column covers.

3. Unscrew the 2 retaining screws and remove the steering column garnish.
4. Turn the ignition key to the **ACC** position.
5. Push the lock cylinder stop in with a small, round object (cotter pin, punch etc.) and pull out the ignition key and the lock cylinder.

→You may find that removing the steering wheel and the combination switch will facilitate easier removal.

6. Withdraw the lock cylinder from the lock housing while depressing the lock tab.
7. To remove the ignition switch, unfasten its securing screws and withdraw the switch from the lock housing.

To install:

8. Align the locking cam with the hole in the ignition switch and insert the switch into the lock housing.
9. Secure the switch with its screws.
10. Make sure that both the lock cylinder and the column lock are in the **ACC** position. Slide the cylinder into the lock housing until the stop tab engages the hole in the lock.
11. Install the steering column garnish and the upper and lower column covers.
12. Connect the negative battery cable.

Steering Linkage

REMOVAL & INSTALLATION

1970–78 Pick-Up—2WD

▶ **See Figures 58 and 59**

1. Raise the front of the vehicle and support it with jackstands.
2. Remove the front wheels.
3. Remove the nut on the pitman arm and using a puller remove it from the steering sector shaft.
4. Unfasten the idler arm support securing bolts and remove the support from the frame.
5. Remove the castle nuts and cotter pins from the tie rod ends and separate them from the steering knuckle arms with a puller.

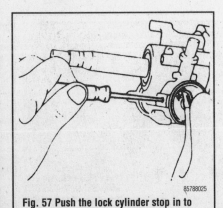

Fig. 57 Push the lock cylinder stop in to remove the cylinder

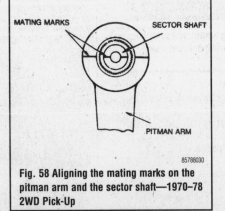

MATING MARKS   SECTOR SHAFT

PITMAN ARM

Fig. 58 Aligning the mating marks on the pitman arm and the sector shaft—1970–78 2WD Pick-Up

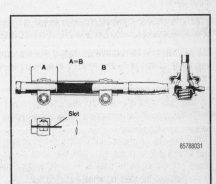

Fig. 59 Adjust the tie-rod ends equally within the tube and the clamp bolt at the tube slot—1970–78 2WD Pick-Up

6. Remove the relay rod complete with the tie rods, pitman arm and idler arm.

To install:

7. Align the marks on the pitman arm and sector shaft before installing the pitman arm.

8. Torque all of the following to 55–79 ft. lbs.: tie rod ends to steering knuckles and relay rod; relay rod to pitman arm. Torque the relay rod to the idler arm to 37–50 ft. lbs. Torque the pitman arm to the sector shaft to 80–90 ft. lbs.

1979–88 Pick-Up—2WD

▶ See Figures 60 thru 71

➡Before working on any of the following steering linkage components, disconnect the battery cable, raise the front of the truck and support it with safety stands.

PITMAN ARM

1. Remove the strut bar.
2. Loosen the pitman arm nut.
3. Using a tie rod end puller or the like, disconnect the pitman arm from the sector shaft.
4. Using a tie rod end puller or the like, disconnect the pitman arm from the relay rod.

To install:

5. Align the marks on the pitman arm and sector shaft and connect them. Tighten the nut to 90 ft. lbs. (123 Nm).

6. Connect the arm to the relay rod and tighten the nut to 67 ft. lbs. (90 Nm).

7. Install the strut bar.

Fig. 60 View of the shimmy damper retaining nut

Fig. 61 Removing the shimmy damper retaining nut

Fig. 62 Removing the shimmy damper with puller type tool

Fig. 63 Removing the shimmy damper assembly

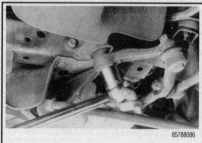

Fig. 64 Removing the pitman arm nut

Fig. 65 Removing the pitman arm with puller tool—matchmark before removal

Fig. 66 Removing the cotter pin from linkage (typical)

Fig. 67 Removing the steering linkage nut

Fig. 68 Removing the steering linkage from idler arm with puller tool

Fig. 69 View of the steering linkage removed from idler arm

Fig. 70 Removing the idler arm from the vehicle

Fig. 71 Removing the idler arm mounting bolts

TIE ROD

▶ **See Figures 72 thru 80**

1. Using a tie rod end puller, disconnect the tie rod from the relay rod.
2. Using a tie rod end puller, disconnect the tie rod from the knuckle arm.
3. Remove the tie rod and remove the tie rod ends.

To install:

4. Screw the tie rod ends onto the tie rod. The tie rod length should be approximately 314.5mm. The remaining length of threads on both ends should always be equal.
5. Turn the tie rod ends so they cross at about 90°. Tighten the clamp nuts to 19 ft. lbs. (25 Nm).
6. Connect the tie rod to the knuckle arm and relay rod and tighten the mounting nuts to 67 ft. lbs. (90 Nm).

RELAY ROD

1. Disconnect the tie rod ends from the relay rod.
2. Using a tie rod end puller, disconnect the pitman arm from the relay rod.
3. Using a tie rod end puller, disconnect the idler arm from the relay rod.
4. Remove the rod and inspect it for cracks or other damage.

To install:

5. Connect the relay rod to the idler arm to the relay rod and tighten the nut 43 ft. lbs. (59 Nm).
6. Connect the relay rod to the pitman arm and tighten the nut to 67 ft. lbs. (90 Nm).
7. Connect the tie rod ends to the relay rod and tighten the nuts to 67 ft. lbs. (90 Nm).

KNUCKLE ARM

1. Remove the front axle hub.
2. Disconnect the tie rod at the knuckle arm and remove the arm.
3. Inspect the arm for cracks or other damage.

To install:

4. Install the arm to the steering knuckle and tighten the nut to 80 ft. lbs. (108 Nm).
5. Connect the tie rod to the knuckle arm and tighten the nut to 67 ft. lbs. (90 Nm).
6. Install the front axle hub.

STEERING DAMPER

1. Disconnect the steering damper at the relay rod.
2. Disconnect the damper at the frame and remove the damper with all washers and cushions.

To install:

3. Install the damper to the frame bracket and tighten the nut to 9 ft. lbs. (13 Nm).
4. Connect the other end of the steering damper to the relay rod and tighten the nut to 43 ft. lbs. (59 Nm).

IDLER ARM BRACKET

1. Disconnect the relay rod from the idler arm.
2. Remove the 3 mounting bolts and remove the idler arm bracket with the arm attached.

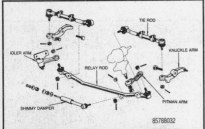

Fig. 72 Steering gear linkage—1979–88 2WD Pick-Up

Fig. 73 Measure the exposed thread before removing the tie-rod end

Fig. 74 View of the exposed thread on the tie-rod end

Fig. 75 Removing the tie-rod end

Fig. 76 Removing the tie-rod from the tube

Fig. 77 Lube the threads before installing the tie-rod end

Fig. 78 Installing the tie-rod in the tube

Fig. 79 Align the tie-rod tube after installation

Fig. 80 Setting the toe adjustment—after installing the tie-rod end

To install:

3. Position the bracket and arm on the frame and tighten the bolts to 48 ft. lbs. (65 Nm).

4. Connect the idler arm to the relay rod and tighten the nut to 43 ft. lbs. (59 Nm).

1970–85 Pick-Up—4WD

▶ **See Figure 81**

1. Jack up the vehicle and support it on stands.
2. Remove the front wheels.
3. Remove cotter pin and nut from the shimmy damper at the tie rod and remove shimmy damper from the tie rod with a puller. Remove the locknut from the other end of the damper. Be sure to note the order of the rubber spacers and washers, and remove damper.
4. Repeat the above procedure where the tie rod ends connect to the steering knuckles. Remove the tie rod.
5. To remove the drag link, remove the cotter pin from the steering knuckle end of the drag, and, using a screwdriver, unscrew the cap at the end of the link.

➡The cap may be tight, so you may have to use a wrench or pliers to turn the screwdriver.

6. When the cap is removed, you should be able to dislodge the spring seat, spring and outer socket holder inside the drag link by working the steering knuckle back and forth. The steering knuckle socket in the drag link can now be removed.

➡Be sure to note the order in which the spring seat, spring and outer socket come out of the drag ling. Their order will be reversed on the side of the drag link that attaches to the pitman arm

7. Repeat Steps 5 and 6 on the pitman arm side of the drag link.
8. Be sure to insert the assemblies in the drag link in their correct orders. On drag links, screw on the caps completely then loosen them 1⅓ turns.

Observe the following torques:
- Shimmy damper-to-axle housing mount: 8–11 ft. lbs.
- Tie rod end-to-steering knuckle arm: 55–79 ft. lbs.
- Shimmy damper-to-tie rod end: 37–50 ft. lbs.

➡Be sure to grease the drag link ends at their grease nipples, and, when installing the drag link end caps, tighten them completely and then loosen them 1⅓ turns.

1986–88 Pick-Up and 4Runner—4WD

➡Before working on any of the following steering linkage components, disconnect the battery cable, raise the front of the truck and support it with safety stands.

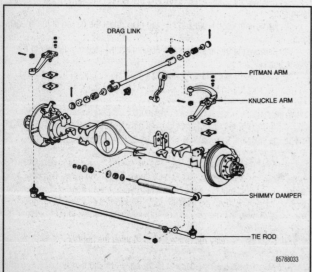

Fig. 81 Steering gear linkage—1970–85 4WD Pick-Up

PITMAN ARM

1. Remove the pitman arm set nut and washer.
2. Using a tie rod end puller or the like, disconnect the pitman arm from the sector shaft.
3. Using a tie rod end puller or the like, disconnect the pitman arm from the relay rod.

To install:

4. Align the marks on the pitman arm and sector shaft and connect them. Tighten the nut to 130 ft. lbs. (177 Nm).
5. Connect the arm to the relay rod and tighten the nut to 67 ft. lbs. (90 Nm). Install a new cotter pin.

TIE ROD

▶ **See Figures 82 and 83**

1. Using a tie rod end puller, disconnect the tie rod from the relay rod.
2. Using a tie rod end puller, disconnect the tie rod from the knuckle arm.
3. Remove the tie rod and remove the tie rod ends.

To install:

4. Screw the tie rod ends onto the tie rod. The tie rod length should be approximately 12.38 (314.5mm). The remaining length of threads on both ends should always be equal.
5. Turn the tie rod ends so they cross at about 90°. Tighten the clamp nuts to 19 ft. lbs. (25 Nm).
6. Connect the tie rod to the knuckle arm and relay rod and tighten the mounting nuts to 67 ft. lbs. (90 Nm).

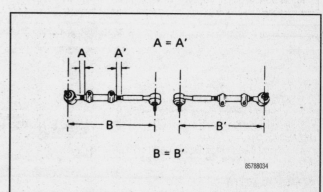

Fig. 82 Measuring the tie-rods—1986–88 4WD Pick-Up and 4Runner

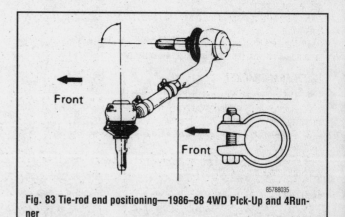

Fig. 83 Tie-rod end positioning—1986–88 4WD Pick-Up and 4Runner

RELAY ROD

▶ **See Figure 84**

1. Disconnect the tie rod ends from the relay rod.
2. Using a tie rod end puller, disconnect the pitman arm from the relay rod.
3. Using a tie rod end puller, disconnect the idler arm from the relay rod.
4. Remove the rod and inspect it for cracks or other damage.

5. Remove the cotter pin and set nut and then disconnect the steering damper from the relay rod.

6. Installation is the reverse of the removal procedure. Tighten the following components:

    a. Relay rod-to-idler arm nut 43 ft. lbs. (59 Nm), with a new cotter pin.

    b. Relay rod-to-pitman arm nut to 67 ft. lbs. (90 Nm). Use a new cotter pin.

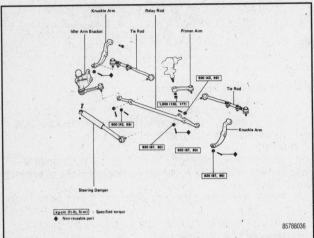

Fig. 84 Steering gear linkage—1986–88 4WD Pick-Up and 4Runner

    c. Tie rod ends-to-relay rod nuts to 67 ft. lbs. (90 Nm) with new cotter pins.

    d. Steering damper-to-relay rod nut to 43 ft. lbs. (50 Nm) with new cotter pins.

KNUCKLE ARM

1. Disconnect the tie rod at the knuckle arm and remove the arm.

2. Inspect the arm for cracks or other damage.

3. Install the arm to the steering knuckle and tighten the nut to 120 ft. lbs. (162 Nm).

4. Connect the tie rod to the knuckle arm and tighten the nut to 67 ft. lbs. (90 Nm).

STEERING DAMPER

1. Disconnect the steering damper at the relay rod.

2. Disconnect the damper at the frame and remove the damper with all washers and cushions.

3. Install the damper to the frame bracket and tighten the nut to 9 ft. lbs. (13 Nm).

4. Connect the other end of the steering damper to the relay rod and tighten the nut to 43 ft. lbs. (59 Nm). Install a new cotter pin.

IDLER ARM BRACKET

1. Disconnect the relay rod from the idler arm.

2. Remove the 3 mounting bolts and remove the idler arm bracket with the arm attached.

3. Position the bracket and arm on the frame and tighten the bolts to 70 ft. lbs. (95 Nm).

4. Connect the idler arm to the relay rod and tighten the nut to 43 ft. lbs. (59 Nm). Install a new cotter pin.

1971–83 Land Cruiser

▶ See Figure 85

1. Remove the hub caps and loosen the lug nuts.

2. Jack up the front of the vehicle and support it on jackstands. Remove the wheels.

3. Unfasten the pitman arm retaining nut.

4. Punch matchmarks on the pitman arm and the sector shaft to aid reinstallation.

5. Remove the pitman arm from the sector shaft with a puller.

6. Detach the drag link from the center arm with a tie rod puller. Remove the link together with the pitman arm.

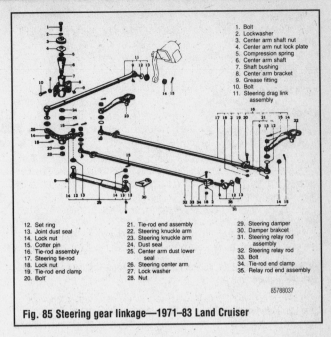

1. Bolt
2. Lockwasher
3. Center arm shaft nut
4. Center arm nut lock plate
5. Compression spring
6. Center arm shaft
7. Shaft bushing
8. Center arm bracket
9. Grease fitting
10. Bolt
11. Steering drag link assembly

12. Set ring	21. Tie-rod end assembly	29. Steering damper
13. Joint dust seal	22. Steering knuckle arm	30. Damper brakcet
14. Lock nut	23. Steering knuckle arm	31. Steering relay rod assembly
15. Cotter pin	24. Dust seal	32. Steering relay rod
16. Tie-rod assembly	25. Center arm dust lower seal	33. Bolt
17. Steering tie-rod	26. Steering center arm	34. Tie-rod end clamp
18. Lock nut	27. Lock washer	35. Relay rod end assembly
19. Tie-rod end clamp	28. Nut	
20. Bolt		

Fig. 85 Steering gear linkage—1971–83 Land Cruiser

7. Detach the tie rod ends from the steering knuckle arm with a puller.

8. Detach the relay rod ends from the center arm. Remove the tie rod/relay rod assembly.

9. Disconnect the end of the steering damper from its brackets on the front crossmember.

10. Remove the center arm attaching nut and use a puller to remove the arm, complete with damper.

11. Remove the skid plate and then remove the center arm bracket from the frame.

To install:

12. Installation is the reverse of removal.

13. Be sure to align the matchmarks, which were made during removal, on the pitman arm and the sector shaft. Tighten the mounting bolt to 120–140 ft. lbs.

14. Lubricate all of the rod ends and damper ends with multipurpose grease.

15. After the linkage is installed, adjust the toe-in to the proper specifications.

1984–88 Land Cruiser

▶ See Figure 86

1. Raise the truck and support it with safety stands. Remove the wheels.

2. Remove the cotter pin and nut and disconnect the relay rod at the pitman arm.

3. Remove the cotter pin and nut and disconnect the tie rod at the knuckle arm.

4. Remove the mounting nut and disconnect the steering damper at the frame bracket.

5. Remove the nut and disconnect the steering damper at the relay rod.

6. Remove the cotter pin and nut and disconnect the relay rod at the tie rod.

To install:

7. To replace the tie rod ends, loosen the clamp and remove the ends. Install the ends and turn them in so they are approximately 1207mm apart. Tighten the clamps.

8. To replace the relay rod ends, loosen the end clamps and remove the ends. Remove the cotter pin. Remove the plug, 2 ball stud seats, link joint knob, spring and spring seat. Coat the parts with grease, install them and tighten the plug completely. Loosen the plug 1-1⅓ turns and install a new cotter pin. Turn the rod ends onto the rod so they are 960mm apart. Tighten the clamp bolts to 33 ft. lbs. (44 Nm).

9. Connect the relay rod to the tie rod, tighten the nut to 67 ft. lbs. (90 Nm) and install a new cotter pin.

10. Connect the steering damper to the relay rod and tighten the nut to 54 ft. lbs. (74 Nm).

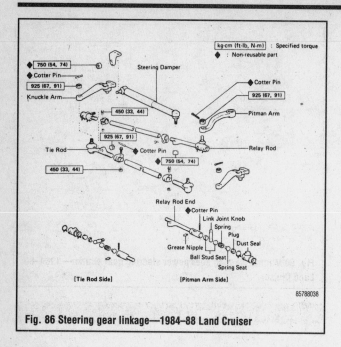

Fig. 86 Steering gear linkage—1984–88 Land Cruiser

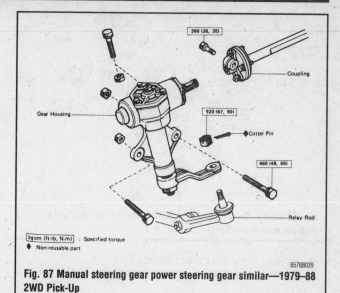

Fig. 87 Manual steering gear power steering gear similar—1979–88 2WD Pick-Up

11. Connect the damper to the frame bracket and tighten the nut to 54 ft. lbs. (74 Nm).

12. Connect the tie rod to the knuckle arm, tighten the nut to 67 ft. lbs. (90 Nm) and install a new cotter pin.

13. Connect the relay rod to the pitman arm, tighten the nut to 67 ft. lbs. (90 Nm) and install a new cotter pin.

14. Install the wheels and lower the truck.

Manual Steering Gear

ADJUSTMENTS

Adjustments to the manual steering gear are not necessary during normal service. Adjustments are performed only as part of overhaul.

REMOVAL & INSTALLATION

1970–78 Pick-Up—2WD

1. Remove the pitman arm from the sector shaft with a puller.
2. Matchmark the flexible coupling and the wormshaft and remove the lock bolt.
3. Unbolt and remove the steering gear housing.
4. Torque the housing bolts to 26–36 ft. lbs., and the pitman arm to 80–90 ft. lbs. Tighten the coupling yoke to 15–20 ft. lbs.

1979-88 Pick-Up—2WD

▶ See Figure 87

1. Remove the steering coupling set bolt where it connects to the worm shaft.
2. Disconnect the relay rod from the pitman arm.
3. Remove the 3 mounting bolts and lift out the steering gear housing.
4. Position the gear housing so that the worm shaft is lined up in the steering coupling and tighten the mounting bolts to 48 ft. lbs. (65 Nm).
5. Tighten the pitman arm mounting nut to 90 ft. lbs. (123 Nm).
6. Connect the pitman arm to the relay rod and tighten the nut to 67 ft. lbs. (90 Nm).
7. Tighten the coupling set bolt to 26 ft. lbs. (35 Nm).
8. Fill the gear housing with gear oil.

1970–85 Pick-Up—4WD

▶ See Figures 88 and 89

1. Remove the pitman arm from the sector shaft with a puller.
2. Matchmark and then loosen the intermediate shaft coupling at the steering gear wormshaft.
3. Loosen the bolt holding the intermediate shaft at the coupling near the fire wall and slide the shaft up off the steering gear wormshaft.
4. Remove the 4 bolts on the steering gear base and remove the steering gear.
5. Install the gear housing and observe the following torques:
- Steering gear housing to frame: 37–47 ft. lbs.
- Pitman arm to sector shaft: 116–137 ft. lbs.
- Wormshaft coupling bolt: 22–32 ft. lbs.

1986–88 Pick-Up and 4Runner—4WD

1. Remove the joint protector set bolt.
2. Matchmark the universal joint to the worm shaft and remove the 2 U-joint bolts. Disconnect the U-joint from the worm shaft.
3. Remove the pitman arm set nut and then disconnect the arm from the gear housing.
4. Remove the 3 housing-to-frame mounting bolts and lift out the gear housing.

To install:

5. Position the housing and tighten the 3 bolts to 70 ft. lbs. (95 Nm).
6. Connect the U-joint to the worm shaft so that the marks are in alignment and tighten the bolts to 26 ft. lbs. (35 Nm).

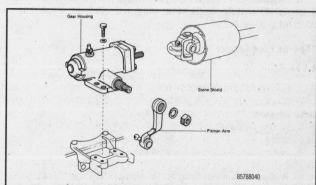

Fig. 88 Manual steering gear for 1970–85 4WD Pick-Up. Power steering gear is similar.

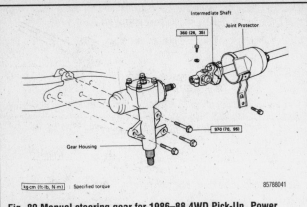

Fig. 89 Manual steering gear for 1986–88 4WD Pick-Up. Power steering gear is similar.

7. Install the joint protector and its bracket set bolt.
8. Connect the pitman arm and tighten the nut to 130 ft. lbs. (177 Nm).

1971–83 Land Cruiser

55 SERIES

1. Remove the worm yoke from the worm and main shaft.
2. Remove the intermediate shaft assembly.
3. Remove the pitman arm from the sector shaft.
4. Unbolt and remove the gear housing.
5. Install the housing and tighten the pitman arm to 119–141 ft. lbs.

➡The intermediate shaft must be installed with the wheels in a straight ahead position and the steering wheel straight ahead.

40 SERIES

1. Remove the horn button assembly and, using a puller, remove the steering wheel.
2. Remove the steering column jacket lower clamp.
3. Remove the turn signal switch assembly.
4. Remove the steering column access plate.
5. Remove the carburetor and oil filter (not necessary on 1975–76 models).
6. Disconnect the No. 1 shift rod and select rod at the ends of the shift controls and select levers.
7. Remove the lower shift control and bracket clamp.
8. Remove the shift control lever, select lever, control shaft lower bracket, control shaft lower speed lever, and control shaft lower bracket.
9. Pull the control shaft out toward the driver's side.
10. Remove the pitman arm with a puller.
11. Remove the steering gear box bracket cap and lift out the gear box.
12. Install the gear housing and tighten the gear box bracket cap to 75–90 ft. lbs. (30–40 for 1975–76); the pitman arm to 120–140 ft. lbs., the steering wheel nut to 30–50 ft. lbs.

1984–88 Land Cruiser

▶ See Figure 90

1. Remove the joint protector set bolt.
2. Matchmark the universal joint to the worm shaft and remove the 2 U-joint bolts. Disconnect the U-joint from the worm shaft.
3. Remove the pitman arm set nut and then disconnect the arm from the gear housing.
4. Remove the 4 housing-to-frame mounting bolts and lift out the gear housing.
5. Position the housing and tighten the 4 bolts to 90 ft. lbs. (122 Nm).
6. Connect the U-joint to the worm shaft so that the marks are in alignment and tighten the bolts to 26 ft. lbs. (35 Nm).
7. Install the joint protector and its bracket set bolt.
8. Connect the pitman arm and tighten the nut to 130 ft. lbs. (177 Nm).

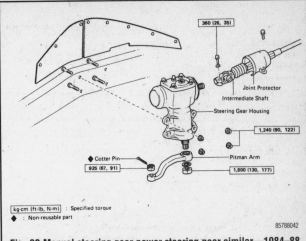

Fig. 90 Manual steering gear power steering gear similar—1984–88 Land Cruiser

Power Steering Gear

REMOVAL & INSTALLATION

1970–78 Pick-Up—2WD and 1970–85 Pick-Up—4WD

1. Disconnect the hydraulic lines from the steering gear.
2. Mark the relationship between the intermediate shaft U-joint yoke and the steering gear wormshaft.
3. Loosen the set bolt of the intermediate shaft U-joint yoke and disconnect the intermediate shaft from the steering gear wormshaft.
4. Using a puller, remove the pitman arm from the steering gear.
5. Remove the steering gear mounting bolts and remove the steering gear through the engine compartment.

To install:
6. Install the housing and be sure to align the marks made during Step 2. Torque the steering gear mounting bolts to 37–47 ft. lbs.; the pitman arm nut to 116–137 ft. lbs.; the U-joint yoke bolt to 22–32 ft. lbs.; the pressure hose fitting to 29–36 ft. lbs.; the return line fitting to 24–30 ft. lbs.

➡During installation of the hydraulic lines, position each line clear of any surrounding components then tighten the fittings.

1979–88 Pick-Up—2WD

1. Remove the hydraulic line clamp bolts and disconnect the 2 lines at the housing.
2. Remove the steering coupling set bolt where it connects to the worm shaft.
3. Disconnect the relay rod from the pitman arm.
4. Remove the 3 mounting bolts and lift out the steering gear housing.

To install:
5. Position the gear housing so that the worm shaft is lined up in the steering coupling and tighten the mounting bolts to 48 ft. lbs. (65 Nm).
6. Tighten the pitman arm mounting nut to 90 ft. lbs. (123 Nm).
7. Connect the pitman arm to the relay rod and tighten the nut to 67 ft. lbs. (90 Nm).
8. Tighten the coupling set bolt to 26 ft. lbs. (35 Nm).
9. Connect the 2 hydraulic lines to the housing and tighten the union bolts to 33 ft. lbs. (44 Nm). Tighten the clamp bolts.
10. Fill the reservoir tank with fluid.

1986–88 Pick-Up and 4Runner—4WD

1. Remove the joint protector set bolt.
2. Matchmark the universal joint to the worm shaft and remove the 2 U-joint bolts. Disconnect the U-joint from the worm shaft.

3. Remove the hydraulic line clamp bolts and disconnect the 2 lines at the housing.

4. Remove the pitman arm set nut and then disconnect the arm from the gear housing.

5. Remove the 3 housing-to-frame mounting bolts and lift out the gear housing.

To install:

6. Position the housing and tighten the 3 bolts to 70 ft. lbs. (95 Nm).

7. Connect the 2 hydraulic lines to the housing and tighten the union bolts to 33 ft. lbs. (44 Nm). Tighten the clamp bolts.

8. Connect the U-joint to the worm shaft so that the marks are in alignment and tighten the bolts to 26 ft. lbs. (35 Nm).

9. Install the joint protector and its bracket set bolt.

10. Connect the pitman arm and tighten the nut to 130 ft. lbs. (177 Nm).

11. Fill the reservoir with fluid.

1971–83 Land Cruiser

1. Disconnect the hydraulic lines from the steering gear.

2. Remove the steering shaft coupling set bolt.

3. Remove the steering column-to-firewall bolts.

4. Loosen the steering column-to-dash bolts.

5. Using a puller, disconnect the relay rod from the pitman shaft.

6. Using a puller, remove the pitman arm from the steering gear.

7. Pull the steering column towards the passenger compartment to uncouple the steering shaft from the steering gear.

8. Remove the steering gear mounting fasteners and remove the steering gear from the vehicle.

To install:

9. Be sure to align the marks on the pitman arm with the corresponding marks on the pitman shaft. Torque the steering gear mounting fasteners to 40–63 ft. lbs.; the pitman arm nut to 120–141 ft. lbs.; the coupling set bolt to 22–32 ft. lbs.; the pressure hose fitting to 29–36 ft. lbs.; and the return hose fitting to 24–30 ft. lbs.

➡**During installation of the hydraulic lines, position each line clear of any surrounding components then tighten the fittings.**

1984–88 Land Cruiser

1. Remove the hydraulic line clamp bolts and disconnect the 2 lines at the housing.

2. Remove the joint protector set bolt.

3. Matchmark the universal joint to the worm shaft and remove the 2 U-joint bolts. Disconnect the U-joint from the worm shaft.

4. Remove the pitman arm set nut and then disconnect the arm from the gear housing.

5. Remove the 4 housing-to-frame mounting bolts and lift out the gear housing.

To install:

6. Position the housing and tighten the 4 bolts to 90 ft. lbs. (122 Nm).

7. Connect the 2 hydraulic lines to the housing and tighten the union bolts to 33 ft. lbs. (44 Nm). Tighten the clamp bolts.

8. Connect the U-joint to the worm shaft so that the marks are in alignment and tighten the bolts to 26 ft. lbs. (35 Nm).

9. Install the joint protector and its bracket set bolt.

10. Connect the pitman arm and tighten the nut to 130 ft. lbs. (177 Nm).

Power Steering Pump

REMOVAL & INSTALLATION

1970–78

1. Remove the fan shroud.

2. Unfasten the nut from the center of the pump pulley.

➡**Use the drive belt as a brake to keep the pulley from rotating.**

3. Withdraw the drive belt.

4. Remove the pulley and the woodruff key from the pump shaft.

5. Detach the intake and outlet hoses from the pump reservoir.

➡**Tie the hose ends up high so the fluid cannot flow out of them. Drain or plug the pump to prevent fluid leakage.**

6. Remove the bolt from the rear mounting brace.

7. Remove the front bracket bolts and withdraw the pump.

To install:

8. Install the pump and tighten the pump pulley mounting bolt to 25–39 ft. lbs.

9. Adjust the pump drive belt tension. The belt should deflect 8–10mm under thumb pressure applied midway between the air pump and power steering pump.

10. Fill the reservoir with Dexron®II automatic transmission fluid. Bleed the air from the system.

1979–88

▸ **See Figure 91**

1. Disconnect the high tension lines at the distributor and then disconnect the air lines at the air valve.

2. Remove some fluid from the reservoir tank.

3. Disconnect the return hose at the power steering pump.

4. Disconnect the pressure line at the pump.

5. Loosen the drive belt pulley retaining nut. Loosen the idler pulley and adjusting bolt and remove the drive belt.

6. Remove the drive pulley and woodruff key.

7. Remove the power steering pump.

To install:

8. Install the pump in its bracket and tighten the nuts to 29 ft. lbs. (39 Nm).

9. Install the drive pulley and belt. Tighten the pulley bolt to 32 ft. lbs. (43 Nm) and check the drive belt tension.

10. Connect the pressure line to the pump and tighten the flare nut to 33 ft. lbs. (44 Nm).

11. Connect the return hose.

12. Connect the air hoses and the high tension leads.

13. Fill the reservoir with fluid, bleed the system and check for leaks.

BLEEDING

1. Raise the front of the truck and support it securely with jackstands.

2. Fill the pump reservoir with Dexron®II automatic transmission fluid.

3. Rotate the steering wheel from lock to lock several times. Add fluid as necessary.

4. With the steering wheel turned fully to one lock, crank the starter while watching the fluid level in the reservoir.

➡**Do not start the engine. Operate the starter with a remote starter switch or have an assistant do it from inside the truck. Do not run the starter for prolonged periods.**

5. Repeat Step 4 with the steering wheel turned to the opposite lock.

6. Start the engine. With the engine idling, turn the steering wheel from lock to lock several times.

7. Lower the front of the truck and repeat Step 6.

8. Center the wheel at the midpoint of its travel. Stop the engine.

9. The fluid level should not have risen more than 5mm. If it does, repeat Step 7.

10. Check for fluid leakage.

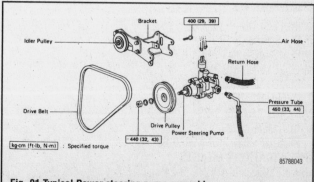

kg·cm (ft-lb, N·m) : Specified torque

85788043

Fig. 91 Typical Power steering pump assembly

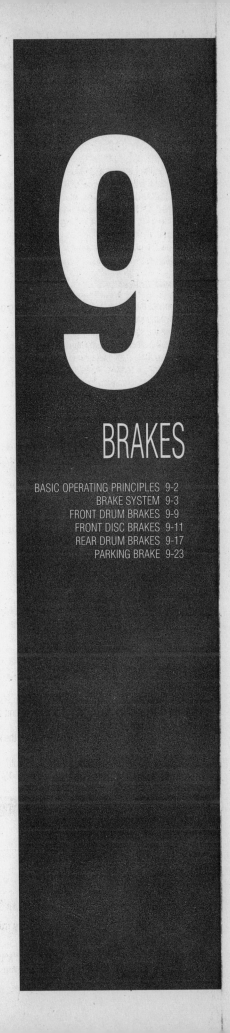

9

BRAKES

BASIC OPERATING PRINCIPLES

Hydraulic systems are used to actuate the brakes of all automobiles. The system transports the power required to force the frictional surfaces of the braking system together from the pedal to the individual brake units at each wheel. A hydraulic system is used for two reasons.

First, fluid under pressure can be carried to all parts of an automobile by small pipes and flexible hoses without taking up a significant amount of room or posing routing problems.

Second, a great mechanical advantage can be given to the brake pedal end of the system, and the foot pressure required to actuate the brakes can be reduced by making the surface area of the master cylinder pistons smaller than that of any of the pistons in the wheel cylinders or calipers.

The master cylinder consists of a fluid reservoir and a double cylinder and piston assembly. Double type master cylinders are designed to separate the front and rear braking systems hydraulically in case of a leak.

Steel lines carry the brake fluid to a point on the vehicle's frame near each of the vehicle's wheels. The fluid is then carried to the calipers and wheel cylinders by flexible tubes in order to allow for suspension and steering movements.

In drum brake systems, each wheel cylinder contains two pistons, one at either end, which push outward in opposite directions.

In disc brake systems, the cylinders are part of the calipers. One cylinder in each caliper is used to force the brake pads against the disc.

All pistons employ some type of seal, usually made of rubber, to minimize fluid leakage. A rubber dust boot seals the outer end of the cylinder against dust and dirt. The boot fits around the outer end of the piston on disc brake calipers, and around the brake actuating rod on wheel cylinders.

The hydraulic system operates as follows: When at rest, the entire system, from the piston(s) in the master cylinder to those in the wheel cylinders or calipers, is full of brake fluid. Upon application of the brake pedal, fluid trapped in front of the master cylinder piston(s) is forced through the lines to the wheel cylinders. Here, it forces the pistons outward, in the case of drum brakes, and inward toward the disc, in the case of disc brakes. The motion of the pistons is opposed by return springs mounted outside the cylinders in drum brakes, and by spring seals, in disc brakes.

Upon release of the brake pedal, a spring located inside the master cylinder immediately returns the master cylinder pistons to the normal position. The pistons contain check valves and the master cylinder has compensating ports drilled in it. These are uncovered as the pistons reach their normal position. The piston check valves allow fluid to flow toward the wheel cylinders or calipers as the pistons withdraw. Then, as the return springs force the brake pads or shoes into the released position, the excess fluid reservoir through the compensating ports. It is during the time the pedal is in the released position that any fluid that has leaked out of the system will be replaced through the compensating ports.

Dual circuit master cylinders employ two pistons, located one behind the other, in the same cylinder. The primary piston is actuated directly by mechanical linkage from the brake pedal through the power booster. The secondary piston is actuated by fluid trapped between the two pistons. If a leak develops in front of the secondary piston, it moves forward until it bottoms against the front of the master cylinder, and the fluid trapped between the pistons will operate the rear brakes. If the rear brakes develop a leak, the primary piston will move forward until direct contact with the secondary piston takes place, and it will force the secondary piston to actuate the front brakes. In either case, the brake pedal moves farther when the brakes are applied, and less braking power is available.

All dual circuit systems use a switch to warn the driver when only half of the brake system is operational. This switch is located in a valve body which is mounted on the firewall or the frame below the master cylinder. A hydraulic piston receives pressure from both circuits, each circuit's pressure being applied to one end of the piston. When the pressures are in balance, the piston remains stationary. When one circuit has a leak, however, the greater pressure in that circuit during application of the brakes will push the piston to one side, closing the switch and activating the brake warning light.

In disc brake systems, this valve body also contains a metering valve and, in some cases, a proportioning valve. The metering valve keeps pressure from traveling to the disc brakes on the front wheels until the brake shoes on the rear wheels have contacted the drums, ensuring that the front brakes will never be used alone. The proportioning valve controls the pressure to the rear brakes to lessen the chance of rear wheel lock-up during very hard braking.

Warning lights may be tested by depressing the brake pedal and holding it while opening one of the wheel cylinder bleeder screws. If this does not cause the light to go on, substitute a new lamp, make continuity checks, and, finally, replace the switch as necessary.

The hydraulic system may be checked for leaks by applying pressure to the pedal gradually and steadily. If the pedal sinks very slowly to the floor, the system has a leak. This is not to be confused with a springy or spongy feel due to the compression of air within the lines. If the system leaks, there will be a gradual change in the position of the pedal with a constant pressure.

Check for leaks along all lines and at wheel cylinders. If no external leaks are apparent, the problem is inside the master cylinder.

Disc Brakes

BASIC OPERATING PRINCIPLES

Instead of the traditional expanding brakes that press outward against a circular drum, disc brake systems utilize a disc (rotor) with brake pads positioned on either side of it. Braking effect is achieved in a manner similar to the way you would squeeze a spinning phonograph record between your fingers. The disc (rotor) is a casting with cooling fins between the two braking surfaces. This enables air to circulate between the braking surfaces making them less sensitive to heat buildup and more resistant to fade. Dirt and water do not affect braking action since contaminants are thrown off by the centrifugal action of the rotor or scraped off the by the pads. Also, the equal clamping action of the two brake pads tends to ensure uniform, straight line stops. Disc brakes are inherently self-adjusting.

There are three general types of disc brake:
1. A fixed caliper.
2. A floating caliper.
3. A sliding caliper.

The fixed caliper design uses two pistons mounted on either side of the rotor (in each side of the caliper). The caliper is mounted rigidly and does not move.

The sliding and floating designs are quite similar. In fact, these two types are often lumped together. In both designs, the pad on the inside of the rotor is moved into contact with the rotor by hydraulic force. The caliper, which is not held in a fixed position, moves slightly, bringing the outside pad into contact with the rotor. There are various methods of attaching floating calipers. Some pivot at the bottom or top, and some slide on mounting bolts. In any event, the end result is the same.

Drum Brakes

BASIC OPERATING PRINCIPLES

Drum brakes employ two brake shoes mounted on a stationary backing plate. These shoes are positioned inside a circular drum which rotates with the wheel assembly. The shoes are held in place by springs. This allows them to slide toward the drums (when they are applied) while keeping the linings and drums in alignment. The shoes are actuated by a wheel cylinder which is mounted at the top of the backing plate. When the brakes are applied, hydraulic pressure forces the wheel cylinder's actuating links outward. Since these links bear directly against the top of the brake shoes, the tops of the shoes are then forced against the inner side of the drum. This action forces the bottoms of the two shoes to contact the brake drum by rotating the entire assembly slightly (known as servo action). When pressure within the wheel cylinder is relaxed, return springs pull the shoes back away from the drum.

Most modern drum brakes are designed to self-adjust themselves during application when the vehicle is moving in reverse. This motion causes both shoes to rotate very slightly with the drum, rocking an adjusting lever, thereby causing rotation of the adjusting screw.

Power Boosters

Power brakes operate just as non-power brake systems except in the actuation of the master cylinder pistons. A vacuum diaphragm is located on the front of the master cylinder and assists the driver in applying the brakes, reducing both the effort and travel he must put into moving the brake pedal.

The vacuum diaphragm housing is connected to the intake manifold by a vacuum hose. A check valve is placed at the point where the hose enters the diaphragm housing, so that during periods of low manifold vacuum brake assist vacuum will not be lost.

Depressing the brake pedal closes off the vacuum source and allows atmospheric pressure to enter on one side of the diaphragm. This causes the master cylinder pistons to move and apply the brakes. When the brake pedal is released, vacuum is applied to both sides of the diaphragm, and return springs return the diaphragm and master cylinder pistons to the released position. If the vacuum fails, the brake pedal rod will butt against the end of the master cylinder actuating rod, and direct mechanical application will occur as the pedal is depressed.

The hydraulic and mechanical problems that apply to conventional brake systems also apply to power brakes, and should be checked for if the tests below do not reveal the problem.

Test for a system vacuum leak as described below:

1. Operate the engine at idle without touching the brake pedal for at least one minute.
2. Turn off the engine, and wait one minute.
3. Test for the presence of assist vacuum by depressing the brake pedal and releasing it several times. Light application will produce less and less pedal travel, if vacuum was present. If there is no vacuum, air is leaking into the system somewhere.

Test for system operation as follows:

4. Pump the brake pedal (with engine off) until the supply vacuum is entirely gone.
5. Put a light, steady pressure on the pedal.
6. Start the engine, and operate it at idle. If the system is operating, the brake pedal should fall toward the floor if constant pressure is maintained on the pedal.

Power brake systems may be tested for hydraulic leaks just as ordinary systems are tested.

BRAKE SYSTEM

✳✳ CAUTION

Brake shoes contain asbestos, which has been determined to be a cancer causing agent. Never clean the brake surfaces with compressed air! Avoid inhaling any dust from any brake surface! When cleaning brake surfaces, use a commercially available brake cleaning fluid.

Adjustment

DISC BRAKES

All disc brakes are inherently self-adjusting. No periodic adjustment is either necessary or possible.

DRUM BRAKES

Front

♦ See Figure 1

1970–74

The front wheels are equipped with two wheel cylinders and two sets of adjusters. Each brake shoe must be adjusted separately to achieve the correct adjustment. The procedure outlined is for the adjustment of one shoe; repeat the procedure on all four shoes of the front wheel brakes.

1. Raise the front of the truck and support the crossmember with jackstands.

✳✳ CAUTION

You will be working under the truck so be absolutely certain that it is firmly supported.

2. Remove the adjusting hole plug from the backing plate.
3. Expand the brake shoe with a starwheel adjusting wrench or a screwdriver. Pump the brake pedal several times while doing this to center the brake shoe.
4. Back off the adjuster just enough so that the wheel will turn with a slight drag. Then back off the adjuster another five notches. The wheel should turn smoothly.
5. If the wheel does not turn smoothly, back off one or two more notches. If the wheel is still dragging, check for worn or defective parts.
6. Pump the brake pedal again to center the shoe.
7. Proceed to the next shoe and repeat the procedure.

Rear

♦ See Figures 2, 3 and 4

➡1975–88 Toyota trucks utilize self-adjusting brakes. The following procedure is necessary only after the brake shoes have been changed.

1. Place blocks under the front wheels so that the truck will not roll forward when it is jacked up at the rear.
2. Fully release the emergency brake.
3. Raise the rear of the truck and support the differential housing with jackstands.
4. Remove the plug from the adjusting hole at the bottom of the backing plate.

➡Unlike the front wheels, the rear brakes have only one wheel cylinder and therefore both shoes on the wheel are adjusted at the same time.

5. Turn the adjusting starwheel to expand the shoes fully. While doing this, have a friend step on the brake pedal occasionally to center the shoes.
6. Tighten the shoes until the wheel will not turn when you release the brake pedal.
7. From this position back off the adjuster until the wheel turns with just a slight drag.
8. Back off the adjuster an additional five notches. The wheel should turn smoothly. If it does not, back off another two or three notches. Should this fail, check for worn or defective parts.
9. Adjust the other wheel in the same manner.

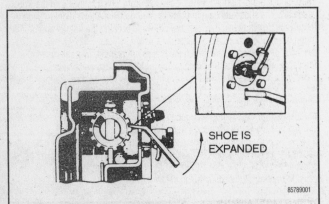

SHOE IS EXPANDED

85789001

Fig. 1 Adjusting the brake shoe clearance-front drum brakes

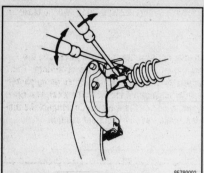

Fig. 2 Adjusting the brake shoe clearance—rear drum brakes (models w/leading-trailing brakes)

Fig. 3 Adjusting the brake shoe clearance—rear drum brakes (models w/duo servo brakes)

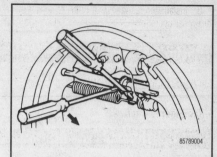

Fig. 4 Adjusting the brake shoe clearance—rear drum brakes 1986–88 4WD Pick-up and 4Runner and 1984–88 Land Cruiser

BRAKE PEDAL

Pedal Height

♦ See Figure 5

1. Measure the distance between the center (upper surface) of the pedal pad and the floor pad.
2. If out of specifications, loosen the brake light switch.
3. Turn the pedal pushrod until the pedal height is within specifications.
4. Move the brake light switch until the body is just touching the pedal stopper. Tighten the switch.
5. Check the brake pedal free-play.

Free-Play

♦ See Figure 6

1. With the engine turned off, depress the brake pedal several times until there is no vacuum left in the brake booster.
2. Push the pedal down until resistance is first felt. Measure this distance.
3. Adjust the free-play by turning the pedal pushrod.
4. Start the engine and recheck the free-play.
5. Recheck the pedal height.

Reserve Distance

♦ See Figure 7

Depress the brake pedal to the bottom of the pedal travel and measure the distance from the center (upper surface) of the pedal pad to the floor mat. If the distance is out of specifications, recheck the other pedal adjustments and the master cylinder.

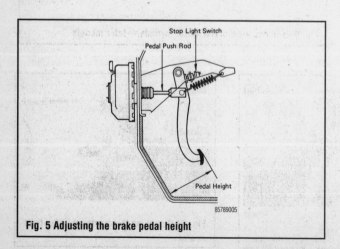

Fig. 5 Adjusting the brake pedal height

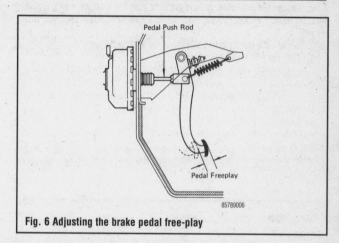

Fig. 6 Adjusting the brake pedal free-play

Brake Pedal Adjustment Specifications

Year	Pedal Height (in.)	Pedal Freeplay (in.)	Pedal Reserve Distance (in.) ①
1980–81	6.18–6.57	0.12–0.24	2 wd : 3.15 4 wd : 3.35 C&C : 2.95
1982–83	6.18–6.57	0.12–0.24	2 wd : 3.00 4 wd : 3.35
1984	5.94–6.14	0.12–0.24	2 wd (½ ton) : 2.56 C&C, 2 wd (¾ ton) : 2.17 4 wd : 2.36
1985	5.67–5.87	0.12–0.24	2 wd (½ ton) : 2.56 C&C, 2 wd (¾ ton) : 2.17 4 wd : 2.36
1986	5.67–5.87	0.12–0.24	2 wd (½ ton) : 2.56 2 wd (22R-TE) : 2.95 C&C, 2 wd (1 ton) : 2.17 4 wd (22R, 22R-E) : 2.17 4 wd (22R-TE) : 1.97
1987–88	②	0.12–0.24	2 wd (½ ton) : 2.56 2 wd (22R-TE) : 2.95 C&C, 2 wd (1 ton) : 2.17 4 wd (22R, 22R-E) : 2.17 4 wd (22R-TE) : 1.97 3VZ-E : 2.36

① More than figure listed, at 100 lbs. pressure
② 4 wd Pick-Up: 5.67–5.87
  2 wd Pick-Up & 4 Runner: 5.91–6.10

Fig. 7 Brake Pedal Adjustment Specifications

Brake Light Switch

REMOVAL & INSTALLATION

1. Disconnect the electrical harness at the switch.
2. Remove the mounting bolt and slide the switch up and down. Remove the switch from the brake pedal.

➡ **It is not necessary to remove the pushrod from the stud.**

3. Installation is the reverse of the removal procedure. Check brake lights for proper operation.

Master Cylinder

REMOVAL & INSTALLATION

▶ **See Figures 8 thru 21**

❊❊ CAUTION

Be careful not to spill brake fluid on the painted surfaces of the vehicle; it will damage the paint.

1. Unfasten the hydraulic lines from the master cylinder. On early models, disconnect the lines running to the master cylinder reservoir.
2. Disconnect the hydraulic fluid pressure differential switch wiring connectors. On models with ESP, disconnect the fluid level sensor wiring connectors, as well.
3. Loosen the master cylinder reservoir mounting bolts.
4. Then do one of the following:
   a. On models with manual brakes, remove the master cylinder securing bolts and the clevis pin from the brake pedal. Remove the master cylinder;
   b. On models with power brakes, unfasten the nuts and remove the master cylinder assembly from the power brake unit.
5. Install the master cylinder and note the following:
   • Certain models have an **UP** mark on the cylinder boot, make sure this is in the correct position.
   • Before tightening the master cylinder mounting nuts or bolts, screw the hydraulic line into the cylinder body a few turns.

• After installation is completed, bleed the master cylinder and the brake system.
• Check and adjust the brake pedal.

➡**To accurately install the master cylinder, the clearance between the booster piston rod and the master cylinder piston should be 3-6mm. This can be done after the master cylinder is installed. The brake pedal should move the specified distance with just a slight touch. Remember, you are only checking the distance in which the rod is traveling to connect the pistons, not to depress it. See the Brake Pedal Adjustment section.**

OVERHAUL

▶ **See Figures 22 thru 38**

1. Place the cylinder securely in a vise. Remove the reservoir caps and floats. Unscrew the bolts which secure the reservoir(s) to the main body.
2. Remove the pressure differential warning switch assembly. Then, working from the rear of the cylinder, remove the boot, snapring, stop washer, piston No. 1, spacer, cylinder cup, spring retainer, and spring, in that order.
3. Remove the end plug and gasket from the front of the cylinder, then remove the front piston stop bolt from underneath. Pull out the spring, retainer, piston No. 2, spacer, and the cylinder cup.
4. Remove the two outlet fittings, washers, check valves and springs.
5. Remove the piston cups from their seats only if they are to be replaced.
   After washing all parts in clean brake fluid, dry them with compressed air (if available). Drying parts with a shop rag can deposit lint and dirt particles inside the assembled master cylinder. Inspect the cylinder bore for wear, scuff marks, or nicks. Cylinders may be honed slightly, but the limit is 0.15mm. In view of the importance of the master cylinder, it is recommended that it is replaced rather than overhauled if worn or damaged.

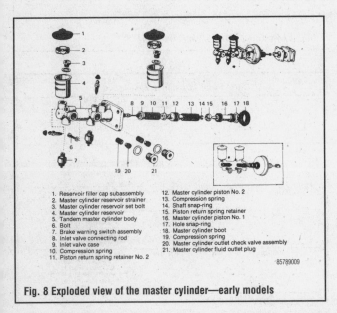

1. Reservoir filler cap subassembly
2. Master cylinder reservoir strainer
3. Master cylinder reservoir set bolt
4. Master cylinder reservoir
5. Tandem master cylinder body
6. Bolt
7. Brake warning switch assembly
8. Inlet valve connecting rod
9. Inlet valve case
10. Compression spring
11. Piston return spring retainer No. 2
12. Master cylinder piston No. 2
13. Compression spring
14. Shaft snap-ring
15. Piston return spring retainer
16. Master cylinder piston No. 1
17. Hole snap-ring
18. Master cylinder boot
19. Compression spring
20. Master cylinder outlet check valve assembly
21. Master cylinder fluid outlet plug

Fig. 8 Exploded view of the master cylinder—early models

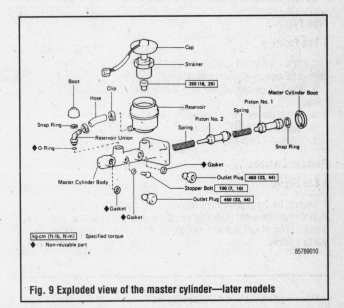

kg-cm (ft-lb, N·m) : Specified torque
◆ : Non-reusable part

Fig. 9 Exploded view of the master cylinder—later models

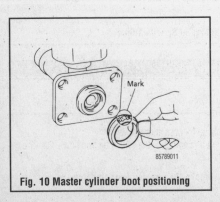

Fig. 10 Master cylinder boot positioning

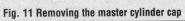

Fig. 11 Removing the master cylinder cap

Fig. 12 Removing the master cylinder fluid strainer

Fig. 13 Removing the master cylinder electrical connection

Fig. 14 Draining the master cylinder

Fig. 15 Removing the front brake line—use the correct type line wrench

Fig. 16 Removing the back brake line—use the correct type line wrench

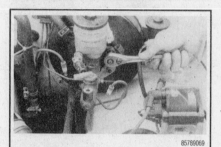

Fig. 17 Removing the master cylinder assembly mounting bolts

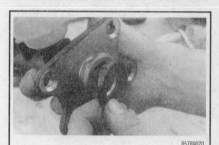

Fig. 18 Install the cylinder boot with UP mark in the correct location

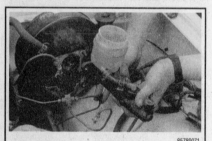

Fig. 19 Installing the master cylinder to the vehicle

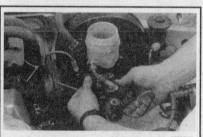

Fig. 20 Installing the master cylinder retaining nuts

Fig. 21 Installing the brake line to the master cylinder—always start thread by hand first

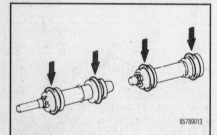

Fig. 22 Apply lithium soap based glycol grease here

Fig. 23 Exploded view of the master cylinder assembly (1987)

Fig. 24 Removing the seal from the piston

Fig. 25 Removing snapring from piston

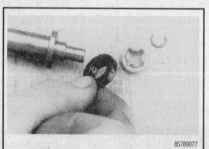

Fig. 26 View of seal and snapring on piston assembly

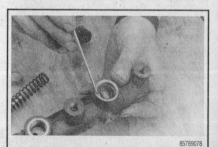

Fig. 27 Removing O-ring from the master cylinder body

Fig. 28 Installing the piston assembly into the cylinder body

Fig. 29 Installing the stopper bolt

Fig. 30 Installing the piston assembly into the cylinder body

Fig. 31 Installing the snapring to hold the piston assemblies

Fig. 32 View of the tool and snapring holding the piston assemblies

Fig. 33 Installing fluid tube onto the cylinder body

Fig. 34 Installing the snapring that holds fluid tube

Fig. 35 Installing the fluid tube boot on cylinder body

Fig. 36 Installing the O-ring for reservoir

Fig. 37 Installing the fluid reservoir

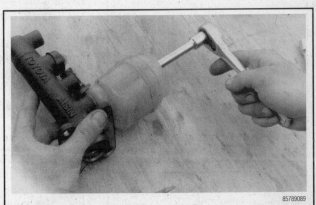

Fig. 38 Tighten the reservoir assembly before installing the cylinder

6. Absolute cleanliness is essential. Coat all parts with clean brake fluid prior to assembly.

7. Bleed the hydraulic system after the master cylinder is installed.

Power Brake Booster

➡Vacuum boosters can be found only on models equipped with power brakes.

REMOVAL & INSTALLATION

♦ See Figure 39

1. Remove the master cylinder as previously detailed.

2. Locate the clevis rod where it attaches to the brake pedal. Pull out the clip and then remove the clevis pin.

3. Disconnect the vacuum hose from the booster.

4. Loosen the four nuts and then pull out the vacuum booster, the bracket and the gasket.

➡ **Many 4WD models have two extra brackets that must be removed when removing the brake booster.**

To install:

5. Install the booster and tighten the mounting bolts to 9 ft. lbs. (13 Nm).
6. Connect the clevis rod to the brake pedal.
7. Install the master cylinder. Check the brake pedal adjustment and bleed the brakes.

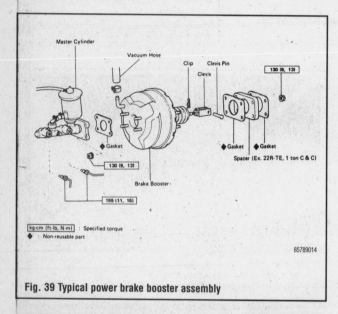

Fig. 39 Typical power brake booster assembly

Load Sensing Proportioning Valve

The purpose of this valve is to control the fluid pressure applied to the brakes to prevent rear wheel lock-up during weight transfer at high speed stops.

➡**This valve can not be rebuilt. It must be replaced.**

REMOVAL & INSTALLATION

1. Disconnect the brake lines going to the valve.
2. Remove the mounting bolt, if used, and remove the valve.
3. Installation is the reverse of removal.
4. Bleed the brake system.

ADJUSTMENT

♦ **See Figure 40**

1. Pull down the load sensing spring to determine that the piston moves slowly.
2. Set the valve body so that the piston lightly touches the load sensing spring.

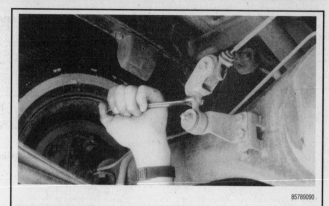

Fig. 40 Load sensing proportioning valve

3. Tighten the mounting bolts.

Brake Hoses and Lines

HYDRAULIC BRAKE LINE CHECK

♦ **See Figures 41, 42 and 43**

The hydraulic brake lines and brake linings are to be inspected at the recommended intervals in the maintenance schedule. Follow the steel tubing from the master cylinder to the flexible hose fitting at each wheel. If a section of the tubing is found to be damaged, replace the entire section with tubing of the same type (steel, not copper), size, shape, and length. When installing a new section of brake tubing, flush clean brake fluid or denatured alcohol through to remove any dirt or foreign material from the line. Be sure to flare both ends to provide sound, leak-proof connections. When bending the tubing to fit the underbody contours, be careful not to kink or crack the line.

Check the flexible brake hoses that connect the steel tubing to each wheel cylinder. Replace the hose if it shows any signs of softening, cracking, or other damage. When installing a new front brake hose, position the hose to avoid contact with other chassis parts. Place a new copper gasket over the hose fitting and thread the hose assembly into the front wheel cylinder. A new rear brake hose must be positioned clear of the exhaust pipe or shock absorber. Thread the hose into the rear brake tube connector. When installing either a new front or rear brake hose, engage the opposite end of the hose to the bracket on the frame. Install the horseshoe type retaining clip and connect the tube to the hose with the tube fitting nut.

Always bleed the system after hose or line replacement. Before bleeding, make sure that the master cylinder is topped up with high temperature, extra heavy duty fluid of at least SAE 70R3 quality.

Bleeding

♦ **See Figures 44, 45, 46, 47 and 48**

➡**Do not reuse brake fluid which has been bled from the brake system. When filling the system, always use clean, fresh brake fluid.**

Fig. 41 View of brake lines at junction block

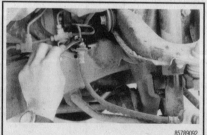

Fig. 42 Removing the brake line at junction block

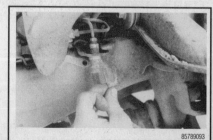

Fig. 43 Removing brake hose retaining clip

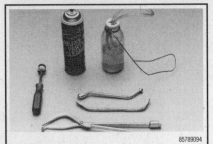

Fig. 44 View of brake tools and brake cleaner

Fig. 45 Removing the bleeder cap off the front caliper

Fig. 46 Bleeding the front caliper

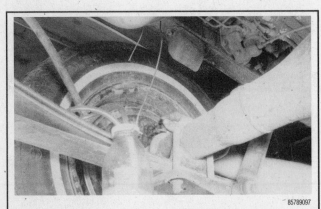

Fig. 47 Removing the bleeder cap off the rear wheel cylinder

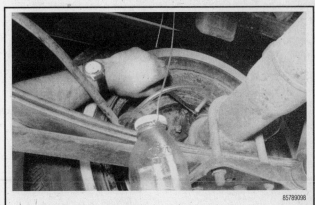

Fig. 48 Bleeding the rear wheel cylinder

1. Insert a clear vinyl tube into the bleeder plug on the master cylinder or the wheel cylinders.

➡️If the master cylinder has been overhauled or if air is present in it, start the bleeding procedure with the master cylinder. Otherwise (and after bleeding the master cylinder), start with the wheel cylinder which is farthest from the master cylinder.

2. Insert the other end of the tube into a jar which is half filled with brake fluid.
3. Have an assistant slowly pump the brake pedal several times. On the last pump, have the assistant hold the pedal to the floor (fully depressed). While the pedal is depressed, open the bleeder plug until fluid starts to run out, then close the plug.

➡️If the brake pedal is depressed too fast, small air bubbles will form in the brake fluid which will be very difficult to remove.

4. Bleed the cylinder before hydraulic pressure decreases in the cylinder.
5. Repeat this procedure until the air bubbles are removed and then go on to the next wheel cylinder.

✳️ CAUTION

Replenish the brake fluid in the master cylinder reservoir, so that it does not run out during bleeding.

FRONT DRUM BRAKES

✳️ CAUTION

Brake shoes contain asbestos, which has been determined to be a cancer causing agent. Never clean the brake surfaces with compressed air! Avoid inhaling any dust from any brake surface! When cleaning brake surfaces, use a commercially available brake cleaning fluid.

Brake Drums

REMOVAL & INSTALLATION

▶ See Figure 49

1. Remove the hub cap and loosen the lug nuts.
2. Raise the front of the vehicle and support it on jackstands.
3. Remove the lug nuts, tire and wheel.
4. Remove the axle hub grease cap.
5. Remove the cotter pin, and then loosen the hub nut. When the nut is close to the end of the spindle, pull the drum and hub assembly toward you. If it does not slide off the brake shoes, loosen the brake shoe adjuster star wheels.

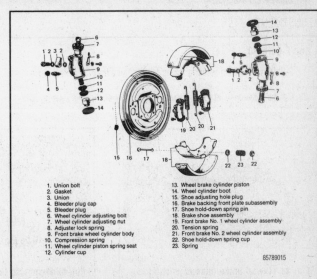

1. Union bolt
2. Gasket
3. Union
4. Bleeder plug cap
5. Bleeder plug
6. Wheel cylinder adjusting bolt
7. Wheel cylinder adjusting nut
8. Adjuster lock spring
9. Front brake wheel cylinder body
10. Compression spring
11. Wheel cylinder piston spring seat
12. Cylinder cup
13. Wheel brake cylinder piston
14. Wheel cylinder boot
15. Shoe adjusting hole plug
16. Brake backing front plate subassembly
17. Shoe hold-down spring pin
18. Brake shoe assembly
19. Front brake No. 1 wheel cylinder assembly
20. Tension spring
21. Front brake No. 2 wheel cylinder assembly
22. Shoe hold-down spring cup
23. Spring

Fig. 49 Exploded view of the front drum brake assembly

Remove the spindle nut, brake drum and hub, the washer, and the wheel bearings.

➡ **Be careful not to get foreign matter in the wheel bearings. The heavy coating of grease will hold many particles. These will damage the bearings.**

6. Inspect the brake drum as outlined below.

✳✳ **CAUTION**

Do not depress the brake pedal with the brake drum removed.

7. Installation is the reverse of the removal procedures. For instructions on preloading the front wheel bearings, see the appropriate section.

INSPECTION

1. Clean the drum with a rag and a little paint thinner.

✳✳ **CAUTION**

Do not blow the brake dust out of the drum with compressed air or lung power. Brake linings contain asbestos, a known cancer causing agent.

2. Inspect the drum for cracks, grooves, scoring and out-of-roundness.
3. Light scoring may be removed with fine emery paper, Heavy scores or grooves will have to be removed by having the drum turned on a lathe. This can be done at many automotive machine shops and some service stations.
4. Before cutting the drum it must be measured to determine whether or not the inside dimension of the drum is within limitations after removing the score marks. The service limits of the brake drums are as follows:
   - 1970–71 w/9 in. drum: 9.134 in.
   - 1972–74 w/10 in. drum: 10.08 in.
5. Check the drum for concentricity. An inside micrometer is necessary for an exact measurement, so unless this tool is available, the drum should be taken to a machine shop to be checked. Any drum which measures more than 0.15mm out of round will result in an inaccurate brake adjustment and other problems, and must be refinished or replaced.

➡ **Make all measurements at right angles to each other and at the open and closed edges of the drum machined surface.**

Brake Shoes

REMOVAL & INSTALLATION

♦ **See Figure 50**

1. Remove the brake drum.
2. Remove the long brake tension (retracting) springs. These have hooks on each end, but you should be able to get them off with a pair of needle nose pliers. Remove the hold-down springs with a brake tool. You can make due with some other tool, but it won't be easy. Pull out the spring pin from the rear, and remove the shoes.

➡ **If the brake shoes are to be reused, mark them so that they may be returned to their original locations.**

3. Clean the backing plate with a wire brush.
4. Inspect the brake springs for deformation and weakness, replace any parts found to be defective.
5. Check the brake linings for wear. The factory limit is 1mm measured at both ends and middle of the shoe. If the limit is exceeded, replace both brake shoes.

➡ **This measurement may disagree with your state inspection laws.**

6. Check to see that no grease or brake fluid is leaking onto the backing plate or the shoes. Fresh grease on the backing plate may indicate a faulty seal in the hub. Brake fluid leakage can be traced to the wheel cylinder or brake line. If there is any leakage, rebuild the wheel cylinders or replace the brake lines. DO NOT DELAY, as a brake failure may result.

➡ **A small trace of fluid may be present to act as a lubricant for the wheel cylinder pistons.**

7. Before proceeding to the installation of the brake shoes, coat all the points of contact on the backing plate with a film of multipurpose grease.

✳✳ **CAUTION**

Do not get grease or oil on the brake shoes.

Install the shoes in the following manner:

8. Fit the upper and lower shoes onto the grooves on the wheel cylinders and adjusting bolts. Install the spring pins and the retaining springs with the aid of a brake spring tool.
9. Hook the brake shoe tension springs on the upper and lower shoes.
10. Install the drum and adjust the brakes.

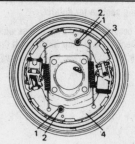

| 1. Hold down spring | 3. Upper brake shoe |
| 2. Spring pin | 4. Lower brake shoe |

85789016

Fig. 50 Remove these parts in the order shown here, after removing the long shoe tension springs

Wheel Cylinders

REMOVAL & INSTALLATION

1. Perform the brake drum and brake shoe removal procedures, as outlined above.
2. Plug the master cylinder reservoir inlet, to prevent fluid from leaking out.
3. Remove the hydraulic lines from the wheel cylinders by unfastening the union bolt.
4. Remove the wheel cylinder attachment screws and remove the wheel cylinders.

➡ **Do not mix the right and left wheel cylinders.**

5. Installation is the reverse of the removal procedure. Keep in mind that the wheel cylinder adjusting nut and bolt on the right side of the brake have left hand threads; those on the left side have right hand threads. Be careful not to mix them.

✳✳ **CAUTION**

Use care to ensure that the hydraulic line is not twisted.

6. Bleed the brake system.

OVERHAUL

Remove the boots, pistons and the cups and closely inspect the bores for signs of wear, scoring and/or scuffing. When in doubt, replace or hone the wheel cylinders with a special brake hone, using clean brake fluid as lubricant. Wash residue from the bores using clean fluid; never use oil or any other solvent on any brake components. Blow dry with air and install with fresh brake fluid. The general limit for a honed cylinder is 0.13mm oversize. Wheel cylinder rebuilding kits are available which include new boots and cups. Never reuse these parts. The adjuster screws should be taken apart and all dirt and rust removed with a wire brush. Lightly coat with brake type grease before assemble; components should turn freely.

FRONT DISC BRAKES

Brake Pads

INSPECTION

➡ For proper inspection, the disc brake pads themselves must be removed. See following section for details.

➡ If a squealing noise occurs from the front brakes while driving a 1986–88 Pick-Up or 4Runner, check the pad wear indicator. If there are traces of the indicator contacting the rotor (disc), the brake pad must be replaced.

REMOVAL & INSTALLATION

1975–83 2WD Pick-Up (Except C & C), 1975–88 4WD Pick-Up and 4Runner and 1975–88 Land Cruiser

▸ See Figures 51 and 52

The front pads must be removed for wear inspection. It is not necessary to remove the caliper.

1. Jack up the front of the truck, support it on jackstands, and remove the front wheel.
2. Pull out the two wire clips at the ends of the pad pins.
3. Pull out the pads and anti-rattle spring.
4. Remove the brake pads. On all 2WD Pick-ups and 1988 4WD Pick-ups and 4Runners, lift out the anti-squeal shims .
5. Check the pad thickness and replace the pads if they are less than 1mm thick. New pads measure approximately 9.6mm thick.

➡ This minimum thickness measurement may disagree with your state inspection laws.

6. Check the pins for straightness and wear, and replace if necessary.
To install:
7. Attach a clear vinyl tube onto the bleeder plug on the brake cylinder, and insert the other end into a jar half filled with brake fluid. Bleed off a small amount of brake fluid.
8. Use a C-clamp or hammer handle and press the caliper pistons back into the housing.

➡ Never press the pistons into the caliper when the pads are out on both sides of the truck.

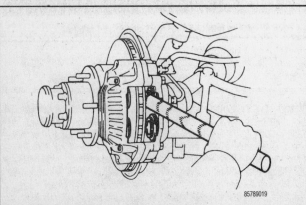

Fig. 51 Seat the caliper pistons in the housing

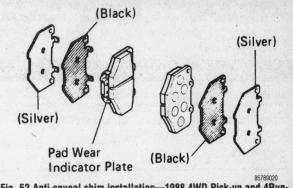

Fig. 52 Anti-squeal shim installation—1988 4WD Pick-up and 4Runner

9. On 2WD Pick-ups, install the anti-squeal shims so that the folded part will face the pad, and the arrows will face the direction of forward rotation. Lightly coat both sides of the shims with anti-squeak lubricant before installation.
10. On 1988 4WD Pick-ups and 4Runner, install the 4 anti-squeal shims so that the black shims are between the silver shims and the brake pad.
11. Install the brake pads. On 1988 models with the V6 engine, the pad with the wear indicator goes on the inside! Be very careful not to get grease or oil on the inner surfaces of the pads.
12. Install the anti-rattle spring.
13. Slide the 2 pad retaining pins through the caliper and pads and install the retaining clip.
14. Install the wheel and lower the truck. Bleed the brakes and road test the vehicle.

1975–83 2WD Pick-Up (C & C Only)

1. Raise the front of the truck and support with safety stands. Remove the wheel.
2. Remove the cylinder guide plates, cylinder support springs and pad support plates.
3. With the outer brake pad still attached, lift the caliper up and away from the caliper mounting frame.
4. Pull out the anti-rattle spring and remove the outer pad from the caliper. Remove the inner pad from the mounting frame.
5. Check the pad thickness and replace the pads if they are less than 1mm thick. New pads measure approximately 9.6mm thick.

➡ This minimum thickness measurement may disagree with your state inspection laws.

To install:
6. Attach a clear vinyl tube onto the bleeder plug on the brake cylinder, and insert the other end into a jar half filled with brake fluid. Bleed off a small amount of brake fluid.
7. Use a C-clamp or hammer handle and press the caliper piston back into the housing.
8. Install the inner pad. Position the outer pad in the caliper and install the anti-rattle spring.
9. Position the caliper and outer pad into the support frame.
10. Install the pad support plates and cylinder support springs. Install the cylinder guide plates and tighten the bolts to 29–44 ft. lbs.
11. Install the wheel and lower the truck. Bleed the brakes and road test the vehicle.

1984–88 2WD Pick-Up w/FS17-Type Brake

▸ See Figures 53 thru 80

1. Remove the hub cap and loosen the lug nuts.
2. Jack up the front of the truck and safely support it with jackstands.
3. Remove the lug nuts and the wheel.

4. Attach a clear vinyl tube onto the bleeder plug on the brake cylinder, and insert the other end into a jar half filled with brake fluid. Bleed off a small amount of brake fluid.

5. Remove the caliper slide pin on the sub-pin (lower) side.

6. Swivel the caliper up and away from the torque plate. Tie the caliper to a suspension member so its out of the way. Do not disconnect the brake line.

7. Lift the 2 brake pads out of the torque plate. Remove the anti-squeal shim.

8. Remove the 4 pad support plates. On 1986-88 trucks, pull the 2 pad wear indicator plates off the pads.

9. Check the pad thickness and replace the pads if they are less than 1mm thick. New pads measure approximately 9.6mm thick.

➡This minimum thickness measurement may disagree with your state inspection laws.

To install:

10. Install the 4 pad support plates into the torque plate.

11. Install a new pad wear indicator plate to the bottom of each pad.

12. Install the anti-squeal shim to the back of the outer pad and then position both pads into the torque plate.

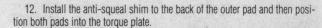
✳✳ CAUTION

When installing new brake pads, make sure your hands are clean. Do not allow any grease or oil to touch the contact face of the pads or the brakes will not stop the truck properly!

13. Use a C-clamp or hammer handle and press the caliper piston back into the housing.

➡**Never press the piston into the caliper when the pads are out on both sides of the truck.**

14. Untie the caliper and swivel it back into position over the torque plate so that the dust boot is not pinched. Install the slide pin and tighten it to 65 ft. lbs. (88 Nm).

15. Check the condition of the cylinder side bushing boot. Pull on it to relieve any air from the cylinder side pin mounting area. Check that the hole

Fig. 53 Swivel the caliper up and out of the way—1984–88 2WD Pick-up w/FS17 type caliper

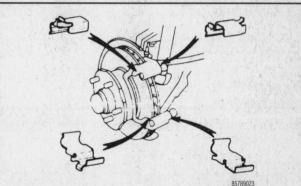
Fig. 55 Installing the pad support plates—1984–88 2WD Pick-up w/FS17 type caliper

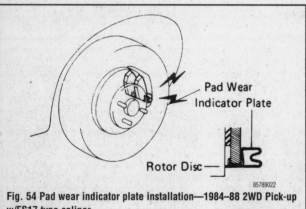
Fig. 54 Pad wear indicator plate installation—1984–88 2WD Pick-up w/FS17 type caliper

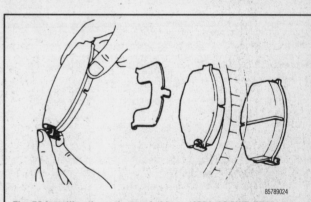
Fig. 56 Installing the anti-squeal shims—1984–88 2WD Pick-up w/FS17 type caliper

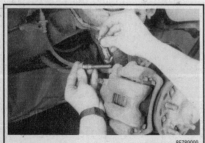
Fig. 57 Remove the caliper mounting bolt or pin

Fig. 58 Swing the caliper assembly back to remove the brake pads

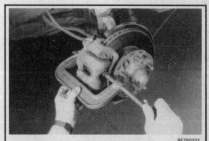
Fig. 59 Using a large C-clamp to compress piston

Fig. 60 Removing the front brake pad

Fig. 61 Removing the rear brake pad

Fig. 62 Removing the caliper assembly

Fig. 63 Removing the pad wear indicator

Fig. 64 View the caliper mounting plate or torque plate

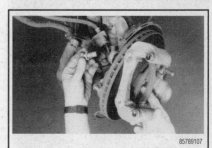

Fig. 65 Removing the caliper mounting plate

Fig. 66 View of the wheel bearing grease cap

Fig. 67 Removing the wheel bearing grease cap with a tool

Fig. 68 Removing the wheel bearing grease cap

Fig. 69 Removing the wheel bearing cotter pin

Fig. 70 Removing the wheel bearing lock ring

Fig. 71 Removing the wheel bearing adjusting nut

Fig. 72 Removing the wheel bearing assembly washer

Fig. 73 Removing the wheel bearing

Fig. 74 Removing the hub/rotor assembly

Fig. 75 View of the wheel bearings and related parts

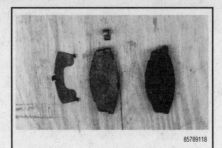

Fig. 76 View of front brake pads and wear indicator

Fig. 77 Apply disc brake quiet before installing brake pads

Fig. 78 Removing the hub from the rotor

Fig. 79 Removing the wheel bearing seal

Fig. 80 Installing the wheel bearing seal

plug on the main pin side is there. Push on the center of the plug to relieve any air from the inner portion of the main pin.

16. Install the wheel and lower the truck. Bleed the brakes and road test the vehicle.

1984–88 2WD Pick-Up w/PD60-Type Brake

▶ See Figures 81, 82, 83 and 84

1. Remove the hub cap and loosen the lug nuts.
2. Jack up the front of the truck and safely support it with jackstands.
3. Remove the lug nuts and the wheel.
4. Attach a clear vinyl tube onto the bleeder plug on the brake cylinder, and insert the other end into a jar half filled with brake fluid. Bleed off a small amount of brake fluid.
5. Remove the two installation bolts from the torque plate.
6. Remove the caliper assembly and suspend it from the suspension with a wire without disconnecting the brake hose.
7. Remove the 2 anti-squeal springs and lift out the brake pads.
8. Remove the 2 anti-squeal shims and the 4 pad support plates. Pull the 2 pad wear indicator off the pads.
9. Check the pad thickness and replace the pads if they are less than 1mm thick. New pads measure approximately 9.6mm thick.

➡This minimum thickness measurement may disagree with your state inspection laws.

To install:

10. Install the 4 pad support plates into the torque plate.
11. Install a new pad wear indicator plate to the bottom of each pad.

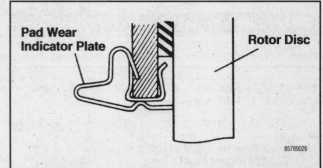

Fig. 82 Pad wear indicator plate installation—1984–88 2WD Pick-up w/PD60-type caliper

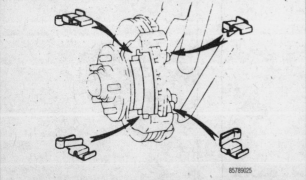

Fig. 81 Installing the pad support plates—1984–88 2WD Pick-up w/PD60-type caliper

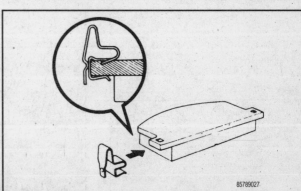

Fig. 83 Installing the anti-squeal shim—1984–88 2WD Pick-up w/PD60-type caliper

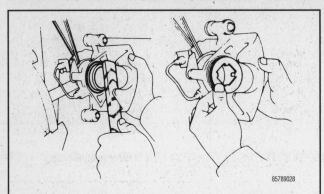

Fig. 84 Press the piston in and install the round anti-squeal shim—1984–88 2WD Pick-up w/PD60-type caliper

12. Install the large anti-squeal shim to the back of the outer pad and then position both pads into the torque plate.

❊❊ CAUTION

When installing new brake pads, make sure your hands are clean. Do not allow any grease or oil to touch the contact face of the pads or the brakes will not stop the truck properly!

13. Use a C-clamp or hammer handle and press the caliper piston back into the housing.

➡️**Never press the piston into the caliper when the pads are out on both sides of the truck.**

14. Press the round anti-squeal shim over the caliper piston and position the caliper over the torque plate so the dust boot is not pinched.
15. Install the 2 mounting bolts and tighten them to 29 ft. lbs. (39 Nm).
16. Install the wheel and lower the truck. Bleed the brakes and road test the vehicle.

Brake Caliper

REMOVAL & INSTALLATION

1975–83 2WD Pick-Up (Exc. C & C), 1975–88 4WD Pick-Up and 4Runner and 1975–88 Land Cruiser

1. Jack up the front of the truck, support it on jackstands, and remove the front wheel.
2. Pull out the two wire clips at the ends of the pad pins.
3. Pull out the pads and anti-rattle spring.
4. Remove the brake pads. On all 2WD Pick-ups and 1988 4WD Pick-ups and 4Runners, lift out the anti-squeal shims .

5. Plug the vent hole on the master cylinder cap to prevent fluid leak. Unbolt the brake line from the caliper, being careful not to deform the fittings.
6. Remove the 2 caliper mounting bolts, and remove the caliper.
To install:
7. Position the caliper and install the mounting bolts. Tighten the caliper mounting bolts to 67–87 ft. lbs. on 2WD Pick-Ups, 55–75 ft. lbs. on 1975–85 4WD Pick-Ups and 90 ft. lbs. on 1986–88 4WD Pick-Ups and all Land Cruisers. Be certain to position the shims correctly.
8. Install the brake pads.
9. Install the wheel and lower the truck. Bleed the brakes and road test the vehicle.

1975–83 2WD Pick-Up (C & C), 1984–88 2WD Pick-Up W/FS17-Type Brakes and 1984–88 2WD Pick-Up W/PD60-Type Brakes

Caliper removal procedures for these models are detailed within the respective "Brake Pad Removal" sections. On models with FS17-type brakes, simply remove the other mounting bolt. Additionally, on all models, disconnect the brake hydraulic line.

OVERHAUL

▶ **See Figures 85, 86, 87 and 88**

1975–83 2WD Pick-Up (Exc. C & C), 1975–88 4WD Pick-Up and 4Runner and 1975–88 Land Cruiser

1. Raise the front of the truck and support with safety stands. Remove the wheels.
2. Remove the caliper.
3. Carefully pry the dust boot set ring out of the caliper. Remove the dust boot.
4. Insert a piece of wood about ½ in. thick between the caliper pistons.
5. Apply compressed air to the brake line union to force the piston out of its bore. Be careful; the piston may come out forcefully!
6. Remove the piston seal from the caliper cylinder bore. Check the piston and cylinder bore for wear and/or corrosion. Replace components as necessary.

❊❊ CAUTION

Do not loosen the four bolts holding the two halves of the caliper together.

To assemble:
7. Coat all components with clean brake fluid or lithium soap base glycol grease.
8. Install the piston seal and then the piston into the caliper cylinder bore. Seat the piston in the bore with your fingers.
9. Fit the boot into the groove in the cylinder bore and press in the set ring.
10. Install the caliper and brake pads.
11. Install the wheels and lower the truck. Bleed the brakes and road test the vehicle.

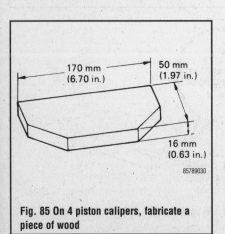

Fig. 85 On 4 piston calipers, fabricate a piece of wood

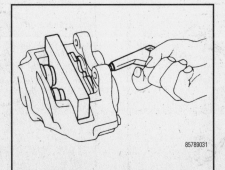

Fig. 86 Force the pistons out of their bores with compressed air—4-piston caliper shown, others similar

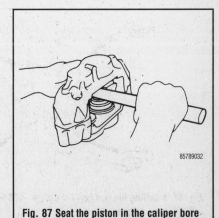

Fig. 87 Seat the piston in the caliper bore

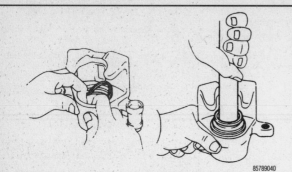

Fig. 88 Install the piston seal and then press the piston into the caliper bore

85789040

1975–83 2WD Pick-Up (C & C), 1984–88 2WD Pick-Up W/FS17-Type Brakes and 1984–88 2WD Pick-Up W/PD60-Type Brakes

▶ **See Figures 89, 90, 91 and 92**

1. Raise the front of the truck and support with safety stands. Remove the wheels.
2. Remove the caliper.
3. Remove the slide bushing (2 on PD60), 2 pin dust boots (4 on PD60) and 2 collars (PD60 only).
4. Carefully pry the dust boot set ring out of the caliper. Remove the dust boot.
5. Insert a piece cloth or rag between the caliper claw and the piston.
6. Apply compressed air to the brake line union to force the piston out of its bore. Be careful; the piston may come out forcefully!
7. Remove the piston seal from the caliper cylinder bore. Check the piston and cylinder bore for wear and/or corrosion. Replace components as necessary.

To assemble:

8. Coat all components with clean brake fluid or lithium soap base glycol grease.
9. Install the piston seal and then the piston into the caliper cylinder bore. Seat the piston in the bore with your fingers.

10. Fit the boot into the groove in the cylinder bore and press in the set ring.
11. On FS17, install the main pin boots to the torque plate. Install the sub pin slide bushing into the torque plate.
12. On PD60, install the collar and dust boots into the caliper. Make sure they are firmly secured to the groove in the caliper. Install the bushing into the boots so that it is firmly set in the boot groove.
13. Install the caliper and brake pads.
14. Install the wheels and lower the truck. Bleed the brakes and road test the vehicle.

Brake Disc

REMOVAL & INSTALLATION

1. Remove the brake pads and the caliper, as detailed in the appropriate section.
2. Check the disc run-out, as detailed following, at this point. Make a note of the results for use during installation.
3. Remove the grease cap from the hub. Remove the cotter pin and the castellated nut.
4. Remove the wheel hub with the brake disc attached.
5. Perform the disc inspection procedure as outlined in this section.

To install:

6. Coat the hub oil seal lip with multipurpose grease and install the disc/hub assembly.
7. Adjust the wheel bearing preload, as detailed following.
8. Measure the disc run-out. Check it against the specifications in the "Brake Specifications" chart and against the figures noted during removal.

➡ **If the wheel bearing nut is improperly tightened, disc run-out will be affected.**

9. Install the remainder of the components as outlined in the appropriate sections.
10. Bleed the brake system.
11. Road test the truck. Check the wheel bearing preload.

Fig. 89 Removing the piston with compressed air

85789123

Fig. 90 Removing the piston from the caliper

85789124

Fig. 91 Removing the dust seal from the caliper

85789125

Fig. 92 Removing the O-ring seal from the caliper

85789126

INSPECTION

Examine the disc. If it is worn, warped or scored, it must be replaced. Check the thickness of the disc against the specifications given in the "Brake Specifications" chart. If it is below specifications, replace it. Use a micrometer to measure the thickness.

The disc run-out should be measured before the disc is removed and again, after the disc is installed. Use a dial indicator mounted on a stand to determine run-out. If run-out exceeds 1.5mm (all models), replace the disc.

➡ **Be sure that the wheel bearing nut is properly tightened. If it is not, an inaccurate run-out reading may be obtained. If different run-out readings are obtained with the same disc, between removal and installation, this is probably the cause.**

For Wheel Bearing removal and installation and adjustment please refer to Sections 1 or 7.

PRELOAD ADJUSTMENT

1. With the front hub/disc assembly installed, tighten the castellated nut to the torque.

2. Rotate the disc back and forth, two or three times, to allow the bearing to seat properly.

3. Loosen the castellated nut until it is only finger tight.

4. Tighten the nut firmly, using a box wrench. Make sure the disc rotates smoothly.

5. Measure the bearing preload with a spring scale attached to a wheel mounting stud.

6. Install the cotter pin.

➡️**If the hole does not align with the nut (or cap) holes, tighten the nut slightly until it does.**

7. Finish installing the brake components and the wheel.

REAR DRUM BRAKES

✳✳ CAUTION

Brake shoes contain asbestos, which has been determined to be a cancer causing agent. Never clean the brake surfaces with compressed air! Avoid inhaling any dust from any brake surface! When cleaning brake surfaces, use a commercially available brake cleaning fluid.

Non self-adjusting brakes were used from 1970-74. Adjustment is covered at the beginning of this section. Self-adjusting brakes were introduced in 1975. Procedures are combined for the two systems in this section for drum removal, installation, and inspection, and brake shoe removal.

Brake Drum

REMOVAL & INSTALLATION

▶ **See Figures 93 thru 116**

1. Remove the hub cap (if used) and loosen the lug nuts. Release the parking brake.

2. Block the front wheels, raise the rear of the truck, and support it with jackstands.

✳✳ CAUTION

Support the truck securely.

3. Remove the wheels.

4. Unfasten the brake drum retaining screws.

5. Tap the drum lightly with a mallet in order to free it. If the drum cannot be removed easily, insert a screwdriver into the hole in the backing plate and hold the automatic adjusting lever away from the adjusting bolt. Using another screwdriver, relieve the brake shoe tension by turning the adjusting bolt clockwise. If the drum still will not come off, use a puller; but first make sure that the parking brake is released. On models with dual rear wheels, the drum is removed along with the rear axle shaft.

✳✳ CAUTION

Do not depress the brake pedal once the brake drum has been removed.

Fig. 93 View of the rear brake drum with retaining screws

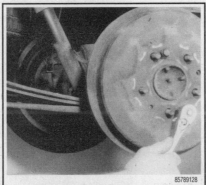

Fig. 94 Removing rear brake drum retaining screws

Fig. 95 Removing the rear brake drum

Fig. 96 Cleaning the rear brake shoes and related parts

Fig. 97 View of the rear brake shoes and related parts

Fig. 98 Removing the brake return spring

Fig. 99 Removing the brake hold-down spring—with special brake tool

Fig. 100 Removing the brake hold-down spring

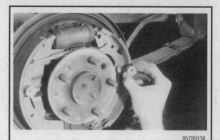

Fig. 101 Removing the brake hold-down spring and washers

Fig. 102 Removing the back brake shoe (secondary)

Fig. 103 Removing the front brake shoe (primary)

Fig. 104 View of the parking brake cable to brake shoe

Fig. 105 Removing the E-clip from the brake shoe

Fig. 106 View of the E-clip on related brake parts

Fig. 107 Removing the spring on brake related parts

Fig. 108 View of the self-adjuster assembly

Fig. 109 Removing the self-adjuster assembly

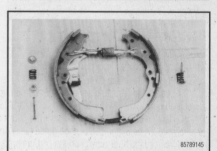

Fig. 110 View of the brake springs in the installed position

Fig. 111 Removing the wheel cylinder assembly

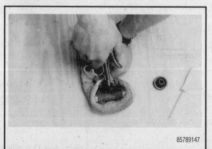

Fig. 112 Removing the wheel cylinder assembly piston

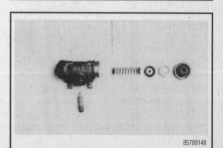

Fig. 113 View of the wheel cyclinder assembly

Fig. 114 Removing the rubber inspection plug from the backing plate

Fig. 115 Adjusting the brake shoes after installation

Fig. 116 Bleeding the brake shoes after installation

6. Inspect the brake drum as detailed in the following section.

7. To install the drum, simply replace the drum on the axle and tighten the retaining screw.

➡Don't forget to adjust the brake shoes.

✳✳ CAUTION

Do not step on the brake pedal with the drum removed.

8. Install the wheels and lower the truck. Bleed the brakes and road test the vehicle.

INSPECTION

1. Clean the drum.

2. Inspect the drum for scoring, cracks, grooves and out-of-roundness. Replace the drum or have it "turned" at a machine or brake specialist shop, as required.

3. Light scoring may be removed by dressing the drum with fine emery cloth.

4. Heavy scoring will require the use of a brake drum lathe to turn the drum.

Brake Shoes

REMOVAL & INSTALLATION

1970–79

♦ See Figures 117, 118 and 119

1. Raise the rear of the truck and support it with safety stands. Remove the wheels.

2. Remove the brake drum.

3. Loosen the retracting spring clamp bolt on non self-adjusting brakes. On self-adjusters, remove the adjusting spring and lever at the bottom.

4. Using a brake spring tool, remove the return springs. On self-adjusters, also remove the adjusting cable, shoe guide plate, and the cable guide.

5. Remove the hold-down springs and the hold-down spring pins. On self-adjusters, first remove the parking brake shoe strut and spring, and the lower retracting spring and adjusting screw set. Then remove the hold down springs and pins.

6. Remove the parking brake shoe strut along with the spring on non self-adjusters only.

7. Grip the brake shoes at the top near the wheel cylinder, spread the shoes apart and draw the shoes, adjusting mechanism, and spring away from the backing plate. On self-adjusters, simply remove the brake shoes, as there should be no spring tension left. If the shoes are hard to remove, check for an obstructing part.

8. Remove the rear shoe and the parking brake shoe lever from the parking brake cable.

9. Remove the shoe lever form the shoe by removing the horseshoe clip form the pin.

To install non self-adjusting brakes:

10. Assemble the rear shoe to the parking brake shoe lever, install a new clip.

➡Coat all contact pints for the shoes and the parking brake mechanism with grease.

✳✳ CAUTION

Do not get grease on the linings or the inside of the brake drum.

11. Assemble the adjusting mechanism between the shoes and install the adjusting spring. The adjuster with left hand threads goes on the left wheel, right hand threads on the right wheel. Install the shoes onto the wheel cylinder and backing plate.

12. Install the hold-down pins and springs.

13. Install the parking brake strut arm and make the necessary connection of the emergency brake cable.

14. Install the return springs.

15. Install the brake drum and adjust the brake shoes.

16. Install the wheels and lower the truck. Bleed the brakes and road test the vehicle.

To install self-adjusting brakes:

17. Assemble the parking brake shoe lever and brake shoe.

18. Connect the parking brake shoe lever to the parking brake cable.

19. Apply a thin coat of grease to the backing plate and shoe contacting surfaces, and anchor pin and shoe end surfaces. Install the brake shoes, shorter lining shoe on the front, and the hold down springs and pins.

20. Install the spring onto the front of the parking brake shoe strut, and install the strut between the brake shoes.

21. Fit the shoe guide plate and automatic adjusting cable onto the anchor pin, and using a brake tool install the brake shoe return spring to the front side.

22. Apply a thin coat of grease to the cable guide sliding surface, and fit the cable guide to the rear shoe. Install the return spring to the rear shoe with a brake tool.

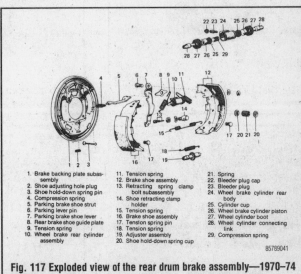

1. Brake backing plate subassembly
2. Shoe adjusting hole plug
3. Shoe hold-down spring pin
4. Compression spring
5. Parking brake shoe strut
6. Parking lever pin
7. Parking brake shoe lever
8. Rear brake shoe guide plate
9. Tension spring
10. Wheel brake rear cylinder assembly
11. Tension spring
12. Brake shoe assembly
13. Retracting spring clamp bolt subassembly
14. Shoe retracting clamp holder
15. Tension spring
16. Brake shoe assembly
17. Tension spring pin
18. Tension spring
19. Adjuster assembly
20. Shoe hold-down spring cup
21. Spring
22. Bleeder plug cap
23. Bleeder plug
24. Wheel brake cylinder rear body
25. Cylinder cup
26. Wheel brake cylinder piston
27. Wheel cylinder boot
28. Wheel cylinder connecting link
29. Compression spring

Fig. 117 Exploded view of the rear drum brake assembly—1970–74 Pick-up

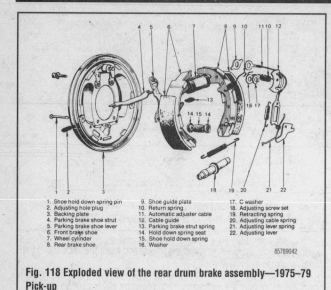

1. Shoe hold down spring pin
2. Adjusting hole plug
3. Backing plate
4. Parking brake shoe strut
5. Parking brake shoe lever
6. Front brake shoe
7. Wheel cylinder
8. Rear brake shoe
9. Shoe guide plate
10. Return spring
11. Automatic adjuster cable
12. Cable guide
13. Parking brake strut spring
14. Hold down spring seat
15. Shoe hold down spring
16. Washer
17. C washer
18. Adjusting screw set
19. Retracting spring
20. Adjusting cable spring
21. Adjusting lever spring
22. Adjusting lever

85789042

Fig. 118 Exploded view of the rear drum brake assembly—1975–79 Pick-up

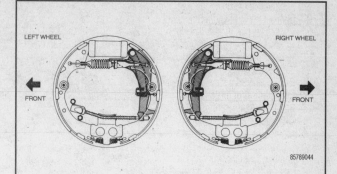

85789044

Fig. 120 Brake shoe installation—1980–88 2WD Pick-up w/leading-trailing brakes

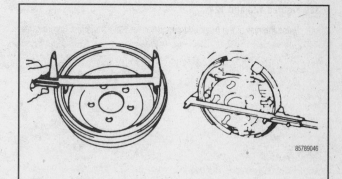

85789046

Fig. 121 Checking the difference between the inner brake drum diameter and the outer brake shoe diameter-all models

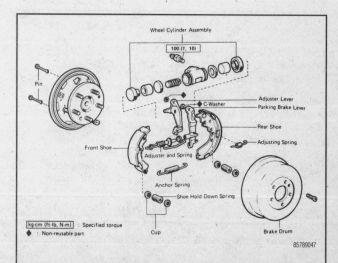

1. Brake drum
2. Shoe hold down springs and pins
3. She return springs
4. Shoe assemblies
5. Wheel cylinders

85789043

Fig. 119 Exploded view of the rear drum brake assembly—1971–83 Land Cruiser

23. Install the adjusting screw set, right hand threads on the right wheel. Apply a coat of grease to the threads, washer, and slots.

➡**Make sure that the threaded portion faces the front.**

24. Install the brake shoe retracting spring at the bottom, longer hook to the rear shoe.

25. Hook the adjusting lever to the adjusting cable spring. Insert the lever slot onto the pivot pin, and hook the adjusting lever spring onto the end of the lever.

26. With the parts assembled, test the auto-adjust mechanism. Insert a screw driver between the anchor pin and the rear shoe end, and move the shoe away from the pin. The adjuster should turn the adjusting screw set to expand slightly.

27. If the adjuster is OK, measure the maximum diameter of the brake drum, and adjust the shoes via the adjusting screw to be 0.012–0.6mm smaller to diameter.

28. Install the brake drum.

29. Install the wheels and lower the truck. Bleed the brakes and road test the vehicle.

1980–88 2WD Pick-Up W/Leading-Trailing Brakes

▶ **See Figures 120, 121 and 122**

1. Raise the rear of the truck and support it with safety stands. Remove the wheels.

2. Remove the brake drum.

3. Using a brake tool, remove the return spring adjuster.

4. Remove the front shoe hold-down spring and pin. Remove the front shoe with the anchor spring.

5. Remove the hold-down spring and pin and pull out the rear shoe.

6. Remove the strut and spring from the parking brake lever. Remove the adjusting lever spring.

7. Remove the parking brake cable from the lever.

To install:

8. Apply high temperature grease to the brake backing plate and the threads and end of the adjuster bolt.

Fig. 122 Exploded view of the rear drum brake assembly—1980–88 2WD Pick-up w/leading-trailing brakes

85789047

9. Pull the parking brake cable out and connect it to the lever.

10. Connect the strut and return spring to the lever.

11. Position the rear shoe so that the upper end of the shoe is in the wheel cylinder and the lower end is in the anchor plate. Install the pin and hold-down spring.

12. Connect the anchor spring to the rear shoe and then stretch it onto the front shoe.

13. Position the front shoe so the upper end is in the wheel cylinder and the lower end is in the strut. Install the pin and hold-down spring.

14. Install the return spring.

15. Check that the adjuster bolt turns while pulling up on the brake lever. Adjust the strut to the shortest possible length and install the brake drum. Pull the parking brake lever (inside the truck) out until the clicks stop.

16. Remove the brake drum and check that the difference between the inner brake drum diameter and the outer brake shoe diameter is no more than 0.6mm.

17. Install the brake drum. Install the wheels and lower the truck. Bleed the brakes and road test the vehicle.

1980–88 2WD Pick-Up and 1980–85 4WD Pick-Up W/Duo-Servo Brakes

▶ **See Figures 123 and 124**

1. Raise the rear of the truck and support it with safety stands. Remove the wheels.

2. Remove the brake drum.

3. Using a brake tool, remove the 2 return springs.

4. Push up on the brake adjusting lever and remove the cable, shoe guide plate and cable guide. Disconnect the spring at the brake lever and remove them both.

5. Using needle-nose pliers, remove the 2 tension springs.

6. Using a brake tool, remove the shoe hold-down springs and pins.

7. Remove the shoes, the adjuster and the strut.

8. Pull the parking brake cable out and disconnect it at the parking brake lever.

To install:

9. Apply high-temperature grease to the brake backing plate.

10. Pull the parking brake cable out and connect it to the lever.

11. Position the rear shoe so that its upper end is in the piston rod. Install the shoe hold-down spring and pin.

12. Install the strut with the spring to the rear. Position the front shoe over the strut so that the upper end in the piston rod. Install the hold-down spring and pin.

13. Grease the threads and end of the brake adjuster and install it between the brake shoes.

14. Install the shoe guide plate and the adjusting cable. Install the front return spring and then install the rear one.

15. While holding the tension spring against the rear shoe, hook the cable into the adjusting lever and install the lever. Pull the adjusting cable backward and release it; the adjusting bolt should turn.

16. Adjust the strut to the shortest possible length and install the brake drum. Pull the parking brake lever (inside the truck) out until the clicks stop.

17. Remove the brake drum and check that the difference between the inner brake drum diameter and the outer brake shoe diameter is no more than 0.6mm.

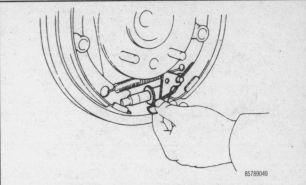

Fig. 124 Connecting the parking brake cable—1980–88 2WD Pick-up and 1980–85 4WD Pick-up w/duo servo brakes

18. Install the brake drum. Install the wheels and lower the truck. Bleed the brakes and road test the vehicle.

1986–88 4WD Pick-Up and 4Runner, 1980–88 Land Cruiser

▶ **See Figures 125, 126, 127, 128 and 129**

1. Raise the rear of the truck and support it with safety stands. Remove the wheels.

2. Remove the brake drum.

3. Remove the tension spring.

4. Remove the rear shoe hold-down spring and pin and then lift out the rear shoe and anchor spring.

5. Remove the front shoe hold-down spring and pin. Disconnect the No. 1 parking brake cable at the bellcrank. Remove the front shoe with the strut. Disconnect the other parking brake cable.

6. Disconnect the adjusting lever spring and remove the adjuster from the front shoe.

To install:

7. Apply high-temperature grease to the brake backing plate and the threads of the adjuster.

8. Position the adjuster in the adjusting lever and then install the adjusting spring.

9. Connect the parking brake cable to the shoe lever. Connect the other side of the cable to the bellcrank. Position the front shoe so the upper end is in the piston rod and install the hold-down spring and pin.

10. Connect the anchor spring to the front shoe and then stretch it onto the rear shoe. Position the rear shoe and install the hold-down spring and pin.

11. Install the tension spring.

12. Pull the bellcrank in direction **A** until there is no slack at **B**. Turn the adjusting bolt so that **C** will be 0.4–0.8mm. Lock the adjusting bolt with the locknut.

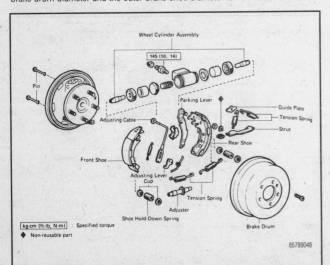

Fig. 123 Exploded view of the rear drum brake assembly—1980–88 2WD Pick-up and 1980–85 4WD Pick-up w/duo servo brakes

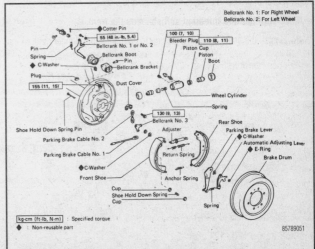

Fig. 125 Exploded view of the rear drum brake assembly—1986–88 4WD Pick-up and 4Runner and 1984–88 Land Cruiser

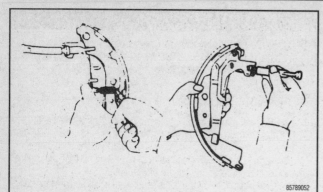

Fig. 126 Positioning the brake shoe adjuster—1986–88 4WD Pick-up and 4Runner and 1984–88 Land Cruiser

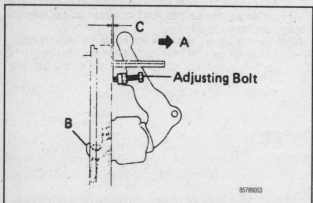

Fig. 127 Bellcrank installation—1986–88 4WD Pick-up and 4Runner

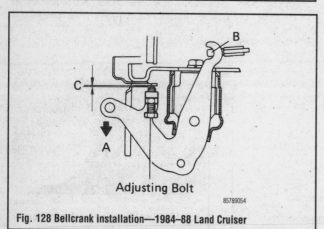

Fig. 128 Bellcrank installation—1984–88 Land Cruiser

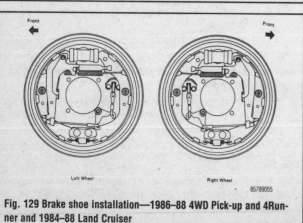

Fig. 129 Brake shoe installation—1986–88 4WD Pick-up and 4Runner and 1984–88 Land Cruiser

13. Connect the parking brake cable to the bellcrank and install the tension spring.

14. Check that the parking brake lever (inside truck) travel is correct and that the adjuster turns while pulling the lever.

15. Turn the adjuster to the shortest possible length and install the brake drum. Pull the parking brake lever (inside the truck) out until the clicks stop.

16. Remove the brake drum and check that the difference between the inner brake drum diameter and the outer brake shoe diameter is no more than 0.6mm.

17. Install the brake drum. Install the wheels and lower the truck. Bleed the brakes and road test the vehicle.

Wheel Cylinders

REMOVAL & INSTALLATION

1. Plug the master cylinder inlet to prevent hydraulic fluid from leaking.

2. Remove the brake drums and shoes.

3. Working from behind the backing plate, disconnect the hydraulic line from the wheel cylinder.

4. Unfasten the screws retaining the wheel cylinder and withdraw the cylinder.

5. Installation is performed in the reverse order of removal. However, on certain older models, once the hydraulic line has been disconnected from the wheel cylinder, the union seat must be replaced.

To replace the seat:

6. Use a screw extractor with a diameter of 2.5mm and having reverse threads, to remove the union seat from the wheel cylinder.

7. Drive in the new union seat with a 8mm bar, used as a drift.

Remember to bleed the brake system after completing wheel cylinder, brake shoe and drum installation.

OVERHAUL

▶ **See Figure 130**

It is not necessary to remove the wheel cylinder from the backing plate if it is only to be inspected or rebuilt.

1. Remove the brake drum and shoes. Remove the wheel cylinder only if it is going to be replaced.

2. Remove the rubber boots from either end of the wheel cylinder.

3. Withdraw the piston and cup assemblies.

4. Take the compression spring out of the wheel cylinder body.

5. Remove the bleeder plug (and ball), if necessary.

6. Check all components for wear or damage. Inspect the bore for signs of wear, scoring, and/or scuffing. If in doubt, replace or hone the wheel cylinder (with a special hone). The limit for honing a cylinder is 0.13mm oversize. Wash all the residue from the cylinder bore with clean brake fluid and blow dry.

To assemble:

7. Soak all components in clean brake fluid, and coat them with the rubber grease supplied in the wheel cylinder rebuilding kit.

8. Install the spring, cups (recesses toward the center), and pistons in the cylinder body, in that order.

9. Insert the boots over the ends of the cylinder.

10. Install the bleeder plug (and ball), if removed.

11. Assemble the brake shoes and install the drum.

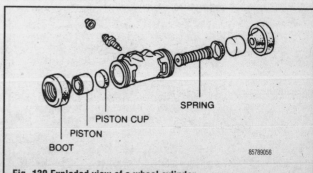

Fig. 130 Exploded view of a wheel cylinder

PARKING BRAKE

Adjustment

PICK-UP AND 4Runner

1970–79

▶ **See Figure 131**

➡**Before attempting to adjust the parking brake, adjust the rear brake shoes as outlined earlier.**

1. Loosen the parking brake warning light switch bracket.
2. Push the parking brake lever in until it is stopped by the pawl.
3. Move the switch so that it will be **OFF** at this position, but **ON** when the handle is pulled out.
4. Tighten the switch bracket and push the bracket lever in again.
5. Working from underneath the vehicle, loosen the locknut on the parking brake cable equalizer.
6. Screw the adjusting nut in, just enough that the brake cables have no slack.
7. Hold the adjusting nut in this position while tightening the locknut.
8. Check the rotation of the rear wheels to make sure that the brakes are not dragging.

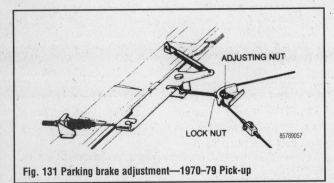

Fig. 131 Parking brake adjustment—1970–79 Pick-up

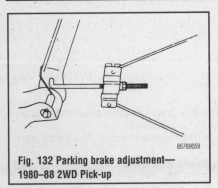

Fig. 132 Parking brake adjustment—1980–88 2WD Pick-up

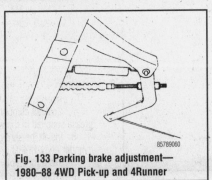

Fig. 133 Parking brake adjustment—1980–88 4WD Pick-up and 4Runner

Fig. 134 View of parking brake adjustment location

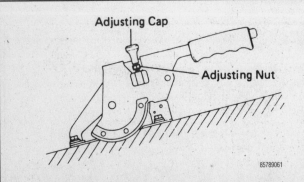

Fig. 135 Parking brake lever adjustment—1984–88 Land Cruiser

9. Pull out the parking lever and count the number of notches needed to apply the brake. If it is between 6 and 9 notches, the brake is properly adjusted.

1980–88

▶ **See Figures 132, 133 and 134**

1. Pull the parking brake lever all the way out and count the number of clicks to the end of travel. 1980–83 models should have 7–15 clicks; 1984–88 2WD models should have 10–16 clicks; 1984–85 4WD models should have 7–15 clicks; and 1986–88 4WD models should have 9–17 clicks. If the parking brake lever is not within these ranges, adjust as follows.

   a. Under the truck on 2WD models, there is an equalizer bar where the 2 cables come together. Tighten or loosen the adjusting nut until the lever travel is within the proper range. Check that the rear brakes are not dragging.

   b. Working under the truck on 4WD models, tighten the bellcrank stopper screw until the play in the rear brake links becomes zero, and then loosen the screw 1 turn. Tighten the locknut.

   Tighten one of the adjusting nuts on the intermediate lever while loosening the other one until the lever travel is correct. Tighten the adjusting nuts.

   After adjustment, check that the bellcrank stopper screw is touching the back of the brake backing plate.

2. Recheck the parking brake travel.

Land Cruiser

▶ **See Figure 135**

1971–83

Land Cruiser models use a separate drum brake assembly, operating on the drive shaft, to serve as a parking brake. Adjust it as follows:
1. Push the parking brake lever all the way in, so that the brake is released.
2. Raise the rear of the vehicle and support it with jackstands.
3. Turn the parking brake adjustment shaft, which is located at the bottom of the parking brake backing plate, counterclockwise until the shoes seat against the drum.
4. Back the adjuster off one notch.

5. Apply the parking brake; the drum should be locked. Release the brake; the drum should rotate freely.

➡**If the drum does not rotate freely with the brake off, loosen the adjuster one more notch.**

6. Adjust the turnbuckles on the parking brake intermediate levers and the adjusting nuts on the end of the parking brake cables, so that 6–9 notches are required to apply the parking brake (1975). Set it for 7–12 notches on the 1976–83 models.

1984–88

Parking brake adjustment procedures for these models are the same as those detailed in the 1980–88 Pick-up section. Use the 4WD steps and adjust the parking brake to 7–9 notches.

BRAKE SPECIFICATIONS
(All measurements given are (in.) unless noted)

Year	Model	Lug Nut Torque (ft. lbs.)	Brake Disk Minimum Thickness	Brake Disk Maximum Run-Out	Brake Drum Diameter	Brake Drum Max. Machine O/S	Brake Drum Max. Wear Limit	Minimum Lining Thickness Front	Minimum Lining Thickness Rear
1970	Pick-Up	65-86	—	—	9.10	9.13	9.15	0.06	0.06
1971	Pick-Up	65-86	—	—	9.10	9.13	9.15	0.06	0.06
	Land Cruiser	65-86	0.750	0.005	11.70	—	11.90	②	0.06
1972	Pick-Up	65-86	0.750	0.005	9.10	9.13	9.15	0.06	0.06
	Land Cruiser	65-86	0.750	0.005	11.70	—	11.90	②	0.06
1973	Pick-Up	65-86	0.750	0.005	10.00	10.07	10.08	0.27	0.06
	Land Cruiser	65-86	0.750	0.005	11.70	—	11.90	②	0.06
1974	Pick-Up	65-86	—	—	10.00	10.07	10.08	0.27	0.06
	Land Cruiser	65-86	0.750	0.005	11.70	10.07	11.90	②	0.06
1975	Pick-Up	65-86	0.453②	0.0059	10.00	10.07	10.08	0.27	0.06
	Land Cruiser	65-86	0.750	0.005	11.70	—	11.90	②	0.06
1976	Pick-Up	65-86	0.453②	0.0059	10.00	10.07	10.08	0.27	0.06
	Land Cruiser	65-86	0.750	0.005	11.70	—	11.90	②	0.06
1977	Pick-Up	65-86	0.453②	0.0059	10.00	10.07	10.08	0.27	0.06
	Land Cruiser	65-86	0.750	0.005	11.70	—	11.90	②	0.06
1978	Pick-Up	65-86	0.453②	0.0059	10.00	—	10.08	0.04	0.04
	Land Cruiser	65-86	0.750	0.005	11.70	—	11.90	②	0.06
1979	Pick-Up	65-86	0.453②	0.0059	10.08	—	10.08	0.039	0.039
	Land Cruiser	65-86	0.750	0.005	11.70	—	11.90	②	0.06
1980	Pick-Up	65-86	0.453②	0.0059	10.00	—	10.08	0.039	0.039
	Land Cruiser	65-86	0.750	0.005	11.70	—	11.90	②	0.06
1981	Pick-Up	65-86	0.453②	0.0059	10.00	—	10.08	0.039	0.039
	Land Cruiser	65-86	0.750	0.005	11.70	—	11.90	②	0.06
1982	Pick-Up	65-86	0.453②	0.0059	10.00	—	10.08	0.039	0.039
	Land Cruiser	65-86	0.750	0.005	11.70	—	11.90	②	0.06
1983	Pick-Up	65-86	0.453②	0.0059	10.00	—	10.08	0.039	0.039
	Land Cruiser	65-86	0.750	0.005	11.70	—	11.90	②	0.06
1984	Pick-Up	65-86	③	0.0059	10.00	—	10.079	0.039	0.039
	Land Cruiser	65-86	0.748	0.0059	11.614	—	11.693	③	0.059
1985	Pick-Up	65-86	③	0.0059	10.00	—	10.079	③	0.059
	4 Runner	65-86	③	0.0059	10.00	—	10.079	0.039	0.039
	Land Cruiser	65-86	0.748	0.0059	11.614	—	11.693	③	0.039
1986	Pick-Up	65-86	③	0.0059	10.00	—	10.079	③	0.059
	4 Runner	65-86	③	0.0059	10.00	—	10.079	0.039	0.039
	Land Cruiser	65-86	0.748	0.0059	11.614	—	11.693	③	0.059

85789C05

BRAKE SPECIFICATIONS
(All measurements given are (in.) unless noted)

Year	Model	Lug Nut Torque (ft. lbs.)	Brake Disk Minimum Thickness	Brake Disk Maximum Run-Out	Brake Drum Diameter	Brake Drum Max. Machine O/S	Brake Drum Max. Wear Limit	Minimum Lining Thickness Front	Minimum Lining Thickness Rear
1987	Pick-Up	65-86	⑤	0.0059	⑥	—	⑦	③	0.039
	4 Runner	65-86	⑤	0.0059	⑥	—	11.693	③	0.039
	Land Cruiser	65-86	0.748	0.0059	11.614	—	11.693	③	0.059
1988	Pick-Up	65-86	⑤	0.0059	⑥	—	⑦	③	0.039
	4 Runner	65-86	⑤	0.0059	⑥	—	11.693	③	0.039
	Land Cruiser	65-86	0.748	0.0059	11.614	—	11.693	③	0.059

85789C06

① K-Type: 0.79, some 1978 Hi-Lux models have front drum brakes, diameter:
10.00 (limit: 10.08), lining thickness: 0.04
② C&C: 0.748
③ Pads: 0.04, shoes: 0.06
④ 2 wd w/PD60: 0.945
　2 wd w/FS17: 0.827
⑤ 2 wd: 0.748
　4 wd: 0.748
⑥ 2 wd: 10.00
　4 wd: 11.64
⑦ 2 wd: 10.079
　4 wd: 11.693

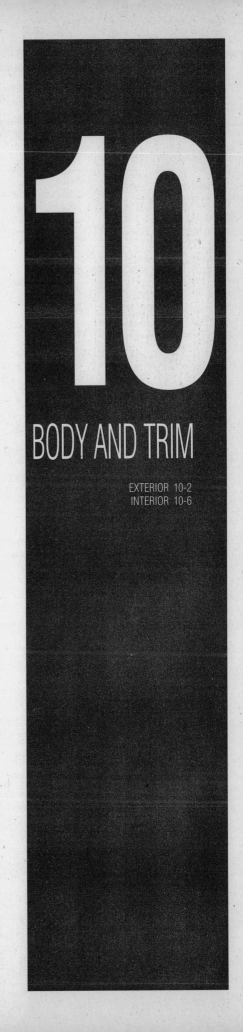

10

BODY AND TRIM

EXTERIOR

Doors

REMOVAL & INSTALLATION

▶ **See Figure 1**

1. Matchmark the hinge-to-body and hinge-to-door locations. Support the door either on jackstands or have somebody hold it for you.
2. On models with a center door check bar, push in on the claw and pull out the stopper pin retainer.
3. Remove the lower hinge-to-door bolts.
4. Remove the upper hinge-to-door bolts and lift the door off the hinges.
5. If the hinges are being replaced, remove them from the door pillar.
6. Install the door and hinges with the bolts finger tight.
7. Adjust the door and tighten the hinge bolts.

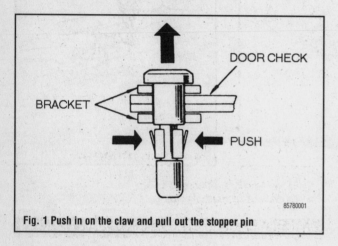

Fig. 1 Push in on the claw and pull out the stopper pin

ADJUSTMENT

▶ **See Figures 2, 3 and 4**

➡**Loosen the hinge-to-door bolts for lateral adjustment only. Loosen the hinge-to-body bolts for both lateral and vertical adjustment.**

1. Determine which hinge bolts are to be loosened and back them out just enough to allow movement.
2. To move the door safely, use a padded pry bar. When the door is in the proper position, tighten the bolts and check the door operation. There should be no binding or interference when the door is closed and opened.
3. Door closing adjustment can also be affected by the position of the lock striker plate. Loosen the striker plate bolts and move the striker plate just enough to permit proper closing and locking of the door.

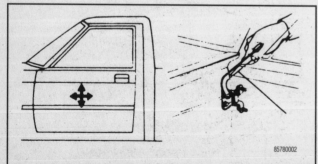

Fig. 2 Adjusting the doors for the forward/rearward and up/down directions

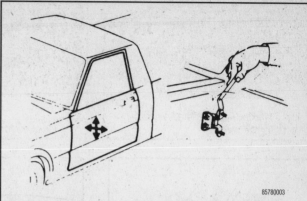

Fig. 3 Adjusting the doors in the left/right and vertical directions

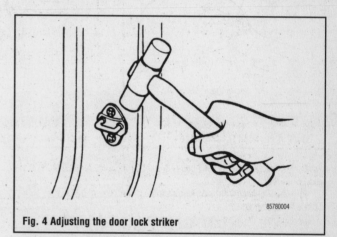

Fig. 4 Adjusting the door lock striker

Hood

REMOVAL & INSTALLATION

▶ **See Figures 5 and 6**

➡**You'll need an assistant for this job.**

1. Open the hood.
2. Remove the 2 link assembly bolts.
3. Matchmark the hood-to-hinge position.
4. Remove the hood-to-hinge bolts and lift off the hood.
5. Installation is the reverse of removal. Loosely install the hood and align the matchmarks. Tighten all bolts.

ADJUSTMENT

▶ **See Figures 7, 8, 9 and 10**

1. Open the hood and matchmark the hinge and latch positions.
2. Loosen the hinge-to-fender bolts just enough to allow movement of the hood.
3. Move the hood as required to obtain the proper fit and alignment between the hood and the top of the cowl panel. Tighten the bolts.
4. Loosen the 2 latch attaching bolts.
5. Loosen the hinge-to-hood bolts just enough to allow movement of the hood.
6. Move the hood forward/backward and/or side-to-side to obtain a proper hood fit.
7. Tighten the hood-to-hinge bolts.

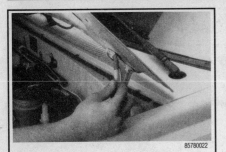

Fig. 5 Marking the hood hinge before removing the hood

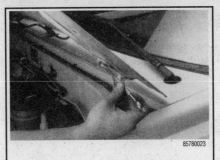

Fig. 6 Removing the hood hinge bolts

Fig. 7 Hood adjustment for the forward/ rearward and right and left directions

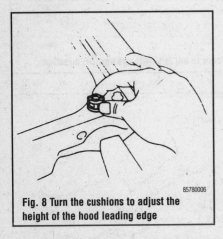

Fig. 8 Turn the cushions to adjust the height of the hood leading edge

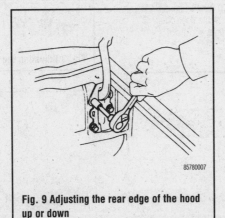

Fig. 9 Adjusting the rear edge of the hood up or down

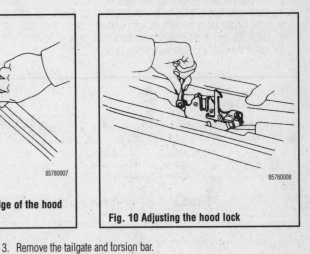

Fig. 10 Adjusting the hood lock

8. The leading edge of the hood may also be adjusted by turning the 2 hood cushions.

9. Move the latch from side-to-side to align the latch with the striker. Torque the latch bolts.

10. Lubricate the latch and hinges and check the hood fit several times.

Tailgate

REMOVAL & INSTALLATION

1. Remove the tailgate support strap at the pillar T-head pivot.
2. Remove the 2 bolts at the tailgate hinge.
3. Remove the tailgate and torsion bar.
4. Installation is the reverse of removal.

Front or Rear Bumper

REMOVAL & INSTALLATION

▶ **See Figure 11**

1. Support the bumper.
2. Remove the nuts and bolts attaching the bumper to the frame.
3. Installation is the reverse of removal.

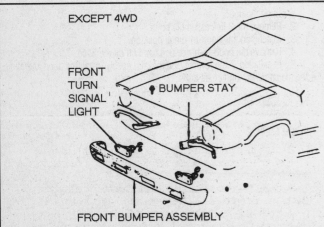

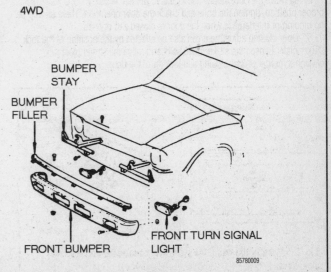

EXCEPT 4WD

FRONT TURN SIGNAL LIGHT

BUMPER STAY

FRONT BUMPER ASSEMBLY

4WD

BUMPER STAY

BUMPER FILLER

FRONT BUMPER

FRONT TURN SIGNAL LIGHT

Fig. 11 Removing the front bumper (typical)

Mirrors

REMOVAL & INSTALLATION

All mirrors are removed by removing the mounting screws and lifting off the mirror and gasket.

Antenna

REMOVAL & INSTALLATION

1. Disconnect the antenna cable at the radio by pulling it straight out of the set.
2. Working under the instrument panel, disengage the cable from its retainers.

➡**On some models, it may be necessary to remove the instrument panel pad to get at the cable.**

3. Outside, unsnap the cap from the antenna base.
4. Remove the screw(s) and lift off the antenna, pulling the cable with it, carefully.
5. Installation is the reverse of removal.

Rear Quarter Window And Rear Windshield

REMOVAL & INSTALLATION

Pick-Up Only

▶ **See Figures 12 and 13**

➡**You'll need an assistant for this job.**

1. Have your assistant stand outside and support the glass.
2. Working from the inside truck, start at one upper corner and work the weather-stripping across the top of the glass, pulling the weather-stripping

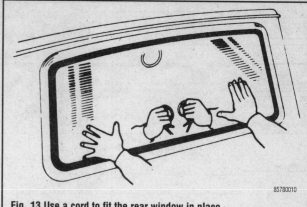

Fig. 13 Use a cord to fit the rear window in place

down and pushing outward on the glass until your assistant can grab the glass and lift it out.

3. Remove the moldings.
4. Remove the weather-stripping from the glass.

To install:

5. Clean the weather-stripping, glass and glass opening with solvent to remove all old sealer.
6. Apply liquid butyl sealer in the glass channel of the weather-stripping and install the weather-stripping on the glass.
7. Install the moldings.
8. Apply a bead of sealer to the opening flange and in the inner flange crevice of the weather-stripping lip.
9. Place a length of strong cord, such as butcher's twine, in the flange crevice of the weather-stripping. The cord should go all the way around the weather-stripping with the ends, about 18 in. long each, hanging down together at the bottom center of the window.
10. Apply soapy water to the weather-stripping lip.
11. Have your assistant position the window assembly in the channel from the outside, applying firm inward pressure.

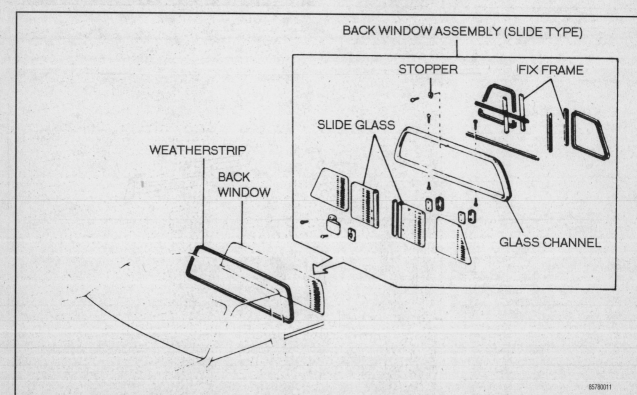

Fig. 12 Rear window assembly—Pick-up only

12. From inside, you guide the lip of the weather-stripping into place using the cord, working each end alternately, until the window is locked in place.

13. Remove the cord, clean the glass and weather-stripping of excess sealer and leak test the window.

DISASSEMBLY

Pick-Up W/Sliding Rear Windows

▶ **See Figure 14**

1. Remove the rear windshield.
2. Remove the sliding glass stopper from the window frame.
3. Remove the mounting screws for the 2 center support frames.
4. While pulling the upper and lower window frame apart, slide the glass into the center of the window and remove each sliding pane from the frame.

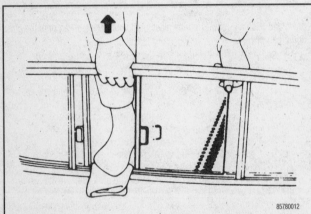

85780012

Fig. 14 Pull the upper and lower window frame channels apart to remove the sliding glass

5. Pull apart the upper and lower frame again and remove the 2 center supports. Slide the stationary glass into the center of the frame and remove it. Repeat for the other side.

6. Coat the mating surfaces of the window frame and the weather stripping with soapy water and slide the 2 stationary window halves into position.

7. Install the 2 center support frames.
8. Install the sliding glass halves, tighten the center frame mounting screws and install the window stopper.
9. Install the entire assembly as previously detailed.

Cover Top

REMOVAL & INSTALLATION

4Runner Only

▶ **See Figure 15**

1. Open the rear window and remove the body garnishes.
2. Disconnect the electrical lead and the hose at the rear washer motor.
3. Remove mounting bolt **B** and then remove the other bolts.
4. Remove the cover top and place it on pieces of wood on the ground.

✳✳ CAUTION

Mounting bolt B controls the cover top switch. Never install it when the cover top is removed!

5. Position the cover top on the truck body and install bolts **E** and **J**. Install bolts **C** and **L**. Tighten all bolts to 10 ft. lbs. (14 Nm).
6. Loosen bolts **E** and **J**.
7. Install and tighten bolts **D** and **K** and then retighten bolts **E** and **J**.
8. Install all remaining bolts and tighten them to 10 ft. lbs. (14 Nm). Install and tighten bolt **B**.
9. Connect the washer motor lead and hose, install the garnishes and close the tailgate. Check for proper operation of the rear window.

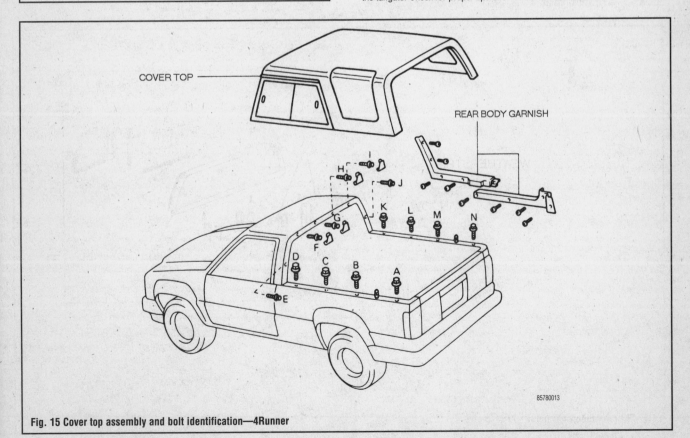

COVER TOP

REAR BODY GARNISH

85780013

Fig. 15 Cover top assembly and bolt identification—4Runner

INTERIOR

Instrument Panel and Pad

REMOVAL & INSTALLATION

See Section 6 for all necessary service procedures.

Door Trim Panels

REMOVAL & INSTALLATION

♦ **See Figures 16, 17 and 18**

1. Remove the bezel from the inside door handle.
2. Remove the armrest or pull handle.

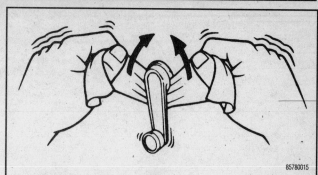

Fig. 17 Using a piece of cloth to remove the window regulator handle

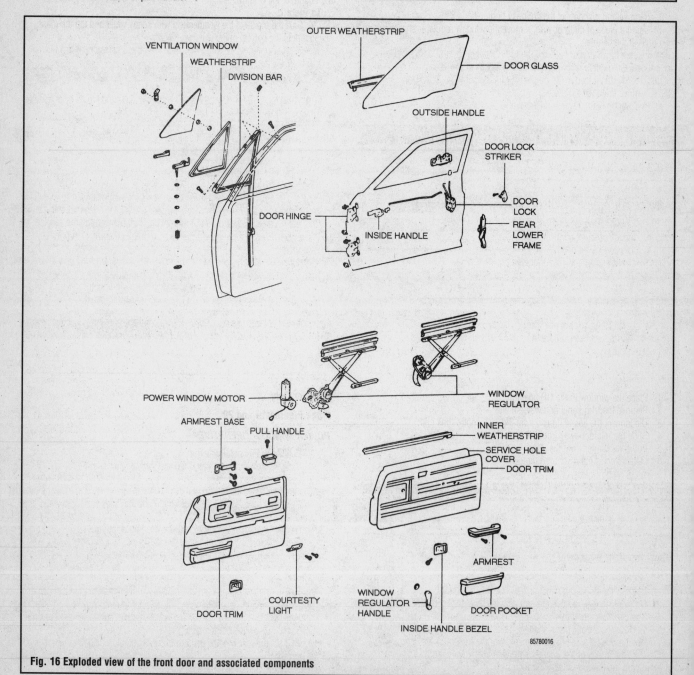

Fig. 16 Exploded view of the front door and associated components

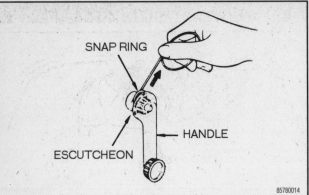

SNAP RING

HANDLE

ESCUTCHEON

85780014

Fig. 18 Using a piece of wire to remove the window regulator handle

3. Remove and disconnect the courtesy light.

4. Using a piece of cloth or wire, remove the window regulator snapring and then pull off the handle.

5. Insert a small prybar between the trim retainers and the door panel and pry it loose. On models with full door trim, pull up the trim and pry it off. Disconnect the electrical lead at the power window switch if equipped.

6. Remove the door trim panel.

7. Installation is the reverse of removal.

Door Locks

REMOVAL & INSTALLATION

1. Remove the door trim panel and the service hole cover.
2. Disconnect the:
   a. inside locking control link
   b. outside opening control link
   c. outside locking control link.
3. Remove the door lock cylinder with a pair of pliers.
4. Install the lock cylinder and connect the links.
5. Loosen the mounting screws for the inside door handle and push it forward until resistance is felt. Move it backwards slightly and tighten the mounting screws.
6. Disconnect the control link form the outside door handle about 1mm from rest. Turn the adjuster on the link until it will fit into the mounting hole of the raised handle.

Door Lock Cylinder

1. Place the window in the UP position.
2. Remove the trim panel and watershield.
3. Disconnect the actuating rod from the lock control link clip.
4. Slide the retainer away from the lock cylinder.
5. Pull the cylinder from the door.
6. Installation is the reverse of removal.

Door Glass and Regulator

REMOVAL & INSTALLATION

Glass w/o Vent Window

1. Lower the window.
2. Remove the door trim panel and the service hole cover.
3. On later models, remove the armrest base and the inside door handle.
4. Remove the inner and outer weather-strips.
5. Remove the 2 door glass channel mounting bolts and pull the window up and out of the door. Pry the glass channel from the bottom of the window.
6. Coat the inside of the weather strip with soapy water and tap the glass channel onto the bottom of the window.

7. Slide the window into the door until the 2 glass channel mounting bolts can be fitted. Tighten the bolts.
8. Install the weather strips. Install the armrest base and inside door handle.
9. Install the service hole cover and the door trim panel.

Glass W/Vent Window

1. Lower the window.
2. Remove the door trim panel and the service hole cover.
3. On later models, remove the armrest base and the inside door handle.
4. Remove the inner and outer weather-strips.
5. Remove the glass run and the rear lower frame.
6. Remove the 2 glass channel mounting bolts and place the window on the bottom of the door cavity.
7. Peel off the weatherstrip on the upper side of the vent window. Remove the 3 screws and the division bar set bolt. Pull the vent window up and out of the door frame.
8. Pull the main window up and out of the door. Pry the glass channel from the bottom of the window.

To install:

9. Coat the inside of the weatherstrip with soapy water and tap the glass channel onto the bottom of the window.
10. Slide the main window into the door until the 2 glass channel mounting bolts can be fitted.
11. Position the vent window and install the 3 mounting screws and the set bolt. Tighten the 2 glass channel mounting bolts.
12. Install the weather-strips. Install the armrest base and inside door handle.
13. Install the service hole cover and the door trim panel.

Regulator

1. Remove the door trim panel.
2. Remove the service hole cover.
3. Remove the window.
4. If the truck has power windows, disconnect the electrical lead from the motor.
5. Remove the regulator mounting bolts and lift it out through the service hole. On models without a vent window, remove the 2 equalizer arm bracket mounting bolts.
6. Install the regulator and tighten the mounting bolts. On models with a vent window, install the 2 equalizer arm bracket mounting bolts.
7. Connect the lead to the power window motor if equipped.
8. Install the window, service hole cover and door trim panel.

Tailgate Window

REMOVAL & INSTALLATION

4Runner Only

▶ See Figures 19 and 20

POWER WINDOW OPERATIVE

1. Remove the inner tailgate trim.
2. Remove the tailgate plate and the service hole cover.
3. Disconnect the control link for the inside handle at the regulator, remove the 2 mounting screws and lift out the door handle.
4. Disconnect the inside lock knob link at the regulator and remove the knob and link.
5. Remove the upper door trim and the weather stripping.
6. Move the locking assembly into the **LOCK** position and then raise the rear window until the regulator arms are in a straight line.
7. Disconnect the electrical lead at the regulator. Disconnect the leads for the rear defogger at the window.
8. Disconnect the door lock control cables at the regulator side. Disconnect the 2 remaining leads and the ground cable at the regulator.
9. Remove the 3 regulator mounting bolts and then shimmy it side-to-side until the arms pull away from the glass.
10. Pull out the rear window and remove the regulator.

To install:

11. Slide the window into the tailgate.

12. Shimmy the regulator side-to-side until the arms position themselves in the glass channel and then install the regulator mounting bolts.

13. Connect the rear defogger leads to the window. Connect the 2 leads and the ground cable at the regulator.

14. Use the original clamps and connect the door lock control cables to the regulator.

15. Connect the power lead to the regulator.

16. Install the upper tailgate trim and weather stripping.

17. Install the inside lock knob and link.

18. Install the inside handle and connect the control link to the regulator.

19. Seal the service hole cover with butyl tape (6mm), insert the lower edge into the panel slit and then seal the slit with cotton tape being careful not to block the trim clip seats.

20. Install the plate and lower tailgate trim.

POWER WINDOW INOPERATIVE

1. Remove the inner tailgate trim.

2. Remove the tailgate plate and the service hole cover.

3. Disconnect the control link for the inside handle at the regulator, remove the 2 mounting screws and lift out the door handle.

4. Disconnect the inside lock knob link at the regulator and remove the knob and link.

5. Remove the upper door trim and the weather stripping.

6. Disconnect the power lead, 2 electrical leads and the ground cable at the regulator.

7. Disconnect the door lock control cables at the regulator.

8. Remove the mounting bolts and lift out the regulator motor. SOMEONE MUST HOLD THE REAR WINDOW while removing the regulator motor!

9. Lower the rear window all the way and open the door by pulling on the control cables. Raise the window until the regulator arms are horizontal and install a small pin into the service hole in the regulator to secure the arms.

10. Disconnect the rear defogger leads at the window.

11. Remove the regulator mounting bolts, slide the regulator side-to-side until the arms pull out of the window channel and then lift out the regulator.

12. Lift out the rear window.

To install:

13. Slide the window into the tailgate.

14. Shimmy the regulator side-to-side until the arms position themselves in the glass channel and then install the regulator mounting bolts.

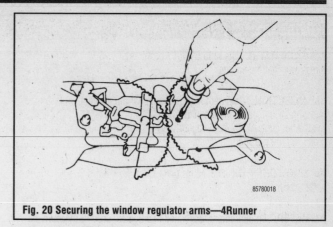

Fig. 20 Securing the window regulator arms—4Runner

15. Connect the rear defogger leads to the window. Connect the 2 leads and the ground cable at the regulator.

16. Use the original clamps and connect the door lock control cables to the regulator.

17. Connect the power lead to the regulator.

18. Install the upper tailgate trim and weather stripping.

19. Install the inside lock knob and link.

20. Install the inside handle and connect the control link to the regulator.

21. Seal the service hole cover with butyl tape (6mm), insert the lower edge into the panel slit and then seal the slit with cotton tape being careful not to block the trim clip seats.

22. Install the plate and lower tailgate trim.

Power Window Motor

REMOVAL & INSTALLATION

1. Remove the window regulator.

2. Disconnect the motor from the regulator.

3. Installation is in the reverse order of removal.

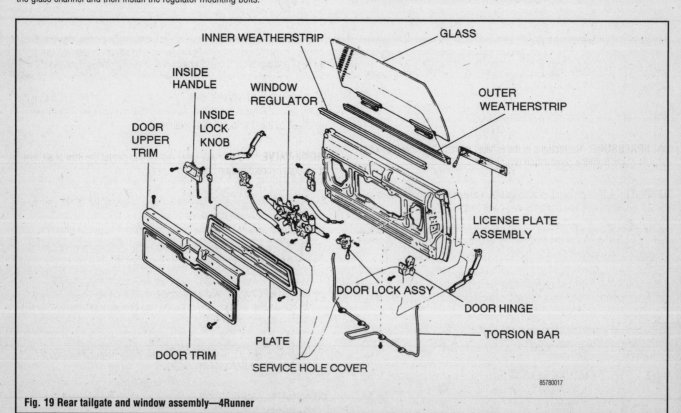

Fig. 19 Rear tailgate and window assembly—4Runner

GLOSSARY

AIR/FUEL RATIO: The ratio of air-to-gasoline by weight in the fuel mixture drawn into the engine.

AIR INJECTION: One method of reducing harmful exhaust emissions by injecting air into each of the exhaust ports of an engine. The fresh air entering the hot exhaust manifold causes any remaining fuel to be burned before it can exit the tailpipe.

ALTERNATOR: A device used for converting mechanical energy into electrical energy.

AMMETER: An instrument, calibrated in amperes, used to measure the flow of an electrical current in a circuit. Ammeters are always connected in series with the circuit being tested.

AMPERE: The rate of flow of electrical current present when one volt of electrical pressure is applied against one ohm of electrical resistance.

ANALOG COMPUTER: Any microprocessor that uses similar (analogous) electrical signals to make its calculations.

ARMATURE: A laminated, soft iron core wrapped by a wire that converts electrical energy to mechanical energy as in a motor or relay. When rotated in a magnetic field, it changes mechanical energy into electrical energy as in a generator.

ATMOSPHERIC PRESSURE: The pressure on the Earth's surface caused by the weight of the air in the atmosphere. At sea level, this pressure is 14.7 psi at 32°F (101 kPa at 0°C).

ATOMIZATION: The breaking down of a liquid into a fine mist that can be suspended in air.

AXIAL PLAY: Movement parallel to a shaft or bearing bore.

BACKFIRE: The sudden combustion of gases in the intake or exhaust system that results in a loud explosion.

BACKLASH: The clearance or play between two parts, such as meshed gears.

BACKPRESSURE: Restrictions in the exhaust system that slow the exit of exhaust gases from the combustion chamber.

BAKELITE: A heat resistant, plastic insulator material commonly used in printed circuit boards and transistorized components.

BALL BEARING: A bearing made up of hardened inner and outer races between which hardened steel balls roll.

BALLAST RESISTOR: A resistor in the primary ignition circuit that lowers voltage after the engine is started to reduce wear on ignition components.

BEARING: A friction reducing, supportive device usually located between a stationary part and a moving part.

BIMETAL TEMPERATURE SENSOR: Any sensor or switch made of two dissimilar types of metal that bend when heated or cooled due to the different expansion rates of the alloys. These types of sensors usually function as an on/off switch.

BLOWBY: Combustion gases, composed of water vapor and unburned fuel, that leak past the piston rings into the crankcase during normal engine operation. These gases are removed by the PCV system to prevent the buildup of harmful acids in the crankcase.

BRAKE PAD: A brake shoe and lining assembly used with disc brakes.

BRAKE SHOE: The backing for the brake lining. The term is, however, usually applied to the assembly of the brake backing and lining.

BUSHING: A liner, usually removable, for a bearing; an anti-friction liner used in place of a bearing.

CALIPER: A hydraulically activated device in a disc brake system, which is mounted straddling the brake rotor (disc). The caliper contains at least one piston and two brake pads. Hydraulic pressure on the piston(s) forces the pads against the rotor.

CAMSHAFT: A shaft in the engine on which are the lobes (cams) which operate the valves. The camshaft is driven by the crankshaft, via a belt, chain or gears, at one half the crankshaft speed.

CAPACITOR: A device which stores an electrical charge.

CARBON MONOXIDE (CO): A colorless, odorless gas given off as a normal byproduct of combustion. It is poisonous and extremely dangerous in confined areas, building up slowly to toxic levels without warning if adequate ventilation is not available.

CARBURETOR: A device, usually mounted on the intake manifold of an engine, which mixes the air and fuel in the proper proportion to allow even combustion.

CATALYTIC CONVERTER: A device installed in the exhaust system, like a muffler, that converts harmful byproducts of combustion into carbon dioxide and water vapor by means of a heat-producing chemical reaction.

CENTRIFUGAL ADVANCE: A mechanical method of advancing the spark timing by using flyweights in the distributor that react to centrifugal force generated by the distributor shaft rotation.

CHECK VALVE: Any one-way valve installed to permit the flow of air, fuel or vacuum in one direction only.

CHOKE: A device, usually a moveable valve, placed in the intake path of a carburetor to restrict the flow of air.

CIRCUIT: Any unbroken path through which an electrical current can flow. Also used to describe fuel flow in some instances.

CIRCUIT BREAKER: A switch which protects an electrical circuit from overload by opening the circuit when the current flow exceeds a predetermined level. Some circuit breakers must be reset manually, while most reset automatically.

COIL (IGNITION): A transformer in the ignition circuit which steps up the voltage provided to the spark plugs.

COMBINATION MANIFOLD: An assembly which includes both the intake and exhaust manifolds in one casting.

COMBINATION VALVE: A device used in some fuel systems that routes fuel vapors to a charcoal storage canister instead of venting them into the atmosphere. The valve relieves fuel tank pressure and allows fresh air into the tank as the fuel level drops to prevent a vapor lock situation.

COMPRESSION RATIO: The comparison of the total volume of the cylinder and combustion chamber with the piston at BDC and the piston at TDC.

CONDENSER: 1. An electrical device which acts to store an electrical charge, preventing voltage surges. 2. A radiator-like device in the air conditioning system in which refrigerant gas condenses into a liquid, giving off heat.

CONDUCTOR: Any material through which an electrical current can be transmitted easily.

CONTINUITY: Continuous or complete circuit. Can be checked with an ohmmeter.

COUNTERSHAFT: An intermediate shaft which is rotated by a mainshaft and transmits, in turn, that rotation to a working part.

CRANKCASE: The lower part of an engine in which the crankshaft and related parts operate.

CRANKSHAFT: The main driving shaft of an engine which receives reciprocating motion from the pistons and converts it to rotary motion.

CYLINDER: In an engine, the round hole in the engine block in which the piston(s) ride.

CYLINDER BLOCK: The main structural member of an engine in which is found the cylinders, crankshaft and other principal parts.

CYLINDER HEAD: The detachable portion of the engine, usually fastened to the top of the cylinder block and containing all or most of the combustion chambers. On overhead valve engines, it contains the valves and their operating parts. On overhead cam engines, it contains the camshaft as well.

DEAD CENTER: The extreme top or bottom of the piston stroke.

DETONATION: An unwanted explosion of the air/fuel mixture in the combustion chamber caused by excess heat and compression, advanced timing, or an overly lean mixture. Also referred to as "ping".

DIAPHRAGM: A thin, flexible wall separating two cavities, such as in a vacuum advance unit.

DIESELING: A condition in which hot spots in the combustion chamber cause the engine to run on after the key is turned off.

DIFFERENTIAL: A geared assembly which allows the transmission of motion between drive axles, giving one axle the ability to turn faster than the other.

DIODE: An electrical device that will allow current to flow in one direction only.

DISC BRAKE: A hydraulic braking assembly consisting of a brake disc, or rotor, mounted on an axle, and a caliper assembly containing, usually two brake pads which are activated by hydraulic pressure. The pads are forced against the sides of the disc, creating friction which slows the vehicle.

DISTRIBUTOR: A mechanically driven device on an engine which is responsible for electrically firing the spark plug at a predetermined point of the piston stroke.

DOWEL PIN: A pin, inserted in mating holes in two different parts allowing those parts to maintain a fixed relationship.

DRUM BRAKE: A braking system which consists of two brake shoes and one or two wheel cylinders, mounted on a fixed backing plate, and a brake drum, mounted on an axle, which revolves around the assembly.

DWELL: The rate, measured in degrees of shaft rotation, at which an electrical circuit cycles on and off.

ELECTRONIC CONTROL UNIT (ECU): Ignition module, module, amplifier or igniter. See Module for definition.

ELECTRONIC IGNITION: A system in which the timing and firing of the spark plugs is controlled by an electronic control unit, usually called a module. These systems have no points or condenser.

END-PLAY: The measured amount of axial movement in a shaft.

ENGINE: A device that converts heat into mechanical energy.

EXHAUST MANIFOLD: A set of cast passages or pipes which conduct exhaust gases from the engine.

FEELER GAUGE: A blade, usually metal, or precisely predetermined thickness, used to measure the clearance between two parts.

FIRING ORDER: The order in which combustion occurs in the cylinders of an engine. Also the order in which spark is distributed to the plugs by the distributor.

FLOODING: The presence of too much fuel in the intake manifold and combustion chamber which prevents the air/fuel mixture from firing, thereby causing a no-start situation.

FLYWHEEL: A disc shaped part bolted to the rear end of the crankshaft. Around the outer perimeter is affixed the ring gear. The starter drive engages the ring gear, turning the flywheel, which rotates the crankshaft, imparting the initial starting motion to the engine.

FOOT POUND (ft. lbs. or sometimes, ft.lb.): The amount of energy or work needed to raise an item weighing one pound, a distance of one foot.

FUSE: A protective device in a circuit which prevents circuit overload by breaking the circuit when a specific amperage is present. The device is constructed around a strip or wire of a lower amperage rating than the circuit it is designed to protect. When an amperage higher than that stamped on the fuse is present in the circuit, the strip or wire melts, opening the circuit.

GEAR RATIO: The ratio between the number of teeth on meshing gears.

GENERATOR: A device which converts mechanical energy into electrical energy.

HEAT RANGE: The measure of a spark plug's ability to dissipate heat from its firing end. The higher the heat range, the hotter the plug fires.

HUB: The center part of a wheel or gear.

HYDROCARBON (HC): Any chemical compound made up of hydrogen and carbon. A major pollutant formed by the engine as a byproduct of combustion.

HYDROMETER: An instrument used to measure the specific gravity of a solution.

INCH POUND (inch lbs.; sometimes in.lb. or in. lbs.): One twelfth of a foot pound.

INDUCTION: A means of transferring electrical energy in the form of a magnetic field. Principle used in the ignition coil to increase voltage.

INJECTOR: A device which receives metered fuel under relatively low pressure and is activated to inject the fuel into the engine under relatively high pressure at a predetermined time.

INPUT SHAFT: The shaft to which torque is applied, usually carrying the driving gear or gears.

INTAKE MANIFOLD: A casting of passages or pipes used to conduct air or a fuel/air mixture to the cylinders.

JOURNAL: The bearing surface within which a shaft operates.

KEY: A small block usually fitted in a notch between a shaft and a hub to prevent slippage of the two parts.

MANIFOLD: A casting of passages or set of pipes which connect the cylinders to an inlet or outlet source.

MANIFOLD VACUUM: Low pressure in an engine intake manifold formed just below the throttle plates. Manifold vacuum is highest at idle and drops under acceleration.

MASTER CYLINDER: The primary fluid pressurizing device in a hydraulic system. In automotive use, it is found in brake and hydraulic clutch systems and is pedal activated, either directly or, in a power brake system, through the power booster.

MODULE: Electronic control unit, amplifier or igniter of solid state or integrated design which controls the current flow in the ignition primary circuit based on input from the pick-up coil. When the module opens the primary circuit, high secondary voltage is induced in the coil.

NEEDLE BEARING: A bearing which consists of a number (usually a large number) of long, thin rollers.

OHM: (Ω) The unit used to measure the resistance of conductor-to-electrical flow. One ohm is the amount of resistance that limits current flow to one ampere in a circuit with one volt of pressure.

OHMMETER: An instrument used for measuring the resistance, in ohms, in an electrical circuit.

OUTPUT SHAFT: The shaft which transmits torque from a device, such as a transmission.

OVERDRIVE: A gear assembly which produces more shaft revolutions than that transmitted to it.

OVERHEAD CAMSHAFT (OHC): An engine configuration in which the camshaft is mounted on top of the cylinder head and operates the valve either directly or by means of rocker arms.

OVERHEAD VALVE (OHV): An engine configuration in which all of the valves are located in the cylinder head and the camshaft is located in the cylinder block. The camshaft operates the valves via lifters and pushrods.

OXIDES OF NITROGEN (NOx): Chemical compounds of nitrogen produced as a byproduct of combustion. They combine with hydrocarbons to produce smog.

OXYGEN SENSOR: Use with the feedback system to sense the presence of oxygen in the exhaust gas and signal the computer which can reference the voltage signal to an air/fuel ratio.

PINION: The smaller of two meshing gears.

PISTON RING: An open-ended ring with fits into a groove on the outer diameter of the piston. Its chief function is to form a seal between the piston and cylinder wall. Most automotive pistons have three rings: two for compression sealing; one for oil sealing.

PRELOAD: A predetermined load placed on a bearing during assembly or by adjustment.

PRIMARY CIRCUIT: the low voltage side of the ignition system which consists of the ignition switch, ballast resistor or resistance wire, bypass, coil, electronic control unit and pick-up coil as well as the connecting wires and harnesses.

PRESS FIT: The mating of two parts under pressure, due to the inner diameter of one being smaller than the outer diameter of the other, or vice versa; an interference fit.

RACE: The surface on the inner or outer ring of a bearing on which the balls, needles or rollers move.

REGULATOR: A device which maintains the amperage and/or voltage levels of a circuit at predetermined values.

RELAY: A switch which automatically opens and/or closes a circuit.

RESISTANCE: The opposition to the flow of current through a circuit or electrical device, and is measured in ohms. Resistance is equal to the voltage divided by the amperage.

RESISTOR: A device, usually made of wire, which offers a preset amount of resistance in an electrical circuit.

RING GEAR: The name given to a ring-shaped gear attached to a differential case, or affixed to a flywheel or as part of a planetary gear set.

ROLLER BEARING: A bearing made up of hardened inner and outer races between which hardened steel rollers move.

ROTOR: 1. The disc-shaped part of a disc brake assembly, upon which the brake pads bear; also called, brake disc. 2. The device mounted atop the distributor shaft, which passes current to the distributor cap tower contacts.

SECONDARY CIRCUIT: The high voltage side of the ignition system, usually above 20,000 volts. The secondary includes the ignition coil, coil wire, distributor cap and rotor, spark plug wires and spark plugs.

SENDING UNIT: A mechanical, electrical, hydraulic or electro-magnetic device which transmits information to a gauge.

SENSOR: Any device designed to measure engine operating conditions or ambient pressures and temperatures. Usually electronic in nature and designed to send a voltage signal to an on-board computer, some sensors may operate as a simple on/off switch or they may provide a variable voltage signal (like a potentiometer) as conditions or measured parameters change.

SHIM: Spacers of precise, predetermined thickness used between parts to establish a proper working relationship.

SLAVE CYLINDER: In automotive use, a device in the hydraulic clutch system which is activated by hydraulic force, disengaging the clutch.

SOLENOID: A coil used to produce a magnetic field, the effect of which is to produce work.

SPARK PLUG: A device screwed into the combustion chamber of a spark ignition engine. The basic construction is a conductive core inside of a ceramic insulator, mounted in an outer conductive base. An electrical charge from the spark plug wire travels along the conductive core and jumps a preset air gap to a grounding point or points at the end of the conductive base. The resultant spark ignites the fuel/air mixture in the combustion chamber.

SPLINES: Ridges machined or cast onto the outer diameter of a shaft or inner diameter of a bore to enable parts to mate without rotation.

TACHOMETER: A device used to measure the rotary speed of an engine, shaft, gear, etc., usually in rotations per minute.

THERMOSTAT: A valve, located in the cooling system of an engine, which is closed when cold and opens gradually in response to engine heating, controlling the temperature of the coolant and rate of coolant flow.

TOP DEAD CENTER (TDC): The point at which the piston reaches the top of its travel on the compression stroke.

TORQUE: The twisting force applied to an object.

TORQUE CONVERTER: A turbine used to transmit power from a driving member to a driven member via hydraulic action, providing changes in drive ratio and torque. In automotive use, it links the driveplate at the rear of the engine to the automatic transmission.

TRANSDUCER: A device used to change a force into an electrical signal.

TRANSISTOR: A semi-conductor component which can be actuated by a small voltage to perform an electrical switching function.

TUNE-UP: A regular maintenance function, usually associated with the replacement and adjustment of parts and components in the electrical and fuel systems of a vehicle for the purpose of attaining optimum performance.

TURBOCHARGER: An exhaust driven pump which compresses intake air and forces it into the combustion chambers at higher than atmospheric pressures. The increased air pressure allows more fuel to be burned and results in increased horsepower being produced.

VACUUM ADVANCE: A device which advances the ignition timing in response to increased engine vacuum.

VACUUM GAUGE: An instrument used to measure the presence of vacuum in a chamber.

VALVE: A device which control the pressure, direction of flow or rate of flow of a liquid or gas.

VALVE CLEARANCE: The measured gap between the end of the valve stem and the rocker arm, cam lobe or follower that activates the valve.

VISCOSITY: The rating of a liquid's internal resistance to flow.

VOLTMETER: An instrument used for measuring electrical force in units called volts. Voltmeters are always connected parallel with the circuit being tested.

WHEEL CYLINDER: Found in the automotive drum brake assembly, it is a device, actuated by hydraulic pressure, which, through internal pistons, pushes the brake shoes outward against the drums.

MASTER
INDEX